Kraus'

Recreation and Leisure
in Modern Society TWELFTH EDITION

Amy R. Hurd, PhD, CPRE
Associate Vice President for Undergraduate Education
Professor
Recreation and Park Administration Program
School of Kinesiology and Recreation
Illinois State University
Normal, Illinois

Denise M. Anderson, PhD
Associate Dean for Undergraduate Studies & Faculty Affairs
Professor
Department of Parks, Recreation, and Tourism Management
College of Behavioral, Social & Health Sciences
Clemson University
Clemson, South Carolina

Tracy L. Mainieri, PhD
Associate Professor
Recreation and Park Administration Program
School of Kinesiology and Recreation
Illinois State University
Normal, Illinois

JONES & BARTLETT
LEARNING

50TH
Anniversary Edition

World Headquarters
Jones & Bartlett Learning
25 Mall Road, 6th Floor
Burlington, MA 01803
978-443-5000
info@jblearning.com
www.jblearning.com

Jones & Bartlett Learning books and products are available through most bookstores and online booksellers. To contact Jones & Bartlett Learning directly, call 800-832-0034, fax 978-443-8000, or visit our website, www.jblearning.com.

Substantial discounts on bulk quantities of Jones & Bartlett Learning publications are available to corporations, professional associations, and other qualified organizations. For details and specific discount information, contact the special sales department at Jones & Bartlett Learning via the above contact information or send an email to specialsales@jblearning.com.

20602-9

Production Credits

VP, Content Strategy and Product Implementation: Christine Emerton
Director of Product Management: Matt Kane
Product Manager: Whitney Fekete
Content Strategist: Carol Brewer Guerrero
Content Coordinator: Andrew LaBelle
Project Manager: Kristen Rogers
Senior Project Specialist: Dan Stone
Senior Digital Project Specialist: Angela Dooley
Director of Marketing: Andrea DeFronzo
VP, Manufacturing and Inventory Control: Therese Connell

Composition: Straive
Project Management: Straive
Cover Design: Kristin E. Parker
Text Design: Kristin E. Parker
Content Services Manager: Colleen Lamy
Senior Media Development Editor: Troy Liston
Rights & Permissions Manager: John Rusk
Rights Specialist: Benjamin Roy
Cover Image: Top Photo: © Jordan Siemens/Getty Images; Bottom Photo: © Lee Cohen/Getty Images
Printing and Binding: LSC Communications

Library of Congress Cataloging-in-Publication Data
LCCN 2021005552 | ISBN 9781284205039 (paperback)
Subjects: LCSH: Recreation—North America—History. | Leisure—Social aspects—North America. | Play—North America—Psychological aspects. | Recreation—Vocational guidance—North America.
Classification: LCC GV51 .M34 2022 | DDC 790.097—dc23
LC record available at https://lccn.loc.gov/2021005552

6048

Printed in the United States of America
25 24 23 22 21   10 9 8 7 6 5 4 3 2 1

Brief Contents

Contents

5   Social Functions of Community Recreation   123

6   The Leisure-Services System   143

Preface

Recreation and leisure touch the lives of almost everyone, whether through participating in sports and games, attending a theater production, visiting an art museum, traveling to another country, attending a street concert, or simply enjoying a local park. A world without recreation and leisure is unfathomable— no parks, no open space, no swimming, no lounging on beaches, and no traveling to other parts of the world just for fun. We often take these things for granted. The purpose of *Kraus' Recreation and Leisure in Modern Society, Twelfth Edition* is to assist students in achieving an understanding and appreciation of the value of leisure and the leisure-service industry from multiple perspectives. This text provides a comprehensive survey of the leisure spectrum and profession, exploring its foundation, history, expansiveness, and continuing evolution. Leisure participation is viewed from the perspective of age, race, gender, and ethnicity and includes societal and personal benefits. It will demonstrate that recreation and leisure is a viable career option employing millions of people in North America. A career overview includes knowledge about public, commercial, and nonprofit recreation, as well as recreation therapy and the growing areas of tourism and sports.

This is the twelfth edition of a text that has been used by hundreds of departments of recreation, parks, and leisure studies at colleges and universities throughout the United States. It is designed for use in courses covering the history and philosophy of recreation and leisure and the role of organized leisure services today in American communities. This text is revised to reflect recent societal changes and the challenges that face leisure-service managers in the twenty-first century. It also provides an in-depth analysis of the basic concepts of recreation and leisure, the motivations and values of participants, and trends in the overall field of organized community services. Throughout the text, several important themes and emerging issues are emphasized, including the following:

- The dynamic dialogue surrounding the nature of the political, economic, and social environment has forced parks and recreation agencies to reevaluate traditional approaches to delivering public park and recreation services by becoming simultaneously innovative, responsive, and entrepreneurial.
- This is a dynamic profession where an understanding of recreation, play, and leisure and what it means to diverse groups of individuals as well as to the professional working in the field is key to facilitating meaningful experiences.
- Wellness continues to be a major issue in the field, with obesity being the most immediate concern facing public parks and recreation agencies. Major efforts are being made to provide health and wellness opportunities, control obesity, and preserve cardiovascular health through parks and recreation. *Well-being* has become an inclusive term, looking beyond traditional wellness indicators.
- Tourism is the world's largest economy. Many communities are presenting themselves as a tourist destination in order to increase resources available to community members through jobs, attractions, and revenue generation.
- The generation commonly referred to as "Baby Boomers" are hitting retirement age at a rate of more than 10,000 per day, and the younger Millennial Generation has become the largest generation.[a] The impact and influence of these two generations on the parks and recreation profession requires organizations to rethink traditional service models. Members of the Baby Boom Generation have more discretionary income than ever before and are willing to spend it on experiences— through travel and tourism, participating in programs, health and fitness activities, and adventure recreation.[*] Some people from other generations are interested in "now" activities and opportunities that simultaneously offer individual and group engagement, and they are eager for change.[b]
- Sport is increasing its influence and importance in the local, national, and international arena. Youth sport is taking on the forms and actions of professional sport, frequently to the detriment of the participants. Sport and tourism have become major community partners

[a]https://www.census.gov/library/stories/2019/12/by-2030-all-baby-boomers-will-be-age-65-or-older.html.
[b]https://www.pewresearch.org/fact-tank/2020/04/28/millennials-overtake-baby-boomers-as-americas-largest-generation/.

emphasizing economic community development. However, youth sport influence and participation has begun to wane as parents have become aware of life-changing injuries happening at young ages that may appear immediately or years later.

- Outdoor recreation has grown as a sector of the profession as an emphasis on recreation in nature, including adventure or experiential recreation, and is seen as necessary for the development of a greater appreciation for natural resources as well as a recognition of the numerous beneficial outcomes of nature-based recreation. Responsible management of these resources is also critical to ensuring their conservation and preservation for years to come.

- Globalization has impacted leisure through the ability to share models, lessons learned, adaptation to local settings, and the greater awareness that a global perspective brings to the profession.

- Multiple sociocultural factors impact leisure through available opportunities, activity choices, and the ways in which leisure is experienced; this is particularly evident when differences in socioeconomic status is considered. Urban communities often provide expanding services at increasing consumer costs, while inner-city urban areas continue to struggle to provide basic leisure services to residents.

- Trends both today and tomorrow from demographic shifts to changes in programming such as esports will continue to impact the field in ways both positive and negative. In addition, large-scale national as well as worldwide events such as climate change and the COVID-19 pandemic must be better understood in order for the professional to effectively meet the recreation and leisure needs of their constituents while having a positive impact on individuals and groups as well as our environments, economies, and societies.

Society is changing so rapidly that it is a challenge to capture the diversity and depth of change. The latest research, trends, and issues in the field are included in this edition. The parks and recreation profession is continually faced with providing services to a diverse population expanding far beyond race and gender. The latest edition of this text focuses on service provision for all people. A considerable amount of discussion is aimed at the role of parks and recreation departments on the health and wellness of our communities, as well as a means to combat the obesity epidemic that is plaguing North America. New case studies incorporated in the chapters allow students to apply knowledge of technology in leisure, the value and benefits of play, and changing family structures, to name a few.

Recreation's expanding roles in health, wellness, the obesity epidemic, quality of life, and environmental awareness and disengagement are examples of the breadth of the profession. Where once recreation professionals delivered programming and provided areas, facilities, and resources, they now face the need to partner, nurture, follow, and lead into new opportunities. Gone are the old socially contrived boundaries between disciplines and professions, replaced by a fluid composite of public, private, and nonprofit organizations and ever-growing numbers of unique stakeholders, all with a claim on recreation and leisure. Expectations of recreation professionals involve knowing about its history and foundations while embracing today's emerging social and physical challenges. It involves simultaneously honoring what was known yesterday and selectively engaging what will be known tomorrow. The fluidity of change in the leisure profession is captured in this text and challenges the reader to look to the past in looking to the future, ultimately learning from that past to strengthen the future. The text concludes with a strong assessment of the challenges and opportunities the future may promise.

Why We Study Recreation and Leisure

This text is intended to provide comprehensive information that will help its readers develop sound personal philosophies, gain a broad awareness of the leisure service field, and answer questions, not with learned-by-rote solutions, but rather through intelligent analysis, critical thinking, and problem solving. Leisure-service professionals should have an in-depth understanding of the full range of recreational needs and motivations as well as agency programs and outcomes. This understanding should be based on a solid foundation with respect to the behavioral and social principles underlying recreation and leisure in contemporary society. To have a sound philosophy of the goals and values of recreation and leisure in modern life, it is essential to understand recreation's history and to be aware of its social, economic, and psychological characteristics in today's society. Should recreation be regarded chiefly as an amenity, or should it be supported as a form of social therapy? What are the recreation needs of populations such as girls and women, those who are aging, those who are disadvantaged, ethnic and racial minorities, persons with disabilities, or others who have not been fully served in the past?

Throughout this text, these contemporary issues are discussed in detail. This text promotes no single philosophical position; its purpose is to clarify the values promoted by recreation and leisure in modern society. What environmental priorities should recreation and park professionals fight to support, and how can outdoor forms of play be designed to avoid destructive ecological outcomes? How can leisure-service practitioners strike a balance between entrepreneurial management approaches, which emphasize fiscal self-sufficiency, and human service programming that responds to individual and community needs? Ultimately, these values are responsible for the field's ability to flourish as a significant form of governmental or voluntary agency service or as a commercial enterprise.

Key Features

- *Learning Objectives:* Guide the reader through the content and set the stage for focused reading. The learning objectives are provided as a guide to assist students in identifying key learning outcomes.

LEARNING OBJECTIVES

1. Defend the importance of a strong conceptual foundation for effective leisure-service professionals.
2. Describe the conceptual evolutions of the terms play, recreation, and leisure.
3. Articulate the meaning of the terms play, recreation, and leisure.
4. Explain the various connections and relationships between the terms play, recreation, and leisure.
5. Accept the challenge to develop your personal "why" for wanting to pursue a career in the field of leisure services by the end of this text.

CASE STUDY: Finding Flow

Csikszentmihalyi's flow principle requires that a person's skill matches the challenge in the activity at hand. If there is not a balance between skill and challenge, negative feelings can occur. The individual experiences boredom if they are too skilled for the challenge or anxiety and frustration if they are under skilled for the challenge. For an individual to experience flow in play several factors must exist. The activity should provide:

- A clear set of goals: The outcomes, or goals, of activities are known. For example, games and sport have clear goals because rules guide play; music is dictated by a score; a marathon runner has a goal to finish. These goals are attainable based on the skill of the individual.
- Immediate feedback: It is clear how well the individual is performing in relation to the activity at hand. A runner knows how well they are progressing, an artist sees his or her work come together, and a team understands how well they are doing in a game.
- A loss of self-consciousness: People do not worry about how they look or are performing; they simply feel good about the activity and their involvement in it.
- A sense of distorted time: The individual loses all sense of time and what seems like minutes can actually be hours.
- An autotelic experience: One participates for the activity itself (intrinsic motivation) and no other reward. Pure enjoyment of the activity is the only justification needed.
- Strong concentration and commitment: The individual totally focuses on the activity and directs all concentration toward it.
- A sense of personal control: The individual feels she or he is in control of the situation and her or his skills to achieve the desired outcome.

Questions to Consider

- Describe an activity that you enjoy. Does it enable you to experience flow? What elements of flow do you most experience with this activity?
- Could work allow you to experience flow? Why or why not?
- Is flow a state that younger people could achieve more so than older people? Justify your answer.

Csikszentmihalyi, M. (1997). *Finding flow: The psychology of engagement with everyday life.* New York: Basic Books.

- *Case Studies:* Provide the reader a basis for in-depth exploration of current issues that are relevant to each chapter. The questions that follow the case studies allow the reader to apply the knowledge gained to real life scenarios, provoking further discussion and exploration.

- *Side Bars:* Highlight important information on current and related topics.

WANT MORE PLAY IN YOUR LIFE? START BY TAKING YOUR PLAY HISTORY

One of the methods Stuart Brown used to inform the conclusions about play he proposed in his 2009 book *Play: How It Shapes the Brain, Opens the Imagination, and Invigorates the Soul,* was to collect "play histories" from over 6,000 people. He encourages adults to use the same method to rediscover play in their own lives. Here are some steps to conduct your own play history:

Step 1: Recall what you did for play when you were younger. What activities really got you excited? Gave you joy?

Step 2: Reflect on those joyful activities to understand your "play temperament." What did it feel like? Who did you do them with or were you alone? Were they more physical or mental activities?

Step 3: Identify activities you could do now that would re-capture that playful spirit. As Brown explained, "Inventory the whole of your life, with an eye toward play, and look for ways to accentuate joy."[2]

Here are some questions to help you conduct your play history:

- When have you felt free to do and be what you choose?
  ○ Is that part of your life now? If not, why not?
  ○ What do you feel stands in the way of your achieving some times of personal freedom?
- Search in your memory for those times in your life when you have been at your very best.
- What have been the impediments to play in your life?
- How and why did some kinds of play disappear from your repertoire?
- Have you discovered ways of reinitiating lost play that work for you now in your life?

Brown, S. (2009). *Play: How it shapes the brain, opens the imagination, and invigorates the soul* (pp. 206–209). New York: Penguin Group.

BEYOND THE NUTS AND BOLTS: STORIES OF PLAY, RECREATION, AND LEISURE

Throughout the chapter you've read stories from real people about their experiences with play, recreation, and leisure. Now it's your turn to tell your story.

Identify something in your life that you do semi- to very regularly that you would label as play, recreation, leisure, or some combination of those ideas.

Write a short story (500–750 words) that describes your thoughts about the play/recreation/leisure thing you just identified. Here are some questions to help guide your storytelling.

1. When did you start doing the play/recreation/leisure thing (we'll call it "it" for the rest of the questions)? How did you get introduced to "it"?
2. How do you feel when you take part in "it"? Have your feelings evolved over the time you've done "it"?
3. Why do you continue to take part in "it"?
4. How do you feel when you're done taking part in "it"? Is there any carryover of feelings to a later time?

Once you've written your story, analyze it based on what you've just learned about the three concepts.

1. What elements of play, recreation, or leisure do you see reflected in your story?
2. Which of the three concepts would you label your "it" with? Is it more play, recreation, or leisure to you?

Want a chance for your "Beyond the nuts and bolts story" to be published in an upcoming edition of this book? Email your completed story to Kraus12e@gmail.com.

■ *Questions for Class Discussion or Essay Examination:* Feature critical thinking questions to spark discussion and classroom engagement with the topics presented in the chapter.

QUESTIONS FOR CLASS DISCUSSION OR ESSAY EXAMINATION

1. What parts of this chapter most resonated with you as you develop your personal "why" for wanting to pursue a career in the field of leisure services?

2. Read one of the Stories of Play, Recreation, and Leisure in the chapter. Conduct an analysis of the story, answering the following questions: (1) Does the experience the author describe in the story sound most like play, recreation, or leisure to you? Why? (2) Identify what you believe to be the play, recreation, and leisure components of the activity, explaining each of the components.

3. If motivation is important in the study of play, recreation, and leisure, explore some of the motivations you identify in leisure participation. How does knowing your motivations for participation in play, recreation, and leisure influence your desire to study the field of leisure services?

4. Compare and contrast the early theories and contemporary theories of play. First, identify the commonalities in the theoretical development of play, and second, the differences.

Organization

In the following chapters, this text focuses on multiple aspects of leisure and recreation. The content provides the reader with an in-depth discussion of present-day recreation, leisure, sports, tourism, outdoor recreation, and parks in American culture. The intended outcome is for the reader to gain an enhanced appreciation and understanding of how leisure affects individuals, groups, and society, and the roles that leisure plays in people's lives and in our society. This text looks at the roles of leisure in everyday life; the impacts of leisure on our culture; and how leisure influences individual choice, society mores, social engagements, the economy, and individual and community quality of life.

Chapter 1 introduces the concept of play, recreation, and leisure. It discusses what play, recreation, and leisure mean to different people, along with who participates in play and recreation and why. It also introduces the reader to theories of play and leisure, focusing on their origins, influences, and importance to earlier and contemporary society. Six views of leisure provide students with insights into how theorists, practitioners, and participants view leisure today. The foundation provided in this chapter prepares the student to understand how leisure fits into our society, is influenced by societal change, and influences society and individuals. The terms *leisure, play,* and *recreation* and their various interpretations are also discussed in this chapter, providing the reader with insights into their use by researchers, practitioners, and participants.

Chapter 2 is an introduction to motivations for participating in leisure and recreation. It includes an in-depth discussion of physical, social, and psychological motivation as it relates to recreation participation. The chapter also examines motivation from the perspective of taboo recreation and serious leisure.

Chapter 3 recognizes the growing influence cultural and social factors have on play, recreation, and leisure. Included in this chapter are discussions of age, family structure, gender, sexual orientation, race and ethnicity, and socioeconomic status. Understanding how these factors have traditionally affected leisure is as important as understanding how the factors are changing the perceptions of leisure and recreation in the twenty-first century.

Chapter 4 narrates the history of recreation and leisure from early civilizations to the present day. It is influenced by a European and North American perspective but recognizes the increasing influences from other cultures emerging in local and national society. The discussions of modern-day leisure are American, focusing on the influences of religion, colonization, and societal organization, and trace how different historical periods have acted on our perceptions of leisure and recreation. The chapter focuses on the dramatic changes that have occurred since World War II, recognizes the growing influence of globalization, and introduces the impact of technology on how people play and recreate.

Leisure and recreation traditionally have been represented from a community perspective and as a community resource. In **Chapter 5**, the 10 social functions of leisure are discussed. Social functions of leisure influence public policy, public commitment to organized leisure and recreation, and community development, all of which are critical in the twenty-first century.

Chapter 6 presents the different types of leisure-service organizations. The three organizational types include government, nonprofit, and commercial. This chapter identifies the three types of organizations, expands on them to address subtypes, compares and contrasts them, discusses their purpose, and generally identifies who is served, types of programming, types of services and areas, and intended outcomes.

The leisure industry, what makes it a profession, and philosophies of leisure service delivery are presented in Chapter 7. This chapter lays the foundation for Chapters 8 through 11 which focus on career areas for leisure services professionals.

Specialized leisure service organizations and areas are discussed in Chapter 8. Included are recreation therapy services for people with disabilities, armed forces recreation for military personnel and their dependents, employee services recreation for corporate employees, campus recreation for university students, private-membership recreation for private club members, meeting and event planning, and faith-based recreation. This chapter concludes with a comparison of the different types of organizations.

Chapter 9 addresses outdoor recreation and natural resources management. The history and legislation that have impacted individuals' ability to utilize natural resources for recreation are outlined followed by an examination of the ways they are used from land and water-based adventure recreation and therapy to opportunities to learn more about the world around us through environmental interpretation. Our understanding of outdoor recreation is further enhanced through an examination of the role sociodemographic factors play in usage as well as issues related to conservation and preservation.

Chapters 10 and 11 explore travel and tourism and sport. While these industries have grown independent of leisure and recreation in recent years, their roots remain firmly within the leisure field. Chapter 10 provides an overview of the travel and tourism aspect of the hospitality and leisure industries. This approach allows the reader to better understand how travel, tourism, and leisure complement each other. Chapter 11 shows how sport has grown into a major commercial enterprise over the last 30 years and is increasingly seen as an economic engine versus a leisure experience. However, much of sport remains strongly fixed in the leisure sector. This chapter explores the growth of sport as a worldwide phenomenon, its place in the business sector, its roots in the leisure context, the role of participation at different levels, and spectating. Finally, it looks at sport from a business perspective as well as the potential for negative outcomes surrounding sport.

Finally, Chapter 12 addresses the future of leisure and recreation and specifically looks at trends, influences, economic impacts, societal impacts, and predictions for the future. The chapter presents the influence of technology; how demographics and the growth of minorities are changing the way leisure is perceived and delivered; the impact of youth and a youth culture on society, especially as it contrasts with the baby boomer culture; global climate change issues, local environmental concerns, and how they relate; and finally, globalization and its influence on leisure and recreation.

New to the *Twelfth Edition*

In marking the 50th Anniversary of the publication of the book, the authors have opened each chapter with a quote from the original edition. In some instances it provides a reflection of the continued importance of the role of play, recreation, and leisure in our lives that we hope will never dim but continue to grow. In other areas a quote may help shine a brighter light on changes that have occurred over the last 50 years that have had a lasting impact on the field.

For the *Twelfth Edition* we have added a new coauthor to provide a fresh view of leisure. Among the most notable changes, we have added a new chapter on outdoor recreation while rearranging other chapters to create a better flow of content. We feel the changes are advantageous to the text and the student and allow the instructor greater flexibility in the delivery of the material.

Many of the case studies have been replaced, with the previous ones now appearing in the instructor materials. Other case studies have been updated to reflect recent trends. In general, chapter content has been updated to reflect changes in the field since the last edition. Multiple chapters address the current COVID-19 pandemic but, as this text goes to press, much is still unknown as to the long-term impacts of this worldwide event.

- Chapter 1 integrates new information throughout the chapter that provides non-Western perspectives on play, recreation, and leisure. It provides updated personal stories about play, recreation, and leisure to illustrate the concepts and a new focus on why foundational concepts are helpful for leisure services professionals. The updated chapter ends with a new charge to readers to discover their "why" for pursuing a career in leisure services.
- Chapter 2 provides updates on physical activity and health data, including obesity rates, across multiple generations and races and incorporates two new case studies. The chapter also expands on the concept of deviant leisure and related examples.
- Chapter 3 features new and expanded information about gender identity and sexual orientation to utilize the latest understandings on those topics, including a new section about transgender people and leisure. The chapter shares updated statistics on all sociocultural factors and new case studies and examples throughout.
- Chapter 4 has added additional information related to the impacts of race on leisure participation and leadership. A new case study has also been added.
- Chapter 5 incorporates a new case study as well as updated data and examples throughout.
- Chapter 6 creates a foundation for the delivery of leisure by looking at 10 major elements of the delivery system. Updates have been incorporated into the sections on different agencies in government providing recreation services, as well as the private and nonprofit sector and a new case study has been added.
- Chapter 7 showcases a new set of professionals and what their careers are like on a day-to-day basis. They are all young professionals that current students can aspire to be in the near future.
- Chapter 8 adjusts terminology to reflect more current practices of referring to therapeutic recreation as recreation therapy. New case studies have been added, and more current information related to campus recreation has been added as well as sections on meeting and event planning as well as faith-based recreation services. The material on outdoor recreation was removed and inserted into a new chapter (Chapter 9) dedicated to outdoor recreation and natural resources management.
- Chapter 9 is a new chapter to this edition with a focus on outdoor recreation and natural resources management with related case studies.
- Chapter 10 includes new statistics on the impact of travel and the ever-evolving trends in the industry as well as new case studies emphasizing these trends. The chapter also addresses both the current state of travel and tourism in light of the COVID-19 pandemic as well as potential future long-term impacts of this event on travel and tourism.
- Chapter 11 views sport from the perspective of the participant and spectator and expands the participant perspective to include a discussion on the structure of sport including recreational and developmental sport, interscholastic sport, intercollegiate athletics, and professional sports. The issues in sport were updated to include the most pressing matters in sport, and section on finding careers in sport was added.
- Chapter 12 features new and updated information that supports the readers in becoming professionals with an eye to the future and provides updated statistics and new examples throughout. The chapter also features new sections addressing eSports and the post-COVID-19 pandemic landscape. Finally, the chapter now concludes with a call for readers to articulate their "why" for pursuing a career in leisure services, first mentioned in the updated Chapter 1.

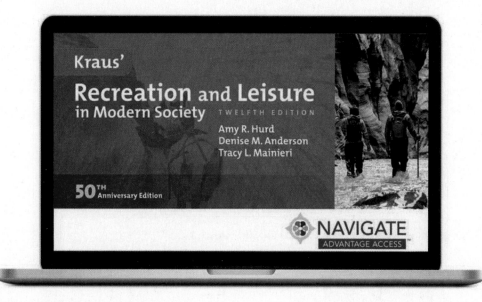

For the Instructor

Qualified instructors can receive access to the full suite of instructor resources, all of which have been revised to reflect the content of the *Twelfth Edition*. These resources include the following:

■ Instructor Manual, including chapter outlines, suggested assignments and projects, and additional case studies
■ Slides in PowerPoint format
■ Test Bank, featuring more than 300 questions
■ Sample Syllabus

For the Student

Additional resources are available online for the student, including the following:

■ Interactive eBook, featuring embedded weblinks and practice Knowledge Check questions tied to specific sections of the text
■ Flashcards
■ Slides in PowerPoint format
■ Lecture Outlines

Recreation and Leisure in Modern Society is meant to make readers think about the field and how it impacts their lives on a daily basis. Its aim is to make the reader appreciate the recreational opportunities that are available in North America and to educate each reader on what it means to be a parks and recreation professional.

Acknowledgments

Completion of this text was more of a challenge than usual with our deadlines being in the midst of a pandemic. That only enhanced our excitement about the end result as we could leave that behind and immerse ourselves in a field that we dearly love. The best part of working on the twelfth edition of the text was gathering the stories, examples, brochures, reports, photos, and information provided by the numerous public, nonprofit, commercial, and other organizations that have given material to us. Although it is difficult to thank everyone who has supported this edition, we truly appreciate the support of Illinois State University and Clemson University, as well as our families who understand the sacrifices needed to complete this project.

We would also like to acknowledge the important contributions and influence a number of practitioners and leading recreation and leisure-studies educators whose work and mentoring influenced our thinking. While it is not possible to name all of these individuals, they include: Karla Henderson, Debra Jordan, Fran McGuire, Dan McLean, Ellen O'Sullivan, Ruth Russell, Kim Shinew, and Robert Toalson.

We welcome Tracy Mainieri from Illinois State University as our new coauthor. She brings a rich knowledge of parks, recreation, and leisure that helps to keep this text current and relevant. Tracy stepped in for Dan McLean, who retired and served as a long-time author for the seventh through eleventh editions. We owe Dan a debt of gratitude for reshaping this text and bringing on a young coauthor fresh out of doc school, bringing on a new author a few years later with innovative ideas and a vision for the future, and setting us up to form this current writing team whose voices and ideas will continue to evolve with each edition.

We thank the reviewers of the *Twelfth Edition,* whose comments and suggestions have truly made this a better text:

- Glen Bishop, PhD, of Arkansas Tech University
- Brooke Burk, PhD, of Minnesota State University – Mankato
- Jonathan Hicks, MS, PhD, of Minnesota State University – Mankato
- Paul Keysaw, of Fresno City College
- Alice Morgan, PhD student, of West Virginia University
- Jodi Murray, MA, of Conestoga College
- Ben F. Tholkes, PhD, of Western Carolina University
- Barbara Vano, MA, of St. Thomas Aquinas College

This text could not have been published without the efforts of the staff at Jones & Bartlett Learning: Whitney Fekete, Product Manager; Carol Guerrero, Content Strategist; Dan Stone, Project Specialist; Benjamin Roy, Rights Specialist; Troy Liston, Senior Media Development Editor; and Andrea DeFronzo, Director of Marketing. Also special thanks to Praveen Babu and team for composition.

We are particularly indebted to the late Dr. Richard Kraus. To carry on his work is both important and critical. His efforts for more than 40 years as a writer, practitioner, and educator helped to shape this profession. This text has become a standard, and, as future editions are prepared, we hope to stay close to the roots that Dr. Kraus nurtured while remaining current with the changes in the profession.

Chapter 1

Conceptual Foundations of the Field of Leisure Services

"Leaders and administrators in recreation and park agencies have become skilled in the planning and development of facilities, personnel policy, and financial management. Yet, in a field intended to meet significant human needs, it is essential that the practitioner become capable of doing more than a 'nuts and bolts' job. [They] must have a thorough and sophisticated understanding of the role of recreation and leisure in human life and the changing functions of recreation in modern society." (pp. xi–xii; original emphasis; pronouns changed for inclusivity)[1]

-From the first edition of Kraus' Recreation and Leisure in Modern Society, published in 1971

LEARNING OBJECTIVES

1. Defend the importance of a strong conceptual foundation for effective leisure-service professionals.

2. Describe the conceptual evolutions of the terms play, recreation, and leisure.

3. Articulate the meaning of the terms play, recreation, and leisure.

4. Explain the various connections and relationships between the terms play, recreation, and leisure.

5. Accept the challenge to develop your personal "why" for wanting to pursue a career in the field of leisure services by the end of this text.

Introduction

Any consideration of the broad field of recreation and leisure should include a clarification of terms and concepts. The words *play, recreation, and leisure* are frequently used interchangeably, as if they mean the same thing. However, although related, they have distinctly different meanings. Leisure theorists struggle to agree on what to call these types of experiences. Is it recreation, leisure, play, free time, available time, creativity, selfishness, or hedonism? One's own perceptions are so important in the defining of play, recreation, and leisure that researchers continue to debate their meaning to society, individuals, and cultures. However, as this text will show, recreation, parks, and leisure services have become an important part of government operations and a vital program element of nonprofit, commercial, private-membership, therapeutic, and other types of agencies. Today, play, recreation, and leisure constitute major forces in our national and local economies and are responsible for millions of jobs in such varied fields as government, travel and tourism, popular entertainment and the arts, health and fitness programs, therapeutic settings, hobbies, and participatory and spectator sports. Beyond their value as a form of sociability, play, recreation, and leisure also provide major personal benefits in terms of meeting physical, emotional, cognitive, and other important health-related needs of participants. In a broad sense, the leisure life of a nation reflects its fundamental values and character. The very games and sports, entertainment media, and group affiliations that people enjoy help to shape the character and well-being of families, communities, and societies at large.

For these reasons, it is the purpose of this text to present a comprehensive picture of the role of leisure services in modern society, including (1) the field's conceptual base; (2) the varied play, recreation, and leisure pursuits people engage in; (3) their social and psychological implications; (4) both positive and negative outcomes of play, recreation, and leisure; (5) the network of community organizations that provide leisure services; (6) the development of leisure services as a rich, diversified field of professional practice; and (7) trends influencing the future of the leisure-services profession.

Why Is a Conceptual Foundation Important for Leisure-Services Professionals?

You may be asking yourself this very question. As a student striving to become a professional in the field of leisure services, why should you care about having a strong understanding of the foundational concepts of our field? Here's one way to think about it. A doctor must know chemistry, anatomy, kinesiology, and other underlying sciences to practice medicine effectively. An entrepreneur must know business, economics, accounting, and customer service philosophies. A farmer must know agriculture, biology, environmental systems, and business. Each profession has a range of foundational concepts, theories, and philosophies that allow someone to be an effective professional in and advocate for their field. This idea is no different for a leisure-services professional. A leisure-services professional must understand the foundational concepts of our field to provide effective, meaningful experiences for our participants and clients. These foundational concepts can act as inspiration for the leisure-services professional and provide deeper meaning for why we do what we do. Indeed, such conceptual understandings allow you, as a future leisure-services professional, to develop your own personal philosophy of leisure services that can motivate you in your work and allow you to advocate for the value of our field to others. As the chapter's starting quotation from the first edition of this textbook argues, the job of the leisure-services professional is more than just the "nuts and bolts"; to move beyond the nuts and bolts, leisure-services professionals need to consider the "why" behind their profession. That's where a solid grounding in our field's foundational concepts comes in. To help us move beyond the nuts and bolts as we explore the three foundational concepts of our field, we have included stories from real people about their experiences with play, recreation, and leisure throughout the chapter. You'll find these stories in boxes titled, "Beyond the nuts and bolts: Stories of play, recreation, and leisure." We hope they help us stay grounded in the "humanness" of our field.

Exploring the Three Major Concepts: Play, Recreation, and Leisure

Our understanding of the three major concepts in leisure services, play, recreation, and leisure, is heavily informed by scholarly writing and research. Writings on the concepts of play, recreation, and leisure are, of course, prominent in the scholarly field of leisure studies, but they also make frequent appearances in the scholarly writings of other fields, such as education, health, psychology, sociology, and child development. As we explore these three main concepts, you will see perspectives from these various fields interwoven into the discussion. When you start to explore the writings about the concepts of play, recreation, and leisure, you may notice that a large majority of these writings originate and describe experiences from Anglo-European Western cultures. Indeed, when Ito, Walker, and Liang reviewed 1,891 articles published in five leisure studies journals between 1990 and 2009, they found that only 4.1% of those articles were non-Western or cross-cultural.[2] The authors noted that the percentage of such articles in the five journals had increased

BEYOND THE NUTS AND BOLTS: STORIES OF PLAY, RECREATION, AND LEISURE

Embracing Joy

Fiona Zachel

The sounds of stomping feet pour from a brightly lit hall, tied together with the tunes of fiddle, flute, and drum. The wood floor, golden and polished from many years of furiously dancing feet, trembles in time with the music, a unified heartbeat of the bodies filling the dance hall. Faces of all ages shine with sweat, smiles blooming across each dancer as they weave between each other in a wondrous pattern of collective joy and connection. All combine into a spell that unleashes a deep yearning in my spirit, to become part of some larger existence. To experience a mere taste of the euphoria I see before me.

This was my introduction to social dancing, the small but dedicated crowd of contra dancers in my Alaskan hometown. I was lucky enough to have friends who were both dancers and musicians and were always eager to welcome a curious soul in search of something different.

I still remember that first night of contra dancing with piercing clarity, where I discovered a new way to converse with my fellow human beings that required no words. Just the touch of a hand, the beat of the music, and the enthusiasm of my own body into a swirling current of collective joy.

I danced until my socks were littered with holes, and bloody blisters began to blossom on my feet. That was my first, true taste of happiness, where my mind, body, and soul seemed to move in perfect harmony for the first time.

To be held, spun, and twirled with such compassion, to feel every concern, worry, or stress evaporate from my mind as I focused solely on another human being. The beat of the music in my bones, the strength of my limbs, all culminating in the soaring of my spirit. Trepidation turns into trust, shyness is exchanged for fearlessness, and if only for a few hours, an unwavering belief in the very best of humanity settles deep in my heart.

When I am dancing with another person, the rest of the world falls away. Nothing exists beyond the connection between me and my fellow dancer. All the fears, doubts, and uncertainties that await me outside the dance hall are banished.

That was many years ago, and I have wandered far from my contra dance days, my favorite dance halls now found in Chicago and Minneapolis. I envelope myself in the rhythms of salsa and bachata, the embrace of Argentine tango, and the recently birthed Brazilian zouk. My euphoria is no less, yet my ability to listen and learn from my fellow dancers has grown. As I move from one dance to another, each is a study in connection, nurturing the ability to communicate with people wherever I go in the world. No words, no borders, just a mutual love of dance and a willingness to hold another human, a stranger with whom you have only exchanged eye contact a few seconds before.

As I gain years and my body begins to wear, I find it is the moments of stillness that are the most cherished. The collective breath before a step, the embrace before the beat drops, precious moments of serenity suspended in time.

Each of us has memories of past dances that we treasure. Moments of magic with another person that transformed us, sent us into spirals of rapture, and ushered us into a more harmonious existence. That is what I strive to become, what fills me with contentment as I leave the dance floor. We carry dances in our hearts forever, stories without words that resonate through our lives years after a dance has ended.

The lights of the dance hall have gone dark and the final notes of music have faded into the dawn. An endless well of joy rests inside my heart, waiting to be unleashed once again.

fivefold in the time period they reviewed, which is encouraging. It remains, however, that a vast majority of the writing about play, recreation, and leisure as concepts in the field of leisure studies centers around Anglo-European, Western voices. As we explore these concepts, we will be intentional in naming this Western bias and bring in voices from other cultures, as we can. We are hopeful that with each edition of our text, our understanding of these concepts from a truly cross-cultural perspective will continue to advance.

Exploring Play

"Many children in public school are getting less and less time outside, despite the documented benefits of free play."[3] Play has long been determined essential for physical and emotional development of children. During the past 2 decades, play fell out of favor among some educators and parents but not among leisure-services professionals. Today, there is a resurgence of research across many fields about the value and importance of play. Researchers are suggesting that play is an organic way of learning, that unstructured play builds skills that will create happy and productive adults, and that under the right conditions, schools that integrate play will enhance the learning, self-awareness, and confidence of their students. Play, long a fabric of cultures across the world, is finding greater evidence to support its importance to children and adults.

ANALYZING THE WORD PLAY

The noun *play* in English is derived from the Old English *plega,* meaning a game or sport, brisk activity, skirmish, fight, or battle. This is related to the Latin *plaga,* meaning a blow, stroke, or thrust. It is illustrated in the idea of striking or stroking an instrument or playing a game by striking a ball. Other Western languages have words derived from a common root (such as the German *spielen* and the Dutch *spelen*) whose meanings include the playing of games, sports, and musical instruments. As a verb, the word *play* is traced to the Old English *plagen,* meaning to frolic, to move about sportively, to divert or amuse yourself. Play also may relate to the Middle Dutch *pleyen,* which means to dance, leap for joy, rejoice, and be glad.

HISTORICAL PERSPECTIVES ABOUT PLAY

Throughout Western history, perspectives about play have swung between a place of value and a force of threat in society. In ancient Greece, play was assigned a valuable role in the lives of children, based on the writings of Plato and Aristotle. The Athenians placed great value on developing qualities of honor, loyalty, and beauty and other elements of productive citizenship in children. For them, play was an integral element of education and was considered a means of positive character development and teaching the values of Greek society. Later, as the Catholic Church gained dominance among the developing nations of western Europe, play came to be regarded as a social threat. The body was thought to detract from more spiritual or work-oriented values, and every effort was made to curb the pleasurable forms of play that had been popular in the Greek and Roman eras. Eighteenth- and 19th-century educators and philosophers such as Froebel, Rousseau, and Schiller came to the defense of play as an important aspect of childhood education. For example, Froebel wrote of play as the highest expression of human development in childhood:

> Play is the purest, most spiritual activity of man at this stage. . . . A child that plays thoroughly with self-active determination, perseveringly until physical fatigue forbids, will surely be a thorough, determined man, capable of self-sacrifice for the promotion of the welfare of himself and others.[5]

Twentieth-century education scholars expanded the notion of the importance of play in society. For example, Vygotsky argued in a 1933 lecture on "Play and its role in the mental development of the child" that, "The child moves forward essentially through play activity. It is in this way that play can be termed a leading activity that determines the child's development."[6] Now, there are concerted efforts in the United States to emphasize the value of play not just to children but throughout the lifespan. For example, the U.S. Play Coalition, the Alliance for Childhood, and numerous regional and local organizations are advocating for play as essential throughout the lifespan.

PLAY IS NOT JUST FOR KIDS! JUST ASK THE Q'ERO PEOPLE OF PERU

As we consider play as a concept, often the concept is associated with children. However, recent research and advocacy has made clear that play is essential across the lifespan. One unique way to illustrate how play can be important past childhood is the concept of *pukllay* (pook-lee-eye), meaning sacred play in English, in the Q'ero people in Peru. Though the word *pukllay* is used more broadly in other areas of Peru, for the Q'ero people, the word takes on a more specific meaning, one that views play as spiritual activity. Ross offers this explanation of *pukllay*:

> For the Q'ero, *pukllay* is a biopsychospiritual relational activity that causes the individual to heal, mature, and learn in order to become a fully developed human. *Pukllay* is exhibited through dancing, singing, playing musical instruments, competing in games, enacting ritual, engaging in healing practices, making offerings, and participating in festivals. These joyful, heart-centred actions help Q'ero individuals, communities, and the earth to evolve in mutually enhancing, symbiotic relationships.[4]

In contrast with Western ideas of play as a temporary state most often associated with children, the play of *pukllay* is a strictly nonchild play and is a state of mind and being integrated throughout life. *Pukllay* can be aimed to provide purification, rejuvenation, relationship building, awakening, and even leadership development and selection.

This example demonstrates that play can be meaningful not just for children but also for adults. What evidence have you seen in your own life that play is not just for kids?

THEORIES TO HELP UNDERSTAND PLAY

Beyond understanding the origins of the word *play* and the evolution of perspectives about play, we can further explore the concept of play by considering the numerous theories about play that have been proposed throughout Western history. A theory is a set of principles that explains how a particular behavior or phenomenon works in society. Theories of play, then, are testable propositions about how play works in the real world. We will first explore some early theories of play then move on to some more contemporary theories and concepts of play.

Early Theories of Play

In the nineteenth and early twentieth centuries, a number of influential scholars evolved comprehensive theories of play that explained its development and its role in human society and personal development.

Catharsis Theory. The catharsis theory is based on the view that play—particularly competitive, active play—serves as a safety valve for the expression of bottled-up emotions. Among the ancient Greeks, Aristotle saw drama as a means of purging oneself of hostile or aggressive emotions; by vicarious sharing in the staged experience, onlookers purified themselves of harmful feelings. Biking a long distance after a hard day at work, playing a musical instrument after an argument with a friend, and hitting a bucket of golf balls to blow off steam after a nonproductive meeting are all examples of the catharsis theory of play.

Surplus-Energy Theory. Similar to the catharsis theory, the English philosopher Herbert Spencer, in his mid-19th-century work *Principles of Psychology,* advanced the view that play was primarily motivated by the need to burn excess energy. This theory asserts that running, playing soccer, or jumping rope on the playground are done because people have excess energy to use. A criticism of this theory is that play also occurs in people with little energy and does not account for nonphysical play.

Coupled with the catharsis theory, the surplus-energy theory suggests a vital necessity for active play to help children and adults burn excess energy and provide a socially acceptable channel for aggressive or hostile emotions and drives.

Relaxation Theory. An early explanation of play that was regarded as the converse of surplus energy was relaxation theory. Rather than to burn excess energy, play was done to restore it. Play was seen as a means to energize a person who was exhausted from work, school, or the stresses of daily life. It was believed that when a person is either mentally or physically tired, play can restore energy. So, exercising after a long day at work can serve to help an individual relax and restore. Spending time on Facebook during a study break or playing after school are both examples of relaxation theory.

Preparation Theory. Preparation theory suggests that play is a means for children to practice adult life. Children who play house, doctor, or school are preparing to experience these things as older children or adults. Preparation theory also suggests that people learn teamwork and role playing in their play. A weakness of this theory is that it does not account for adult play.

Contemporary Theories and Concepts of Play

During the 20th century, a number of psychologists and educators examined play, particularly as a developmental and learning experience for children.

Self-Expression Theory. Two leading physical educators, Elmer Mitchell and Bernard Mason, saw play primarily as a result of the need for self-expression. Humans were regarded as active, dynamic beings with the need to find outlets for their energies, use their abilities, and express their personalities. The specific types of activity that an individual engaged in were, according to Mitchell and Mason, influenced by such factors as physiological and anatomic structure, physical fitness level, environment, and family and social background.[7]

Stimulus-Arousal Theory. This approach is based on the observation that both humans and animals constantly seek stimuli of various kinds, both to gain knowledge and to satisfy a need for excitement, risk, surprise, and pleasure. Often this is connected with the idea of fun, expressed as light amusement, joking, and laughter. However, the expectation that play is always light, enjoyable, pleasant, or humorous can be misleading. Often, play activities can be frustrating, boring, unpleasant, or even physically painful—particularly when they lead to addiction (as in the case of drug, alcohol, or gambling abuse) and subsequent ill health or economic losses.

Competence-Effectance Theory. A closely related theory holds that much play is motivated by the need of the player to test the environment, solve problems, and gain a sense of mastery and accomplishment. Typically, it involves experimentation or information-seeking behavior, in which the player—whether human or animal—observes the environment, tests or manipulates it, and observes the outcome. Beyond this, the player seeks to develop competence, defined as the ability to interact effectively with the environment. Often this is achieved through repetition of the same action even when it has been mastered. The term *effectance* refers to the player's need to be able to master the environment and, even when uncertainty about it has been resolved, to produce desired effects in it.

Csikszentmihalyi "Flow" Principle. Related to the competence-effectance theory is Mihaly Csikszentmihalyi's view of play as a process in which ideally the player's skills balance the challenge level of the tasks. If the task is too simple, it may become boring and lacking in appeal. If it is too difficult, it may produce anxiety and frustration, and the player may discontinue the activity or change the approach to it so that it becomes more satisfying. This balance between skill and challenge results in what is called "flow." Csikszentmihalyi suggests that a sense of flow is a unique element in true play, which he identifies as a sense of flow. This is the sensation players feel when they are totally involved with the activity. It includes a feeling of harmony and full immersion in play; at a peak level, players might tend to lose their sense of time and their surroundings, and experience an altered state of being. Such flow, he argues, could be found in some work situations, but it is much more commonly experienced in play such as games or sport.[8]

Play as a Social Necessity. During the late 19th century, leaders of the public recreation movement called for the provision of organized play for all children. Joseph Lee, who is widely regarded as the father of the play movement in the United States and who promoted the establishment of numerous playgrounds and recreation centers, was instrumental in the public acceptance of play as an important force in child development and community life. Jane Addams, founder of

If the waves match the surfer's ability, surfing is an optimal activity in which an individual might experience flow.
© iStockphoto/Thinkstock/Getty.

the Hull House Settlement in Chicago and a Nobel Peace Prize winner, advocated the need for organized play opportunities that served as an alternative to the difficult life children living in poverty faced. These values continue to be embraced by contemporary communities, as is evidenced by

CASE STUDY: Finding Flow

Csikszentmihalyi's flow principle requires that a person's skill matches the challenge in the activity at hand. If there is not a balance between skill and challenge, negative feelings can occur. The individual experiences boredom if they are too skilled for the challenge or anxiety and frustration if they are under skilled for the challenge. For an individual to experience flow in play several factors must exist. The activity should provide:

- A clear set of goals: The outcomes, or goals, of activities are known. For example, games and sport have clear goals because rules guide play; music is dictated by a score; a marathon runner has a goal to finish. These goals are attainable based on the skill of the individual.
- Immediate feedback: It is clear how well the individual is performing in relation to the activity at hand. A runner knows how well they are progressing, an artist sees his or her work come together, and a team understands how well they are doing in a game.
- A loss of self-consciousness: People do not worry about how they look or are performing; they simply feel good about the activity and their involvement in it.
- A sense of distorted time: The individual loses all sense of time and what seems like minutes can actually be hours.
- An autotelic experience: One participates for the activity itself (intrinsic motivation) and no other reward. Pure enjoyment of the activity is the only justification needed.
- Strong concentration and commitment: The individual totally focuses on the activity and directs all concentration toward it.
- A sense of personal control: The individual feels she or he is in control of the situation and her or his skills to achieve the desired outcome.

Questions to Consider

- Describe an activity that you enjoy. Does it enable you to experience flow? What elements of flow do you most experience with this activity?
- Could work allow you to experience flow? Why or why not?
- Is flow a state that younger people could achieve more so than older people? Justify your answer.

Data from Csikszentmihalyi, M. (1997). *Finding flow: The psychology of engagement with everyday life*. Basic Books.

public and private support of parks and recreation departments, community recreation programs, after-school programs, and other play-based activities.

Huizinga's Theories of Play and Culture. Probably the most far-reaching and influential theory of play as a cultural phenomenon was advanced by the Dutch social historian Johan Huizinga in his provocative work *Homo Ludens* (*Man the Player*). Huizinga presented the thesis that play pervades all of life. He saw it as having certain characteristics: It is a voluntary activity, marked by freedom and never imposed by physical necessity or moral duty. It stands outside the realm of satisfying physiological needs and appetites. It is separate from ordinary life both in its location and its duration, being "played out" within special time periods and in such special places as the arena, the card table, the stage, and the tennis court. Play is controlled, said Huizinga, by special sets of rules, and it demands absolute order. It is also marked by uncertainty and tension. Finally, it is not concerned with good or evil, although it has its own ethical value in that its rules must be obeyed.

In Huizinga's view, play reveals itself chiefly in two kinds of activity: contests for something and representations of something. He regarded it as an important civilizing influence in human society and cited as an example the society of ancient Greece, which was permeated with play forms. He traced historically the origins of many social institutions as ritualized forms of play activity. For example, the element of play was initially dominant in the evolution of judicial processes. Law consisted of a pure contest between competing individuals or groups. It was not a matter of being right or wrong; instead, trials were conducted through the use of oracles, contests of chance that determined one's fate, trials of strength or resistance to torture, and verbal contests. Huizinga suggested that the same principle applied to many other cultural institutions:

> In myth and ritual the great instinctive forces of civilized life have their origin: law and order, commerce and profit, craft and art, poetry, wisdom, and science. All are rooted in the primeval soil of play.[9]

Caillois's Theories for Categorizing the Play Experience. The French sociologist Roger Caillois examined the play experience itself by classifying the games and play activities that were characteristic of various cultures and identifying their apparent functions and values. In doing so, he established four major types of play and two contrasting styles of play.

Caillois's four major types of play and game activity were:

1. *Agon* refers to activities that are competitive and in which the equality of the participants' chances of winning is artificially created. Winners are determined through such qualities as speed, endurance, strength, memory, skills, and ingenuity. Agonistic games may be played by individuals or teams; they presuppose sustained attention, training and discipline, perseverance, limits, and rules. Most modern games and sports, including many card and table games involving skill, are examples of agon.

2. *Alea* includes games of chance—those games or contests over whose outcome the contestant has no control; winning is the result of fate rather than the skill of the player. Games of dice, roulette, and baccarat, as well as lotteries, are examples of alea.

3. *Mimicry* is based on the acceptance of illusions or imaginary universes. Children engage in mimicry through pretend play. This category includes games in which players make believe, or make others believe, that they are other than themselves. For children, Caillois writes:

> The aim is to imitate adults. . . . This explains the success of the toy weapons and miniatures which copy the tools, engines, arms and machines used by adults. The little girl plays her mother's role as cook, laundress and ironer. The boy makes believe he is a soldier, musketeer, policeman, pirate, cowboy, Martian, etc.[10]

4. *Ilinx* consists of play activities based on the pursuit of vertigo or dizziness. Historically, ilinx was found in primitive religious dances or other rituals that induced the trancelike state necessary for worship. Today it may be seen in children's games that lead to dizziness by whirling rapidly and in the use of swings and spring riders. Among adults, ilinx may be achieved through amusement park rides such as roller coasters and a variety of adventure activities, including skydiving and bungee jumping.

Caillois also suggested two contrasting styles of play behavior. The first of these, *paidia*, involves exuberance, freedom, and uncontrolled and spontaneous gaiety. The second, *ludus*, is characterized by rules and conventions and represents calculated and contrived activity. Each of Caillois's four major types of play (agon, alea, mimicry, and ilinx) may be conducted at either extreme of paidia or ludus or at some point on a continuum between the two.

Brown's Theories about Play and the Brain. Stuart Brown, a medical doctor and psychiatrist, advanced the understanding of play by connecting the study of play with the latest advancements in the field of neuroscience (study of the brain). In his 2009 book, *Play*, he proposed the following properties of play:

- Apparently purposeless (done for its own sake)
- Voluntary
- Inherent attraction (fun)
- Freedom from time
- Diminished consciousness of self
- Improvisational potential
- Continuation desire[11]

WANT MORE PLAY IN YOUR LIFE? START BY TAKING YOUR PLAY HISTORY

One of the methods Stuart Brown used to inform the conclusions about play he proposed in his 2009 book *Play: How It Shapes the Brain, Opens the Imagination, and Invigorates the Soul*, was to collect "play histories" from over 6,000 people. He encourages adults to use the same method to rediscover play in their own lives. Here are some steps to conduct your own play history:

Step 1: Recall what you did for play when you were younger. What activities really got you excited? Gave you joy?

Step 2: Reflect on those joyful activities to understand your "play temperament." What did it feel like? Who did you do them with or were you alone? Were they more physical or mental activities?

Step 3: Identify activities you could do now that would re-capture that playful spirit. As Brown explained, "Inventory the whole of your life, with an eye toward play, and look for ways to accentuate joy."[11]

Here are some questions to help you conduct your play history:

- When have you felt free to do and be what you choose?
  - Is that part of your life now? If not, why not?
  - What do you feel stands in the way of your achieving some times of personal freedom?
- Search in your memory for those times in your life when you have been at your very best.
- What have been the impediments to play in your life?
- How and why did some kinds of play disappear from your repertoire?
- Have you discovered ways of reinitiating lost play that work for you now in your life?

Brown, S. (2009). *Play: How it shapes the brain, opens the imagination, and invigorates the soul* (pp. 206–209). Penguin Group.

Though the first property he listed for play was its apparent lack of purpose, Brown goes on to argue that play, in fact, has great purpose for humans throughout the lifespan. Indeed, he argued that the fact play is, at its core, purposeless or nonessential allows it to be a powerful force of brain development. Ideas, actions, and connections made in play are made in a relatively "safe" space, without huge threats to physical or mental well-being or "real world" consequences. Play, then, is a space to simulate life and test things out.

BENEFITS OF PLAY

In addition to developing the variety of theories describing play, the work of scholars and researchers over the past half century has documented the benefits of play to children, in particular, and adults. The American Academy of Pediatrics (AAP) released a report about the importance of play that highlighted the importance of play to the holistic well-being of youth, including physical, mental, social, and emotional development.[12] The AAP later went on to encourage pediatricians to give prescriptions for play, arguing that play is essential to prosocial brain development of youth, especially when it involves play with peers and adults. Indeed, play can be a vital resource for building healthy relationships between youth and their caregivers.[13] Let's explore some of the benefits that play produces for children and adults.

Personality is shaped by play in many different ways. Play prompts enjoyment, freedom, and fun. It prompts self-expression, creativity, imagination, and self-confidence. Play allows children to learn to interact with others through cooperative, sharing, and conflict-resolution activities. All of these experiences affect an individual's personality and contribute to the type of person the individual will become.

Play also aids in the psychological development of children, outlined in depth by Sigmund Freud. Freud saw play as a medium through which children are able to gain control and competence and to resolve conflicts that occur in their lives. He believed that children are frequently overwhelmed by their life circumstances, which may be confusing, complex, and unpleasant. Through play, they are able to reexperience threatening events and thus to control and master them. In this sense, play and dreams serve a therapeutic function for children. In general, Freud thought that play represented the child's way of dealing with reality—in effect, by playing with it, making it more acceptable, and exerting mastery over it.

> Might we not say that every child at play behaves like a creative writer, in that he creates a world of his own, or, rather, rearranges the things of his world in a new way which pleases him? It would be wrong to think he does not take his play seriously; on the contrary he takes his play very seriously and he expends large amounts of emotion on it. The opposite of play is not what is serious but what is real.[14]

A recent focus has been put on the value of play to healthy development. Play can prevent and combat a number of conditions that can have a negative impact on a child's health including childhood obesity, anxiety and depression, and weak bone development.[15] Play helps children develop motor skills, balance, and coordination. Organizations such as the U.S. Play Coalition, Voice of Play, the Centers for Disease Control and Prevention, and many others are providing resources and information on the health benefits of play to parents, community leaders, and parks and recreation professionals.

Because of what we now know about how play affects healthy brain development, play also provides cognitive benefits that are essential for children in contemporary society. The AAP argues that "play is fundamentally important for learning 21st-century skills, such as problem solving, collaboration, and creativity, which require the executive functioning skills that are critical in adult success."[13] Indeed, a recent study indicated that play can be essential for children to release and play out the emotions they hold in relation to recent societal events such as the COVID-19 pandemic or the social injustices and protests that occurred throughout the summer of 2020.[16] Importantly, these brain benefits of play are not limited to children. Brown argued that play can have important, similar impacts for adults, particularly at work, including increased creativity, innovation, and skill mastery.[11]

A WORKING DEFINITION OF PLAY

As you can see, what we may consider, at first, the simple concept of play actually has numerous associated theories, benefits, and concepts that have been developed over a couple of centuries of thought. It is difficult to arrive at a single definition of play because it takes so many forms and appears in so many contexts. However, a general definition would describe play as a form of human or animal activity or behavioral style that is self-motivated and carried on for intrinsic, rather than external, purposes. It is generally pleasurable and often is marked by elements of competition, humor, creative exploration and problem solving, and mimicry or role playing. It appears most frequently in free time activities but may be part of work. It is typically marked by freedom and lack of structure but may involve rules and prescribed actions, as in sport and games.

Exploring Recreation

The second major foundational concept for the field of leisure services is recreation. Of the three concepts, many may find recreation to be the most concrete and understandable. Having said that, the concept of recreation has a variety of historical and contemporary nuances that are important for leisure-services professionals to consider.

ANALYZING THE WORD RECREATION

The term itself stems from both the French *recreation*, meaning the action or process of creating again or anew and the Latin word *recreātiō*, meaning the action or process of restoring. When you look up the noun *recreation* in the

Recreation occurs in many forms with group involvement highly desirable for some individuals.
© Germanskydiver/Shutterstock.

modern dictionary, interestingly you see two versions of the noun. The first version, *recreation*, means the action of refreshing or entertaining oneself through a pastime or, more simply, an activity or pastime pursued for pleasure. The second version, though, is important to note as you explore your own "why" for being a professional in the field of recreation, as we started talking about at the beginning of this chapter. The second definition of the noun recreation you will find in the dictionary appears as *re-creation*, meaning the action or process of creating again or in a new way. Though we focus primarily on the first meaning here, you will notice that both versions retain the idea that recreation has something meaningful to do with helping people to refresh, or re-create, themselves.

HISTORICAL PERSPECTIVES ABOUT RECREATION

Historically, recreation was often regarded as a period of light and restful activity, voluntarily chosen, that permits one to regain energy after heavy work and to return to work renewed. This point of view lacks acceptability today for two reasons. First, as most work in modern society becomes less physically demanding, many people are becoming more fully engaged, both physically and mentally, in their recreation than in their work. Thus, the notion that recreation should be light and relaxing is far too limiting. Second, the definition of recreation as primarily intended to restore one for work does not cover the case of persons who have no work, including the growing retiree population, but who certainly need recreation to make their lives meaningful.

In contrast to work, which is often thought of as tedious, unpleasant, and obligatory, recreation has traditionally been thought of as light, pleasant, and revitalizing. However, this contrast too should be reconsidered. A modern, holistic view of work and recreation would be that both have the potential for being pleasant, rewarding, and creative and that both may represent serious forms of personal involvement and deep commitment.

BEYOND THE NUTS AND BOLTS: STORIES OF PLAY, RECREATION, AND LEISURE

How I Discovered Backpacking

Rocio Rivadeneyra

My family was on an amazing road trip the summer before my younger two children started kindergarten in 2012. We had excavated dinosaur fossils in Montana because my three young kids loved dinosaurs. Following the dig, we saw similar fossils displayed in the Museum of the Rockies, spent a few days in Yellowstone, and we were now spending our nights in a tent in Grand Teton National Park. The scenery was spectacular. Jenny Lake reminded me of a beautiful puzzle we had when I was a kid. I remember looking at the beautiful, jagged mountains and clear lake. As we were heading back to our minivan after hiking and a dip in the lake, we got passed by a group of Boy Scouts. They were in uniform and loaded with their packs. I remember one of the boys taking off his pack, kneeling to the ground dramatically, raising his arms above him and exclaiming, "Finally! Civilization!" I laughed, but I was also impressed at what they had seemingly accomplished.

I looked at my two daughters, both Girl Scouts in troops that I led. We were celebrating 100 years of the organization that year and had traveled to Washington, DC earlier in the summer to celebrate. I loved what the Girl Scout movement had given us: Skill development, community engagement, and leadership opportunities. It had given me the opportunity to gain outdoor skills that I had not developed having grown up in Los Angeles. Because of Girl Scouting, I had pushed myself to become comfortable outdoors and had started to take my older troop camping on Girl Scout property. As I saw this troop of Boy Scouts come down the mountain, I wondered if I could ever feel as comfortable as their leaders seemed leading young people into the wilderness. I made a vow right there and then not to let my discomfort and inexperience keep any of my Girl Scouts from experiencing all they could.

When I got home, I started to research primitive and back country camping. I subscribed to *Backpacker* magazine. I read the book *Wild* by Cheryl Strayed. I became fascinated by what could be gained on a backpacking trip. Not only did I want to learn backpacking skills for my girls, but now I also became fascinated by the promise of adventure. I signed up for a Backpacking 101 class with a friend and we headed into the Smoky Mountains with a guide who demystified the entire process for us. That year all my Christmas gifts were backpacking gear. I had an acquaintance who was section hiking the Appalachian Trail and I asked her to join me on a trip. Another acquaintance had heard about our plans and invited herself on our trip. That summer of 2015, three acquaintances went into the woods and emerged as close friends.

There is nothing like backpacking to bring you closer to others. You are reliant on each other for your survival. You often sleep in close quarters. You are each other's entertainment and when you stop and take in a jaw-dropping view, you have only each other to truly share that moment. That summer started a tradition of taking annual trips together. We love our adventures. We have been worried about bears, a falling tree in a big windstorm, or the strange sounds we hear in the middle of the night. We have laughed so hard we cried. We have lifted each other up (figuratively and literally). We have shared birthdays and anniversaries on the trail. We have developed traditions on our trips. For example, we always start our first night with wine and cheese. It may be box wine and Babybels but it feels extravagant when you combine the beautiful locations where they are consumed. Our friendship developed in the back country.

Six years after seeing that Boy Scout exclaim words of gratitude for reaching civilization, I took five junior high Girl Scouts into the wild. It only took multiple trips with friends, a Wilderness First Aid class, and years of research, to finally feel ready. Nothing beat watching these girls pitch their tents near a beach, filter water, practice Leave No Trace principles, cook on a small backpacking stove, and hang their bear bags. They learned how to take it slow and enjoy each other's company without the competing distraction of electronics. They hiked over 22 miles, worked as a team, and learned to depend on each other. They made memories, rose to the challenge, and earned their Primitive Camper badge. These girls are now in high school and have become such experts they just taught their own Backpacking 101 workshop to junior high girls. This includes my younger daughter and her troop of Girl Scouts who are now ready for their first back country trip!

CONTEMPORARY DEFINITIONS OF RECREATION

Typically, definitions of recreation found in the professional literature have included the following elements:

- Recreation is widely regarded as activity (including physical, mental, social, or emotional involvement), as contrasted with sheer idleness or complete rest.

Recreation may include an extremely wide range of activities, such as sport, games, crafts, performing arts, fine arts, music, dramatics, travel, hobbies, and social activities. These activities may be engaged in by individuals or by groups and may involve single or episodic participation or sustained and frequent involvement throughout one's lifetime.

- The choice of activity or involvement is voluntary, free of compulsion or obligation.
- Recreation is prompted by internal motivation and the desire to achieve personal satisfaction rather than by extrinsic goals or rewards.
- Recreation is dependent on a state of mind or attitude; it is not so much what one does as the reason for doing it, and the way the individual feels about the activity, that makes it recreation.
- Although the primary motivation for taking part in recreation is usually pleasure seeking, it may also be meeting intellectual, physical, or social needs. In some cases, rather than providing "fun" of a light or trivial nature, recreation may involve a serious degree of commitment and self-discipline and may yield frustration or even pain.

Most modern definitions of recreation fit into one of three categories: (1) recreation has been seen as an activity carried on under certain conditions or with certain motivations; (2) recreation has been viewed as an outcome—a specific set of emotions or psychological states that results from participation in recreation pursuits; and (3) recreation has been perceived as a social institution, a body of knowledge, or a professional field.

Recreation as Activity under Certain Conditions or Motives

The first category of modern definitions of recreation in the professional literature aligns well with the first dictionary definition we discussed: recreation as an activity carried on under certain conditions or with certain motives. Although it is generally accepted that recreation participation should be voluntary and carried out without any degree of pressure or compulsion, often this is not the case. We tend to be influenced by others, as in the case of the child whose parents urge him to join a Little League team, or the gymnast or figure skater who is encouraged in the thought that he or she

Recreation can occur anyplace and includes a variety of activities.
© Trevor Buttery/Shutterstock.

might become a professional performer. Although ideally recreation is thought of as being free of compulsion or obligation, once one has entered into an activity—such as joining a company bowling league or playing with a chamber music group—one accepts a set of obligations to the other members of the team or group. Thus, recreation cannot be entirely free and spontaneous and, in fact, assumes some of the characteristics of work in the sense of having schedules, commitments, and responsibilities.

Definitions of recreation generally have stressed that it should be conducted for personal enjoyment or pleasure—ideally of an immediate nature. However, many worthwhile activities take time to master before they yield the fullest degree of satisfaction. Some complex activities may cause frustration and even mental anguish—as in the case of the golf addict who is desperately unhappy because of poor putting or driving. In such cases, it is not so much that the participant receives immediate pleasure as that they are absorbed and challenged by the activity; pleasure will probably grow as the individual's skill improves.

What about the view that recreation must be carried on for its own sake and without extrinsic goals or purposes? It is essential to recognize that human beings are usually goal-oriented, purposeful creatures.

James Murphy and his coauthors identified different recreational behaviors that suggest the kinds of motives people may have when they engage in activity:

- *Socializing behaviors:* Activities such as dancing, dating, going to parties, or visiting friends, in which people relate to one another in informal and unstereotyped ways.
- *Associative behaviors:* Activities in which people group together because of common interests, such as street rod car clubs; stamp-, coin-, or gem-collecting groups; or hobbyists.
- *Competitive behaviors:* Activities including all of the popular sport and games and also competition in the performing arts or in outdoor activities in which individuals compete against the environment or even against their own limitations.
- *Risk-taking behaviors:* An increasingly popular form of participation in which the stakes are often physical injury or possible death.
- *Exploratory behaviors:* In a sense, all recreation involves some degree of exploration; in this context, it refers to such activities as travel and sightseeing, hiking, scuba diving, spelunking, and other pursuits that open up new environments to the participant.[17]

To these may be added the following motives:

- *Vicarious experiences:* Activities such as watching movies or sports events.
- *Sensory stimulation:* Activities that might include drug use, sexual involvement, or listening to rock music.

- *Physical involvement:* Activities that are done for their own sake, as opposed to competitive games.
- *Creative arts:* Activities that stimulate creativity and imagination through such mediums as the visual or performing arts.
- *Intellectual pursuits:* Activities that require cognitive skill such as reading, puzzles, strategic games, playing a musical instrument, or crocheting.

Recreation as an Outcome

Recognizing that different people may have many different motives for taking part in recreation, Gray and Greben suggest that it should not be considered simply as a form of activity. Instead, they argue that recreation should be perceived as the outcome of participation—a "peak experience in self-satisfaction" that comes from successful participation in any sort of enterprise.

> Recreation is an emotional condition within an individual human being that flows from a feeling of well-being and self-satisfaction. It is characterized by feelings of mastery, achievement, exhilaration, acceptance, success, personal worth, and pleasure. It reinforces a positive self-image. Recreation is a response to aesthetic experience, achievement of personal goals, or positive feedback from others. It is independent of activity, leisure, or social acceptance.[18]

Historically, researchers have focused on the social-psychological outcomes of recreation. More recently, significant attention has been given to physical outcomes. Researchers and practitioners are particularly interested in the relationship between recreation participation and physical health outcomes, including reduction of obesity and other chronic health conditions.

Recreation as a Social Institution

Recreation is identified as a significant institution in the modern community, involving a form of collective behavior carried on within specific social structures. It has numerous traditions, values, channels of communication, formal relationships, and other institutional aspects.

Once chiefly the responsibility of the family, the church, or other local social bodies, recreation in contemporary society is the responsibility of a number of major agencies in today's society. These may include public, nonprofit, or commercial organizations that operate parks, beaches, zoos, aquariums, stadiums, or sports facilities. Recreational activities may also be provided by organizations such as hospitals, schools, correctional institutions, and branches of the armed forces. Clearly, recreation emerged in the 20th century as a significant social institution, complete with its own national and international organizations and an extensive network of programs of professional preparation in colleges and universities.

Beyond this development, over the past century, there has been general acceptance of the view that community recreation, in which citizens take responsibility for supporting organized leisure services to meet social needs, contributes significantly to democratic citizenship. Community recreation is offered through city or county park and recreation departments.

A WORKING DEFINITION OF RECREATION

Acknowledging these contrasting views of the meaning of recreation, the following definition of the term is offered.

People are motivated to engage in high-adventure activities because of the risk involved.
Courtesy of Billy Heatter/U.S. Air Force.

Gardening is an example of a recreation activity that is freely chosen and has elements of intrinsic and extrinsic motivation.
© Photodisc/Getty.

BEYOND THE NUTS AND BOLTS: STORIES OF PLAY, RECREATION, AND LEISURE

Bike Riding

Beth Venable, MS, LPC

Living in New York City in the late 90s was an incredible life adventure. Having grown up in a family that valued outdoor activity, moving to the Big Apple was a big change of pace. It was challenging to figure out how to integrate outdoor play into what quickly became a very indoor life. Walking and running in my local parks was fun and convenient. But, it was the decision to step into my local Brooklyn bike shop that brought the pieces together. Having not really ridden a bike since I was a kid, I made the life-changing purchase of a commuter bike in my favorite shade of green.

One of the great pleasures of cycling is the speed at which I get to move through a landscape. Soon after buying that first "grown-up bike," my route became a new freedom lifting me over the Brooklyn Bridge, up the West Side Highway along the Hudson to the gardens of the Upper West Side. Flying along the edge of the city gave me a different perspective, a chance to sort through the mental clutter of the week. More than 20 years later, this is still the most compelling reason for me to ride, to lift up and out, to gain a different perspective.

Over the years, the commuter bike gave way to a mountain bike, a road bike, and a gravel bike. Athleticism entered the equation. Growing up I was an arts kid. While other kids went to practice, I went to dance class or rehearsal. Other high schools had Friday night football, while mine had performances and gallery openings. It was surprising to wake up one day in my thirties and self-identify as an athlete. Although cycling allows my mind to clear, it allows my body to take root in something tangible, measurable, and empowering.

In 2019, after I had more than a year of treatment for breast cancer, my brother noticed I was looking like myself again and asked me what had gotten me through. I said, "My bike." "Yeah," he replied, "But, what else?" Again I answered, "My bike." Of course, there is a longer answer to this question that includes family, friends, and a ton of medical intervention. What no one told me about chemo, surgery, and radiation was how much it would challenge my identity. The reduction to "cancer patient," the loss of privacy, agency, and the overwhelming grief and fear eroded my confidence in that internal knowing of who I was. Every pedal stroke I took during treatment and for the year after was a tiny bit of taking back my own whole self.

Every 10 years my "why" seems to grow a bit. Freedom and clarity gave way to empowerment and then to healing. More recently it has shifted to include community and social justice. On the bike, I am forced to lift my eyes and really look around at the rural southern city I call home. I try to reconcile how the thread of my ride through this community relates to the larger tapestry. Sometimes that means frustration and futility. Other times it leads to compassion and understanding. Over a hundred years ago the bike was instrumental in providing women access to transportation so that they could organize for the right to vote. Bikes continue to be the most affordable, environmentally friendly transportation for millions making their way to work or school. They also offer developmentally appropriate adventure and independence for children.

Reflecting on the impact of cycling in my life, I feel compelled to leverage whatever influence I have to fostering ways bikes can positively influence the health and well-being of others. When we find our favorite recreation, I believe it transcends our own personal benefit to the benefit of those around us. For me, biking lifts, empowers, heals, and creates more empathy just like a wheel generating power with each stroke of the pedals.

Recreation consists of human activities or experiences that are voluntarily chosen for intrinsic purposes and are pleasurable, although they may involve a degree of compulsion, extrinsic purpose, and discomfort, or even pain or danger. Recreation may also be regarded as the emotional state resulting from participation or as a social institution, a professional career field, or a business.

Exploring Leisure

The third foundational concept of the field of leisure services is, perhaps, the most abstract. What exactly is leisure? Leisure is a term we hear a lot in everyday use—people discussing their leisure time, taking a leisurely walk, or dreaming about living a "life of leisure." But what is leisure when considered through the eyes of a leisure-services professional or a leisure studies scholar? How can these specialized views about leisure advance our everyday understanding of the concept? Let's explore the answers to these questions together.

ANALYZING THE WORD LEISURE

The English word *leisure* seems to be derived from the Latin *licere*, meaning to be permitted or to be free. Also derived from *licere* were the French *loisir*, meaning free time, and such English words as *license* (originally meaning immunity from public obligation) and *liberty*. These words are all related; they suggest free choice and the absence of compulsion.

The early Greek word *scole* or *skole* meant "leisure." It led to the Latin *scola* and the English *school* or *scholar*—thus implying a close connection between leisure and education. The word *scole* also referred to places where scholarly discussions were held. One such place was a grove next to the temple of Apollo Lykos, which became known as the *lyceum.* From this came the French *lycée,* meaning "school"—again implying a bond between leisure and education.

It's useful to look beyond the English word for the concept of leisure as we start our exploration of our third foundational concept. Indeed, as we analyze the word for leisure outside of Western word origins, we find that though the concept of leisure appears in many non-Western cultures, the word itself is not as easily translatable. For example, let's look a term closely related to, but not a direct translation of, leisure in Chinese, *Xiū xián*, and its origins. The Chinese characters (休闲 or 休閒) that represent *Xiū xián* can be traced back at least 3,000 years. In ancient Chinese, the first character represented a person leaning on a tree and has evolved to mean taking a rest, relaxing, or fine quality. The second character represented the concept of moonlight coming through the planks of a door in ancient meaning, with its contemporary meaning being free and unoccupied.[19] In the evolution of the term *Xiū xián*, we see that the concept of leisure in Chinese culture, tracing back 3 millennia, has representations of physical rest, psychological feelings, and freedom in time. This brief exploration of a leisure-like term highlights the need for leisure scholars and professionals to try to look beyond conventional, Western views of not just leisure but play and recreation as well. In doing so, we can start to understand the definitions and value different people place on the concept of leisure through different cultural lenses, allowing us to have a deeper appreciation for these foundational concepts of our field.

HISTORICAL PERSPECTIVES ABOUT LEISURE

The Western classical view of leisure centered largely on ancient Greece. Aristotle regarded leisure as "a state of being in which activity is performed for its own sake." It was sharply contrasted with work or purposeful action, involving instead such pursuits as art, political debate, philosophical discussion, and learning in general. The Athenians saw work as ignoble; to them it was boring and monotonous. A common Greek word for work is *ascholia,* meaning the absence of leisure—whereas we do the opposite, defining leisure as the absence of work.

How meaningful is this classical view of leisure today? Although the Greek view of leisure as a necessary and integral piece of a holistic life has merit, this view has two flaws. First, it is linked to the idea of an aristocratic class structure based on the availability of a substantial underclass and slave labor. When Aristotle wrote in his *Treatise on Politics* that "it is of course generally understood that in a well-ordered state, the citizens should have leisure and not have to provide for their daily needs," he meant that leisure was given to a comparatively few patricians and made possible through the strenuous labor of the many. In modern society, leisure cannot be a privilege reserved for the few; instead, it must be widely available to all. It must exist side by side, and integrated, with work that is respected in our society, and it should have a meaningful relationship to work.

A leading American sociologist of the late 19th century, Thorstein Veblen, showed how, throughout history, ruling classes emerged that identified themselves sharply through the possession and use of leisure. In his major work, *The Theory of the Leisure Class,* he points out that in Europe during the feudal and Renaissance periods and finally during the industrial age, the possession and visible use of leisure became the hallmark of the upper class. Veblen attacks the "idle rich"; he sees leisure as a complete way of life for the privileged class, regarding them as exploiters who lived on the toil of others. He coined the phrase "conspicuous consumption" to describe their way of life throughout history. This theory is dated because of the rise of greater working-class leisure and because many members of extremely wealthy families work actively in business, politics, or other demanding professions.

To some degree, however, Veblen's analysis is still relevant. The wealthy or privileged class in modern society continues to engage in a wide variety of expensive, prestigious, and sometimes decadent leisure activities even though its members may not have an immense amount of free time. They tend to travel widely, entertain, patronize the arts, and engage in exclusive and high-status pastimes. Recent scholars have characterized contemporary leisure in Western cultures as consumerist and motivated by the pursuit of diversionary experiences that can be purchased. Ramsey expresses the following critique of consumerist leisure:

> So the nasty face of consumerist leisure expresses acquisitiveness, possessiveness, what the ancient Greeks called *plenoxia:* the desire for more than one's appropriate share. . . . The paradox around obligation-free leisure time is the drive quality, the compulsions and obsessions around purchase and use, to which many people are vulnerable due to the sheer vastness and success and ease of consumerism.[20]

We can also learn about historical perspectives about leisure from non-Western civilizations. Both Taoism and Confucianism developed around the same time as the philosophers we discussed from ancient Greece, in the fifth and fourth centuries BCE. The ancient writings from these two systems of thinking both contained insights about leisure-like concepts and both have strong influences on many Eastern cultures today.

For example, a primary figure in the development of Taoism was Chuang Tzu (369–286 BCE). In his writings, he encouraged withdrawing from world affairs and reconnecting with nature. In doing so, he believed that people could live more authentically. Chuang Tzu also talked about the great use in seemingly useless things.[21] His writings emphasized living a leisurely lifestyle and finding happiness in being completely unoccupied.[19] Kong Tzu (known in the West as Confucius; 551–479 BCE), the founder of Confucianism, also included in his writings insights about leisure-like concepts. He emphasized the value of striving for a life of leisure. He wrote about a need for both a free and leisurely mind and care for people and the nation. Indeed, he postulated that one can only obtain a true leisurely lifestyle if the nation is governed well; if it is, then everyone could live such a life.[21]

Confucianism and Taoism both influenced a later Chinese scholar, Wen Zhuenheng (1585–1645). Passages of his *Zhang Wu Zhi (Treatise on Superfluous Things)* describe the leisure thoughts and interests of the Chinese literati (the educated class of China between the 17th and early 20th centuries). In this work, he proposed that leisure involved withdrawing from society, escaping mainstream ideology, and countering national politics. By refusing involvement in government and retiring to the countryside, the literati avoided being under control of the centralized government, allowing them freedom, calm, and happiness. Leisure activities like playing the ancient instrument Guqin, drinking tea, and appreciating painting and calligraphy provide comfort and reflect interests of individuals. Like Veblen, Wen Zhuenheng cautioned against extravagance in the leisure life of the literati.[20]

LEISURE-LIKE CONCEPTS IN CONFUCIUS'S *THE ANALECTS*

The Analects represent a collection of passages that tell of the teachings and experiences of Confucius and his disciples. The work was compiled after the death of Confucius by his disciples and is considered one of the core texts of Confucianism. It also offers a classic passage that has been associated with the concept of leisure. In this passage, the Master (Confucius) is asking four of his disciples what their deepest wish would be. The wish expressed by Dian is the one scholars point to as reflecting notions of leisure. Give the passage a read:

Zi Lu (You), Zi Xi (Qiu), Zan You (Chi), and Gong Xihua (Dian) were sitting with the Master. Confucius said, "Although I am a day or so older than you fellows, forget about it for the time being. You are all always saying: 'Our talents are unrecognized.' Suppose your abilities were fully acknowledged. What would you do then?"

Zi Lu jumped to reply first, saying: "I would like to be in the position of the charge of a thousand-carriage state (a relatively small state) which was being threatened by the armies of the surrounding larger states, and suffering from crop failure. If I were in this position, within three years my people would be fearless and know how to take care of themselves."

Confucius laughed at him.

He turned to Qiu and said, "What about you?"

Qiu said, "Let me have the government of a territory of 60 to 70 *li*, or maybe 50 to 60 *li*, for three years, and the people would have all they need. As for handling the affairs of ritual and music, I would seek the services of a noble man."

"Chi, what about you?"

Chi said, "I cannot say I am capable of what the other two have proposed, though I would like to work toward it. At the services at the ancestral hall, or at the audiences with the Prince, I would like to serve as a minor assistant, dressed in the ceremonial gown and cap."

"Dian, what about you?"

Dian set his lute down with its strings still ringing, and stood up. "What I would like to do," he said, "is quite different from these three." The Master said, "What harm can there be? Please speak as the others have."

Dian said, "At the height of spring, all decked out in spring clothes, I would like to take five or six young men, and six or seven youngsters to go for a swim in the Yi river, enjoying the cool breeze at the Rain Dance Festival, and make our way back home, singing."

Confucius sighed, and said, "Ah, lovely. I am with you, Dian."[22]

Questions to Consider

1. What connections do you see between Dian's wish and the concept of leisure?
2. How is the concept of leisure in Dian's wish similar to your own ideas about leisure? Different?

CONTEMPORARY DEFINITIONS OF LEISURE

Now that we've explored some of the historical perspectives about leisure, let's delve into current definitions of leisure. As we discuss these definitions, be on the lookout for hints about how the historical perspectives we just explored have affected our current understandings of the concept of leisure. As with the definitions of play and recreation, narrowing leisure down to one definition is extremely difficult. Indeed, some leisure scholars argue that leisure is a concept that defies definition! However, if we as leisure-services professionals are going to advocate for the value of our field, we must be able to offer a definition of this primary concept. The literature about leisure does contain some common themes that help us to understand how we might go about defining leisure today. These themes can be organized into two categories: objective and subjective definitions of leisure. Walker, Kleiber, and Mannell offered this method of categorizing leisure phenomena.[23] The definitions in the objective category (leisure as time, leisure as activity, and leisure as setting) describe what, when, and how people do leisure whereas the subjective category (leisure as spiritual expression and leisure as state of mind) describes what people think and feel before, during, and after experiencing leisure. We will explore both categories before offering a working definition of leisure.

Objective Definitions of Leisure

Leisure as Discretionary Time. The most common approach to defining leisure is to regard it as unobligated or discretionary time. Discretionary time is time that is not used for work obligations and personal maintenance. This view of leisure sees it essentially as time that is free from work or from such work-related responsibilities as travel, study, or social involvements based on work. It also excludes time devoted to essential life-maintenance activities, such as sleep, eating, and personal care. Its most important characteristic is that it lacks a sense of obligation or compulsion. This approach to defining leisure is most popular among economists or sociologists, who are particularly concerned with trends in the economic and industrial life of the nation. Other scholars, including feminists, have found this definition useful in the study of time constraints faced by working adults in contemporary society.

Although this definition appears to be convenient and largely a matter of arithmetic (subtracting work and other obligated tasks from the 24 hours that are available each day and coming out with a block of time that can be called leisure), it has some built-in complexities. For example, is it possible to say that any time is totally free of obligation or compulsion or that any form of leisure is totally without some extrinsic purpose? Is it also possible to say that all unobligated time is intrinsically rewarding and possesses the positive qualities typically associated with leisure? For example, some uses of free time that are not clearly work or paid for as work may contribute to success at work. A person may read books or articles related to work, attend evening classes that contribute to work competence, invite guests to a party because of work associations, or join a country club because of its value in establishing business contacts or promoting sales. Within community life, those nonwork occupations that have a degree of obligation about them—such as serving on a school board or as an unpaid member of a town council—may also be viewed as part of a person's civic responsibility.

The strict view of leisure as time that lacks any obligation or compulsion is suspect. If one chooses to raise dogs as a hobby or to play an instrument in an orchestra, one begins to assume a system of routines, schedules, and commitments to others. When this happens one has to question if it is really leisure by this definition of unobligated time. This dichotomy between unobligated leisure time and obligated nonleisure time becomes even more suspect when we look outside of Western cultures. For example, when Iwasaki, Bartlett, Gottlieb, and Hall conducted interviews with urban-dwelling Aboriginal people in Canada, they found that those participants did not categorize leisure as something separate from other aspects of their lives or completely free of obligation. Instead, they reported that the times they would label as leisure-like, including family, friend, and relationship pursuits, helping people in the community, and spiritual and cultural activities, were enjoyable and meaningful ways to live their culture throughout their everyday lives. Many of the examples they shared that were leisure-like simply did not follow the notions of leisure as unobligated time and nonleisure as obligated time.[24]

Leisure as Activity. Another common understanding of leisure is that it is activity in which people engage during their free time or nonwork activities. Obviously, this concept of leisure is closely linked to the idea of recreation because it involves the way in which free time is used for activity purposes. Early writers on recreation stressed the importance of activity; for example, Jay B. Nash urged that the procreative act be thought of as an active, "doing" experience. Recuperation through play, he wrote, isn't wholly relegated to inertia—doing nothing—but is gained through action.

For many individuals, Nash's view of leisure would be too confining. They would view relatively passive activities, such as reading a book, going to a museum, watching a film, or even dozing in a hammock or daydreaming, to be appropriate leisure pursuits, along with forms of active play.

Feminist scholars have criticized conceptualizations of leisure as activity as irrelevant for many women whose everyday life experiences cannot be easily categorized into a work/leisure dichotomy. For example, when conducting research with women in Uganda, Adams et al. found that the ways that those women described their leisure-like experiences confirmed that we cannot discount activities that are strenuous or that have productive outcomes as possibilities for leisure, particularly for women who carry a large proportion of the burden of child-rearing and home maintenance.[25]

Furthermore, definitions of leisure as activity do not accommodate individual perceptions about particular activities. Some individuals may view preparing a meal as a pleasurable activity of self-expression, whereas others view the activity as a monotonous, domestic obligation. In response to this criticism, contemporary scholars who study leisure as activity are primarily concerned with the outcomes of a particular activity rather than the activity itself.

Leisure as Setting or Place. Closely related to, and sometimes hard to separate from, the notion of leisure as activity, is the concept of defining leisure based on the setting in which it occurs. We can probably all think about typical "venues" where leisure-type activities or experiences often occur such as recreation facilities, arenas, fields, outdoor spaces, parks, and so on. The setting, or environment, can have important impacts on people's experiences in relation to leisure. And such settings can take on important personal meanings for people in themselves, becoming places of meaning that people become attached to or identify with. Having acknowledged those realities, we can see that defining leisure strictly by the setting can become problematic, particularly when we consider that different people have different amounts of access to traditional leisure settings.

Subjective Definitions of Leisure

Leisure as Spiritual Expression. Another way of conceptualizing leisure today sees it in terms of its contribution to spiritual expression or religious values. Newly founded faith-based social welfare organizations in the late 19th century were a driving force behind the growth of public and philanthropic leisure services during that time. During the early decades of the 20th century, play and recreation were often referred to as uplifting or holy kinds of human experiences.

A more modern approach to spirituality moved beyond religion to an inner peace, understanding of the values that drive a person, and the meaning people assign to their lives. Leisure's connection to spirituality may not seem immediately obvious. The most commonly cited spiritual leisure pursuits are outdoor and nature activities. Walking through the woods, sitting on the bank of a creek, or paddling a canoe across a calm lake are means to spirituality for some. Others may prefer meditation, yoga, or other relaxation and contemplative exercises.

Leisure as a State of Mind. The final concept of leisure places the emphasis on the role of leisure involvement in helping the individual achieve personal fulfillment and self-enrichment. Often this definition of leisure is related to the perceived freedom of the activity. Neulinger writes:

> To leisure means to be engaged in an activity performed for its own sake, to do something which gives one pleasure and satisfaction, which involves one to the very core of one's being. To leisure means to be oneself, to express one's talents, one's capacities, one's potentials.[26]

This concept of leisure implies a mental experience that is holistic, in the sense that one's view of life is not sharply fragmented into a number of spheres such as family activities, religion, work, and free time. Instead, all such involvements are seen as potentially providing a leisure experience in which the individual explores their capabilities, develops enriching experiences with others, and seeks "self-actualization" in the sense of being creative, involved, expressive, and fully alive.

In Western concepts of leisure as a state of mind, this definition places great emphasis on the need for perceived freedom. Recognizing the fact that some constraints always exist, Godbey defines leisure in the following way:

> Leisure is living in relative freedom from the external compulsive forces of one's culture and physical environment so as to be able to act from internal compulsion in ways which are personally pleasing and intuitively worthwhile.[27]

Such contemporary leisure theorists stress the need for the true leisure experience to yield a sense of total freedom and absence from compulsion of any kind. Realistically, however, there are many situations in which individuals are pressured to participate or in which the activity's structure diminishes their sense of freedom and intrinsic motivation.

Recent investigations into leisure-like concepts in non-Western cultures has also illustrated that what may be the most important factors in the "leisure state of mind" may diverge from Western scholars' emphasis on perceived freedom. For example, Chinese in mainland China may prioritize a sense of belonging more than perceived freedom.[28] For Ugandan women, perceived choice was most defining:

> Rather than being defined by non-obligated time, in many cases, leisure was a mental time–space where Ugandan women experienced personal choice, achievement, building relationships, a sense of accomplishment, stress relief, and a sense of enjoyment. Both discretionary time and productive time were only considered leisure when women perceived they were engaging by choice.[25]

Regardless of what is the primary emphasis that defines leisure as a state of mind, it seems that the subjective concept of leisure as mental state that happens within the individual seems to connect across cultures in the limited cross-culture explorations that have happened so far. For example, when surveying what Chinese university students in China and Euro-Canadian university students in Canada defined as leisure and as not leisure, both groups seem to find the subjective definitions, such as leisure as state of mind, to be the most unique to leisure. In other words, these subjective definitions of leisure seemed most essential as these two groups of students sorted through what leisure was to them, in their own cultural terms.[28]

A Working Definition of Leisure

Each of the definitions of leisure discussed here has its strengths and its limitations, meaning that if we were to define leisure strictly from one of them, we may miss essential defining factors of leisure. Further, as we've seen, concepts of leisure can not only vary from person to person but also may vary greatly depending on the culture within which an individual is situated. To counter these shortcomings, Gui, Walker, and Harshaw devised what they view as a cross-cultural definition of leisure, based on their research. Their definition says leisure is, "positive mental states (e.g., fun, relaxed, related) experienced through typically unobligated activities (e.g., media use, outdoor recreation, travel, sports) that take place during free time with little time pressure."[28] We will use their definition as the basis for our working definition in this text. Therefore, leisure is a positive mental state individuals experience internally that typically, though does not have to, takes place during unobligated activities and during discretionary time. Leisure-like experiences are often characterized by some combination of perceived freedom, pleasure, belonging, self-growth, and motivation.

Connecting the Three Major Concepts

Obviously, the three terms discussed in this chapter are closely interrelated. All three concepts involve some discussion of the concept in objective terms (what people do) and in subjective terms (what people think or feel). Of the three, recreation is the concept that seems to be most related to objective terms as it's more defined as activity, whereas play and leisure seem more defined by being a type of mental state. All three concepts tend to be associated with positive feelings or described as beneficial experiences, though all three can involve discomfort in the moment and can produce negative outcomes. All three have been topics of debate in terms of the concept of time, with all three being most likely to occur during people's discretionary time, though both play and leisure can be experienced during work or other nondiscretionary time. All three concepts also have been linked to the

ideas of freedom and motivation. With all three concepts, times when people experience high perceived freedom and intrinsic motivation seem to be most likely to be labeled as play, recreation, and/or leisure, though people may experience structure, compulsion, or constraint in all three. Of the three, play seems to be the concept most defined by intrinsic motivation, carried out for its own purpose. Recreation obviously includes many forms of play, but it also may involve distinctly nonplay-like activities such as traveling, reading, going to museums, and pursuing other cultural or intellectual activities.

There are also clearly things that make each of the three concepts distinct from one another, which we have explored in detail. Beyond what we've already discussed, two further distinctions are important for us to note. First, recreation is the concept that has been most recognized as a distinct social institution or as a practitioner career field. Second, leisure seems to be the most abstract of the three concepts. Although we would be likely to say that participation in recreation may result in people experiencing a leisure state of mind, we might be less likely to say, for example, that leisure results in a recreation state of mind. In this way, it seems that the experience of leisure may be an ideal state to strive for. Leisure also seems to be the experience that can occur across the widest range of life spheres—during work, nonwork, passive activities, active activities, education activities, religious activities, community service…even housework! We have chosen to refer to our broad field in this text as "leisure services" because of these distinctions, though we acknowledge that some of the specific career paths within our field may occur in institutions that do not have leisure as a primary concern, such as the armed forces or business concerns, and in institutions that often provide other social or environmental services.

Volunteers form Adopt-a-Park programs to enhance local parks and build social capital within the community.
Courtesy of Deb Garrahy.

BEYOND THE NUTS AND BOLTS: STORIES OF PLAY, RECREATION, AND LEISURE

Coming Home

Courtesy of Ania Pathak.

Dance greets me—often literally—like a warm hug from an old friend. It has shaped who I am, how I exist in space and time, and how I connect to others. Dance also appears across cultures and history, creating a sense of taking part in something timeless, fundamentally human, and bigger than oneself.

Specifically, dance gives me presence and connection to myself, others, and the world around me. I find presence and connection to the ground, gravity, momentum; with the space that surrounds me, the sound filling that space, the movement of others; with the moods of the people and music and movement, the culture and history of the dance, and the ambience. Incredibly, dance exists only in the people who do it, emphasizing the role and creation of community and interpersonal connection through shared experience.

Dance brings me into the present, allowing me to escape everything that is not the here and now, cultivating something restorative and meditative. Dancing requires awareness and presence of both my entire body and its surroundings. Aware of space and sound enveloping me, I am present with how they morph as time passes between two beats—creating an acutely present moment void of anything other than existing in harmony with the world around me. Listening to fellow dancers—this feeling keeps many of us coming back. Dance feels like the harmonizing of the human body with both time and space through movement to sound.

This restorative present creates room for reflection, growth, and healing. I am able to process existence and experience. There is room for curiosity. It is play—but in the deeply significant and needed for development and growth kind of way—the way play is fundamental and critical for the healthy development of children. Play that allows for exploration, and facilitates growth, while connecting and synthesizing and processing experience more totally, leaving us better, happier, and more able and ready to both be ourselves and give to the world.

There was always a natural draw to dance for me, an undercurrent that makes itself evident when I look back on my childhood in retrospect. I took ballet when I was 3 or 4, and remember a Christmas gift from those years being an illustrated book of the famous ballet, Giselle. I have wisps of memories of twirling to music at family gatherings, receiving coos and accolades the way only a 4-year-old can elicit when they are truly immersed in experience and freedom of expression that comes with not yet knowing self-consciousness. What a freeing thing to reflect upon and to witness—a child so honestly present in the world they're in, unabashedly swept up by song. What a beautiful simplicity—to lack regard for and capacity to comprehend not just the judgment of others, but the judgment of ourselves. I suspect dance as adults brings us back to this state.

I could say I inherited it. My grandmother was nearly adopted by traveling dancers wanting to develop her talent after they saw her dance as a child in her small Polish village's festival. My great grandparents declined. My big brother ballroom danced competitively in college. And boy, did I look up to him. When he came home from school to visit, he would dance with me, and it felt like magic.

I shared what he taught me in a single high school talent show performance, and then off to college I went. Overhearing a conversation about ballroom in the dorm cafeteria, I sat down with a junior who would found the Michigan State University ballroom dance team that year. I also joined the salsa club because it met in my building, and I had interested friends.

Within a few years, I served as co-president of both those clubs and dabbled in swing dancing. I developed a competitive ballroom partnership, started taking private lessons, grew tremendously as a competitive dancer, and made friends across the Midwest traveling to compete. I was hooked, and poured my heart and soul into it. I danced from 10 p.m. to midnight, 4 nights a week. Then I'd head back to my dorm, finish my homework, and go to bed at 3 a.m. I traveled for private lessons on weekends if we could afford them, taught community lessons, and attended four or five competitions a year. The whole experience taught me dedication and skill and cultivated an insatiable desire to never live without the freedom of flying, unweighted, suspended in time, in harmony with time and space and the character of a dance with another person, to music. It also solidified my love for sharing that with others.

When we graduated our ballroom partnership ended. Missing dancing really wore on me. Transitioning from a dedicated, 5-year, competitive partnership to social dancing was difficult. I always left feeling like no one was my partner and no one danced with me like he did (because they weren't and didn't). But in time, I kept coming back.

BEYOND THE NUTS AND BOLTS: STORIES OF PLAY, RECREATION, AND LEISURE (*CONTINUED*)

I rekindled my love for dance through new dances and techniques: blues and fusion, some west coast swing. I joined a modern dance company for a year. I dived back into salsa, bachata. All while courting zouk and kizomba before I even knew what they were called, exposed to them through videos from people I had danced with in college. I went through an Argentine tango bout, too. And now, I spend most of my time dancing zouk and kizomba, with some bachata, salsa, and Argentine tango.

I feel immense happiness being part of these communities and calling these dances home. They're part of me. They're a refuge, a space for both meditation and play. And play is development, leisure is healing, community is support, and sensory integration is the making of knowledge and meaning and connection. Dance has given me all of that, over my entire lifetime—growth, healing, support, meaning. Now a part of me, dance is no longer a matter of always coming back, but of knowing I'll always have a home.

BEYOND THE NUTS AND BOLTS: STORIES OF PLAY, RECREATION, AND LEISURE

Throughout the chapter you've read stories from real people about their experiences with play, recreation, and leisure. Now it's your turn to tell your story.

Identify something in your life that you do semi- to very regularly that you would label as play, recreation, leisure, or some combination of those ideas.

Write a short story (500–750 words) that describes your thoughts about the play/recreation/leisure thing you just identified. Here are some questions to help guide your storytelling.

1. When did you start doing the play/recreation/leisure thing (we'll call it "it" for the rest of the questions)? How did you get introduced to "it"?
2. How do you feel when you take part in "it"? Have your feelings evolved over the time you've done "it"?
3. Why do you continue to take part in "it"?
4. How do you feel when you're done taking part in "it"? Is there any carryover of feelings to a later time?

Once you've written your story, analyze it based on what you've just learned about the three concepts.

1. What elements of play, recreation, or leisure do you see reflected in your story?
2. Which of the three concepts would you label your "it" with? Is it more play, recreation, or leisure to you?

Want a chance for your "Beyond the nuts and bolts story" to be published in an upcoming edition of this book? Email your completed story to Kraus12e@gmail.com.

A Challenge for Readers

Before moving on, we need to return to where we started – Why is a conceptual foundation important for leisure-services professionals? Why should you, as a student aiming for a career in this field, care about these foundational concepts? At the start of the chapter, we provided our own thoughts about how these ideas are useful for professionals in moving past the "nuts and bolts" and consider the "why" of our profession. We've offered you stories throughout the chapter that highlight the "humanness" of play, recreation, and leisure. Though we hope our thoughts are useful for you, ultimately, it's up to each leisure-services professional to determine and articulate their own "why" for what they do. So we offer each of you a challenge here. As you consider all of the topics in this text, keep this question in the back of your mind: What parts of this text most resonate with you as your personal "why" for wanting to pursue a career in the field of leisure services? Track the things that most resonate with you. Write them down. These items can form the basis for your own "why" of our profession. When we reach the end of the text, we will help you articulate your "why."

In the meantime, the themes that have just been introduced here in this chapter are explored more fully throughout this text, as the historical development of play, recreation, and leisure and the evolution of the present-day leisure-service system are described. Throughout, the social implications of play, recreation, and leisure and the role of leisure-services professionals are fully discussed, along with the challenges that face practitioners in this field in the 21stcentury.

SUMMARY

Play, recreation, and leisure represent important foundational concepts that are essential aspects of the overall field of organized leisure services. They have been explored by philosophers, psychologists, historians, educators, and sociologists from ancient civilizations to the present.

Play may best be understood as a form of activity or behavior that is generally nonpurposeful in terms of having serious intended outcomes but that is an important element in the healthy growth of children and in other societal functions. The chapter presents various theories of play, ranging from the classical views of Herbert Spencer to more contemporary concepts that link play to advancing knowledge about brain development.

Recreation is also explored from different perspectives, with a consideration of historical conceptions of recreation and contemporary definitions. The role of recreation as an important contemporary social institution and force in economic life is also discussed.

The concept of leisure is discussed in terms of its historical context in different cultures as well as the primary contemporary definitions of the concept. These contemporary definitions can be categorized into objective (leisure as time, leisure as activity, leisure as setting) and subjective (leisure as spiritual expression and leisure as state of mind).

QUESTIONS FOR CLASS DISCUSSION OR ESSAY EXAMINATION

1. What parts of this chapter most resonated with you as you develop your personal "why" for wanting to pursue a career in the field of leisure services?

_____

_____

2. Read one of the Stories of Play, Recreation, and Leisure in the chapter. Conduct an analysis of the story, answering the following questions: (1) Does the experience the author describe in the story sound most like play, recreation, or leisure to you? Why? (2) Identify what you believe to be the play, recreation, and leisure components of the activity, explaining each of the components.

_____

_____

3. If motivation is important in the study of play, recreation, and leisure, explore some of the motivations you identify in leisure participation. How does knowing your motivations for participation in play, recreation, and leisure influence your desire to study the field of leisure services?

_____

_____

4. Compare and contrast the early theories and contemporary theories of play. First, identify the commonalities in the theoretical development of play, and second, the differences.

_____

_____

_____

5. Discuss the contrasting meanings of play, leisure, and recreation, and show how individually and collectively they overlap and differ from each other in their meanings. Which of the three do you feel is the more useful term as far as public understanding of leisure services is concerned?

_____

_____

_____

6. Play is considered by many to be the domain of youth, and yet we see the creation of senior playgrounds, adult sport activities, and participation by adults in more and more recreation activities that could be called "play." Explain why play is defined as a youth activity and adults use the term recreation. Are they really that different? Are the motivations similar? Expand on this discussion.

_____

_____

_____

7. Examine your free time as a student. Do you have more or less free time than you did before college? Explain how your free time has changed. Compare it with your parents' or older siblings' free time and explain the difference. What causes these differences?

_____

_____

_____

ENDNOTES

1. Kraus, R. (1971). *Recreation and leisure in modern society*. Meredith Corporation.
2. Ito, E., Walker, G. J., & Liang, H. (2014). A systematic review of non-Western and cross-cultural/national leisure research. *Journal of Leisure Research, 46*(2), 226–239.
3. Westervelt, E. (2014). Scientists say child's play helps build a better brain. National Public Radio. https://www.npr.org/sections/ed/2014/08/06/336361277/scientists-say-childs-play-helps-build-a-better-brain
4. Ross, S. L. (2020). Sacred play: An ancient contribution to contemporary play. *Annals of Leisure Research*. Advance online publication. https://doi.org/10.1080/11745398.2020.1742751.
5. Friedrich Froebel, cited in Torkildsen, G. (1992). *Leisure and recreation management* (pp. 48–49). E. and F. N. Spon.
6. Vygotsky, L. S. (2016). Play and its role in the mental development of the child (N. Veresov & M. Barrs, Trans.). *International Research in Early Childhood Education, 7*(2), 3–25. (Original work published 1966).
7. The original source of this theory was W. P. Bowen and Elmer D. Mitchell, *The Theory of Organized Play* (New York: A. S. Barnes, 1923).
8. Csikszentmihalyi, M. (2007). *Flow: The psychology of optimal experience*. HarperCollins Publishers.
9. Huizinga, J. (1944/1960). *Homo ludens: A study of the play element in culture* (p. 5). Beacon Press.
10. Caillois, R. (1961). *Man, play, and games* (p. 21). Thames and Hudson.
11. Brown, S. (2009). *Play: How it shapes the brain, opens the imagination, and invigorates the soul.* Penguin Group.
12. Ginsburg, K. R. (2007). The importance of play in promoting healthy child development and maintaining strong parent-child bonds. *Pediatrics, 119*(1), 182–191. http://pediatrics.aappublications.org/content/119/1/182.short.
13. Yogman, M., Garner, A., Hutchinson, J., Hirsh-Pasek, K., & Golinkoff, R. M. (2018). The power of play: A pediatric role in enhancing development in young children. *Pediatrics, 142*(3), e20182058. https://pediatrics.aappublications.org/content/142/3/e20182058.
14. Sigmund Freud, quoted in Ellis, M. J. (1973). *Why people play* (p. 60). Prentice Hall.
15. Almond, J. (2018). *Improving children's health through play: Exploring issues and recommendations.* Alliance for Childhood and U.S. Play Coalition. https://usplaycoalition.org/wp-content/uploads/2018/04/Play-and-Health-White-Paper-FINAL.pdf.
16. Voice of Play. (2020). *2020 survey on the importance of play and the mental impacts of social injustice in the U.S.* https://voiceofplay.org/2020-survey/.
17. Murphy, J. et al. (1973). *Leisure service delivery systems: A modern perspective* (pp. 73–76). Lea and Febiger.
18. Gray, D., & Greben, S. (1974, July). Future perspectives. *Parks and Recreation*, 49.
19. Liu, H., Yeh, C-K, Chick, G., & Zinn, H. C. (2008). Exploration of meanings of leisure: A Chinese perspective. *Leisure Sciences, 30*, 482–488. .
20. Ramsey, H. (2005). *Reclaiming leisure: Art, sport and philosophy*. Palgrave Macmillan.
21. Wei, X. (2019). An exploration of the leisure thoughts of Confucianism and Taoism in *Zhang Wu Zhi*

(Treatise on Superfluous Things). Leisure Sciences. Advance online publication. https://doi.org/10.1080/01490400.2019.1686444.

22. Muller, A. C. (Trans.). (2020). *The analects of Confucius.* Retrieved January 14, 2021, from http://www.acmuller.net/con-dao/analects.html.

23. Walker, G. J., Kleiber, D. A., & Mannell, R. C. (2019). *A social psychology of leisure* (3rd ed.). Sagamore-Venture.

24. Iwasaki, Y., Bartlett, J. G., Gottlieb, B., & Hall, D. (2009). Leisure-like pursuits as an expression of Aboriginal cultural strengths and living actions. *Leisure Sciences, 31,* 158–173. http://doi.org/10.1080/01490400802686011.

25. Adams, E. V., Taniguchi, S. T., Hite, S. J., Ward, P. J., Mugimu, C. B., & Nsubuga, Y. K. (2018). Leisure defined by perceiving choice: perspectives of Ugandan women. *World Leisure Journal, 60*(4), 265–280. http://doi.org/10.1080/16078055.2018.1517106.

26. Neulinger, J. (1974). *The psychology of leisure* (p. xi). Charles C. Thomas.

27. Godbey, G. (1981). *Leisure in your life: An exploration* (p. 10). W. B. Saunders.

28. Gui, J., Walker, G. J., & Harshaw, H. W. (2019). Meanings of *Xiū Xián* and leisure: Cross-cultural exploration of lay people's definition of leisure. *Leisure Sciences.* Advance online publication. http://doi.org/10.1080/01490400.2019.1571968.

Chapter 2
Leisure Motivation

Mentally healthy people participate in some form of volitional activity to supplement their required daily work . . . Their satisfaction from these activities meets deep-seated psychological demands, quite beyond the superficial rationalization of enjoyment . . . There is considerable scientific evidence that the healthy personality is one who not only plays, but who takes his play seriously. Furthermore, there is also evidence that the inability and unwillingness to play reveals an insecure or disordered aspect of personality.

. . . the youngster who gets plenty of exercise . . . is more likely to do better academic work and be freer from tension than his passive, non-athletic roommate . . . Participation in sports relaxes and challenges the student and enables him [sic] to concentrate more intensely.[1]

-From the first edition of Kraus' Recreation and Leisure in Modern Society, published in 1971

LEARNING OBJECTIVES

1. Define and provide examples of physical, social, and psychological motivators to leisure.

2. Discuss the utilization of motivators in recreation programming.

3. Explain serious leisure as a unique form of leisure.

4. Define deviant recreation and identify examples of activities that would be classified as deviant recreation.

Introduction

Having reviewed the foundations of leisure and recreation, we now examine them from personal and social perspectives. This chapter outlines the varied motivations that impel individuals to take part in a wide range of recreational activities. These motivations are examined from the perspective of positive leisure experience, recreation activities that involve extreme risks, and those activities that are considered to be deviant, such as illegal drug use and gambling.

Motivation: What Is It?

Why do people choose to watch television for hours on end, play competitive sports, or conquer Mount Everest? The reasons are as varied as people are. Recreation enthusiasts derive different qualities from their activities, and these qualities are what drive them to participate. These driving factors are called *motivators*. Motivation can be defined as an internal or external element that moves people toward a behavior. A recreation-related motivator could be the desire to develop soccer skills or to learn about the visual arts.

When discussing motivation at the theoretical level, the names Edward L. Deci and Richard M. Ryan always emerge. They have studied motivation for many years and developed Self-Determination Theory (SDT). SDT is a general psychological theory that assumes that "humans are inherently motivated to grow and achieve and will fully commit to and engage in even uninteresting tasks when their meaning and value is understood." SDT focuses on the intrinsic motivation of the activity and not the extrinsic (defined shortly).[2]

Ryan and Deci outline six different types of motivation on a self-determination continuum that spans from no control over a situation to complete autonomy:

- *Amotivation:* Performance done without any intention of doing so. For example, amotivation is present when a parent takes a child to see a baseball game when the child has no desire or interest in seeing it. The child goes along because he has no choice and it is beyond his control.
- *Extrinsic motivation:* Performance of an activity because of an external force or reward. For example, a professional athlete receives compensation for playing for his or her team. This compensation is an external reward and is most likely one of the driving factors behind the athlete's participation. Another example of an extrinsic motivator is that of the golfer who plays with a regular foursome and bets $5 per hole with her friends. If she plays because of the money involved, this is an extrinsic motivator.
- *Introjected motivation:* Performance of an activity to alleviate guilt and anxiety or to enhance ego. Participation occurs in an activity because others desire that participation and the individual would feel guilty or anxious about letting people down. In terms of enhancing the ego, some participate in activities simply because they can demonstrate their skills to others. A professional athlete may continue playing the sport because of the admiration from the fans when in reality the athlete does not really enjoy playing.
- *Identified motivation:* Performance is done because the individual sees the value in the activity and gets something out of it. This could be building skills or increasing physical fitness. For example, if a person is running to enhance her fitness level and increase weight loss and not for the pure love of running, she is experiencing identified motivation.
- *Integrated motivation:* Performance of an activity matches the individual's values and desires, yet there are external reasons too. For example, the individual who runs for fitness and weight loss understands the need for physical health and has chosen running as an activity to achieve it.
- *Intrinsic motivation:* Performance of an activity for the behavior itself and the feelings that result from the activity. For example, completing a half-marathon for the first time could lead to a sense of accomplishment and pride in the fact that a goal was reached. These feelings are intrinsic motivators. The half-marathon was done because of the benefits of the activity and not because an external reward was dictating or influencing the person's behavior. The rewards are internal to the person, and the activity is done for its own sake.[3]

In leisure services, intrinsic motivation is most desired. Ryan and Deci summarize the importance of intrinsic motivation by saying, "Perhaps no single phenomenon reflects the positive potential of human nature as much as intrinsic motivation, the inherent tendency to seek out novelty and challenges, to extend and exercise one's capacities, to explore, and to learn."[4] Intrinsic motivation is enhanced and more likely to occur when there is a sense of autonomy, competence, and relatedness. Autonomy is the freedom to determine your own behavior, to guide your own actions, and to be in control of the situation. Competence occurs when an individual feels capable, skilled, and able to meet an acceptable level of challenge. Feelings of competence result from effective and positive feedback from performance. Last, relatedness is a sense of belonging, security, and connection with others. These three things enhance the likelihood of intrinsic motivation. The following sections look at motivation from a variety of perspectives.

Although there is a plethora of ways to look at motivation, including by activity type, age, and gender, it is important to look at broad motivating factors that relate to leisure preferences. In describing the major areas of human development, behavioral scientists use such terms as *cognitive* (referring to mental or intellectual development), *affective* (relating to emotional or feeling states), and *psychomotor* (meaning the broad area of motor learning and performance). Because these terms are somewhat narrow in their application, this chapter instead uses the following more familiar terms: (1) *physical*, (2) *social*, (3) *psychological*, and (4) *emotional*. Most, if not all, motivators of leisure participation can fit into one or more of these four categories.

Physical Motivators

Active recreational pursuits such as sport and games, dance, and even such moderate forms of exercise as walking or gardening have significant positive effects on physical development and health. The value of such activities obviously will vary according to the age and developmental needs of the participants. For children and youth, the major need is to promote healthy structural growth, fitness, endurance, and the acquisition of physical qualities and skills. It is essential

Youth baseball serves as a physical motivator where health, wellness, and other physical qualities are gained.
© Creatas/Thinkstock/Getty.

that children learn the importance of fitness and develop habits of participation in physical recreation that will serve them in later life. This is particularly important in an era of electronic games, labor-saving devices, and readily available transportation, all of which save time and physical effort but encourage a sedentary way of life.

Physical motivators can best be summarized as control of obesity and preserving cardiovascular health. Although each is discussed separately, they are intertwined. Most of what drives people who are motivated by the physical aspects of leisure is achieving wellness. A means to wellness is cardiovascular health and reduced obesity. Society is changing and starting to realize how important an active lifestyle is, and parks and recreation play an active role in this.

Control of Obesity

The Centers for Disease Control and Prevention (CDC) defines overweight and obesity in terms of body mass index (BMI). BMI is a calculation of height and weight. Table 2-1 demonstrates the level of BMI in an adult 5'9".

BMI for children is calculated a bit differently and takes into account age- and sex-specific percentiles. However, as a measurement of obesity, BMI has its critics as it can incorrectly flag people who are muscular as overweight and it can result in "normal" scores for people who carry excess weight in body areas that are more risky. For this reason, other key measures of weight and health risk include waist circumference as well as risk factors including high blood pressure, high-density lipoprotein (HDL; good) cholesterol, low-density lipoprotein (LDL; bad) cholesterol, heart disease, type 2 diabetes, high blood sugar, high triglycerides, family history of heart disease, smoking, and physical inactivity.[5] Scientists agree that physical activity plays a major role in weight control. Obesity among American adults has grown steadily and is now a serious health problem in this country as well as in Canada. Nearly 72% of the U.S. population is overweight, and of those the percentage considered obese is

TABLE 2-1	Sample Adult BMI Chart		
Height	**Weight Range (lbs)**	**BMI**	**Considered**
5' 9"	124 or less	Less than 18.5	Underweight
	125–168	18.5–24.9	Healthy weight
	169–202	25.0–29.9	Overweight
	203 or more	30 or higher	Obese

Data from Centers for Disease Control and Prevention. (n.d.). *Defining adult overweight and obesity.* https://www.cdc.gov/obesity/adult/defining.html

approaching 40%. Children are not exempt from this weight problem because one in three children is considered overweight and 18.5% of these children are obese.[6] In Canada 61% of adults are overweight or obese with almost 27% classified as obese while 12% of children and youth are classified as obese.[7]

Not only is there a difference in obesity rates based on age, but race and geography also show differences. The obesity rate among Hispanic people is 47%, followed by non-Hispanic black people at 46.8%, non-Hispanic white people at 37.9%, and non-Hispanic Asian people at 12.7%.[8] The states with the highest percentage of population (greater than or equal to 35% of the population) who are overweight or obese include North Dakota, Iowa, Missouri, Louisiana, Mississippi, West Virginia, Arkansas, Alabama, and Kentucky. The healthiest states with 20% to less than 34% of the population overweight or obese are Colorado, Hawaii, and the District of Columbia. In general, the states in the south have a tendency to be fattest, and the states in the West and Northeast are the slimmest.[9]

The main reason for obesity is inactivity. In 2018, only a small percentage over half (53.3%) of Americans aged 18 to 64 met the 2008 federal physical activity guidelines for aerobic activity, and only 23.2% of them met the guidelines for aerobic activity and muscle-strengthening activity.[10] Although these numbers are not stellar, they are, however, higher than they were in 2015. For both categories, the highest levels of inactivity for every age group were found among women, with 58% of men meeting aerobic activity guidelines compared to 50.5% of women.[11] The numbers are similar when adding muscular strengthening exercise into the mix, with 27.3% of men meeting the guidelines, whereas only 20.7% of women did.[12] Age is also a factor; whereas

64.8% of adults aged 18 to 24 meet aerobic guidelines, the number plummets to 32.3% for those aged 75 and older.[13] The same is true for the combination of aerobic and muscle-strengthening activity, with a drop from 34% of those aged 18 to 24 to 10.2% of those aged 75 and older meeting guidelines.[14] With respect to race, 47.6% of Hispanic people met the guidelines for aerobic activity compared to 46.4% of non-Hispanic black people and 57.4% of non-Hispanic white people.[15] The trend is similar for a combination for aerobic and muscle-strengthening activity, with 21.3% of Hispanic people meeting guidelines compared to 25.6% of non-Hispanic black people and 20.1% of non-Hispanic white people who met the guidelines.[16] Each of these percentages is also trending in a positive direction since 2015.

Education is also an indicator of regular physical activity levels. As education increases, so does physical activity. People without a high school diploma or General Educational Development (GED) certificate are least likely to meet federal recommended guidelines for aerobic and muscle-strengthening activities at only 9%, followed by those with a high school diploma or GED (15.1%) and those with some college or more (28.1%).[17] The benefits of getting regular physical activity are proven for both children and adults, with decreased obesity rates and decreased incidences of coronary disease, diabetes, high blood pressure, and stroke. Although many of these diseases do not occur in children, obese children are more likely to become obese adults.

Because of these statistics, public, nonprofit, and commercial agencies have come together to offer programs and education to help people become more active. For example, the Healthy People 2030 Framework, as the next stage of the Healthy People initiative, is dedicated to helping people live longer and have a better quality of life. It

---

CASE STUDY: Calculating Your Waist Circumference

Waist circumference helps screen for possible health risks associated with overweight and obesity by taking into consideration where a person carries excess fat. Go to the National Heart, Lung, and Blood Institute website (http://www.nhlbi.nih.gov/health/educational/lose_wt/risk.htm) to calculate your waist circumference as well as your BMI.

Questions to Consider

- Were you surprised by your waist circumference or BMI? Do you have any risk factors as described by the National Heart, Lung, and Blood Institute?
- What changes, if any, need to be made for you to reduce any risk factors you may currently have?
- If you are at a healthy weight, what do you do on a regular basis to maintain that healthy weight?
- Think about your family, including grandparents, parents, aunts, and uncles. Is there a weight issue within the family as a whole? Explain.
- What do you first think when you see an obese younger child?

Data from National Heart, Lung, and Blood Institute. (n.d.). *Assessing your weight and health risk*. Retrieved January 22, 2021, from https://www.nhlbi.nih.gov/health/educational/lose_wt/risk.htm.

includes 10 indicators as to what makes a person healthy, and physical activity is woven throughout the overarching goals.[18]

Preserving Cardiovascular Health

Of all the fitness-related aspects of active recreation, maintaining cardiovascular health may represent the highest priority. Cardiovascular diseases include such things as high blood pressure, heart failure, stroke, and coronary heart disease. Johns Hopkins Medicine reported that approximately 121.5 million people in the United States have cardiovascular disease, causing about 840,678 deaths in 2016. Furthermore, about approximately one-third of cardiovascular disease deaths occur before age 75.[19]

Even with these known statistics, physical inactivity is the main culprit, with a sedentary lifestyle being every bit as bad for one's heart as smoking, high cholesterol, or high blood pressure. The American Heart Association suggests that adults need 150 minutes of moderate-intensity aerobic activity per week or 75 minutes per week of vigorous-intensity aerobic physical activity. Moderate-intensity aerobic activity increases a person's heart rate and can be accomplished by participating in activities that increase the heart rate in episodes of at least 10 minutes. As such, a person could walk briskly or ride a bike three times a day for 10 minutes each time to achieve the standard. Vigorous-intensity activity, such as running or riding a bicycle at an accelerated speed, causes rapid breathing and a substantial increase in heart rate. It is also recommended that adults

---

CASE STUDY: Kids Can Bike!

Knoxville, Tennessee's Childhood Obesity Coalition launched the Kids Can Bike! program in the spring of 2012. The 7-week bicycling program was designed to increase physical activity, teach safe cycling skills, and explore local parks and greenways while having fun. After-school and summer program participants in third–fifth grades were eligible for the program. Once a week, the children were transported to a safe riding location while the City of Knoxville Department of Parks and Recreation transported bicycles to the corresponding location. The Department of Parks and Recreation provided staffing and the University of Tennessee provided student volunteer assistants. The instructors were trained to deliver a safe cycling curriculum that included both physical activity and education components. With a focus on the impact of the program on bicycle knowledge as well as the children's experience with the program, the Obesity Coalition surveyed the children at the beginning and end of the 7-week program with results indicating an increase in knowledge as well as high satisfaction. With a goal of building lifelong bicyclists, the program provided youth with the equipment they needed, a safe location for practicing, as well as a fun program to motivate continuation of what they had learned.

Questions to Consider

- What other kinds of physical activity programs for youth are you aware of either in your hometown or surrounding communities? What ages do they target and what activities do they offer?
- Why might a cycling program in particular be a good way to encourage physical activity among all ages?

Data from Chandler, J. L., Flynn, J. I., Bassett, D. R., Aaron, K., Walsh, J., Manual, K., Fernandez, R., Epperson, E., & Zavisca, E. (2015). A community-based after-school program to promote bicycling skills and knowledge: Kids Can Bike! *Journal of Park and Recreation Administration, 33*(4), 90–99. https://doi.org/10.18666/JPRA-2015-V33-I4-6083.

HEALTHY PEOPLE 2020

Healthy People is a governmental organization under the auspices of the U.S. Department of Health and Human Services that is dedicated to providing science-based national objectives to improve the health of Americans. This group has published three reports, or 10-year agendas, that give guidelines and strategies for building healthy people and communities—Healthy People 2000, Healthy People 2010, and Healthy People 2020. Healthy People 2020 strives to:

- Identify nationwide health improvement priorities.
- Increase public awareness and understanding of the determinants of health, disease, and disability, and the opportunities for progress.
- Provide measurable objectives and goals that are applicable at the national, state, and local levels.
- Engage multiple sectors to take actions to strengthen policies and improve practices that are driven by the best available evidence and knowledge.
- Identify critical research, evaluation, and data collection needs.

Data from U.S. Department of Health and Human Services. Office of Disease Prevention and Health Promotion. (n.d.). *About Healthy People*. Retrieved January 22, 2021, from http://www.healthypeople.gov/2020/about/default.aspx

NATIONAL PHYSICAL ACTIVITY RECOMMENDATIONS

The American College of Sports Medicine recommends 30 minutes of moderate physical activity five times per week as well as training each major muscle group 2 or 3 days each week through resistance training. However, it likely takes more than the minimum activity levels to facilitate weight loss or weight maintenance.

select activities that will increase muscle strength and endurance at least twice per week.

In 2018, just over half (53.3%) of Americans aged 18 and older met the guidelines for aerobic activity and 23.2% for both aerobic and muscle-strengthening activities.[20]

The U.S. Department of Health and Human Services recommends children aged 6 years and older should get at least 1 hour a day of moderate-to-vigorous-intensity physical activity. The American Heart Association lowers this age to 2 years and older. Three days per week a child should do activities that are muscle strengthening, and another 3 days should include activities that are bone strengthening. Muscle-strengthening activities work the major muscle groups such as the legs, arms, and chest. These can include rope climbing, tree climbing, swinging, climbing walls, or cross-country skiing. Bone-strengthening activities put a force on the bones and help them grow and strengthen through impact with the ground. Bone-strengthening activities include such things as hopping, skipping, jumping, running, volleyball, and gymnastics.[21]

However, recent research involving thousands of men and women indicates that even moderate forms of exercise, including such activities as walking, stair climbing, gardening, and housework, have a beneficial long-term effect on one's health. Although high-intensity, pulse-pounding workouts yield the most dramatic benefits, more modest forms of exercise do yield significant benefits. Beyond these findings, other research demonstrates that regular exercise reduces the incidence of other diseases such as diabetes, colon cancer among men and breast and uterine cancer among women, stress, osteoporosis, and other serious illnesses.

Although there is a plethora of reasons why people should be physically active and the implications of not being active are widely known, the obesity rate is still quite high. A line of research on the constraints to physical activities demonstrates some of the reasons why. Constraints are things that keep people from participating in leisure activities or participating as much as they would like or that compromise the quality of participation. A few findings that researchers uncovered about physical activity suggest the following:

- The healthier a person is, the less likely that person will find reasons not to participate in physical activity.[22]
- The more people see the benefits of being physically active, the more likely they are to choose these types of activities.[23]
- Time, family obligations, and lack of energy are the main reasons people give for not participating in physical activity.[24]
- Enjoyment of an activity is a major predictor of selecting an activity, including sedentary activities.[25]
- Cost, work obligations, time, and other priorities diminish the likelihood of participating in physical activity.[26]
- An increased preference for sedentary activities has been found among children who are overweight or obese.[27]

Given all of this, the most effective forms of physical activity are those that are most enjoyable to different people. The challenge comes with those who prefer sedentary over physical activities.

If people are motivated to participate in parks and recreation activities based on physical motivators, then there are plenty of opportunities to be found. More and more employers have fitness facilities, offer discounted memberships at local clubs, or give paid time off for employees to participate in fitness activities. Organizations such as the Y, Young Women's Christian Association (YWCA), local parks and recreation agencies, and hospitals all provide activities to get people moving. Even the travel industry is trying to help. Seeing the value of health and fitness, the travel industry is taking action by making health easier for guests. Many hotels offer more healthy options on room service menus, but more important, they are catering to the health conscious and expanding beyond the typical fitness facility with a half dozen pieces of equipment. For example, Omni Hotels brings a workout kit to the guest's hotel room. The Get Fit Kit arrives in a canvas bag and includes a floor mat, dumbbells, exercise bands, and a workout booklet. The Hilton McLean Tysons Corner and the Hilton San Francisco Union Square have yoga and cardio rooms where guests can stay. These rooms have a king-sized bed and the equipment needed to work out. Other hotels are offering boot camp classes daily.[28]

Social Motivators

The need to be part of a social group and to have friends who provide companionship, support, and intimacy is at the heart of much recreational involvement. It helps to explain why people join sororities, fraternities, or other social clubs, sports leagues, tour groups, or other settings where new acquaintances and potential friends may be met. It is an underlying element in sport in terms of the friendships and bonds that are formed among team members. There are a number of specific social motivators that must be mentioned, including being with others, reducing loneliness, and developing social norms among people.

Being with Others and Reducing Loneliness

Many adults today find their primary social contacts and interpersonal relationships not in their work lives but in

Building social relationships through leisure helps reduce loneliness.

© Rubberball Productions.

voluntary group associations during leisure hours. Even in the relatively free environment of outdoor recreation, where people hike, camp, or explore the wilderness in ways of their own choosing, interaction among participants is a key element in the experience. Only 2% of all leisure activities are done alone. This indicates that people like to participate in activities with others.

Social contact, friendship, or intimacy with others is key to avoiding loneliness. Loneliness is a widespread phenomenon among all ages. Typically, as many as three-quarters of all college students report being lonely during their first term away from home. As adults age, they begin to experience increased loneliness as significant others and friends begin to pass away and children leave home. Loneliness can have unpleasant and even life-threatening consequences and often is directly linked to depression, obesity, high blood pressure, and heart problems.[29]

Involvement in recreation activities with others can alleviate feelings of loneliness. People can join the Y, YWCA, their local recreation center, or take classes at their local parks and recreation department where they can learn new skills or exercise while also meeting others who enjoy these same activities. Keep in mind, there is a difference between loneliness and solitude. Russell suggests that time spent alone is an important part of our lives and can be a much desired state. People participate in certain activities to reduce loneliness, but they also do things to escape or focus totally on themselves such as the case with solitude.[30]

Social Norms

Clearly, different types of recreation groups and programs impose different sets of social norms, roles, and relationships that participants must learn to accept and that contribute to their own social development. For children, play groups offer a realistic training ground for developing cooperative, competitive, and social skills. Through group participation, children learn to interact with others, to accept group rules and wishes, and, when necessary, to subordinate their own views or desires to those of the group. They learn to give and take, to assume leadership or follow the leadership of others, and to work effectively as part of a team.

THE RELATIONSHIP BETWEEN HAPPINESS AND SOCIALIZING

In a survey of 140,000 Americans, it was found that people are happiest when they spend 6 to 7 hours per day socializing. People who are alone all day are least happy and experience higher levels of stress than those who are more social. Furthermore, there is a weekend effect where people experience more happiness and less stress than during the week.

Data from Harter, J., & Arora, R. (2008, June 5). *Social time crucial to daily emotional well-being in U.S. Gallup Poll*. Retrieved January 22, 2021, from https://news.gallup.com/poll/107692/social-time-crucial-daily-emotional-wellbeing.aspx.

As children age, their social groups increase in importance in their lives. Social peer groups for teens are a major sense of support and help them form their social identity. Into adulthood, social groups reflect our social status and position in society, whether it is playing golf at the country club or camping with family and friends. As people reach senior adulthood (65+), social connections increase in importance as the social group starts to decrease, and loneliness and isolation become more prevalent as our social networks diminish. Although social connections change throughout our lives, they always remain a significant part of our leisure lives.[31]

Introverts and extroverts view social interaction differently. It was found that people were happier when they were interacting with others.[32] However, this does not mean that introverts are unhappy or should force themselves to go to parties, hang out with large groups of people, or engage in other social activities. The difference in the two types of personalities is our tolerance for social stimulation. Extroverts need more social interaction, and introverts need less. Each need to get their own desired level to achieve happiness through social interactions.[33]

The social aspect of leisure is a significant motivator for many people. It may be a terrific opportunity to participate in activities with a friend or significant other or to participate in a setting to increase the possibility of meeting people for friendship or more.

Psychological Motivators

Often, recreational activities are seen as a means of providing excitement and challenge, as a means of relaxation and escape, as a way to relieve stress, or as a way to balance work and play. These are psychological motivators that contribute to our mental health.

People often seek adventure and challenge in their leisure activities.

© Dudarev Mikhail/Shutterstock.

Sense of Adventure, Excitement, and Challenge

A great deal of recreational involvement today is based on the need for excitement and challenge, particularly in such outdoor recreation activities as skiing, mountain climbing, or hang gliding, or in active, highly competitive individual or team sports. These activities are a part of adventure recreation, also called risk recreation. Adventure recreation is activity in the natural environment that has challenge, personal risk, uncertainty, and a reasonable chance for success.[34] People choose some of these leisure activities because they have an inherent risk associated with them. Participants thrive on the adrenaline rush, the challenges they are taking, and the thrill they get from completing the activity. As people participate in these types of activities, their perception of risk decreases and perception of skill increases.[35] In other words, people become less afraid while doing such things as backcountry backpacking or rock climbing, while they also feel their skills are increasing. Adventure recreation activities have also been shown to enhance psychological well-being for people.

In addition to outdoor recreation, there has been tremendous growth in adventure sports because of the need for adventure, excitement, and challenge. For example, the 2018 X Games had competition sites in Aspen, Minneapolis, Shanghai, and Norway. X Games include competitions in such sports as BMX, skateboarding, Moto X, snowboarding, and others.[36] For those who are less skilled but who still crave that rush from adventure recreation, tourism companies are capitalizing on this motivational aspect. Some companies specialize in whitewater rafting, sea kayaking, off-road vehicle trips, snowmobiling, and mountain trekking.

For many people, the urge for adventure, excitement, and challenge is met through spectatorship—by watching action-oriented movies or television shows—or in the form of video games based on high-speed chase or conflict. For others, ballooning, skydiving, parasailing, amateur stock car racing, or scuba diving satisfy risk-related motivations. Although varied forms of deviant social behavior, such as gang fighting, vandalism, or other types of juvenile crime, are not commonly considered as leisure pursuits, the reality is that they often are prompted by the same need for thrills, excitement, and challenge that other, more respectable recreation pursuits satisfy. This is discussed later in the chapter.

Stress Management

A closely related value of recreation is its usefulness in stress reduction. A leading authority on stress, Dr. Hans Selye, defines stress as the overall response of the body to any extreme demand made upon it, which might include threats, physical illness, job pressures, and environmental extremes—or even such life changes as marriage, divorce, vacations, or taking a new job. Increasing amounts of stress in modern life have resulted in many individuals suffering from pain, heart disease, sleep deprivation, excessive tiredness, and depression.

Once it was thought that the best approach to stress was rest and avoidance of all pressures, but today, there is an awareness that some degree of stress is desirable and healthy. Today, researchers point out that physical activity can play a significant role in stress reduction. Typically, people work off anger, frustration, and indignation by taking long walks or engaging in some kind of physical activity such as exercise. All of the body's systems—the working muscles, heart, hormones, metabolic reactions, and the responsiveness of the central nervous system—are strengthened through stimulation. Following periods of extended exertion, the body systems slow, bringing on a feeling of deep relaxation. Attaining this relaxed state is essential to lessening the stress reaction.

Relaxation and Escape

When you consider the positive side of leisure and why people choose the activities they do, often relaxation and escape are mentioned as key benefits to leisure. Escaping from work, home, or the everyday pressures of life can be done by taking a bike ride, going for a hike, or becoming absorbed in a creative activity through art or drama.

Relaxation allows people to forget the stresses they face. They can temporarily forget about upcoming deadlines, the need to find a job, or pressure to select a good graduate school. Choosing relaxing activities allows individuals to forget about these issues and become absorbed in the activity itself. Relaxation and escape can come from activities or doing nothing at all. Sitting in the backyard, lying on the beach, and taking a nap in the middle of the day are means for relaxation and escape resulting from use of leisure time. Relaxation experts often suggest deep breathing, meditation, exercise, sex, music, and yoga as ways to relax from stress.[37]

Healthy Balance of Work and Play

The role of work and leisure in our lives has changed dramatically from the thinking of the Greeks and Romans to whom leisure was the root of happiness and something enjoyed by those who did not have to work. Today, society sees leisure as something for all, and for most people,

CASE STUDY: Take Back Your Time

Take Back Your Time is a nonprofit that seeks to challenge the epidemic of overwork, overscheduling, and time famine in the United States and Canada that threatens individuals' health, relationships, communities, and the environment. The organization's goal is to help others better appreciate the value of leisure time—particularly through vacation time—and the costs of time stress in our lives and workplaces.

Although 9 out of 10 people report that their happiest memories are from vacation, 52% do not take all of their paid vacation time in a year. Although 71% of vacationers are satisfied at work and 46% are not, 27% report taking less vacation time than 5 years ago, 54% do not take vacation time—saving it in case of an emergency that would require time off—and 34% never take vacation with family. In fact, 23% of people who get vacation time reported taking no vacation time in the past 12 months. Unfortunately, 25% of Americans get no paid vacation time at all.

Through events such as the annual "Take back your time day" and the "Vacation Commitment Summit," Take Back Your Time works to share the benefits of vacation time, as well as other types of paid leave (e.g., paid parental leave, limits on compulsory overtime work) that allow for more balance in people's lives. According to a broad array of researchers, among other benefits, vacations can:

- Relieve stress
- Help prevent heart diseases
- Help maintain focus
- Help prevent illness
- Make you happier
- Strengthen relationships
- Make you more productive at work

Questions to Consider

- Should all employers be mandated to provide at least 1 week of paid leave to their full-time employees? What are reasons why they might not want to?
- Should employers actually make employees take all of their paid vacation time? Why or why not?

Data from Take Back Your Time. (n.d.). *Home page*. Retrieved January 22, 2021, from http://www.takebackyourtime.org

emotional well-being is greatly strengthened if they are able to maintain a healthy balance of work and recreation in their lives. Today, we recognize that there can be too much commitment to work, resulting in the exclusion of other interests and personal involvements that help to maintain mental health.

The emphasis on work and leisure is shifting in the United States. Much has been said in the news about the different generations and how the baby boomers (born in 1940–1964) are affecting our lives. The baby boomers are often today's upper management. They live to work and view themselves as having a strong work ethic. A strong work ethic is characterized by this group as working long hours and weekends to meet customer demands. This group likes recognition for a job well done and sees working long hours as a way of getting this reward. It was with the baby boomer group that the divorce rates and stress levels skyrocketed and the number of latchkey kids increased.[38]

The tendency to place excessive emphasis on work, at the expense of other avenues of expression, has been popularly termed workaholism. While not a trait of all baby boomers, for some people, work is an obsession, and they are unable to find other kinds of pleasurable release. For those who find their work a deep source of personal satisfaction and commitment, this may not be an altogether undesirable phenomenon.

The idea of workaholism will always be prevalent in society, but Generation X (born in 1965–1980) and the Millennial generation (born in 1981–1997) will most likely decrease this phenomenon. Many Generation Xers prefer a balance of work and play. They are today's middle and upper managers who were the latchkey kids coming home to find their parents still at work. They feel work productivity is important but not at the cost of what is most important to them—their leisure, family, and friends. Much of the Millennial generation works to live. They have a job so that they can make money to do the things they really want to do. They have been involved in a number of leisure activities their whole lives, from soccer to piano lessons, and they enjoy these things. This group sees the value of leisure and plans to take advantage of it rather than work excessive hours.[39] Only time will tell what attitudes Generation Z (born after 1997), raised with the Internet and social media, will ultimately bring to work and play as more enter the workforce. However, members of Generation Z appear to be more than willing to engage in business travel and enjoy the "bleisure" phenomena where a business trip is extended so the employee can enjoy leisure time in a destination.[40]

Leading authorities on business management and personnel practices now stress the need for business executives to find outside pleasures that open up, diversify, and enrich their lives. The guilt that successful people too often have about play must be assuaged, and they must be helped to realize that, with a more balanced style of life, they are likely to be more productive in the long run—and much happier in the present. Generation X and the Millennial generation already know this and are probably better than their older supervisors and coworkers at taking advantage of the services offered by recreation professionals.

Emotional Motivators

Emotional health is typified by positive self-esteem, a positive self-concept, ability to deal with stress, and a person's ability to control emotions and behaviors. Emotionally healthy people handle the daily stresses of life, build healthy relationships, and lead productive lives. Leisure is a major contributor to emotional well-being.

Leisure activity can provide strong feelings of pleasure and satisfaction and can serve as an outlet for discharging certain emotional drives that, if repressed, might produce emotional distress or even mental illness. The role of pleasure is increasingly recognized as a vital factor in emotional well-being. Some researchers have begun to analyze the simple concept of fun, defined as intense pleasure and enjoyment and an important dimension of social interactional leisure.

In leisure, people predominantly seek fun in their free time. Why do a leisure activity if it is not fun? Fun is the reason we play, enjoy the outdoors, and socialize with others. Associated with fun is laughter. There are a number of benefits of laughter, including binding people together, enhancing intimacy, providing stress relief, and because it simply feels good. Fun and laughter can enhance emotional well-being and can be experienced through such activities as going to a comedy show, trying a brand-new activity with friends, or having a game night with family.[41]

In addition to fun and laughter, self-actualization has been linked to emotional well-being. Self-actualization is a term that became popular in the 1970s chiefly through the writings of Abraham Maslow, who stressed the need for individuals to achieve their fullest degree of creative potential. Maslow developed a convincing theory of human motivation in which he identified a number of important human needs, arranging them in a hierarchy. As each of the basic needs is met in turn, a person is able to move ahead to meet more advanced needs and drives. Maslow's theory includes the following ascending levels of need:

- *Physiological needs:* Needed for human survival, physiological needs include food, rest, shelter, sleep, and other basic survival needs.

- *Safety needs:* Safety needs encompass self-protection needs such as health and well-being and physical safety from danger and threats.
- *Social needs:* Sometimes labeled as love/belonging, these needs include association with others, friendship, intimacy, and connection with family.
- *Esteem needs:* People have a need for self-esteem, confidence, recognition, achievement, attention, and the respect of and for others.
- *Self-actualization:* The highest level of the hierarchy is the need for being creative and for realizing one's maximum potential in a variety of life spheres, and the need for spontaneity.

The lower-level needs—physiological, safety, social, and esteem needs—are considered deficiency needs and come from a lack of something in our lives. Unless something in these three areas is missing, these needs are considered met and are rarely acknowledged. When they do not exist, people experience unpleasant feelings. The higher-level need, self-actualization, is a growth need and results in a drive to grow and develop as individuals, to master something and to reach our full potential.

Obviously, play and recreation can be important elements in satisfying at least the last three levels of need in Maslow's hierarchy. Much discussion has already been attributed to social needs. Esteem needs can be met from participating in team sports, enhancing fitness levels, or building skills in an activity such as skiing, soccer, or diving. Self-actualization can be realized in both work and leisure. In leisure, creativity can come from art, theater, or drama. Continued participation can continually build self-esteem to the point of self-actualization, or continued participation and drive can help people become self-actualized by reaching a self-imposed goal of completing a marathon or climbing Mount McKinley.

A discussion of the emotional and psychological implications of leisure must also include the work of Mihaly Csikszentmihalyi, who developed flow theory. Csikszentmihalyi posited that people are most happy and content when they reach a state of flow. Flow is a state of mind that occurs when the challenge and skill in an activity are in synch with each other.[42] In other words, the person has the skill to meet the challenges presented in participating in the activity. When these two are out of balance, a range of emotions occurs. For example, when there is a low skill and low challenge required, a person will experience apathy and boredom, whereas low skill and high challenge can result in worry and anxiety because the individual is anxious about his or her ability to meet the challenge ahead. Activities that

A group of backpackers seek to achieve social, ego, and self-actualization needs through a backpacking trip on the Appalachian Trail.

Courtesy of the Appalachian Trail Conservancy.

trigger flow in a person vary. It may be nighttime kayaking, creating an oil painting, or playing the guitar that leads a person to experience flow. Notice that flow encompasses several motivational issues already discussed, including intrinsic motivation. However, one of the major benefits is escape because of the total absorption in the activity itself.

Happiness and Well-Being

In general, people want to be happy. Happiness is "frequent positive affect, high life satisfaction, and infrequent negative affect."[43] Lyubomirsky and colleagues analyzed many studies on the subject and learned that happiness generates many positive rewards including obtaining a positive state of mind, higher marriage success rates, having more friends and social connections, superior work outcomes, increased mental health, more activity and energy, and experiencing flow more often. They also found that happiness is determined from three sources. First, 50% of happiness is established by our genetics and is set with little chance of changing it. Another 10% is established by the circumstances we find ourselves in. This could be the part of the world we live in, our personal demographics, life events that we experience, and circumstantial factors such as marital status, job, and income levels. The last piece of happiness, which makes up 40%, is determined by intentional activity. Based on this model, 40% of happiness is determined by the actions we purposefully do. Recreation can play a major role in these intentional activities. The activities in which we participate general are likely to contribute to happiness.

In addition to happiness, life satisfaction is also a motivator in leisure. Life satisfaction, or one's emotions and feelings about their directions and options in life, suggests a favorable attitude toward one's life. Jordan, Gagnon, Anderson, and Pilcher found that participation in leisure education can contribute to the life satisfaction of college students when they found an increase in both school and student life satisfaction as well as greater levels of self-esteem.[44]

This insight into happiness and well-being demonstrates that leisure plays a major role in people's ability to be happy and feel good emotionally. Because intentional activities influence 40% of individuals' happiness and happiness enhances well-being, choosing leisure activities that fit well for individuals is an important motivator.

Intellectual Outcomes

Of all the personal benefits of play and recreation, probably the least widely recognized are those involving intellectual or cognitive development. Play is typically considered physical activity rather than mental and has by definition been considered a nonserious form of involvement. How then could it contribute to intellectual growth? Researchers have come to realize that physical recreation tends to improve personal motivation and make mental and cognitive performance more effective. Numerous studies, for example, have documented the effects of specific types of physical exercise or play on the development of young children. Other research studies show a strong relationship between physical fitness and academic performance. Although a number of these studies focus on formal instructional programs, others use less structured experimental elements. Several studies show that playfulness as a personal quality is closely linked to creative and inventive thinking among children.

Children learn so much through play such as colors and shapes, how to build using blocks, and how to connect with other children and build social relationships. As they grow, they learn such things as how to follow rules, make up their own rules, build consensus, and solve problems.[45]

In the early age of games in North America, the sole purpose of playing was for intellectual stimulation. Although the focus has moved away from learning to a means of having fun, many games still have an intellectual aspect. For example, Monopoly was first developed so that people could begin to understand economic principles, and Snakes and Ladders (later renamed Chutes and Ladders) taught about morality and ethical behavior. Today, games also have been used to help children learn simple scientific, mathematical, and linguistic concepts. Games like Payday and Head Full of Numbers focus on math. Children and adults learn about geography from games such as Sequence—States & Capitals; logic and strategy from Clue, Sudoku, and Battleship; vocabulary from Scrabble and Boggle; and general knowledge from games such as Cranium or the vast array of Trivial Pursuit games on the market.

On another level, a reporter for *Forbes* magazine points out that business executives frequently enjoy high-level competitive play in games such as contract bridge, chess, or backgammon and that they value competence in these pastimes in the people they employ. Investment advisors in particular recognize the risk-taking elements involved in such games and the need for strategic flair in taking calculated risks. Whether the game is poker, gin rummy, bridge, backgammon, or chess, the skills involved are all equally important in business.[46]

Spiritual Values and Outcomes

A final area in which recreation and leisure make a vital contribution to the healthy growth and well-being of human beings is within the spiritual realm. The term spiritual is commonly taken to be synonymous with religion, but here it means a capacity for exhibiting humanity's higher nature—a sense of moral values, compassion, and respect for other humans and for the earth itself. It is linked to the development of one's inner feelings, a sense of order and purpose in life, and a commitment to care for others and to behave responsibly in all aspects of one's existence.

How does recreation contribute in this respect? Josef Pieper, in his 1963 book *Leisure: The Basis of Culture*, and others suggest that in their leisure hours, humans are able to express their fullest and best selves. Leisure can be a time for contemplation, for consideration of ultimate values, for disinterested activity. This means that people can come together simply as people, sharing interests and exploring pleasure, commitment, personal growth, beauty, nature, and other such aspects of life.

Outdoor recreation is often linked to the spiritual side of leisure. The peace and serenity of the outdoors allows people to escape and experience a sense of freedom. Jensen and Guthrie suggest that nature-based recreation is a spiritual source, and "spiritual sources can help people navigate through life . . . spirituality often represents a person's higher nature—moral values and a respect for humanity, the environment, and the earth itself."[47]

So far, this chapter has examined the important personal values of recreation and leisure involvement from three different perspectives: physical, social, and psychological. It is essential to recognize that these are not distinctly separate components of motivation but are instead closely interrelated from a holistic perspective. Furthermore, it must be understood that leisure means different things to different people. The motivators behind one-person bicycling may be completely different from what another gets out of it. The same is true for the outcomes from participation. The first individual may feel great after biking because of the exercise element, whereas the second person may not think about the exercise portion but the feeling of joy he or she gets from contributing to a healthy environment by biking to work rather than driving. Leisure motivators are as unique as the participants themselves.

Serious Leisure

Much of the discussion so far on leisure motivation focuses on the average person who enjoys leisure time for a multitude of reasons, from physical and social to intellectual and spiritual. A different perspective on leisure is serious leisure. Serious leisure is "the systematic pursuit of an amateur, hobbyist, or volunteer activity sufficiently substantial and interesting for the participant to find a career there in the acquisition and expression of a combination of its special skills, knowledge, and experience."[48] People who undertake a leisure activity to the point it extensively extends into their everyday lives could consider that activity to be serious leisure. On the other hand, most people participate in what is labeled as casual leisure. Casual leisure is an "immediately, intrinsically rewarding, relatively short-lived pleasurable activity requiring little or no special training to enjoy it."[49] The difference for most between casual and serious leisure is time, money, and effort dedicated to the activity. For example, a musician who plays with friends a couple of times a month in someone's garage would be a casual participant. If that same person practiced every night, arranged for gigs every weekend, and invested many hours in music each week, that could be considered serious leisure.

Serious leisure has six defining qualities:

- *Perseverance:* Serious leisure is defined by the need to persistently persevere through adverse conditions over time. This may mean a runner must work through pain, fatigue, or poor weather conditions. A performer must deal with stage fright or embarrassment. People are willing to overcome what some would see as negative situations because of the positive feelings they ultimately get from the activity.
- *Leisure career:* Although the individual is most likely not paid for participation, serious leisure emulates a career in that it has stages of achievement. Individuals exhibit a career-like commitment to the leisure activity, where they work to improve and achieve set goals.
- *Significant effort:* Serious leisure is characterized by people developing special knowledge, skills, or abilities. This requires considerable effort that is beyond the ordinary skill development of casual leisure.
- *Durable outcomes:* Serious leisure pursuits are steeped in outcomes including enrichment, self-actualization, self-expression, enhanced self-image, self-gratification, recreation, and sometimes financial returns. Although these attributes can be found in casual leisure, it is the depth that distinguishes serious leisure. These activities may not be fun at times, but the skills people are developing are used and these durable outcomes emerge and make the activity more positive for the individual.
- *Unique ethos:* A unique ethos is a subculture among those who participate in serious leisure. These people share similar ideals, values, norms, and beliefs that pertain to the activity. Social relationships and networks emerge that focus on the leisure pursuit.
- *Identification with the pursuit:* The individual strongly identifies with the leisure activity. These people talk excitedly about their activity, are proud of the activity, and are quite committed to it.[50]

Given these six distinguishable characteristics, you can see that the commitment and motivation for serious leisure are far more intense than for casual leisure.

Deviant Leisure

So far, this chapter has examined leisure motivation from the physical, social, psychological, and emotional perspectives. All of these motives have been positive, yet there is a negative side of leisure that requires some discussion. Russell suggests that leisure is not always done for the person's well-being, and these types of activities are considered deviant leisure, also referred to as taboo leisure.[51] Deviant leisure is leisure behavior that is restricted by law or society's norms or in some cases may be entirely legal but have harmful impacts that might not be initially evident. Because societal norms are subjective and change from group to group and culture to culture, it is difficult to decide what falls under deviant leisure and what are simply fringe activities. For example, some sects of the Catholic Church and some Scottish politicians have claimed that the Hokey Pokey was written to mock the actions and language of priests leading the Latin mass.[52] Other religious groups denounce dancing as evil.

According to Stebbins, deviant leisure can fall into the categories of casual or serious deviant leisure. Casual deviant leisure is rooted in sensory simulation and the desires it invokes with examples including heavy drinking and betting money on games of chance. Although a casual participant needs a basic level of knowledge to engage in these activities (e.g., where to buy illicit alcohol), they need a much greater knowledge base for serious deviant leisure such as knowing conventions of behavior at a nudist park or the rules of skilled, face-to-face gambling.[53] For some, deviant leisure is identified by different types of harmful outcomes attached to the activities. For instance, environmental harms associated with strains from tourism in underdeveloped countries or islands or carbon emissions from airline flights might be considered deviant leisure because of the larger impact of the activities.[54]

Most deviant leisure is typically viewed as tolerable and thus there is no serious attempt for society to control it. However, there is a smaller list of activities that some may deem as personal leisure but that society would agree are intolerable and thus are governed by the legal system including activities such as vandalism and sexual assault.[55] Because of the disagreement on a clear delineation of what constitutes deviant leisure, three common "tolerable" pursuits are discussed as examples.

Sexual Activity

Sexual activity by some can be classified as deviant leisure. Engaging in recreational sexual activity with a casual acquaintance, one-night stands, having "friends with benefits," or engaging in sexual activity outside of a marriage may be deemed inappropriate by some in society. In fact, the phrase "Netflix and chill" has become slang not for enjoying a streaming video at home but for casual sexual encounters. Deviant sex can also encompass such things as viewing pornography, visiting sex clubs, or engaging in swinging or partner swapping. Although these recreational activities are not illegal, some sectors of society may view them as negative recreational activities. These judgments are often driven more by religious-based moral ideologies than legal ones although questions regarding harm to others often enter the discussion about whether activities such as pornography should be classified as deviant. Like other activities that will be discussed, sex is one that is classified as positive or negative based on the beliefs of the individual.

Motivation for these sexual activities is as varied as those engaging in them. Deviant sexual activity can be motivated by pleasure, social status, revenge, or power.[56]

Gambling

Gambling is wagering money or something of value on a preselected outcome. Examples of gambling include betting on horse races, buying lottery tickets, and entering a National Collegiate Athletic Association (NCAA) Final Four Tournament pool. Gambling has a storied past and actually began during colonial times when lotteries were implemented to generate revenues. Lotteries were also used to fund some of the most prestigious universities in the United States, including Harvard, Yale, and Princeton, and today are often used to support scholarship funds for university students such as the South Carolina Education Lottery. It did not take long for gambling to become illegal and an underground activity. Gambling made a resurgence during the Great Depression because it was seen as a way to stimulate the economy.[57] Also at this time, Nevada legalized most forms of gambling. In these early years, gambling was infiltrated with organized crime. In the 1950s, the federal government cleaned up gambling and organized crime got out of the business. The variety of opportunities to gamble has increased across the United States. What started out as a few casinos has expanded to include pari-mutuel betting, Internet gambling, and riverboat casinos. In addition, because land owned by Native American tribes have tribal sovereignty, the federal government cannot forbid gambling there and thus many have profited from the development of casinos, bingo halls, and other gambling operations.[58]

Because the focus of this chapter is not on gambling, per se, but motivation, the question arises as to why people gamble. Research shows a wide variety of reasons including fun, risk, excitement, challenge, adrenaline rush, and relaxation—all motivators that were previously discussed. If it stops at this, there would be no reason to discuss gambling separately from any other activity. However, gambling is deviant when it becomes a problem. Gamblers Anonymous defines someone with a gambling addiction as a compulsive gambler. Compulsive gambling is an illness that progressively worsens, can never be cured, but that can be stopped. The motivation to gamble at this point in a person's life is where it becomes deviant leisure.

Substance Abuse

Substance abuse is a pattern of using substances that alter mood and behavior beyond what they were originally intended. These substances include such things as legal and illegal drugs, inhalants, solvents, and alcohol.

For those using illegal drugs, binge drinking, or consuming alcohol underage, the deviant leisure label fits this behavior. Social drinking, on the other hand, is not considered deviant leisure until it becomes a problem. Just like sex and gambling, alcohol and drug use have signs that indicate when this activity becomes problematic. Also, like sexual activity and gambling, there are motives for engaging in this activity. It could be for escape, relaxation, to fit in with a group, to socialize, to take risks, or to be more outgoing.

Social drinking is a major subculture in North America and not considered deviant leisure by most. A few examples are as follows:

- Young adults go to clubs and drink socially around their friends and to meet people.

GAMBLING STATISTICS

- The largest percentage of visitors to Las Vegas were in the age group of 65 and older (22%).
- Forty-eight states have some form of legal gambling. Only Hawaii and Utah do not.
- Gambling generates more revenue than movies, spectator sports, theme parks, cruise ships, and recorded music combined.
- Gambling has become a $40 billion dollar a year industry in the United States.
- Eighty million Americans visit casinos annually.

Data from Iowa PBS. (n.d.). *Gambling facts & stats*. Retrieved January 22, 2021, from https://www.pbs.org/wgbh/pages/frontline/shows/gamble/etc/facts.html.

CASE STUDY: Nude Recreation . . . Is It Deviant?

The American Association for Nude Recreation (AANR) serves over 213,000 individuals who feel life is enhanced "by the naturalness of social nudity." Nudists feel that they are comfortable in their own skin and see the human body as a vessel that carries it through life.[a]

AANR focuses on protecting places for nude recreation to happen, including sanctioned nude beaches, public lands set aside for nude recreation, resorts, and campgrounds, among others. Nude recreation is legal in these designated areas.[a]

The AANR stresses that nude recreation is about the family and is not considered an "adults only" activity. They promote body acceptance regardless of age or other factors and strongly oppose sexual exploitation of any kind.[a]

Traditionally thought of as an activity for older generations, nude recreation organizations have recently emerged that target 18- to 35-year-olds. The Florida Young Naturists have emerged to bring together a younger generation of adults interested in nude recreation. Both groups plan gatherings, trips, and other adventures to enjoy a clothes-free experience.[b]

Questions to Consider

- Is nude recreation considered deviant leisure? Why or why not?
- Should children be allowed to participate in nude recreation with their parents and other adults?
- A local nude recreation organization wants to rent out the indoor pool at the recreation center after hours. What are the pros and cons of allowing this?
- Should public land be designated specifically as clothing optional? Why or why not?
- A hotel several blocks from a popular Florida beach is declaring bankruptcy. The AANR wants to buy it and convert it to a clothing-optional resort. What are the pros and cons of doing this?
- The Florida Young Naturists are coming to your campus to promote their upcoming spring break trip. How would this be received on campus by the students? Would students be more accepting because it is a group targeting 18- to 35-year-olds rather than the general population?

[a]American Association for Nude Recreation: www.aanr.com/
[b]Florida Young Naturists: www.floridayoungnaturists.com/

- Wine tasting and beer making are leisure activities and social events.
- Tourism capitalizes on trips to wineries.
- Beermakers and restaurants are partnering to present beer and dinner events.
- Wine glass making is an art form.

Although each year more states pass laws allowing for recreational marijuana use (as of January 2021 the number stood at 15 plus the District of Columbia), it is too early to determine if this form of substance use will follow the trends of alcohol use.[59] There are far more examples of potentially deviant leisure pursuits that could be discussed here. For example, viewing pornography, adult entertainment and erotica, vandalism, dog fighting, or excessive Internet use can be deemed deviant by some portions of our society. To many people some sexual activities, gambling, the use of legal drugs and limited use of alcohol are no different than any other leisure activity. For those who see these activities as morally wrong or abuse any of them, the deviant leisure label emerges. Regardless of whether an individual sees these activities as acceptable and at what level they are acceptable, the motivation to participate varies for each person but focuses strongly on the social and psychological motivations for leisure.

SUMMARY

Beyond the familiar motivations of seeking fun, pleasure, or relaxation, people engage in leisure pursuits for a host of different reasons. Recreational motivations include personal goals such as the need for companionship, escape from stress or the boredom of daily routines, and the search for challenge.

The outcomes of recreational involvement may be classified under four major headings: physical, social, psychological, and emotional.

Physical motivators have never been as important as they are in today's society. The obesity rates of both children and adults continue to grow. Recreational activities help people control weight, fight against obesity, and improve cardiovascular health. The social motivation for leisure results in reduced loneliness, strengthens relationships, and promotes social bonding. The psychological motivations for leisure are quite extensive. People seek adventure, relaxation, escape, stress reduction, and overall well-being and happiness. The emotional motivators involve fun, happiness, intellectual outcomes, and spiritual values. Leisure can bring all of these rewards to a person.

Serious leisure requires a person to be highly motivated to participate in their chosen activity. Those engaged in serious leisure have their leisure activities consume a major part of their lives and are quite committed to participation.

Although all of these motives are viewed as having positive outcomes, there is a part of leisure that not everyone sees as positive. Deviant leisure, or leisure that is seen as negative based on societal standards, can include such activities as some sexual activities, gambling, illegal drug use, and excessive use of alcohol. Society's views vary and some see any involvement in these activities as deviant whereas others base judgment on the frequency and extent to which participation occurs.

This chapter focused on why people choose the activities that they do and what outcomes they receive from participation. These motives are subjective and vary from person to person. No one activity provides the same outcomes for everyone. Because of this, people must assess their own needs and choose activities that meet these needs.

QUESTIONS FOR CLASS DISCUSSION OR ESSAY EXAMINATION

1. Define obesity. Give an overview of childhood and adult obesity. What is the role of parks and recreation in the fight against obesity? What things in society contribute to the obesity epidemic?

   _____

   _____

   _____

2. The chapter describes some of the specific contributions of recreation to emotional or mental health. What are they? On the basis of your own experience, can you describe some of the positive emotional outcomes resulting from recreational involvement?

   _____

   _____

   _____

3. Recreation centers are increasingly adding fitness equipment designed for children. This equipment includes such tools as smaller treadmills and stationary bicycles. Do you think this is a good use of money and will stimulate physical activity in children? Why or why not? What other activities could recreation centers implement to help fight childhood obesity? What role do parents play in this problem?

   _____

   _____

   _____

4. Define deviant leisure. What motives do people have for participating in these types of activities? Give examples of other deviant activities that were not discussed in this text.

_____

_____

_____

5. A number of psychological motivators were discussed. What are they? How do they relate to your choices for leisure activities?

_____

_____

_____

6. Think of an activity that you could see yourself engaging in to the point of it being serious leisure. Describe your participation level and what would make that activity serious leisure.

_____

_____

_____

7. Select your five favorite recreational activities and then answer the following question: Why do you participate in these activities (motives)? Predict how this list will change in the next 10, 20, 30, and 50 years.

_____

_____

_____

ENDNOTES

1. Kraus, R. (1971). *Recreation and leisure in modern society*. New York: Appleton-Century-Crofts.
2. Stone, D., Deci, E. L., & Ryan, R. M. (2009). Beyond talk: Creating autonomous motivation through self-determination theory." *Journal of General Management*, 34, 75–91.
3. Ryan, R. M., & Deci, E. L. (2000). Self-determination theory and the facilitation of intrinsic motivation, social development, and well-being. *American Psychologist*, 55(1), 68–78.
4. Ibid., p. 70.
5. National Heart, Lung, and Blood Institute. (n.d.). *Assessing your weight and health risk*. Retrieved April 13, 2020, from https://www.nhlbi.nih.gov/health/educational/lose_wt/risk.htm.
6. Centers for Disease Control and Prevention. (2021). *Obesity and overweight*. Retrieved September 9, 2019, from https://www.cdc.gov/nchs/fastats/obesity-overweight.htm.
7. Vogel, L. (2017). Overweight or overfat? Many Canadians are both. *Canadian Medical Association Journal*, 189(37). doi: 10.1503/cmaj.109-5472.
8. Hales, C. M., Carroll, M. D., Fryar, C. D., & Ogden, C. L. (2017). *Prevalence of obesity among adults and youth: United States, 2015–2016*. NCHS Data Brief No. 288. Hyattsville, MD: National Center for Health Statistics. Retrieved April 12, 2020, from https://www.cdc.gov/nchs/data/databriefs/db288.pdf.
9. Centers for Disease Control and Prevention. (2020). *Prevalence of self-reported obesity among U.S. adults by state and territory, BRFSS, 2017–2019*. Retrieved April 12, 2020, from https://www.cdc.gov/obesity/data/prevalence-maps.html#hispanic-adults.
10. Centers for Disease Control and Prevention. (2018). *Participation in leisure-time aerobic and muscle-strengthening activities that meet the federal 2008 Physical Activity Guidelines for Americans among adults aged 18 and over, by selected characteristics: United States, selected years 1998–2017*. Retrieved April 12, 2020, from https://www.cdc.gov/nchs/data/hus/2018/025.pdf.
11. National Health Information Survey. (2019). *Percentage of adults aged 18 and over who met 2008 federal physical activity guidelines for aerobic activity through leisure-time aerobic activity: United States, 2006–2018*. Retrieved April 13, 2020, from https://public.tableau.com/profile/tina.norris#!/vizhome/FIGURE7_1/Dashboard7_1.

12. National Health Information Survey. (2019). *Percentage of adults aged 18 and over who met 2008 federal physical activity guidelines for both aerobic and muscle-strengthening activities through leisure-time aerobic and muscle-strengthening activities: United States, 2018.* Retrieved April 12, 2020, from https://public.tableau.com/profile/nhis#!/vizhome/FIGURE7_5/Dashboard7_5.

13. Ibid., p. 11.

14. Ibid., p. 11.

15. Ibid., p. 11.

16. Ibid., p. 12.

17. Ibid., p. 10.

18. Office of Disease Prevention and Health Promotion. (n.d.). *Development of the National Health Promotion and Disease Prevention Objectives for 2030.* Retrieved April 12, 2020, from https://www.healthypeople.gov/2020/About-Healthy-People/Development-Healthy-People-2030.

19. American Heart Association. (2019). *Nearly half of all Americans have cardiovascular disease.* Retrieved April 12, 2020, from https://www.sciencedaily.com/releases/2019/01/190131084238.htm.

20. U.S. Department of Health and Human Services. (2018). *Physical activity guidelines for Americans* (2nd ed.). Washington, DC: U.S. Department of Health and Human Services. Retrieved April 12, 2020, from https://health.gov/paguidelines/second-edition/pdf/Physical_Activity_Guidelines_2nd_edition.pdf.

21. Ibid., p. 19.

22. Son, J. S., Kerstetter, D. L., & Mowen, A. J. (2009). Illuminating identity and health in the constraint negotiation of leisure-time physical activity in mid to late life. *Journal of Park and Recreation Administration, 27*(3), 96–115.

23. Ibid.

24. Wilhelm Stanis, S. A., Schneider, I. E., Chavez, D. J., & Shinew, K. J. (2009). Visitor constraints to physical activity in parks and recreation areas: Differences by race and ethnicity. *Journal of Park and Recreation Administration, 27*(3), 78–95.

25. Salmon, J., Owen, N., Crawford, D., Bauman, A., & Sallis, J. F. (2003). Physical activity and sedentary behavior: A population-based study of barriers, enjoyment, and preference. *Health Psychology, 22*(2), 178–188.

26. Ibid.

27. Wardle, J., Guthrie, C., Sanderson, S., Birch, L., & Plomin, R. (2001). Food and activity preferences in children of lean and obese parents. *International Journal of Obesity and Related Metabolic Disorders, 25*, 971–977.

28. Trejos, N. (2012, October 10). Hotels make it easier to stay fit on the road. *USA Today*, Retrieved January 15, 2021, from https://www.usatoday.com/story/travel/hotels/2012/10/10/hotel-gyms-workouts/1622289/.

29. Scott, E. (2020, January 8). *17 highly effective stress relievers.* Retrieved January 15, 2021, from http://stress.about.com/od/generaltechniques/tp/toptensionacts.htm.

30. Russell, R. (2009). *Pastimes: The context of contemporary leisure* (4th ed.). Champaign, IL: Sagamore Publishing.

31. Jordan, D. J. (2007). *Leadership in leisure services: Making a difference* (3rd ed.). State College, PA: Venture Publishing.

32. Fleeson, W., Malanos, A. B., & Achille, N. M. (2002). An intra-individual process approach to the relationship between extraversion and positive affect: Is acting extraverted as "good" as being extraverted? *Journal of Personality and Social Psychology, 83*(6), 1409–1422.

33. Cain, S. (n.d.). *When does socializing make you happier?* Retrieved January 15, 2021, from http://www.quietrev.com/when-does-socializing-make-you-happier/.

34. Jensen, C. R., & Guthrie, S. P. (2006). *Outdoor recreation in America.* Champaign, IL: Human Kinetics.

35. Priest, S., & Carpenter, G. (1993). Changes in perceived risk and competence during adventurous leisure experiences. *Journal of Applied Recreation Research, 18*(1), 51–71.

36. ESPN X Games. (2020, April 14). Retrieved January 22, 2021, from http://xgames.com.

37. WebMD. (2017, May 24). *Stress management: Ways to relieve stress.* Retrieved January 15, 2021, from https://www.webmd.com/balance/stress-management/stress-management-relieving-stress.

38. Raines, C. (2003). *Connecting generations.* Menlo, CA: Crisp Publications.

39. Ibid.

40. Whitmore, G. (2019, September 23). How Generation Z is changing travel for older generations. *Forbes.* Retrieved April 14, 2020, from https://www.forbes.com/sites/geoffwhitmore/2019/09/13/how-generation-z-is-changing-travel-for-older-generations/#7de98b6278f7.

41. Helpguide.org. (2020). *"Laughter is the best medicine: The health benefits of humor and laughter.* Retrieved January 15, 2021, from https://www.helpguide.org/articles/mental-health/laughter-is-the-best-medicine.htm.

42. Csikszentmihalyi, M. (1997). *Finding flow: The psychology of engagement with everyday life.* New York: Basic Books.

43. Lyubomirsky, S., Sheldon, K. M., Schkade, D. (2005). Pursuing happiness: The architecture of sustainable change. *Review of General Psychology, 9,* 111–131.

44. Jordan, K. A., Gagnon, R. J., Anderson, D. M., & Pilcher, J. J. (2018). Enhancing the college student experience: Outcomes of a leisure education program. *Journal of Experiential Education, 41*(1), 90–106.

45. Elkind, D. (2008, June 9). Cognitive and emotional development through play. *Greater Good Magazine.* Retrieved from January 15, 2021, from https://www.sharpbrains.com/blog/2008/06/09/cognitive-and-emotional-development-through-play/.

46. Hurd, A. (2004). Board games. In G. Cross (Ed.), *Encyclopedia of recreation and leisure in America.* New York: Charles Scribner's Sons.

47. Jensen, C. R., & Guthrie, S. P. (2006). *Outdoor recreation in America* (6th ed., p. 41). Champaign, IL: Human Kinetics.

48. Stebbins, R. A. (1992). *Amateurs, professionals, and serious leisure.* Montreal: McGill-Queen's University Press.

49. Stebbins, R. A. (1997). Casual leisure: A conceptual statement. *Leisure Studies, 16,* 17–25.

50. Gould, J., Moore, D., McGuire, F., & Stebbins, R. (2008). Development of the Serious Leisure Inventory and Measure. *Journal of Leisure Research, 40*(1), 47–69.

51. Russell, R. V. (2013). *Pastimes: The context of contemporary leisure* (5th ed., p. 165). Champaign, IL: Sagamore Publishing.

52. Cramb, A. (2008, December 21). Doing the hokey cokey "could be hate crime." *The Telegraph.* Retrieved January 15, 2021, from https://www.telegraph.co.uk/news/newstopics/howaboutthat/3883838/Doing-the-Hokey-Cokey-could-be-hate-crime.html.

53. Stebbins, R. A. (2019). Consumptive and non-consumptive leisure and its fit with deviance. In T. Raymen and O. Smith (Eds.), *Deviant leisure: Criminological perspectives on leisure and harm* (pp. 17–44). Cham, Switzerland: Springer Nature.

54. Raymen, T., & Smith, O. (2019). The deviant leisure perspective: A theoretical introduction. In T. Raymen and O. Smith (Eds.), *Deviant leisure: Criminological perspectives on leisure and harm* (pp. 17–44). Cham, Switzerland: Springer Nature.

55. Ibid.

56. Kashdan, T.B. (2016, January 22). *The 13 reasons we have sex.* Psychology Today. Retrieved February 8, 2021 from https://www.psychologytoday.com/us/blog/curious/201601/the-13-reasons-we-have-sex

57. *History of gambling in the United States.* Retrieved from February 8, 2021 from http://www.worldcasinodirectory.com/united-states/history.

58. National Indian Gaming Commission. (n.d.). *Indian Gaming Regulatory Act.* Retrieved April 14, 2020, from https://www.nigc.gov/general-counsel/indian-gaming-regulatory-act.

59. DISA. (2020, November 4). *Map of marijuana legality by state.* Retrieved October 21, 2020, from https://disa.com/map-of-marijuana-legality-by-state.

Chapter 3

Sociocultural Factors Affecting Leisure Experiences

One of the most familiar guides in the professional literature in recreation service has been the dictum that all community residents should be provided with equal opportunity for participation in recreation (p. 290; original emphasis).[1]
-From the first edition of Kraus' Recreation and Leisure in Modern Society, published in 1971

LEARNING OBJECTIVES

1. Describe how the age of participants can affect leisure experiences.

2. Explain gender identity differences in the experience of leisure.

3. Describe how sexual orientation can affect leisure experiences.

4. Explain race and ethnicity factors influencing leisure.

5. Describe differences in leisure participation among socioeconomic statuses.

6. Identify how leisure-services agencies and professionals can better serve and meet the needs of all members of their diverse communities.

Introduction

Many sociocultural factors affect personal leisure values and involvement today including age, gender identity, sexual orientation, racial and ethnic identity, and socioeconomic status.

It is easy to see the major changes that children experience as they grow. The same thing holds true for adults. Albeit, we change at a much slower pace, but differences exist based on age. Our leisure preferences evolve. We try new activities. Some of them remain activities for a lifetime and others stay with us until we reach a certain point in our lives. Interests may influence these changes as well as physical abilities, family status, education, or work, among others.

Progress in this field has been striking with respect to expanded recreational opportunities for girls and women in sport and outdoor recreation. Although the chief concern has been about females and leisure, the role of boys and men in contemporary leisure has also been an issue. Further, leisure-services professionals must expand their abilities to serve gender identities beyond male and female; people who identify as transgender, for example, experience a variety of constraints and opportunities in their play, recreation, and leisure.

Sexual orientation affects leisure pursuits in a number of ways. Focus is changing from ignoring or marginalizing those who don't identify as straight to seeing them as a viable market as the numbers of identified lesbian, gay, and bisexual people become more visible.

Racial and ethnic identity also has limited many individuals from full participation in organized recreation in the past and continues to influence the leisure involvement of black, Indigenous, and people of color (BIPOC). With continuing waves of immigration from other parts of the world, religion linked to ethnic identity will pose new policy questions as Muslims, as well as other people who are neither Christian nor Jewish, continue to shape the national landscape.

Socioeconomic status shapes leisure participation as well as where people participate in leisure activities. Those who are from lower socioeconomic status (SES) backgrounds have fewer opportunities and get most of their services from the nonprofit and public sector, whereas those from higher SES backgrounds experience relatively unlimited access to services and use commercial services almost exclusively.

All of these interactions between one's various identities and their opportunities, constraints, and access to leisure have important implications for leisure-services professionals if they are going to equitably serve an increasingly diverse clientele.

Constraints to Leisure

To help us better understand the impact of sociocultural factors on people's play, recreation, and leisure, let's first explore the concept of constraints.

It is evident that people experience issues that affect their leisure participation. These issues have been labeled as constraints to leisure. An entire body of research examines these constraints and their impact. Constraints to leisure occur when an individual is unable to participate in a leisure activity, is unable to participate as much as the individual would like, or when the quality of the experience is diminished for some reason. Constraints are categorized as interpersonal, intrapersonal, and structural.

Intrapersonal constraints are factors that affect an individual's preference for, or interest in, an activity. For example, a person may not feel skilled at an activity and, as a result, will choose not to participate. Another example is having feelings of self-consciousness. For example, people sometimes feel self-conscious about their bodies. If this self-consciousness leads to a person not joining a gym, they are experiencing an intrapersonal constraint. Likewise, if a person has interest in an activity but doesn't feel that activity is for them, they will most likely avoid that activity because they see it as an activity for someone else, despite their interest in the activity. For example, boys in the United States who have an interest in ballet may feel a constraint to participating because it is not seen as an activity for boys.

Interpersonal constraints are associated with the individual's relationship with others. The constraint occurs because of this relationship with friends, family, or even coworkers. An example of an interpersonal constraint would be not having another person to participate with or participating in an activity because of the desires of others rather than an actual desire to do so. If a person goes along with friends to see a baseball game but really has no interest in the game, this is considered an interpersonal constraint.

Finally, *structural constraints* are factors that intervene between the desire to participate and actual participation in an activity. The most common structural constraint is a lack of time. Other examples include lack of transportation, money, or access to safe facilities.

As we discuss the sociocultural factors that affect play, recreation, and leisure, we consider all of these constraints and how different people experience them.

Age Factors Influencing Play, Recreation, and Leisure

For many years, scholars have analyzed the influence of one's age on values, motivators, and patterns of participation in play, recreation, and leisure. There are key periods of the life span as well as growth processes and development tasks to be accomplished at each stage. People develop physically, socially, and cognitively throughout their lives, and play, recreation, and leisure activities must reflect these changes and be age appropriate.[2]

Apart from differences in individual personalities within each age group, there is also the reality that developments in modern technology, economic and social trends, and shifts in family relationships have been responsible for major changes in age-related norms of human behavior. For example, children today are exposed to the realities of life and mature physically at a much earlier point than in the past. At the same time, paradoxically, they have a longer period of adolescence and schooling before entering the adult workforce. Adults now tend to marry later and have fewer children, and many adults are choosing not to marry at all. Older people have a much longer period of retirement, and a significantly greater number of older persons live more active and adventurous leisure lives today than in the past.

To fully understand these interactions between individual age development, societal trends, and leisure experiences and services, it is helpful to examine each major age group in turn, including children, adolescents, young adults, middle adults, and older adults. We will explore each age group with a focus on the particular opportunities and challenges presented to that age group as they pursue play, recreation, and leisure amid current societal norms.

Play, Recreation, and Leisure in the Lives of Children

Childhood is the age group that includes youth from early infancy through the preteen years. Throughout this period, play satisfies important developmental needs in children—often helping to establish values and behavior patterns that will continue throughout a lifetime. Psychologists have examined the role of play at each stage of life, beginning with infancy and moving through the preschool period, middle and late childhood, and adolescence.

Children typically move through several stages: (1) solitary play, carried on without others nearby; (2) parallel play, in which children play side by side without meaningful interplay; (3) associative play, in which children share a common game or group enterprise but concentrate on their own individual efforts rather than group activity; and (4) cooperative play, beginning at about age 3, in which children actually join together in games, informal dramatics, or constructive projects. By the age of 6 or 7, children tend to be involved in loosely organized play groups, leading to much more tightly structured and organized groups between 8 and 12.[3]

Play contributes to children's physical, social, and cognitive development in a variety of ways, such as the following:

- Physical growth through play contributes to fine and gross motor development; body awareness; and physical growth, such as building or maintaining energy and increasing joint flexibility and muscular strength.
- Social skills are developed through interacting with other children and adults, including language, personal awareness, emotional well-being, and negotiation skills.
- Cognitive development in children improves creativity, problem solving and decision making, the ability to engage successfully in new situations, and learning ability. When young children use their imaginations in play, they are more creative, perform better at school tasks, and develop a problem-solving approach to learning.[4,5]

Although these developmental benefits of play for children are well documented, they are complicated by a number of societal realities contemporary children face today.

CHANGE OF THE FAMILY STRUCTURE

For decades, the definition of a "typical family structure," with two parents or guardians raising their children together, has been changing. For example, the proportion of U.S. children living in single-parent households has been increasing, with 23% of children under the age of 18 living with only one parent. This figure means that the United States has the highest rate of children living in single-parent households out of 130 countries.[6] Of unmarried parents, 53% are solo mothers, 12% are solo fathers, and 35% are cohabiting with a partner.[7] About 4% of children under 18 years old are living in households without either of their parents.[8] In 2019, of coupled households with children, 41% were married opposite-sex couples, 22% were married same sex couples, 38% were unmarried opposite sex couples, and 14% were unmarried same sex couples.[9] Among families with children and married parents, 64.2% of families have both parents working, and 97.5% have at least one parent working.[10] These realities of family structure in the United States mean that families are ever more in need of responsive leisure services that fit their family situation, including such things as after-school and before-school programming, child and grandchild activities, and mentoring programs for children with single parents.

Children develop physically, emotionally, and socially through play and recreation.

© Fuse/Thinkstock/Getty.

OVERSCHEDULED CHILDREN

The overscheduling of children is becoming a problem in today's culture. For example, there are increasing opportunities for youth to participate in sport clinics, camps, and leagues for children as young as age 4. Many go on to be a part of traveling sport teams that go to different communities on the weekends to play in tournaments. Parents and guardians feel if they do not start their children in sports this young, they will be left behind. Couple this with the demands of household responsibilities, school assignments, and any number of other recreation activities, classes, and clubs and the result is dwindling unstructured time for today's youth.

Although art and music lessons as well as sport and other educational activities may be beneficial to the child, there comes a point when the child has too many things going on in their life. Such overscheduling can result in damage to a children's self-esteem because they see that their parents are always trying to push them to do more, which can send a message that they are not good enough the way they are. This overscheduling can add unnecessary stress to a child's life and quite possibly lead to escalated incidences of depression, anxiety, and a lack of creativity and problem-solving skills. Experts on overscheduled children suggest a need for a balance between athletics, academics, and character-building activities. Athletics and academic achievement cannot be thrust upon children to the point they worry about not measuring up to adult expectations. These activities should be fun and meaningful. Free time with family and time to just do nothing builds character, reduces stress, and shows children they are loved.[11]

INTENSIVE PARENTING

Each generation seems to increase its role of parenting and obsession with protecting its children. The terms "helicopter parenting" and "snowplow parenting" are becoming more common in our language, and fall under the umbrella of intensive parenting. Helicopter parents are very involved in their child's education, experiences, and issues. They have a tendency to hover and are never far away from their children. Helicopter parents try to solve problems for their children, and, as a result, the children become reliant on their parents to do this for them. The snowplow parents are ones who plow right through any obstacles that stand in their child's way. Intensive parents are raising children to believe they have few faults and will always be successful. These same parents are the first to confront a teacher or coach about unfair treatment of their child. In shielding children from failure, these intensive parents are also inhibiting their children's abilities to learn how to solve problems and cope with frustration.

Intensive parenting hinders children's ability to make decisions for themselves—and not just young children but also young adults. The impacts and practices of intensive parenting linger into young adulthood, with college students feeling overwhelmed by independence and parents continuing to clear the way at college and work.[12] Interestingly, though extreme forms of intensive parenting such as the behaviors reported in the 2019 college admissions scandal remain most prevalent amongst families from high socioeconomic backgrounds, the more everyday forms of intensive parenting are supported by parents from all socioeconomic

---

INTENSIVE PARENTING BEYOND HIGH SCHOOL GRADUATION

When people hear the terms "helicopter parents" or "intensive parenting," they tend to think only of parents and guardians of youth in grades K-12. But college campuses are increasingly experiencing intensive parenting habits by parents and guardians of their enrolled college students. Below, you'll see some of the behaviors colleges are experiencing from parents and guardians. Do any of these behaviors sound familiar to you?

- Remaining in near constant communication via phone, email, or text message
- Contacting their student's professor or advisor to discuss an assignment or course grade
- Asking their student to put them on speaker phone while the student meets with their academic advisor
- Using their student's log in information to check the student's university email, learning management system, or to register the student for their classes
- Contacting college deans or presidents in regards to concerns they have, without the student knowing
- Calling their student to remind them to go to class
- Tracking their student's due dates and reminding their student of upcoming deadlines

Questions for Discussion

- Did any of the above behaviors sound familiar to you? Do you think you have parents or guardians who practice intensive parenting some or a lot of the time? If so, what do you think about that?
- How do you view intensive parents and their relationship with their child?
- At what age do you consider yourself an adult and not need/want this level of help from parents?

backgrounds.[13] Although intensive parenting is often portrayed as a negative thing, and most parents and guardians deny they are helicopter or snowplow parents, there are positives. A close relationship with a child and one where the parent or guardian helps a child make good decisions is beneficial to the child becoming a self-sufficient adult.

INFLUENCE OF COMMERCIAL MEDIA: VIOLENCE AND SEX

Another important influence on the lives of children today stems from the overwhelming barrage of violence and sexual content contained in movies, television shows, video games, and music that saturate their environment. Because children spend more time watching television than any other activity, discussions about media portrayal of violence and sex have prevailed. Seventy-one percent of 8 to 18 year olds in the U.S. have a television in their bedroom, which increases watch time per day by about an hour. In 1998, the American Psychiatric Association estimated that by age 18, children and teens will have seen 16,000 simulated murders and 200,000 acts of violence through media.[14] Since then, multiple national task forces and professional organizations have similarly concluded that violence is prevalent in content on television, interestingly with the highest rates of violence frequently being reported in cartoons and animated movies. These realities become even more complicated when we account for the explosion of streaming services, available on multiple devices, and video games that are becoming more and more prevalent in homes. Streaming services have little consistency in their age-based content ratings and child-friendly programming often appears amid selections for adult programming.[15] For the past 30 years, the American Psychological Association has posited that media increases aggressive behavior in children. Further, in a study that surveyed researchers, pediatricians, and parents, 66% of researchers, 67% of parents, and 90% of pediatricians agreed or strongly agreed that exposure to media violence can increase aggression in children.[16]

LACK OF OUTDOOR PLAY

Children are staying inside and spending more and more time with their computers, video games, and televisions rather than being outside experiencing all that nature has to offer. Richard Louv authored a book in which he explains how children do not have the same outdoor experiences previous generations had.[17] Parents and guardians keep a closer watch over children and limit where they can play and explore. They prefer structured, supervised activities to unstructured play in the outdoors. The radius that children are allowed to roam outside of their home is one-ninth of what it was 20 years ago. Much of this is because of safety concerns when in actuality child safety has steadily improved during the past decade, and they are far safer than they were 40 years ago.[18]

Learning a new skill, expressing creativity through art, or experiencing nature all lead to enhanced personal well-being.
© sonya etchison/Shutterstock.

Louv reviewed research on the positive effects of children being close to nature. It was determined that nature can improve a child's emotional health. Children who spend time outdoors may experience increased learning, increased attention span, decreased stress, more self-discipline, increased physical activity, and enhanced social connections.[19] Further, unstructured, free play in nature has been shown to have positive impacts on physical activity and cognitive development in children.[20]

Attention deficit hyperactivity disorder (ADHD) is a growing phenomenon among today's youth. More and more children are taking prescription drugs to curb the symptoms of ADHD that include a difficulty in paying attention, focusing, listening, and following directions. Researchers have claimed that being in nature can boost a child's attention span and relieve symptoms of ADHD.[21] Something as simple as taking a walk in the woods, playing in an open space such as a park, or spending time in the backyard can have tremendous rewards, yet these types of activities are on the decline.

Play, Recreation, and Leisure in the Lives of Adolescents

The teenage population, which began to climb in the early 1990s following years of decline, is expected to keep growing until at least 2045, according to U.S. Census Bureau projections. By then, it is projected there will be more than 51 million Americans between the ages of 10 and 19.

Adolescence is a challenging time for teens, their friends, and their families. They are struggling with self-identity issues, emotional swings, puberty, greater reliance on friends, and a greater need for privacy and independence.[22] They are concerned with being popular; they challenge the status quo; they are concerned with their appearance; and they are strongly influenced by their peers.[23] Parents and adolescents may both feel this is a challenging time.

This group of young people matures faster, is technologically savvy, and knows what they want from their leisure. The group is proving to be quite challenging for leisure-services professionals for many different reasons, some of which are discussed here.

TEEN EMPLOYMENT

The teen labor force has remained fairly steady since 2010 with teens working mostly in the summer months. In July 2019, 24% of employed youth worked in the leisure and hospitality industry, the largest percentage industry for employed youth, followed by 17% in retail, and 13% in education and health services.[24] Obviously this is a prime population to fill recreation jobs such as lifeguards or camp counselors. Although many teens are employed, there are still many who do not have jobs until after they graduate from high school. This may be because of parents or guardians wanting teens to focus on a sport or academics. It could be a lack of viable jobs within the community or several other reasons. What this employment outlook means for parks and recreation departments is the continuing need to offer programs and services for this age group.

RISKY BEHAVIORS

Risky leisure pursuits by teens include such things as drug and alcohol use, gambling, and sex, among others. Participation rates are changing with each one. For example, the National Institute on Drug Abuse saw a decline in alcohol, cigarette, and illegal drug consumption in teens over the last 5 years. However, there has been a dramatic increase in the occurrence of vaping, particularly for nicotine and marijuana. Indeed, between 2017 and 2020, the percentage of 12th graders who reported vaping in the past month rose from 16.6% to 28.2%.[25]

Alcohol is also a problem with adolescents. The problem is not so much social drinking as it is binge drinking. Binge drinking is consuming a large amount of alcohol over a short period of time. This means that at least twice within the past 2 weeks males have consumed five drinks in a row and females four.[26] Promisingly, the percentage of 8th, 10th, and 12th graders reporting alcohol use and binge drinking in the past year has been on a significant long-term decline since 2009.[27] The results or consequences of binge drinking are fighting, aggressiveness, blackouts, increased sexual activity, and memory loss.

Teen gambling is also on the rise. It is estimated that 60%–80% of all teens have gambled at least once in the last year.[28] That may include buying lottery tickets, small bets with friends, online gambling, or participating in a National Collegiate Athletic Association (NCAA) basketball tournament pool. If gambling turns into an addiction for adolescents, they may experience negative impacts on their work and school responsibilities, their finances, their relationships, their sleep, and their mood.[29] Online gambling may be a major player in teen gambling behaviors because tens of thousands of websites are available to them as well as advertisements running on television and social media. There is never a lack of exposure to gambling opportunities for this age group.

In 2013, the Planned Parenthood Federation reported that the United States had the highest rate of teen pregnancies among Western developed nations. However, teen pregnancy rates are at their lowest level in the United States in 40 years because of increased contraception use.[30] In 2019, 38% of all high school students reported ever having sex, which is a decline from 54% in 1991. Eight percent report having had sexual intercourse with four or more partners in their life, and 27% report being currently sexually active. Twenty-one percent reported using alcohol or drugs during their most recent sexual encounter.[31]

"Sexting," a compound of "sex" and "texting," where people share messages and/or photos containing sexual content or behavior via technology, has been in the news over the last several years. By analyzing 39 studies published between 1990 and 2016, Madigan, Ly, Rash, Van Ouytsel, and Temple found that 14.8% of youth reported sending sexts and 27.4% reported receiving sexts. Further, they reported that these percentages have increased over time and increase as youth got older.[32] Sexting gains media attention when it is used as a bullying tactic or results in negative consequences such as teen suicide.

TECHNOLOGY AND SOCIAL MEDIA

Teens are avid users of cell phones and other technology. Ninety-five percent of U.S. teens ages 13 to 17 either have a smartphone or have access to a smartphone and 45% of teens report being online on an almost continuous basis, with YouTube, Instagram, and Snapchat being the most used platforms.[33] With this shift in cell phone use, teens are constantly connected. Teens text friends more than any other form of non-face-to-face communication and reserve phone calls for their closest friends.[34] Because of the amount of time teens spend with their phones, parents and guardians are concerned about relationships established through social media, cyber bullying, the impact their online activity will have on their future academic or employment opportunities, and unsafe sharing of personal information.

BOREDOM AND THE NEED FOR EXCITEMENT

Since the last decades of the 19th century, the perceived need to provide positive recreation programs and facilities for children and youth has been based on the belief that constructive free-time alternatives help prevent risky behaviors that otherwise might result from boredom. Again and again, adolescents apprehended for criminal activity report that they were bored, that there was nothing else to do, or that their risky behaviors were a form of fun. Often, however, such forms of thrill-seeking play end in episodes of violence, drug- and alcohol-fueled accidents, or other self-destructive experiences.

CASE STUDY: The Challenge of Recreation Programming for Teens

Many of the teen issues discussed here influence their recreational needs. For many leisure-services agencies, teens are one of the most difficult groups to develop programs, activities, and events for. Because of the changing teen experiences already discussed, agencies have tried many different approaches, including establishing teen centers and teen advisory boards. For example, the City of Palo Alto (California) Recreation Department established the Teen Advisory Board and the Youth Council. The Teen Advisory Board is a group of high school students who plan and lead activities for their peers. They also have a teen center specifically for these activities. The Youth Council was established to give teens a voice in the community. They work closely with the Recreation Department and the City Council and study problems, activities, and concerns of youth in the community.

Questions for Discussion/Tasks to Complete

- What were your recreation experiences as a teenager in your community? Were they focused on school, family, friends, or the neighborhood? Were these activities part of an agency such as the local parks and recreation department or the Y?
- What challenges would leisure-services agencies face in providing recreation opportunities for teens? How could they overcome some of these challenges?
- Search and find three teen advisory boards across the country. Compare and contrast them.
- Select a community without a teen advisory board. Outline how you would establish a board and how it would operate.

Data from City of Palo Alto. (2020). *Teen leadership.* https://www.cityofpaloalto.org/gov/depts/csd/recreation/teens/teen_leadership/default.asp.

GENERATIONS

Generations are groups of people who share similar formative years by experiencing similar history, fads, and events. One way to divide the generations is as follows:

- *Silent generation:* Born between 1928 and 1945, they experienced the Depression, World War II, Amelia Earhart's solo flight across the Atlantic, and the passage of the Social Security Act.
- *Baby boomer generation:* Born between 1946 and 1964, this group saw Woodstock, the Korean War, Jackie Robinson break into Major League Baseball, and the assassinations of Bobby and President John Kennedy and Martin Luther King Jr.
- *Generation X, or Gen X:* Born between 1965 and 1980, they experienced Watergate, the peak of Michael Jackson, break dancing, and Madonna.
- *Generation Y, or Millennial generation:* Born between 1981 and 1996, this group experienced the technology boom with MP3 players, cell phones, and handheld computers, lived through the September 11, 2001 terrorist attacks and the great recession, and saw the first Black American president.
- *Generation Z:* Born between 1997 and 2012, this group is exposed to highly diverse environments in their community, school, and play; they have never known a world without the Internet, cell phones, or terrorism.

Data from Dimock, M. (2019). *Defining generations: Where Millennials end and Generation Z begins.* https://www.pewresearch.org/fact-tank/2019/01/17/where-millennials-end-and-generation-z-begins.

Play, Recreation, and Leisure in the Lives of Adults

The adult population in modern society, defined as those in their late teens and older, may logically be subdivided into several age brackets, lifestyle patterns, or generations. Although many life experiences occur in this broad age range, it is important to look at an overall picture of how people progress through these years.

YOUNG ADULTS

The population of young adults, extending from late teens through late 30s, currently includes Gen Y and Gen Z. For them, the single population has exploded. People are marry-ing later, if at all. In the past, the word *single* usually meant a lonely person or someone whose solitary status was a temporary sidetrack on the way to happy matrimony. However, singlehood has come to be regarded as a happy ending in itself—or at least an enjoyable prolonged phase of post-adolescence. When this trend became obvious, a vast number of singles-only institutions sprang up to meet the needs of this newly recognized population that had an estimated $40 billion of annual spending power. Singles apartment complexes, bars, weekends at resort hotels, social groups at local churches, cruises, and a variety of other leisure programs or services emerged—including online dating services.

As a subgroup of the young adult population, college students are usually strongly influenced in their choice of leisure activities by their status as students. Students living at home are likely to have relatively little unstructured time, often holding jobs and traveling back and forth to school, and they frequently find much of their recreation with friends in their neighborhoods. Students living on college campuses generally take part in social or religious clubs, athletic events, fraternity or sorority functions, college union programs, and entertainment or cultural activities. Many young college students regard their first experience in living away from home for a sustained period of time as an opportunity to engage in hedonistic forms of play without parental supervision. In part, this appears to be a response to the stress that challenges many first-year college students. All genders of first-year students suffer from higher levels of anxiety and stress than in past generations. Many worry about the debt they are incurring for their college education, job prospects upon graduation, having to work part time, and the pressure for success. This stress has resulted in steady increases in the percentage of college students reporting lifetime diagnoses of a mental health condition, depression, and suicidal ideation over the past decade.[35]

The majority of young single adults are able to use their leisure time in positive and constructive ways. Particularly for those who have finished school and are financially independent, travel, participation in sport or fitness clubs, social clubs, or forms of popular entertainment and involvement in hobbies and creative activities enrich their lives, both in college and in community settings.

Although millions of young adults have joined the trend toward a continuing single lifestyle, a majority of young adults today choose marriage and family life. Leisure behavior is markedly affected when people marry and have children. Social activities tend to center around the neighborhood in which the couple lives, and the home itself becomes a recreation center for parent and child activities. The family takes part in social programs sponsored by religious agencies, civic and neighborhood associations, or parent–teacher organizations (PTOs). As children move into organized community programs, parents and guardians begin to use their leisure time for volunteer service as adult leaders for scout groups, coaches and managers of sport teams, or in similar positions.

The group in this age bracket that is most deprived of leisure consists of single parents who often must work, raise a family under difficult economic and emotional circumstances, and try at the same time to find needed social outlets and recreational opportunities for themselves.

MIDDLE ADULTS

The current middle adult age group is considered Gen X and baby boomers. They are approximately 40–65 years old and make up the largest section of the population.

Middle adults have immense diversity in their lifestyles. Some are devoted to their families; others remain unattached. Some are sport minded or wilderness oriented, whereas others are committed to the arts, hobbies, or literary pursuits. Growing numbers of this age group have begun to place a high value on the creative satisfaction found in work or to devote a fuller portion of their time to family and personal involvements.

For parents and guardians in the middle adult years, patterns of leisure involvement begin to change as children become more independent and even establish their own families. Many nonworking parents, who have devoted much time and energy to the family's needs, begin to find these demands less pressing. They have more available time, as well as a need to find a different meaning and fulfillment in life through new interests and challenges.

Play, Recreation, and Leisure in the Lives of Older Adults

Older adults are defined here as people in their mid-60s and older. Given the increase in life expectancy, this group is quite large and diverse. They pass through several stages, much like those in the adult category do.

ACTIVE OLDER ADULTS

Recreation and leisure assume a high priority in the lives of most older adults, particularly for those in their late 60s and beyond who have retired from full-time jobs. Without work to fill their time and often with the loss of partners or friends, such persons find it necessary to develop new interests and often to establish new relationships.

It is now popular to assert that older adults are far more active, vigorous, economically secure, and happier than had been assumed in the past. Older adults in the United States experience a wide range of financial security, housing security, health, retirement status, and mobility. Research has shown that many older adults continue to enjoy sexual relations and to maintain active and creative lives well into their 70s and 80s.

Leisure for young adults often encompasses both family and friends.

© Monkey Business/Fotolia.com.

CASE STUDY: Programming for Baby Boomers

Baby boomers have financial resources to spend, are retiring at rapid rates, are not afraid of technology, and want to travel and have new experiences. This makes them a prime target market for leisure services. Because of this, the local parks and recreation agency has recognized a significant need for increased programs for this group. You have been hired as the new director of adult activities in your community. Your charge is to develop programs targeted at the 65+ age group.

Tasks to complete:

- Without doing any research, make a list of activities and events that you would like to offer for baby boomers. Compare your list to others in the class. How many of the activities are sedentary vs. active? How many are stereotypically for "old people"?
- Find five agencies online that offer programs specifically for the baby boomer population. Gather the following information:
    - What are these programs called (e.g., Senior Adults)?
    - Are there active and sedentary programs?
    - What type of fees are assessed?
    - What programs do you consider to be stereotypical for older adults?
    - What programs surprised you?
- Select the best and most creative programs you found in your research. Develop a schedule of activities you would like to initially offer.

The lives of older adults have changed dramatically over the past 3 or 4 decades. Not only can they expect to live much longer, but their living circumstances are likely to be radically different from those of past generations in terms of familial roles, social activities, economic factors, and other important conditions.

CHANGES IN FAMILY STRUCTURE

In the past, it was common for several generations of family members to live together. Older persons continued not only to receive the affection and support of their children and grandchildren, but also to play meaningful roles in family life. An increasing number of older adults continue to live by themselves for longer periods of time. Although many do not want to live in a nursing home, there is still need for some additional care as people age. The number of senior living communities, retirement communities, and assisted-living environments is growing. Depending on the level of care needed (from no care at all to full-time nursing care), these types of living situations can meet the needs of people as they age. These communities provide nursing care, daily living assistance, socialization, and recreation opportunities for the residents. Many see this as a better alternative than living with grown children and their families. Some retirement facilities have graduated living quarters where the level of care increases based on what the individual needs. An older adult may enter the facility being totally self-sufficient and, as health declines, can be moved to other areas within the same facility. This living arrangement lends itself to continuity and familiarity to the individual.

POSITIVE HEALTH INDICATORS

Most older people are living longer, happier, and healthier lives than in the past. Indeed, there is striking new evidence that the very old are enjoying remarkably good health in comparison with other age groups. The average annual Medicare bill for people who live to their late 80s and 90s is significantly lower than that for those who die sooner. Part of the reason is that older adults tend to be relatively robust. Cancer and heart disease, the two chief killers of retired persons in the younger age brackets, tend not to affect the very old, and Alzheimer's disease also attacks slightly younger men and women. Today, there are more and more centenarians in the United States—people who have made it to their 100th birthday—72,197 in 2016, an increase of 44% since 2000.[36]

With improved medical care, people are not just living longer, healthier lives—they are living them differently. Particularly in the so-called retirement states of New Mexico, Arizona, Nevada, and Florida, which have fast-growing populations of older men and women, they are engaging in active sports, volunteering, going back to school, and developing new networks of friends and relationships.

Older adults are breaking away from stereotypical leisure pursuits and engaging in a variety of activities.

© M.G. Mooij/Shutterstock.

WHY NOT? HOW I MET AND FELL IN LOVE WITH ARGENTINE TANGO

Karen Jackson

How was I so lucky to get introduced to Argentine tango dancing at the age of 55?

It was a dark and stormy night—really it was. I was home alone and happy to be home on a very rainy Saturday evening. It was a time in my life when I usually liked going out on the weekend evenings. However, on this rare night I was very content to be at home alone. Then the phone rang and a girlfriend of mine was calling to ask me to go out with her. I told her that I was very happy to be spending this particular Saturday night at home and suggested she call someone else. She said that she wanted to go out dancing and not many of her other friends enjoyed dancing—I did. So, I agreed to go before I asked her where she wanted to go—she wanted to go to a ballroom dance event—my least favorite because in our area most of the ballroom dancers came with their own partners. I had already committed so I went, only to find out that the reason she wanted to go to this event was that there was a man that she wanted to meet there. She met the man, and I sat and watched others dance until a man I did not know came and asked me to dance. Joe was new to the area and saw that I was alone and he also did not come with a partner. So, we danced a few dances, enjoyed ourselves, and then he asked if I would go to a dance workshop with him the following weekend. I am a "why not" kind of gal so said yes. Later in the evening I asked what type of dance we would be learning and when he said Argentine tango, I quickly responded that I have never even heard of Argentine tango and he may want to ask someone else. He said it was new to him also and would really like me to join him. I am always up for an adventure and always looking to learn something new so the following weekend started my love affair with Argentine tango. I am so thankful to Joe for starting me on an adventure that has lasted 15 years so far.

The workshop was conducted by a young Argentine couple who over the years of return trips to teach tango in Iowa have become dear friends. I give them and Joe full credit for igniting a passion I did not know I had. From the moment I saw Lorena and Ariel dance and listened to the music, I was captivated. It is not an easy dance to learn, but once the basics are mastered, there is limitless pleasure to be experienced on many levels. When I am dancing tango, I feel a deep connection to my partner—even a stranger with whom I am dancing for the first time. The essence of tango is connection: physically, mentally, emotionally. Argentine tango is a dance of improvisation in which both partners surrender to each other and the music. It is a physical conversation of movement without words. There is no wrong step or move, just a new creation. While dancing tango I have 100% concentration on my feelings and those of my partner to create a beautiful conversation.

When an evening of dancing Argentine tango comes to an end, I leave the milonga (Argentine tango dance event) always happier, more satisfied, and more fulfilled than when I entered. If you truly allow yourself to surrender to the beauty of the movement, the music, and the partner connection, you are left wanting more. Thus, the never-ending chase for a repeat of those feelings begins.

I have been dancing Argentine tango for 15 years and the pleasure has only increased as I have traveled worldwide to chase the elusive feeling of connection where two people move, think, and breathe as one through the dance. It is a dance for people of all ages.

Implication for Leisure-Services Professionals

Clearly, as people develop throughout their lifespan, their needs, challenges, and contexts in relation to play, recreation, and leisure evolve. As a result, age of participants or clients must be a primary consideration as leisure-services professionals plan programs and spaces for people to pursue their play, recreation, and leisure activities in. Knowledge of participants' and clients' age can help us understand what types of activities may be the most appealing, what types of leadership are required, what outcomes people are seeking from their activities, and what constraints people may face in accessing or completing their activities. Let's explore just a few examples.

When considering that U.S. children are increasingly experiencing overscheduling and intensive parenting, along with decreases in outdoor play, leisure-services professionals can aim to counteract the potential negative impacts of these trends. Incorporating more unstructured, outdoor play becomes a natural path. Because we are learning that intensive parenting can negatively affect children for the long term, leisure-services professionals can consider creating spaces and experiences that introduce children to risk taking, failure, decision making, and resiliency skills.

When planning experiences for teens, their increasing involvement with technology and social media can affect leisure-services professionals' choices. On one hand, interest in technology can be an asset to leverage. If activities or experiences incorporate technology to engage teens, it could help them try out new experiences they might otherwise avoid. On the other hand, it may be important to offer activities and experiences that help teens have a break from their technology.

When thinking about young and middle adults, recognizing the increasing demands on their time, including the demands of family, offers leisure-services professionals valuable information. Such knowledge indicates what times of the day or week these participants may most pursue activities or experiences so professionals can make informed scheduling decisions. Professionals can also consider the challenges of pursuing play, recreation, and leisure activities as parents by offering childcare or family experience opportunities to get everyone in the family involved.

Finally, the knowledge we have about how the aging process is changing helps leisure-services professionals ensure that their programming and spaces are relevant for older adult participants. For example, because people are living longer, healthier, leisure-services professionals need to break free from the stereotypes they may hold about older adult participants' abilities and needs. One of the key problems affecting older adults is that they tend to become isolated and lose a sense of playing a significant role in family life or in the community at large. Therefore, community service and volunteerism are useful leisure activities for older adults. How can leisure professionals leverage this group's desire for social and community connection?

These examples are just a sampling of the types of implications age factors can have for leisure-services professionals. What other examples can you think of?

Gender Identity Factors Influencing Play, Recreation, and Leisure

A second factor that plays an important role in leisure has to do with gender identity. Throughout history, distinctions among gender identities have been made that extend beyond the procreative functions. These distinctions encompass family or marital roles, educational status, career opportunities, political influences, and all other aspects of daily life.

Among younger children, play often has served to reinforce gender-related stereotypes. Little boys were given toy guns or cowboy outfits and encouraged to playact in stereotypically masculine roles such as doctors, fire fighters, or airline pilots. Girls were given dolls or play equipment designed to encourage stereotypically feminine roles such as caring for babies, cooking and sewing, or playing as nurses or flight attendants. Only after the resurgence of the feminist movement following World War II did society begin to question these roles and assumptions and challenge such sexist uses of play in childhood.

Defining Terms

As U.S. society learns more about gender and sex, it can be overwhelming to sift through all of the related terms. Let's explore these terms together. First, a distinction should be made between the two terms *sex* and *gender*. These terms are often, mistakenly, used interchangeably and lack specificity. For the purposes of this text, instead of *sex* and *gender*, we use the more specific terms *sex assigned at birth* and *gender identity*. *Sex assigned at birth* refers to a biological or physical classification in terms of the hormones and body parts present at birth. Some of the common categories associated with sex assigned at birth are intersex, female, and male. In contrast, the word *gender identity* refers to a person's internal sense of themselves as male, female, a combination of both, neither male nor female, or unrelated to the binary system. Some people's gender identity matches their sex assigned at birth, which we would call *cisgender*, and others have a gender identity that differs from their sex assigned at birth. Some ways that people label their gender identities are female, male, nonbinary, transgender, gender nonconforming, gender fluid, and all, none, or a combination of these. Gender identity is self-defined and its expression is influenced by the complex interactions between a person's inner sense of who they are, societal structures, and cultural expectations associated with gender norms. For example, at the time of early European contact, researchers have identified over 100 concepts of gender identities within the Native American societies,[37] a cultural reality that would have influenced people's internal processes in comprehending their own gender identities.

Women and Leisure

During the early decades of the 20th century, leadership roles and activities assigned to those who identified as girls and women, as well as the expectations regarding their

Leisure for girls and women has changed and improved from the impact of the feminist movement.

Courtesy of Deb Garrahy.

THE GENDER UNICORN

The Gender Unicorn is a helpful graphic to understand the endless combinations of ways people can identify themselves in terms of gender identity, sex assigned at birth, and sexual orientation, which we discuss later in the chapter. It also reminds us that these different identities are separate from each other. The graphic originates from a youth-led organization called Trans Student Educational Resources. You can even map your own identities by placing dots on each of the arrows based on how you identify. A dot placed all the way to the left on one of the arrows indicates you do not identify at all on that item and a dot all the way to the right indicates you fully identify with that item. You can place your dot all the way to either side or anywhere in between!

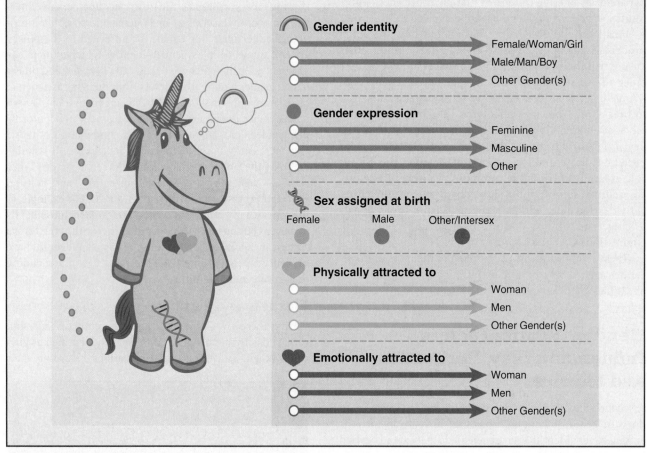

Data from Trans Student Educational Resources. (2015). *The gender unicorn.* https://transstudent.org/gender.

ability to work well in groups, reflected past perceptions of women as weak and inferior in skills and lacking drive, confidence, and the ability to compete. Victorian prudery and misconceptions about physical capability and health needs also limited programming for girls and women.[38] Physical activity was seen as detracting from womanliness, having a negative effect on motherhood, and being detrimental to women's mental health.[39]

IMPACT OF THE FEMINIST MOVEMENT

Although times have changed since the Victorian age, there are still differences in experiences, attitudes, and expectations of women's participation in sport and recreation versus that of men. A major influential factor in the changes toward equality was the feminist movement.

Feminism is defined as political, social, and economic equality among men and women. This equality first came to light politically with women wanting the right to vote just as men could. With the passage of the Nineteenth Amendment in 1920 giving women this right, feminism virtually disappeared until women entered the workforce in large numbers starting in the 1950s. As women entered the workforce, they wanted equal pay as well as access to jobs that were stereotypically labeled as a "man's job." Political and economic

TITLE IX

Title IX of the Education Amendments of 1972 states that "No person in the United States shall, on the basis of sex, be excluded from participation in, be denied the benefits of or be subjected to discrimination under any education program or activity receiving Federal financial assistance."[a] Although many associate Title IX with athletics, it also covers education (including career and vocational programs), admissions and employment policies, standardized testing, and treatment of pregnant and parenting teens.

Title IX has been instrumental in improving opportunities for female athletes at both the high school and collegiate levels. Those opposed to Title IX often argue that it decreases athletic opportunities for men. However, this is not an accurate assessment. Here are the numbers of athletes from 1982–2020:

	1982	1992	2002	2012	2020
Men	167,055	183,675	209,890	257,690	282,411
Women	64,390	94,922	153,601	195,657	221,212

Note: The NCAA currently uses the binary system of gender identity (men and women only) to classify athletes.
Data from National Collegiate Athletic Association. (2020). *NCAA sports sponsorship and participation rates database*. Retrieved January 26, 2021, from http://www.ncaa.org/about/resources/research/ncaa-sports-sponsorship-and-participation-rates-database.

[a] U.S. Department of Education. (2015). *Title IX and sex discrimination*. https://www2.ed.gov/about/offices/list/ocr/docs/tix_dis.html#:~:text=Title%20IX%20states%20that%3A,activity%20receiving%20Federal%20financial%20assistance

aspects of feminism still exist today, but it is the social aspect of feminism that is most affected by leisure.

What did this mean for leisure? Feminism empowered women that they had freedom in their choices of activities and participation. Limits and stereotypes could be removed. Furthermore, it advocated for women the same opportunities as men in terms of leisure.

IMPLICATIONS FOR LEISURE-SERVICES PROFESSIONALS

Women's leisure has been a prominent topic in research for more than 20 years. By examining what scholars have learned, there are several implications regarding women's leisure that are important for leisure professionals to keep in mind.

- Women's participation in physical activity continues to grow. Women are moving beyond traditional physical fitness classes and staying active through activities such as outdoor recreation pursuits, cycling, running, and intense fitness programs such as CrossFit.
- Leisure has changed for women from being centered around family and household responsibilities to women also taking time for their own recreational activities. They still enjoy attending their child's soccer game but want their own activities as well.
- The difference between men's and women's leisure is diminishing. Once stereotypical activities have more blurred gender lines. Men can enjoy yoga as much as women can have a poker night with friends.

- Women value the social aspects of leisure. Although time is a constraint to leisure for many, the resulting social opportunities with others and physical benefits drive women to pursue leisure activities.

Men and Leisure

Although most of the professional literature and research studies dealing with gender identity in recreation and leisure focuses on discrimination against girls and women and the efforts made to strengthen their opportunities today, it is essential to examine the changing role of males in this area as well. Generally, men have been portrayed as the dominant gender identity within most areas of community life and have been seen as responsible for denying women access to a full range of leisure pursuits and professional advancement. However, it would be misleading to assume that men's lives are invariably richer and more satisfying than those of women. Moreover, traditional gender roles continue to break down. For example, men are spending more time in the home sharing day to day tasks, whereas more and more women are spending time outside the home with work and other demands.

SHIFTING MASCULINE IDENTITIES

Parents, guardians, family, friends, and teachers all play a major role in helping a child define what it means to be masculine. The media portrays males as being in control of themselves and situations around them, aggressive, physically desirable, and heroic. Male-oriented magazines show men with muscular bodies, well dressed, and successful. Although these images encourage men to behave in certain ways, not all men buy into this image. Increasingly, men are breaking free of these rigid stereotypes and behaving as they want, regardless of the associated stereotypes.

THE ROLE OF FATHERHOOD

A man's role as father has changed drastically over the past 2 decades. With more women entering the workforce, fathers are taking more responsibility for raising children and contributing to the household responsibilities. More men are beginning to take on childcare responsibilities, for reasons ranging from rising daycare costs to the growth in the number of working women. In addition, stay-at-home dads are not quite so rare as they once were. As women's salaries are rivaling men's, many families are finding it just as beneficial if the father stays home to raise the children. Fathers increasingly see parenting as a crucial aspect of their own identity, experience societal pressure and constraints when taking time off work to care for their children, worry that they are not doing enough with their kids, and are simply more involved in childcare than they were 50 years ago.[40] No longer is it a given that in a divorce the mother is automatically granted custody. The quality of parenting has a larger influence on such decisions than gender identity of the parent in most states.

Men, and fathers in particular, are using leisure as a means to build social relationships. For men in general, similar interests such as watching sports, engaging in outdoor pursuits, playing card games or sports, or pursuing music interests can be used as social outlets to connect with others. Fathers are participating in leisure activities to share experiences with their children. They may coach their child's sports team, play video games with their children, or engage in activities with their kids at a family picnic. Like mothers, fathers sometimes face interpersonal constraints in the fact that they choose leisure activities not because they particularly want to participate, but because their child wants to participate or the father understands the value of participating with the child. Another constraint that men face can be a misconception that men do not wish to establish emotional or supportive relationships with each other. Furthermore, men can feel the constraints of gendered activities. Stereotypically labeled "female" activities are often seen as prohibited for male participants because of the fear of being perceived as less than masculine.

IMPLICATIONS FOR LEISURE-SERVICES PROFESSIONALS

What are the implications of these trends in masculine identity and lifestyle values that leisure-services professionals should keep in mind? First, many boys and men who formerly felt pressured to be involved heavily in sports, both as participants and as spectators, may now feel free to break from this traditional masculine image. Further, growing numbers of males are increasingly likely to take part in domestic functions or hobbies, the creative arts, or other leisure pursuits that in the past might have raised questions about their degree of "maleness."

It is important to note that some of the barriers that separated males and females in the past have been weakened in recent years. For example, a number of leading youth organizations that formerly were separate in terms of membership have now joined forces, as in the case of Boys and Girls Clubs of America. In other cases, national organizations such as the Y not only have substantial numbers of members who are girls and women, but also in many communities are directed by women executives and division heads.

Transgender People and Leisure

Consideration of gender identity's impact on experiences with play, recreation, and leisure must not and does not stop with men and women. Recent considerations have pushed past the binary view of gender to contemplate the experiences of a wide range of gender identities, particularly the experiences of those who identify as transgender. Though we focus here on transgender people, many of the experiences and implications for leisure services extend to other nonbinary gender identities as well.

DISCRIMINATION AGAINST TRANSGENDER PEOPLE

Transgender people experience high rates of discrimination and violence in their everyday lives. Results from a national survey of transgender people indicate that for those in K-12 school, 54% reported being verbally harassed, 24% reported being physically attacked, and 13% reported being sexually assaulted because they identified as transgender. In the broader population, 46% reported being verbally harassed and 9% reported being physically attacked because they were transgender. Twenty-nine percent reported living in poverty, a rate almost 2.5 times higher than the U.S. population. Such levels of discrimination have alarming impacts on the mental health of transgender people. The lifetime suicide attempt rate among the transgender population in 2014 was 40%, nearly nine times the 4.6% national average.[41] All of these numbers escalate for transgender BIPOC.

IMPLICATIONS FOR LEISURE-SERVICES PROFESSIONALS

In their article encouraging dialog about the experiences of transgender and intersex athletes, Krane and Barak argued:

> While sport often reinforces traditional notions of gender and gendered expectations, it can also be a place for transformation and growth.[42]

As a result of the discrimination they face in larger society, we can imagine that transgender people can face many constraints to participating in their desired play, recreation, and leisure activities. These constraints can range from intrapersonal (e.g., feelings of discomfort or fear in traditionally gendered spaces) to structural (e.g., inadequate or unwelcoming gendered changing facilities and programs). Consequently, there are a multitude of intentional steps leisure-services professionals can take to help transgender participants and clients navigate around these constraints. A sample of such actions are:

- Rethinking the layout of bathrooms, locker rooms, and sleeping quarters to be more inclusive for people who do not identify within the binary gender system
- Implementing gender identity training for staff to ensure participants experience an inclusive environment in which to recreate
- Reconsidering how gender identity is captured on registration forms so there are more options beyond male and female
- Critically examining gender-specific programming, its necessity, and how participants are assigned to such programming
- Including an antidiscrimination policy specific to gender identity and expression into company policies, marketing, and paperwork
- Asking participants and staff members their pronouns, rather than assuming people's pronouns from their physical appearance
- Eliminating pronouns and other wording in organization marketing and communications that reinforce the binary system of gender

These steps, and many others, can ensure that transgender people experience equitable and safe opportunities for play, recreation, and leisure.

Sexual Orientation Factors Influencing Play, Recreation, and Leisure

Leisure is affected by sexual orientation as well as by gender identity. It's important to emphasize that one's sex assigned at birth and gender identity do not imply anything about someone's sexual orientation. A person's sexual orientation refers to someone's emotional, romantic, and/or physical attraction to other people. Some ways people identify in terms of their sexual orientation are gay, lesbian, straight, homosexual, heterosexual, pansexual, bisexual, queer, asexual, fluid, and all, none, or a combination of these. Often this community is referred to with the acronym LGBTQIA+ (lesbian, gay, bisexual, transgender, queer/questioning, intersex, asexual, with the plus sign indicating inclusion of other identities not already mentioned). This acronym includes both gender identities and identities related to sexual orientation. As we've already discussed gender identities, let's focus on sexual orientation, specifically the experiences of gay people (i.e., people whose physical, romantic, and/or emotional attractions are to people of the same sex). This group of people faces constraints in their leisure and their life as a whole as a result of their sexual orientation that those who identify as straight do not experience.

Experiences of Gay People in the United States

Members of this group have had a difficult past in terms of acceptance by the mainstream population. In the 1930s and 1940s, a backlash developed against gay forms of entertain-

CREATING A FITNESS SPACE FOR TRANSGENDER PEOPLE: THE CITY GYM MOMENTUM PROGRAM

City Gym in Kansas City, Missouri, believes that a gym should be more than a place to work out; it should be a place to feel like you belong. The gym has taken this belief one step further with their Momentum program. The Momentum program is a health and fitness group specifically designed to serve transgender people who were assigned female at birth and identify as male. The 90-day program is designed for the specific body needs of people who have transitioned from female to male. Momentum, which has been featured in *Men's Journal*[a] and in a Google "My Business" ad, is a partnership between City Gym and The Union, A Midwest Transguy Coterie, which is a nonprofit organization designed to be "a support, social, and resource group that caters to the female-to-male, transgender community."[b] One additional way that City Gym ensures a welcoming environment for people of all gender identities is that instead of traditional, gendered locker rooms, they have private shower suites.

[a] Sturtz, R. (2015). The ultimate transformation: Meet the trans men who are redefining their lives through fitness. *Men's Journal*. Retrieved January 26, 2021, from https://www.mensjournal.com/health-fitness/transformation-trans-men-fitness-city-gym-momentum/.

[b] The Union—A Midwest Transguy Coterie. (n.d.). Retrieved January 26, 2021, from https://www.theunionkc.com.

Data from City Gym. (n.d.). *City gym momentum*. Retrieved January 26, 2021, from https://www.citygymkc.com/lifestyle/real/momentum

ment, with state assemblies barring the performance of plays dealing with sexual "degeneracy" and Hollywood agreeing not to depict homosexuality in movies. State liquor authorities closed many bars that catered to gay and lesbian clientele, and in the 1950s, gay government employees lost their jobs because it was assumed that they could be easily blackmailed into spying for other countries on the basis of their hidden identities.

In the 1960s and 1970s, the effect of the Stonewall Riot in New York City (a mass protest against police persecution of gay people), the impact of the counterculture movement with its emphasis on sexual freedom, and the activism of leaders such as Harvey Milk, a San Francisco city supervisor who was assassinated in 1978, all converged to help gay people gain a greater measure of public acceptance. A major change in attitudes toward the gay community resulted in the U.S. Supreme Court ruling 5–4 in favor of legalizing same-sex marriage on Thursday, June 25, 2015, making it the 21st country to legalize marriage for all gay couples.

As a nation, we have seen tremendous improvements in acceptance of gay people. Much of this can be attributed to the millennial generation who are more open to different sexual orientations than their older counterparts. There are several reasons for this. For example, there are more people who are open about their sexuality, so millennials may be raised around someone who identifies as gay; there are LGBTQIA+ characters regularly seen on television; millennials have access to technology to answer questions and keep them more informed; and more people talk about LGBTQIA+ issues than ever before.[40]

Although today there are more identified gay people than ever before—an estimated 29 million—and there has been progress on social acceptance, there are still many who do not openly identify as gay for a variety of different reasons. It could be fear of not being accepted by friends and family, fear of losing their family support system, concerns about harassment and discrimination, or worry about losing a job. Indeed, those in the LGBTQIA+ community experience discrimination and violence. One of the recent examples occurred when a gunman attacked Pulse, a gay nightclub in Orlando, Florida. The nightclub, according to customers, was a place people gathered for fun and entertainment, in a space where they could be themselves. The attack specifically targeted members of the LGBTQIA+ community during Pride Month, leaving 49 people dead and 53 people injured.

Implications for Leisure-Services Professionals

There are several issues to consider with this group in terms of the work of leisure-services professionals. First, LGBTQIA+ people have been labeled a gold mine for recreation companies and agencies. This group is more highly educated and has a higher income level than the national average. It is estimated that they have $884 billion per year in buying power[44] and the LGBTQIA+ travel and tourism industry is valued at $211 billion.[45] Second, on a more negative note, teens who identify as gay have a higher than average suicide rate among their peers. They often feel isolated and rejected by family or friends and have very few outlets for social and recreational opportunities where they feel comfortable. Third, gay people are increasingly becoming parents through past marriages, adoptions, or other means. All of these factors affect their leisure in a number of ways.

The following are a few examples of how these issues have sparked leisure-services professionals to welcome and support LGBTQIA+ people:

- In Boulder, Colorado, a play group has been established for young children of gay and lesbian couples.
- Olivia Cruise Lines focuses solely on cruises for gays and lesbians. R Family Vacations offers family cruises for gay people with children.[46]
- Key West, Florida, Portland, Oregon, New York City, and Palm Springs, California, specifically target gay and lesbian tourists by promoting the city as a tourism destination and providing information on gay/lesbian-friendly hotels, resorts, restaurants, and recreational opportunities.
- LYRIC is a recreation center for youth aged 24 and younger. It was opened in 1988 and offers social and recreational programs and services for LGBTQIA+ youth. The center provides community, education, and recreation programs and events.[47]
- In New York City, there is a nonprofit group called Services and Advocacy for LGBTQIA+ Elders (SAGE). SAGE started in 1977 for adults, serving as a drop-in center and offering discussion groups and various recreational activities such as arts, exercise, dances, and trips.[48]
- Fountaingrove Lodge is an LGBTQIA+ retirement community that focuses on wellness and active lifestyles to maintain health for older adults. The community features such recreation amenities as a fitness center and classes, walking trails, pet park, golf course, and movie theater.[49]
- The Seattle Parks and Recreation Department has a specifically designated LGBTQIA+ resource page to connect people with LGBTQIA+-specific opportunities, such as All Gender Swims at public pools, teen programming, "Rainbow Recreation" programming for LGTBQ adults ages 50 and older, and wedding/ceremony information.

Given the growing numbers and acceptance of LGBTQIA+ people, the economic impact of this group, and the constraints they can face, it is important that leisure-services agencies understand the need to offer programs, activities, and events that serve the LGBTQIA+ community from youths through older adults.

Race and Ethnicity Factors Influencing Play, Recreation, and Leisure

A fourth major sociocultural factor is of key importance in determining leisure values and behaviors. A succession of past research studies shows that recreational involvement in the United States is heavily influenced by one's racial or ethnic identity. The provision of public, nonprofit, and other forms of leisure-services facilities and programs is also affected by these demographic factors, and the broader fields of popular culture—including the sport and entertainment worlds—continue to reflect their impact.

Defining Terms

Before examining the actual influence of race and ethnicity on play, recreation, and leisure, it is helpful to clarify the meaning of the two terms. Although they are often used interchangeably, social scientists distinguish between them. *Ethnicity* refers to one's social and cultural heritage that is passed on from one generation to another. Ethnic groups are often identified by patterns of language, family life, religion, recreation, and other customs or traits that are used to distinguish them from other groups. *Race* refers to a socially constructed categorization of people into different groups, usually based on visible characteristics people display such as eye shape, hair texture, and skin color. On the 2020 U.S. Census, the categories offered for race were White, Black or African American, American Indian or Alaska Native, Asian, Native Hawaiian and Pacific Islander, and Some Other Race. The census also asked people to identify whether the respondent was of Hispanic, Latino, or Spanish origin to capture their ethnic or national identity.[50]

Dance is an important aspect of Indigenous Hawaiian cultures.
© Jose Gil/Shutterstock.

CASE STUDY: LGBTQIA+ Sports League to Form?

A group of 10 LGBTQIA+ people in the community come into the local parks and recreation department to discuss sport opportunities for those who identify as part of the LGBTQIA+ community. They are requesting that a volleyball league and a co-ed softball league be formed. They also guarantee that they can put together at least six teams in each league and that they will not limit players to just people who are LGBTQIA+. Your agency already has adult sports leagues, but this group wants their own league.

Questions to Consider

- Assume you are part of the LGBTQIA+ group seeking a league. What arguments would you use to convince the agency to start a league for you?
- Take the other side of the argument. List potential reasons why forming the league would not be a good idea.
- Because this is an adult sports league, it will generate revenue from the players and not rely on tax support. Does this make a difference in whether or not you would start this league? Why or why not?
- You have decided to go ahead and run the softball league as a trial. You have two choices in location. One open field is in a complex of three other diamonds and is one of the best fields in the city. The other location is a decent field, but it is a standalone diamond on the edge of town. Which diamond would you choose for the league and why?

Race, as conceptualized throughout the history of the United States, has no basis in biology or genetics. Instead race, and to some extent ethnicity, has been a social construct that has evolved over time in the United States. In most cases, the evolution of the concept of race has aligned with shifting concepts of who is and is not considered "White" in U.S. society, typically for purposes of oppression of BIPOC.[51,52] Having acknowledged the limitations and troubling past associated with the concepts of race and ethnicity, the reality is that, in the United States, race and ethnicity act as powerful forces that affect people's experiences and constraints because people ascribe different value to different races and apply stereotypes about one group or the other. This reality is particularly significant for leisure services because our traditional patterns of facility development and program planning were essentially based on the assumption that the public being served was predominantly a White, middle-class population familiar with the literature, traditions, and customs that came to North America from the British Isles.

Changing Racial and Ethnic Demographics in the United States

Understanding how race and ethnicity affect play, recreation, and leisure is essential for leisure-services professionals for a variety of reasons, including the reality that the racial and ethnic landscape in the United States is changing. By 2055, the Pew Research Center projects that there will be no numerical racial or ethnic majority group in the United States, primarily driven by immigration of people who identify as Asian or Latinx. Consider the numbers in Figure 3-1.[53]

The United States is also seeing an increase in the number of people identifying as multiracial. In 2015, 6.9% of adults reported having two or more races in their background, the proportion of marriages that are multiracial has grown fourfold since 1980, and the percentage of babies who are multiracial has increased tenfold since 1970.[54]

In addition to race, ethnicity can have a major impact on leisure preferences. One guiding force in ethnicity is religion. The United States continues to be dominated by Protestants (46.57%) and Catholics (20.87%). However, Christian religions overall are on a 7.8% decline from 2007 and 2014. During this same time period, people identifying with non-Christian faiths (e.g., Jewish, Islamic) and nonaffiliated (e.g., atheist, agnostic, no religion) have both increased. Non-Christian religions grew by 1.2% and nonaffiliated grew by 6.7%.[55] The 2008 American Religious Identification Survey (ARIS) found that there are 1,349,000

The Holi Festival of Colors in Malaysia is one of the largest traditional Indian cultural celebrations.
© Dimitry Berkut/Shutterstock.

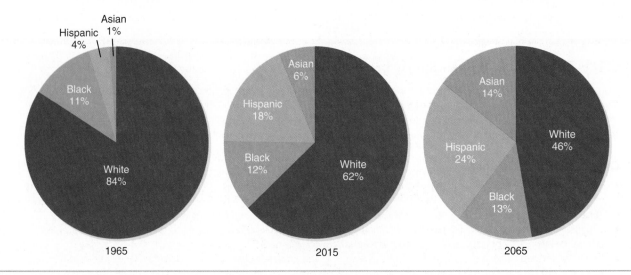

FIGURE 3-1 Estimated and projected U.S. population by race and Hispanic origin. **A.** 1965 **B.** 2015. **C.** 2065 (projected)

Data from Pew Research Center. (2015, September 28). *Modern immigration wave brings 59 million to U.S., driving population growth and change through 2065: Views of immigration's impact on U.S. society mixed.* https://www.pewresearch.org/hispanic/2015/09/28/modern-immigration-wave-brings-59-million-to-u-s-driving-population-growth-and-change-through-2065/.

Muslims in the United States, which is a 156% growth since 1990. The number of Buddhists has grown 194% in that same time period, and that religion has 1,189,000 followers in the United States. Fifteen percent of the population claims no religion. This is an increase of 138% since 1990.[56]

The racial and ethnic composition of the United States is rapidly changing. Beyond the sheer numbers, it is evident that growing minoritized populations are also exerting powerful influences on the nation's cultural scene and recreational life. No longer is it acceptable to offer programs from a predominantly White, middle-class perspective and interest level. Leisure services need to be more inclusive than that.

Implications for Leisure-Services Professionals

The approach to delivering services to people from different racial and ethnic backgrounds has changed and improved over time but still has incredible room for growth. Scott suggested that recreation services need to be accessible, affordable, safe, culturally relevant, and welcoming in order to meet the needs of all racial and ethnic groups.[57]

Accessible

The importance of access to parks and recreation is immeasurable. People who live near a park are more physically active, healthy, and have higher levels of psychological well-being.[58] Accessibility can refer to financial resources, transportation, and physical access; accessibility to parks is not equal in most communities. The research on accessibility is limited, but BIPOC are less likely to live near a park, or the parks they do live near are smaller with fewer amenities than are found in predominantly White neighborhoods. Accessibility via transportation could be problematic both in terms of getting to local recreation opportunities as well as the ability to travel to rural locations for outdoor recreational activities. If there are no parks within walking distance, public transportation is limited, or there is little family discretionary income, people living in these areas face significantly more obstacles to using parks than anyone else.

Affordable and Safe

Many research studies have shown that racial and ethnic minorities are limited in their recreation participation because of affordability and safety issues. Those who have lower levels of discretionary income do not have the financial resources to travel to a national park, go skiing in Jackson Hole, Wyoming, go to the Texas Rangers game, or pay the fee to take a cooking class. The link between income and safety is significant. For example, lower income neighborhoods often have elevated crime rates and residents who are concerned about their safety. This fear can diminish use of public spaces for many. Low-income neighborhoods often have high traffic roads, railroads, or other barriers making access to parks difficult and unsafe, especially for those with limited transportation options.[59]

Culturally Relevant and Welcoming

Many cultural factors prohibit the use of recreation facilities and programs. Some may not feel welcome because they view activities as being planned by and for Whites, or that their own religious or personal values do not match those of others. For example, agencies that are not mindful of significant non-Christian religious holidays or lack understanding of requirements regarding modesty and mixing of genders in activities for such religions as Islam will not draw these groups into their facilities. Essentially, some people do not feel there is anything for them and see no need to participate. However, working with different groups to learn what activities they want and involving them in the planning can help them feel they have a voice and are welcome. Skokie, Illinois, does this well through the Skokie Festival of Cultures. This citywide event has a planning committee with representatives from 24 different racial and ethnic groups residing in the community. Each group is represented and plans its facet of the event including food, art, entertainment, and activities.

Agencies must continually review their program offerings, marketing, administration, and staffing to best meet the needs of the community. Schneider, Shinew, and Fernandez[60] provide several suggestions for agencies to better serve the entire community:

- Show diversity in marketing materials through photos, content, and distribution to locations that reach diverse populations.
- Work with the city, public transportation agencies, schools, and nonprofit organizations to coordinate transportation options.

DEFINING WHO IS HISPANIC IN THE CENSUS

The United States Census 2020 indicated that included in those who identify as Hispanic, Latino, or Spanish origin are those with ethnic or national origins in Mexico, Puerto Rico, Cuba, Central or South America, and other Spanish cultures, regardless of race. Examples they provide for this category are Mexican, Mexican American, Puerto Rican, Cuban, Salvadoran, Dominican, Columbian, Guatemalan, Honduran, Spaniard, Ecuadorian, Venezuelan, and so on.

Data from United States Census Bureau. (n.d.). *2020 census questions: Hispanic origin*. https://2020census.gov/en/about-questions/hispanic-origin.html.

CASE STUDY: Pokémon GO: Where Augmented Reality, Culture, and Race Intersect

Though Pokémon GO experienced an expected dip in its popularity after its record-breaking launch in July 2016, the game still experiences tremendous use. It has reached over $3 billion in lifetime revenue and, as of March 2019, had 1 billion downloads. In January 2019, its parent company Niantic had a valuation of $4 billion.[a] The game has gotten people outside, traveling to places they wouldn't have visited previously; however, the game has also had some challenging incidents when considering interactions with race, ethnicity, and culture.

First, controversy has arisen based on the real world locations in which people play the game. Players or "trainers" use a GPS map to locate Pokémon or "pocket monsters." When a character is tapped, the smartphone camera is launched by the app for a mini-game where the Pokémon appear in the real world. Once Pokémon are captured, trainers use them to battle in specialized locations called Pokémon gyms. Pokémon can be found anywhere in the world including "Pokémon stops" that are cultural and historic landmarks. Although this component adds to the educational benefits of the game, not everyone is pleased to be a stop. For example, the Holocaust Museum in Washington, DC, and the Auschwitz and Birkenau Concentration Camp sites in Poland have requested they be removed from the game because they feel the game dishonors Holocaust victims.[b]

Second, preexisting racial inequities in our society still affect players of the game. A *USA TODAY* article interviewed four Black men who felt recent racial tensions have become an issue for some who play the game. Pokémon GO was released at the same time that two Black men were shot and killed by police officers in Baton Rouge and a suburb of Minneapolis, followed by a fatal shooting of five police officers in Dallas who were working at a peaceful rally for the men. Those interviewed expressed their concerns that people could call the police on them because they look suspicious as they walk by a window three or four times trying to catch a character. One player said, "my brain started combining the complexity of being Black in America with the real-world proposal of wandering and exploration that is designed into the game play of Pokémon GO, there was only one conclusion. I might die if I keep playing."[c]

Questions to Consider

- Should the Holocaust museum officials have asked that it be removed from the game as a location for a character? Why or why not?
- Can games like Pokémon GO have an impact on physical activity for the players? Why or why not?
- Read the Guynn article in *USA TODAY* listed in the sources. Discuss the points made in the article.

[a]Iqbal, M. (2020). *Pokémon Go revenue and usage statistics.* Retrieved January 26, 2021, from https://www.businessofapps.com/data/pokemon-go-statistics/.
[b]Akhtar, A. (2016, July 13). Holocaust Museum, Auschwitz want Pokémon Go hunts out. *USA TODAY.* Retrieved January 26, 2021, from http://www.usatoday.com/story/tech/news/2016/07/12/holocaust-museum-auschwitz-want-pokmon-go-hunts-stop-pokmon/86991810/.
[c]Guynn, J. (2016, July 13). Playing Pokémon GO while black: Fear stifles the fun. *USA TODAY.* Retrieved January 26, 2021, from http://www.usatoday.com/story/tech/news/2016/07/12/playing-pokemon-go-while-black/86989554/.

MUSLIM RECREATION PARTICIPATION

Islam is a worldwide religion with more than 1 billion followers. Leisure is closely connected with religious activities for Muslims because free time is allotted to be spent with family and on religious activities and festivals.[61] Activity and sport are encouraged in Islamic countries for the purpose of a healthy body and mind. Livengood and Stoldolska found that Muslim Americans participate in the same mainstream leisure activities that the rest of Americans do, but their leisure style, location of leisure, and the individuals with whom they participate are different.[62] Lack of participation by Muslims in leisure has been attributed to such issues as disapproval from family, concern over contact between people with different gender identities (which is discouraged), unacceptable facilities, immodest sport clothes, agency dress codes for participation that go against religious beliefs about what parts of the body should be covered, lack of experience in an activity, and obligations to family.

- Conduct an access assessment and include safety as a factor. Outline ways to increase access to parks, programs, and facilities.
- Build culturally competent staff through ongoing equity training. One-time training is insufficient, as employees must continue to learn about their community and the people within it.

- Develop social activities that can build relationships among community members, especially helpful to those new to the neighborhood such as recent immigrants.
- Hire a diverse staff. A customer seeing staff from their same racial or ethnic group can be an opening for groups to feel welcome.

A Muslim family plays cricket in London's Kensington Gardens.
Courtesy of Deb Garrahy.

Leisure services do not exist in isolation from the racial and ethnic changes, discord, progress, and inequities that exist in our larger society. These issues influence and shape participants' and clients' experiences within our leisure-services spaces. Consequently, leisure-services professionals must be aware of their own biases, learn about other backgrounds, and incorporate inclusive practices into their work. It is also essential that leisure-services professionals continue to strive to overcome the long-standing patterns of racial prejudice, discrimination, and oppression that still exist in our communities.

Socioeconomic Factors Influencing Play, Recreation, and Leisure

Socioeconomic status is a means of classifying people based on their income, education, occupation, and household size. Although sociologists have developed several labels for the different categories of SES, there are three common ones: low, middle, and high.

A person's SES affects leisure in a number of ways. The amount of education and/or the amount of money a person has dictates the amount of free time and discretionary income available for leisure, creating clear structural constraints for some people. Traditionally, people from lower socioeconomic backgrounds are underrepresented in recreation activity participation. It was seen previously that this was particularly true for health and fitness programs. On the other hand, those with higher SES usually have more education and money and look for more refined and prestigious leisure.[58]

In the United States, those from low or middle SES backgrounds historically have been the dominant users of public and nonprofit leisure services. Logically, as income and other SES indicators increase, so does the ability to pay more for services; thus, those from high SES backgrounds will use commercial services almost exclusively, for a number of reasons. For example, it may be an attitude of "you get what you pay for" where the commercial sector is seen as higher quality. Arguably, this assessment is not accurate at all because many public and nonprofit leisure-services agencies offer recreation services that rival commercial agencies. Another reason for using commercial services over the other two sectors may be a prestige or status issue. Status is assigned to such things as exclusive club memberships or exotic travel destinations booked through a travel agency.

Implications for Leisure-Services Professionals

Although there are activities that transcend all SES categories such as watching television, reading, sports, or socializing, many others could be placed within each SES category almost exclusively. For example, yachting, attending the symphony, or having a second home in the Hamptons would most likely be assigned to the high SES category, whereas a trip to Disney World or playing golf at a public course would more likely be activity choices of the middle SES category.

Sometimes there are activities that are popular among all SES categories, but the way in which they are enjoyed differs. Travel is a common activity to all. However, those from low SES backgrounds may take short day or overnight trips and stay with family and friends; those from middle SES may vacation in a popular tourism destination in the United States and stay at a Holiday Inn; whereas those from high SES backgrounds may take an extended cruise, travel abroad, or stay in a luxury hotel where a night's stay is equal to a month's rent for people with low SES.

In ancient Greece, leisure and upper classes were supported by the poor, slaves, and women. In some ways, this reality has not changed in modern society. The leisure pursuits of the middle and high SES categories are often supported by those from low SES backgrounds. Take tourism, for example: The economically stable classes travel to destinations and enjoy activities where the workers are making minimum wage. In today's economy, minimum wage is below the poverty level. In addition, when an area is tourism dependent, there is a tendency to drive up the cost of living, including housing and food, making it difficult for the workers to live in these communities that provide leisure for the middle and upper classes.

The Slow Progress of Alleviating Constraints to Play, Recreation, and Leisure

Age, gender identity, sexual orientation, race, and SES all affect leisure activity choices and experiences, and it is the responsibility of leisure professionals to understand these impacts and provide services that meet the needs of the community. Because it is not feasible for all agencies to provide services to all people, the different segments and agencies must find their niche and work to understand the leisure needs, constraints, patterns, and preferences of their intended populations so that no group is underrepresented or denied leisure opportunities.

Although this chapter deals in detail with many of the constraints people encounter in their leisure because of their age, gender identity, sexual orientation, race, ethnicity, and/or SES, it must also be stressed that progress has been made over the past several decades.

Although we have seen changes at all age levels, one age group has had a significant impact over the last 20 years. The aging baby boomers and their economic impact have driven leisure-service providers to rethink traditional services. The need for experiences; desire for physical activity, health, and wellness; and the ability to pay have created a whole new array of program opportunities as people age.

Women and people who identify as part of the LGBTQIA+ community continue to experience increased social acceptance and have access to a wide range of play, recreation, and leisure opportunities that were not available to them in the past. Furthermore, people of all gender identities have been more accepted in activities that, traditionally, have been gendered for males or females. We see more and more people disregarding past stigmas and choosing activities of interest rather than what society says they "should" choose.

In terms of race, similar gains have been achieved—particularly for BIPOC—even though there remains a tremendous amount of work to dismantle the systems of oppression and discrimination present in U.S. society. In many cities, particularly in such states as Florida, Texas, and California, large Latinx American populations have begun to achieve economic success and a degree of political power. Agencies increasingly are recognizing this growth and the need to provide specialized services.

Ability to pay for leisure services by individuals and the ability of agencies to fund free programs for low-income people are issues. With the economy the way it is today, many agencies have to generate income to stay in business, even nonprofit and public entities. So, "pay to play" becomes the norm and, in turn, eliminates opportunities for those from low SES backgrounds. However, great strides have been made by nonprofit and public agencies to offer services to those who cannot afford them. Many agencies offer program scholarships, programs that are free to the public and supported by sponsors or tax dollars, or programs funded by local, state, and federal grants. Although access to play, recreation, and leisure is not equitable yet, leisure-services professionals must continue to seek ways to break down the barriers and constraints so many people face simply because of their identity.

SUMMARY

Major influences on play, recreation, and leisure in contemporary society are the sociocultural factors of age, gender identity, sexual orientation, race and ethnicity, and SES. This chapter defines these terms and shows how they have affected play, recreation, and leisure participation in the past and continue to do so today.

As people age, their leisure preferences and patterns change. Children experience a tremendous amount of growth and try different leisure activities. As people enter and move through adulthood, family has a major influence on leisure participation. In an individual's latter years, physical abilities and social elements are key factors in leisure.

As the chapter notes, women and girls have historically been denied many of the leisure opportunities open to men and boys. However, the feminist movement has succeeded in urging colleges, school systems, and community recreation agencies to provide more support to female participants in a wide range of sports and physical activities. This helps women to develop positive self-images and feelings of empowerment. In addition, many women have overcome barriers to professional advancement in various types of agencies in the leisure-service field. Women are also being admitted to business and social groups that had excluded females in the past.

The status of males with respect to recreation and leisure is also discussed. In the past, many men were pressured to adopt stereotypical "macho" roles in leisure activities. Today, they are being encouraged to play a more open, sensitive, and creative role in their recreational pursuits, as well as in domestic life and their relationships.

People who identify as transgender experience unique constraints when it comes to play, recreation, and leisure, including fear of discrimination and violence and challenges related to facilities and programs designed to recognize only two genders. Leisure-services professionals can take a multitude of steps to break down the binary system of gender in their spaces, welcoming people of all genders to experience their services.

The issue of sexual orientation is dealt with as well. LGBTQIA+ people are increasingly gaining acceptance in the United States and are considered a key demographic for leisure-services providers. Not only are they forming their own social and recreational groups, but commercial recreation agencies and tourism bureaus in particular are targeting this group.

There is rapid change going on in the United States in relation to race and ethnicity. Given that legacies of discrimination and oppression are still prevalent in our society, it is essential that organized leisure services contribute to positive intergroup relations in community life. To better include all groups, leisure services need to be accessible, affordable, safe, culturally relevant, and welcoming. Involving different groups in the planning of programs is a step in the right direction.

Socioeconomic status plays a powerful role in what leisure opportunities are available to people. There is a major difference in the leisure lives of those from low and high SES backgrounds, with the latter experiencing more access to a wider variety of leisure services. However, the public and nonprofit sectors understand their responsibility in providing services to a group of people who have a great need for quality recreation near their homes and at a price they can afford.

QUESTIONS FOR CLASS DISCUSSION OR ESSAY EXAMINATION

1. Select one of the following age groups: children, teens, young adults, middle adults, or older adults. What are this group's special needs for recreation in modern society, and what constraints or problems does it face in the appropriate choice of satisfying leisure activity?

_____

_____

_____

2. Older adults make up a rapidly growing segment of the population. How has society traditionally considered the aging process and the role of older persons in community life? What new views have developed in recent years? What are the implications of these changes for leisure-services professionals working with older persons?

_____

_____

_____

3. How have women's roles with respect to recreation and leisure differed from those of men, in terms of societal attitudes and constraints, throughout history? How have they changed from the past?

_____

_____

_____

4. Although there is still discrimination toward the LGBTQIA+ community, there has been progress in terms of their legal standing and status in community life. What issues do you perceive as critical in terms of involving people who identify as part of this community as identifiable groups in leisure-services programs and facilities?

_____

_____

_____

5. How do you think race, ethnicity, and socioeconomic status interrelate? How are play, recreation, and leisure affected by these sociocultural factors?

_____

_____

_____

6. Define the three categories of leisure constraints. What constraints do transgender people face? Men? Women?

_____

_____

_____

7. BIPOC have experienced discrimination and oppression since the founding of the United States. What methods are most effective if leisure-services professionals want to ensure their programs and facilities are places where people of color do not experience such constraints as they pursue leisure experiences?

_____

_____

_____

8. Define socioeconomic status. Compare and contrast the leisure opportunities of the those from low, middle, and high SES backgrounds.

_____

_____

_____

9. This chapter explored the variety of constraints people, especially people from minoritized groups, face as they pursue play, recreation, and leisure. What do you see as the role of the leisure-services professional in breaking down those constraints?

_____

_____

_____

ENDNOTES

1. Kraus, R. (1971). *Recreation and leisure in modern society*. New York: Appleton-Century-Crofts.

2. Garrahy, D. A. (2011). Motor development and recreation. In A. R. Hurd & D. M. Anderson, *The parks and recreation professional's handbook* (pp. 39–56). Human Kinetics.

3. Payne, G. V., & Isaacs, L. D. (2012). *Human motor development: A lifespan approach* (8th ed.) McGraw-Hill.

4. Isenberg, J. P., & Jalongo, M. R. (2020). *Why is play important? Social and emotional development, physical development, creative development*. Retrieved January 25, 2021, from https://www.education.com/download-pdf/reference/22193/.

5. Montessori, M. (n.d.). *Play is the work of the child*. Child Development Institute. Retrieved January 25, 2021, from https://childdevelopmentinfo.com/child-development/play-work-of-children/.

6. Kramer, S. (2019, December 12). *U.S. has world's highest rate of children living in single-parent households*. Pew Research Center. Retrieved January 25, 2021, from https://www.pewresearch.org/fact-tank/2019/12/12/u-s-children-more-likely-than-children-in-other-countries-to-live-with-just-one-parent/.

7. Livingston, G. (2018, April 25). *The changing profile of unmarried parents: A growing share are living with a partner*. Pew Research Center. Retrieved January 25, 2021, from https://www.pewsocialtrends. org/2018/04/25/the-changing-profile -of-unmarried-parents/.

8. U.S. Census Bureau. (2019). *America's families and living arrangements: 2019*. Retrieved January 25, 2021, from https://www.census.gov/data/tables/2019/demo/families/cps-2019.html

9. United States Census Bureau. (2021). *Same-sex couple households: 2019*. Retrieved June 17, 2021 from, https://www.census.gov/library/publications/2021/acs/acsbr-005.html

10. U.S. Bureau of Labor Statistics. (2020). *Employment characteristics of families summary*. Retrieved January 25, 2021, from https://www.bls.gov/news.release/famee.nr0.htm.

11. Mason, K. C. (2015, July 2). *The downside of no downtime for kids*. PBS Newshour. http://www.pbs .org/newshour/updates/whats-conflicted-parent-scheduling-childs-summer/.

12. Miller, C. C., & Bromwich, J. E. (2019, March 16). How parents are robbing their children of adulthood: Today's "snowplow parents" keep their children's futures obstacle-free—even when it means crossing ethical and legal boundaries. *New York Times*. Retrieved January 25, 2021, from https://www. nytimes.com/2019/03/16/style/snowplow-parenting-scandal.html.

13. Ishizuka, P. (2019). Social class, gender, and contemporary parenting standards in the United

States: Evidence from a national survey experiment. *Social Forces, 98*(1), 31–58. https://doi.org/10.1093/sf/soy107.

14. Muscari, M. (2002). Media violence: Advice for parents. *Pediatric Nursing, 28*(6), 585–591.

15. Henson, M. (2017). *Over-the-top or a race to the bottom: A parent's guide to streaming video.* Parents Television Council. Retrieved January 25, 2021, from https://www.parentstv.org/resources/OTT2017_D.pdf.

16. Bushman, B. J., Gollwitzer, M., Cruz, C., Kaufman, J. C., & Sumerson, J. B. (2015). There is broad consensus: Media researchers agree that violent media increase aggression in children, and pediatricians and parents concur. *Psychology of Popular Media Culture, 4*(3), 200–214. https://doi.org/10.1037/ppm0000046.

17. Louv, R. (2005). *Last child in the woods: Saving our children from nature-deficit disorder.* Algonquin Books of Chapel Hill.

18. Land, K. C. (2014). *Child and Youth Well-Being Index (CWI) report.* Retrieved January 25, 2021, from https://childandfamilypolicy.duke.edu/wp-content/uploads/2014/12/Child-Well-Being-Report.pdf.

19. Kuo, M. (2019, June 7). Six ways nature helps children learn. *Greater Good Magazine.* Retrieved January 25, 2021, from https://greatergood.berkeley.edu/article/item/six_ways_nature_helps_children_learn.

20. Dankiw, K., Tsiros, M. D., Baldock, K. L., & Kumar, S. (2020). The impacts of unstructured nature play on health in early childhood development: A systematic review. *PLoS ONE, 15*(2), 1–22. https://doi.org/10.1371/journal.pone.0229006.

21. CHADD. (2017). *Spend time outside to improve ADHD symptoms.* Retrieved January 25, 2021, from https://chadd.org/adhd-weekly/spend-time-outside-to-improve-adhd-symptoms/.

22. DelCampo, D. S. (2012). *Understanding teens, bringing science to your life* (Guide F-122). Retrieved January 25, 2021, from http://aces.nmsu.edu/pubs/_f/F-122.pdf.

23. Welker, E. (2016, June 22). *Understanding teens: Opening the door to a better relationship.* News for Parents. Retrieved January 25, 2021, from http://www.newsforparents.org/expert_understanding_teens.html.

24. U.S. Bureau of Labor Statistics. (2019, August 16). *Employment and unemployment among youth– Summer 2019.* Retrieved January 25, 2021, from https://www.bls.gov/news.release/archives/youth_08162019.htm.

25. National Institute on Drug Abuse. (2020). *Monitoring the Future Study: Trends in prevalence of various drugs.* Retrieved January 25, 2021, from https://www.drugabuse.gov/publications/drugfacts/monitoring-future-survey-high-school-youth-trends.

26. TeensHealth. (2016, June 22). *Binge drinking.* Retrieved January 25, 2021, from http://kidshealth.org/en/teens/binge-drink.html.

27. National Institute on Drug Abuse. (2019, December 18). *Monitoring the Future 2019 survey results: Overall findings.* Retrieved January 25, 2021, from https://www.drugabuse.gov/drug-topics/trends-statistics/infographics/monitoring-future-2019-survey-results-overall-findings.

28. National Council on Problem Gambling. (2016, June 22). *High school gambling fact sheet.* Retrieved January 25, 2021, from http://www.ncpgambling.org/files/HS_Fact_Sheet.pdf.

29. California Council on Problem Gambling. (2021). *Impacted youth.* Retrieved January 25, 2021, from https://calpg.org/impacted-youth/.

30. Planned Parenthood Federation of America. (2013). *Reducing teenage pregnancy.* Retrieved January 25, 2021, from https://www.plannedparenthood.org/files/6813/9611/7632/Reducing_Teen_Pregnancy.pdf.

31. Centers for Disease Control and Prevention. (2019). *Trends in the prevalence of sexual behaviors and HIV testing national YRBS: 1991–2019.* Retrieved January 25, 2021, from https://www.cdc.gov/healthyyouth/data/yrbs/factsheets/2019_sexual_trend_yrbs.htm.

32. Madigan, S., Ly, A., Rash, C. L., Van Ouytsel, J, & Temple, J. R. (2018). Prevalence of multiple forms of sexting behavior among youth: A systematic review and meta-analysis. *JAMA Pediatrics, 172*(4), 327–335. https://doi.org/10.1001/jamapediatrics.2017.5314.

33. Anderson, M., & Jiang, J. (2018, May 31). *Teens, social media, and technology 2018.* Pew Research Center. Retrieved January 25, 2021, from https://www.pewresearch.org/internet/2018/05/31/teens-social-media-technology-2018/.

34. Anderson, M. (2015, August 20). *How having smart-phones (or not) shapes the way teens communicate.* Pew Research Center. Retrieved January 26, 2021, from http://www.pewresearch.org/fact-tank/2015/08/20/how-having-smartphones-or-not-shapes-the-way-teens-communicate/.

35. Lipson, S. K., Lattie, E. G., & Eisenberg, D. (2019). Increased rates of mental health service utilization by U.S. college students: 10-year population-level trends (2007–2017). *Psychiatric Services*, *70*(1), 60–63. https://doi.org/10.1176/appi.ps.201800332.

36. Tavernise, S. (2016, January 21). Centenarians proliferate, and live longer. *New York Times*. Retrieved January 26, 2021, from https://www.nytimes.com/2016/01/21/health/centenarians-prolif-erate-and-live-longer.html?_r=0.

37. National Park Service. (2018). *Gender and sexuality in Native America: Many people, many meanings.* Retrieved January 26, 2021, from https://www.nps.gov/articles/gender-and-sexuality-in-native-america.htm.

38. Dulles, F. R. (1965). *A history of recreation: America learns to play*, (p. 96). Appleton-Century-Crofts.

39. Henderson, K. A., Bialeschki, M. D., Shaw, S. M., & Freysinger, V. J. (1996). *Both gains and gaps: Feminist perspectives on women's leisure*. Venture Publishing.

40. https://www.usatoday.com/story/college/2015/04/03/study-millennials-more-accepting-of-homosexuality-than-casual-sex/37401793/

41. Livingston, G., & Parker, K. (2019, June 12). *8 facts about American dads*. Pew Research Center. Retrieved January 26, 2021, from https://www.pewresearch.org/fact-tank/2019/06/12/fathers-day-facts/.

42. Krane, V., & Barak, S. K. (2012). Current events and teachable moments: Creating a dialog about transgender and intersex athletes. Journal of Physical Education, Recreation, & Dance, 83(4), 38–43. https://doi.org/10.1080/07303084.2012.10598761.

43. Krane, V., & Barak, S. K. (2012). Current events and teachable moments: Creating dialog about transgender and intersex athletes. *Journal of Physical Education, Recreation, & Dance*, 83(4), 42.

44. Gaily Grind Staff. (2015, June 25). *America's LGBT buying power in 2014 estimated at $884 billion.* Retrieved January 26, 2021, from http://www.thegailygrind.com/2015/06/25/americas-lgbt-buying-power-in-2014-estimated-at-884-billion/.

45. Geosure. (2019, February 28). *The $211 billion LGBTQ travel industry is getting serious about safety.* Retrieved January 26, 2021, from https://geosureglobal.com/blog/the-211-billion-lgbtq-travel-industry-is-getting-serious-about-safety.

46. R Family Vacations. (2016). Retrieved January 26, 2021, from http://www.rfamilyvacations.com/.

47. LYRIC Center for LGBTQQ+ Youth. (2020). Retrieved January 26, 2021, from https://lyric.org/.

48. *SAGE*. (2020). Retrieved January 26, 2021, from https://www.sageusa.org.

49. FountainGrove Lodge LGBT Retirement Community. (2020). Retrieved January 26, 2021, from http://www.fountaingrovelodge.com/.

50. United States Census 2020. (2020). *Questions asked on the form*. Retrieved January 26, 2021, from https://2020census.gov/en/about-questions.html.

51. Coates, T.-N. (2013, May 15). What we mean when we say "race is a social construct." *The Atlantic*. Retrieved January 26, 2021, from https://www.theatlantic.com/national/archive/2013/05/what-we-mean-when-we-say-race-is-a-social-construct/275872/.

52. Onwuachi-Willig, A. (2016, September 6). Race and racial identity are social constructs. *New York Times*. Retrieved January 26, 2021, from https://www.nytimes.com/roomfordebate/2015/06/16/how-fluid-is-racial-identity/race-and-racial-identity-are-social-constructs.

53. Pew Research Center. (2015, September 28). *Modern immigration wave brings 59 million to U.S., driving population growth and change through 2065: Views of immigration's impact on U.S. society mixed*. Retrieved January 26, 2021, from https://www.pewresearch.org/hispanic/2015/09/28/modern-immigration-wave-brings-59-million-to-u-s-driving-population-growth-and-change-through-2065/.

54. Parker, K., Horowitz, J. M., Morin, R., & Lopez, M. H. (2015). *Multiracial in America: Proud, diverse, and growing in numbers*. Retrieved January 26, 2021, from https://www.pewsocialtrends.org/2015/06/11/multiracial-in-america/#fn-20523-2.

55. Pew Research Center. (2015, May 12). *America's changing religious landscape: Christians decline sharply as share of population; unaffiliated and other faiths continue to grow*. Retrieved January 26, 2021, from http://www.pewforum.org/2015/05/12/americas-changing-religious-landscape/.

56. Kosmin, B. A., & Keysar, A. (2009). *American Religious Identification Survey (ARIS 2008)*. Trinity College. Retrieved January 26, 2021, from http://commons.trincoll.edu/aris/files/2011/08/ARIS_Report_2008.pdf.

57. Scott, D. (2014). Race, ethnicity, and leisure services: Can we hope to escape the past? In M. Stodolska, K. J. Shinew, M. F. Floyd, & G. J. Walker (Eds.), *Race, ethnicity, and leisure: Perspectives on research, theory and practice,* (pp. 37–50). Human Kinetics.

58. van Eijck, K. (2004) "Leisure, lifestyle, and the new middle class," *Leisure Sciences*, 26, 373-392.

59. Noonan, D. S. (2005). Neighbours, barriers and urban environments: Are things "different on the other side of the tracks"? *Urban Studies, 42*, 1817–1835.

60. Schneider, I. E., Shinew, K. J., & Fernandez, M. (2014). Leisure constraints. In M. Stodolska, K. J. Shinew, M. F. Floyd, & G. J. Walker (Eds.), *Race, ethnicity, and leisure: Perspectives on research, theory and practice*, (pp. 165–176). Human Kinetics.

61. Martin, W., & Mason, S. (2003). Leisure in three Middle Eastern countries. *World Leisure, 45(1)*,35–44.

62. Livengood, J., & Stodolska, M. (2004). The effects of discrimination and constraints negotiation on leisure behavior of American Muslims in the post–September 11 America. *Journal of Leisure Research, 36*, 183–208.

Chapter 4

History of Recreation and Leisure

As one examines the role of recreation and leisure in modern society, it is helpful first to view it through the lens of historical perspective. Throughout history, one must ask: What has been the nature of humankind's play? How much leisure have we had? How was work regarded, in contrast to recreation? Did the educational system of each period make use of play activities? How did philosophers regard leisure and its uses? Did the state make provision for the entertainment or recreation of the various classes of society?[1]

-From the first edition of Kraus' Recreation and Leisure in Modern Society, published in 1971
(pronouns changed for inclusivity)

LEARNING OBJECTIVES

1. Describe changing perceptions of leisure from ancient civilizations through modern day.

2. Describe the impact that religion had on recreation and leisure tolerance.

3. List forms of recreation activities popular during each major time period.

4. Describe current trends in recreation and leisure.

5. Describe differences in recreation access for participants of diverse backgrounds.

Introduction

To provide a meaningful background for the study of recreation and leisure in modern society, it is helpful to have a clear understanding of its role in the past. We can trace the origins of many of our contemporary views of leisure and related cultural customs to the traditions and practices of ancient cultures. The history of recreation and leisure is a rich tapestry of people, places, events, and social forces, showing the role of religion, education, and government and the customs and values of different cultures, their arts, sport, and pastimes. By becoming familiar with the evolution of our recreation and leisure, we are better able to understand and deal effectively with the present.

The Play of Early Societies

Relatively little is known about the nature of leisure and play in the early periods of the Paleolithic and Neolithic epochs. However, between archaeologists' discovery of artifacts providing evidence of leisure activities and societal accounts by missionaries and anthropologists, we have some understanding of early play.

Origins of Games and Sport

In primitive societies, play may have had many sources. Popular games were often vestiges of warfare, practiced as a form of sport. Musical instruments were likely created for use in religious rituals. Pottery, painting, drawings, and other early art provided a record of both daily life and cultural mythology. Beads and other types of jewelry were created as external symbols of individual status and group affiliations. When an activity was no longer useful in its original form (such as archery for hunting or warfare), it became a form of sport.

Some indigenous groups offer an example of how play was used to equip the young for adult life. Children practiced warriors' skills, were taught to survive unarmed and unclothed in the wilderness, and were taught household crafts. Through dancing, singing, and storytelling, everyone learned the history and religion of their cultures.

Early Chinese societies developed highly organized cultural events.
© IMAGEMORE Co, Ltd./Getty.

Recreation and Leisure in Ancient Civilizations

As prehistoric societies advanced, they developed specialization of functions. Humans learned to domesticate plants and animals, which permitted them to shift from a nomadic existence based on hunting and food gathering to a largely stationary way of life. Ultimately, ruling classes developed, along with soldiers, craftsmen, peasants, and slaves. As villages and

TRIBAL VIEW OF WORK AND LEISURE

Tribal people do not make the same sharp distinction between work and leisure that more technologically advanced societies do. Whereas the latter set aside different periods of time for work and relaxation, a tribal, pretechnological society has no such precise separations. Instead, work is customarily done when it is available or necessary, and it is often infused with rites and customs that lend it variety and pleasure. In such tribal societies, work tends to be varied and creative, rather than being a narrow, specialized task demanding a sharply defined skill, as in modern industry. Work is often accompanied by ritual that is regarded as essential to the success of the planting or harvesting or to the building or hunting expedition. The ritual may involve prayer, sacrifice, dance, or feasting, which thus becomes part of the world of work.

ARCHAEOLOGISTS UNCOVER ANCIENT FLUTES USED IN CULTURAL CELEBRATION

In a period ranging from May 1986 to June 1987, archaeologists at the early Neolithic site of Jiahu in Henan Province, China, uncovered 25 flutes between 7,000 and 9,000 years old, most at grave sites. Six of the instruments were intact and are now believed to be the earliest, playable multinote instruments. The flutes, which were made of bone, contain seven holes that correspond to a scale similar to the Western eight-note scale. This tone scale indicates that musicians living in 7000 BCE could compose and play music. Some believe that the flutes were part of religious rituals; others believe that music was simply a part of community life.

Data from Juzhong, Z., & Kuen, L. Y. (2005). The magic flutes. *Natural History, 114*(7), 43.

The highest form of leisure usually occurred among the elite in ancient societies.

© Pavel Mitrofanov/Dreamstime.com.

cities evolved and large estates were farmed by lower-class workers, the upper classes gained power, wealth, and leisure. Thus, in the aristocracy of the first civilizations that developed in the Middle East during the 5 millennia before the Christian era, we find for the first time in history a leisure class.

Ancient Egypt, Assyria, and Babylonia

The Egyptian culture, lasting from about 5000 BCE into the Roman era, was a rich and diversified one; it achieved an advanced knowledge of astronomy, architecture, engineering, agriculture, and construction. The culture was richly recorded in paintings, statuary, and hieroglyphic records. The ancient Egyptians engaged in many sports as part of education and recreation, including wrestling, gymnastic exercises, lifting and swinging weights, and ball games. Music, drama, and dance were forms of religious worship as well as social entertainment with complex orchestras that included various stringed and percussive instruments.

Until the invasion by Alexander the Great in 330 BCE, Middle Eastern countries Assyria and Babylon were also powerful empires. Like the ancient Egyptians, the Assyrians and Babylonians had many popular recreation activities, such as boxing, wrestling, archery, and a variety of table games. In addition to watching dancing, listening to music, and giving banquets, Assyrians, particularly nobles, were also devoted to hunting, often in established parks.

Ancient Israel

Among the ancient Israelites, music and dancing were performed for ritual purposes as well as for social activities and celebrations as referenced in the Old Testament. Like other ancient societies, the ancient Hebrews also engaged in hunting, fishing, wrestling, and the use of such weapons as the sword and javelin for both recreational and defensive purposes. As for leisure itself, their major contribution was to set aside the Sabbath as a time for people to rest from work and to worship.

Ancient Greece

In the city-states of ancient Greece, particularly in Athens during the so-called Golden Age of Pericles from about 500 to 400 BCE, humankind reached a new peak of philosophical and cultural development. The Athenians took great interest in the arts, in learning, and in athletics. These pursuits were generally restricted to aristocratic noblemen. Craftsmen, farmers, and tradespeople were also citizens but had limited rights and less prestige, and labor was performed by slaves and foreigners.

The amenities of life were generally restricted to the most wealthy and powerful citizens, who represented the Athenian ideal of the balanced man—a combined soldier, athlete, artist, statesman, and philosopher. In fact, Athenian philosophers believed strongly in the unity of mind and body and that play activity was essential to the healthy physical and social growth of children. This ideal was furthered through education and the various religious festivals, which occupied about 70 days of the year. The arts of music, poetry,

WOMEN IN ANCIENT GREECE

Women did not enjoy the leisurely pursuits of men in ancient Greece, although there are some historical accounts of women receiving modest education and young girls participating in some athletic competitions. Citizens were, by definition, men.

theater, gymnastics, and athletic competition were combined in these sacred competitions.

The ancient Greeks developed the art of town planning and customarily made extensive provisions for parks and gardens, open-air theaters and gymnasiums, baths, exercise grounds, and stadiums. Early Athens had many public baths and some public parks, which later gave way to privately owned estates.

A gradual transition occurred in the Greek approach to leisure and play. At first, all citizens were expected to participate in sports and games, and the Olympic Games were restricted to free-born Greeks only. Gradually, however, the religious and cultural functions of the Olympic Games and other festivals were weakened by athletic specialization, corruption, and commercialism. In time, sport and other forms of activity such as drama, singing, and dance were performed only by highly skilled specialists drawn from the lower classes or slaves.

Ancient Rome

Like the Greek city-states, the Roman republic during its early development was a vigorous and nationalistic state. The Roman citizen, although part of a privileged class, was required to defend his society and fight in its wars. Citizens participated in sport and gymnastics, intended to keep the body strong and the spirit courageous. Numerous games held in connection with the worship of various Roman gods later developed into annual festivals. The most important of the Roman games were those that celebrated military triumphs, usually held in honor of the god Jupiter, head of the Roman pantheon.

Like the early Greeks, young Roman children had toy carts, houses, dolls, hobbyhorses, stilts, and tops and engaged in many sports and games. The Romans, however, had a different concept of leisure than the Greeks. Although the Latin words for "leisure" and "business" are *otium* and *negotium*, suggesting the same view of leisure as a positive value (with work defined negatively as a lack of leisure), the Romans supported play for utilitarian rather than aesthetic or spiritual reasons.

Even more than the Greeks, the Romans were systematic planners and builders. Their towns generally included provisions for baths, open-air theaters, amphitheaters, forums for public assemblies, stadiums, gymnasiums, and sometimes parks and gardens. Wealthier Romans often had private villas, many with large gardens and hunting preserves.

The Roman Colosseum is considered one of the greatest architectural achievements of antiquity. Built almost 2000 years ago, the Colosseum is a monument to the achievements and culture of ancient Rome.
© Tan, Kim Pin/Shutterstock.

As the empire grew more powerful, the simple agricultural democracy of the early years, in which all male Romans were citizens and free men, shifted to an urban life with sharply divided classes. There were four social levels: the richest, land-holding *senators*; the *curiae*, who owned more than 25 acres of land and were officeholders or tax collectors; the *plebs*, or free common people, who owned small properties or were tradesmen or artisans; and the *coloni*, who were lower-class tenants of the land. In time, a huge urban population of plebs lived in semi-idleness because most of the work was done by *coloni* and slaves brought to Rome. Gradually, it became necessary for the Roman emperors and senate to amuse and entertain the *plebs*; they did so with doles of grain and with public games—in other words, "bread and circuses."

As early as the reign of the Emperor Claudius in the first century CE, there were 159 public holidays during the year, 93 of which were devoted to games at public expense. By CE 354, there were 200 public holidays each year, including 175 days of games. Even on working days, the labor began at daybreak and ended shortly after noon during much of the year.

As leisure increased with the necessity for military service and other forms of physical effort declining for the Roman citizen, the normal practice was for the citizen to be entertained or to follow a daily routine of exercise, bathing, and eating. No longer as active in sport as they once had been, the men now sought to be amused and to entertain their guests with paid acrobats, musicians, dancers, and other artists. Athletes performed as members of a specialized profession with unions, coaches, and training schools.

CORRUPTION OF ENTERTAINMENT

Gradually, the focus on the traditional sports of running, throwing, and jumping gave way to an emphasis on human combat—first boxing and wrestling and then displays of cruelty in which gladiators fought to the death for the entertainment of mass audiences. Imported wild beasts, such as tigers and elephants, were pitted against each other or against human antagonists, often Christians.[2] Both animals and humans were maimed and butchered in cruel and horrible ways. By this time, competitive sport had become completely commercialized. To maintain political popularity and placate the poor masses, the emperors and the senate provided great parades, circuses, and feasts. Spectacles were often lewd and obscene, leading to mass debauchery, corruption, and perversion that profoundly weakened the Roman state.

Early Christian Era: Dark and Middle Ages

Under attack by successive waves of northern European tribes, the Roman Empire finally collapsed. For a period of several centuries, Europe was overrun with warring tribes and shifting alliances. The organized power of Rome, which had built roads, extended commerce, and provided civil order, was at an end. Gradually, the Catholic Church emerged to provide a form of universal citizenship within Europe. Having suffered under the brutal persecutions of the Romans, the early Christians condemned all that their pagan oppressors had stood for—especially their hedonistic way of life. Indeed, the early church fathers believed in a fanatical asceticism, which in the Byzantine, or Eastern, Empire was marked by the Anchorite movement, with its idea of salvation through masochistic self-deprivation.

Pastimes in the Middle Ages

Despite disapproval from the church, many forms of play continued during the Middle Ages. Medieval society was marked by rigid class stratification; below the nobility and clergy were the peasants, who were divided into such ranks as freemen, villeins, serfs, and slaves.

Life in the Middle Ages, even for the feudal nobility, was crude and harsh. Manors and castles were little more than stone fortresses. Knights were responsible for fighting in the service of their rulers; between wars, their favorite pastimes were hunting and hawking, with hunting serving as a useful preparation for war. Other pastimes during the Middle Ages were various types of games and gambling, music and dance, sport, and jousting. Gambling was popular, although forbidden by both ecclesiastical and royal authority.

As the chaos of the Dark Ages yielded to greater order and regularity, life became more stable. Travel in reasonable safety became possible, and by the 11th century, commerce was widespread. The custom of jousting emerged within the medieval courts, stemming from the tradition that only the nobility fought on horseback.

GAMES OF THE COMMON PEOPLE

Edward Hulme suggests that life was not all work for the lower classes. There were village feasts and sport, practical joking, throwing weights, cockfighting, bull baiting, and other lively games. As life in the Middle Ages became somewhat easier, a number of pastimes emerged. Many modern sports were developed at this time in rudimentary form. Peasants usually went to bed at dark, reading was a rare accomplishment, and there was much drinking and crude brawling.

The people of the Middle Ages had an insatiable love of sightseeing and would travel great distances to see entertainment. When the kings of France assembled their principal retainers once or twice a year, they distributed food and liquor among the common people and provided military displays, court ceremonies, and entertainment by jugglers, tumblers, and minstrels.

CHANGE COMES TO ROMAN LIFE IN THE DARK AND MIDDLE AGES

Many aspects of Roman life were forbidden during the Dark and Middle Ages. The stadiums, amphitheaters, and baths that had characterized Roman life were destroyed. The Council of Elvira ruled that the rite of baptism could not be extended to those connected with the stage, and in 398 CE, the Council of Carthage excommunicated those who attended the theater on holy days. The Roman emphasis on leisure was replaced by a Christian emphasis on work. It would be a mistake, however, to assume that the Catholic Church eliminated all forms of play. Many early Catholic religious practices were based on the rituals of earlier faiths. Priests built churches on existing shrines or temple sites, set Christian holy days according to the dates of pagan festivals, and used such elements of pagan worship as bells, candles, incense, singing, and dancing.

The Renaissance

Following the Dark Ages (400–1000 CE) and High Middle Ages, the Renaissance is said to have begun in Italy about 1350, in France about 1450, and in England about 1500. It marked a transition between the medieval world and the modern age. The term renaissance means rebirth and describes the revived interest in the scholarship, philosophy, and arts of ancient Greece and Rome. More broadly, it also represented a new freedom of thought and expression, a more rational and scientific view of life, and the expansion of commerce and travel in European life.

As the major European nations stabilized during this period under solidly established monarchies, power shifted from the church to the kings and their nobles. Particularly in Italy and France, the nobility became patrons of great painters, sculptors, musicians, dancers, and dramatists.

Play as Education

Varied forms of play became part of the education of the youth of the nobility at this time. The Athenian philosophy that had supported play as an important form of education was given fuller emphasis during the Renaissance, with an emphasis on the need for physical exercises and games as well as singing, dancing, modeling and painting, nature study, and manual training.

Influence of the Protestant Reformation

The Reformation was a religious movement of the 1500s that resulted in the establishment of a number of Protestant sects whose leaders broke away from Roman Catholicism. It was part of a broader stream that included economic, social, and political currents. In part, it represented the influence of the growing middle classes, who allied with the nobility in the emerging nations of Europe to challenge the power of the church.

The "Protestant work ethic" that emerged during the Reformation led to periods of strict limitations on leisure and recreation throughout the history of many Christian cultures, including societies in North America. This same ethic has heavily influenced our contemporary Western views of the relative value of work and leisure.

Puritanism in England

The English Puritans waged a constant battle to limit or condemn sport and other forms of entertainment during the period from the 16th to the 18th century. Maintaining strict observation of the Sabbath was a particular issue. Anglican clergy during the Elizabethan period bitterly attacked stage plays, church festival gatherings, dancing, gambling, bowling, and other "devilish pastimes" such as hawking and hunting, holding fairs and markets, and reading "lascivious and wanton books."

Types of Major Parks

During the Middle Ages, park planning was characterized in the city by a lack of space or open areas, and as residents moved out from the city, a lack of planning for satellite communities. However, as the Renaissance period began, European town planning was characterized by wide avenues,

The English natural park school of thought emphasized using nature as the primary tool of creating a park rather than adding non-native species of plants to a park.
© Chris Lofty/Dreamstime.com.

THE PROTESTANT PURITANISM

The new Protestant sects tended to be more solemn and austere than the Catholic Church. Calvin established an autocratic system of government in Geneva in 1541 that was directed by a group of Presbyters, who were considered morally upright men and who controlled the social and cultural life of the community to the smallest detail. They ruthlessly suppressed heretics and burned dissenters at the stake. Miller and Robinson describe the unbending Puritanism in Geneva:

"Purity of conduct" was insisted upon, which meant the forbidding of gambling, card playing, dancing, wearing of finery, singing of gay songs, feasting, drinking and the like. There were to be no more festivals, no more theaters, no more ribaldry, no more light and disrespectful poetry or display. Works of art and musical instruments were removed from the churches.[3]

long approaches, handsome buildings, and similar monumental features, with nobility decorating their estates with elaborate gardens.

Three major types of large parks came into existence during the late Renaissance. In almost every instance, they were derived from private estates of nobles or the elite. The first were royal hunting preserves or parks, some of which have become famous public parks today, such as the 4,000-acre Prater in Vienna and the Tiergarten in Berlin. Second were the ornate and formal garden parks designed according to the so-called French style of landscape architecture. Third were the more naturalistic English garden parks.

In England, efforts at city planning began during the 18th century. Business and residential streets were paved and street names posted. Because it was believed that overcrowding led to disease (in the 17th century, London had suffered from recurrent attacks of the plague), an effort was made to convert open squares into gardens and to create more small parks. Deaths from contagious disease declined during each successive decade of the 18th century, and this improvement was believed to have been the result of increased cleanliness and ventilation within the city.

Popular Diversions in England

Great outdoor gardens were established in England to provide entertainment and relaxation. Vauxhall, a pleasure resort founded during the reign of Charles II, was a densely wooded area with walks and bowers, lighting displays, water mills, fireworks, artificial caves and grottoes, entertainment, eating places, and tea gardens. The park was supported by the growing class of merchants and tradesmen, and its admission charge and distance from London helped to "exclude the rabble."

Among the lower classes, tastes in entertainment varied according to whether one lived in the country or city. Countrymen continued to engage vigorously in such sport as football, cricket, wrestling, or "cudgel playing" and to enjoy traditional country or Morris dancing and the singing of old folk songs.

Concerns About Leisure: Class Differences

Gradually, concerns about the growing number of holidays and the effect of leisure activities on the working classes began to be voiced. For example, in France during the 18th century, wealthy individuals had the opportunity for amusement all week long—paying social visits, dining, and passing evenings at gaming, at the theater, ballet, opera, or clubs. In contrast, the working classes had only Sundays and fête days, or holidays, for their amusements. La Croix points out, however, that these represented a third of the whole year. This excess in time off led many economists and men of affairs to argue that the ecclesiastic authorities should be called upon to reduce the number.[4]

Recreation in America: The Colonial Period

We now cross the Atlantic to examine the development of recreation and leisure in the early American colonies. First, it needs to be recognized that when English and other European settlers established colonies, they did not entirely divorce themselves from the customs and values of the countries they had left. Commerce was ongoing; governors and military personnel traveled back and forth; and newspapers, magazines, and books were exchanged regularly.

The first need of 17th-century colonists was for survival. They had to plant crops, clear forests, build shelters, and in some cases defend themselves against attack by Indigenous tribes, whose land they were developing. In such a setting, work was all important; there was little time, money, or energy to support amusements or public entertainment. Without nobility possessing the wealth, leisure, and inclination to patronize the arts, there was little opportunity for music, theater, or dance to flourish—but the most important hindrance to the development of recreation was the religious attitude.

Restrictions in New England

The Puritan settlers of New England came to the New World to establish a society based on a strict Calvinist interpretation of the Bible. Although the work ethic had not originated with the Puritans, they adopted it enthusiastically. Idleness was detested as the "devil's workshop," and a number of colonies passed laws binding "any rougs, vagabonds, sturdy beggards, masterless men

The U.S. southern economy was built on the labor of slaves who had little time for recreation, which allowed slave owners to create a life of leisure and luxury.

Courtesy of Library of Congress, Prints & Photographs Division [reproduction number LC-USZ62-76385].

PLAY ATTACHED TO WORK GAINS ACCEPTANCE

Gradually, restrictions against play were relaxed in New England and elsewhere. Recreation became more acceptable when amusements could be attached to work, and thus country fairs and market days became occasions for merrymaking. Social gatherings with music, games, and dancing were held in conjunction with such work projects as house raisings, sheep shearing, logrolling, or cornhusking bees. Many social pastimes were linked to other civic occasions such as elections or training days for local militia.

or other notorious offenders" over to compulsory work or imprisonment.[5]

Puritan magistrates attempted to maintain curbs on amusements long after the practical reasons for such prohibitions had disappeared. Early court records show many cases of young people being fined, confined to the stocks, or publicly whipped for such "violations" as drunkenness, idleness, gambling, dancing, or participating in other forms of "lascivious" behavior. However, despite these restrictions, many forms of play continued. Football was played by boys in Boston's streets and lanes, and although playing cards (the "devil's picture-books") were hated by the Puritans, they were freely imported from England and openly on sale.

Other ordinances banned gambling, drama, and nonreligious music, with dancing—particularly between men and women—also condemned. There was vigorous enforcement of the Sabbath laws: Sunday work, travel, and recreation—even "unnecessary and unseasonable walking in the streets and fields"—were prohibited.

Leisure in the Southern Colonies

A number of the southern colonies had similar restrictions during the early years of settlement. The laws of Virginia, for example, forbade Sunday amusements and made imprisonment the penalty for failure to attend church services. Sabbath-day dancing, fiddling, hunting, fishing, and card playing were strictly banned. Gradually, however, these stern restrictions declined in the southern colonies. There, the upper classes had both wealth and leisure from their large estates and plantations, on which the labor was performed by indentured servants and slaves. As southern settlers of this social class became established, plantation life for the upper class became marked by lavish entertainment and hospitality.

The lifestyles of slaves in the colonies were a stark contrast to the lavish lifestyles of their owners. The majority of slaves in the colonies were of West African ancestry and leisure had been used as a trap for their enslavement. Slaves were enticed to perform their native dances in exchange for food and drink aboard their would-be captors' boats and then, drunk and unable to defend themselves, they found themselves headed to America and the slave markets. They were able to bring nothing with them to the colonies other

than language and customs, both of which they were compelled to disregard upon arrival. The customs that thrived in the harsh life of the colonies included music, folktales and storytelling, and dance. In the colonies, and later in the southern states, slaves had very few opportunities for leisure. Slave masters used free time as a "reward" to improve morale and often enforced strict rules about what could happen during that free time. Although white people subscribed to the "universal law of slavery" that African American people were inferior, their talents were clear as they were instrumental in the development of some of the world's most famous art forms such as in woodworking and weaving.[6]

Decline of Religious Controls

Despite the stern sermons of New England ministers and the severe penalties for infractions of the established moral code, it is clear that play became gradually tolerated in the colonies. The lottery was introduced during the early 1700s and quickly gained the sanction and participation of the most esteemed citizens. Towns and states used lotteries to increase their revenues and to build canals, turnpikes, and bridges. This "acceptable" form of gambling helped to endow leading colleges and academies, and even Congregational, Baptist, and Episcopal churches had lotteries "for promoting public worship and the advancement of religion."

The climate around drinking began to change despite the fact that under Puritan law, drunkards were subject to fines and imprisonment in the stocks, and sellers were forbidden to provide them with any liquor thereafter. By the early part of the 18th century, taverns were widely established throughout New England. By the mid-1700s, the stern necessity of hard work for survival had lessened, and religious antagonism toward amusements had also declined.

Parks and Conservation in the Colonial Era

Early American colonies showed little concern for developing parks in cities and towns with open space so plentiful around the isolated settlements. The earliest planned outdoor spaces were "commons" or "greens," found in many New England communities and used chiefly for pasturing cattle and sheep but also for military drills, market days, and fairs. Similar open areas such as plazas were established in towns settled by the Spanish in the South and Southwest. As urban areas grew, cities such as Philadelphia, Savannah, and Washington, DC were among the first to give attention to the need for preserving or establishing parks and open spaces.

Early Conservation Efforts

From the early days of settlement, there was concern for the conservation of forests and open land in the New England countryside. As early as 1626 in the Plymouth Colony, the cutting of trees without official consent was prohibited by law. The Massachusetts Bay Colony passed the Great Ponds Act in 1641, which set aside 2,000 bodies of water for such public uses as "fishing and fowling." Pennsylvania law in 1681 required that for every five acres of forest land that were cleared, one was to be left untouched.

As early as the late 17th century, Massachusetts and Connecticut defined hunting seasons and established rules for hunting certain types of game. As wildlife populations sharply fell, provinces such as New York started providing for closed seasons to protect different species. It is apparent that the colonists had shown a concern for the establishment of parks and urban open spaces and for the conservation of forests and wildlife in early days.

The Boston Common, often credited as the first community park in the United States because of its 1634 creation, continues to provide opportunities for recreation and park experiences.
© Marcos Carvalho/Shutterstock.

Nineteenth-Century Changes: Impact of the Industrial Revolution

During the late 18th through the 20th century, great changes took place in both Europe and the United States. It was a time of growing democratization, advancement of scientific knowledge and technology, and huge waves of immigration from Europe to America. More than any other factor, the Industrial Revolution changed the way people lived. By the early 20th century, leisure was more freely available to all, and a widespread recreation movement had begun in the United States.

Science and capital combined to increase production, as businessmen invested in the industrial expansion made possible by newly invented machines. Industry moved from homes and workshops to new mills and factories with mechanical power. The invention of such devices as the spinning jenny, the weaving machine, and the steam engine (all during the 1760s) drastically altered production methods and increased output.

Urbanization

Throughout the Western world, there was a steady shift of the population from rural areas to urban centers. Because factory wages were usually higher than those in domestic industry or agriculture, great numbers of people migrated to the cities. Millions of European peasant families emigrated because of crop failures, expulsion from their land, religious or social discrimination, or political unrest. During the latter part of the 19th century, tens of thousands of African American people, disillusioned by the failed Reconstruction, immigrated to northern cities in search of a better quality of life.

The American population increased rapidly during this period. From 1829 to 1860, America's population had grown from 12.5 to 31 million. In the large cities, the proportion of foreign-born inhabitants was quite high: 45% of New York City's population in 1850 was foreign born, mostly Irish and German. Although 85% of the population in 1850 was still rural, as more and more people moved into factory towns and large cities, the United States became an urban civilization.

THE CHANGING WORKWEEK

Overall, the average workweek declined from 62 hours per week for all industries (including agriculture) in 1870 to 58.3 hours in 1913, and to 42.4 hours in 1950 (see Figure 4-1). As a consequence, during the last half of the 19th century, concerns about increases in free time began to appear—including fears about the dangers of certain forms of play and the broader question of what the potential role of leisure might be in the coming century.

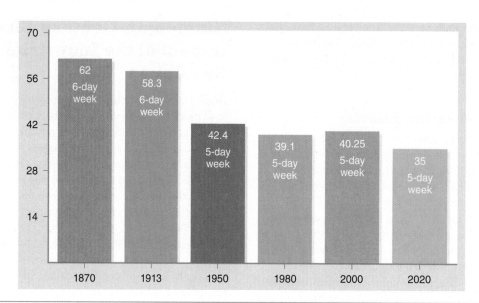

FIGURE 4-1 How the Average Workweek Has Changed (in hours)

Data from Giattino, C., Ortiz-Ospina, E., & Roser, M. (2020). *Working hours. Our world in data*. Retrieved February 9, 2021, from https://ourworldindata.org/working-hours; and Statista. (n.d.). *Monthly change of the average working week of all employees in the United States from March 2020 to March 2021*. Retrieved February 9, 2021, from https://www.statista.com/statistics/215643/average-weekly-working-hours-of-all-employees-in-the-us-by-month.

TRAVELING WHILE AFRICAN AMERICAN

In order to navigate travel in areas where segregation and racial hostilities were the norm, through the first half of the 20th century African American people relied on two resources to guide their plans, the *Green Book* and the *Travel Guide*. Both resources provided a compilation of hotels, restaurants, and other amenities that African American people could frequent. In fact, in 1946 the *Travel Guide*'s motto was "vacation and recreation without humiliation."

Rural townspeople and foreign immigrants moved into the congested tenement areas of growing cities, living in quarters that were inadequate for decent family life with slums marked by congestion and disease. Their residents were oppressed by low wages and recurrent unemployment and by monotonous and prolonged labor, including the use of young children in mills, mines, and factories and at piecework tasks at home.

Reduction in Work Hours

Throughout this period, there was steady pressure to reduce the workweek, both through industry-labor negotiation and legislation. Benjamin Hunnicutt points out that the effort to obtain shorter work hours was a critical issue in reform politics in the United States throughout the 19th century and up until the period of the Great Depression.

The 8-hour day had been a union objective for many years in the United States, paralleling efforts to reduce the workweek in other countries. In 1868, Congress established the 8-hour day for mechanics and laborers employed by or under contracts with the federal government. Following the 1868 law, labor unions made a concerted effort to obtain the 8-hour day in other areas and in 1890 began to achieve success.

Religious Revivalism and Recreation

Fueled by a religious revival before the Civil War, there was a strong emphasis on the importance of "honest toil" during the middle and latter parts of the 19th century. Many Americans believed, and continue to believe, that hard work alone is sufficient for an individual to improve their social and economic status. Clergy, policy makers, civic leaders, and scholars were particularly concerned that new immigrants and the urban poor develop appropriate social values through hard work and appropriate, disciplined use of leisure time.

Churches Attack Leisure

Work was considered the source of social and moral values, and therefore the proper concern of churches, which renewed their attack upon most forms of play. The churches condemned many commercial amusements as "the door to all the sins of iniquity."

Despite antiamusement efforts, the first half of the 19th century saw an expansion of popular amusements in the United States. The theater, which had been banned during the American Revolution, gradually gained popularity in cities along the eastern seaboard and in the South. Large theaters were built to accommodate audiences of as many as 4,000 people. Local stock companies throughout the country presented serious drama as well as lighthearted entertainment, which later became burlesque and vaudeville. By the 1830s, about 30 traveling shows were regularly touring the country with menageries and bands of acrobats and jugglers, ultimately evolving into circuses.

Drinking remained popular as the majority of American men were taverngoers. Printed street directories of American cities listed tavern keepers in staggering numbers, and taverns were the nation's most popular centers of male sociability.

Growing Interest in Sport

A number of sports gained their first strong impetus during the early 19th century. Americans enjoyed watching amateur wrestling matches, foot races, shooting events, and horse races during colonial days and along the frontier. In the early 1800s, professional promotion of sport events began as well.

PROFESSIONALISM IN SPORT

Crowds as large as 50,000 from all ranks of society attended highly publicized boating regattas and 5- and 10-mile races of professional runners during the 1820s. The first sport promoters were owners of resorts or of commercial transportation facilities such as stagecoach lines, ferries, and later, trolleys and railroads. These new sport impresarios initially made their profits from transportation fares and accommodations for spectators; later, they erected grandstands and charged admission. Horse racing, boxing, and basketball were among the first sports to gain large followings.

Changing Attitudes Toward Play

During the last half of the 19th century, the Industrial Revolution was flourishing, with factories, expansion of urban areas, and railroads crisscrossing the country. Free public education had become a reality in most areas, and health care and life expectancy were improving. As the industrial labor force began to organize into craft unions, working conditions improved, levels of pay increased, and

Sailing regattas were a popular form of recreation and a popular spectator sport in the early 1800s.
Courtesy of Library of Congress, Prints & Photographs Division [reproduction number LC-DIG-pga-00437].

the hours of work were cut back. Children who had worked long, hard hours in factories, mines, and big-city sweatshops were freed of this burden through child labor legislation while the strong disapproval of play that had characterized the colonial period began to disappear.

By the 1880s and 1890s, church leaders recognized that religion could no longer arbitrarily condemn all play and offered "sanctified amusement and recreation" as alternatives to undesirable play. Many churches made provisions for libraries, gymnasiums, and assembly rooms.

Popular hobbies such as photography caught on and were frequently linked to new outdoor recreation pursuits. Sport was probably the largest single area of expanded leisure participation, with increasing interest being shown in tennis, archery, bowling, skating, bicycling, and team games such as baseball, basketball, and football.

The Muscular Christianity movement—so named because of the support given to it by leading church figures and because sport and physical activity were thought to build morality and good character—had its greatest influence in schools and colleges, which began to initiate programs of physical education and athletic competition.

RISE OF SPORT

As the country neared the end of the 19th century, a series of athletic crazes swept through the eastern states.

On its path to becoming as American as hot dogs and apple pie, the popularity of baseball soared in the late 1800s. Beyond baseball, lawn games such as croquet, lawn tennis, and archery gained a level of popularity not seen prior. In addition to these lawn games, roller-skating also saw a rise in participation rates across the country.[8]

College Sport

In the United States, colleges initiated their first competitive sports programs. In colonial New England, students had engaged in many pastimes, with some tolerated by college authorities and others prohibited. The first college clubs had been founded as early as 1717, and social clubs were in full swing by the 1780s and 1790s. By the early 19th century, most U.S. colleges had more or less recognized clubs and their social activities. The founding of social fraternities in the 1840s and the building of college gymnasiums in the 1860s added to the social life and physical recreation of students.

Intercollegiate sport competition in rowing, baseball, track, and football was organized. The first known intercollegiate football game was between Princeton and Rutgers in 1869; interest spread rapidly, and by the late 1880s, college football games were attracting as many as 40,000 spectators.

Amateur Sport

Track and field events were widely promoted by amateur athletic clubs, some of which, like the New York Athletic Club, had many influential members who formed the Amateur Athletic Union and developed rules to govern amateur sport competition. Gymnastic instruction and games were sponsored by the German turnvereins, the Czech sokols, and the Young Men's Christian Association (YMCA), which had established some 260 large gymnasiums around the country by the 1880s and was a leader in sport activities.

Other Activities

Women began to participate in recreational pastimes, enjoying gymnastics, dance, and other athletics in school and college physical education programs. Bicycling was introduced in the 1870s, and within a few years, hundreds of thousands of people had become enthusiasts. Moving outdoors, Americans also began to enjoy hiking and mountain climbing, fishing and hunting, camping in national forests and state parks, and nature photography.

Growth of Commercial Amusements

Particularly in larger cities, new forms of commercial amusement sprang up or expanded during the 19th century. The theater was more popular than ever. Dime museums, dance halls, shooting galleries, bowling alleys, billiard parlors, beer gardens, and saloons provided a new world of entertainment for pay. In addition to these, many cities had "red light districts" where prostitution flourished. Drinking, gambling, and commercial vice gradually became serious social problems, particularly when protected by a tacit alliance between criminal figures and big-city political machines.

Amusement parks grew on the outskirts of cities and towns, often established by new rapid transit companies offering reduced-fare rides to the parks in decorated trolley cars. Amusement parks featured such attractions as parachute jumps, open-air theaters, band concerts, professional bicycle races, freak shows, games of chance, and shooting galleries. Roller coasters, fun houses, and midget-car tracks also became popular.[9]

Although new commercial recreation ventures opened up new opportunities for many, access for African American people was limited. Swimming pools, amusement parks, and skating rinks in particular provided the backdrop for continuous struggles by African American people to be permitted to use facilities both in the Jim Crow south as well as the north where segregation in many places was not "de jure" or mandated by law but "de facto" in that it existed in reality. Leaders promoted the idea that violence would be inevitable should races comingle, particularly men and women. Authorities used this belief, drawing on the findings in *Plessy v Ferguson*, the landmark 1896 Supreme Court decision that upheld the constitutionality of racial segregation under the "separate but equal" doctrine, to maintain separate facilities that were anything but equal.[10]

Concerns About Leisure

Intellectual and political leaders raised questions about the growing amusement industry and new forms of recreation affected by the growing urban centers of population. The English author Lord Lytton commented, "The social civilization of a people is always and infallibly indicated by the intellectual character of its amusements."[11] In 1876, American journalist Horace Greeley observed that although there were teachers for every art, science, and "elegy," there were no "professors of play." He asked, "Who will teach us incessant workers how to achieve leisure and enjoy it?"[12] And, in 1880, President James Garfield declared in a speech at Lake Chautauqua, "We may divide the whole struggle of the human race into two chapters: first, the fight to get leisure; and then the second fight of civilization—what shall we do with our leisure when we get it."[13]

The Beginning Recreation Movement

The period extending from the mid-19th through the early 20th century is referred to by recreation scholars as the public recreation movement. The period was characterized by the widespread development of organized recreation activities and facilities by government and voluntary agencies with the intent of achieving desirable social outcomes. There were four major streams of development during the public recreation movement: the adult education movement; the development of national, state, and municipal parks; the establishment of voluntary organizations; and the playground movement.

The Adult Education Movement

During the early 19th century, there was considerable civic concern for improving intellectual cultivation and providing continuing education for adults. Again, this was found in other nations as well; in France, workers' societies were determined to gain shorter workdays and more leisure time for adult study and cultural activities.

In the United States, there was a growing conviction that leisure, properly used, could contribute to the idealistic liberal values that were part of the American intellectual heritage. One of the means of achieving this took the form of the Lyceum movement, a national organization with more than 900 local chapters. Its program consisted chiefly of lectures, readings, and other educational events, reflecting the view that all citizens should be educated to participate knowledgeably in affairs of government.

A closely related development was the expansion of reading as a recreational experience, which was furthered by the widespread growth of free public libraries that supported the increasing need for better educated workers. As an example of the growing interest in cultural activity, the arts and crafts movement found its largest following in the United States in the beginning of the 20th century.

The Development of National, State, and Municipal Parks

Concern for preservation of the natural heritage of the United States in an era of increasing industrialization and despoilment of natural resources began in the 19th century. The first conservation action was passed in 1864, when Congress set aside an extensive area of wilderness primarily for public recreational use, consisting of the Yosemite Valley and the Mariposa Grove of Big Trees in California. This later became a national park. The first designated national park was Yellowstone, founded in 1872. In 1892, the Sierra Club was founded by John Muir, a leading Scottish-born conservationist who, along with Theodore Roosevelt, encouraged national interest in the outdoors and ultimately the establishment of the National Park Service.[14]

The primary purpose of the national parks at the outset was to preserve the nation's natural heritage and wildlife. This contrasted sharply with the Canadian approach to wilderness, which saw it as primitive and untamed. Parks, as in Great Britain and Europe, were seen as landscaped gardens, and intensive development for recreation and tourism guided early Canadian policy. Indeed, Banff National Park was initially a health spa, and early provincial parks were designed to be health resorts.[15]

STATE PARKS

As federal park development gained momentum in the United States, state governments also became concerned with the preservation of their forest areas and wildlife. As early as 1867, Michigan and Wisconsin established fact-finding committees to explore the problem of forest conservation; their example was followed shortly by Maine and other eastern states. Between 1864 and 1900, the first state parks were established, as were a number of state forest preserves and historic parks.

MUNICIPAL PARKS

Until the 19th century, North America lagged far behind Europe in the development of municipal parks, partly because this continent had no aristocracy with large cultivated estates, hunting grounds, and elaborate gardens that could be turned over to the public. The first major park to be developed in an American city was Central Park in New York.

There long had been a need for open space in New York City. During the first 30 years of the 19th century, plans were made for several open squares to total about 450 acres, but these were not carried out completely. By the early 1850s, the entire amount of public open space in Manhattan totaled only 117 acres. Pressure mounted among the citizens of the city for a major park that would provide relief from stone and concrete.

When the public will could no longer be denied, legislation was passed in 1856 to establish a park in New York City. Construction of the 843-acre site began in 1857. Central Park, designed by landscape architects Frederick Law Olmsted and Calvert Vaux, was completely man-made and planned with purpose. The park was to be heavily wooded and to have the appearance of rural scenery, with roadways screened from the eyes of park users wherever possible. Recreational pursuits permitted in the park included walking, pleasure driving, ice skating, and boating—but not organized sport.

Local, state, and national park access was not always equal opportunity. Many African American people, while allowed to walk through local parks, often were not allowed to sit or use equipment within a park. In 1962 the state of South Carolina shut down all state parks to avoid having to integrate until the passage of the Civil Rights Act of 1964. In 1963, seven African American people filed a lawsuit to desegregate Jekyll Island State Park in Georgia. These barriers to access could also be found at the national level. As just one example, Shenandoah National Park in Virginia offered only separate campgrounds for African American people well into the 1960s.[16]

County Park Systems

Planning for what was to become the nation's first county park system began in Essex County, New Jersey. Bordering the crowded industrial city of Newark, it was outlined in a comprehensive proposal in 1894 that promised that the entire cost of the park project would be realized through tax revenues from increased property values. The Essex County park system proved to be a great success and set a model to be followed by hundreds of other county and special district park agencies throughout the United States in the early 1900s.

Establishment of Voluntary Organizations

During the 19th century, a number of voluntary (privately sponsored, nonprofit) organizations were founded that played an important role in providing recreation services, chiefly for children and youths. In many cases, voluntary organizations were the outgrowth of their founders' desires to put religious principles into action through direct service to the underprivileged. One such body was the YMCA, founded in Boston in 1851 and followed by the Young Women's Christian Association (YWCA) 15 years later. At

Old Faithful and the geysers of Yellowstone have made this first national park a popular destination since 1872.
Courtesy of the National Park Service. Photographed by Ed Austin and Herb Jones.

Central Park was America's first large urban park and was the prototype for other large city parks across the nation for the next 50 years.
© Christopher Walker/Shutterstock.

first, the Ys provided fellowship between youths and adults for religious purposes. They gradually enlarged their programs, however, to include gymnastics, sport, and other recreational and social activities.

Another type of voluntary agency that offered significant leisure programs was the settlement house—neighborhood centers established in the slum sections of the East and Midwest. Among the first were University Settlement, founded in New York City in 1886, and Hull House, founded in Chicago in 1889. Their staffs sought to help poor people, particularly immigrants, adjust to modern urban life by providing services concerned with education, family life, and community improvement.

CASE STUDY: Types and Uses of Urban Parks, 1850–1965

Early urban parks in the United States were places seen as an antidote to the problems of cities, which were perceived as dangerous, dirty, and unhealthy places. Parks formed an important component of the urban environment, and cities embraced them. Those same parks today provide a type of precursor to the emerging sustainable park of the 21st century. Cranz and Boland define three periods of park development beginning in 1850 and continuing through 1965. The three periods include the following:

- Pleasure ground (1850–1900)
- Reform park (1900–1930)
- Recreation facility (1930–1965)

Each of the park types is described in terms of social goal, activities, size, relation to city, elements, promoters, and beneficiaries.

The importance of understanding the different park movements from 1850 to the mid-1960s is to gain a greater appreciation of how citizens, politicians, and social and environmental movements affected park design and use. The first wave saw the large urban parks created all across the country, including such places as Central Park in New York City, Golden Gate Park in San Francisco, and Grant Park in Chicago. These large urban parks became major components of large urban areas, most becoming the core of larger and more diverse park and recreation systems.

The three park systems described in Table 4-1 show how the movements shifted, as did the population. In most cases, the park movement followed, rather than led, public needs and desires. As social reform advanced, the pleasure ground gave way to a more active and focused reform park, many of which still boast the same services and benefits today, although they have been changed several times. The recreation facility, a continuing popular model, was an expression of efforts to move from the city core to the suburbs.

Questions to Consider

- Discuss how the three park movements mirrored society in the United States.
- What were the actual benefits to the beneficiaries of the different types of parks?
- How many of these types of parks have you visited? How have they changed?

TABLE 4-1 Typology of Urban Parks, 1850–1965			
	Pleasure Ground (1850–1900)	**Reform Park (1900–1930)**	**Recreation Facility (1930–1965)**
Social goal	Public health and social reform	Social reform, children's play, assimilation	Recreation service
Activities	Strolling, carriage racking, bike riding, picnics, rowing, classical music, nondidactic education	Supervised play, gymnastics, crafts, Americanization classes, dancing, plays and pageants	Active recreation, basketball, tennis, team sports, spectator sports, swimming
Size	Very large, 1,000+ acres	Small, city blocks	Small to medium, follow formula
Relation to city	Set in contrast	Accepts urban patterns	Suburban
Elements	Woodlands and meadow, curving paths, placid water bodies, rustic structures, limited floral displays	Sandlots, playgrounds, rectilinear paths, swimming pools, fieldhouses	Asphalt or grass play area, pools, rectilinear paths, standard play equipment

CASE STUDY: Types and Uses of Urban Parks, 1850–1965 (*Continued*)

TABLE 4-1	Typology of Urban Parks, 1850–1965 (*Continued*)		
	Pleasure Ground (1850–1900)	**Reform Park (1900–1930)**	**Recreation Facility (1930–1965)**
Promoters	Health reformers, transcendentalists, real estate interests	Social reformers, social workers, recreation workers	Politicians, bureaucrats, planners
Beneficiaries	All city dwellers (intended), upper-middle class (reality)	Children, immigrants, working class	Suburban families

Data from Cranz, G., & Boland, M. (2004). Defining the sustainable park: A fifth model for urban parks. *Landscape Journal, 23*(2), 102–140. http://lj.uwpress.org/content/23/2/102

The Playground Movement

To understand the need for playgrounds in cities and towns, it is necessary to know the living conditions of poor people during the latter decades of the 19th century.

The wave of urbanization that had begun earlier now reached its peak. The urban population more than doubled—from 14 to 30 million—between 1880 and 1900 alone. By the century's end, there were 28 cities with more than 100,000 residents because of the recent waves of migration. A leading example was New York, where nearly five of every six of the city's 1.5 million residents lived in crowded tenements in 1891, characterized by dark hallways, filthy cellars, and inadequate cooking and bathroom facilities. In neighborhoods populated by poor immigrants, there was a tremendous amount of crime, gambling, gang violence, and prostitution.

CASE STUDY: The YMCA as the Prototype of the Social Movement of the Late 1800s

The Young Men's Christian Association was founded in London, England, in 1844 and migrated to the United States in 1851. George Williams was the founder of the YMCA, working with friends to find a way to get people off of London's streets. "The YMCA idea, which began among evangelicals, was unusual because it crossed the rigid lines that separated all the different churches and social classes in England in those days. This openness was a trait that would lead eventually to including in YMCAs all men, women and children, regardless of race, religion or nationality. Also, its target of meeting social needs in the community was clear from the start."[a]

As the growth of the YMCA was quick, it soon spread beyond Boston. While at the start only young men who were members of evangelical churches could join, this requirement was soon dropped. Those is management positions, however, were required to maintain membership in an evangelical church.

There were a number of likely explanations for the quick growth of the association. During a time of religious revivals, the Christian values and related programming (e.g., prayer meetings, Bible readings) of the YMCA were attractive to many. In addition, it is likely that the association also grew thanks to its decentralized approach to management which allowed growth to follow local interest in the movement thus helping ensure a healthy membership base in a community. Finally, the presence of a physical space operated by the local YMCA in each community that might include a reading room, a coffee shop, and information boards related to local jobs provided stability to their efforts while meeting a need for local young, single males.[b]

It became obvious to the leaders that if the YMCA was going to grow and serve a broader population it needed to adapt. Therefore, the association pivoted from a focus on evangelism to a more inclusive approach that allowed for a broad array of religions and ages as well as both men and women. With these adjustments, programmatic changes were also evident as the YMCA was committed to the development of a well-rounded individual from the mental to the physical and social abilities of participants. Unfortunately, at times programming around physical training produced conflict over what were acceptable forms of recreation from those with a more conservative mind-set.[b]

One of the other factors that has made the YMCA successful was the effort to avoid politics. YMCA services have focused on prevention rather than rehabilitation. With a focus on improving the individual client, rather than taking a stand with respect to potential outside influences in the political or social spheres, the YMCA has generally remained out of the political spotlight.[b]

Questions to Consider

- Explain the importance of the YMCA changing from an evangelical type of organization to a social organization.
- It is suggested that the YMCAs grew "by a diffusion process based on local enthusiasm." Discuss how this is similar to movements created via social networks today. How do you think this diffusion process occurred in the late 19th century?
- Discuss the differences between a preventive and rehabilitative organization.

[a]YMCA. (n.d.). *About us.* Retrieved January 24, 2021, from http://www.ymca.net/about-us/.
[b]Zald, M. N., & Denton, P. (1963). From evangelism to general service: The transformation of the YMCA. *Administrative Science Quarterly*, 8(2), 214–234. https://doi.org/10.2307/2390900

BOSTON SAND GARDEN: A BEGINNING

Within poor working-class neighborhoods, there were few safe places where children might play. The first such facility—and the one that is generally regarded as a landmark in the development of the recreation movement in the United States—was the Boston Sand Garden. The city of Boston has been the arena for many important developments in the park and recreation movement in the United States. The Boston Common, established in 1634, generally is regarded as the first municipal park; a 48-acre area of green, rolling hills and shade trees, it is located in the heart of the city.

The famous Boston Sand Garden was the first playground in the country designed specifically for children. A group of public-spirited citizens had a pile of sand placed behind the Parmenter Street Chapel in a working-class district. Supervision was voluntary at first, but by 1887 when 10 such centers were opened, women were employed to supervise the children. Two years later, the city of Boston began to contribute funds to support the sand gardens.

NEW YORK'S FIRST PLAYGROUNDS

In the nation's largest city, Walter Vrooman, founder of the New York Society for Parks and Playgrounds, directed the public's attention to the fact that in 1890 there were 350,000 children without a single public playground. Although the city had almost 6,000 acres of parkland, none was set aside for children. Civic leaders pointed out that children of working parents lacked supervision and were permitted to grow up subject to various temptations. Vrooman wrote that such children

are driven from their crowded homes in the morning … are chased from the streets by the police when they attempt to play, and beaten with the broom handle of the janitor's wife when found in the hallway, or on the stairs. No wonder they learn to chew and smoke tobacco before they can read, and take a fiendish delight in breaking windows, in petty thievery, and in gambling their pennies.[17]

Gradually, the pressure mounted. Two small model playgrounds were established in poor areas of the city in 1889 and 1891 by the newly formed New York Society for Parks and Playgrounds, with support from private donors. Gradually, the city assumed financial and legal responsibility as many additional playgrounds were built in the years that followed, often attached to schools.

The period between 1880 and 1900 was of critical importance to the development of urban recreation and park programs. More than 80 cities initiated park systems; a lesser number established sand gardens, and, shortly after, playgrounds. Illinois passed a law permitting the establishment of local park districts in which two or more municipalities might join together to operate park systems.

Effects of Racial and Ethnic Discrimination

Throughout this period, public and nonprofit youth-serving organizations often discriminated against members of minoritized racial or ethnic groups.

Prejudice Against Minoritized Groups

Generally, the most severe discrimination was leveled against African American people, who, though no longer slaves, were kept in a position of economic servitude through the practice of sharecropping, and were without civil, political, or judicial rights in the southern and border states. African American people were increasingly barred from social contact, economic opportunity, or recreational involvement with white people by a wave of state legislation and local ordinances in the late 19th and early 20th centuries.

There was also an extreme degree of prejudice against Mexican Americans and other Hispanics of mixed racial origins. For example, Anglo settlers in Texas regarded Mexicans as savage "heathens" who historically practiced human sacrifice and saw them as a decadent and inferior people.

There was also widespread prejudice expressed against Asian Americans, mostly Chinese nationals who began to arrive in California in the mid-1800s and who worked on the transcontinental railroad. As the number of Asians grew, so did xenophobia. Americans viewed them as heathens who could not readily be assimilated within the nation's essentially Anglo-Saxon framework and condemned them as unsanitary, immoral, and criminal. In fact, Chinese were barred from entry into the United States by the Oriental Exclusion Acts of 1882 and 1902.

Recreation and Parks: Early 20th Century

For the majority of Americans, however, the beginning of the 20th century was an exciting period marked by growing economic and recreational opportunity. By 1900, 14 cities had made provisions for supervised play facilities. Among the leading cities were Boston, Providence, Philadelphia, Pittsburgh, Baltimore, Chicago, Milwaukee, Cleveland, Denver, and Minneapolis.

At the same time, municipal parks became well established throughout the United States. In addition to the parks mentioned earlier, the first metropolitan park system was established by Boston in 1892. In the West, San Francisco and Sacramento in California as well as Salt Lake City, Utah, were among the first to incorporate large open spaces in town planning before 1900. The New England Association of Park Superintendents, the predecessor of the American Institute of Park Executives, was established in 1898 to bring together park superintendents and promote their professional concerns.

Growth of Public Recreation and Park Agencies

Gradually, the concept that city governments should provide recreation facilities, programs, and services became widely accepted. By 1906, 41 cities were sponsoring public

Playgrounds became more popular in the early decades of the 20th century in large urban areas.

Courtesy of Library of Congress, Prints & Photographs Division, Detroit Publishing Company Collection [reproduction number LC-D4-18183].

recreation programs, and by 1920, the number was 465. More and more states passed laws authorizing local governments to operate recreation programs, and between 1925 and 1935 the number of municipal recreation buildings quadrupled. Municipalities were also discovering new ways to add parks, including through mandated land dedications and gifts.

Federal Park Expansion

As president, Theodore Roosevelt, a dedicated outdoorsman, encouraged the acquisition of numerous new areas for the federal park system. Thanks in part to his assistance and support, the Reclamation Act of 1902, which authorized reservoir-building irrigation systems in the West, was passed, along with the Antiquities Act of 1906, which designated the first national monuments. Establishment of the U.S. Forest Service in 1905 and of the National Park Service 11 years later helped place many of the scattered forests, parks, and other sites under more clearly defined policies for acquisition, development, and use (see Figure 4-2).

Emergence of the Recreation Movement: Four Pioneers

As the recreation field developed during the first 3 decades of the 20th century, several men and women emerged as influential advocates of play and recreation. Four of the most effective were Joseph Lee, Luther Halsey Gulick, Jane Addams, and Ernest Attwell.

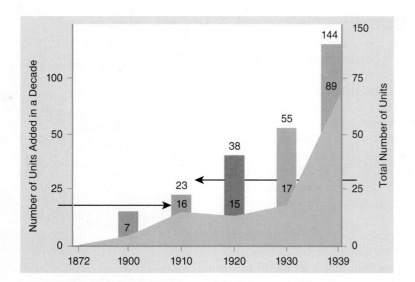

FIGURE 4-2 Growth of the National Park System 1900–1939

Data from National Park Service. (n.d.). *National park system areas listed in chronological order of date authorized under DOI*. Retrieved October 7, 2010, from http://www.nps.gov/applications/budget2/documents.chronop.pdf.

Known as the Father of the Playground Movement, Joseph Lee was an advocate for the importance of play.
©Library of Congress, LC-DIG-ggbain-50026.

Joseph Lee

Regarded as the "father" of the playground movement, Joseph Lee was a lawyer and philanthropist who came from a wealthy New England family. Born in 1862, he took part in a survey of play opportunities conducted by the Family Welfare Society of Boston in 1882. Shocked to see boys arrested for playing in the streets, he organized a playground for them in an open lot. In 1898, Lee helped create a model playground on Columbus Avenue in Boston that included a play area for small children, a boys' section, a sport field, and individual gardens. With Lee's influence expanding, he served as vice president of public recreation for the American Civic Association. President of the Playground Association

Luther Halsey Gulick, M.D., was a staunch supporter of girls' and women's right to access recreation.
©Library of Congress, LC-DIG-hec-25912.

of America for 27 years, he was also the president and leading lecturer of the National Recreation School, a 1-year program for carefully selected college graduates, as well as author of *Play in Education*.

Luther Halsey Gulick

Another leading figure in the early recreation movement was Luther Halsey Gulick. A physician by training, he developed a special interest in physical education and recreation. Beginning in 1887, Dr. Gulick headed the first summer school of "special training for gymnasium instructors" at the School for Christian Workers (now Springfield College) in Massachusetts. He was active in the YMCAs in Canada and the United States, was the first president of the Camp Fire Girls, and was instrumental in the establishment of the Playground Association of America in 1906. He also vigorously promoted expanded recreation programs for girls and women.

Gulick distinguished play from recreation. He defines play as "doing that which we want to do, without reference primarily to any ulterior end, but simply for the joy of the process." But, he goes on to say, play is not less serious than work:

> The boy who is playing football with intensity needs recreation as much as does the inventor who is working intensely at his invention. Play can be more exhausting than work, because one can play much harder than one can work. No one would dream of pushing a boy in school as hard as he pushes himself in a football game. If there is any difference of intensity between play and work, the difference is in favor of play. Play is the result of desire; for that reason it is often carried on with more vigor than work.[18]

Jane Addams

Jane Addams was a social work pioneer who established Hull House in Chicago. Her interest in the needs of children and youths, and in the lives of immigrant families and the poor in America's great cities, led her to develop programs of educational, social, and recreational activities. Beyond this, she was a leading feminist pioneer and so active a reformer that she was known as "the most dangerous woman in America."

Mary Duncan points out that Jane Addams was part of a wider radical reform movement in America's cities. Joining with muckraking editors, writers, ministers, and other social activists, they continually fought city hall, organized labor strikes, marched in the street, gave public speeches, and wrote award-winning articles deploring the living conditions of the poor. The issues and problems they faced were well defined: slavery, the aftermath of the Civil War, thousands of new immigrants, slums, child labor, disease, the suffrage movement, World War I, and a rapidly industrializing nation.[19]

Ernest T. Attwell

Ernest T. Attwell extended the "quality as well as quantity" focus on recreational opportunities for minoritized groups in the first half of the 20th century. After working with the

Jane Addams worked tirelessly to support immigrants and the poor.
©Library of Congress, LC-USZ62-13484.

Ernest Attwell was instrumental in expanding recreation opportunities for minority groups.
Courtesy of National Recreation and Park Association.

U.S. Food Administration during World War I, in March 1919 Attwell was invited to join the Playground and Recreation Association of America (PRAA), later known as the National Recreation Association. The following year he began to lead the association's Bureau of Colored

Work with a mission to encourage the participation in and the expansion of the recreation opportunities, facilities, and leadership available to African American citizens.

Attwell's early work focused on developing the temporary War Camp Community Service Centers into permanent recreation centers in 27 cities as well as establishing recreation centers and training African American recreation leaders at a time when there were very few options for such training. After 9 years, 75 more cities had African American recreation leaders and the number of such leaders increased from 35 to 400.

Working with local citizen councils and armed with data to make recreation recommendations, Attwell had to convince the "majority" group who controlled the tax monies that there was wisdom in providing "wholesome" recreation programs for the "minority" citizens. Attwell often found it effective to quote President Theodore Roosevelt who declared, "This country will not be a good place for any of us to live in unless we make it a good place for all of us to live in."

In 1924 Attwell was invited to President Coolidge's National Conference on Outdoor Recreation held in Washington, DC. Following this, with his understanding of African American social and recreational needs, Attwell was a delegate to President Hoover's Conference on Child Health and Protection in 1930, the chair of the Committee on Recreation and Leisure Time at the Conference on Fundamental Problems in Education of Negroes in 1934, and a leader in the National Conference on the Problems of the Negro and Negro Youth in 1939.[20]

Emerging New Lifestyles

Such views of recreation, play, and leisure were not shared by the entire population. The early 20th century was a time when the traditional Victorian mindset that had been taught and enforced by the home, school, and church was being challenged. For the first time, many young women took jobs in business and industry in cities throughout the country. With relative freedom from disapproving, stern parental authority, and with money to spend, they frequented commercial dance halls, boat rides, drinking saloons, social clubs, and other sources of popular entertainment.[21]

Part of what appealed to young people were the playgrounds, parks, public beaches, and picnic grounds. However, often these were considered too tame and unexciting, and more and more young people became attracted to commercial forms of entertainment involving liquor, dancing, and sex that were viewed by the establishment as immoral and dangerous. Increasingly, organized recreation programs were promoted by churches, law enforcement agencies, and civic associations in an attempt to resist the new, hedonistic forms of play.

Public Concerns About the Use of Leisure

To some degree, the support for public recreation was based on the fear that without public programs and facilities, adult leisure would be used unwisely. When the 8-hour workday laws first came under discussion, temperance societies prepared for increased drunkenness, and social reformers held international conferences on the worker's spare time and ways to use it constructively.

The major concern, however, was for children and youths in the large cities and their need for healthful and safe places to play. Indeed, much "juvenile delinquency" arose from children being arrested for playing on city streets. Authorities during this period reported reduced rates of juvenile delinquency in slum areas where playgrounds had been established.

Concern About Commercial Amusements

At this time, there was also fear that unregulated and unsupervised places of commercial amusement posed a serious threat to children and youths. Commercially sponsored forms of entertainment and recreation had grown rapidly during the early 20th century, with many new pool and billiard parlors, dance halls, vaudeville shows and burlesque, and other amusement attractions. There was much concern about movies and stage performances, with frequent charges that they were immoral and led to the sexual corruption of youth.

A high percentage of privately operated dance halls that were freely patronized by young girls were attached to saloons and rooming houses. Dancing seemed to be only a secondary consideration. Pickups occurred regularly, often of young girls who had come to cities from the nation's farms and small towns with a presumed degree of innocence; so-called white slavers, who trapped or recruited girls and women into prostitution, appeared to ply their trade with little interference.

An examination of socially approved forms of recreation found that in many cities the schools were closed in the evening and throughout the summer, that libraries closed at night and on weekends, that churches closed for the summer, and that publicly provided forms of recreation were at a minimum. Jane Addams concluded that the city had "turned over the provision for public recreation to the most evil-minded and the most unscrupulous members of the community." Gradually, pressure mounted for more effective control of places of public amusement. In city after city, permits were required for operating dance halls, pool parlors, and bowling alleys, and for the sale of liquor.

There was also a fear that Americans were moving away from the traditional active ways of using their leisure to pursuits in which they were passive spectators. Some critics commented that instead of believing in the wholesome love of play, Americans now had a love of being "played upon."

Emerging Mass Culture

Such complaints and fears were the inevitable reactions of civic leaders to what they perceived to be a threat to traditional morality and values. The reality is that the United States in the early decades of the 20th century was undergoing massive changes in response to changing economic and social conditions. These included the emergence of new middle-class and working-class people who had the time and money to spend on leisure, as well as a steady infusion of immigrants from a variety of cultures who contributed new ideas and values to American society. Part of the change involved a growing rejection of authoritarian family structures and church-dominated social values, as well as a readiness to accept new kinds of roles for young people and women. All of these influences resulted in a new mass culture that emerged during the new century.

Defining Popular/Mass Culture

Popular culture (or pop culture) is the totality of ideas, perspectives, attitudes, memes, images, and other phenomena that are deemed preferred by an informal consensus within the mainstream of a given culture. Popular culture is heavily influenced by mass media and becomes ingrained in everyday life.[22]

Defining *popular* and *culture* is complicated with multiple competing definitions. The preceding definition represents mainstream perceptions of popular culture. Yet the definition of popular culture is often muddied with varying opinions on "high culture" versus "popular culture" as well as equating pop culture with mass culture or commercial culture, which is focused on items produced for mass consumption. Regardless, what is known for sure is that popular culture changes constantly and occurs uniquely in place and

time. Items of popular culture typically appeal to a broad spectrum of the public.

Major Forces Promoting Organized Recreation Services

At the same time that mass culture was providing new pastimes that challenged traditional community values and standards, the forces that sought to guide the American public in what they regarded as constructive uses of leisure were becoming active.

Growth of Voluntary Organizations

In the opening decades of the 20th century, a number of important youth-serving, nonprofit organizations were formed, either on a local basis or through nationally organized movements or federations. The National Association of Boys' Clubs was founded in 1906, the Boy Scouts and the Camp Fire Girls in 1910, and the Girl Scouts in 1912. Major civic clubs and community service groups such as the Rotary Club, Kiwanis Club, and the Lions Club were also founded between 1910 and 1917.

By the end of the 1920s, these organizations had become widely established in American life and were serving substantial numbers of young people. One of every seven boys in the appropriate age group in the United States was a Scout. The YMCA and YWCA had more than 1.5 million members in 1926.

Playground Association of America

In the early 1900s, leading recreation directors called for a conference to promote public awareness of and effective practices in the field of leisure services. Under the leadership of Luther Halsey Gulick, representatives of park, recreation, and school boards met in Washington, DC, in April 1906. Unanimously agreeing upon the need for a national organization, the conference members drew up a constitution and selected Gulick as the first president of the Playground Association of America.

A basic purpose of the Playground Association was to develop informational and promotional services to assist people of all ages in using leisure time constructively. Field workers traveled from city to city, meeting with public officials and citizens' groups and helping in the development of playgrounds and recreation programs. To promote professional training, the association developed The Normal Course in Play, a curriculum plan of courses on play leadership on several levels.

In keeping with its broadening emphasis, the organization changed its name in 1911 to the Playground and Recreation Association of America and in 1926 to the National Recreation Association. It sought to provide the public with a broader concept of recreation and leisure and to promote recreation as an area of government responsibility.

Billiard parlors, also known as pool halls, were often frequented by youths and adults alike as a form of entertainment.
Courtesy of Library of Congress, Prints & Photographs Division, National Child Labor Collection [reproduction number LC-DIG-nclc-04662].

DEVELOPMENT OF THE AMUSEMENT PARK

As a single example of the new craze for excitement and freedom in leisure, a host of amusement parks were developed close to various cities around the country. Typically, they put together a mélange of popular attractions, including bathing facilities, band pavilions, dance halls, vaudeville theaters, sideshows, circus attractions, freak displays, food and drink counters, and daredevil rides of every description.

The Boy Scouts have provided outdoor recreation experiences for youths since 1910.

Courtesy of the Library of Congress, Prints & Photographs Division, LC-USZ62-109741.

Recreation Programs in World War I

The nation's rapid mobilization during World War I revealed that communities adjacent to army and navy stations and training camps needed better programs of recreation. The Council of National Defense and the War Department Commission on Training Camp Activities asked the Playground and Recreation Association to assist in the creation of a national organization to provide wartime community recreation programs. The association established the War Camp Community Service (WCCS), which used the recreation resources of several hundred communities near military camps to provide recreation activities for both military personnel and civilians.

Role of the Schools

As indicated earlier, a number of urban school boards initiated after-school and vacation play programs as early as the 1890s. This trend continued in the 20th century. Playground programs were begun in Rochester, New York, in 1907; in Milwaukee, Wisconsin, in 1911; and in Los Angeles, California, in 1914. These pioneering efforts were strongly supported by the National Education Association, which recommended that public school buildings and their resources such as playgrounds, gymnasiums, pools, and art

rooms be used for community recreation and social activities.

With such support, public opinion encouraged the expansion of organized playground and public recreation programs. Between 1910 and 1930, thousands of school systems established extensive programs of extracurricular activities, particularly in sport, publications, hobbies, and social and academic-related fields. In 1919, the first college curriculum in recreation was established at Virginia Commonwealth University.

Outdoor Recreation Developments

The role of the federal and state governments in promoting outdoor recreation was enlarged by the establishment of the National Park Service in 1916 and an accelerated pattern of acquisition and development of outdoor areas by the U.S. Forest Service. In 1921, Stephen Mather, director of the National Park Service, called for a national conference on state parks. This meeting made it clear that the Park Service was primarily to acquire and administer areas of national significance; it led to the recommendation that state governments take more responsibility for acquiring sites of lesser interest or value.

Park administrators began to give active recreation a higher priority in park design and operation.

The End of Shorter Hours

As the recreation movement continued to gain impetus, a reverse trend took place as the movement to shorten the workweek and provide workers with more free time gradually slackened. Benjamin Hunnicutt points out that the most dramatic increase in free time occurred in the period between 1901 and 1921, when the average workweek dropped from 58.4 to 48.4 hours, a decline never before or since equaled.[23]

Since the mid-19th century, shorter hours and higher wages had been a campaign issue for progressive politicians. Union pressure, legislation, and court decisions achieved the 8-hour day in jobs under federal contracts, sections of the railroad industry, and certain hazardous occupations. The policy was supported by the findings of scientific management experts such as Frederick Taylor, who argued that workers' efficiency declined significantly after 8 hours.

Impact of the Great Depression

Following the flourishing 1920s, the Great Depression of the 1930s mired the United States—and much of the industrial world—in a period of almost total despair. By the end of 1932, an estimated 15 million people, nearly one-third of the labor force, were unemployed. Individuals who were employed also experienced greater free time as the average

Civilian Conservation Corps camps were located throughout the United States during the Depression.

Courtesy of the Franklin D. Roosevelt Library and Museum.

workweek declined. During this period, scholars and public officials became concerned that leisure had become too commercial and passive and would contribute to the decline of American culture. Furthermore, there was widespread concern that excessive free time was linked to crime.

In response to these concerns and in conjunction with a broad plan to combat the effects of the Depression, the federal government soon instituted a number of emergency work programs related to recreation. The Federal Emergency Relief Administration, established early in 1933, financed construction of recreation facilities such as parks and swimming pools and hired recreation leaders from the relief rolls. A second agency, the Civil Works Administration, was given the task of finding jobs for four million people in 30 days! Among other tasks, this agency built or improved 3,500 playgrounds and athletic fields in a few months.[24]

Both the National Youth Administration and the Civilian Conservation Corps (CCC) carried out numerous work projects involving the construction of recreational facilities. During the 5 years from 1932 to 1937, the federal government spent an estimated $1.5 billion developing camps, buildings, picnic grounds, trails, swimming pools, and other facilities. The CCC helped to establish state park systems in a number of states that had no organized park programs before 1933. The Works Progress Administration allocated $11 billion or 30% of their budget to recreation-related projects that spanned the nation and included 12,700 playgrounds, 8,500 gymnasiums or recreation buildings, 750 swimming pools, 1,000 ice skating rinks, and 64 ski jumps.[25]

CASE STUDY: President Franklin D. Roosevelt's Legacy for Parks and Recreation

During the Great Depression of the 1930s, President Franklin D. Roosevelt created a legacy that has had enduring and significant influence on parks and recreation. It can be argued that Roosevelt's New Deal was a tool that initiated a growth of public parks and recreation areas, state parks, national parks, conservations, and wildlife areas.

The New Deal was a product of one of the most difficult periods in American history. Roosevelt was elected after the 1929 stock market crash and came to office in 1933. He saw the need to put Americans to work. The term "New Deal" was introduced during Franklin Roosevelt's 1932 Democratic presidential nomination acceptance speech, when he said, "I pledge you, I pledge myself, to a new deal for the American people."[a] Roosevelt summarized the New Deal as a "use of the authority of government as an organized form of self-help for all classes and groups and sections of our country."[a]

The New Deal represented a major shift in government involvement in everyone's lives. Its main purpose was to put people back to work and improve the economy. It is important to remember that during this period unemployment hovered at 30% nationwide. Among the important initiatives created, two significantly influenced parks and recreation. They were the CCC and the Works Progress Administration (WPA).

The CCC initially targeted putting three million young men, between the ages of 18 and 25 years, to work. The CCC was involved in road building, forest maintenance and restoration, and flood control. The West saw the heavy use of CCC and the WPA's workers in national forests, national parks, on Indian reservations, and in municipal and state parks for work on natural resource–related projects.[b] During the existence of the CCC, members planted nearly three billion trees to help reforest America and constructed more than 800 parks nationwide that would become the start of many state parks.[c]

At the height of the program, 47 of 48 states participated in CCC programs, and in 1935 there were 475 CCC camps on state park lands. By the end of the CCC program, 405 state parks directly benefited from the program. In some cases, whole state parks were turned over to appreciative states. Georgia, as an example of a benefiting state, in 2010 identified 11 state parks that still had CCC-constructed facilities. The structures include a bathhouse, casino, dam, pumphouse, residences, comfort stations and picnic shelters, springhouse, bridge and walkways, museum building, blacksmith shop, and group shelters, to name a few. Georgia's legacy of the CCC is similar to many states that point to the WPA and CCC as an unexpected boon.[d]

The WPA, established in 1935 and renamed in 1939 as the Work Projects Administration, similarly focused on creating jobs for the unemployed. It became the largest of the New Deal programs carrying out public works projects that involved the construction of public buildings and roads, and it operated large arts, drama, media, and literacy projects. It fed children and redistributed food, clothing, and housing. Almost every community in the United States had a park, bridge, or school constructed by the agency. The WPA spent billions of dollars on reforestation, flood control, construction of facilities and parks and recreation areas, and many other conservation and community projects. From a municipal and state perspective, the WPA had a significant impact on communities and their ability to provide park and recreation resources and services. For example, the WPA hired artists, actors, and musicians to provide programming, create art, and hold concerts for local communities. In some cases, the park shelters, restrooms, picnic shelters, swimming pools, and other facilities that were constructed remain today. An example WPA project from New York City is McCarren Pool, located in Brooklyn. McCarren Pool was the eighth of 11 giant pools built by the WPA, opening during the summer of 1936. With a capacity of 6,800 swimmers, the pool served as the summertime social hub. The pool was closed in 1984, but in 2006, the abandoned pool was the site of a series of Sunday afternoon concerts. After the mayor of New York announced in 2007 that major renovations would be undertaken to reopen the pool, in 2012, with a $50 million renovation, the pool reopened with no admission fees for users.[e]

The National Park Service (NPS) has done the most effective job of chronicling the CCC and WPA involvement with their areas. The NPS budget was $10.8 million in 1933, and yet NPS took advantage of the New Deal, receiving $218 million for emergency conservation projects between 1933 and 1939. The NPS said, "Almost all federal conservation activities after 1933, including those in the national parks and monuments, were designed in part as pump-priming operations that would not only protect our national resources but also indirectly stimulate the economy."[c]

The work of New Deal organizations from 1933 to 1942 provided a foundation that would be expanded upon throughout the remainder of the 20th century.

Questions to Consider

- How do you think recreation areas, national parks, and wildlife areas would be different today without the New Deal?
- Prepare a series of justifications for implementation of a New Deal program today.
- Go on the Internet and find a state or community that is still using CCC- or WPA-constructed facilities and report on how they are used, how they were changed, and the legacy it has left upon the community or state. (Hint: do a search for "New Deal" facilities.)

[a]The New Deal: A Speech Delivered by President Franklin D. Roosevelt (1932). Retrieved February 9, 2021, from http://www.danaroc.com/guests_fdr_021609.html.
[b]The National Archives. (2016, August 15). The Great Depression and the New Deal. Retrieved March 31, 2017, from https://www.archives.gov/seattle/exhibit/picturing-the-century/great-depression.html.
[c]Unrau, H., & Williss, G. F. (1982). Expansion of the National Park Service in the 1930s: Administrative history. Washington, DC: National Park Service. Retrieved March 31, 2017, from https://www.nps.gov/parkhistory/online_books/unrau-williss/adhi.htm.
[d]Georgia Department of Natural Resources. Retrieved January 24, 2021, from http://www.georgiastateparks.org.
[e]Foderaro, L. W. (2012, June 28). Empty about 3 decades, pool from the depression era reopens to cool off Brooklyn. New York Times. Retrieved January 24, 2021, from https://www.nytimes.com/2012/06/29/nyregion/mccarren-pool-in-brooklyn-reopens-after-28-years.html.

Data from Roosevelt, F. D. (2017). Roosevelt's nomination dress. http://newdeal.feri.org/speeches/1932b.htm; The National Archives. (2017). The great depression and the new deal. https://www.archives.gov/seattle/exhibit/picturing-the-century/great-depression.html; Unraw, H., & Williss, G. F. (1982). Expansion of the National Park Service in the 1930s: Administrative history. https://www.nps.gov/parkhistory/online_books/unrau-williss/adhi.htm; Georgia Department of Natural Resources. (n.d.). Home page. http://www.georgiastateparks.org; Foderaro, L. W. (2012, June 29). Empty about 3 decades, pool from the depression era reopens to cool off Brooklyn. New York Times. https://www.nytimes.com/2012/06/29/nyregion/mccarren-pool-in-brooklyn-reopens-after-28-years.html

Sharpened Awareness of Leisure Needs

The Depression helped to stimulate national concern about problems of leisure and recreational opportunity. For example, a number of studies in the 1930s revealed a serious lack of structured recreation programs for young people, especially African American youth, girls, and rural youth. In the early 1930s, the National Education Association carried out a major study of leisure education in the nation's school systems and issued a report, *The New Leisure Challenges the Schools*, that urged the educational establishment to take more responsibility for this function and advocated enlarging the school's role in community recreation.

Shortly thereafter, the National Recreation Association examined the public recreation and park programs in a number of major European nations with nationalized recreation programs and published a detailed report that included implications for American policy makers. The American Association for the Study of Group Work examined the overall problem and in 1939 published an important report, *Leisure: A National Issue*. In the report, Eduard Lindeman, a leading social work administrator who had played a key role in government during the Depression, stated that the "leisure of the American people constitutes a central and crucial problem of social policy."[26]

Lindeman argued that in the American democracy, recreation should meet the true needs of the people. Pointing out that American workers were gaining a vast national reservoir of leisure estimated at 390 billion hours per year, he suggested that the new leisure should be characterized by free choice and a minimum of restraint. He urged, however, that if leisure were not to become "idleness, waste, or opportunity for sheer mischief," a national plan for leisure had to be developed, including the widespread preparation of professionally trained recreation leaders.

Recreation during the Depression came in many forms and frequently was family oriented.

A Nation at War

World War II, in which the United States became fully involved on December 7, 1941, compelled the immediate mobilization of every aspect of national life. The Special Services Division of the U.S. Army provided recreation facilities and programs on military bases throughout the world, making use of approximately 12,000 officers, even more enlisted personnel, and many volunteers. About 1,500 officers were involved in the Welfare and Recreation Section of the Bureau of Naval Personnel, and expanded programs were offered by the Recreation Service of the Marine Corps. These departments were assisted by the United Service Organizations (USO), which was formed in 1941 and consisted of the joint effort of six agencies: the Jewish Welfare Board, the Salvation Army, Catholic Community Services, the YMCA, the YWCA, and the National Travelers Aid. The American Red Cross established approximately 750 clubs in wartime theaters of operations throughout the world and about 250 mobile entertainment units, staffed by more than 4,000 leaders. Its military hospitals overseas and in the United States involved more than 1,500 recreation workers as well.

Many municipal directors extended their facilities and services to local war plants and changed their schedules to provide programs around the clock. Because of the rapid increase in industrial recreation programs, the National Industrial Recreation Association (later known as the National Employee Services and Recreation Association) was formed in 1941 to assist in such efforts. Also, the Federal Security Agency's Office of Community War Services established a recreation division to assist community programs. The Women's Bureau of the U.S. Department of Labor developed guidelines for recreation and housing for women war workers, based on their needs in moving from their home environments into suddenly expanded or greatly congested areas.

By the end of World War II, great numbers of servicemen and servicewomen had participated in varied recreation programs and services and thus had gained a new appreciation for this field. Many people had been trained in recreation leadership (more than 40,000 people were in the Special Services Division of the U.S. Army alone) and were ready to return to civilian life as professionals in this field.

Post–World War II Expectations

Immediately after World War II, expectations for the growth of leisure in the United States were high. In the 1950s and 1960s, it was predicted that leisure—usually defined as nonwork or discretionary time—would expand dramatically and have an increasing influence on the lives of Americans in the years ahead.

Think tanks such as the Rand Corporation and the Hudson Institute and special planning bodies such as the National Commission on Technology envisioned futurist scenarios with such alternatives as lowering the retirement age to 38, reducing the workweek to 22 hours a week, or extending paid vacations to as many as 25 weeks a year. Other authorities predicted that the 3-day or 4-day workweek, which some companies had been experimenting with, would soon be widespread.

In the early and mid-1990s and again on a much broader scale in 2008 and beyond, widespread company downsizing and other business trends led to the firing of millions of employees and an atmosphere of economic pessimism. There was a strong business recovery in the late 1990s, unemployment declined sharply, prosperity was widespread, and government budgets began to show surpluses on every level. By early 2009, however, there was a new decline with more far-reaching impact on personal income and government budgets, layoffs and unemployment at levels not seen since the Great Depression, loss of homes, and closing of businesses nationwide and a general sense of hopelessness among many.

Expansion of Recreation and Leisure

Over the last 60 years, recreation and leisure witnessed an immense growth in participation. There was a steady increase in sport, the arts, hobbies, outdoor recreation, and fitness programs, along with a parallel expansion of home-based entertainment through the use of computer, television, media players, handheld devices, and other electronic equipment.

Influence of National Affluence

An important factor in the growth of recreational participation was the national affluence of the postwar years. The gross national product rose from $211 billion in 1945 to more than a trillion dollars annually in 1971. In the late 1950s, it was reported that Americans were spending $30 billion a year on leisure—a sum that seemed huge then but that is dwarfed by the $841 billion spent in 2007.[27]

Involvement in varied forms of recreation exploded during this period. Visits to national forests increased by 474% between 1947 and 1963, and to national parks by 302% during the same period. Overseas pleasure travel increased by 440%, and attendance at sports and cultural events also grew rapidly. Sales of golf equipment increased by 188% and tennis equipment by 148%, and use of bowling lanes by 258%. Hunting and fishing, horse-racing attendance, and copies of paperback books sold all gained dramatically, and—most strikingly—the number of families with television sets grew by 3,500% over this 16-year period.[28]

Government recreation and park agencies dramatically expanded their budgets, personnel, facilities, and programs until the mid-1970s. Then, many federal, state, and local agencies were forced by funding cuts to cut back or freeze budgets. At the same time, the recreation and park profession continued to grow in numbers and public visibility. Preprofessional curricula were established in many colleges and universities during the 1960s and 1970s, and several national organizations, including the National Recreation Association, the American Recreation Society, and the American Institute of Park Executives, merged to form the National Recreation and Park Association.

Effect of Demographic Changes: Suburbanization and Urban Crises

In the years immediately after World War II—which had disrupted the lives of millions of servicemen and women—great numbers of young couples married. Within a few years, many of these new families with young children moved from the central cities to new homes in surrounding suburban areas. Most suburbs were quick to establish new recreation and park departments, hire personnel, and develop programs and facilities to serve all age groups—often in concert with local school districts.

At the same time, the population within the inner cities changed dramatically. With the rapid mechanization of agriculture in the South and the abandonment of the sharecropper system, millions of African American people moved from the South to the cities and industrialized areas of the Northeast, the Midwest, and the West in search of jobs and better opportunities. Growing numbers of Hispanic immigrants moved into the cities from the Caribbean islands and Central America. Generally, these new residents faced economic hardships, including limited employment opportunities, resulting in health, housing, and welfare concerns for cities. In addition, as people of color grew in numbers in urban areas, a sense of unease grew among white people, often leading to confrontation in recreation settings as the number of African American residents grew into a numerical majority in some locales. Efforts to keep recreation facilities, both public and commercial, segregated left recreation sites fraught with tension that often boiled over into violence or simply led to the closure of facilities by white owners or management rather than desegregation.

Trends in Program Sponsorship

As a result of such population shifts and changes in lifestyle, a number of trends in recreation program functions and in the role to be played by government emerged. These included (1) programs aimed at improving physical fitness, (2) emphasis on environmental concerns, (3) activities and services designed to meet specific age group needs, (4) recreation for persons with disabilities, (5) increasing programming in the arts, (6) services for people living in poverty,

© Jim David/Shutterstock.

Affluence is evidenced by the increase in attendance at resorts.
© Digital Vision/Photodisc/Thinkstock/Getty.

and (7) programs concerned with the needs of racial and ethnic minorities.

Emphasis on Physical Fitness

Beginning in the 1950s, there was a strong emphasis on the need to develop and maintain the physical fitness of youth. In both world wars, a disappointingly high percentage of male draftees and enlistees had been rejected by the armed forces for physical reasons. Then, after World War II, comparative studies such as the Kraus-Weber tests showed that American youths were less fit than the youths of several other nations. Vice President Richard Nixon convened the President's Conference on the Fitness of American Youth at the United States Naval Academy in Annapolis, Maryland, in 1956. The recommendations from the conference included increasing public awareness, increasing public

funding of community recreation, supporting nonprofit youth-serving agencies through private and public funds, increasing and improving community recreation facilities, improving fitness opportunities for girls, and improving leadership for physical activity. In 1956, President Dwight Eisenhower also established the President's Council on Youth Fitness to serve as a catalyst for motivating communities and individuals to adopt active lifestyles. In response to the conference, schools strengthened their programs of physical fitness, and many public recreation departments expanded their leisure activities to include fitness classes, conditioning, jogging, and sports for all ages. Yet, despite these measures, today we are continuing to fight an obesity epidemic, with 72% of adults older than 20 years overweight and 40% those obese. The statistics for children are concerning as well, as one-third are categorically overweight or obese.[29]

THE IMPACT OF ECONOMIC DECLINES ON SPENDING FOR LEISURE AND RECREATION

Over the course of the last quarter of the 20th century and the first decade of the 21st century, the U.S. economy experienced periodic economic declines. The declines are called recessions and take place when the economy contracts, or gets smaller. Recessions are characterized by high unemployment, stagnant wages, and falls in retail sales. Most recent recessions have been short lived and their impact on public parks and recreation is documented elsewhere in this chapter. The impact on personal and public spending for recreation has broader implications. Not only does it affect public parks and recreation but also nonprofits providing recreation programs, the arts, and commercial recreation enterprises. The major recessions of the last 30 years occurred in 1981 (14 months), 1990 (8 months), 2001 (8 months), and 2007 (19 months). It was generally assumed that personal spending declines during a recession. However, spending data do not support that assumption. Between 1981 and 2009, there was only one quarter showing a decline in personal spending, and that occurred in 2001, during the dot-com bust. Through the early part of the 21st century, personal spending continued to increase in every quarter. That ended with the 2009 recession. This was the most broad-based recession since 1929, with a majority of Americans affected. Some economists suggested that as a result of the 2009 recession, personal spending declined in excess of 3%, which translates into $300–$400 billion annually. Spread over the three plus years of the recession, spending declines had a major impact on public and nonprofit organizations. In 2010, evidence suggested people had continued to cut expenses and reduce personal spending. The Internet, which was a nonfactor in previous recessions, was a source individuals turned to for ways to reduce costs. Consumers bargain shopped, looked for coupons and special offers, did research on products, and so forth, all in an effort to reduce their spending.

Before the recession of 2009, conventional wisdom suggested that some spending reluctance would occur but would be short term. The widespread impact of the 2009 recession, although the recession was declared officially over in 2010, continued to affect states well into 2016. For leisure and recreation, the impact was felt in a variety of ways. From a positive perspective, public agencies experienced high levels of program demand from families and individuals replacing more costly commercial enterprises they used to patronize. Commercial enterprises also focused on cost effectiveness and efficiency, engaged in more effective marketing, and ensured that their products and experiences were perceived as a value.

Simultaneous with the increase in demand, public and nonprofit-based parks and recreation agencies faced the most significant funding crisis since the tax revolt of the early 1970s. Agencies laid off staff, closed recreation centers, raised fees for programs, and looked for partnerships, all focused on meeting the needs of citizens who were demanding more services.

As of publication of this edition, the entire world has felt the economic impact of the COVID-19 pandemic. Although it is too early to forecast the long-term economic ramifications of the ongoing pandemic, there is little doubt that they have been catastrophic for many recreation outlets in all sectors. Commercial agencies, especially travel, were hit hard as doors were shuttered during lockdowns and reopening to date has been slowed at best and stalled at worst as providers seek to offer programming and travel opportunities with new safety precautions in place.

The President's Council on Physical Fitness and Sport was created by President Eisenhower in 1956 and continues into the 21st century.

© Photodisc/Getty Images.

Environmental Concerns

A key concern of the recreation field has been the environment. In the postwar period, it became evident that there was a critical need to preserve and rehabilitate the nation's land, water, and wildlife resources. U.S. citizens permitted the country's great rivers and lakes to be polluted by waste, forests to be razed by lumbering interests, and wildlife to be ravaged by overhunting, lack of adequate breeding areas, chemical poisons, and invasion of their environments. Greater and greater demands had been placed on the natural resource bank, with open space shrinking at an unprecedented rate.

In the late 1950s, President Dwight Eisenhower and the Congress formed the Outdoor Recreation Resources Review Commission to investigate this problem. The result was a landmark, heavily documented report in 1962 that helped to promote a wave of environmental efforts by federal, state,

A SHORT HISTORY OF THE LAND AND WATER CONSERVATION FUND

The legislation creating the Land and Water Conservation Fund (LWCF) was passed by Congress in 1964 and became law in 1965. The LWCF became the primary source of revenue for park and recreation agencies at the federal, state, and local levels and continues to play an important role. The LWCF initially had three sources of revenue: proceeds from sales of federal properties, motorboat fuel taxes, and user fees for recreational use of federal lands. This raised $100 million annually, but it quickly became evident the level of funding was inadequate to meet the goals of the program. In 1968, the funding level was raised to $200 million per year for 5 years, and an additional funding source, revenues from leasing of the Outer Continental Shelf oil and gas resources, was added. Congress gradually raised the funding level to $900 million annually.

Currently, approximately $900 million is annually accumulated into the fund. Through 2006, the fund accumulated $29 billion with 62% of the allocation going to federal land acquisition, 28% to state grant programs, and 10% to other programs. The major roadblock preventing greater success of the fund is that the allocation is not automatic but must be authorized annually by Congress. The president recommends a level of spending for the LWCF and in some years has recommended low levels of spending. Congress can override this recommendation and sometimes has. However, allocated funds (actual dollars spent) have often been below levels authorized by Congress (dollars appropriated by Congress). In 2019, the LWCF was permanently authorized yet funding, at $495 million, still fell far short of the aforementioned $900 million annual allowance.[30]

Appropriations from the fund have been made for three general purposes: (1) federal acquisition of land and waters and interests therein; (2) grants to states for recreational planning; acquiring recreational lands, waters, or related interests; and developing outdoor recreation facilities; and (3) other federal purposes.

One of the key provisions of the fund is a requirement that every state create a "state comprehensive outdoor recreation plan" to be eligible to receive monies from the fund. Another important aspect of the program requires that all grants made to states be matched by state or local dollars. At the state level, funding is administered through a state organization, with some money going to state parks, wildlife, and other outdoor recreation managers. The remainder of the funding is provided to cities and counties on a competitive basis. Between 1965 and 2016, over 40,000 grants were made to states. "This figure includes 10,600 grants for acquisition; 26,420 grants for developing recreation facilities; 2,760 grants for redeveloping older recreational facilities; and 641 state planning grants for studies of recreation potential, need, opportunity, and policy."[31] From these funds the National Park Service reported that the grants have supported "purchase and protection of 3.0 million acres of recreation lands and over 29,000 projects to develop basic recreation facilities in every State and territory of the nation."[32]

Results at the federal level have been equally impressive as the four recipient federal agencies (National Park Service, Forest Service, Fish and Wildlife Service, and Bureau of Land Management) have protected more than 4.5 million acres.

and municipal governments. The Federal Water Pollution Control Administration divided the nation into 20 major river basins and promoted regional sewage treatment programs in those areas. The Water Quality Act of 1965, the Clean Water Restoration Act of 1966, the Solid Waste Disposal Act of 1965, the Highway Beautification Act of 1965, and the Mining Reclamation Act of 1968 all committed the United States to a sustained program of conservation and protection of its natural resources. Another major piece of legislation was the Wilderness Act of 1964, which gave Congress the authority to declare certain unspoiled lands permanently off limits to human occupation and development.

Many states and cities embarked on new programs of land acquisition and beautification and developed environmental plans designed to reduce air and water pollution. Nonprofit organizations such as the American Land Trust, the Nature Conservancy, and the Trust for Public Lands took over properties encompassing hundreds of thousands of acres—many of them donated by large corporations—for preservation or transfer to public agencies for recreational use. Such programs were accompanied by efforts within federal agencies such as the National Park Service, the Forest Service, the Fish and Wildlife Service, and the Bureau of Land Management.

In the early 1980s, federal expenditures for parks and environmental programs were sharply reduced, the rate of land acquisition was cut back, and government policies regulating the use of wild lands for mining, timber cutting, grazing, oil drilling, and similar commercial activities were dramatically relaxed.

Meeting Age-Group Needs

In addition to the demographic trends cited earlier, three important changes in the nation's population that gathered force in the postwar decades were (1) the dramatic rise in the birth rate, with millions of children and youths flooding the schools and community recreation centers; (2) the lengthening of the population's life span, resulting in a growing proportion of older adults in society, at times resulting in increased demands of adult children to provide elder care; and (3) the increasing pressures on families with children because of growing numbers of single-parent households and the entrance of millions of women into the workforce.

In response to these trends, thousands of governmental and nonprofit organizations expanded their programs for children and youths, and numerous youth sport leagues such as Little League, Biddy Basketball, and American Legion Football recruited millions of participants. At the other end of the age range, public and nonprofit organizations, including many municipal park and recreation agencies, developed golden age clubs or senior centers, often

Outdoor recreation and nature areas have benefited from the environmental efforts that began with Yellowstone National Park and continue today.
© djgis/Shutterstock.

with funding from the federal government through the Administration on Aging.

Changing family households confirmed the need for recreation programs to provide day care services for children of working parents and to meet other leisure-related needs. Religious organizations in particular are stressing family-oriented programming in an effort to strengthen marital bonds and parent–child relationships.

Special Recreation for Persons with Disabilities

An area of increased emphasis in the postwar era was the provision of supportive services for persons with physical and mental disabilities. Various government agencies concerned with rehabilitation were expanded to meet the needs of individuals with physical disabilities, especially the large numbers of returning veterans who sought to be integrated into community life.

To better serve people with developmental disabilities, the federal government sharply increased its aid to special education. In recreation, assistance was given to programs serving children, youths, and adults with developmental disabilities. Beginning in the mid-1960s, there was an increased emphasis on developing social and recreational programs for aging persons in both institutional and community settings. Overall, the specialized field of what came to be known as recreation therapy service expanded steadily in this period. With the establishment of the National Therapeutic Recreation Society in the mid-1960s and the American Therapeutic Recreation Association in the 1980s, professionalization in recreation therapy service developed rapidly. The establishment of curriculum guidelines for professional preparation, the setting of program standards, and the development of registration and certification plans all served to make this field a significant specialized area within the broad leisure-service field.

Persons with disabilities engage in a variety of sport and recreation activities today, including Special Olympics, tennis, basketball, and snow skiing.
© Bikeworldtravel/Shutterstock.

Increased Interest in the Arts

Following World War II, the United States embarked on an expansion of cultural centers, museums, and art centers. In part, this represented a natural follow-up to the stimulus that had been given to art, theater, music, and dance by emergency federal programs during the Great Depression. Another element, however, was that Americans had come to enjoy the arts as both spectators and participants. Through the 1970s and early 1980s, community arts activities continued to flourish, with the assistance of federal funding through the National Endowment for the Arts, which helped to support state arts units, choreographers and composers, and individual performers and companies.

In the mid- and late-1980s, seeing declines in attendance at music, drama, and dance events, as well as a need to increase funding for many museums, libraries, and similar institutions, new methods of fundraising led to diversification of offerings and marketing them to a broader community audience. As an example, art, natural history, and science museums today offer lectures, tours, films, innovative displays, special fundraising dinners, and other events designed to attract a wide spectrum of patrons.

Recreation's Antipoverty Role

During the 1930s and 1940s, a number of federal housing programs provided funding to support small parks, playgrounds, or centers in public housing projects. In the 1960s, as part of President Lyndon Johnson's "war on poverty," a new wave of legislation, such as the Economic Opportunity Act of 1964, the Housing and Urban Development Act of 1964, and the Model

THE SPECIAL OLYMPICS

In 1968, Eunice Kennedy Shriver (1921–2009) organized the first International Special Olympic Games in Chicago, Illinois. The Special Olympics were an outgrowth of a day-camp program started in 1962 by Shriver for people with developmental disabilities. During the first international games, 1,000 athletes from the United States and Canada competed. In 1977, the first winter games were held in Steamboat Springs, Colorado, and included 500 athletes. Today, over 3 million athletes from 220 countries compete in local, state, national, and international Special Olympics events. The Special Olympics movement and the tireless work of Shriver have had an extraordinary impact on the public's understanding of people with developmental disabilities and creation of supportive public policy. Her comments at the 1987 Special Olympics have become a rallying cry for the rights of individuals with disabilities:

The right to play on any playing field?

You have earned it.

The right to study in any school?

You have earned it.

The right to hold a job?

You have earned it.

The right to be anyone's neighbor?

You have earned it.[33]

Segregation and Integration in Recreation

As previously mentioned, the public recreation movement of the late 19th and early 20th centuries did not equally benefit all Americans. Throughout most of the United States, separate recreation facilities had been built for African and white Americans. As with public education, the result of this segregation was highly disparate opportunities. The first widespread attempts at racial integration were in the late 1950s and early 1960s following the Supreme Court's landmark *Brown v. Board of Education* decision. However, even after that decision was rendered, African American people still found many previously public facilities converted to "private clubs" in order to restrict access.

Unfortunately, it was not until the late 1960s, following escalated racial tensions in many cities, that the federal government dedicated serious financial resources to serving African American people, particularly those living in impoverished urban centers, and often for youth programs. These included sports and social activities, cultural pursuits, job training and tutorial programs, and trips and similar recreation activities. On a national scale, the Job Corps, VISTA, Neighborhood Youth Corps, and an aggregate of special projects known as Community Action Programs continued into the 1970s but were gradually terminated in the years that followed.

Red Rock Conservation Area is an example of an outdoor recreation resource located just minutes from the Las Vegas strip. It is a popular visitors site for tourists and residents and provides numerous free days each year so all residents can visit.

Courtesy of U.S. Bureau of Land Management.

Cities program approved in 1967, provided assistance for locally directed recreation programs to be conducted by disadvantaged citizens themselves in depressed urban neighborhoods. Other federal programs, such as the Job Corps, VISTA (Volunteers in Service to America), and the Neighborhood Youth Corps, also included recreation-related components.

CASE STUDY: Integration and Commercial Recreation

Although numerous commercial recreation sites served as the background for racial tensions as African American people demanded equal access, amusement parks, skating rinks, and swimming pools were often the sites of the most violent of clashes between white people and people of color. Because of the potential for interracial mixing between men and women, these recreation facilities were fraught with tension as white people aggressively worked to keep the facilities segregated. Coney Island provides just one example of the fight for integration of amusement parks.

In Ohio, it took activists like Marian Spencer to lead to change. Spencer, listening to her radio in 1952, heard an ad that stated, "Come on kiddies. Come on out. Meet Uncle Al! Come out to Coney Island!" Excited, she called the park and had the following conversation with the person on the other end of the line:

"Are all kids welcome?"

"Oh yes, all children."

"Ours is a negro family."

"Well, now of course, that's not my doing, it's management's decision, but I don't think it means negro children."

Hanging up the phone, Spencer's call to the National Association for the Advancement of Colored People (NAACP) and a local civil rights group put additional pressure on Coney Island to desegregate.

Marketed as a "white utopia," Coney Island, situated on the Mason-Dixon line in Cincinnati, Ohio, is just one example of the extent to which amusement parks worked to keep out African American customers. Well before Marian's phone call, the 1930s saw the Girl Scouts boycotting the park over its refusal to allow anyone but white customers entrance to the park. Even if they somehow made it past the entrance, they were met rude park employees, and in some cases physical violence. The park's collusion with local police supported the park's ability to keep out "undesirable" customers. Although parks often skirted the law by selling day-long rentals to private companies and groups to control who could access the park on any given day, there were plenty of instances when public access was denied to African American customers for no reason other than the color of their skin. Transportation options to the park played a role in managing access to the park.

Coney Island had long had a tradition of ferrying customers to the park via a steamboat, the Island Queen, that linked the park to the city. In 1922 the steamboat caught fire, thus jeopardizing the viability of the park until they built a new boat. During this time, the park enhanced its offerings adding two new attractions to the park, the Moonlite Gardens, a deluxe dance palace, and the 400' x 200' Sunlite Pool. However, as mentioned earlier, these attractions put owners and white customers on high alert as they amped up efforts to keep the park segregated and not risk interracial mingling between men and women.

Once again, in 1947 the "new" Island Queen burned, forcing the park to rely on charter buses to shuttle groups but this did not allow for control of private autos. In the 1950s civil rights activists targeted the public automobile entrances, forcing Coney Island to guard all entrances to the park to control access. It was not until 1955, after numerous activists such as Marian Spencer continued to push for integration of Coney Island, that full integration became a reality.

Questions to Consider

- Explain the importance of civil rights activists to integration of swimming pools, amusements parks, and roller rinks.
- When swimming pools were forced to integrate, often the city would choose to just fill in the site of the pool rather than keep it open. What were the long-term impacts of these actions on citizens of color?
- Coney Island was not the only amusement park to resist integration. What are other examples of amusement parks or commercial recreation entities that engaged in active obstruction to integration and what were the reasons they gave for doing so?

Data from Wolcott, V. W. (2012). *Race, riots and roller coasters*. University of Pennsylvania Press.

PROTESTANT WORK ETHIC REJECTED

The rejection of the Protestant work ethic was widely expressed in the music, art, and literature of the 1960s. The historical record of the baby boomers of the 1960s, however, indicates that the demise of Americans' obsession with work is more myth than reality. A study published by the Families and Work Institute in 2006 indicates that baby boomers are more likely to live work-centric lifestyles than the generations that preceded and follow them. A 2004 study by the same institute indicates that baby boomers work longer hours and are more likely to feel overworked than employees of other generations.

Counterculture: Youths in Rebellion

During the late 1960s, what came to be known as the counterculture made its appearance in America. The term counterculture, as John Kelly points out, is generally applied to a movement that develops in opposition to an established and dominant culture—often in political, religious, or lifestyle terms—and that manifests itself in language, symbols, and behavior.

Rejection of the Work Ethic

A significant aspect of the counterculture movement was its rejection of work as the be-all and end-all of one's life, and of the widely accepted goal of "making it" in the business or professional world. A deep-rooted belief in the value of hard work, which was linked to an essentially conservative, industrious, and moralistic view of life, had long been a fundamental tenet of American society.

However, since World War II, there had been a retreat from the stern precepts of the Protestant work ethic. As establishment values and monetary success were undermined in the thinking of young people during the counterculture period, leisure satisfactions assumed new importance.

The counterculture movement in the United States during the 1960s was part of a larger youth movement that challenged the political, economic, and educational establishments in a number of other nations around the world. Here, it symbolized the rebellion of young people against parental authority and the curricular and social controls of schools and colleges. Much of it stemmed from mass protests against the Vietnam War. Rock music and lyrics that challenged traditional values became popular, and some young people joined "hippie" communes or fled to neighborhoods like Haight-Ashbury in San Francisco or the East Village in New York City, where they experimented with drugs and a variety of alternative lifestyles.

Drives for Equality by Minoritized Groups

Another important aspect of the counterculture movement was that it provided a climate within which various populations in American society that had historically been minoritized were encouraged to press vigorously for fuller social and economic rights.

Racial and Ethnic Minoritized Groups

For racial and ethnic minoritized groups, there was a strong thrust during the 1960s and 1970s toward demanding fuller recreational service in terms of facilities and organized programs. In response, many public recreation and park departments not only upgraded these traditional elements but also began to provide mobile recreation units that would enter affected neighborhoods to offer cultural, social, and other special services. Building on projects that had been initiated during the war on poverty and in response to escalating racial tensions in cities, many departments initiated classes, workshops, festivals, and holiday celebrations designed to promote ethnic pride and intercultural appreciation.

Through legislation, Supreme Court decisions, other judicial orders, and voluntary compliance, public, nonprofit, and commercial facilities were gradually desegregated through the 1970s and 1980s. Major youth and adult social membership organizations such as the Girl Scouts and the YMCA, which had tended either to maintain segregated units for racially minoritized groups or not to serve them at all, opened up their memberships and in some cases identified racial justice as a high-priority mission for the years ahead. In terms of the broader culture, greater numbers of racial and ethnic minorities began to achieve great success in such leisure-related areas as college and professional sports and popular entertainment such as music, television, and motion pictures.

Progress for Women

In the 1960s and 1970s, feminist groups mobilized to address two major areas of gender-based discrimination in recreation and leisure: employment practices and program involvement. In response to equal opportunity laws and other pressures, governmental recreation and park departments and other agencies began to hire more women.

Rock concerts began in earnest in the 1960s and continue today.
© Guitarsimo/Dreamstime.com.

A fundamental principle in community recreation has been that all persons should be given an equal opportunity, regardless of sex, religion, race, or other personal factors. However, in the postwar decades, it became evident that this principle had not been applied to participation of girls and women in public recreation programs in the United States. In 1972, growing pressure from women's groups led to the approval of groundbreaking legislation, Title IX of the Education Amendments Act. Title IX was the first legislation to prohibit sex discrimination in educational institutions. Although Title IX prevents discrimination in all aspects of public education, including recruitment, admission, and employment, the primary focus of public discourse over the past 50 years has been equality in athletics.

During the 1970s and 1980s, community recreation organizations joined the nationwide effort to offer equal opportunities for girls and women. A significant development at this time was the merger of formerly sex-separated organizations into organizations serving both sexes, such as the Boys and Girls Club of America. As a result of these changes, girls and women today have a far greater range of sport and physical recreation opportunities than they did in the past.

Lesbians, Gays, Bisexual, Transgender, and Queer/ Questioning+

Lesbians, gays, bisexual, transgender, and queer/questioning+ (LGBTQIA+) individuals compose a third group who traditionally have been disadvantaged in American society. During the counterculture era, gay activists began to mobilize as an economic and political force. In the 1960s and 1970s, many gay and lesbian groups began to organize and promote their recreational and social activities openly on college campuses and in community life.

CASE STUDY: Designing for Ethnically Minoritized Groups

One of the key concerns of outdoor recreation resource managers is the low number of people from racially and ethnically minoritized groups visiting and participating in programs at outdoor recreation areas. Although not a new issue, land management agencies continue to struggle to find ways to engage these groups, especially as their population increases as a percentage of the total U.S. population. In a report prepared by the NPS in 2008, five research hypotheses were reported that attempt to explain the lack of involvement in outdoor recreation. The hypotheses are marginality, subculture/ethnicity, discrimination, opportunity, and acculturation.

The *marginality* hypothesis suggests the differences in racial/ethnic minority representation are a result of socioeconomic factors caused by historical discrimination and include barriers such as limited financial resources, lower levels of education, and limited employment opportunities. The subculture/ethnicity hypothesis recognizes the influence of marginality on leisure and recreation patterns but argues the differences in park visitation, at least partially, are a result of cultural norms, value systems, social organizations, and socialization practices. Examples of cultural values or norms can include size of recreational groups, preferred activities (e.g., hiking, biking, swimming, picnicking), and development level of sites (e.g., bathrooms, pavilions, visitor centers).

The *discrimination* hypothesis places importance on contemporary, post–civil rights discrimination that occurs from interpersonal contact with other visitors or park personnel or through institutional policies. The *opportunity* hypothesis examines the relationship between the residential location of minoritized populations, recreational sites, and recreation preferences. The *acculturation* hypothesis examines the relationship between cultural assimilation into the majority culture and recreational choices. According to this hypothesis, as a minoritized culture assimilates into the majority culture, they begin to take on the recreational patterns of the majority culture.[a]

Understanding the hypotheses is important, and moving from hypotheses to action is much more challenging. It frequently requires agencies to rethink how they do business, change organizational culture, recognize the organization is not representative of the population it is designated to serve, and finally, strive to overcome bureaucratic inertia that promotes preservation of the norm over change. Each outdoor management agency deals with the challenge in its own way, and often in multiple ways. Federal agencies initiate plans and actions at the director, regional, and local levels. Much of the actual work falls to the local level because, at this level, the situation is direct and immediate. For example, in the mid-1990s, the Pacific regional director for the NPS determined that the public relations programs were focusing only on traditional media resources such as major newspapers, television, and radio stations. He organized a task force charged with identifying alternative media outlets in the San Francisco Bay area. In a short period of time, they identified more than 300 media outlets focusing on specific racially and ethnically minoritized groups, as well as women, people who identify as LGBTQIA+, and persons with disabilities.

The U.S. Army Corps of Engineers approached the development and renovation of recreation sites with a focus on providing facilities, amenities, and programs designed to meet the expressed needs of racially and ethnically minoritized groups. In 2002, the Army Corps of Engineers published a report titled *Managing for Ethnic Diversity: Recreation Facility and Service Modifications for Ethnic Minorities* in which the premise was that ethnically universal designs can meet the needs of a progressively more diverse population. Ethnically universal design focuses on creation of programs and facilities that are more inclusive of ethnic cultural diversity. Specifically, the report suggests moving away from the traditional design model, called an ethnically neutral design, which focuses wholly on white middle-class nuclear families with the assumption that other ethnic groups would adapt to the design model. The new approach moves toward a model of embracing cultural pluralism. Further, the report argues that the development of day-use facilities are essential to the success of this model.[b]

The report suggests a variety of facilities and services that appeal to Hispanic, Asian, and African American people. These services include the following:

- Group shelters to provide shade and protection from inclement weather
- Larger tables, or modular movable tables, to accommodate large family groups
- Larger and easier-to-maintain grills and cookers for recreational cooking for large groups
- Shade trees in picnic sites
- Playgrounds (kid zones) near picnic areas
- Open grassy play areas for sports that can accommodate a wide variety of activities
- Facilities for community events (e.g., large group shelter, gazebo, amphitheaters)
- Use of universal symbols on signs
- Interpretive signs on walking trails in Spanish and other dominant languages of the region
- Mass transportation facilities (bus loading areas) at the most popular areas
- Improved security through increased ranger patrols, bilingual rangers, and improved gatehouses at park entrances[b]

Questions to Consider

- How has the move away from ethnically neutral design intended to improve attendance at outdoor areas?
- Why is it important to understand the reasons why ethnic populations may not see the outdoors as a special place?
- Put yourself in the role of a resource manager and determine how you would increase participation by racial and ethnic minorities.

[a]McCowan, R. S., & Laven, D. N. (2008). *Evaluation research to support National Park Service 21st century relevance initiatives* (p. 3). Washington, DC: National Park Service.
[b]Dunn, R. A. (2002). *Managing for ethnic diversity: Recreation facility and service modifications for ethnic minorities.* ERDC/EL TR-02-14. Vicksburg, MS: U.S. Army Research and Development Center.

WOMEN'S WORLD CUP SOCCER

From an international perspective, the Olympic Games were among the first true competitive events for women. Yet, it was Women's World Cup Soccer that captured the imagination of the world and firmly placed women as equals on the international sport stage. The International Federation of Association Football (FIFA) is the governing body for international football (soccer) and has been responsible for the men's World Cup since 1930. FIFA initiated the first Women's World Cup in 1991, and the event was held in China with 12 teams participating. Although it had an inauspicious start, the FIFA Women's World Cup has become an icon for women's equality in sport. The 1995 World Cup, held in Sweden, had a total attendance of 112,213 with one match drawing only 250 spectators. The 1999 World Cup, held in the United States, was the breakout World Cup with more than 1.1 million spectators and more than 1 billion television viewers. The Women's World Cup provided the U.S. team's first international success, with championships in 1991 and 1999 and players such as Mia Hamm and Brandi Chastain becoming overnight household names. The success of the U.S. women's national soccer team, which resulted in four World Cups and four Olympic gold medals from 1990 to 2019, has helped earn soccer a place in the hearts of American society. Beyond that, it has opened women's sport on an international basis in areas where it might not otherwise have flourished as attendance at the 2019 World Cup in France reached 1,131,312.

In other cases, when LGBTQIA+ groups sought to participate in big-city St. Patrick's Day parades, or when they held a huge festival at Florida's Walt Disney World, a number of conservative Christian organizations protested. In response, when Cobb County, Georgia, passed a resolution condemning the LGBTQIA+ lifestyle as incompatible with its values, LGBTQIA+ groups and their allies pressured the International Olympic Committee to withdraw some of its featured events from the county after they had been scheduled to take place there as part of the 1996 Olympics. In advance of the 2014 Sochi winter Olympics Russian anti-gay laws raised enough cause for concern to lead some to call for a U.S. boycott of the games. Discussions related to transgender individuals' right to compete based on their gender identity rather than biological sex assigned at birth are ongoing.

Older Adults in Community Life

Although the counterculture was primarily a youth movement in the United States and abroad, it also prompted many middle-aged and older persons to examine their value systems and their status in community life.

Older adults at this time represented a fourth group of minoritized persons in the sense that they were generally regarded and treated as powerless individuals who were both physically and economically vulnerable. However, under the leadership of such growing organizations as the American Association of Retired Persons and the much smaller Gray Panthers, older adults began to mobilize and exert political clout to obtain improved benefits. With support from various federal programs, including the Administration on Aging, senior citizens' groups and golden age clubs around the United States began to offer diversified programs of health care, social services, nutrition, housing and transportation assistance, and recreation.

Programming for Persons with Disabilities

Although significant progress had been made following World War II, both treatment-centered and community-based programming for persons with disabilities received a major impetus during the counterculture period. Like other minoritized groups that had essentially been powerless, persons with disabilities began to act as their own advocates, demanding their rights and opportunities. Persons with disabilities began to mobilize politically to promote positive legislation and increased community services for those with physical, mental, or social disabilities.

At the same time that recreation therapy specialists began to include a broader range of disabilities within their scope of service, numerous organizations went one step further and promoted such innovative programming as theater arts for people with physical disabilities, skiing for individuals with visual impairments, and a full range of sports and track-and-field events for people with mobility impairments.

Austerity and Fiscal Cutbacks: 1970s and 1980s

Despite this general picture of positive progress, the recreation, parks, and leisure-service field faced a serious threat in the 1970s and 1980s as mounting costs of government led to tax protests and funding cutbacks in states and cities across the United States. As early as the mid-1970s, a number of older industrial cities in the nation's Rust Belt, an area of the Midwest where iron and steel are produced and manufactured, began to suffer from increased energy costs, welfare and crime problems, and expenses linked to rising infrastructure maintenance problems. Along with some suburban school districts confronted by skyrocketing enrollments and limited tax bases, such communities experienced budget deficits and the need to freeze expenditures.

In 1976, a tax limitation law was passed in New Jersey, and in 1978 California's much more radical Proposition 13 sharply reduced local property tax rates and assessment increases. A "tax revolt" soon spread rapidly across the United States. By the end of 1979, statutory provisions had been approved in 36 states that either reduced property, income, or sales taxes or put other types of spending limits in place. Austerity budgets had to be adopted in many communities, counties, and other governmental units. Typically, Proposition 13 resulted in major funding cutbacks for parks, libraries, recreation, social services, and street sweeping and maintenance, while police and fire departments tended to be protected against cuts.[34]

Expanding Use of Revenue Sources

Many local recreation and park agencies adopted the policy of instituting or raising fees and charges for participation in programs, for use of the facilities, for rental of equipment, and for other types of uses. In the past, it generally had been the practice to provide all basic play opportunities, particularly for children and youths, without charge and to impose fees only for classes with special expenses or for admission to facilities such as skating rinks, swimming pools, golf courses, or tennis courts—often with arrangements made for annual permits at modest cost.

ACCEPTANCE OF MARKETING ORIENTATION

Directly linked to this trend was the widespread acceptance of an entrepreneurial, marketing-oriented approach to recreation and park programming and administration. It was argued by both educators and practitioners that it was necessary to be aggressive in seeking out new program

In periods of austerity and fiscal cutbacks, states sometimes close state parks as a cost-saving measure.
Courtesy of Alan Levine.

opportunities and creative in responding to fiscal challenges.

It was argued that managers of recreation and park programs, directors of nonprofit youth organizations, and operators of commercial play facilities were all essentially in the same "business"—that of meeting the public's leisure needs and interests. Therefore, recreation was increasingly referred to as an "industry."

It was often argued that to compete, public recreation agencies had to adopt the philosophy and businesslike methods of successful companies. At every stage of agency operations—from assessing potential target populations and planning programs to pricing, publicizing, and distributing services—sophisticated methods of analysis and businesslike approaches to attracting and satisfying "customers" were to be used.

Privatization of Recreation and Park Operations

As a second type of response to the era of austerity that began in the 1980s, many recreation, park, and leisure-service agencies resorted to privatization—subcontracting or developing concession arrangements with private organizations—to carry out functions that they could not themselves fulfill as economically or efficiently.

Numerous parks and recreation departments have contracted with private businesses to operate golf courses, tennis complexes, marinas, and other facilities under agreements that govern the standards they must meet and the rates they may impose. Particularly in the construction of massive new facilities such as sports stadiums and arenas, similar arrangements have been made with commercial developers or businesses for private funding of all or part of

PROMINENCE OF FEES AND CHARGES FOR ACTIVITIES

Even when recreation programs are provided by public local or nonprofit agencies, price tags are placed today on almost every kind of sponsored recreational opportunity. Typically, the annual or seasonal program brochures of public recreation and park agencies list various classes, aquatic or sport facilities, camps, tournaments, or special events—invariably with attached fees and charges that may run into several hundreds of dollars.

construction expenses, with long-term leases being granted to owners of major sports teams.[35]

Impact of Funding Cuts

In 1978, the National Urban Recreation Study reported that hiring freezes and staff cutbacks had taken place in a majority of urban park and recreation departments during the preceding 5 years. Two years later, a study of U.S. cities with populations greater than 150,000 found that a majority of the responding recreation and park departments experienced cutbacks that necessitated personnel freezes, staff discharges, program elimination, rejection of bond issues, and reduced facility maintenance.

Some reports suggested that many municipal and county recreation and park agencies weathered the financial crisis that followed the tax revolt and reached a point of relative stability. A study of small-town public recreation departments in several Western and Midwestern states by Ellen Weissinger and William Murphy found that although these departments experienced somewhat similar cutbacks to those reported in larger cities, they generally avoided drastic reductions in staff and programs.[36]

However, the reality is that in many larger cities, which have the greatest number of poor families and are marked by high welfare statistics, school dropouts, drug and alcohol abuse, youth gangs, and random violence, recreation and park programs today offer only the most minimal opportunities.

Beyond this, Jack Foley and Veda Ward point out that in the early 1990s the most severely disadvantaged communities, such as South Los Angeles, nonprofit sports groups like Little League, Pony League, Amateur Athletic Union swimming, and gymnastic and track clubs (which use public facilities but rely on volunteer leaders and membership fees) do not exist. There is also no commercial recreation in the form of movie theaters, malls, skating rinks, or bowling alleys. They continue:

> Boys and Girls Clubs, YMCAs and YWCAs, Scouts, and so forth, which rely on business and community support, are underrepresented and financed in poor communities. A market equity policy (one gets all the recreation one can buy) has created a separate, unequal, and regressive City of Los Angeles recreation system. City parks in wealthier neighborhoods raise from $50,000 to $250,000 annually

from user fees and donations, whereas recreation centers in South Los Angeles exist on small city subsidies and money they can squeeze out of the parents of poor children.[37]

Expansion of Other Recreation Programs

In sharp contrast with this negative picture, other forms of recreation services have flourished over the past 3 decades. Today, the largest single component of leisure services is the diversified field of commercial recreation businesses. Travel and tourism; fitness spas; professional sport and sport equipment; the manufacture and sale of hobbies, toys, and games; and varied forms of popular entertainment represent only part of this major sector of leisure involvement.

Similarly, most of the other areas of specialized recreation programming, such as recreation therapy, employee services, campus recreation, and private-membership and residential leisure services, have expanded steadily. These fields have sharpened their own identities by developing professional societies or business associations, sponsoring national and regional conferences, publishing newsletters and magazines, and in some cases establishing continuing education and certification programs.

Trends in the 1990s and Early 21st Century

This section describes several important demographic, social, economic, and technological trends beginning in the 1990s that influenced the provision of recreation and leisure services in the years immediately before and after the turn of the century. We deal with these and more trends in greater detail elsewhere in the text.

Economic Stratification: Income Gaps and "Luxury Fever"

Historically, the United States was viewed as a land of opportunity, in which every individual might climb the socioeconomic ladder and in which the middle class represented the backbone of society. During the 1990s and into the 21st

THE IMPORTANCE OF INDIVIDUAL DONORS TO NONPROFITS

Nonprofit organizations are dependent upon the goodwill of individuals and organizations to provide financial donations. This is especially true when the nonprofit desires to renovate existing buildings or to construct new buildings. The annual operating budget of a nonprofit is highly dependent upon individual donations. Many organizations gain a share of their operating budget from the United Way, but this is rarely sufficient to maintain day-to-day operations, and to improve its physical facilities an organization is wholly dependent upon contributions and grants. Physical facilities can be as simple as furniture for a meeting room and a softball complex for girls and women or can be major structures, such as multisport facilities, community centers, hospitals, and the like. The Salvation Army was the recipient of such a goodwill gift in 1998 and the gift has allowed it to change the way it delivers community services in some communities.

In 1998, Joan Kroc, widow of McDonald's founder Ray Kroc, in making a $90 million donation to the Salvation Army of San Diego, California, started what would become a nationwide impact on the services provided to communities by the Salvation Army through funds designed to build comprehensive community centers. With the goal of developing centers that would bring together diverse community members to engage in a wide variety of activities that otherwise might not be available to them, the first Kroc Center in San Diego was completed in 2001. The San Diego facility offers an ice arena, gymnasium, three pools, rock climbing walls, a theatre, internet-based library, computer lab and school of visual and performing arts. In 2003, upon Mrs. Kroc's death, $1.5 billion was bequeathed to the Salvation Army, ultimately growing to $1.8 billion, to continue to grow the building of community centers across the country. Today, there are 26 centers in cities such as San Fran, California; Atlanta, Georgia; Ashland, Ohio; Coeur d'Alene, Idaho; Omaha, Nebraska; Salem, Oregon; Dayton, Ohio; Grand Rapids, Michigan; Kerrville, Texas; Guayama, Puerto Rico; and Phoenix, Arizona with each having substantial economic and social impacts on their community.[38]

An example of the success of the Kroc Centers comes from Greenville, South Carolina, whose Kroc Center opened in 2011.

Conservatively, the Greenville Kroc Center contributed over $5,482,934 annually (2014) in local value, bringing economic and social vitality to the community through its programming, spending, and support of community members and organizations. The Greenville Kroc Center's spending results in a local impact of $3,124,995. In total, participants in center events and activities infuse $814,881 into the local economy annually. It is estimated that the value to the community of the Greenville Kroc Center's fitness programming totals $637,695 annually. The estimated annual value of the Greenville Kroc Center's safety net is $905,363.[39]

The Kroc Centers, operated by the Salvation Army, are major community centers that provide multiple services, including recreation.
Courtesy of Bryan E. Smith.

century, these assumptions were sharply reversed. Several new studies on the growing concentration of U.S. wealth and income challenged the nation's cherished self-image. Bradsher writes:

They show that rather than being an egalitarian society, the United States has become the most economically stratified of industrial nations. Indeed the drive under the so-called Contract with America to reduce federal welfare programs and cut taxes is expected to widen disparities between rich and poor.[40]

In part, this development stemmed from the emergence of a winner-take-all mentality in American business and public life, as more and more Americans compete for ever fewer and bigger prizes. In fact, a tiny fraction of the population controls much of the financial resources in America as just 1% of Americans control 40% of the wealth.[41]

The growth of the number of wealthy families in the United States in the 1990s was not accompanied by reduction of families living in poverty. In 1993, the nation's poverty rate rose to a 10-year high of 15.1%. In 2018, 11.8% of U.S. citizens, or 38.1 million people, lived in poverty. Although the poverty rate fluctuates a few percentage points across each decade, there has been very little change since the mid-1960s when a number of antipoverty social programs were implemented (see Figure 4-3).[42]

Starting in the 1990s, there were growing concerns about the ability of the middle class to make ends meet. Meanwhile,

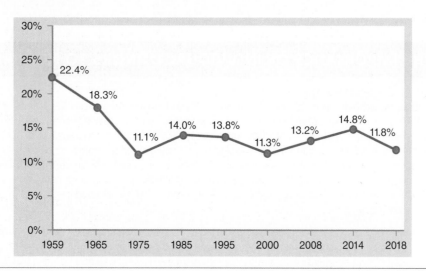

FIGURE 4-3 Poverty Level in the United States, 1959–2018

Data from Bishaw, A., & Renwick, T. J. (2009). *Poverty: 2007 and 2008 American Community Surveys*. American Community Service Reports. https://www2.census.gov/library/publications/2009/acs/acsbr08-01.pdf; Dalaker, J. (2005). *Alternative poverty estimates in the United States: 2003*. Current Population Reports. https://www2.census.gov/library/publications/2005/demo/p60-227.pdf; Semega, J., Kollar, M., Creamer, J., & Mohanty, A. (2019). *Income and poverty in the United States: 2018* (Report number P60-266). https://www.census.gov/library/publications/2019/demo/p60-266.html.

STRATIFICATION OF SALARIES AND THE MIDDLE CLASS

Much has been written about the stratification of salaries, including in this chapter. Less has been written about the impact on the middle class. Robert Frank's book *Falling Behind* is among several books addressing the effects of salary stratification on middle-class Americans.[43] A key premise of the book looks at the income gains at the highest level. Frank suggests that although the rich have gotten richer, the middle class has not kept up with income increases. There is no accepted definition of the middle class, so when annual income is considered as a measure, and individuals are asked if they are part of the middle class, people with annual incomes ranging from $40,000 to $250,000 say yes, they are middle class. These respondents typically say that they are stretched to make ends meet. They have not seen their salaries grow at a pace with the rich, yet they are purchasing more expensive homes, engaging in more expensive activities, and appear to be enjoying it less. Frank addresses the "rising cost of adequate" and uses homes as an example. When the rich build new homes or mansions, those at the top of the middle class begin to build larger homes, sometimes stretching what they can afford. There is a trickle-down effect to other levels of middle class as families see the community expectation for middle class rise. It is what Frank calls a cascading effect, where what top income earners spend their money on influences the spending patterns of the group directly below them, and on down until the effect reaches individuals at the bottom of the middle-class spectrum.

the middle class was declining, both in terms of numbers, income, and morale. In fact, between 1979 and 2007, while the income of the top 1% rose 278%, the median family income rose by just 35%. Furthermore, families in the middle class have achieved income gains by working longer hours, increasing their labor supply with more women in the workplace, and increasing household debt as wages failed to keep pace with inflation. Undoubtedly each of these are likely to have implications for leisure.[44]

IMPLICATIONS FOR LEISURE

What does this growing separation of U.S. society into rich and poor mean for recreation and leisure? First, a growing number of individuals have become immensely wealthy. In 1999, it was reported that 4.1 million of the nation's 102

million households had a net worth of $1 million or more and today that number is up to 18.6 million households. In addition, "one-percenters" or those who are a member of the top 1% of the population by wealth, are close to surpassing the wealth of the middle class as defined by those in the 50th to 90th percentile at a rate of 35.4% versus 36.9%.[45]

In what seemed to be a vivid replay of Thorstein Veblen's view of "conspicuous consumption," these individuals were caught up in what Cornell economist Robert Frank described as luxury fever—a rage to spend wildly on vehicles, clothing, toys and hobbies, and a host of other possessions.[46]

Meanwhile, children in less affluent neighborhoods or school districts often attended schools that lacked even the most minimal resources for play, as well as spaces and equipment for classes. Throughout the nation at the century's end, the growing gap between rich and poor evidenced itself in jarring contrasts in terms of recreation, parks, and leisure opportunities.

Growing Conservatism in Social Policy

Accompanying the nation's division into rich and poor social classes, there was a pronounced shift in the late 1980s and the 21st century toward more conservative social and economic policies. This trend took many forms, including a sharp withdrawal of assistance for welfare and for inner-city programs serving the economically disadvantaged. Particularly in the mid-1990s (and again in the early 21st century), there were renewed efforts to open the nation's parks and forests to economic exploitation and to reduce support for environmental education programs.

The election of President Barack Obama and the initiation of the 2009 great recession for a short time loosened the growing social conservatism. However, once the initial crisis was over, Congress and the public became gridlocked in ideological discussions. There were continuing assaults on federal support for the National Endowment for the Arts and other cultural programs.

Throughout the past 3 decades, newspaper headlines illustrated the impact of conservative political thrusts on

Participation in recreation activities does not need to occur in large recreation centers; it can occur in almost any setting.
© Gennadiy Titkov/Shutterstock.

American life in such areas as mandates for child welfare, nursing home beds for the elderly, health care, environmental protection enforcement, legal help for the urban poor, and youth programs. The widespread decline in support for needed public services and the harsh resistance to government policies benefiting minoritized people and the poor inevitably posed a severe challenge to many public and nonprofit leisure-service organizations.

Commodification and Privatization of Leisure Services

There is a continued blurring of functions among different types of organizations in American society: governmental, nonprofit, private, and commercial. Instead of having clearly marked areas of responsibility and program operations in the leisure-service field, these separate kinds of organizations overlap each other through partnerships or cosponsorship arrangements; privatization by expanding their missions and undertaking new, innovative ventures; by adopting new fiscal policies; and by turning their operations over to the private sector. This overall trend had two related components: commodification and privatization.

COMMODIFICATION

Simply defined, commodification describes the process of taking any product or service and commercializing it by designing and marketing it to yield the greatest degree of financial return or profit. On the national scene, as part of the effort to gain fuller financial support in an increasingly consumer-oriented society, art museums, libraries, and theater, orchestra, and ballet companies all have become centers of popular entertainment, offering chartered trips abroad, film series and lecture programs, social events, and jazz concerts.

PRIVATIZATION

As described earlier, privatization refers to the growing practice of having private corporations take on responsibility for providing services, maintaining facilities, or performing other functions formerly carried out by government agencies.

During the 1990s, privatization grew increasingly widespread. In terms of public recreation and park privatization, the most striking event was the 1998 contract for a private group, the Central Park Conservancy, to operate New York City's Central Park, with joint public and private funding. A more common approach to privatization is to contract with a nonprofit to provide recreation services. This has been a frequent model in smaller communities where a nonprofit exists and no public recreation agency exists. The same model is present in large cities where existing recreation and park agencies cannot provide the level of service requested. A major recreation center is built, at public expense, and then leased to a nonprofit for operation. In many cases, the nonprofit continues to require a membership fee and may exclude some lower-income users.

THE NEW REALITIES: NEW, REVISITED, OR JUST PESSIMISM?

A consistent theme appearing in the literature of public and nonprofit recreation and leisure publications is that the recession of 2009–2010 has changed funding models forever. It is true that the recession diminished funding for public and nonprofit organizations. These organizations are almost always negatively affected by a recession, even when for-profit enterprises appear to be less affected.

One of the dilemmas faced by public and nonprofit organizations when the economy is in recession is an increasingly greater need for public services. People turn to public agencies for basic and recreational needs. Unfortunately, as demand increases, public agencies are facing similar financial challenges, frequently resulting in budget cuts and reduction of services. What was particularly challenging in the 2009 recession was the loss of revenue from multiple funding sources. Cities count on property, income, and sales taxes for the bulk of their operating revenues. Each source is somewhat volatile, but for the last 30 years property taxes have steadily increased until 2010, when property values dropped across major portions of the country. The new reality for recreation agencies may be that funding has changed forever. It did in the early 1970s when the tax revolt affected many states and communities. However, it is easy to assume things will not get better. That is a wrong-thinking attitude. Government funding sources, although traditionally stable, have not always been so, and to approach change from a negative perspective guarantees that opportunities such as those that can be provided through stimulus packages and other unique mechanisms will be missed.

It is important that public organizations and nonprofits maintain quality and focus on the future. In Las Vegas, Nevada, where more than 150 park and recreation employees were laid off and five community centers were closed, the director stated, "We will be a smaller, more efficient, and more responsive organization in the future." The new realities are that in the short term, public and nonprofit organizations will rethink, reorganize, and reprioritize their services and programs. Simultaneously, however, they need to plan for and aggressively act on the future.

The City of Rock Hill, South Carolina, offers a great example of using a unique funding opportunity to develop recreation facilities. In 2000, Congress established the New Markets Tax Credits (NMTC) Program to incentivize new development in low-income communities by permitting investors to receive a tax credit against their federal income tax return in exchange for making equity investments in specialized financial institutions called Community Development Entities. With the opportunity to be part of a larger effort to develop the abandoned site of a former cellulose acetate manufacturing facility with housing, commercial, and recreation facilities, the city identified NMTC as the most cost-effective avenue to fund a velodrome, BMX/supercross, cyclocross, and mountain biking trails as their part of the project. In essence, in taking advantage of the NMTC, the City of Rock Hill was able to ultimately reduce the cost of what was a $7,500,000 project (including interest) to $5,125,000 as they financed the deal as a NMTC with a Recovery Zone Designation.

Maturation of Organized Leisure-Services Field

The nature of municipal, state, and federal governments has changed dramatically in the almost 140 years of organized recreation in the United States. Government is more dependent on alternative income sources and less reliant on taxes. Where few fees once existed, now public agencies depend on fees and charges to make up as much as 90% of their operating budget. Parks and recreation agencies cannot serve all who either desire or have a need for services. Nonprofit and commercial agencies often fill the gap. In today's environment of rapidly changing demand for different types of leisure activities, public, commercial, and nonprofit organizations strive to respond, but often public agencies and nonprofits do not have the resources, financial capital, or ability to respond effectively. Commercial enterprises typically respond more quickly to what initially may appear to be fringe activities such as paintball, skateboarding, laser tag, and the like.

Maturation does not suggest the organized leisure-services field is not changing but rather that growth in the public and nonprofit sector is constrained by available funds, politics, public interest, and the perceived opportunity for growth. Public and nonprofit agencies have developed an infrastructure of parks, recreation centers, sports fields, cultural centers, and others that become a burden to agencies' ability to rapidly respond to change. The traditional programming of public and nonprofit agencies remains in place, although there is less of it and more of the emerging programs, but change is coming slowly. Where communities once built a 50-meter swimming pool, today they build a small to medium waterpark—except when politicians or other influential groups intervene and demand a traditional or old-fashioned approach. The leadership is changing and new, younger leaders are emerging. Values are being reassessed, commitments rethought, demands evaluated, and expectations challenged.

Commercial recreation is present in or near national parks as evidenced by the new glass walkway over the Grand Canyon—it exists on Native American land.

Courtesy of Grand Canyon Skywalk Development, LLC

New Environmental Initiatives

As this chapter has shown, the nation's support for environmental protection and the recovery of polluted lakes and streams, as well as the continuing acquisition and preservation of wilderness areas, faced a sharp challenge through the end of the 20th century.

Several decades of neglect and overcrowding left the nation's park system and forests in a precarious state. With national concern mounting, park authorities have instituted new fees to gather additional revenue and restricted automobile traffic into interior sections. Increasingly, corporate sponsors were recruited to assist in park maintenance, and major environmental organizations such as the National Park Trust provided support for the acquisition of new parks and wildlands.

Although public concerns focused chiefly on the ecological recovery of parks and wilderness areas, they also were directed to problems of clean air and water that affected major metropolitan areas. At the same time, major efforts were made in such older cities as Baltimore and Boston to revive waterfront and disused industrial areas. In such settings, cities developed new harbor facilities such as aquariums, museums, sport stadiums, marinas, theme parks, and other attractions—both to improve their image and attract tourists and to serve their own residents with appealing leisure programs.

Technological Impacts on Leisure

Beyond the effects of technological innovation described, a number of other scientifically based advances had a major impact on American leisure in the final decades of the 20th century. Many of these had to do with forms of travel. Apart from the use of computers in tourism planning and reservations, global positioning system (GPS) services became able to direct an automobile trip through every turn until reaching the desired destination. Electronic navigation simulators created by companies such as Maptech, Inc., provided piloting assistance for boating enthusiasts. For the vacationing family, movies and video games replaced license-plate Bingo, as cars became entertainment centers with the latest audio and video technology.

Home environments became increasingly "smart." Home theater systems can control lighting; digital, CD, and MP3 systems; window shades; satellite service; and Blu-Ray players, while other lines wirelessly accommodate the family's telephones and computers—all at a distance.

Television, video games, and children's toys represent impressive examples of technology's impact on family leisure. As of the late 1990s, almost 80% of homes had cable or satellite television, and many studies reported that about 40% of Americans' free time was spent watching the home screen.

Into the 21st century, television watching has continued to be the most popular form of viewing media; however, it is receiving stiff competition from Internet-based sources used with computers and handheld devices. The Internet has had a huge impact on viewing. In the past, almost all viewing was on the television. Now television viewing is shared with watching television or videos on the Internet with a surge in on-demand services such as Netflix, Hulu, and Amazon Prime. The availability of handheld video devices means that individuals no longer need to be at home to watch videos. The most current figures suggest people watch 3.5 hours of video each month on their mobile phone.[47]

Recreation and Wellness Revisited

Public health officials have recognized that the sedentary lifestyles led by a large percentage of adults and children in the United States are directly contributing to a prevalence of obesity in the population that approaches epidemic levels.[48] Unfortunately, the rise in childhood obesity has coincided with a decline in student time spent in physical education classes, recess, and outdoors.

Today, recreation and leisure-service providers and the federal government recognize the role of community recreation in encouraging physical activity. Federally funded initiatives include the establishment of community trail systems and support of after-school programs. The Surgeon General's Office recommended the development of public policy that addresses community access to safe physical activity. A growing number of nonprofits focusing on childhood obesity, lack of fitness orientations and programs, and the decline in children's contact with the outdoors and nature have emerged and are providing leadership.

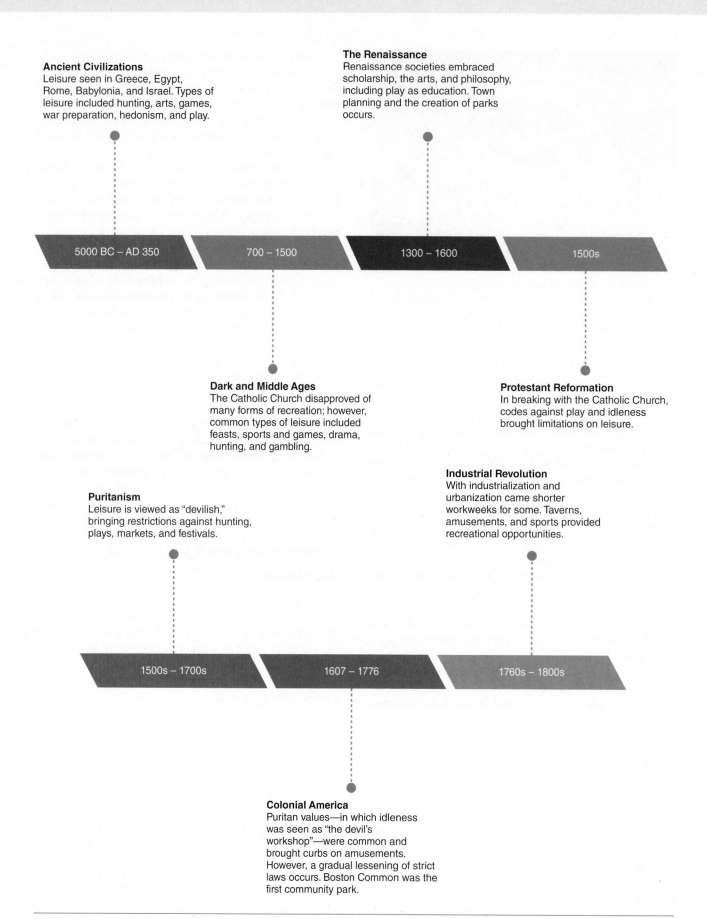

Ancient Civilizations
Leisure seen in Greece, Egypt, Rome, Babylonia, and Israel. Types of leisure included hunting, arts, games, war preparation, hedonism, and play.

The Renaissance
Renaissance societies embraced scholarship, the arts, and philosophy, including play as education. Town planning and the creation of parks occurs.

5000 BC – AD 350

700 – 1500

1300 – 1600

1500s

Dark and Middle Ages
The Catholic Church disapproved of many forms of recreation; however, common types of leisure included feasts, sports and games, drama, hunting, and gambling.

Protestant Reformation
In breaking with the Catholic Church, codes against play and idleness brought limitations on leisure.

Industrial Revolution
With industrialization and urbanization came shorter workweeks for some. Taverns, amusements, and sports provided recreational opportunities.

Puritanism
Leisure is viewed as "devilish," bringing restrictions against hunting, plays, markets, and festivals.

1500s – 1700s

1607 – 1776

1760s – 1800s

Colonial America
Puritan values—in which idleness was seen as "the devil's workshop"—were common and brought curbs on amusements. However, a gradual lessening of strict laws occurs. Boston Common was the first community park.

History of Recreation and Leisure Timeline

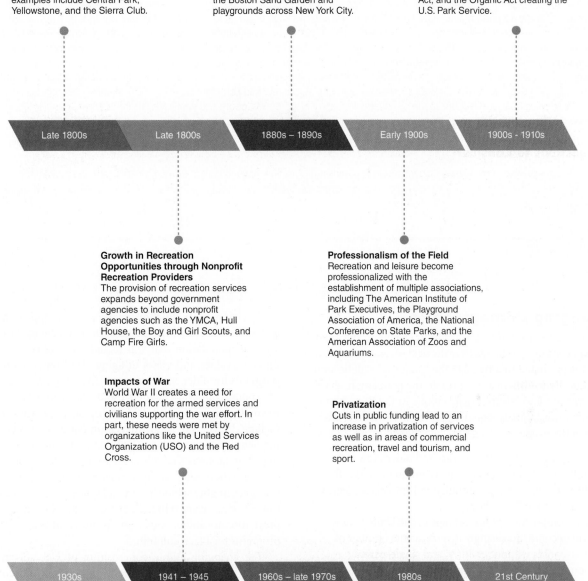

Conservation Movement
All levels of government, as well as nonprofits, recognized the importance of protecting open space. Key examples include Central Park, Yellowstone, and the Sierra Club.

Playground Movement
With changes to child labor laws, it was recognized that youth needed safe spaces for play. Cities moved toward developing play areas such as the Boston Sand Garden and playgrounds across New York City.

Federal Acts of Significance
Several acts are passed at the federal level that impacted the profession, including the Transfer Act creating the U.S. Forest Service, the Antiquities Act, and the Organic Act creating the U.S. Park Service.

Late 1800s   Late 1800s   1880s – 1890s   Early 1900s   1900s - 1910s

Growth in Recreation Opportunities through Nonprofit Recreation Providers
The provision of recreation services expands beyond government agencies to include nonprofit agencies such as the YMCA, Hull House, the Boy and Girl Scouts, and Camp Fire Girls.

Professionalism of the Field
Recreation and leisure become professionalized with the establishment of multiple associations, including The American Institute of Park Executives, the Playground Association of America, the National Conference on State Parks, and the American Association of Zoos and Aquariums.

Impacts of War
World War II creates a need for recreation for the armed services and civilians supporting the war effort. In part, these needs were met by organizations like the United Services Organization (USO) and the Red Cross.

Privatization
Cuts in public funding lead to an increase in privatization of services as well as in areas of commercial recreation, travel and tourism, and sport.

1930s   1941 – 1945   1960s – late 1970s   1980s   21st Century

Great Depression
Roosevelt's New Deal programs, designed to address mass unemployment, helped lead to the creation of thousands of parks and recreation centers, specifically through the Civilian Conservation Corps and Works Progress Administration.

Legal Impacts on Recreation Services
Local, state, and federal legislation such as Proposition 13, the Land and Water Conservation Act, and Title IX have major implications for funding parks and recreation services across the country.

Current Trends and Impacts
National and global crises—including 9/11, global terrorism, global pandemic and the housing crisis and resulting recession—resonated with service providers, as issues related to globalization, technology, diversity, and the economy impact all sectors of the field.

CASE STUDY: Smoking Policies in Public Parks

Although physical activity is a hot button item with regard to parks and recreation programming, there are other health-related concerns at the forefront of professionals' minds. As more and more communities pass no smoking laws for indoor venues such as restaurants and bars, parks managers are frequently examining the issue of smoking regulations for their outdoor facilities. In 2015 the Office of Recreation and Park Resources, housed in the Department of Recreation, Sport, and Tourism at the University of Illinois, Urbana-Champaign, worked with the Illinois Department of Natural Resources to gain a greater understanding of how parks and recreation agencies in the state were regulating smoking in their outdoor parks and facilities. A total of 208 park districts, 119 municipalities, and 16 forest preserves completed a written survey asking about park policies and implementation of policies, with 42% indicating they had formal outdoor smoke-free policy areas, but few had complete bans. For most agencies the policies were specific to areas that saw frequent usage by children including playgrounds, pools, and youth athletic fields. Most agencies enforced behaviors in one of three ways: signage, citizen enforcement, and staff monitoring.

Questions to Consider

- With an upswing in the use of e-cigarettes do you think agencies will move to limit their use on park property as well?
- As states such as Colorado move to legalize marijuana, do you think its use should be allowed in outdoor park areas? Why or why not?

Data from Owens, M. (2016, March). Outdoor smoke-free policy development and enforcement in parks." *Parks & Recreation, 51*(3), 24–26. https://ezine.nrpa.org/html5/reader/production/default.aspx?pubname=&edid=144db82d-88e5-4bd4-b855-d511c7a7d1b0.

Changing Demographics

The face of the United States began to change in the 1990s and will continue to change over the next several decades. In fact, it is predicted that by 2043 the "majority" will become the minority in America. As a result, the population served by recreation and leisure organizations in the 21st century will differ substantially from that served in the 20th century. Some of the primary changes include the following:

- The number of adults 65 years and older grew from 25 million in 1980 to more than 41 million in 2011. By 2050, the 65-and-over population is projected to grow to more than 70 million.
- The composition of households in the United States will become increasingly diverse, as the number of households without children and single-parent households continue to grow.
- The growth of the Hispanic population in the United States will continue throughout the next few decades as Hispanic Americans become the largest ethnic minority group in the United States.

A changing population requires new approaches to delivery of leisure services. Agencies are challenged to serve an older population that will include several cohorts with different values and views of aging. Traditional recreation programs for older adults may not appeal to baby boomers, who highly value independence and resist aging stereotypes. Examples of the impact of a changing population might include decisions in facility development that reflect changing family structures that might demand alternative changing areas or areas that allow for more modesty for certain cultures where religion dictates its necessity. Programming examples might include health and safety programs targeted toward ethnic groups in light of risk factors such as diabetes prevention for Indigenous communities and Learn to Swim programs for Black children.

The changing ethnic composition of U.S. society will require leisure-service providers to examine the cultural framework that underlies programs and services. Agencies in certain geographic areas and some urban areas currently are responding to the need for truly multicultural programming.

SUMMARY

This chapter shows the long history of recreation, play, and leisure by discussing their roles in the ancient civilizations of Assyria, Babylonia, and Egypt; then in the Greek and Roman eras; during the Middle Ages and the Renaissance in Europe; and from the pre-Revolutionary period in the North American colonies to the 21st century.

Religion and social class were major factors that influenced recreational involvement in terms of either prohibiting certain forms of activity or assigning them to one class or another throughout history. From the Catholic Church placing a strong value on work and worship to the Puritans that identified idleness as "the devil's workshop" to the impact of the Protestant Reformation and the related emphasis on work, religion continues today to have an impact on how we define appropriate leisure.

The chapter traces the influence of the Industrial Revolution, which brought millions of immigrants from Europe to America, where they lived in crowded tenements in large cities or in factory towns.

By the middle of the 19th century, however, religious opposition to varied types of play and entertainment began to decline. Sport became more popular and accepted and, after reaching a high point at midcentury, work hours began to decline. Four major roots of what was ultimately to become the recreation and park movement appeared: (1) the establishment of city parks, beginning with New York City's Central Park, and the later growth of county, state, and national parks; (2) the growing interest in adult education and cultural development; (3) the appearance of playgrounds for children, sponsored first as charitable efforts and shortly after by city governments and the public schools; and (4) the development of a number of nonprofit, youth-serving organizations that spread throughout the country.

Popular culture gained momentum during the Jazz Age of the 1920s, with college and professional sport, motion pictures and radio, new forms of dance and music, and a host of other crazes capturing the public's interest. Although the Great Depression of the 1930s had a tragic impact on many families, the efforts of the federal government to build recreation facilities and leisure services to provide jobs and a morale boost for the public at large meant that the Depression was a powerful positive force for the recreation movement in general.

By the early 1940s, organized recreation service was firmly established in American life, and both government officials and social critics began to raise searching questions about its future role in postwar society.

The years following World War II represented a period of immense change in the lives of Americans. From 1945 to the early 1970s, it was a time of prosperity and optimism for most families. As great numbers of young people—generally white and working or middle class—moved into suburban areas, recreation and park programs flourished, and leisure was seen as part of the good life.

Recognizing that a substantial part of the population continued to live in urban slums, with limited economic and social opportunities, the federal government launched a "war on poverty," in which recreation played a significant role. Under pressure from the civil rights movement, many recreation and park agencies began to give a higher level of priority to serving minorities. With the inner-city riots of the mid- and late-1960s, this effort was expanded throughout the country. At the same time, the counterculture movement, which saw young people rebelling against traditional authority and establishment values, transformed society with its resistance to the work ethic and its acceptance of drugs.

The late 1960s and 1970s were also a time when minority groups—including women, older adults, persons with disabilities, and those who are lesbian, gay, bisexual, or transgender—began to demand greater social, economic, political, and leisure opportunities. For them, recreation represented a means of gaining independence and achieving their fullest potential.

Beginning in the 1970s and intensifying during the decade that followed, recessions, inflation, rising costs of welfare and crime, and declining tax bases created an era of austerity that affected many government agencies. With sharp cutbacks in their budgets, many recreation and park agencies imposed severe staffing and maintenance cuts and relied more markedly on fees and privatization to maintain their programs. The entrepreneurial marketing strategy that prevailed widely at this time meant that many public departments were forced to give less emphasis to socially oriented programming.

At the same time, political conservatism in areas related to race relations, the criminal justice system, services for the poor, and environmental programs gained support. Studies in the 1980s and 1990s indicate that many Americans were working longer hours because of changes in family patterns and technological influences on business. At the end of the 1990s, with economic prosperity and more positive social and environmental concerns gaining acceptance, the place of recreation and leisure in contemporary life appeared to be more secure than ever.

Parks and recreation agencies face new challenges and opportunities in the 21st century. The population has started to change dramatically, requiring parks and recreation professionals to develop appropriate programs and services. Growing health concerns have provided an opportunity for agencies to play a greater role as public health advocates. The rapidly growing older population has time and resources for leisure but may reject traditional senior programs for more youthful and diverse opportunities. Changing household composition, including an increase in the number of singles, has challenged agencies that have historically focused on providing programs for families with children. Increasing ethnic diversity provides an opportunity for agencies to increase multicultural programming. In addition to changing demographics, parks and recreation agencies have experienced growing pressure to provide evidence of financial accountability through outcomes assessment. In the early 21st century, the place of recreation and leisure as a cultural and social institution seems secure.

QUESTIONS FOR CLASS DISCUSSION OR ESSAY EXAMINATION

1. Contrast the attitudes toward sport and other uses of leisure that were found in ancient Greece with those found in the Roman Empire. How did their philosophies differ, and how did the Roman philosophy lead to a weakening of that powerful nation? Could you draw a parallel between the approach to leisure and entertainment in ancient Rome and that in the present-day United States? _____

_____

2. Trace the development of religious attitudes and policies regarding leisure and play from the Dark and Middle Ages, through the Renaissance and Reformation periods, to the colonial era in 17th- and 18th-century North America. What differences were there in the approach to recreation between the northern and southern colonies at this time? _____

3. Do you feel that it was appropriate that religion had such an impact on how individuals spent their free time in Colonial America? Why or why not? _____

4. In the second half of the 19th century, the roots of what was to become the modern recreation and park movement appeared. What were these roots (e.g., the adult education or Lyceum movement), and how did they relate to the broad social needs of Americans? _____

5. Four important pioneers of the early recreation movement in the United States were Lee, Gulick, Addams, and Attwell. Summarize some of the key points of their philosophies and their contributions to the playground and recreation developments. Describe the conflict between the traditional Victorian values and code of morality and the emerging popular culture, especially during the 1920s. _____

6. What do you feel are the three most influential events in history that have had a lasting impact on the provision of recreation services today? Explain. _____

7. Trace the expanding role of government in terms of sponsoring recreation and park programs during the first half of the 20th century, with emphasis on federal policies in wartime and during the Depression of the 1930s. What were some of the growing concerns about leisure during this period? _____

8. The federal government has progressively pushed for stronger regulation of the environment since the mid-1950s. Explain how these efforts have affected, in positive and negative ways, the nation's perceptions and commitment to the environment and parks and recreation. _____

9. Explain the role that recreation and leisure had in helping to bridge the challenges of racial unrest and the counterculture movement of the 1960s and 1970s, and describe the influence recreation and leisure have on today's issues._____

_____

_____

_____

_____

10. What are the current events occurring in society (e.g., elections, international political unrest, growth in conservatism, economic challenges) that you feel have a direct impact on the provision of recreation as we continue to move further into the 21st century?_____

_____

_____

11. Explain why free time has not met expectations. Take a position in favor of or against increased free time and defend your position._____

_____

_____

_____

12. Discuss the impact of the fluctuating economy on parks and recreation over the past 20 years._____

_____

_____

_____

13. Explain counterculture. How has the counterculture affected parks and recreation?_____

_____

_____

_____

ENDNOTES

1. Kraus, R. (1971). *Recreation and leisure in modern society.* New York: Appleton-Century-Crofts.
2. Kirstein, L. (1935). *Dance: A short history of classical theatrical dancing* (p. 57). New York: G. P. Putnam.
3. Miller, N. P., & Robinson, D. M. (1963). *The leisure age,* (p. 66). Belmont, CA: Wadsworth, p. 66.
4. Paul La Croix, *France in the Middle Ages* (New York: Frederick Ungar, 1963).
5. Richard B. Morris, *Government and Labor in Early America*, 1946. Chapter: Compulsory Labor. http://www.ditext.com/morris/toc.html (retrieved February 8, 2021)
6. Holland, J. W. (2002). *Black recreation: A historical perspective.* Chicago: Burnham, Inc.
7. Will, G. (1996, April 7). Review of G. Edward White, "Creating the National Pastime." *New York Times Book Review*, p. 11.
8. Dulles, F. R. (1965). *A history of recreation: America learns to play* (p. 182). New York: Appleton-Century-Crofts.
9. Nasaw, D. (1993). *Going out: The rise and fall of public amusements* (p. 2). New York: Basic Books.
10. Ibid., p. 5.
11. Thomas P. Hughes (1896). The stage from a clergyman's standpoint. *The Forum, Vol. 20,* p. 703.
12. Horace Greeley. (1869) *Recollections of a busy life: Reminiscences of American politics and politicians.* New York: JB Ford & Co. p. 121.
13. Jesse Lyman Hurlbut (1921). *The story of Chautauqua.* New York: G. P. Putman's Son. P. 184
14. Muir, J. (1981). *Our national parks* (p. 40). Madison: University of Wisconsin Press. (Original published 1901)
15. Heintzman, P. (1997). Wilderness and the Canadian mind: Impact upon recreation development in Canadian parks. NRPA Research Symposium, p. 75.
16. Jearold Winston Holland, *Black Recreation: A Historical Perspective* (Chicago: Burnham, Inc.)
17. Vrooman, W. (1894, July). Playgrounds for children. *The Arena*, 286.
18. Knapp, R. (1973, July). Play for America: The New Deal and the NRA. *Parks and Recreation*, 23.
19. Duncan, M. (1980). Back to our radical roots. In T. L. Goodale & P. A. Witt (Eds.), *Recreation and leisure: Issues in an era of change* (pp. 287–295). State College, PA: Venture Publishing.

20. Ernest J. Attwell. *Play and playground encyclopedia*. Retrieved October 15, 2020, from https://www.pgpedia.com/a/ernest-t-attwell.

21. Kathy Peiss, *Cheap Amusements: Working Women and Leisure in Turn-of-the-Century New York*. Philadelphia: Temple University Press, 1986.

22. Art and popular culture. (2017, May 26). *Popular culture*. Retrieved January 18, 2021, from http://www.artandpopularculture.com/Popular_culture.

23. Hunnicutt, B. (1980). Historical attitudes toward the increase of free time in the twentieth century: Time for leisure, for work, for unemployment. *Loisir et Societe 3*, 196.

24. Ibid., p. 14

25. Currell, S. (2005). *The march of spare time: The problem and promise of leisure in the Great Depression* (p. 51). Philadelphia: University of Pennsylvania Press.

26. Lindeman, E. (1939). *Leisure: A national issue* (p. 32). New York: American Association for the Study of Group Work.

27. U.S. Census Bureau. (2011). *Statistical abstract of the United States: 2012*. Retrieved January 18, 2021, from https://www.census.gov/library/publications/2011/compendia/statab/131ed.html.

28. Kraus, R. (1994). *Leisure in a changing America: Multicultural perspectives* (p. 61). New York: Macmillan College Publishing.

29. National Center for Health Statistics. (2021). Obesity and overweight. Retrieved May 14, 2020, from https://www.cdc.gov/nchs/fastats/obesity-overweight.htm.

30. The Land and Water Conservation Fund Coalition. Retrieved October 15, 2020, from https://www.lwcfcoalition.com.

31. National Park Service. *Land and Water Conservation Fund. State and local grant funding*. Retrieved October 15, 2020, from https://www.nps.gov/subjects/lwcf/stateside.htm.

32. Ibid.

33. Eunice Kennedy Shriver, home page. Retrieved January 18, 2021, from http://www.eunicekennedyshriver.org.

34. O'Leary, K. (2009, June 27). The legacy of Proposition 13. *Time*.

35. Kraus, R. (1980). *New directions in urban parks and recreation: A trends analysis report* (p. 6). Philadelphia, PA: Temple University and Heritage Conservation and Recreation Service.

36. Weissinger, E., & Murphy, W. (1993). A survey of fiscal conditions in small-town public recreation departments from 1987 to 1991. *Journal of Park and Recreation Administration, 11*(3), 61–71.

37. Foley, J., & Ward, V. (1993, March). Recreation, the riots and a healthy L.A. *Parks and Recreation*, 68.

38. Salvation Army. (2015, May 18). *National study quantifies impact of Salvation Army Ray and Joan Kroc Corps Community Centers*. Retrieved October 15, 2020, from https://www.salvationarmyusa.org/usn/news/study_quantifies_impact_of_salvation_army_ray_and_joan_kroc_corps-community_centers/.

39. Amanda Chastiain, *Greenville, SC Kroc Center creating positive long-term impact*. https://www.salvationarmycarolinas.org/greenvillesc/blog/2015/05/18/kroccenterreport/ (Retrieved February 20, 2021)

40. Bradsher, K. (1995, April 17). Gap in wealth in U.S. called widest in West. *New York Times*, 1.

41. Frank, R., & Cook, P. (1995). *The winner take all society*. New York: Free Press.

42. Poverty USA. (2020). *The population of Poverty USA*. Retrieved October 14, 2020, from http://www.povertyusa.org/facts.

43. Frank, R. H. (2007). *Falling behind: How rising inequality harms the middle class*. Berkeley: University of California Press.

44. Boushey, H., & Hersh, A. S. (2012, May). *The American middle class, income inequality, and the strength of our economy*. Retrieved February 10, 2021, from https://cdn.americanprogress.org/wp-content/uploads/2012/05/93905594-The-American-Middle-Class-Income-Inequality-and-the-Strength-of-Our-Economy.pdf

45. Tanzi, A. (2019, November 12). *Richest 1% of Americans close to surpassing wealth of middle class*. Retrieved January 18, 2021, from https://www.bloombergquint.com/global-economics/one-percenters-close-to-surpassing-wealth-of-u-s-middle-class

46. Frank, R. (1999). *Luxury fever: Why money fails to satisfy in an era of excess*. New York: Free Press.

47. Fottrell, Q. (2018, August 4). People spend most of their waking hours staring at screens. *Marketwatch*. Retrieved January 18, 2021, from https://www.marketwatch.com/story/people-are-spending-most-of-their-waking-hours-staring-at-screens-2018-08-01.

48. Centers for Disease Control and Prevention. (2020). *Overweight and obesity*. Retrieved January 18, 2021, from https://www.cdc.gov/obesity/index.html.

Chapter 5

Social Functions of Community Recreation

The casual interpersonal relationships of the metropolis cause problems of isolation and unhappiness; often individuals find themselves in the state described as anomie, or alienation. The loneliness of the city, particularly for large numbers of unattached young adults, is illustrated by the rapid increase of computerized dating services, which match single adults in terms of their background, age, and interests. This indicates the need for more meaningful ways in which people can make contact with each other in the modern metropolis, in direct, open, and friendly forms of group involvement. While recreation cannot provide a total solution for the pathological loneliness and lack of communication that characterize much of modern urban life, there certainly is an important need for activities and groups in which people may find personal enrichment and social involvement.[1]

-From the first edition of Kraus' Recreation and Leisure in Modern Society, published in 1971

LEARNING OBJECTIVES

1. Define community.

2. Discuss the factors that contribute to community well-being.

3. Identify and discuss each of the 10 functions of community recreation.

Introduction

Early definitions of recreation suggested that it served to restore participants' energy for renewed work but did not seek to achieve other, extrinsic purposes. Today, it is quite clear that this is no longer the case. Contemporary recreation programs and services—whether sponsored by public, nonprofit, or commercial agencies—are goal oriented and intended to achieve constructive outcomes for both participants and the community at large. These outcomes range from improving the quality of life for all community residents and reducing antisocial and destructive uses of leisure to promoting the arts, serving special populations, and protecting the environment. This chapter outlines the societal benefits of organized recreation service and provides a strong rationale for supporting recreation as an essential community function.

Emphasis on Community Benefits

Thus far in this text, recreation and leisure have been described conceptually as important aspects of human experience. We now examine their contribution to community well-being on a broader scale. The term *community* is used here to mean a significant clustering of people who have a common bond, such as the residents of a city, town, or neighborhood. It may also refer to other aggregations of people, such as the employees of a company or those who live and work on an armed forces base.

As community recreation has evolved and changed over the years, we have seen different philosophies emerge regarding the value of parks and recreation. What began as a social entity in the 1800s that provided services free of charge for the betterment of society has changed and grown. Although agencies still provide these services, they must also justify their value as well as the economic efficiency of services. Our country has seen periods of economic austerity, such as after the September 11, 2001 attacks that forced many public and nonprofit agencies to cut programs and services, during the recession from 2008 to 2011, and in other times of economic uncertainty including the 2020 coronavirus pandemic. At those times, it becomes necessary to document the positive benefits derived from organized recreation programs and services to secure support for them. Although communities often call for more police and fire protection, park and recreation agencies have to show how they contribute to communities and how they can make their community a better place to live, work, and play.

Many agencies have placed an emphasis on showing economic and social value for their services. For example, Virginia Beach Parks and Recreation Department (VBPRD) understood their value to the community and tourism but needed a means to communicate it to the public with facts.

Agencies like the Young Men's Christian Association (YMCA) of Greater Des Moines offer summer camps for youths that focus on setting values, building character, and enhancing creativity.
© Felix Mizioznikov/Shutterstock.

To do this they did a study on this value and included seven major factors: clean air, clean water, tourism, direct use, health, property value, and community cohesion. They learned that VBPRD adds $701,814,399 in direct and indirect value to their community each year.[2] The City of New York Parks and Recreation Department calculated the tree benefits for the city and found that through positive impacts on air quality ($5.3 million), energy savings ($27.8 million), reduction in CO_2 emissions ($753,000), reduction in stormwater runoff ($36 million), and impacts on property values and other benefits ($52 million), the total economic impact of trees was $122 million.[3]

Given this understanding, we now examine 10 major areas of recreation's contribution to community life. In several cases, the benefits cited are similar to those presented in other chapters dealing with the personal values of recreation. However, here they apply to broader community needs and benefits.

Function 1: Enriching the Quality of Life

Purpose: To enrich the quality of life in the community setting by providing enjoyable and constructive leisure opportunities for all residents.

Quality of life encompasses elements that together contribute to the general well-being of individuals as well as communities as a whole including physical health, family, education, employment, safety, and others. Assessing quality of life looks at very quantifiable items as well as a personal perspective of the community. In terms of the quantifiable aspects of quality of life, Mercer's Quality of Living Survey is released annually and rates cities across the world on their perceived livability based on such factors as safety, education, health care, and political and economic environments. It also looks at factors such as recreation, the natural environment, and sociocultural environment.[4] In addition, International Living rates the livability of countries.[5] They use categories of cost of living, culture and leisure, economy, environment, freedom, health and safety, infrastructure, and climate. In this index, recreation and tourism fall under the culture category.

As mentioned, some things contribute to quality of life that are not as quantifiable and are personal to the individual. In terms of recreation, these include such things as available social opportunities, cultural activities, special events, parks, trails, lakes, restaurants, streetscaping, and facilities to enjoy ample recreation programs. Recreation's most obvious value is the opportunity that it provides for fun, relaxation, and pleasure through active participation in leisure experiences.

Parks provide a vivid illustration of the social value of leisure. During the warmer months of the year, they provide outdoor living spaces that are used by people of all ages and

Parks, activities, and special events enhance the quality of life for community members of all ages and abilities.
© iStockphoto/Thinkstock/Getty Images.

backgrounds. In swimming pools, zoos, playgrounds, nature centers, and sports facilities, community residents enjoy vigorous and sociable forms of group recreation. In community centers, children and adults can join clubs and special interest groups, take courses on a variety of enriching hobbies or self-development skills, and find both relaxation and challenge. The personal perspective of quality of life can be affected by family and friends, neighborhood, culture of the community, sense of well-being, love of a job, and overall life satisfaction. People place different values on these items and the indicators listed previously. Different people would view a 50-mile biking path, 5-minute access to a beach, and a premier theatrical venue quite differently, thus influencing their quality of life. In many ways, organized leisure services contribute significantly to the overall quality and enjoyment of community life.

Function 2: Contributing to Personal Development

Purpose: To contribute to a person's healthy physical, social, emotional, intellectual, and spiritual development, and well-being.

Recreation does far more than simply provide fun or pleasure for participants. It also makes an important contribution to their growth and development at each stage of life. Although we often tend to focus on such obvious goals as improving physical fitness or social adjustment, recreation participation also can help people reach their full potential as integrated human beings. For example, psychologists point out that many individuals have vivid memories of sports experiences in their childhood. Such experiences often play a key role in developing positive self-concepts and, beyond this, help to strengthen the bonds between parents and their children. In addition to providing benefits for children, these experiences may also contribute to a parent's own sense of well-being and mental health.

Varied types of community-sponsored recreation programs provide a rich setting in which children and youth are

---

CASE STUDY: Finding a New Community

You have recently graduated with your degree in recreation. You have decided to be adventurous, pack up all of your belongings and move to a new community in another state. You are leaving behind family and friends and want a new place to start your career. Your degree has made you marketable, and you are not worried about finding a job in your field. Let the search begin.

Tasks to complete:

- List 10 factors you will look for when evaluating your community options.
- Rank your factors from most to least important. Why did you rank the factors in this order?
- What role does recreation play in your choice of factors?
- Select three potential communities. Using your factors, rate these cities. Did your factors change as you started doing your research? Why or why not?
- Which city did you choose?

able to explore and confirm their personal values, experience positive peer relationships, discover their talents, and achieve other important personal benefits. For example, Camp Fire, originally called the Campfire Girls of America, has expanded its services, mission, and goals from its inception

Learning a new skill, expressing creativity through art, or experiencing nature all lead to enhanced personal well-being.
© Layland Masuda/Shutterstock.

in 1910. Today Camp Fire is committed to providing activities and services to all youth and their families in the United States and has as its core purpose to help youth prepare for life through environmental and camp programs, out-of-school-time programs, and teen service and leadership programs.[6] Furthermore, the St. Louis Children's Museum, The Magic House, has as its mission "To engage all children with hands-on learning experiences that spark imagination, pique curiosity, enhance creativity, and develop problem-solving skills within a place of beauty, wonder, joy and magic."[7]

Although it is easy to focus on personal development for children, adults benefit from community-based recreation as well. For example, the City of Portland, Oregon Parks and Recreation Department has programs and facilities specifically designed with adult recreation in mind, including such things as 3 art centers, 6 golf courses, a motorsports raceway, 57 community gardens, 158 miles of trails, and 35 dog parks.[8] This is not a unique agency with a special emphasis on adults. They have a special interest in the community as a whole and provide services for everyone. Military bases, concerned with providing armed service members a sense of community, also offer a variety of recreation facilities that may include swimming pools, bowling facilities, golf courses, recreation centers, trails, libraries, movie theaters, and outdoor and recreation rental centers.[9]

How effective are programs such as Camp Fire programs and children's museums? There is much research that demonstrates the effectiveness of these programs. Arguably, one of the better organizations at measuring their outcomes is the Girl Scouts of America. They outline end results for their programs, establish measurements, and compile data to

CASE STUDY: A Planned Recreation Community

Bella Vista (BV) is a 36,000-acre recreational community in Northwest Arkansas. Bella Vista has a population of approximately 31,000 people in almost 12,200 households. Governed by a city government and supported by the Bella Vista Property Owners Association, this planned recreation community offers a large number of amenities to its members.

BV owns and operates 6 golf courses, 7 lakes, and over 50 miles of trails. In addition, the community boasts eight outdoor tennis courts, three fitness centers, a dog park, an 18-hole disc golf course, one indoor and two outdoor pools, a beach, a historical museum, a camping/recreational vehicle park, a gun range, and multiple parks and pavilions throughout the community. They offer passive and active recreation opportunities for adults year-round. Two types of property lots are available: membership lots that are small parcels of land in the original subdivision and would not be approved for a typical building permit and building lots in over 300 other subdivisions that would likely be approved for new home construction. This planned recreation community is an exemplary example of enhancing the quality of life and contributing to the personal development of its residents.

Questions for Discussion

- Review the information on BV at https://bellavistapoa.com. Summarize what you learned.
- Did any program offerings surprise you? Why or why not?
- Look at the membership structure. Is this a good structure? If someone does not want to use the facilities, should they have to pay the fees? Why or why not?
- Would you want to live in a community such as this one? Why or why not?

Data from Bella Vista. (n.d.). Website. https://bellavistapoa.com

show what they do works. For example, the Girl Scout Leadership Experience has 15 outcomes, including such things as developing a strong sense of self, gaining practical life skills, and advancing diversity in a multicultural world.[10]

There are several studies that have looked at outcomes of different types of programs. For example, when youths participate in out-of-school-time programs, juvenile delinquency reduces in the community, youths are exposed to less violence, and their education performance improves, which ultimately increases their economic contributions as adults.[11]

The National Endowment for the Arts showed that involvement in the arts increases academic achievement, high school graduation rates, college enrollment, and college graduation rates.[12] Research on community gardening programs has demonstrated that gardens bring neighbors of various ages, races, and ethnic backgrounds together; they offer educational opportunities and vocational skills for youth; increase physical activity; and provide open space for community gatherings and family events.[13] All of these programs within a community contribute to personal development throughout the lifespan.

Function 3: Making the Community a More Attractive Place to Live and Visit

Purpose: To improve the physical environment and make the community a more attractive place to live and visit by providing a network of parks and open spaces, incorporating leisure attractions in the redesign and rehabilitation of run-down urban areas, and fostering positive environmental attitudes and policies.

In local governments, the recreation function is closely linked to the management of parks and other open spaces, historical sites, and cultural facilities. Together, they help to

The gardens at Temple Square in Salt Lake City, Utah, serve as an attraction for both residents and visitors.
Courtesy of Deb Garrahy.

make cities and towns more appealing as places to live. Inner cities and other communities have areas that have deteriorated over time. Gradually, we have come to realize that we no longer can permit our urban centers to be congested by cars, poisoned by smog, cut off from natural vistas, and scarred by the random disposal of industrial debris, ugly signs, auto junkyards, decaying railroad yards, and burned-out slum tenements. It is essential to protect and grace rivers with trees, shaded walkways, boating facilities, and cafés; to eliminate auto traffic in selected areas by creating pedestrian shopping centers; and to provide increased numbers of malls, playgrounds, and sitting areas that furnish opportunities for both passive and active uses of leisure.

Over the past few decades, numerous cities throughout the world have adopted ambitious projects of promoting recreation and tourism through the revitalization of their waterfronts—both in the redevelopment of decayed harbor areas and in the recreational uses of formerly polluted rivers. In a number of American cities, once abandoned freight yards, wharves, waterfront ports, or junk-filled streams winding through inner-city slums have been dramatically transformed into new, attractive open plazas and parklike settings. Frequently with the help of the business community, these eyesores have been rebuilt into condominium housing, offices, upscale shopping centers, marinas for boating or waterfront play, and outdoor amphitheaters for various forms of entertainment throughout the year. Run-down architectural masterpieces have been restored, and older ethnic neighborhoods preserved while adding restaurants, art galleries, and other cultural activities that appeal to tourists and residents.

Beyond recreation's role in helping to maintain and improve the environment in the central cities themselves, it also is a key player in helping to reclaim or protect natural areas within the larger framework of surrounding county or metropolitan regions. Environmental planners and park authorities are collaborating in many communities on remodeling abandoned railway corridors and establishing greenways to permit outdoor play or environmental education, provide hiking trails, or protect historic sites.

There are numerous examples of redeveloping land into usable space across North America. The Tampa Bay, Florida, waterfront, once an industrial port, has been transformed into a major destination for community members and tourists. It has been labeled as an "active, pedestrian friendly environment for commerce, transportation, entertainment and fitness—all to enhance the city center."[14] Tampa Bay neighborhood parks were developed and later connected by a linear park for pedestrians, runners, and cyclists. Restaurants, cultural institutions, hotels, a convention center, and a dog park have been added to make the waterfront a focal point of the community.[15] In Manhattan, the High Line was opened in 1934 as a railway for transporting goods

---

PEDESTRIAN MALLS SPARK TOURISM AND LIVABILITY

The Charlottesville (Virginia) Historic Downtown Mall is a park within the Charlottesville Parks and Recreation Department system. This pedestrian mall is closed to automobile traffic and is a space where people walk from store to store without the hassle of traffic. The Charlottesville Historic Downtown Mall Pedestrian Mall is home to a vibrant collection of more than 120 shops and 30 restaurants, half-a-dozen art galleries, two historic theaters, multiple venues for live music, a movie theater, and an ice skating rink located in the historic buildings on and around old Main Street. The area has been called the "Community Living Room" and is a primary destination for locals and tourists.[18]

Also situated in Charlottesville, the University of Virginia has implemented sustainability practices through recreation programming for students, faculty, and staff. From its bike share program and bike maintenance classes to its pilot of powerless treadmills in the University's recreation center, UVA continues to work to complement the work done by the city in improving livability through sustainable practices.

---

within the city. The High Line was discontinued in 1980, leaving an unused railway bed in the midst of a bustling urban area. After 10 years of planning, fundraising, and construction, the first section of the High Line linear park opened to the public in 2009, followed by the second section in 2012, and the third section in 2014.[16] The High Line sees an average of 5 million visitors per year; it has increased property values near the park by 10%. The city recouped construction costs within a year through increased property values. In addition, the park led to more than $2 billion in private investments: restaurants, luxury apartment buildings, hotels, clubs, and a Whitney Museum branch all opened near the High Line.[17]

To foster environmental attitudes, the University of Colorado at Colorado Springs new Campus Recreation Center has earned Leadership in Energy and Environmental Design (LEED) Gold Certification. LEED certification requires buildings to be constructed and operated according to standards that are environmentally sustainable. The facility achieved the following to receive the certification:

■ Low-flow toilet and sink fixtures cut down on facility water use, and the rec center uses 38% less water than comparable buildings.
■ Where possible, unused construction materials were recycled instead of being added to a landfill.
■ Highly efficient heating and cooling systems reduce energy expenditures, making the recreation center 30% more energy efficient than comparable buildings.
■ Efficient landscaping reduces need for watering.

Function 4: Providing Positive Opportunities for Youth Development

Purpose: To provide positive recreation opportunities and experiences for youth to help them overcome or avoid negative use of free time.

Keeping youths engaged in recreation activities can reduce incidences of risky behavior.
© Photodisc/Getty Images.

One of the major objectives of the early recreation movement in the United States was to help prevent or reduce juvenile delinquency. Indeed, during the last decades of the 19th century and for much of the first half of the 20th century, it was widely accepted that vigorous group activities were helpful in burning up the excess energy of youth, diverting their aggressive or antisocial drives, and "keeping them off the streets" and sheltered from exposure to criminal influences.

In the United States, there was widespread support for playgrounds, community centers, and other recreation programs for city youth by the police, juvenile court judges, and other youth authorities. A number of sociologists pointed out that much delinquent behavior on the part of younger children stemmed from the search for excitement, risk taking, and the need to impress their peers. It was argued that if other, more challenging, forms of constructive play could be offered to youngsters at this stage, it would be possible to divert them from more serious involvement in criminal activities.

This diversion concept has grown and changed over the past couple of decades. It was not until the mid-1980s that a strong focus on youth development and recreation emerged in the recreation research. Many terms have been used for the concept, such as *youth at risk*. This term in particular had a tendency to be applied only to minoritized, inner-city, and low-income youth. In actuality, all children can benefit from recreation programs and focus should not be limited to those traditionally labeled as "at risk." Needing a broader and better perspective, the term *positive youth development* emerged and has been accepted in the profession. Peter Witt, a leading researcher in youth development, suggests that *youth development* is efforts made to "create organizations and communities that enable youth to move along the pathways to adulthood by supplying the support and opportunities necessary to develop beyond simple problem prevention."[20] The definition of youth development pushes recreation professionals beyond simply getting kids off the streets, as was the idea in the early recreation movement. Youth development challenges recreation professionals to provide programs with a purpose and goal in mind.

Youth sports have been seen as a means to provide positive experiences for youth, despite some of the negatives seen in sport such as overly critical parents, adults fighting with officials, and crowds getting out of control. Extensive research in youth sports has shown that sport involvement often leads to improved academic performance, greater personal confidence and self-esteem, stronger peer relationships, development of an appreciation for diversity, and more restraint in participating in risky behavior.[21] Sports should be designed so that specific outcomes occur. Developing sport programs with specific benefits in mind can lead to sport programs that have moral, physical, mental, and cognitive development outcomes that contribute to positive youth development;[22] that reduce obesity and increase health;[23] and that build character.[24]

One model that has been used nationwide to develop youth is the Search Institute's 40 Developmental Assets for Adolescents. These assets are said to contribute to healthy, caring, and responsible young adults. The 40 assets are broken down into four age groups covering children 3–18 years of age.[25] Here are a few examples for 12- to 18-year-olds regarding what they should do as it relates to recreation:

- *Creative Activities.* Young person spends 3 or more hours per week in lessons or practice in music, theater, or other arts.
- *Youth Programs.* Young person spends 3 or more hours per week in sports, clubs, or organizations at school and/or in community organizations.
- *Time at Home.* Young person is out with friends "with nothing special to do" two or fewer nights per week.[25]

Here are a few examples of programs specifically designed to provide positive experiences for youth:

- Outward Bound's mission is to change lives through challenge and discovery. This nonprofit organization offers outdoor expeditions and programs such as canyoneering, backcountry skiing and snowshoeing, and sailing. Expeditions are designed to be challenging and character developing. The high impact skills learned will teach leadership, communication, and teamwork.[26]
- The Alex Fiore Thousand Oaks Teen Center is for 7th through 12th graders and features a gymnasium, soundproof music room, computer lab, classrooms, and a 1700-square-foot game room complete with three pool tables, two Ping-Pong tables, air hockey, foosball, assorted video games, and a 50-inch high-def plasma TV. Programs include sports leagues, surfing lessons, dance, fitness, music lessons, snowboarding, Los Angeles Lakers excursions, and a wide variety of special events.[27]
- Seattle (Washington) Parks and Recreation Department offers Late Night Recreation Programs for teens. The goal of the program is to provide a safe place for teens to hang out between 7 p.m. and midnight on Friday and Saturday. The city has 10 recreation centers with late evening programs such as tutoring, cultural and ethnic dance, and sport.[28]
- Peace Players International (PPI) has as its mission to unite divided communities through sport. With a focus on leadership skills, building long-term relationships, and engagement through sport, PPI has programs in five U.S. cities as well as in Northern Ireland, the Middle East, Cyprus, and South Africa with a focus on uniting communities from opposite sides of religious, ethnic, and cultural divides.[29]

Function 5: Educating and Uniting Community Members

Purpose: To improve and develop positive relationships within the community by educating residents about similarities and differences on such things as culture, race, ethnicity, age, gender identity, sexual orientation, religion, income, and more.

Our personal identity is formed by a variety of things including race, ethnicity, culture, gender identity, sexual orientation, education, and income, among others. Community parks and recreation serve as a conduit to bring a variety of groups together in order to experience someone else's perspective. Special events, museums, programs, and sports leagues are used across the country to teach people about other cultures and shape our own leisure-related values and behaviors. Clearly, this presents a challenge to recreation and park professionals in terms of the need to provide program opportunities suited to the tastes and traditions of the various groups within the community.

CASE STUDY: Role of Recreation and America's Promise Alliance

America's Promise Alliance is a nonprofit organization that leads the nation's largest network of organizations and individuals dedicated to improving the lives of young people. The Alliance is committed to creating the conditions of success for all children and youth through Five Promises.

The Five Promises include the following:

- Caring Adults: They are the centerpieces of children's development. They serve as guides, caretakers, and advisers and give positive and productive guidance throughout their development.
- Safe Places: To develop intellectually and emotionally, young people need physical and psychological safety at home, at school, and in the community. Without such "safe places"—environments that support and encourage inquiry, exploration, and play without fear of harm—children are not able to get support, form positive relationships, and concentrate on school.
- A Healthy Start: Children grow and learn better when they are born healthy and practice healthy habits throughout childhood, including proper nutrition and exercise, and have access to high-quality learning opportunities. Healthy and well-nourished children are more able to develop their minds and bodies as they should, and they are far more capable of concentrating, learning, and thriving throughout their school years.
- Effective Education: Our increasingly knowledge-driven world demands people who have the education and skills to thrive in a competitive marketplace and to understand the increasingly complex world in which they live. That means in order to compete and succeed, all young people will need an effective education that prepares them for work and life.
- Opportunities to Help Others: Through service to others and their communities, young Americans develop the character and competence they need to be helpful, hopeful, and civically engaged all their lives, regardless of their own life circumstances. The chance to give back teaches young people the value of service to others, the meaning of community, and the self-respect that comes from knowing that one has a contribution to make in the world.

Questions for Discussion

- What role can recreation play in each of these promises?
- Look at programs offered in the following cities. Compare and contrast the communities and the demographic information provided. What programs have they implemented that are recreation related?
  - Charleston, SC (http://www.americaspromise.org/charleston-south-carolina-0)
  - Missoula, MT (http://www.americaspromise.org/missoula-montana)
  - Bedford, MA (http://www.americaspromise.org/bedford-massachusetts-0).

Reproduced from America's Promise Alliance. (n.d.). *The 5 promises*. Retrieved January 31, 2021, from http://www.americaspromise.org/promises

ATLANTA ARAB FESTIVAL

The Atlanta, Georgia–based Alif (first letter of the Arabic alphabet) Institute is a nonprofit organization whose mission is to foster understanding and appreciation of Arab culture. They do this through education, culture, arts, and enrichment programs. The Atlanta Arab Festival is held by the Alif Institute each year and features cultural and educational exhibits related to the Arab culture and Arab Americans, music and dance performances, a fashion show, games, food, and shopping at the souk (market).[34]

Part of the role of a community-oriented parks and recreation agency is to provide people with different opportunities to try new activities, play a new sport, or learn a new game. Agencies should provide opportunities that encourage people to go beyond their socially constructed boundaries, which might allow them to see themselves and the world a bit differently.[30] In order to do this, Chavez suggests that if agencies want to make all groups feel welcome and want to participate in recreation activities, agencies need to invite, include, and involve these groups.[31] Parks and recreation agencies cannot assume people feel welcome and that professionals know what people want without asking them and involving them in planning and providing programs.

Special events in particular represent a major area of opportunity for sharing cultural traditions and increasing the self-knowledge and pride of different racial and ethnic populations. These events are designed to celebrate culture because they are planned by people within the specific

Recreation activities are an important means to developing intergenerational connections among families and community members.

© Blend Images/Shutterstock.

culture, but they are designed for everyone regardless of race or ethnicity. As an example, Milwaukee, Wisconsin, is well known for its ethnic festivals on the lakefront at Henry Maier Festival Park. Each year they hold such festivals as German Fest, Polish Fest, Irish Fest, Mexican Fiesta, and Festa Italiana.[32] The Skokie, Illinois, Park District sponsors the Skokie Festival of Cultures, which features food, music, merchandise, and activities representing many of the

80 languages spoken in Skokie. Cultures represented at the festival include Armenian, Assyrian, Bangladeshi, Chinese, Cuban, Danish, Filipino, Finnish, Hellenic, Indian, Israeli, Japanese, Korean, Lebanese, Mexican, Pakistani, Scottish, Swedish, Thai, Turkish, West Indian, and more.[33]

In some cases, leisure-service agencies and programs may focus on problems of intergroup hostility and prejudice through meetings, staff training programs, workshops, and similar efforts. Organizations such as the Young Women's Christian Association (YWCA) have focused on the elimination of prejudice and discrimination as a key program goal, and in some cases youth camping programs have been established to promote intercultural friendship and understanding. In one such camp, the Seeds of Peace, teens from Egypt, Israel, Jordan, Palestine, and others are selected each year from their respective governments to participate in the camp, which is based on academic achievement and leadership abilities. The youth come together to share cultural traditions and to begin to build respect, friendship, and leadership skills and to confront their prejudices and deep-seated fears and tackle the issues that fuel violence, hatred, and oppression at home.[35]

Many larger communities host gay pride events, with one of the largest being in New York City. In fact, New York was chosen as the host of 2019 World Pride. The festivities commemorate the Stonewall riots, which launched the gay rights movement in 1969. Events include such things as LGBTQIA+ Pride March, family movie night, and a fundraiser for Broadway Cares/Equity Fights AIDS. All of these events are open to the general public to learn about the history and progress of the LGBTQIA+ community.[36]

The City of Chicago has developed itineraries for visitors and community members to follow to learn about different cultures. For example, they have itineraries posted to learn about African American heritage, and Asian culture, as well as budget-friendly attractions and family-orientated activities. The African American heritage tour includes

CASE STUDY: Religion and Recreation

You have had various religious groups in your community complain about the name and content of some of your events because they focus on Christian religious affiliation to the exclusion of other religions. For example, the community offers an Easter egg hunt, a festival of Christmas lights, and a Christmas tree lighting ceremony. The local Jewish community has expressed concern about youth sports games being played on major Jewish holidays but cancelled on major Christian holidays.

Questions to Discussion

- Should the community schedule around major holidays for all religions? If yes, why and how will this affect a local agency? If no, where do you draw the line on deciding what holidays warrant a change to program/league schedules?
- Would you change the name of the events? Why or why not?
- How could these events be made more inclusive of others outside the Christian faith?
- Should a community recreation service provider respect the predominant religion in the community and exclude others? Why or why not?

stops at public art displays, restaurants and jazz clubs, the DuSable Museum, the Black Ensemble Theater, and historic places such as the homes of heavyweight boxer Louis Armstrong and President Barack Obama.[37]

Community recreation is a place where people come together. They get to experience new things, see people who may be different from themselves, learn about the history of a group, acquire skills in a new sport such as cricket, develop salsa dancing skills, and simply build understanding through education. Given all of this, recreation is a pretty powerful component in a community seeking a high quality of life for all of its residents.

Function 6: Strengthening Neighborhood and Community Ties

Purpose: To strengthen neighborhood and community life by involving residents in volunteer projects, service programs, and special events to enhance civic pride and morale.

An important tenet of the early recreation movement was that shared recreational experiences helped to strengthen neighborhood and community ties by giving residents of all backgrounds a sense of belonging and common purpose, helping them to maintain social traditions and cultural ties and enabling them to join together in volunteer service roles. Recreation's role in strengthening neighborhood and community ties lies in the concepts of human and social capital. Human capital is the tools and training that can enhance individual or collective productivity. When people give their time and talent to the workforce or the community, they are using human capital. Although human capital is important, using it with social capital enriches the lives of those in the community. Social capital is defined as "connections among individuals— social networks and the norms of reciprocity and trustworthiness that arise from them."[38] Communities are made up of networks of people through schools, employment, the neighborhoods we live in, and of course recreation. These networks of people form valuable relationships that bond them together. Recreation and parks provide a plethora of opportunities for the human and social capital to merge and strengthen the community. Here are a few examples of how recreation and parks strengthen and improve communities:

> In 2003, a group of residents in southwest Florida banded together to protect the bays, beaches, barrier islands, and watersheds in the area.[39] They formed the Conservation Foundation of the Gulf Coast. One example of the group's impact since its inception over a decade ago was saving 150 acres of land from residential development and adding to the existing Robinson Preserve.

The New York Restoration Project (NYRP), founded by actress Bette Midler, strives to reclaim, restore, and redevelop parks, open space, and community gardens in New York City primarily in economically disadvantaged neighborhoods.[40] For example, Fort Tryon Park fell victim to neglect by the city in the 1980s and 90s. The NYRP stepped in and removed debris, downed trees, and uncovered and repaired paths that had been obscured under mounds of trash for many years. Within this park are the Cloisters Museum and Gardens and the New Leaf Restaurant and Bar. The New Leaf is a popular fine dining establishment, and net proceeds support the maintenance and beautification of NYRP's 55 community gardens and six New York City parks.[41]

More and more leisure-services providers are realizing the value of volunteers to the agency, the individual, and the community. For example, the Champaign Park District in Illinois, which was one of the first public parks and recreation agencies to hire a volunteer coordinator, uses volunteers in all aspects of its operations, from recreation to maintenance.[45] Each year, volunteers spend more than 20,000 hours working in day camps, at special events, planting flowerbeds, and coaching youth sports. In addition, the Champaign Park District has an adopt-a-park program in which neighborhoods take ownership of their area parks through such things as building flowerbeds, planting flowers, holding their own special events, raising money for playground equipment, and working with staff on park decisions. The adopt-a-park program allows the parks to be maintained at a higher level than ordinarily possible.

In many communities, recreational projects related to sports, the environment, the arts, people with disabilities, and similar concerns serve to promote civic pride and neighborhood cooperation.

Street rod owners form their own social community through a common hobby.
© Jamie Roach/Shutterstock.

COMMUNITY INVOLVEMENT IN PARKS

Joshua's Park, a project of the Amherst Land Trust and Amherst Community Foundation, brought together citizens of Amherst, New Hampshire to build a 4-acre park that was described as a chance to give kids a new place to play, to give adults a new place to garden, and to keep old farmland open. The park was funded 100% through volunteer fundraising and community volunteers with expertise in real estate law, contracting, landscape design, and environmental science laid the groundwork, and hundreds of community volunteers contributed funds and labor to build the park that serves as a memorial to 9-year-old Joshua Savyon, an Amherst resident who was tragically killed in 2013.[42]

In times when disaster strikes, the communities affected and those who simply want to help come together to provide immediate emergency relief and assist in long-term rebuilding efforts. When Hurricane Sandy hit the eastern seaboard in late October 2012, major damage and flooding affected 24 states from Florida to Maine, in particular New York and New Jersey. Many communities opened their recreation centers to serve as emergency shelters for displaced residents. After the immediate danger of the hurricane lessened, staff and volunteers worked to rebuild parks and recreation areas such as the Gateway National Recreation Area. A 1000-person staff from the National Park Service worked to stabilize the area and over the next 6 months 1700 volunteers dedicated 6250 hours in the effort to restore numerous parts of the park.[43] Following the Category 5 Hurricane Irma in 2017, Miami-Dade (Florida) opened recreation facilities for residents' use including swimming pools. Free admission to the pools allowed the residents something fun to do during a difficult time and provided access to showers and lounges as well as an escape from oppressive heat with lengthy power outages.[44]

Unselfish involvement in civic betterment activities is particularly important today, when many Americans see the signs of a spreading social and moral breakdown around them. At such a time, it is critical that every means be explored to develop a true sense of community, of sharing and mutual support in neighborhood life. Clearly, volunteerism and the kinds of projects just described help to promote such values and positive interactions among community residents.

Function 7: Meeting the Needs of Special Populations

Purpose: To serve special populations such as those with physical or cognitive disabilities, both through recreation therapy service in treatment settings and through community-based programs serving individuals with a broad range of disabilities.

All people need diversified recreational opportunity; those with disabilities are no different. It is estimated that one in five people in the United States, or over 85 million, has a disability, and as adults age, this number is likely to increase.[46] Add to these the number of military servicepeople who are returning from serving in Iraq and Afghanistan with disabilities ranging from amputations and visual impairments to traumatic head injuries and post-traumatic stress disorder. As such, it is important to focus special attention on providing leisure services in the community to these groups.

Recreation for people with disabilities is provided from three different standpoints. First, recreation can be used to assist with physical or cognitive improvement and delivered in a hospital, a residential facility, or outpatient programs that focus on purposeful intervention to achieve a healthy leisure lifestyle. This form of recreation is often referred to as *recreation therapy*. Recreation therapy programs have been used to assist clients to become more independent,

increase self-esteem, improve functional status, learn social skills, or learn to use leisure wisely. A second form of recreation for people with disabilities focuses on participation for the activity itself rather than as a means of therapy. This form of recreation is called *inclusive recreation*. Inclusive programs provide opportunities for people from different ability levels to interact together. The third form focuses on recreation programs designed for people with disabilities and is called *special recreation*. Opportunities for people with disabilities are as varied as the agencies that provide these services: Easter Seals, Special Olympics, and Disabled Sports USA.

Both inclusive recreation and special recreation can be found in community settings offered typically by public or nonprofit agencies. For example, the South Suburban Special Recreation Association (SSSRA) is a public agency that provides programs for people with disabilities from eight park districts and three recreation and parks departments in Illinois. It is organized to provide individuals with disabilities or special needs the opportunity to be involved in year-round recreation. SSSRA programs are for individuals from birth through adult who are in special education classes, sheltered workshops, or who have recreational needs not met by traditional parks and recreation programs. This could include individuals who have varying degrees of physical disabilities, cognitive impairments, learning disabilities, emotional difficulties, hearing or visual impairments, and developmental delays. SSSRA offers Special Olympics programs, programs for veterans, adapted sports, trips, and special events each season.[47]

Many of the opportunities for people with disabilities arose because of federal legislation. The Americans with Disabilities Act (ADA), passed in 1990 and amended in 2016, mandated that people not be denied opportunities, segregated, or discriminated against because of their disability. Recreation-service providers had to ensure that equal opportunities were available for all constituents, and, if some specialized services were available, that people with disabilities had a choice of participating in the general or the special program. The ADA also stipulates that facilities should be accessible and that programs be offered for all residents regardless of abilities. Furthermore, if a person has a disability, reasonable accommodations for participation must be made for that individual.

Conflicts have contributed to an increased need for programs for people with disabilities. Many military servicepeople return home injured in the line of duty, the most prevalent injury being traumatic brain injuries. Often referred to as "wounded warriors," these people initially receive services through the military medical centers and hospitals. Once released, some participate in recreation programs through parks and recreation departments and other nonprofits such as Wounded Warriors in their communities. In addition to these opportunities, special programs are being designed to accommodate wounded warriors. Here are three examples:

- U.S. Paralympics has expanded to include programs for the United States Army Warriors Transition Units (WTU). The sports and fitness programs were created to help these servicepeople by providing postrehabilitation support. These programs are also done in partnership with local parks and recreation, as is the case with the Fort Bragg WTU and the Fayetteville-Cumberland Parks and Recreation Department.[48]
- Founded in London in 2014, the Invictus Games used the power of sport to inspire recovery, support rehabilitation, and generate a wider understanding and respect for wounded, injured, and sick servicepeople. Established by Prince Harry, the Invictus Foundation manages the games, including the 2018 competition held in Sydney, Australia, which featured 13 competitive events including archery, golf, indoor rowing, powerlifting, road cycling, sailing, sitting volleyball, swimming, track and field, wheelchair basketball, wheelchair rugby, wheelchair tennis, and a Land Rover Driving Challenge. The event drew 491 competitors and over 1,000 friends and family.[49]
- The Wounded Warrior Project Physical Health & Wellness program provides inclusive sports such as water skiing, snowboarding, and golf; fitness programs for weight management, strength, and overall health; nutrition education; and wellness.[50]

As our culture continues to be more inclusive, recreation provides both a means of therapy and a source of diversion for varied populations, both in clinical and community settings. Trends include not only serving the needs of veterans but also baby boomers, individuals with Autism Spectrum Disorder, our aging population, and many others.

Function 8: Maintaining Economic Health and Community Stability

Purpose: To maintain the economic health and stability of communities by acting as a catalyst for business development and a source of community or regional income and employment and by keeping neighborhoods desirable places to live.

Recreation has become a major focus of business investment and an essential element in the total national economy. It is estimated that leisure is a $400 billion industry annually; it is the nation's third largest retail industry and the second largest employer behind the health industry. Communities with commercial, public, and nonprofit agencies have benefited economically from recreation. Such economic benefits may arise through taxes, such as bed taxes at hotels or taxes from the lottery that go to support local parks and recreation. Shoppers have indicated that they will travel greater distance to an area with high-quality trees and spend more time once they arrive.[51] Furthermore, recreation increases property values, such as for homes on lakes, by parks, or on golf courses. A home adjacent to a passive park will see a 20% increase in value on average and residences next to a larger and longer "greenbelt" area can see an average of a 32% increase. Furthermore, people like trees specifically—tree-covered nearby acreage can increase a home price by 22% on average and lots bordering suburban wooded preserves were 19% to 35% higher in value on average.[52]

Some cities have set out deliberately to transform themselves into centers of entertainment, culture, and sports. Indianapolis, Indiana, built nine major sports arenas between 1974 and 2008 to revitalize the city. These included a 10,000-square-foot tennis facility, a 12,111-seat track and field facility, a natatorium, a minor league ballpark, Bankers Life Fieldhouse (home of the Indiana Pacers and Fever), and Lucas Oil Stadium (home of the Indianapolis Colts). In addition, the cultural and entertainment opportunities were expanded. For example, White River State Park was built to connect city parks and cultural attractions—including the Indianapolis Zoo, White River Gardens, the Eiteljorg Museum of American Indians and Western Art, the NCAA Hall of Champions, the IMAX Theater, the Indiana State Museum, Victory Field, and Farm Bureau Insurance Lawn at White River State Park.[53]

To expand the convention opportunities in Indianapolis, once the Colts moved from the RCA Dome to Lucas Oil Stadium, the Indiana Convention Center was renovated and

The Ice Rink at Rockefeller Center is an economic stimulant for New York City because of the large number of visitors throughout the winter holiday season.

Courtesy of Deb Garrahy.

expanded into the RCA Dome.[54] In other cases, cities depend on special events and attractions to stimulate economic activity.

Economic activity is better known as economic impact, or the measure of the amount of new dollars infused into the community by the agency. Economic impact is usually examined from the standpoints of direct and indirect. Direct economic impact is the amount of money that is directly generated by the event such as staff salaries, concessions, program fees, construction costs, and operating expenditures. Indirect impact is the money spent that results from the program or event. Examples are the money spent by a staff person or money spent at a hotel or in restaurants when a team is playing at a local softball tournament.

Here are some examples of economic impact from leisure services:

- The St. Louis Zoo, which has free admission, generates over $200 million for the local economy. This includes revenues from food, lodging, programs, and souvenir sales from its 3.2 million annual visitors and its 330 full-time employees and 950 seasonal part-time employees.[55]
- The Portland, Oregon, Rose Festival attracts over 1 million people and generates an estimated $75 million annually for the local and state economies.[56]

- Americans for the Arts conducted a study on the economic impact of nonprofit arts and cultural organizations (for example, museums) and found they had a $135.2 billion economic impact on communities across the country: $61.1 billion was from spending by the organizations, and the remaining $74.1 billion by the audience for event-related purchases. This industry also supports 4.1 million full-time jobs.[57]
- The Swamp Rabbit Trail, a rails to trails project in Greenville, South Carolina, creates an estimated $7 million economic impact in Greenville County each year.[58]
- Broadway shows and musicals generated nearly $12 billion in spending for the New York City economy during the 2012–13 season.[59]

In summary, evidence shows that public, private, and commercial leisure attractions and resources of cities are key elements in their economic health and stability, not only in bringing tourism revenues but also in the positive picture they present to potential residents and companies that are seeking to relocate.

Function 9: Enriching Community Cultural Life

Purpose: To enrich cultural life by promoting fine and performing arts, special events, and cultural programs and by supporting historic sites, folk heritage customs, and community arts institutions.

It is generally recognized that the arts provide a vital ingredient in the culture of nations. Through the continued performance and appreciation of the great works of the past, in the areas of symphonic and choral music, opera, ballet, theater, painting, and sculpture, or through contemporary ventures in newer forms of expression,

Dance is a popular means to experiencing and understanding other cultures.

© Boykov/Shutterstock.

MURAL ARTS PHILADELPHIA

Mural Arts Philadelphia was established in 1984 as part of the city's antigraffiti initiative. Those who were creating the unwanted graffiti were contacted and given an opportunity to put their artistic talents to work by creating murals throughout the city. The murals they created instantly added color, beauty, and life to an old, industrial city struggling with decades of economic distress and population loss. Since it began, Mural Arts Philadelphia has produced over 3,600 murals, which have become a cherished part of the civic landscape and a great source of inspiration to the millions of residents and visitors who encounter them each year.

Reproduced from Mural Arts Philadelphia. (n.d.). *Art ignites change: 35 years of impact.* http://muralarts.org/ignite.

such as modern dance or experimental art forms, people of every age and background gain a sense of beauty and human creativity. Arts and culture manifest themselves in many different ways in communities. Art and culture can be found in the architecture of buildings, the design of parks, in museums, through educational programs, or by attending concerts. Enriching a community through art and culture does not require that one be an artist or have talent in the areas of drawing, painting, or music. A community benefits when art and cultural opportunities are available to be appreciated or to educate the community. In addition, art and culture are not just for the rich; opportunities should be available for all ages and income levels.

As such, it is imperative that community agencies, both public and nonprofit, play a strong role in presenting programs in the arts that improve the level of popular taste and provide an opportunity for direct personal expression through music, dance, theater, and arts and crafts. One such program is found in Prince George's County Department of Parks and Recreation (Maryland), which has four community recreation centers dedicated to the visual, performing, and literary arts. They offer such programs and facility space for art galleries, a store for local artisans to sell their work, learning studios for classes, a concert hall with several music series, and a public playhouse.[60]

In 2013 the City of Indianapolis debuted the Indianapolis Cultural Trail. The 8-mile trail is a curbed, buffered, beautifully paved, richly landscaped, and artfully lighted bike and pedestrian pathway that connects to every arts, cultural heritage, sports, and entertainment venue in the urban core. The inspiration for the idea was that it was going to connect to six designated cultural districts downtown in order to make those districts more vibrant and viable by connecting them and giving people a way to get to them that was walkable and bikeable.[61]

Seattle, Washington, has the Olympic Sculpture Park that was opened in 2006. What once was an industrial site has been transformed into an 8.5-acre park on the waterfront that contains classic, modern, and contemporary

Many public parks and recreation agencies sponsor summer concerts in the park featuring music that appeals to many different populations within the community.
© pcruciatti/Shutterstock.

permanent sculptures, temporary art installations, art-related musical and theatrical performances, and year-round educational programming in the arts.[62] Without parks such as these, many people would never be exposed to art at this level.

Art is not just for the rich. It benefits the entire community. As shown in these examples, art does not have to be in a museum. Art can be found in the parks, as murals on buildings, in flower gardens, and even in the architecture of buildings. Art enhances the livability and beauty of the community as a whole.

Function 10: Promoting Health and Wellness

Purpose: To promote community health and wellness by offering needed services, programs, and facilities to encourage active lifestyles for community members.

Parks offer unlimited opportunities for both children and adults to be physically active to improve their health.

© Seiya Kawamoto/Lifesize/Thinkstock/Getty Images.

Public parks and recreation departments as well as other recreation providers such as nonprofits and Morale, Welfare, and Recreation (MWR) can be leaders in promoting health and wellness in their communities. They can combat some of the community's most pressing problems—poor nutrition, hunger, obesity, and physical inactivity.[63]

Many communities have developed programs such as fitness classes, dance programs, and sports leagues for all ages and abilities to promote health and fitness. Although these programs most likely have a fee attached to them, these same communities also are promoting free opportunities for health through their parks and trails so that all residents can become physically active and healthier. Parks and trails allow for close-to-home, low-cost activities. With any community, the key is to get people to use the parks. A National Recreation Foundation study found that people living near a park were twice as likely to use the park as those who do not live near one.[64]

In addition to parks, trails are also an important part of many cities. Walking and biking trails have been built through and around cities all over the United States. Trails have been built along rivers and streams, where railroads once stood, and on utility right of ways. These trails are used for fitness purposes as well as for transportation on foot, bike, or inline skates. People who live near trails are 50% more likely to get enough physical activity to help them stay healthy, and people who live in walkable neighborhoods are twice as likely to get enough physical activity as people who do not. Installing bike lanes within communities has increased cyclists by 69% in Portland, Oregon and by 225% in New Orleans, Louisiana.[65]

Whether it is playing tennis with a friend, participating in a sand volleyball league, playing with a child on the playground, or biking on a trail, people who are in parks are physically active. There are thousands of examples of what local parks and recreation agencies are able to do in their communities to make their residents healthier. Here are a few examples:

- Many cities boast of their extended bike/walking trails built for residents as well as visitors to communities. For example, what once was a railroad bed connecting Chicago and Milwaukee has now become a continuous 100-mile bike trail that is promoted as a healthy tourism destination.
- Named the 2019 Best Park System in the United States by the Trust for Public Lands, the Washington, DC, park system contributes to the health of its residents as well as visitors in that 98% of DC residents are within a 10-minute walk of a public park. In fact, 21% of the city area is composed of parks. With an investment of over $200 million, the city ranks high on spending per resident at $270.40. Additional amenities that earned the park system top honors included the availability of 3.5 dog parks per 100,000 residents and 7.8 basketball hoops per 10,000 residents.[66]

In addition to physical and mental health and wellness, parks and recreation can contribute to the safety of its residents. Many community programs are focused on teaching safety skills through programs and events. These programs include such things as swim lessons, basic water safety programs, and boater and hunter safety programs. For example, the Chehalem, Oregon, Park and Recreation District and

Park and recreation professions are instrumental in keeping children safe on playgrounds by adhering to national safety standards.

© iStockphoto/Thinkstock/Getty Images.

Newberg-Dundee Police offer a weeklong summer camp for K–1 focused on safety, including personal safety, water, fire, electric, animal, pedestrian, bicycle, poison, and school bus safety.[67] The Deer Park,[68] Texas, Parks and Recreation Department offers hunter education courses, and many different local agencies offer programs such as wilderness first aid, lifeguard training, and swim lessons.

Health and wellness are increasingly being seen as a major factor in the quality of life in a community. Cities and towns are making a concerted effort to provide programs and activities as well as facilities and open spaces to increase physical activity and mental health. When cities are planning for the future, they are more likely than ever to build biking/walking trails, add bike lanes to the streets, add parks to neighborhoods that do not have them, and promote the abundance of opportunities that keep people moving.

Leisure-services providers often offer programs to help people learn proper techniques of activities such as kayaking so that they can safely participate on their own.
© Bochkarev Photography/Shutterstock.

FITTEST AND FATTEST U.S. CITIES

Men's Health Magazine ranked the fittest cities in the United States. Rankings are determined by such indicators as fitness guidelines as defined by the Centers for Disease Control and Prevention, percentage of the population reporting inactivity, and general health that included state and county health records as well as self-reported data about health and obesity. In 2019, San Francisco finished first followed by Madison, Wisconsin; Seattle; Denver; and San Diego.[69] On the flip side, WalletHub, in an attempt to identify the "fattest" cities, used 19 key indicators of weight-related problems including physical inactivity, projected obesity rates by 2030, and access to healthy foods. They concluded that the fattest cities were McAllen-Edinburg-Mission, Texas; Shreveport-Bossier City, Louisiana; Memphis, Tennessee; Jackson, Mississippi; and Knoxville, Tennessee.[70]

CASE STUDY: Make Your Community a More Fit City

You have been placed on a committee within your city to improve its overall fitness with the goal of becoming the fittest city in the state. As the committee develops, it plans to achieve this goal, and you have been given the following tasks to complete:

- Look at the fitness opportunities that currently exist in your community. Make a list of those that have fees associated with them and those that are free.
- Develop a list of criteria that you feel measure a fit city. Look at what other polls (e.g., *Men's Health*) measure.
- Choose four of the criteria you selected above and gather data about your city.
- Review two cities that are considered to be fit cities such as Portland, Oregon, and Minneapolis, Minnesota. What do these cities have that you could realistically suggest to make your city more fit?
- Make a priority list of changes you would suggest be made to your community to increase its overall fitness level.

SUMMARY

Far from simply providing casual or superficial amusement, organized recreation services help to satisfy a number of significant community needs, including the following:

- *Quality of life.* Constructive and enjoyable leisure for people of all ages and backgrounds contributes significantly to their quality of life and satisfaction with their communities.
- *Personal development.* Organized recreation promotes healthy personal development in physical, emotional, social, intellectual, and spiritual terms, thus contributing to overall community well-being.
- *Attractive community.* Recreation and park agencies maintain parks, nature reserves, riverfronts, and other natural areas and may assist in rehabilitating or sponsoring historic and cultural settings.
- *Positive opportunities for youth development.* As an important element in the community's educational, social, and other services for youth, organized recreation assists in preventing or reducing delinquency and other deviant forms of play and giving youth positive alternatives to develop into health adults.
- *Educating and uniting community members.* Recreation serves as a useful tool in promoting understanding and cooperation of cultural, ethnic, racial, and other sociodemographic characteristics.
- *Strengthening community ties.* Volunteerism and taking part in neighborhood efforts to improve the community environment and similar involvement help to build civic togetherness.
- *Needs of special populations.* In both treatment settings and in the community at large, recreation therapy service promotes inclusion and independence for persons with physical and cognitive disabilities.
- *Maintaining economic health.* As a growing form of business enterprise, recreation employs millions of people today. By helping to attract tourists, industries that are relocating, or new residents, it also provides income and promotes community stability.
- *Enriching cultural life.* Many public and nonprofit leisure-services agencies today assist or sponsor programming in the various artistic and cultural fields, strengthening this important dimension of community life.
- *Promoting health and wellness.* Increasingly, recreation is recognized as a health-related discipline by helping individuals to maintain sound lifestyles and by helping to promote physical activity and safe access to leisure.

QUESTIONS FOR CLASS DISCUSSION OR ESSAY EXAMINATION

1. This chapter presents 10 different areas in which recreation, parks, and leisure services contribute to community life. If you had to present a positive argument for establishing or expanding a community recreation and park department, which of these areas would you emphasize and why?

   _____

   _____

   _____

2. Explain and discuss the importance of community recreation within one of the following areas: (1) economic contribution; (2) health-related benefits; (3) promoting the cultural arts; or (4) educating and uniting residents of different socioeconomic, racial, or cultural backgrounds.

   _____

   _____

   _____

3. Think about the community in which you live. Give examples of how the 10 functions of community recreation are demonstrated in that community. Which ones are missing?

   _____

   _____

   _____

4. Think about the 10 functions of community recreation as they apply to your college campus. What are strengths and weaknesses of the campus in providing these 10 functions? Provide examples of each function that is demonstrated on campus.

_____

_____

_____

_____

ENDNOTES

1. Kraus, R. (1971). *Recreation and leisure in modern society*. Appleton-Century-Crofts.

2. Trust for Public Land. (2011). *The economic benefits of the park and recreation system of Virginia Beach, Virginia*. Retrieved January 26, 2021, from http://cloud.tpl.org/pubs/ccpe-va-beach-park-analysis-report.pdf.

3. City of New York Parks & Recreation. (2019, November 12). *Calculating tree benefits for New York City*. Retrieved January 26, 2021, from https://www.nycgovparks.org/sub_your_park/trees_greenstreets/images/treecount_report.pdf.

4. Mercer. (2019, March 13). *Vienna tops Mercer's 21st quality of living ranking*. Retrieved January 26, 2021, from https://www.mercer.com/newsroom/2019-quality-of-living-survey.html.

5. International Living. Retrieved February 24, 2021, from https://internationalliving.com/

6. Camp Fire. Retrieved January 26, 2021, from http://campfire.org.

7. The Magic House St. Louis Children's Museum. (n.d.). *Our mission*. Retrieved January 26, 2021, from https://www.magichouse.org/about-us.

8. Portland Parks & Recreation Department. (n.d.). "*Park system by the numbers*. Retrieved January 26, 2021, from http://www.portlandoregon.gov/parks/article/422533.

9. Military One Source. (2020, April 9). *Morale, welfare and recreation: Your source for affordable fun*. Retrieved January 26, 2021, from https://www.militaryonesource.mil/recreation-travel-shopping/recreation/single-life/morale-welfare-and-recreation-your-source-for-affordable-fun.

10. Girl Scouts of the United States of America. (2008). *Transforming leadership: Focusing on outcomes of the new Girl Scout leadership experience*. Retrieved January 26, 2021, from https://www.girlscouts.org/content/dam/girlscouts-gsusa/forms-and-documents/about-girl-scouts/research/transforming_leadership.pdf.

11. Witt, P. A., & Caldwell, L. L. (2010). *The rationale for recreation services for youth: An evidenced [sic] based approach*. National Recreation and Park Association. Retrieved January 26, 2021, from http://www.nrpa.org/uploadedFiles/nrpa.org/Publications_and_Research/Research/Papers/Witt-Caldwell-Full-Research-Paper.pdf.

12. Catterall, J. S. with S. A. Dumais and G. Hampden-Thompson. (2012). *The arts and achievement in at-risk youth: Findings from four longitudinal studies* (Research Report #55). National Endowment for the Arts. Retrieved January 26, 2021, from https://www.arts.gov/sites/default/files/Arts-At-Risk-Youth.pdf.

13. Local Government Commission. (2017, May 29). *Cultivating community gardens: The role of local government in creating healthy, livable neighborhoods*. Retrieved January 26, 2021, from http://lgc.org/wordpress/docs/freepub/community_design/fact_sheets/community_gardens_cs.pdf.

14. *Friends of the Riverwalk*. Retrieved May 16, 2016, from http://www.thetampariverwalk.com/.

15. Drinkard, S. (2016, February 11). *Tampa Riverwalk. Project for Public Spaces*. Retrieved May 16, 2016, from http://www.pps.org/places/tampa-riverwalk/.

16. *Friends of the High Line*. Retrieved January 26, 2021, from http://www.thehighline.org/about.

17. New York's high line fuels wave of urban renewal projects. (2014, October 7). *Free Enterprise*. Retrieved January 26, 2021, from http://www.freeenterprise.com/new-yorks-high-line-inspires-wave-of-urban-renewal-projects/.

18. *Visit Charlottesville, VA*. Retrieved May 16, 2016, from http://www.visitcharlottesville.org.

19. University of Virginia Sustainability Annual Report 2016-2017. Retrieved April 13, 2021 from https://sustainability.virginia.edu/sites/sustainability/files/2019-08/UVASustainabilityAnnualReport2016-2017.pdf.

20. Witt, P. A. (2002). Youth development: Going to the next level. *Parks & Recreation, 37*(3), 52–59.

21. U.S. Anti-Doping Agency. (2012). *True sport: What we stand to lose in our obsession to win*. Retrieved January 26, 2021, from http://www.truesport.org/

library/documents/about/true_sport_report/ True-Sport-Report.pdf.

22. Bean, C., & Forneris, T. (2016). Examining the importance of intentionally structuring the youth sport context to facilitate positive youth development. *Journal of Applied Sport Psychology, 28*(4), 410–425. https://doi.org/10.1080/10413200 .2016.1164764.

23. Hedstrom, R., & Gould, D. (2004). *Research in youth sports: Critical issues status.* Institute for the Study of Youth Sports.

24. Coakley, J. (2004). *Sports in society: Issues and controversies* (8th ed.). McGraw-Hill.

25. Search Institute. 40 Developmental Assets for Adolescents. Retrieved January 26, 2021, from http:// www.search-institute.org/content/40-developmental -assets-adolescents-ages-12-18.

26. *Outward Bound. Our mission.* Retrieved May 18, 2016, from http://www.outwardbound.org/about -Outward-bound/outward-bound-today/.

27. Thousand Oaks Teen Center. Retrieved May 18, 2016, from http://www.thousandoaksteencenter. com/.

28. Seattle Parks and Recreation Department. (n.d.). *Teen life centers and late night programs.* Retrieved January 26, 2021, from https://www.seattle.gov/ parks/find/teen-programs.

29. Peace Players. Retrieved November 12, 2019, from https://www.peaceplayers.org/about-ppi/.

30. Kivel, P., & Kivel, B. D. (2016). Beyond cultural competence: Building allies and sharing power in leisure, recreation, and tourism settings. In I. Schneider & B. Kivel (Eds.), *Diversity and inclusion in the recreation profession: Organizational perspectives* (3rd ed., pp. 339–356). Sagamore Publishing.

31. Chavez, D. J. (2000). Invite, include, and involve! Racial groups, ethnic groups, and leisure. In M. T. Allison & I. E. Schneider (Eds.), *Diversity and the recreation profession: Organizational perspectives* (pp. 179–191). Venture Publishing.

32. Henry Maier Festival Park Calendar of Events. Retrieved November 21, 2019, from http://www. milwaukeeworldfestival.com/find-events/calendar.

33. Skokie Park District Festival of Cultures. Retrieved November 8, 2019, from http://www.skokiecul- turefest.org.

34. Alif Institute. Retrieved September 17, 2019, from http://www.alifinstitute.org.

35. Seeds of Peace. Retrieved September 19, 2019, from http://www.seedsofpeace.org.

36. Metrosource. (2020). *World pride guide 2020.* Retrieved January 26, 2021, from https:// metrosource.com/?s=world+price+guide.

37. Chicago: Choose Chicago. *Explore Black culture and history in Chicago.* Retrieved February 23, 2021, from http://www.choosechicago.com/articles/view/ african-american-heritage/944/.

38. Putnam, R. D. (2000). *Bowling alone: The collapse and revival of American community* (p. 19). Simon & Schuster.

39. Conservation Foundation of the Gulf Coast. Robinson Preserve. Accessed February 23, 2021, from https://www.conservationfoundation.com/ robinson-preserve/

40. New York Restoration Project. Retrieved September 17, 2019, from https://www.nyrp .org/about.

41. New York Restoration Project. (2021). *Fort Tryon Park.* Retrieved September 17, 2019, from https:// www.nyrp.org/green-spaces/park-details/ fort-tryon-park/.

42. Planning for Play. (2017). *Case study: Joshua's Park, Amherst, NH.* Retrieved February 25, 2021, from https://www.nashuarpc.org/files/2015/1379/0460/ Full_Guidebook_FINAL_12.18.17.pdf.

43. National Park Service. (2015, February 26). *Hurricane Sandy—Six months later.* Retrieved May 19, 2016, from http://www.nps.gov/gate/parknews/ sandy-6.htm.

44. Batchelor, A. (2017). *Miami-Dade parks continue to open facilities for residents after Hurricane Irma.* Retrieved November 13, 2019, from https://www. local10.com/weather/hurricane-irma/miami -dade-parks-continues-to-open-facilities-for -residents-after-hurricane-irma.

45. Champaign Park District. Retrieved February 23, 2021, from https://champaignparks.com/

46. Taylor, D. (2018, November 29). *Americans with disabilities: 2014.* Retrieved November 21, 2019, from https://www.census.gov/library/publications/2018/ demo/p70-152.html.

47. South Suburban Special Recreation Association. Retrieved November 21, 2019, from http://www. sssra.org.

48. Vaira, D. (2009). A soldier's story. *Parks & Recreation, 44*(12), 32–36.

49. Invictus Games. Retrieved November 21, 2019, from https://invictusgames2018.com/games-hq/ results/.

50. Wounded Warrior Project. (n.d.). Health and wellness. Retrieved November 19, 2019, from https://

www.woundedwarriorproject.org/programs/
physical-health-wellness.

51. Green Cities: Good Health. (2018, August 16). *Local economics*. Retrieved November 15, 2019, from http://depts.washington.edu/hhwb/Thm_Economics.html.

52. Caston, R. (2018, October 12). *Research shows parks add significant boost in home values nearby*. Retrieved November 15, 2019, from https://www.theparkcatalog.com/blog/parks-homes-values/.

53. White River State Park. Retrieved May 19, 2016, from http://www.visitindy.com/indianapolis-white-river-state-park.

54. Rosentraub, M. M. S. (2010). *Major league winners: Using sports and cultural centers as tools for economic development*. CRC Press.

55. St. Louis Zoo, (2016). *About economic impact*. Retrieved January 26, 2021, from http://www.stlzoo.org/about/economicimpact/.

56. Portland Rose Festival, 2018 Portland Rose Festival Advertising Kit. (November 21, 2019). http://www.rosefestival.org/wp-content/uploads/2016_Advertising-Kit.pdf.

57. Americans for the Arts. (2012). *Arts and economic prosperity IV*. Americans for the Arts. Retrieved November 21, 2019, from https://www.americansforthearts.org/arts-and-economic-prosperity-iv-economic-impact-measurements.

58. Coyle, A. (2016, September 16). Swamp Rabbit Trail helps Travelers Rest businesses boom. *Greenville News*. Retrieved November 21, 2019, from https://www.greenvilleonline.com/story/news/local/2016/09/16/swamp-rabbit-trail-helps-travelers-rest-businesses-boom/89968190/.

59. Cox, G. (2014, May 30). Broadway's $12 billion impact on New York economy matches film and TV biz. *Variety*. Retrieved January 26, 2021, from http://variety.com/2014/legit/news/broadway-economic-impact-on-new-york-2012-13-1201199054/.

60. Prince George's County Department of Parks and Recreation. (n.d.). *Art centers*. Retrieved November 21, 2019, from http://www.mncppc.org/1735/Art-Centers.

61. Indianapolis Cultural Trail. (n.d.). *Trail facts*. Retrieved January 26, 2021, from http://indyculturaltrail.org/alongthetrail/facts-and-figures/.

62. Seattle Art Museum. (n.d.). Olympic Sculpture Park. Retrieved January 26, 2021, from http://www.seattleartmuseum.org/visit/olympic-sculpture-park.

63. National Recreation and Park Association. (n.d.). *Health and wellness*. Retrieved May 29, 2017, from http://www.nrpa.org/our-work/Three-Pillars/health-wellness/.

64. Brownson, R. C., Baker, E. A., Housemann, R. A., Brennan, L. K., & Bacak, S. J. (2001). Environmental and policy determinants of physical activity in the United States. *American Journal of Public Health*, *91*(12), 1995–2003.

65. National Recreation and Park Association. (n.d.). *Active transportation, parks and public health*. Retrieved January 26, 2021, from http://www.nrpa.org/uploadedFiles/nrpaorg/Tools_and_Resources/Parks_and_Health/Fact_Sheets/Active-Transportation-Parks-Public-Health.pdf.

66. Moyer, J. W. (2019, May 21). D.C. has the nation's best park system, study says. Arlington isn't far behind. *Washington Post*. Retrieved October 15, 2019, from https://www.washingtonpost.com/local/dc-has-the-nations-best-park-system-study-says-arlington-isnt-far-behind/2019/05/21/ecbd528c-7b1f-11e9-a3dd-d481bcdabfe6_story.html.

67. Chehalem Park & Recreation District. (n.d.). *Safety Town Kids Summer Camp*. Retrieved January 26, 2021, from https://www.cprdnewberg.org/general/page/safety-town-kids-summer-camp-0.

68. Deer Park Parks & Recreation. Hunter Education. Accessed February 23, 2021, from https://www.deerparktx.gov/1231/Hunter-Education

69. These are the 20 fittest cities in America. (2019, September 18). *Men's Health*. Retrieved December 16, 2019, from https://www.menshealth.com/fitness/a28945130/healthiest-fittest-cities-united-states/#https://wallethub.com/edu/fattest-cities-in-america/10532/.

70. McCann, A. (2020, March 4). *Most overweight and obese cities in the U.S.* Retrieved January 26, 2021, from https://wallethub.com/edu/fattest-cities-in-america/10532/.

Chapter 6

The Leisure-Services System

Man [sic] has always had, since the earliest recorded civilizations, some degree of unobligated time. History describes countless forms of recreative pursuits which have been used to fill leisure hours—particularly by the wealthy and influential social classes of each era. But it has only been within the past century, particularly among the highly industrialized Western nations, that both leisure and economic growth have made it possible for recreation to be widely available to all social classes.

Within the United States, there has been a vast expansion of recreational programs, services, and facilities under four different types of sponsorship. These categories of sponsors which provide pleasurable leisure opportunities to the American people may be regarded as the institutional basis of the twentieth-century recreation movement. They are found on four levels: government, voluntary agency, private, and commercial.[1]

--From the first edition of Kraus' Recreation and Leisure in Modern Society, published in 1971

LEARNING OBJECTIVES

1. Identify the key elements in the leisure-services delivery system.

2. Explain the role of each of the elements in the leisure-services delivery system.

3. Selecting a leisure-services agency and program from that agency, assess how the program influences the steps in the leisure-services delivery system.

4. Understand the uniqueness and commonality of the leisure-services delivery system in the different types of agencies: public, nonprofit, and private.

5. Recognize the multiple agencies delivering leisure services and explain their unique and common goals.

Introduction

We now turn to a detailed examination of the overall leisure-services system in the United States at the turn of the 21st century. This chapter deals with three major types of recreation providers that share a broad responsibility for sponsoring recreation, park, and related leisure facilities and programs for the public at large: governmental agencies, nonprofit community organizations, and commercial recreation enterprises. In each case, the background, mission, and chief program elements of sponsoring agencies are described, with numerous examples drawn from the field that illustrate recreation and leisure services today.

Key Elements in the Leisure-Services System

There are 10 different types of leisure-services organizations in modern society, as shown in Table 6-1. Of these, three of the major types that meet a broad range of public needs are described in this chapter, with the other seven elsewhere in the text.

Understanding the 10 Major Elements in the Modern Leisure-Services Delivery System

Understanding the modern leisure-services delivery system is the essence of this chapter. Table 6-1 provides a matrix of how leisure services are structured and delivered. The table is a simple representation of a complex process of relationships, interchanges, and decisions leading to outcomes in the form of benefits.

Across the top of the table are the five categories representing the major processes (A through D) and outcomes of the delivery (E) of a leisure program by an organization. In the columns, each of the major processes is separated into more specific descriptors. These in turn allow processes to be classified as the examples will show.

The major processes are described as follows:

- The *types of recreation sponsoring organizations* (A) are categories reflecting types of groups or organizations that offer recreation programs. The 10 areas are the major providers in a modern leisure-services delivery system. Most delivery types can be grouped within this list of 10 types of sponsors.
- The *partnered with support groups and services* (B) is present when a program sponsor is working with one or more additional program sponsors to deliver a program.
- The *process to provide leisure programs* (C) category consists of types of delivery approaches. The delivery approaches represent traditional delivery models.

- To *satisfy public needs for* (D) represents (1) types of program areas and (2) variables that influence demand for leisure services and public needs and desires.
- The *yielding major benefits* (E) category addresses the importance of leisure activities in providing measurable benefits to individuals, groups, organizations, and communities.

Using Table 6-1

Step 1: Beginning with column A, Types of Recreation-Sponsoring Organizations, select an agency that provides a program. For example, the Boys and Girls Club provides an after-school basketball clinic. In column A, nonprofit (2) is selected as the type of sponsoring organization.

Step 2: Are there any sponsoring organizations (column B)? In this case a local sporting goods store has offered to provide basketballs. The sporting goods company is a small business (8) and a sponsor of the Boys and Girls Club.

Step 3: The Boys and Girls Club are providing the basketball clinic (column C), taking on the role of direct program leadership (1).

Step 4: The basketball clinic satisfies a public need (column D) for games and sport as well as personal enjoyment (1). In this case, more than one spectrum of involvement is considered. The decision to offer the program was influenced by a number of factors such as age, gender, physical and emotional health, socioeconomic status, and ability (2). Other benefits unique to the situation could also have been considered.

Step 5: Participation in the basketball clinic should result in tangible and intangible benefits to the participant and potentially to others (column E). This can include personal values (1) and social outcomes (2).

Table 6-2 shows how the basketball clinic moved through Table 6-1. The table allows the reader to look at the variables influencing leisure-services delivery and track the relationships of those variables. It is not a neat and clean process but rather often is messy. What the table does is provide an improved understanding of the complexity of the delivery of leisure-services programs and offerings.

Public Recreation, Park, and Leisure Services

Public, or government, leisure-services agencies have the following characteristics: (1) They were the first type of agency to be formally recognized as responsible for serving the public's recreation needs and, as such, have constituted the core of the recreation movement; (2) the primary means of support for most government recreation and park agencies traditionally has been tax funding, although in recent years other revenue sources have begun to be used more extensively; (3) government agencies have a major responsibility

TABLE 6-1   The 10 Major Elements in the Modern Leisure-Services Delivery System

(A) Types of Recreation-Sponsoring Organizations	(B) Partnered with Groups and Services	(C) Provide Leisure Programs Consisting of	(D) To Satisfy Individual and Public Needs for	(E) Yielding Major Benefits
① Public agencies	① Trade associations	① Direct program leadership	① Full spectrum of involvement in:	① Personal values (health, emotional wellness, mental development, well-being)
② Nonprofit organizations	② Professional associations	② Provision of facilities and open spaces for undirected public use	Games and sport	② Social and community-based outcomes
③ Commercial recreation enterprises	③ Special-interest groups	③ Education for leisure	Outdoor recreation	③ Economic benefits, employment, taxes, and other fiscal returns
④ Employee service and recreation programs	④ Sponsors of special programs and events	④ Information referral services	Cultural activities	④ Environmental values, both natural and urban settings
⑤ Armed Forces morale, welfare, and recreation	⑤ Professional preparation institutions	⑤ Enabling facilitation	The arts	
⑥ Private membership organizations	⑥ Private groups that subcontract leisure functions	⑥ Advocacy and leadership in special areas	Hobbies	
⑦ Campus recreation programs	⑦ Other civic agencies and citizen groups	⑦ Jointly sponsored campaigns and events	Special events	
⑧ Recreation therapy services	⑧ Corporations	⑧ Authentic leisure experiences	Club and other social groups	
⑨ Sport management organizations	⑨ Small business enterprises	⑨ Opportunities for well-being	Personal enjoyment	
⑩ Tourism and hospitality industry	⑩ Individuals		Travel	
			Electronic media	
			Other social services	
			② With needs influenced by:	
			Age group	
			Gender	
			Socioeconomic status	
			Educational background	
			Racial/ethnic factors	
			Residential and regional factors	
			Physical and emotional health	
			Ability/disability	
			Family status	

TABLE 6-2　Simple Version

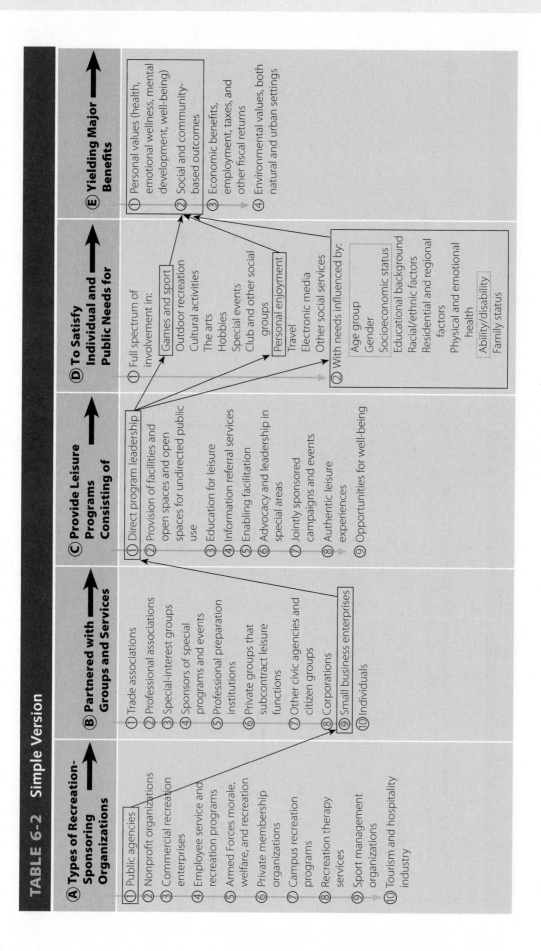

(A) Types of Recreation-Sponsoring Organizations

1. Public agencies
2. Nonprofit organizations
3. Commercial recreation enterprises
4. Employee service and recreation programs
5. Armed Forces morale, welfare, and recreation
6. Private membership organizations
7. Campus recreation programs
8. Recreation therapy services
9. Sport management organizations
10. Tourism and hospitality industry

(B) Partnered with Groups and Services

1. Trade associations
2. Professional associations
3. Special-interest groups
4. Sponsors of special programs and events
5. Professional preparation institutions
6. Private groups that subcontract leisure functions
7. Other civic agencies and citizen groups
8. Corporations
9. Small business enterprises
10. Individuals

(C) Provide Leisure Programs Consisting of

1. Direct program leadership
2. Provision of facilities and open spaces and open spaces for undirected public use
3. Education for leisure
4. Information referral services
5. Enabling facilitation
6. Advocacy and leadership in special areas
7. Jointly sponsored campaigns and events
8. Authentic leisure experiences
9. Opportunities for well-being

(D) To Satisfy Individual and Public Needs for

1. Full spectrum of involvement in:
   - Games and sport
   - Outdoor recreation
   - Cultural activities
   - The arts
   - Hobbies
   - Special events
   - Club and other social groups
   - Personal enjoyment
   - Travel
   - Electronic media
   - Other social services
2. With needs influenced by:
   - Age group
   - Gender
   - Socioeconomic status
   - Educational background
   - Racial/ethnic factors
   - Residential and regional factors
   - Physical and emotional health
   - Ability/disability
   - Family status

(E) Yielding Major Benefits

1. Personal values (health, emotional wellness, mental development, well-being)
2. Social and community-based outcomes
3. Economic benefits, employment, taxes, and other fiscal returns
4. Environmental values, both natural and urban settings

for the management of natural resources; and (4) they are obligated to serve the public at large with socially useful or constructive programs because of their tax-supported status.

Role of the Federal Government

The federal government's responsibility for managing parks and recreation areas and providing or assisting other leisure services evolved gradually. The growth of the parks and recreation movement began with the early immigrants to New England, with Boston Common being an archetype of future park development across the United States. National and state parks grew differently from urban parks, and recreation evolved still differently—yet people talk of parks and recreation as if they are one. The parks systems, including urban, state, and national parks, are uniquely American and range from Central Park in the late 1850s to the formation of the first national park in 1872. The growth of government and nonprofit involvement, beginning with experiences such as the Boston Sand Gardens and expanding dramatically under Franklin Roosevelt's New Deal policies, solidified government's role in parks and recreation.

The federal government in the United States developed a great variety of programs related to recreation in dozens of different departments, bureaus, or other administrative units. Typically, recreation functions evolved in federal agencies as secondary responsibilities. For example, the initial purposes of the Tennessee Valley Authority lakes and

Providing interpretive services to visitors is essential to individuals understanding parks and natural settings.

Courtesy of John and Karen Hollingsworth/U.S. Fish and Wildlife Service.

reservoirs were to provide flood control and rural electrification; only over time did recreation uses become important. The following list examines the responsibilities and roles of the federal government.

- *Direct management of outdoor recreation resources:* The federal government, through such agencies as the National Park Service, the National Forest Service, and the Bureau of Land Management, owns and operates a vast network of parks, forests, lakes, reservoirs, seashores, and other facilities used extensively for outdoor recreation.
- *Conservation and resource reclamation:* Closely related to the preceding function is the government's role in reclaiming natural resources that have been destroyed, damaged, or threatened and in promoting programs related to conservation, wildlife, and antipollution control.
- *Assistance to open space and park development programs:* Chiefly with funding authorized under the 1965 Land and Water Fund Conservation Act, the federal government has provided billions of dollars in matching grants to states and localities to promote open-space development. Also, through direct aid to municipalities carrying out housing and urban development projects, the federal government subsidized the development of local parks, playgrounds, and centers.
- *Direct programs of recreation participation:* The federal government operates a number of direct programs of recreation service in Veterans Administration hospitals and other federal institutions and in the armed forces on permanent and temporary bases throughout the world.
- *Advisory and financial assistance:* The federal government provides varied forms of assistance to states, localities, and other public or voluntary community agencies. For example, many community programs serving economically and socially disadvantaged populations have been assisted by the Departments of Health and Human Services, Housing and Urban Development, Labor, and others.
- *Aid to professional education:* Federal agencies concerned with education and the needs of special populations have provided training grants for professional education in colleges and universities throughout the United States.
- *Promotion of recreation as an economic function:* The federal government has been active in promoting tourism, providing aid to rural residents in developing recreation enterprises, and assisting Native American tribes in establishing recreational and tourist facilities on their reservations. Such agencies as the Bureau of the Census and the Coast Guard also provide needed

information for those interested in travel, boating, and similar pastimes.

- *Research and technical assistance:* The federal government has supported a broad spectrum of research on topics ranging from outdoor recreation trends and needs and the current status of urban recreation and parks to specific studies of wildlife conservation, forest recreation, or the needs of special populations.
- *Regulation and standards:* The federal government has developed regulatory policies with respect to pollution control, watershed production, and environmental quality. It has also established standards with respect to rehabilitative service for those who are ill or those with disabilities and architectural standards to guarantee access to facilities for persons with disabilities.

The first two areas of responsibility (one, direct management and conservation, and two, resource reclamation) are carried out by seven major federal agencies that are either service units or bureaus in cabinet departments or separate authorities. They are the National Park Service, the U.S. Forest Service, the Bureau of Land Management, the Bureau of Reclamation, the U.S. Fish and Wildlife Service, the Tennessee Valley Authority, and the U.S. Army Corps of Engineers.

The National Park Service

The leading federal agency with respect to outdoor recreation is the National Park Service (NPS) (www.nps.gov), housed in the Department of the Interior. Its mission has been stated as follows:

The National Park Service preserves unimpaired the natural and cultural resources and values of the national park system for the enjoyment, education, and inspiration of this and future generations.[2] The Park Service cooperates with partners to extend the benefits of natural and cultural resource conservation and outdoor recreation throughout this country and the world.

Most of the property administered by the NPS in its early years was west of the Mississippi, and it has since added major seashore parks and other areas throughout the country and closer to urban centers. For example, East Coast sites now include the Fire Island National Seashore on Long Island, Acadia National Park in Maine, Assateague National Seashore on the Maryland coast, Cape Hatteras National

The Appalachian Trail is an example of a national trail used by tens of thousands of people annually for 1-day to multiday trips.
Courtesy of the Appalachian Trial Conservancy.

WHO REALLY OWNS THE WESTERN LANDS

The federal government is the largest land owner in the United States, and this is especially true in the western states. The federal government owns 61.3% of Alaska and 47% of the 11 coterminous western states, including 79.6% of Nevada, 63.1% of Utah, 61.6 percent of Idaho, and 53% of Oregon. By contrast, in the remaining states the federal government only owns an average of 4% of each state.[3] For years, the western states have argued that the vast tracts of lands in their states should be state controlled rather than federally controlled. What's called the "sagebrush rebellion" see these vast tracts of land as revenue sources for mining, oil drilling, expanding ranches, and the like. Most of the states have smaller populations and need additional revenue sources to provide basic services such as schools, roads, and jobs. Western Congressmen have pushed this agenda for many years, but more recently activist ranchers have had standoffs with the Bureau of Land Management and other federal agencies. Simultaneously, western state legislatures, especially in the intermountain west, have become more aggressive in challenging federal control over so much of their land. The question of who really would provide the best stewardship is open for debate. In fact, the question of managing the land, as well as working and living on it, is longstanding with roots as far back as the late 1700s when Native Americans were often forcibly relocated from these lands and others to "Indian Territory." It seems as though this contentious debate, in its various forms, is likely to continue for decades into the future.

Data from National Park Service. (2016). *Overview*. https://www.nps.gov/aboutus/upload/NPS-Overview-04-12-16.pdf

Seashore in North Carolina, and Gateway East in the New York and New Jersey harbor area.

The national park system consists of 85 million acres (34.4 million hectares) of land, about 5% of which remains in private ownership. The system generates a huge volume of tourism, with appeal for both domestic travelers and foreign visitors that yields major benefits for the nation's economy and the balance of trade with other countries. In 2018, the national park system experienced 318.2 million visitors, spread across the 419-unit system. The level of usage in the national parks has created overcrowding at what are frequently called the "crown jewels" including Glacier National Park, Death Valley, the Grand Canyon, and Yellowstone.[4]

The Forest Service

A second federal agency that administers extensive wilderness preserves for public recreation use is the U.S. Forest Service (USFS) (www.fs.usda.gov) within the Department of Agriculture. The resource management responsibilities of the NPS and USFS have blurred in recent years, even though their management mandates have not. Both agencies had responsibilities for managing national monuments, recreation areas, trails, and wild and scenic rivers. The USFS is best known for its management of huge areas of forests and grasslands. The USFS was a predecessor to the NPS and had a very different role. It adopted the multiple-use concept of federally owned land under its control; mining, grazing, lumbering, recreation, and hunting are all permitted in the national forests.

The recreation function of the USFS has continued to grow steadily. It currently manages 193 million acres of forest and grasslands (78 million hectares) and is the lead agency responsible for management of six national trails as well as portions of 16 National Scenic and Historic Trails, and numerous National Recreation Trails for a total of 158,000 miles of trails. Additionally, the USFS is responsible for 5,000 wild and scenic river miles out of the total of 12,700 miles. On average the USFS recreation sites combined record 148 million visits. Its major recreational uses include relaxation and viewing scenery; camping, picnicking, and swimming; hiking, horseback riding, and water travel; winter sports; and hunting and fishing.[5]

Forest service-administered lands face many threats. The USFS identified four main threats: fires and fuels, invasive species, loss of open space, and unmanaged recreation. Data suggest the loss of more than 3000 acres a day over a 6-year period, mostly to development, in lands near or adjacent to USFS areas. The loss of open space will place greater stress on forest service lands. Unmanaged recreation comes mostly in the form of off-highway vehicles (OHV). There were a reported 36 million OHV owners in 2000, a number that climbed until gas prices and the recession devastated the market. The use of OHVs in USFS lands has resulted in increased erosion, creation of new unplanned roads, and watershed and habitat degradation. The USFS has established action plans for each of the threats.

Other Federal Agencies

The Bureau of Land Management (BLM) (www.blm.gov) administers more than 245 million acres (99.1 million hectares), chiefly in the western states and Alaska. Its properties are used for a variety of resource-based outdoor recreation activities (including camping, biking, hunting and fishing, mountain climbing, and cycle racing), as well as mining, grazing, and lumbering activities that yield more than $800 million a year in revenues, much of it returned to state and local governments.

The U.S. Fish and Wildlife Service (USFWS) (www.fws.gov) originally consisted of two federal bureaus, one dealing

 2016: 100TH ANNIVERSARY OF THE NATIONAL PARK SERVICE

On August 25, 2016, the NPS celebrated its 100th anniversary. The first national organization of its kind, the NPS has been the champion of preservation of unique natural, historical, and cultural sites in the United States. The NPS was created by an act of Congress in 1916, signed into law by President Woodrow Wilson, and championed by John Muir, a naturalist often called "The Father of our National Parks." The NPS has been the world leader in conservation and preservation. In the beginning, the NPS was hampered by small budgets and a small core of dedicated people. In 2016, it had over 20,000 employees and 412 administered areas ranging from national parks to local historical and cultural sites. The original "Organic Act" states, "the service thus established shall promote and regulate the use of the Federal areas known as national parks, monuments, and reservations … which purpose is to conserve the scenery and the natural and historic objects and the wild life therein and to provide for the enjoyment of future generations." Throughout the NPS system, special events are planned. Hawai'i Volcanoes National Park also celebrated its 100th anniversary in 2016, created just weeks before the National Park Service. From an international perspective, the National Park System has been touted as "America's best idea" and if not that, it does represent America's best ideals.[6]

with commercial fisheries (which was transferred to the Department of Commerce) and the other dealing with sports fisheries and wildlife (which remained in the Department of the Interior). Its functions include restoring the nation's fisheries, enforcing laws, managing wildlife populations, conducting research, and operating the National Wildlife Refuge System (www.fws.gov/refuges). This system includes 560 units comprising 150 million acres (60.7 million hectares) with at least one site in every state and vast acreages in the Caribbean and Pacific Ocean. In addition to meeting the ongoing needs of hunters and fishers, the USFWS particularly has been active in helping to ensure the survival of endangered species, conserving migratory birds, and administering federal aid programs that assist state wildlife programs and tribal lands programs. Its 2017 visitation exceeded 53 million with an economic impact of $3.2 billion.[7]

The federal Bureau of Reclamation (BOR) (www.usbr.gov) is responsible for water resource development, primarily in the western states. Although its original function was to promote irrigation and electric power, it has accepted recreation as a responsibility since 1936. The policy of the BOR is to transfer reservoir areas wherever possible to other federal agencies; often these become classified as National Recreation Areas and are assigned to the NPS for operation. The emphasis is on active recreational use such as boating, camping, hiking, hunting, and fishing rather than sightseeing. The NPS, USFS, USFWS, and BOR have provided employment opportunities for thousands of young men and women through the Youth Conservation Corps (YCC), which has habilitated or built campgrounds and boating facilities at recreation areas throughout the West.

The Tennessee Valley Authority (TVA) (www.tva.gov) operates extensive reservoirs in Kentucky, North Carolina, Tennessee, and other southern or border states. The TVA

Participation in outdoor recreation continues to increase. The variety of outdoor activities increases demand on existing natural resource areas.
© Ammit Jack/Shutterstock.

does not manage recreation facilities itself, but it makes land available to other public agencies or private groups for development.

The U.S. Army Corps of Engineers civilian side (www.usace.army.mil) is responsible for the improvement and maintenance of rivers and other waterways to facilitate navigation and flood control. It constructs reservoirs, protects and improves beaches and harbors, and administers more than 12 million acres (4.9 million hectares) of federally owned land and water impoundments. This includes 460 reservoirs and lakes; the majority of these are managed by the corps, and the remainder are managed by state and local agencies under lease. These sites totaled 370 million annual visits. Army Corps of Engineers recreation sites are heavily used by the public for boating, camping, hunting, and fishing

Several other agencies in the U.S. Department of Agriculture (USDA) have important recreation functions. The Farm Service Agency's (www.fsa.usda.gov) conservation programs focus on several areas, three of which are relevant to parks and recreation. The Conservation Reserve Program is a state and federal partnership with farmers. "In exchange for a yearly rental payment, farmers enrolled in the program agree to remove environmentally sensitive land from agricultural production and plant species that will improve environmental health and quality."[9] The Farmable Wetlands Program "reduces downstream flood damage, improves surface and groundwater quality, and recharges groundwater supplies by restoring wetlands." Finally, the Grassland Reserve Program "helps landowners restore and protect grassland, and provides assistance for rehabilitating grasslands."[10] The former Farmers Home Administration, now USDA Rural Development (www.rd.usda.gov), gives credit and management advice to rural organizations and farmers in developing recreation facilities. The Extension Service aids community recreation planning in rural areas and advises states on outdoor recreation development, working in many states through extension agents at land grant agricultural colleges.

The Bureau of Indian Affairs (www.bia.gov) exists primarily to provide service to Native American tribes in such areas as health, education, economic development, and land management. However, it also operates (under civilian control in the Department of the Interior) Native American–owned properties of about 55 million surface acres, with 57 million subsurface mineral estates, and more than 5500 lakes that are used heavily for recreational purposes, including camping, museum visits, hunting, and fishing.

Programs in Health and Human Services, Education, and Housing

A number of federal agencies related to health and human services, education, and housing and urban development have provided funding, technical assistance, and other forms of aid to recreation programs designed to meet

BLM'S CONTRIBUTION TO AMERICA'S NATURAL HERITAGE

The BLM manages 245 million acres (99.1 hectares), almost all of it in the western United States. The BLM's management program is called the National Landscape Conservation System (See Table 6-3), and includes more than 850 units dedicated to preserving natural resources. The BLM-managed lands are home to approximately 30,000 free-roaming wild horses and burros; approximately 31,000 additional animals are cared for in short-term and long-term holding facilities. Managed areas include Wilderness and Wilderness Study Areas, Wild and Scenic Rivers, National Scenic and Historic Trails, National Monuments, and National Conservation Areas.

Additionally, the BLM manages 16,000 miles of multiple-use trails, including approximately 5300 miles of trails classified within the National Trails System; a vast array of geologic, historic, and archaeological sites, including 800 caves and 271,000 archaeological and historic recorded sites such as lighthouses, ghost towns, petroglyphs, pictographs, and cliff dwellings; and more than 117,000 miles of fisheries habitat and 4 million acres (1.6 billion hectares) of reservoirs and lakes.[8]

TABLE 6-3   BLM's National Landscape Conservation System

Category	Areas	Number	BLM Acres	BLM Miles
National monuments and national conservation areas	National monuments National conservation areas Similar designations	28 17 6	11,958,369	
Wilderness	Wilderness areas Wilderness study areas	260 491	9,977,599 11,616,634	
Wild and scenic rivers		81	1,207,694	2698
Trails	National historic trails National scenic trails	13 5		5080 683
Conservation lands of the California desert			4,200,000	
Totals		**901**	**Approximately 39 million**	**8461**

Data from U.S. Department of the Interior, Bureau of Land Management. (2020). *Nationaal landscape conservation system summary tables.* http://www.blm.gov/files/ NLCS Summary Table_Q2_2020.

various social needs in U.S. communities. Within the federal Department of Health and Human Services (www.hhs.gov), such units as the Administration for Children and Families (www.acf.hhs.gov), and the Public Health Service (www.usphs.gov) have been active in this area. For example, the Administration on Aging, authorized by the Older Americans Act of 1965 and reauthorized in 2016, promotes comprehensive programs for older persons and supports training programs and demonstration projects intended to prepare professional personnel to work with older people. It also gathers information on new or expanded programs and services for the aging and supports research projects in this field.

The Rehabilitation Services Administration (rsa.ed.gov) administers the federal law authorizing vocational rehabilitation programs designed to help persons with physical or mental disabilities gain employment and lead fuller lives. It has oversight of formula and discretionary grant programs. Other federal legislation, such as Section 504 of the Rehabilitation Act of 1975 (often called the "nondiscrimination clause") and the Americans with Disabilities Act of 1990, have been instrumental in pressuring school systems, units of local government, and other agencies to provide equal opportunity for persons with disabilities in a wide range of community opportunity fields.

The federal Department of Housing and Urban Development (HUD) (www.hud.gov) was established in 1965, with responsibility for a range of federally assisted programs, including urban renewal and planning, public housing, and open space. HUD's primary responsibility lies with urban development. Its mission is to increase home ownership, support community development, and increase access to affordable housing free from discrimination. Through its $44.1 billion budget, it administers a wide variety of programs focusing on community development. The Community Development Block Grant (CDBG) Entitlement Program, first authorized in 1974, is HUD's most valuable and effective community development program. Examples of use of CDBG funds include roads, sewers, and other infrastructure investments, or for community centers and parks. HUD also funds housing development and rehabilitation through CDBG, HOME, Youthbuild, and Lead Hazard Control grants.

Arts and Humanities Support

Another area of federal involvement in leisure pursuits in the United States has reflected public interest in the arts and a wide range of cultural activities. The National Foundation on the Arts and the Humanities Act of 1965 resulted in the creation of the National Endowment for the Arts (NEA) (www.arts.gov), and it celebrated 50 years of service in 2015. It functions as an independent federal agency supporting and encouraging programs in the arts (including dance, music, drama, folk art, creative writing, and the visual media) and humanities (including literature, history, philosophy, and the study of language).

Although there was strong conservative resistance to some controversial programs in the 1990s, the NEA administered a $162 million budget in 2020.[11] Over its 40-year history, NEA has awarded more than 120,000 grants to communities, arts groups, and artists. In 2002, the NEA initiated the National Initiative Program and by 2021, 15 initiatives were available. They included both short- and long-term initiatives lasting from a single year to many years. The initiatives include Shakespeare in American Communities, Poetry Out Loud, NEA Big Read, Mayors' Institute on City Design, Art and Human Development Task Force, Arts Education Partnership, Citizens Institute on Rural Design, Creative Forces: NEA Military Healing Arts Network, International, Musical Theater Songwriting Challenge, NEA Research Labs, Save America's Treasures, Blue Star Museums, Sound Health Network, and Women's Suffrage Centennial.[12] Creativity Connects, an initiative honoring and moving the arts forward, was initiated during NEA's 50th anniversary celebration in 2015 "to show how the arts contribute to the nation's creative ecosystem and how the arts can connect

Attendance at cultural events is an important component of public services provided by leisure-services and cultural arts agencies.
© Susan Montgomery/Shutterstock.

with other sectors that want and utilize creativity."[13] The initiative plans to address key resources that artists need in order to produce their best work and includes a grant program supporting partnerships between arts organizations and the nonarts sectors.

Physical Fitness and Sports Promotion

Another recreation-related federal program has been the President's Council on Sports, Fitness & Nutrition (www.fitness.gov). Created in 1956 to help upgrade the fitness of the nation's youth, and broadened in 1968 to include the promotion of sport participation, the council has operated to encourage public awareness of fitness needs and to stimulate school and community-based sport and fitness programs. It has conducted nationwide promotional campaigns through the media and sponsored many regional physical fitness clinics. This effort continued through the 2000s, with a Presidential Youth Fitness Program providing for state and federal goals and guidelines, school championships, and participant fitness awards. Along with community school systems, many local recreation and park agencies and professional groups have assisted in such fitness programs.

Recreation-Related Functions of State Governments

The role of state governments in recreation and parks generally has rested on the Tenth Amendment to the Constitution, which states, "The powers not delegated to the United States by the Constitution, nor prohibited by it to the States, are reserved to the States respectively, or to the people." This amendment, commonly referred to as the "states' rights amendment," is regarded as the source of state powers in such additional areas as public education, welfare, and health services.

Outdoor Recreation Resources and Programs

Each state government today operates a network of parks and other outdoor recreation resources. The National Association of State Park Directors (NASPD) (www.state-parks.org) developed categories of facilities and areas:[14]

- *State parks areas:* Containing a number of coordinated programs for the preservation of natural and/or cultural resources and provisions of a variety of outdoor recreation activities supported by those resources.
- *State recreation areas:* Where a clear emphasis is placed on the provision of opportunities for primarily active recreation activities; this category includes recreational beaches, water theme parks, and so forth.
- *State natural areas:* Where a clear emphasis is placed on protection, management, and interpretation of natural resources or features; this category includes wilderness areas, nature preserves, natural landmarks, and sanctuaries.
- *State historic areas:* Where a clear emphasis is placed on protection, management, and interpretation of historical and/or archaeological resources or features; this category includes monuments, memorials, shrines, museums, and so forth dealing with historical and/or archaeological subjects, as well as areas that actually contain substantive remains (e.g., forts, burial mounds) and areas where historic events took place (e.g., battles, discoveries, meetings).
- *State environmental education sites:* Used exclusively or primarily for conducting educational programs on environmental subjects, natural resources, and conservation; this category includes nature centers, environmental education centers, "outdoor class-rooms," and so forth.
- *State scientific areas:* Set aside exclusively or primarily for scientific study, observation, and experimentation involving natural objects, processes, and interrelationships; any other allowable uses are secondary and incidental.
- *State trails:* Linear areas outside any other unit of the state park system that provide primarily for trail-type recreational activities (hiking, cycling, horseback riding, etc.); they normally do not contain any land areas large enough to support nontrail activities.

During the 1960s and early 1970s, most state governments expanded their recreation and park holdings, primarily with funding assistance from the Land and Water Conservation Fund but also through major bond issues totaling hundreds of millions of dollars in many cases. In the 1990s, many states again secured major bond issues for park renovation, new construction, and land acquisition. Open space and natural beauty were widely supported concepts, and the public enthusiastically supported programs of land acquisition and water cleanup. State parks are perceived as a close-to-home outdoor recreation experience available to most residents. Attendance at state parks exceeds all national agencies except the USFS. Attendance at state parks in 2018 was 807 million on 18 million acres (7.3 million hectares). State park acreage is only 18% of the size of the national park system and yet state parks have more visitors. State parks are essential to outdoor recreation activities of many citizens. (See Table 6-4.)

Other State Functions

An important function of state government is to assist and work with local governments in environmental efforts. Just as no single municipality can clean up a polluted stream that flows through a state, so in the broad field of urban planning, recreation resource development, and conservation, problems must be approached on a statewide or even a regional basis. In such planning, as in many other aspects of federal relationships with local communities, the state acts as a catalyst for action and as a vital link between the national and local governments.

Many state governments have offices or sponsor arts councils that distribute funds to nonprofit organizations and performing groups or institutions in various areas of creative and cultural activity. A unique aspect of state-sponsored or state-assisted recreation is the state fair. This term covers a wide variety of fairs and expositions held each year throughout the United States and includes carnivals and midways, displays and competitions of livestock and produce, farm equipment shows, and a host of special presentations by corporations of every type. The majority of such fairs are run by nonprofit organizations that are publicly owned and operated, including a number of bona fide state agencies. Attended by about 160 million persons each year, they promote civic and state boosterism, offer a showcase for agricultural and other regional industries or attractions, and provide varied forms of entertainment.

An important function of state governments is to promote all aspects of leisure involvement that support economic development. Many states assist with or coordinate outdoor recreation ventures, tourism campaigns, regional recovery projects, and other efforts to attract visitors and revive local economies. Travel and tourism to urban and rural areas have become increasingly important to economies. States are providing leadership, assistance, and funding to local levels.

TABLE 6-4 Areas, Acreage, and Visitation for Selected Outdoor Recreation Agencies

Agency	Areas	Acreage[a]	Visitation[a]
National Park Service	419	85	318
U.S. Forest Service	14,077[b]	193	205
U.S. Fish and Wildlife Service[c]	567	147	54
Bureau of Land Management	238[d]	245	62
Army Corps of Engineers	460[e]	12	250
State Parks (all 50 states)	8,565	18	807

[a] number in millions—45 means 45 million
[b] recreation sites (may be more than one per area)
[c] National Wildlife Refuge System
[d] wilderness areas and national monuments
[e] reservoirs and lakes

Data from America's State Parks. (n.d.). *State Park Facts*. Retrieved May 27, 2021, from https://www.americasstateparks.org; Bies, L. (2019, July 10). *U.S. Fish and Wildlife Service releases Banking on Nature report*. Wildlife Society. https://wildlife.org/u-s-fish-and-wildlife-service-releases-banking-on-nature-report; Bureau of Land Management. (n.d.). *About us*. Retrieved February 7, 2021, from https://www.blm.gov/about; Bureau of Land Management. (n.d.). *Data resources*. Retrieved February 7, 2021, from https://www.blm.gov/about/data; Fish and Wildlife Service. (2019). *Statistical data tables for Fish & Wildlife Service lands* (as of 9/30/2019). https://www.fws.gov/refuges/land/PDF/2019_Annual_Report_Data_Tables(508-Compliant).pdf; National Environmental Education Foundation. (n.d.). *US Army Corps of Engineers recreation—Closer than you think!* Retrieved February 7, 2021, from https://www.neefusa.org/nature/land/us-army-corps-engineers-recreation-closer-you-think; National Park Service. (2021). *Frequently asked questions*. Retrieved February 7, 2021, from https://www.nps.gov/aboutus/faqs.htm; Public Lands Interpretive Association. (n.d.). *Public lands maps of the West*. Retrieved February 7, 2021, from http://publiclands.org/agencies/USACE.php; U.S. Army Corps of Engineers. (n.d.). *Recreation overview*. Retrieved February 7, 2021, from http://www.usace.army.mil/Missions/Civil-Works/Recreation; U.S. Forest Service. (n.d.). *By the numbers*. Retrieved February 7, 2021, from https://www.fs.usda.gov/about-agency/newsroom/by-the-numbers.

CASE STUDY: Alabama State Parks "Dirt Pass"

Every public park and recreation agency struggles to meet the demands and expectations of their constituents. State park systems as well as the National Park System are historically underfunded. With pressing infrastructure and social needs and demands, states often let their natural resources take a back seat during the funding process. As a result, state parks frequently have a medium to large unfunded maintenance and repair backlog. It is sometimes easier to convince state legislatures to fund new projects rather than provide funds to maintain and renovate older facilities and parks. In 2016, Alabama's state park system faced an unusual challenge—even for a state park system—with five parks scheduled to be closed because of anticipated budget cuts.[a]

Alabama's budget crisis was very real. Over a 5-year period, almost $30 million had been transferred from the state parks budget to cover what the state legislature deemed as essential services. Some communities and counties have negotiated with the state to keep parks in their area open. Fees have also been raised to aid in keeping the park system open. By 2016, the state park system was generating most of its meager operating budget from self-generated funds (such as entrance fees) and from federal earmarked funds, which have decreased significantly in recent years.[a]

Even those parks that have remained open have reduced staffing significantly and have an almost nonexistent operations and repair budget. In 2016, an amendment to the Alabama state constitution (Amendment 2) was approved by a ballot initiative with a majority vote of 79.7% of those voting. The amendment prohibits the state legislature from reallocating state park funds for other uses and allows the parent state government organization, the Department of Conservation and Natural Resources, to contract with nonstate entities for the operation and maintenance of land and facilities that are part of the state park system.[b]

The state park system has looked for creative ways to increase park revenue. One approach has been the "Dirt Pass," a voluntary contribution to the state park system's trails program that individuals can purchase for $35. In return, donors can display their membership with the Dirt Pass Trail Crew with a rubber wristband and t-shirt; they also receive a trails gift. The fees are used for activities such as organizing trail work days, supporting a full-time trail crew, new trail building, and surveying needs of trail users. These monies are enhanced by other state level efforts to build support for the state parks such as state park license plates from which 80% of the sales go directly to supporting the parks.[c]

Questions to Consider

- How is your state park system funded?
- Do you think states should use their tax dollars toward maintaining a state park system?
- Is it appropriate to ask people who use the state parks to pay an additional fee, above their taxes, to enter and use parks? Explain the rationale for your answer.
- Would you be willing to pay a voluntary fee to show your support of your state parks if the fee was going back into the state park for operations and maintenance?
- What ideas might be considered to increase alternative funding for state parks?

[a] Alabama State Parks Division. (2015). *5 Alabama State Parks to close due to budget cuts.* https://abc3340.com/news/local/5-alabama-state-parks-to-close-due-to-budget-cuts.
[b] Ballotpedia. (n.d.). *Alabama rules governing allocation of state park funds, Amendment 2 (2016).* Retrieved August 2, 2017, from https://ballotpedia.org/Alabama_Rules_Governing_Allocation_of_State_Park_Funds,_Amendment_2_(2016).
[c] Alabama State Parks. (n.d.). *Dirt pass trail crew program.* Retrieved March 1, 2021 from https://www.alapark.com/trails/dirt-pass-trail-crew-program.

Individuals with disabilities actively engage in sports, sometimes with individuals without disabilities.
© Shariff Che'Lah/Dreamstime.com.

RECREATION THERAPY SERVICE

Each state government provides direct recreation services within the institutions or agencies it sponsors, such as mental hospitals or mental health centers, special schools for people with cognitive disabilities with mental retardation, and penal or correctional facilities. Many of the largest networks of facilities that employ recreation therapy specialists are tax-supported state mental health systems or similar organizations, although their overall numbers have been reduced because of deinstitutionalization policies.

PROMOTION OF PROFESSIONAL ADVANCEMENT

Although states promote effective leadership and administrative practices in recreation and parks by developing personnel standards and providing conferences and research support, their major contribution lies in the professional preparation of recreation practitioners in state colleges and universities. Of the colleges and universities in the United States with professional recreation and park curricula, a substantial majority are part of state university systems.

Many state agencies also assist professional development by conducting annual surveys of municipal and county recreation and parks departments and publishing their findings on facilities, fiscal practices, and personnel.

DEVELOPMENT AND ENFORCEMENT OF STANDARDS

States also have the function of screening personnel by establishing standards and hiring procedures, or by requiring Civil Service examinations, certification, or personnel registration programs in recreation and parks.

Some also have developed standards relating to health and safety practices in camping and similar settings. State departments enforce safety codes, promote facilities standards, ensure that recreation resources can accommodate persons with disabilities, regulate or prohibit certain types of commercial attractions, and in some cases carry out regular inspections of camps, pools, or other facilities.

The Role of County and Local Governments

Although federal and state governments provide major forms of recreation service in the United States, the responsibility for meeting year-round day-to-day leisure needs belongs to agencies of local government. These range from counties, special park districts, and townships (which embrace larger geographical areas) to cities, villages, and other political subdivisions.

For recreation and parks in the United States, all powers that are not vested in the federal government belong to the states. In turn, local governments must get their authority through enabling laws passed by state legislatures or through other special charter or home rule arrangements. Of all branches of government, the local government is closest to the people and therefore most able to meet the widest range of recreation needs.

THE ILLINOIS PARK DISTRICT SYSTEM

The Illinois Park District system is not unique in its organization but is among the largest collection of park districts in the United States. A *park district* is a geographically and politically bounded separate taxing district, serving a distinct population with recreation, park and leisure services, and programs. The districts are created by state enabling legislation and voted into creation at the local level. Each district has an elected board that is responsible for the operations of the park district. Typically, they are policy-setting boards that hire an executive director and staff to run day-to-day operations. They are unique because most municipal park and recreation systems operate under a city government organization in which they compete for resources with other city agencies. A park district's independent status allows it to make investments and provide services with less conflict and competition than agencies that are part of city and county government. This does not remove the park districts from needing to create relationships with cities, counties, planning agencies, and the like. Park districts do not necessarily conform to traditional political boundaries such as cities and school districts. The Illinois Association of Park Districts (www.ilparks.org) has membership from 294 park districts, 9 forest preserve districts, 5 conservation districts, 25 special recreation associations, 25 city park and recreation agencies, 2 water conservancy districts, and 87 corporate members.[15]

County and Special Park District Programs

As an intermediate stage between state and incorporated local government agencies, county or special district park and recreation units provide large parks and other outdoor recreation resources as a primary function. They may also sponsor services for special populations; that is, programs for those aging or who have a disability, as well as services for all residents of the county, such as programs in the fine and performing arts.

During the early decades of the century, county governments had relatively limited functions. However, since World War II, the rapid growth of suburban populations around large cities has given many county governments new influence and power. Counties have become a base for coordinating and funneling numerous federal grants-in-aid programs. As a result, county park and recreation departments expanded rapidly.

Regional and Special Park Districts

Several states, including California, Illinois, Oregon, and North Dakota, have enabling legislation that permits the establishment of special park and recreation districts. Illinois has more than 300 such districts, including forest preserve and conservation districts. Other states with park and recreation districts include Ohio and Washington.

Many special recreation and park districts are in heavily populated areas; in some cases, they may encompass a number of independent, separate counties and municipalities in a single structure. Frequently, special park districts and counties are able to carry out vigorous programs of land acquisition in a combined effort, or to impose other means of protecting open space. Many counties enacted laws requiring home developers to set aside community recreation areas. Pennsylvania, for example, authorizes municipalities and counties to receive land from developers as "mandatory dedication" or other alternatives as outlined in the state code. Examples of alternatives include allowing the developer to pay a fee, making close-by park and recreation facilities accessible to development, construction of recreational facilities, or to privately reserve land within a subdivision for park and recreation purposes.[16]

Another common approach used by cities and counties to secure funds and lands is to require owners of new homes to pay an impact fee. The impact fee is based on the concept that current taxpayers should not have to pay for new development; it should be the responsibility of the new owner to pay for community improvements to the neighborhood. Park and recreation departments have been recipients of these funds. Some county governments are establishing permanently protected greenbelts to halt or lessen the tide of construction. Strengthened zoning policies and more flexible building codes that permit cluster zoning of homes with larger and more concentrated open spaces are also helpful.

Municipal Recreation and Park Departments

Municipal government is the term generally used to describe the local political unit of government, such as the village, town, or city, that is responsible for providing the bulk of direct community service such as street maintenance, police and fire protection, and education. Most areas depend on municipal government to provide many important recreation and park facilities and program opportunities, in addition to those provided by voluntary, private, and commercial agencies.

COUNTY PARK AGENCIES

County park systems across the United States are very common. King County, Washington, which includes Seattle, is representative of many county park agencies, with the majority of its efforts focused on natural resource management. Its mission is to foster environmental stewardship and strengthen communities by providing regional parks, protecting the region's water, air, land and natural habitats, and reducing, safely disposing of and creating resources from wastewater and solid waste.[17] King County Parks has evolved from a relatively small 150 acres in 1938 to over 32,000 acres in 2021, and includes 205 parks, 175 miles of regional trails, and 215 miles of backcountry trails. In addition to managing major natural resources, the system has had to change its approach to financing by becoming more entrepreneurial, increasing accountability for its operating budget, and establishing performance measures for the system and its employees.[17] County park systems across the United States are being challenged to develop new funding sources, become more efficient, and increase the use and effectiveness of partnerships.

With the widespread recognition of this responsibility, municipal recreation and park agencies expanded rapidly in the United States during the period following World War II, with a steady increase in the number of departments, amount of acreage in park and recreation areas, number of full- and part-time or seasonal personnel, and total expenditures.

Functions and Structure of Municipal Agencies

The most common structure for delivery of services is a combined parks and recreation department. In a few cases, parks and recreation may include other social service organizations such as libraries, assistance agencies, and the like. Some remain separate departments.

Other municipal agencies may also sponsor special leisure services that are linked to their own missions. They may include (1) police departments, which often operate youth service centers or leagues; (2) welfare departments or social service agencies, which may operate daycare centers or senior centers; (3) youth boards, which tend to focus on out-of-school youth or teen gangs; (4) health and hospital agencies, which sometimes operate community mental health centers or similar services; (5) public housing departments, which sometimes have recreation centers in their projects; (6) cultural departments or boards, which frequently sponsor performing arts programs or civic celebrations; and (7) school systems and local community colleges.

Programs of Municipal Agencies

Municipal recreation and parks departments operate programs within several categories of activity: games and sports, aquatics, outdoor and nature-oriented programs, arts and crafts, performing arts, special services, social programs, hobby groups, and other playground and community center activities.

In addition, public recreation and parks departments often sponsor large-scale special events such as holiday celebrations, festival programs, art and hobby shows, and sport tournaments. These departments also assist other community agencies to organize, publicize, and schedule activities. Frequently, sport programs for children and youth, such as Little League or American Legion baseball, are cosponsored by public departments and associations of interested parents who undertake much of the actual management of the activity, including coaching, fundraising, and scheduling. Similarly, many cultural programs, such as civic opera or little theater associations, are affiliated with and receive assistance from public recreation departments.

Varied Program Emphases

Cities tend to have common and unique emphases in their recreation and park operations. Henderson, Nevada, a city of over 310,000 residents, is an example of an established community and parks and recreation department that includes 4 year-round aquatic centers, 6 seasonal swimming pools, 8 multiuse recreation centers (including a senior center), 5 major outdoor sports parks, a bird preserve, 2 disc golf courses, and over 65 parks ranging from small vest-pocket parks to large parks, an outdoor events center and pavilion with an amphitheater, and a stand-alone convention center.[18]

Louisville, Kentucky, has a rich heritage of parks and recreation with major early developments in their park system designed by Frederick Law Olmsted and considered one of the four ultimate park systems of his career. Since that time Louisville has kept the Olmsted legacy alive with rich investment in park development and simultaneously developing a strong recreation system with community recreation centers, golf courses, athletic fields, historic properties, and recreation programs focusing on seniors, the arts, youth, athletics, programs for individuals with disabilities, summer camps, and the like.

FITNESS PROGRAMMING

Many cities have undertaken special programs to promote health, fitness, and sport. The Parks and Recreation Department in San Antonio, Texas, sponsors a broad range of programs under the title, "Fitness in the Parks," all of which are free. The variety of programs available includes Boot Camp, Circuit Training, Pediatrics in the Park, Mommy and Me Fitness, Body Combat, Zumba, Kettle Bell Conditioning, Yoga, Pilates, and many more. Classes target people of all ages, fitness levels, and ability levels, including those with disabilities. Some classes target specific groups such as seniors, expectant mothers, and youth. Beginning in 2011 the city focused on the installation of fitness equipment in parks and fitness programs. The project was a joint initiative of the mayor's fitness council, the city parks and recreation department, and the metropolitan health district.

CASE STUDY: The Next Generation of Urban Parks

Urban parks have been part of the American fabric since the creation of the Boston Common in the mid-17th century and New York's Central Park in the early 19th century. Each defined parks in different ways, but it was the ideal of Central Park that brought about the large urban park movement. A movement that has defined public parks for 175 years, it has been rethought, discussed, challenged, but remains the ideal for many communities.

With burgeoning populations, the resurgence of urban areas, the recognition that communities must rethink how they provide public parks, and the desire to ensure that green spaces are available to many, the concept of the urban park in the 21st century is receiving much attention.[a] Traditionally park and recreation professionals have led the discussion, but increasingly the push for change is coming from nonprofits, community organizations, and community members, all devoted to their communities. Within the past decade there have been some creative approaches to transforming city park access through greenway corridors, including the High Line in New York City, Klyde Warren Park in Dallas, Rail Park in Philadelphia, and The 606 in Chicago.

At a cost of $153 million, the High Line is a 1.5 mile linear park on a former railroad in lower Manhattan in the Chelsea neighborhood. Plagued by crime and other unsavory activities, in 1999 many people were calling the High Line an ugly eyesore but few of these critics saw what had secretly taken over the structure: a thriving garden of wild plants. Inspired by the beauty of this hidden landscape, Joshua David and Robert Hammond founded Friends of the High Line, a nonprofit conservancy, to advocate for its preservation and reuse as a public space. Friends of the High Line remains the sole group responsible for maintenance and operation of the High Line, raising millions each year through private donations that cover 90% of its costs. By 2003, Friends of the High Line hosted an "ideas competition," receiving 720 ideas from over 36 countries for ways the park might be used (including ideas that were neither realistic nor practical, like a rollercoaster or a mile-long lap pool). With strong support from then-Mayor Bloomberg and the City Council, a special zoning area was proposed: The West Chelsea Special District facilitated the use of the High Line as a public park. In 2009, 4 years after CSX Transportation donated ownership of the structure to the City of New York, and 3 years after first breaking ground (in April 2006), the first section of the High Line opened to the public from Gansevoort to 20th streets with two additional sections added since. The High Line is now one, continuous, 1.45-mile-long greenway featuring 500+ species of plants and trees. The park is maintained, operated, and programmed by Friends of the High Line in partnership with the New York City Department of Parks & Recreation.[b]

A 5.2-acre park situated over a freeway overpass. The Klyde Warren Park in Dallas connects part of uptown to the downtown Arts District. The $110 million price tag was partially paid through $20 million in bonds secured by the city, $20 million in state highway funds, and $16.7 million in stimulus dollars with the nonprofit group the Woodall Rodgers Park Foundation working tirelessly to secure private funds for continued support of the park. With plans to expand to an additional 1.2 acres, the park currently has walking trails, a dog park, and children's park.[c]

The Rail Park in Philadelphia has completed phase one at a cost of $11 million secured through private and public funding including a Redevelopment Assistance Capital Program Grant ($3.5 million), funding raised by the Friends of the Rail Park group, the City of Philadelphia, and multiple foundations. Built on an abandoned railroad line, the Reading Viaduct, two different nonprofit groups, the Reading Viaduct Project and Viaduct Greene, had been working independently to develop the area for recreational purposes. Merging in 2013 to become the Friends of the Rail Park, the two groups supported efforts that led to the completion of the first phase of the project, a quarter mile of trail that includes walking space, seating areas, and greenery while also highlighting the history of the railroad line.[d]

The story of The 606 in Chicago begins just after the Great Chicago Fire. In their efforts to rebuild the city, the Chicago City Council gave permission for the Chicago & Pacific Railroad to lay tracks down the middle of Bloomingdale Ave. on Chicago's Northwest side. Because of multiple conflicts between residents and the rail, in 1893 the City Council passed an ordinance mandating that railroads elevate their tracks. The embankments created by elevating the line are essentially enormous concrete bathtubs filled with soil, stones, and other drainage material, 7 feet thick at the base, the walls have proved sturdy for 100 years and form a firm foundation for the centerpiece of The 606, the Bloomingdale Trail. As activity on the line slowed to a trickle by the mid-1990s, the few trains that used the corridor were rerouted, and freight service ceased completely with the neighborhoods of Wicker Park, Bucktown, Humboldt Park, and Logan Square below and nature reclaimed the former rail line above. Official plans for converting the

Bloomingdale Line into a public space date back to the late 1990s, when it was included in the city's Bike Plan. In 2003, the city's Department of Planning and Development held a series of public meetings to determine how to bring new open space to the city's underserved Northwest side, forming the basis of what would become The 606. The 2004 Logan Square Open Space Plan called for an ambitious reuse of the former industrial rail corridor. An alliance among the Friends of the Bloomindale Trail, the City of Chicago, Chicago Park District, The Trust for Public Land, and dozens of groups generated the idea for the park and trail system. The system, which connects four Chicago neighborhoods serves both residents and visitors and is the signature project of Mayor Rahm Emanuel who had pushed for the creation of 800 new parks, recreation areas, and green spaces throughout Chicago.[e]

Crime reduction and greater access to recreation spaces are just two of the benefits of these types of parks. Although there is widespread support for urban park spaces, it is important to remember that with these greenways not all impacts are positive for all groups and issues of inclusion and equity need to be examined in order to gain a greater understanding of usage and impact. Although gentrification brought about by development of these green spaces and the resulting increases in property values are often seen as positive, they may at the same time force out the community members who had long called those parts of the community home. As parks and recreation professionals work to provide greater resources for community members, it is important to closely examine consequences of these changes, both intentional and unintentional.

Questions to Consider

- Does your community have an urban park or greenway?
- Would it benefit from an urban park or greenway? If so, how would it benefit?
- How could you help your community begin to think about creating or renewing its urban parks or revitalizing urban areas in a way that would offer more open space access to all community members?

[a] City Parks Alliance, Why City Parks Matter. Retrieved May 27, 2021, from https://cityparksalliance.org/about-us/why-city-parks-matter/
[b] High Line. Retrieved January 28, 2021, from https://thehighline.org.
[c] Klyde Warren Park. Retrieved January 28, 2021, from https://www.klydewarrenpark.org.
[d] Rail Park. Retrieved January 28, 2021, from https://www.centercityphila.org/ccd-services/streetscape/rail-park.
[e] The 606. Retrieved January 28, 2021, from https://www.the606.org/about.

Denver, Colorado, opened its first truly urban recreation facility in 2018 at a cost of $44 million. Named after a community advocate who had recently died, the Carla Madison Recreation Center has 67,000 square feet of space and houses such amenities as an indoor leisure and lap pools for recreation and competitive purposes, a large fitness/training area, a multicourt gymnasium, multipurpose classrooms, a childcare/toddler area, a rooftop deck for rental, and a large group exercise room.[19] From the opposite end of the spectrum, White Pine County, Nevada—the 17th largest county by area (8,897 square miles) and with a population of 10,000, opened a new aquatic facility in Ely, in 2013. It was the first new facility in decades, and focuses on serving the population with a variety of aquatic recreation and fitness activities. Rural counties frequently struggle to provide recreation and park services to their residents.[20]

HUMAN SERVICE FUNCTIONS

Many local recreation and park agencies have moved vigorously into the area of programming to meet human and social service needs. The Recreation and Human Services Department of the city of Gardena, California, for example, offers many services, including youth services; individual, family, and group counseling; tutoring workshops; alcohol and drug abuse programs; after-school activities; licensed family childcare; youth and adult counseling; senior citizen outreach and meals programming; and care for those suffering from Alzheimer's or mental disease.

Exercise classes are frequently offered at local recreation centers.
© iStockphoto/Thinkstock/Getty Images.

A trend of the last 2 decades has been to develop multiservice departments in which recreation and park programs play a leading role. Thus, a merged department of community services might have responsibility for beaches, parking meters, special housing units, libraries, and other special public facilities or programs. Larger urban recreation and park departments may include management responsibilities for stadiums, convention centers, piers and marinas, or even municipal airports.

Fee-Based Programs

In response to government efforts to become more business oriented, including seeking expanded revenue sources, fee-based programs have gained popularity with recreation and park departments. The trend toward imposing substantial fees for many program elements or facilities membership in public recreation and parks is firmly established. Those who favor it argue that it provides a logical means of developing rich programs and services and strengthens the role of the recreation and agency in community life. As tax revenues available for recreation and parks continue to decline, many agencies find fee-based programs a survival tool. Other agencies have implemented fee-based programs to offer services that would otherwise not be available through government funding.

Some critics argue that placing heavy reliance on fee structures discriminates against children and youth, people who are elderly, persons with disabilities, and poor people, who cannot afford to pay significant fees for participation in public recreation programs. As such, it represents a retreat from the fundamental mission of public recreation and leisure programs. In some cases, cities or other public recreation and park agencies have provided fee discounts, "scholarships," or variable pricing policies to enable partici-

pation by poorer families. Although such policies are generally acceptable in well-to-do towns or suburban areas, they are obviously not workable in socially and economically disadvantaged inner-city neighborhoods or in less affluent communities. Some cities developed models in which they assess the social priority that should be attached to recreation facilities or programs and base fee-charging policies on this assessment.

Innovative Developments in Larger Cities

Problems related to inadequate budgets, increasing crime, and declining infrastructure and maintenance services tend to be most severe in older cities with limited public, nonprofit, and commercial leisure resources—yet, even in these communities, recreation and park administrators are working to expand and improve leisure facilities, programs, and maintenance. In 2014, Seattle, Washington, residents approved the creation of the Seattle Park District with funding coming from property taxes. The park district was a response, in part, to the need for a more stable funding source for parks. In 2016, the first full year of funding, a $47 million budget was proposed for operations and capital improvements; by 2020, the total funds approved from the park district was $53 million out of the total budget for Seattle Parks and Recreation of $262 million. Like many American cities, funding for maintenance of parks and recreation facilities has not kept up with maintenance demands and expectations. When maintenance is not performed because of lack of funding it is called "deferred maintenance." Deferred maintenance can become an overwhelming budget and operations issue for an organization with limited fiscal resources. The long-term capital budget (funds dedicated to major projects over several years) has targeted $48 million for "Fix it First" deferred projects with $17 million from the park district fund.[21]

Aquatic centers with a variety of amenities have become popular year-round activities incorporated into public park and recreation agencies, commercial enterprises, and resorts.

Courtesy of Amy Hurd.

City parks allow residents to enjoy leisure time relaxing in open spaces.

© Siri Stafford/Lifesize/Thinkstock/Getty Images.

In addition to maintenance operations, construction of new facilities, and renovation of facilities, the Seattle Park District has set targets to improve community member experiences in community centers; create partnerships to provide more recreation opportunities; place a focus on enhancing arts in the parks through public performances and events; focus on programming for older adults as well as young people; and to meet the needs of persons with disabilities. An additional source of creative funding for some of these projects comes from a municipal tax on sweetened beverages that provided a total of $600,000 in funding in 2020.[22]

Along with such environmental and marketing-based efforts, many municipal recreation and park agencies also have moved vigorously in the direction of benefits-based programming as a means of documenting and providing direction to their overall services.

CASE STUDY: How Are Public Parks and Recreation Funded?

Funding public parks and recreation is very different from operating a private enterprise. Governments are run by elected decision-makers and federal, state, and local elected legislators, county officials, and city councils who enact laws and ordinances within bounds set by state governments for funding parks and recreation. Funding for public parks and recreation can come from multiple sources, including the community, county, state, or federal levels. This creates a complicated approach to achieve an adequate level of funding for public agencies. Parks and recreation rarely has its own funding base and is more likely in competition with other city, county, or state agencies for the local revenue sources. For the purposes of this case study, the four primary sources of income for a public agency (e.g., a city or county) are compulsory income, earned income, contractual receipts, and partnerships and collaborations. Compulsory income includes funds governments secure from taxes, licensing, or other sorts of government instituted income sources. The most common compulsory income includes property taxes, sales tax, and state and/or local income taxes. Other frequently used sources of compulsory income include special assessment taxes such as for street or sewer construction but can also include parks and recreation development, dedication ordinances where a specific geographic area of the community is taxed such as a new housing development, which is taxed for the creation of a neighborhood park. Earned income includes cash revenues generated from fees and charges instituted by the public organization. These can include admission fees, program fees, entrance fees, charges for use of area and facilities, income from sales of supplies and equipment, gift shop sales, rental fees, and special user fees. Contractual receipts are funds generated from legal agreements with private and nonprofit organizations. Agreements can include the management of public properties (such as a tennis center), rental of facilities, rental of equipment, management of special operations (such as golf course, an indoor facility, or a marina). Partnerships and collaborations are agreements between two or more organizations who chose to work for a mutual goal. The partnership can be for a fixed or indeterminate length of time. The success of a partnership is dependent upon each organization clearly understanding and identifying their needs. In contrast, a collaboration is where organizations work together to achieve the common goal but may not have the same vision, resources, or risks.

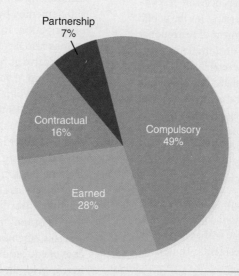

FIGURE 6-1 Example revenue sources for municipal park and recreation department

A public agency uses all of the sources of income to varying degrees. Figure 6-1 depicts an example of revenue sources, contribution to the revenue budget. For example, compulsory income is a primary source of income for all public agencies but is rarely present in the nonprofit sector. Earned income is an essential source of income to public park and recreation agencies and includes fees for classes, golf course fees, admission fees to swimming pools or other facilities, membership fees, and much more. It has become a key source of income for public agencies as tax dollars are not sufficient to meet public demands. Contractual receipts are common for almost all agencies but vary in the importance of operations. For example, some communities have negotiated contracts with for profit or nonprofit organizations to manage golf courses, recreation centers, aquatic centers, and programs and services. Partnerships and collaborations focus on working with other organizations in sharing costs and resources to achieve a common goal, such as a special event (a sporting event, cultural event, or community event). Partnerships allow public, commercial, and nonprofit organizations to work together to meet community needs.

Public agencies construct their annual budget based on anticipated sources of income. For example, compulsory income typically is the single largest source followed by earned income and contractual receipts. Partnerships may or may not involve income. A budget might include 40% compulsory income, 36% earned income, and 24% contractual. Within the broad classes of income there are many different sources and will vary from state to state. Budgeting for public parks and recreation is a complex mix of different local sources of income with the occasional addition of state and federal funds. Increasingly, public parks and recreation has relied less on tax dollars (compulsory income) for operations and increasingly on noncompulsory income sources.

Questions to Consider

- Select a community or county park and recreation agency and explore its income sources. What is its balance of income sources? You should be able to find this on their website.
- Do the same process for a nonprofit organization, which will have no compulsory sources of income. This will be available on their website or possibly from the local United Way.
- Find a partnership between a public agency and/or a private company, nonprofit, or another public agency. Identify the goals and outcomes for each agency, and if possible, the financial commitment each agency made to the partnership.
- Explain how the four income sources complement each other.

Data from Brayley, R. E., & McLean, D. D. (2008). *Managing financial resources in sport, tourism, and leisure services.* Sagamore Publishing.

Nonprofit Organizations: Organizing the Voluntary Sector

Whereas government recreation and park agencies are responsible for providing a floor of basic leisure services for the public throughout the United States, a major segment of recreational opportunities is sponsored by nonprofit organizations, often called *voluntary agencies.* These consist of several different types of youth-serving, special-interest, and charitable organizations.

Organizations in this category may be completely independent or may be part of national or regional federations. Often they are described as "quasi-public" or "public/private." In some cases, they must meet government-imposed standards as charitable organizations to retain tax-exempt status. They tend to share the following characteristics:

- Usually established to meet significant social needs through organized citizen cooperation, community organizations represent the voluntary wishes and expressed needs of neighborhood residents. Thus, they are voluntary in origin.
- Governing boards of directors or trustees are usually public-spirited citizens who accept such responsibilities as a form of social obligation; thus, membership and administrative control are voluntary.

- For funding, voluntary agencies usually rely on public contributions, either directly to the agency itself or to Community Chest, United Way, or similar shared fundraising efforts. Contributed funds are usually supplemented by membership fees and charges for participation. In recent years, many voluntary organizations also have undertaken special projects for which they receive government funding.
- Leadership of voluntary agencies is partly professional and partly voluntary. Management is usually by directors and supervisors professionally trained in social work, recreation, education, or other related areas. At other levels, leadership is by nonprofessionals, part-time or seasonal personnel, and volunteers.
- In some cases, nonprofit organizations in the overall leisure-services system do not sponsor recreation activities directly but rather represent organizations that do or that manufacture equipment or provide services, often on a for-profit basis. However, as in the case of educational institutions or professional societies in this field, they are nonprofit and tax exempt.

Nonprofit voluntary agencies regard recreation as part of their total spectrum of services rather than their sole function. Typically, they recognize the importance of creative and constructive leisure and see recreation as a threshold activity that serves to attract participants to their agencies. In addition, they see it as a means of achieving significant social goals, such as building character among youth, reducing social pathology, enriching educational experience, strengthening community unity, and similar objectives. In general, even though voluntary agencies do not describe themselves as recreation agencies, this often tends to be the largest single component in their programs.

Nonprofits rely on volunteers for much of their work. Americans provide more volunteer service than any other society. In 2018, 77.3 million people, or 30.3% of all Americans, volunteered to serve organizations or other programs. Parents volunteer 48% more than nonparents with working moms logging the highest rate at 46.7%. Generation X volunteers at the highest rate at 36.4% although baby boomers give more time at 2.2 billion hours a year. Who are they volunteering for? Religious groups top the list (32%) followed by sports or arts (25.7%), and education or youth-serving groups (20%).[23]

Nonprofit But Fee Charging

Many voluntary organizations, though they are nonprofit and interested in meeting important social goals, may charge substantial fees. For example, Y's (formerly known as Young Men's Christian Associations or YMCAs) or Young Women's Christian Associations (YWCAs) in suburban areas are likely to have fees that are as high as several hundred dollars a year for full family memberships and charge impressive sums for varied program activities. However, such fees are intended simply to help the organization maintain financial stability, without making a profit, and are frequently used to subsidize other services to marginalized populations who cannot afford to pay fees for membership or participation.

Because of the word *voluntary*, some assume incorrectly that such agencies are staffed solely by volunteer workers. The reality is that, although some nonprofit organizations such as the Boy Scouts and Girl Scouts rely heavily on volunteer leaders, most of them have full-time, paid professionals in their key management or supervisory posts.

It was estimated in 2016 that nonprofit organizations employed 10.2% of working Americans, involving 12.3 million paid workers.[24] Salaries for professional employees of nonprofits such as the Boy Scouts and Girl Scouts, the Y and YWCA, Junior Achievement, and Big Brothers/Big Sisters of America all have risen steadily in recent years.

Types of Nonprofit Youth-Serving Agencies

Although voluntary nonprofit organizations fit under many headings—including the arts, education, health, and social service—the largest segment of such groups with strong

recreational components is generally youth oriented. Included in this segment are the following:

- Nonsectarian youth-serving organizations
- Religiously affiliated youth-serving or social agencies
- Special-interest organizations in such fields as sport, outdoor recreation, and travel
- Conservation and outdoor recreation
- Organizations promoting youth sports and games
- Arts councils and cultural organizations
- Service and federal clubs
- Promotional and coordinating bodies

Nonsectarian Youth-Serving Organizations

Nationally structured organizations that function directly through local branches, nonsectarian youth-serving groups have broad goals related to social development and good citizenship and operate extensive programs of recreational activity. There are hundreds of such organizations. Many of them are junior affiliates of adult organizations, whereas others are independent. Sponsorship is by such varied bodies as civic and fraternal organizations, veterans' clubs, rural and farm organizations, and business clubs. Several examples follow.

BOY SCOUTS OF AMERICA

Founded in the United States in 1910, the Boy Scouts of America is a powerful and widespread organization. In 2018, its youth membership consisted of 2.2 million youth, ranging from Tiger Cubs to Explorers with a total of 262 councils. Together with adult leaders, a total of 3.2 million were involved in Boy Scouts of America.[25] In addition to its membership in the United States, Boy Scouts of America is part of a worldwide scouting movement involving more than 100 other countries. The program emphasizes mental and physical fitness, vocational and social development, and the enrichment of youth hobbies and prevocational interests, relying heavily on adventure and scouting skills and service activities.

The Boy Scouts of America has been regarded as a middle-class organization in U.S. society and as a small town or suburban rather than a big city phenomenon. As the urban environment has changed, so has scouting's impact among youth living in large metropolitan areas and among diverse populations. For example, scouting has special focus programs for African American, Asian American, and American Indian groups. In addition, they have developed multicultural partnerships.

GIRL SCOUTS OF THE UNITED STATES OF AMERICA

The largest voluntary organization serving girls in the world, the Girl Scouts of the United States of America is open to girls between the ages of 5 and 17 who subscribe to its ideals as stated in the Girl Scout Promise and Law. It is part of a worldwide association of girls and adults in more than 90 countries through its membership in the World Association of Girl Guides and Girl Scouts. Its membership in 2018 consisted of 1.7 million members and 750,000 adults, including volunteers, board members, and staff specialists.[26]

Founded in 1912, the Girl Scouts provides a sequential program of activities centered around the arts, the home, and the outdoors, with emphasis on character and citizenship development, community service, international understanding, and health and safety. Senior Girl Scouts in particular may take on responsibilities in hospitals, museums, childcare, or environmental programs. Like the Boy Scouts of America, the Girl Scouts today conducts special programs for the poor; those with physical, emotional, or other disabilities; and similar populations.

BOYS AND GIRLS CLUBS OF AMERICA

The Boys and Girls Clubs movement is the fastest-growing youth-serving organization in the United States today. Originally composed of two separate organizations, the merged club movement holds a U.S. congressional charter and is endorsed by 21 leading service, fraternal, civic, veteran, labor, and business organizations. Today, the Boys and Girls Clubs movement serves almost 4 million youth members in more than 4,100 club locations with a staff of 67,000 full-time trained professionals and more than 239,000 adult volunteers. Its members are from underrepresented populations (70%), 6–9 years old (36%), 10–12 years old (30%),

The Girl Scouts are involved in their local communities through a variety of community service activities.
Used by permission of Girl Scouts of the United States of America.

and 13 and older (29%), and are closely equal gender wise.[27] Programs include sport and games, arts and crafts, social activities, and camping, as well as remedial education, work training, and job placement and counseling. The national goals of the Boys and Girls Clubs of America include the following: citizenship education and leadership development; health, fitness, and preparation for leisure; educational vocational motivation; intergroup understanding and value development; and enrichment of both family and community life.

With the help of special funding from corporations, foundations, and government agencies, the organization has developed program curricula for several key projects in the social services area. Although each club is an independent organization with its own board and professional staff, the national headquarters and seven regional offices provide essential services to local clubs in such areas as personnel recruitment and management training, program research and development, fundraising and public relations, and building design and construction assistance.

POLICE ATHLETIC LEAGUES

In hundreds of communities today, law enforcement agencies sponsor Police Athletic Leagues (PALs). Operating in poverty areas, the league programs rely primarily on civilian staffing and voluntary contributions for support, although they sometimes receive technical assistance from officers on special assignment from cooperative municipal police departments. In a few cities, police officers provide the bulk of full-time professional leadership in PAL programs. PALs typically provide extensive recreation programming, indoor centers, and summer play streets, with strong emphasis on sport and games, creative arts, drum and bugle corps, and remedial education. Many leagues also maintain placement, counseling, and job training programs and assist youth who have dropped out of school.

The PAL is one of the few youth organizations that continues to have resisting juvenile delinquency as a primary thrust. One of its principal purposes has been to promote favorable relationships between young people and the police in urban settings, and it has been markedly successful in this effort. Like other voluntary agencies, PALs rely on varied funding sources, including the United Way, independent fundraising campaigns, contracts with government, and often partial police department sponsorship.

BEST BUDDIES

Established in 1989 by Anthony Kennedy Shriver, Best Buddies focuses on creating one-to-one friendships, integrated employment, and leadership development for people with intellectual and developmental disabilities.[28] The program currently has chapters on more than 1,800 middle school, high school, and college campuses across the United States. There are six programs focusing on bringing one-to-one relationships to people with intellectual and developmental disabilities with community members. The programs include Best Buddies Citizens, including the corporate and civic communities; Best Buddies Colleges; High Schools; Middle Schools; Best Buddies Jobs with supported employment; and e-Buddies focusing on an email pen pal program.

Best Buddies Massachusetts and Rhode Island, an example state chapter, has an active program including participants and fundraising. In 2019, for example, its events included the Sweat for Inclusion group workout and in 2020 numerous virtual events included a prom and Halloween dance as well as numerous golf tournaments. [29] As with most nonprofits, there is a mix of activities for participants and fundraising to secure funding for operation of the program.

Religiously Affiliated Youth-Serving or Social Agencies

Many religious organizations sponsor youth programs with recreational components today, including activities sponsored by local churches or synagogues and activities sponsored by national federations that are affiliated with a particular denomination.

Recreation programs provided by local churches or synagogues tend to have two broad purposes: (1) to sponsor recreation for their own members or congregations to meet their leisure needs in ways that promote involvement with the institution and (2) to provide leisure opportunities for the community at large or for a selected population group in ways that are compatible with their own religious beliefs. Typical activities offered by individual churches and synagogues may include the following:

- Day camps, play schools, or summer Bible schools, which include recreation along with religious instruction
- Year-round recreation activities for families, including picnics, outings, bazaars, covered dish suppers, carnivals, single-adult clubs, dances, game nights, and similar events
- Programs in the fine and performing arts, including innovative worship programs involving dance and folk music
- Fellowship programs for various age levels, including discussion groups on religious and other themes
- Varied special-interest or social service programs, including daycare centers for children, senior citizens clubs or golden age groups, and recreation programs for persons with disabilities
- Sport activities, including bowling and basketball leagues, or other forms of instructional or competitive participation

On a broader level, such organizations as the Y, YWCA, the Catholic Youth Organization (CYO), and the Young Men's

Nonprofit organizations such as the Y provide important services for members, including fitness programs.
© muzsy/Shutterstock.

and Young Women's Hebrew Association (YM-YWHA) provide a network of facilities and programs with diversified recreation, education, and youth service activities. Although their titles include the words *young* or *youth*, they tend to serve a broad range of children, youth, adult, and aging members.

THE Y AND YWCA

Voluntary organizations affiliated with Protestantism in general rather than with any single denomination, both the Y and YWCA are devoted to the promotion of religious ideals of living, and view themselves as worldwide fellowships "dedicated to the enrichment of life through the development of Christian character and a Christian society." However, the actual membership of both associations is multireligious and multiracial. In 2020, there were 2,700 Ys with 22 million members in 10,000 communities, making it one of the largest nonprofits providing recreation. There were an additional 600,000 volunteers and 20,000 full time staff.[30]

In many communities, the Y offers facilities and leadership for indoor aquatics, sport and games, physical fitness, social and cultural programs, and family-centered programs. These activities are usually aggressively marketed and bring in substantial revenues. Both the Y and YWCA derive funding from varied sources: membership fees, corporate and private contributions through the United Way, fundraising drives, and government and foundation grants.

MUSLIM YOUTH GROUPS

There is no single national organization providing leadership for Muslim youth groups; rather, multiple groups are providing leadership, all with partial or total emphasis on youth. These include the Islamic Society of North America, Muslim American Society, and Young Muslims. The Islamic Society of North America (ISNA) provides information on aging, domestic violence, matrimony, leadership, and youth.

There are Muslim youth groups concentrated in local communities and regions. The Islamic Center of Southern California, for example, provides an educational, social, spiritual, and moral environment, and physical activities to motivate young American Muslims to live by and serve Islam and to identify themselves as Muslims, creating a nurturing learning environment in which a basic core knowledge of Islam is provided. In addition, they encourage education, self-expression, the creation of a social environment to build healthy interaction, and foster an American Muslim identity.

Catholic Youth Organization

The leading Catholic organization concerned with providing spiritual, social, and recreational services for young people in the United States is the CYO. CYO originated in the early 1930s, when a number of dioceses under the leadership of Bishop Sheil of Chicago began experimenting with varied forms of youth organizations. It was established as a national organization in 1951 as a component of the National Council of Catholic Youth. Today, the National CYO Federation has an office in Washington, DC, as well as many citywide or diocesan offices. The parish, however, is the core of the CYO, which depends heavily on the leadership of parish priests and the services of adult volunteers from the neighborhood for direction and assistance.

Young Men's and Young Women's Hebrew Association

Today, there are more than 275 YM-YWHAs, Jewish Community Centers, and camps serving more than 1 million members throughout the United States. Like the Ys and YWCAs, the Jewish Ys do not regard themselves primarily as recreation agencies but rather as community organizations devoted to social service and having a strong Jewish

Ethnic background affects the types of activities individuals participate in but does not diminish participation.

© Robert Kneschke/Shutterstock.

cultural component. Specifically, the YM-YWHA has defined its mission in the following way:

- To meet the leisure-time social, cultural, and recreational needs of its membership, embracing both sexes and all age groups
- To stimulate individual growth and personality development by encouraging interest and capacity for group and community participation
- To teach leadership responsibility and democratic process through group participation
- To encourage citizenship education and responsibility among its members and, as a social welfare agency, to participate in community-wide programs of social betterment

Special-Interest Organizations

Numerous other types of voluntary nonprofit organizations can best be classified as special-interest groups, concerned with promoting a particular area of activity or social concern. Their functions may include leadership training, public relations, lobbying and legislation, establishing national standards or operational policies, or the direct sponsorship of program activities. Special-interest organizations may be free of commercial involvement or may represent manufacturers of equipment, owners of facilities, schools, or other businesses that seek to stimulate public interest and support and, ultimately, to improve their own business success.

Conservation and Outdoor Recreation

Numerous nonprofit organizations seek to educate the public and influence governmental policies in the areas of conservation and outdoor recreation. In some cases, they lobby, conduct research, and sponsor conferences and publications. In others, their primary thrust is to mount projects and carry out direct action on state or local levels.

Sierra Club

Founded in 1892, Sierra Club was headed initially by the famous naturalist John Muir with an original focus on the conservation of the California's Sierra Nevada mountains. "Since then, the Sierra Club has evolved into an organization that works to advance climate solutions and ensure everyone has access to clean air, clean water, and a healthy environment."[31] The Sierra Club has gained an international focus, emphasizing issues of global warming and the effects of recent disasters such as the tsunami in south Asia and Hurricane Katrina. Its activities are not restricted to conservation; it is also the nation's largest skiing and hiking club, operating a major network of ski lodges and "river runners," numerous wilderness outings, and ecological group projects.

Appalachian Mountain Club

This organization has a regional focus and is the oldest outdoor recreation and conservation organization. At its core,

"AMC promotes the protection, enjoyment, and understanding of the mountaints, forest, waters, and trails of the Northeast outdoors."[32] Since its inception, it has explored and mapped many of the wildest and most scenic areas in Massachusetts, New Hampshire, and Maine, in addition to promoting such sports as skiing, snowshoeing, mountain climbing, and canoeing.

Although practical conservation remains a primary concern of the club, it also has acquired various camp properties, published guides and maps, and maintained hundreds of miles of trails and a network of huts and shelters throughout the White Mountains for use by its members. It promotes programs of instruction and leadership training in such activities as snowshoeing, skiing, smooth and whitewater canoeing, and rock climbing.

Outdoor Leadership Programs

A number of other national nonprofit organizations teach outdoor leadership skills and promote sound environmental practices in the wilderness. The National Outdoor Leadership School sponsors a variety of courses in backpacking, mountaineering, rock climbing, sea kayaking, and other outdoor adventure activities in settings throughout the western states, Alaska, and such foreign countries as Australia, Mexico, Argentina, Chile, and Kenya. Outward Bound uses five core programs for character development and self-discovery through challenge and adventure. Initiated in the early 1960s, early programs trained the first Peace Corps volunteers. Since that time it has become a worldwide organization providing training and experiences to more than 500,000 people. The Association for Experiential Education is a professional membership association focusing on experiential education for students, educators, and practitioners. It provides program resources, a national conference, and accreditation for environmental education sites.

Organizations Promoting Youth Sport and Games

There are thousands of national, regional, and local organizations promoting and regulating sport of every kind. Although many of these govern professional play or high-level intercollegiate competition, others are concerned with sports and games on a purely amateur basis. One example of such an organization is Little League.

Founded in Williamsport, Pennsylvania, in 1939, Little League International is the largest youth sports program in the world today. In its various leagues, including softball, it serves more than 2 million players in more than 80 countries. In 2020, there were about 6,500 organized leagues.[33] Vietnam was one of the most recent nations initiating a Little League program. Before the Little League Baseball World Series, up to 16,000 tournament games are played in a 6-week time frame. Little League operates an impressive

Nonprofits, art centers, and civic organizations offer art classes.
© Layland Masuda/Shutterstock.

headquarters complex and stadium in Williamsport, where camps, conferences, and the annual World Series are held. It has standardized rules of play, requirements for financial operation and fee structures, insurance coverage, approved equipment, and other arrangements for member leagues and teams. Little League also conducts research into youth sport and carries out a great variety of training programs for league officials, district administrators, umpires, managers, and coaches, as well as a series of publications.

Youth sports in general are assisted by national organizations that set standards and promote effective, values-oriented coaching approaches, such as the National Alliance for Youth Sports and the Positive Coaching Alliance. Examples of organizations that are particularly concerned with individual sport include Youth Basketball of America, the Young American Bowling Alliance, and the United States Tennis Association (USTA). The latter organization has mounted a vigorous campaign to promote tennis to children and youth through the schools and public recreation agencies. USTA has awarded more than $4 million to support community park and recreation tennis programs.

Arts Councils and Cultural Organizations

Another major area of activity for voluntary agencies is the arts. In addition to nonprofit schools and art centers that offer painting, drawing, sculpture, and similar programs, there are literally thousands of civic organizations that sponsor or present performing arts. These include symphony orchestras, bands of various types, choral societies, opera or operetta companies, little theater groups, ballet and modern dance companies, and similar bodies.

In many communities, special-interest organizations in the arts are coordinated or assisted by umbrella agencies that help to promote their joint efforts. The Pasadena Arts Council was the first umbrella organization chartered in California. It provides a number of services to its members and the community, including a resource guide for artists, a business center for artists and new arts organizations, an information clearinghouse, networking events, financial sponsorship, an arts calendar, and a bimonthly publication. The Pasadena Arts Council efforts are similar to those in communities across the United States.

Service and Fraternal Clubs

Another category of nonprofit organizations that provide recreation for their own membership and sponsor programs for other population groups is community service clubs and fraternal organizations.

These include service clubs such as the Kiwanis, Lions, or Rotary clubs, which represent the business and professional groups in the community and which have as their purpose the improvement of the business environment and contributing to social well-being. A number of organizations established specifically for women, such as the Association of Junior Leagues, the General Federation of Women's Clubs, and the Business and Professional Women's Club, have similar goals.

The goals of such groups may include publicizing environmental concerns or issues, promoting the arts and other cultural activities, helping disadvantaged children and youth, and providing programs for persons with disabilities. For example, many Kiwanis organizations are involved in providing camping programs for special populations.

Promotional and Coordinating Bodies

A final type of nonprofit organization in the recreation, parks, and leisure-services field consists of associations that serve to promote, publicize, or coordinate activities within a given recreational field. In bowling, for example, the American Bowling Congress is composed of thousands of individuals whose careers or livelihoods depend on bowling and who therefore seek to promote and guide the sport as aggressively as possible, including setting standards and regulations and sponsoring a range of major tournaments each year.

There are hundreds of such nonprofit organizations in the fields of travel, tourism, entertainment, and hospitality, covering the range from associations of theme park or waterpark management to associations of tour directors or cruise ship operators. As an example, the Outdoor Amusement Business Association works to upgrade standards and services throughout the carnival and outdoor show industry. Its membership consists chiefly of manufacturers and distributors of trailers, tents and tarps, games supplies, and similar materials, as well as operators of many different kinds of traveling shows, concessions, and carnivals. Similarly, the International Association of Amusement Parks and Attractions conducts market studies, publishes standards and guidelines, and sponsors huge conventions

and trade shows for thousands of companies worldwide in the tourism, entertainment, and amusement field. The World Waterpark Association assists waterparks with trend analysis, customer satisfaction, business skills, training, publications related to the waterpark industry, and an annual trade show.

Within local communities, there are often several types of coordinating groups that serve to exchange information, conduct studies, identify priorities, develop planning reports, provide technical assistance, train leadership, and organize events related to recreation and leisure. In some cases, these include councils of social agencies, including religious, healthcare, youth-serving, and social work groups.

Commercial Recreation

We now turn to the type of recreation sponsor that provides the largest variety of leisure opportunities in the United States today—commercial, profit-oriented businesses. Such organizations have proliferated in recent years, running the gamut from small "mom-and-pop" operations to franchised programs and services; large-scale networks of health and fitness clubs, theme parks, hotels, and casino businesses; manufacturers of games, toys, and hobby equipment; and various other entertainment ventures.

The Nature of Commercial Recreation

Commercial recreation focuses on the retail provision of recreation opportunities for individuals. The retail orientation suggests that recreation enterprise has a goal of generating a profit for its owners.

The profit motive distinguishes a recreation business from any other type of leisure-services sponsor. Although public or voluntary agencies may charge for their services and may seek to clear a profit on individual program elements—or at least to run them on a self-sustaining basis where possible—their overall purpose is to meet important community or social needs. However, the commercial recreation organization has as a primary thrust the need to show a profit on the overall operation. Without commercial businesses that provide a host of important and high-quality leisure experiences, our recreational opportunities would be sharply diminished.

Commercial recreation sponsors today have the following characteristics: (1) they must constantly seek to identify and capitalize on recreational interests that are on the rise to ensure a constant or growing level of participation; (2) they are flexible and independent in their programmatic decisions and are not subject to the policy strictures of a city or town council or an agency board of trustees; (3) they constantly seek to promote and create experiences by packaging a product that will appeal to the public, by systematic marketing research, and by creative advertising and public relations; and

Amusement parks are a growth industry serving millions of people annually.
© Edwin Verin/Shutterstock.

(4) to be successful, they depend on effective entrepreneurship—a creative and aggressive approach to management that is willing to take risks to make gains.

Some of the most significant, creative, and cutting-edge facilities are provided by commercial recreation. Amusement parks, waterparks, mega-theaters, speedways, and sports stadiums may be the first to come to mind, but commercial recreation is present in almost every community. It may be the local dance studio, the combative-arts studio, or a crafts store that offers classes. Enterprises large and small continue to flourish in most communities. Quilt stores regularly have a room full of sewing machines, longarm quilting machines, and the like, and classes are full. Stop by the Arthur Murray Dance Studio (arthurmurray.com) and see more full classes. Slot car tracks exist in many communities, as well as hobby shops, scuba shops, skydiving enterprises, tour buses, family recreation centers—the list could go on for pages. These commercial enterprises, regardless of their size, stay in business because they meet a need for recreation participation. It is not uncommon for commercial recreation enterprises to partner with public and nonprofit agencies.

Categories of Service

Commercial recreation services may be classified under several major headings, including the following:

- Admission to facilities, either for self-directed participation (as in the use of a rented tennis court, an ice skating rink, or a billiard parlor) or for participation with some degree of supervision, instruction, or scheduling (as in admission to a ski center with use of a ski tow).
- Organized instruction in individual leisure activities or areas of personal enrichment, such as classes in arts and crafts, music, dance, or other hobbies.
- Membership in a commercially operated club, such as a for-profit tennis, golf, or boat club.

- Provision of hospitality or social contacts, ranging from hotels and resorts to bars, casinos, singles clubs, or dating services, which may use computers, videotaping, telephone contacts, or other means to help clients meet each other. At the socially less acceptable end of this spectrum of services are escort services, massage parlors, and sexually oriented telephone conversation operations.
- Arranged tours or cruises, domestic or foreign, which may consist solely of travel arrangements or which may also include a full package of travel, housing accommodations, meals, special events, side trips, and guide services.
- Commercial manufacture, sale, and service of recreation-related equipment, including sport supplies, electronic products, boats, off-road vehicles, toys, games, and hobby equipment.
- Entertainment and special events, such as theater, rock concerts, circuses, rodeos, and other such activities, when they are sponsored by a for-profit business, rather than a nonprofit, tax-exempt group.

Several of these types of commercial recreation businesses are described in the concluding section of this chapter. Others, such as sport and games and travel and tourism, are presented elsewhere in the text.

Family Entertainment Centers

Another recently evolved for-profit recreation enterprise includes family entertainment centers that combine children's play activities and equipment, video games, and other computerized activities with refreshments.

These businesses developed as an outgrowth of such "kiddie exercise" programs as Gymboree, which expanded as franchised chains that were usually situated in shopping malls. Family fun centers such as Malibu Grand Prix broadened their appeal, by adding more family-slanted activities, such as miniature golf, bumper cars, video games, and other indoor games, and packaged them with fast food options such as pizza, hot dogs, and soft drinks for birthday party and other group visits.

Theme Parks, Waterparks, and Marine and Wildlife Parks

Closely linked to the growth of tourism as a form of recreation has been the expansion of theme parks such as California's famous Disneyland. This major entertainment complex was built at a cost of more than $50 million in the 1950s and covers 65 acres in Anaheim, California. Its success led to the construction of a second major Disney complex, Walt Disney World, at Lake Buena Vista, Florida, and ultimately 11 parks worldwide by 2016.

Growing with the amusement park industry is the International Association of Amusement Parks and Attractions (IAAPA). Started in 1918, it now boasts more than 4,500 members from 93 countries and is the largest organization in the world that supports amusement parks. Its membership is associated with some areas of the amusement park industry. They include family entertainment centers, large parks and theme parks, museums, waterparks, zoos and aquariums, resorts, hotels, and casinos, small parks and attractions, and manufacturers and suppliers. IAAPA has an international perspective, hosting three international trade shows: one each in Europe, Asia, and the Americas. Each is called an *Attractions Expo* with content focusing on the industry, management, safety, education, marketing, operations, and products.

The list of top 10 performing amusement parks worldwide by yearly visitors, in 2018, helps demonstrate how large this marketplace is and the dominance of the Disney brand:

- Magic Kingdom (Florida)—20,559,000
- Disneyland (California)—18,666,000
- Tokyo Disneyland (Japan)—17,907,000
- Universal Studios (Japan)—14,300,000
- Tokyo Disney Sea (Japan)—14,651,000
- Disney's Animal Kingdom (Florida)—13.750,000
- EPCOT (Florida)—12,444,000
- Shanghai Disneyland (China)– 11,800,000
- Disney's Hollywood Studios (Florida)—11,258,000
- Chimelong Ocean Kingdom (China)—10,830,000[34]

EXPANSION OF DISNEY ENTERTAINMENT EMPIRE

None of the other chains of theme parks or outdoor play centers could match the diversity and inventiveness of the Disney planners. In 1982, Disney opened EPCOT (an acronym for Experimental Prototype Community of Tomorrow), an $800 million, 260-acre (105.2 hectares) development that was conceived as being more than a theme park. Instead, EPCOT was intended to be a place that would offer an environment where people of many nations might meet and exchange ideas. It consists of two sections: Future World, which contains corporate pavilions primarily concerned with technology; and World Showcase, which has international pavilions designed to show the tourist attractions of various nations around the world.

Since then, Disney World has added a number of other spectacular and imaginative attractions, including Typhoon Lagoon, the Disney Hollywood Studios, and in 2012, Cars Land based on the popular *Cars* movies. In 1983, a Disneyland opened in Japan on 202 acres (81.7 hectares) of landfill in Tokyo Bay. It featured the traditional Disney characters and popular rides and attractions. Although the attraction was owned by a Japanese corporation, Disney provided technology and guidance during the construction and operation of Tokyo Disneyland for a share of the gross ticket take. Then, with the opening of Disneyland Paris, formerly known as Euro Disney, the company created the largest theme park in Europe.

Throughout the 1990s, Disney continued to add new attractions and program features. In 1997, Disney's 200-acre (80.9-hectare) Wide World of Sports offered a 7500-seat stadium and other facilities as a venue for the Atlanta Braves, the Harlem Globetrotters, and the Indiana Pacers as well as thousands of other competitors on every age level in several different sports. Through a cooperative arrangement with the Amateur Athletic Union, national youth tournaments in baseball, basketball, softball, and tennis, among others, are held at this facility.

Disney continued its expansion into the 21st century with acquisition of Pixar, Marvel Comics, and Lucasfilm, all major participants in the movie industry. More recently, Disney opened a new 14-acre Star Wars themed area, Galaxy's Edge, with its newest attraction, Rise of the Resistance, welcoming its first riders in 2019.

WHAT'S NEXT FOR THEME PARKS?

Today, visitors to theme parks expect more than just a decade ago. What was good enough for their parents is rarely acceptable to younger generations. They are accustomed to the presence of technology and set high expectations for their experiences. As a result, theme parks are becoming more tech savvy and integrating experiences for the millennial generation. This period has been characterized as the golden age of technology. Visitors and potential visitors are looking for the next big thing. Virtual reality, frequently talked about, has made its appearance in theme parks. Disney created the first virtual reality experience in 1955, operating on what today would be called dinosaur technology. Virtual reality is available in many attractions as a part of the total experience. This is expected to continue to expand. Another example of the use of technology and LED digital technology is Disney's Rivers of Light, based on traditional Asian lantern festivals, focusing on the use of technology to present a visual experience for guests. The technology controls the lighting, creating stunning visual effects, and provides guidance for various part of the event such as boats and barges and sound. All of the technological components provide the visitor with a unique and engaging experience as a spectator. Other parks are experimenting and implementing virtual experiences that allow the participant to control the level and intensity of the experience, as opposed to just being a spectator.

New Kinds of Theme Parks

Other entertainment entrepreneurs soon followed the Disney example, and by 1976 at least three dozen parks of similar scale had been built around the United States. Some parks concentrate on a single theme, such as Opryland, U.S.A. in Nashville, Tennessee, and Holiday World and Splashing Safari in Indiana. Others incorporate moving rides through settings based on literary, historical, or international themes; entertainment; and typical amusement park "thrill" rides such as roller coasters and parachute jumps. In 2018 there were over 400 theme parks reporting in excess of 501 million annual visits[35] and in the United States alone revenue was estimated at $22 billion in 2019.[36]

Another unusual facility, opened in the early 1980s by Busch Gardens, is Adventure Island in Tampa, Florida. This 30-acre waterpark provides vistas of white sand beaches, glistening waters, palm trees, and tropical plants. Built on varied levels with complex waterfalls, slides, pools, cliffs, and rocks, Adventure Island provides an all-inclusive water experience in which visitors slide down twisting water chutes.

Other Parks

There are literally hundreds of theme parks in the United States today. Orlando, Florida, can be considered the theme park capital of the United States. Universal's Orlando Islands of Adventure is typical of many of today's large theme parks. The park has five distinctive themes, similar to those Disneyland introduced. The themes are linked to Universal Studios films, cartoons, or specific activities. For example, Toon Lagoon, a waterpark, has rides named for different cartoon characters, such as Dudley Do-Right's Rip Saw Falls.

Cedar Point, located in Sandusky, Ohio, is an example of a regional theme park that provides multiple experiences on a single site. Typical of a growth industry in theme parks is the roller coaster. Cedar Point boasts 17 different roller coaster rides, ranging from the Wicked Twister, a 215-foot-tall (65.5 meters), 72-mph (115.9-kph) steel stunner, to the Millennium Force, a 310-feet-tall (94.5 meters) roller coaster with a top speed of 93 mph (149 kph) that is targeted toward young riders.

However, not all theme parks rely on such forms of entertainment. Dollywood, for example, a complex of shops, rides, shows, craft centers, restaurants, and other theatrical features based on folk themes, is an outstanding tourist attraction in the Great Smoky Mountain National Park Region. Linked to the image of Dolly Parton, the popular movie actress and country music star, Dollywood offers gospel music performances, harvest celebrations, a "showcase" series of well-known performers, and other programs attuned to its traditional Appalachian Mountain environment.

Waterparks

A specialized type of theme park today consists of waterparks—tourist destinations that feature wave pools, slides, chutes, shows, and other forms of water-

Amusement parks are present in almost every major community; the parks provide locally available thrill experiences for participants.
© Sergey Ivanov/Shutterstock.

based play and entertainment. There are almost 1,000 waterparks today that provide such outdoor play in the United States. The largest concentration of waterparks is located in the Midwest, with the south a close second. They are not restricted to warmer areas, however. The Wisconsin Dells, for example, is famous for the number of indoor and outdoor waterparks in the region. One of the largest waterparks is located inside the West Edmonton Mall in Canada. Public agencies are the largest source of waterparks.

Often, water attractions are part of larger theme park operations. In Universal's Islands of Adventure, for example, the Jurassic Park River Adventure and Popeye and Bluto's Bilge Rat Barges offer either whirling and steep whitewater rides and sluice falls or swirling vortexes that spray riders thoroughly. Each year, dozens of new waterparks open, with the latest technology, marketing, and management skills taught to their operators at conventions held by the American Waterpark Association.

Zoos, Marine Parks, and Wildlife Parks

The addition of rides and other entertainment features to animal attractions is making marine and wild animal parks increasingly popular among tourists. Annually, members of the American Zoo and Aquarium Association in the United States receive approximately 200 million visitors. Wild animal parks have seen steady growth in recent years where visitors of all ages are offered the opportunity to view big game and exotic animals in natural (or semiwild) settings.

Other Fun Centers

In heavily populated metropolitan areas throughout the United States, other entrepreneurs have developed a variety of indoor fun centers, ranging from children's play, gymnastics, and exercise chains to family party centers, video game arcades, and huge restaurants with game areas. Fun centers are not just for children but adults as well. Dave and Buster's, an immensely successful chain of adult "fun and food" offerings in Dallas, Houston, Atlanta, Chicago, Philadelphia, and expanding into 30 states, Canada, and Mexico, offers a host of simulated fun experiences: golf, motorcycling, race car driving, space combat, and virtual reality, among others.

Similarly, the children's and family play centers that have been established in thousands of suburban neighborhoods and shopping malls around the United States offer a combination of computer and video games, billiards and other table games, miniature golf, entertainment by clowns and magicians, music, and popular fast-food refreshments. Offering packaged birthday parties and other family play services, they illustrate commercial recreation's success in providing attractive play activities that have supplanted more traditional home-based and "do it yourself" kinds of recreation.

Outdoor Recreation

The broad field of outdoor recreation—defined as leisure pursuits that depend on the outdoor environment for their special appeal or character—represents an important area of commercially sponsored services. Although a major portion of outdoor recreation is carried on in government-managed settings, many activities are provided by for-profit enterprises.

In 2016 the U.S. Fish and Wildlife Service reported that 101.6 million Americans aged 16 and older, including 38.8 million anglers and 11.5 million hunters, fished, hunted, or participated in wildlife-associated activities. The number of wildlife watchers increased from 71.80 million in 2011 to 86 million in 2016. Participants in these outdoor sports spent $46.1 billion on fishing related expenses, $25.6 billion on hunting expenses, and $75.9 billion on wildlife-watching related expenses. Expenses encompass such things as equipment, trips, licenses, and membership dues.[37]

Commercial recreation in the outdoors takes many forms, including hunting preserves and guide services; charter fishing and other private fishing operations; marinas and other boating services; ski centers and schools; campgrounds, adventure recreation, vacation ranches, and farms; paintball centers; and numerous other pursuits.

In many cases, a single company, such as Pocono Whitewater Adventures in Jim Thorpe, Pennsylvania, may offer several different types of adventure activities, such as river rafting, whitewater kayaking, family biking excursions, or paintball, at different seasons of the year. Numerous hunting businesses throughout the United States offer the opportunity to shoot big game and in some cases exotic species imported from other continents. Both inland and ocean fishing represent another huge industry. Boating alone represents a major segment of the outdoor recreation market, with annual retail sales and service in 2018 estimated at almost $41 billion. It was estimated that 87 million adults went boating in 2018.[38] The Great Lakes has the largest concentration of boaters in the nation, while Florida led the nation in registered boats, followed by California, Minnesota, Michigan, Wisconsin, Texas, New York, South Carolina, Ohio, and North Carolina.

Health Spas and Fitness Clubs

Commercial fitness centers and health clubs constitute a major source of leisure spending in the United States. Although those who join such facilities may have varying kinds of motivations, ranging from actual health concerns to a cosmetic concern with appearance, the reality is that health spas often offer an attractive social setting, particularly for single men and women.

This overall field includes a variety of program emphases, such as aquatic and fitness centers with varied pool facilities, exercise equipment rooms, aerobics and Jazzercise classes, yoga, conditioning counseling or remedial services, and similar options with annual fees that may range up to thousands of dollars.

As a variation of such health-connected services, many nonprofit hospitals or long-term care facilities have established for-profit subsidiary companies that offer a wide range of exercise programs, physical therapy, aerobic classes, and innovative techniques that include hypnosis, pain management, acupuncture, and other alternative forms of treatment serving the public at large. They may also focus on holistic and homeopathic treatment, including meditation groups, clubs dealing with specific forms of illness such as arthritis, overeaters anonymous, living with loss, and massage and reflexology methods.

Other For-Profit Ventures

Beyond the examples just cited, commercial recreation today includes a host of other kinds of social and hobby activities and amusement or entertainment ventures. Private golf or tennis clubs, bowling alleys and billiard parlors, contract bridge or chess clubs, night clubs and dance halls, and even dating services and gambling casinos are all part of this picture. In a sense, movies, television, video games, book publishing, and electronic devices are all aspects of popular culture that represent forms of commercialized leisure. A growing marketplace is quilting. Long thought to be the domain of grandmothers, quilting stores are present in many communities. They sell material, quilting-related items, and specialized quilting machines, and sponsor classes, tours, cruises, exhibitions, and competitions.

In addition, both amateur sport participation and professional spectator sport and travel and tourism involve huge elements in the commercial recreation field and are discussed in detail elsewhere in this text.

Differences and Similarities Among Agencies

This chapter describes the provision of organized recreation services today by three types of organizations: public or governmental, nonprofit or voluntary, and commercial recreation businesses. Each of these types of leisure-services organization simultaneously provides unique and similar services.

Public recreation and park agencies, for example, have a major responsibility for maintaining and operating outdoor resources such as parks, forests, playgrounds, sport and aquatic facilities, and, in many cases, indoor centers, performing arts centers, conference or convention venues, stadiums, and similar facilities. Their obligation is to serve the public at large, including individuals and families at all socioeconomic levels and without regard to ethnic, religious, or other demographic differences. However, given the intensified use of marketing-based fees and charges for many recreation programs, many government recreation and park agencies today are not reaching community groups with limited economic capability.

Nonprofit voluntary agencies are generally most concerned with social values and with achieving constructive outcomes either for the community or for specific population groups. They see recreation both as an end in itself and as a means to an end, are generally respectful of the social environment, and are sensitive to gender-, ethnicity-, and race-related issues. Particularly in terms of serving young people and special recreation interests, they are able to offer

Amateur sporting events in major urban centers are frequently integrated into existing parks where activities share spaces.
© Wendy Nero/Shutterstock.

richer programs than many public agencies. Nonprofits fill voids that public and commercial agencies cannot or will not fill.

Of the three types of sponsors, commercial recreation sponsors provide the greatest range of recreational services and opportunities today, and they represent a steadily growing sphere of organized leisure programming. In some ways, profit-oriented businesses are similar to public and nonprofit recreation and park agencies in terms of their offerings and the leisure needs they satisfy. What distinguishes them is their ability to commit substantial sums to developing facilities and programs that will attract the public. Huge corporations that are able to design and build theme parks, aquatic complexes, stadiums, health and fitness clubs, and other types of specialized equipment or programs obviously have a tremendous advantage in appealing to those who are able to pay the necessary fees and charges. Commercial recreation sponsors have harnessed technology and industry in creating spectacular environments for play and have used the most subtle and sophisticated public relations and advertising techniques to market their products successfully.

Social Values in Recreation Planning

It would be wrong to assume that commercial recreation businesses are entirely free to provide any sort of leisure activity without considering its social impact.

Health clubs, camps, amusement parks, theaters, dance halls, gambling casinos, taverns, and a host of other facilities are subject to regulation under state, county, and municipal laws. These may include provisions regarding the sale of liquor, sanitary conditions, service to minors, safety practices, hours of operation, and similar restrictions. Many enterprises that require licenses may have these withdrawn if the operators do not conform to approved practices. Similarly, trade associations often influence practices, even though they may not have the legal power to enforce their rulings. Public attitudes—as expressed in the press, through the statements of leading citizens, civic officials, or religious organizations, or through consumer pressure—often are able to influence the operators in desired directions. For example, when Time Warner was sharply criticized in the press for its promotion of violent, racist, and sexist rap music products, it divested itself of the involved recording label.

The competition of other organizations and products is another key factor in the management of commercial recreation agencies. Often, better products and services within a branch of the industry will serve to drive out inferior competitors. The entire field of recreation service and participation may be viewed as a marketing system in which the economic forces of supply and demand work so that as a new product or service appears, existing products and services are threatened. Within this framework, there is a constant pruning and reshuffling of recreation enterprises as competing sponsors seek to maintain public interest and attendance.

Partnerships Among Major Leisure-Services Agencies

Although public, nonprofit, and commercial leisure-services agencies are dealt with separately in this chapter, it is important to emphasize that in actual practice they often join together in cooperative ventures. For example, a survey of more than 100 cities found that almost all municipal recreation and parks departments conducted programs with other agencies and organizations; more than half of the respondents had 10 or more synergetic programs during the year. They worked closely with voluntary agencies, schools and colleges, service clubs, and business and industry to promote sport, cultural, and other types of events and projects.

Partnering among public, nonprofit, and commercial recreation providers is commonplace. Where these agencies once jealously guarded their own areas, they have embraced the concept that partnering better serves the public and individual agencies. Public and nonprofit agencies are frequently judged on their effectiveness by the number and quality of the partnerships they establish.

Many forms of partnerships are created by park and recreation agencies working with nonprofits, commercial organizations, other government agencies, private individuals, special-interest groups, and others. They can be as simple as the city parks and recreation department providing space for a model airplane club to construct a runway or as complex as multiple agencies working together to manage a unique natural resource. There is a long history of the National Park Service working with state park agencies and local parks and recreation departments. The Bureau of Land Management has transferred land to public agencies, such as the Grand Junction, Colorado, Parks and Recreation Department, to help maintain a buffer between urban development and natural areas. Special recreation associations, initially unique to Illinois, are the creation of multiple park districts joining together to develop a professional organization with the primary purpose of providing services to persons with disabilities. The special recreation associations operate as a separate service, yet integrate their services into existing park district programs using the resources of the association that exceed those of any individual park district.

There are numerous examples of partnerships in the areas of open space acquisition and environmental recovery. The Trust for Public Land (TPL) annually takes on

Sponsorship of recreation programs is increasing, as sponsors frequently have their organizations depicted at events.
© Joyce Vincent/Shutterstock.

numerous projects working with local public agencies, nonprofit, and neighborhood groups. TPL partnered with Cascade Bicycle Club in Puget Sound, Washington to start the remake of a defunct rail corridor which was 42 miles in length, completing it one section at a time. For example, Lakeview Elementary School allows students to ride their bicycles to school away from traffic corridor. Over 350,000 residents live within easy reach of the East Side Rail Corridor.[39] Two-thirds of the way across the country in Cleveland, Ohio, TPL is working with the Cuyahoga Metropolitan Housing Authority to bring together segments of urban trails into a greenway network that will ultimately bring users and residents to Cleveland's waterfront parks.[40] Table 6-5 depicts TPL's impacts over a 2-year period.

Similarly, nonprofit organizations are frequently involved in collaborative program efforts. Typically, Boy and Girl Scout troops often work closely with churches and religious organizations or with school boards. The Y encourages numerous partnership arrangements with local parks and recreation departments, schools and colleges, public housing boards, hospitals, and even correctional institutions. In the mid-2000s the Y initiated in more than 160 communities' collaborative projects working jointly with the Centers for Disease Control and Prevention and 20 other national organizations, nonprofits, and local community organizations, including parks and recreation departments, to expand community ability and to identify or create programs that establish positive health-related behavior change. The Healthier Communities Initiative has focused efforts on making healthy living available to community residents.

TABLE 6-5	Trust for Public Land Impacts—Two-Year Period				
Year	Acres Protected	Ballots Help Pass	Projects Completed	Fitness Zones	Members, Friends, Volunteers
2015	92,978	19	140	70	192,744
2016	62,134	12	128	78	453,966

Data from The Trust for Public Land. (2015). *2015 annual report*. https://www.tpl.org/2015-annual-report; The Trust for Public Land. (2016). *2016 annual report*. https://www.tpl.org/2016-annual-report.

Different types of collaborations are beginning to emerge as agencies begin serving an older American population. Lewisburg, Pennsylvania, created the first multigenerational park as a destination designed to bring together different age groups to enjoy experiences while in close proximity. The emphasis was on the environment, families, and activity, recognizing that such an approach met the needs of many different age groups. Many communities are now recognizing that older Americans use parks more frequently than other age groups do and are beginning to cooperate within their communities to modify parks to fit the needs of older adults. The University of Illinois is working with a variety of groups, including parks and recreation agencies, to develop New Active Green Environments facilities that strive to improve the cardiovascular health, muscle strength, and flexibility of older Americans, understanding that the new older generation is different from all previous aging generations.[41]

Finally, the National Recreation and Park Association has successfully initiated a number of partnerships. These include joint ventures with NFL PLAY60 After-School Kickoff program; the United States Tennis Association; Soccer5 in the development of parks allowing more children to play soccer in a smaller space; and the National Basketball Association's "Jr. NBA" program for boys and girls 6–14, focusing on skills, sportsmanship, and values of the game. Collaborative arrangements of this type are growing in number and variety and are helping to build a climate of mutual assistance among the different elements that constitute the leisure-services system.

Revisiting the Major Elements in the Leisure-Services Delivery System

Early in this chapter, Tables 6-1 and 6-2 depicted how agencies, partnerships, programs, participants, and outcomes interact to create recreation and leisure opportunities.

This chapter has demonstrated the diversity of recreation opportunities and the value of partnering to achieve greater opportunities for individuals to experience leisure. Table 6-6 provides a more complex example of the interaction of these elements. The community orchestra is performing at the city's major outdoor park performance center. The city is cosponsoring the event with the orchestra. A local bank has agreed to pay for the labor to set up the sound, lights, and security for the performance. The city and orchestra have contracted with a local caterer who will provide food for purchase at the event. The parks and recreation department is advertising the event on its website and in its seasonal brochure and the local public television station is assisting the orchestra by webcasting the concert.

The perspective depicted in Table 6-6 is that of the city parks and recreation department. The initiating organization was a community orchestra and the venue is managed by the parks and recreation department. These two organizations have a long-standing relationship. The bank is a sponsor of the community orchestra. The food caterer is approved by the parks and recreation department and contracted with by the community orchestra. The community orchestra has a partnership with the food vendor and receives a share of the profit of sales during the event. The webcasting of the performance is handled through the community orchestra, the parks and recreation department, and the local public television station, which determines what special needs the webcast may require.

By diagramming the program process in Table 6-6, it becomes easier to see the relationships and dependencies that are present. Seeing the type of agencies involved (A), the types of partnerships in place (B), the types of services provided (C), the reasons the programs or services are offered (D), and the influencers allows the agency to predict benefits (E).

TABLE 6-6 Complex Version

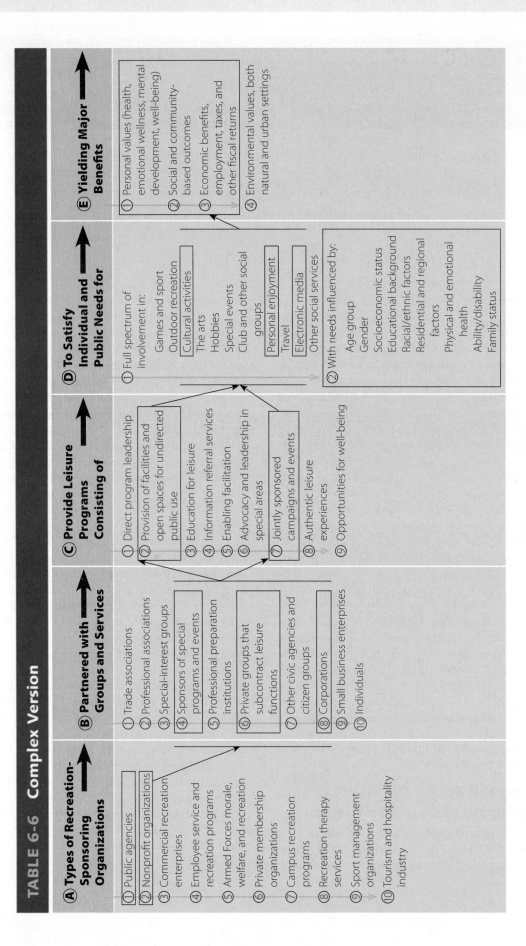

(A) Types of Recreation-Sponsoring Organizations

① Public agencies
② Nonprofit organizations
③ Commercial recreation enterprises
④ Employee service and recreation programs
⑤ Armed Forces morale, welfare, and recreation
⑥ Private membership organizations
⑦ Campus recreation programs
⑧ Recreation therapy services
⑨ Sport management organizations
⑩ Tourism and hospitality industry

(B) Partnered with Groups and Services

① Trade associations
② Professional associations
③ Special-interest groups
④ Sponsors of special programs and events
⑤ Professional preparation institutions
⑥ Private groups that subcontract leisure functions
⑦ Other civic agencies and citizen groups
⑧ Corporations
⑨ Small business enterprises
⑩ Individuals

(C) Provide Leisure Programs Consisting of

① Direct program leadership
② Provision of facilities and open spaces for undirected public use
③ Education for leisure
④ Information referral services
⑤ Enabling facilitation
⑥ Advocacy and leadership in special areas
⑦ Jointly sponsored campaigns and events
⑧ Authentic leisure experiences
⑨ Opportunities for well-being

(D) To Satisfy Individual and Public Needs for

① Full spectrum of involvement in:
    Games and sport
    Outdoor recreation
    Cultural activities
    The arts
    Hobbies
    Special events
    Club and other social groups
    Personal enjoyment
    Travel
    Electronic media
    Other social services

② With needs influenced by:
    Age group
    Gender
    Socioeconomic status
    Educational background
    Racial/ethnic factors
    Residential and regional factors
    Physical and emotional health
    Ability/disability
    Family status

(E) Yielding Major Benefits

① Personal values (health, emotional wellness, mental development, well-being)
② Social and community-based outcomes
③ Economic benefits, employment, taxes, and other fiscal returns
④ Environmental values, both natural and urban settings

SUMMARY

Government's role with respect to organized leisure services is diversified. On the federal level, government is concerned with the management of outdoor recreation resources, either as a primary function or within a multiple-use concept, through such agencies as the National Park Service, U.S. Forest Service, Bureau of Land Management, and the Tennessee Valley Authority. The federal government also assists states and local political units through funding and technical assistance for programs serving children and youth, those with disabilities, older adults, and similar groups.

State governments operate major park systems and play an important role in promoting environmental conservation and outdoor recreation opportunities. They also set standards and pass enabling legislation defining the role of local governments in the area of recreation and parks. In addition, states have traditionally maintained networks of state hospitals and special schools for those with disabilities, although this function has been reduced in recent years as a result of deinstitutionalization trends that involve placing many such individuals in community settings.

The chief sponsors of government recreation and park programs are on the local level—city, town, county, and special district government agencies. They operate many different types of facilities and offer a wide range of classes, sport leagues, special events, the arts, social activities, and other leisure areas. They also provide or assist in many programs in the human services area. Although many municipal departments have expanded their revenue source operations, departments in other larger and older cities suffer from depleted staff resources and have limited program and maintenance potential.

Voluntary agencies place their greatest emphasis on using leisure to achieve positive social goals. Several types of youth-serving organizations are described, including both sectarian and nonsectarian groups. Such agencies rarely consider themselves to be primarily recreation organizations; instead, they generally prefer to be regarded as educational, character-building, or youth-serving organizations. However, recreation usually does constitute a sector of their program activities.

A second type of nonprofit leisure-services agency consists of special-interest groups, which usually promote a particular area of activity in outdoor recreation, sport, the arts, or hobbies. Such groups, although they may include many enthusiasts as members, are often formed to promote business interests within the particular leisure specialization.

Commercial recreation businesses offer an immense number of public recreation opportunities in such areas as travel and tourism, outdoor recreation, sport, popular entertainment, the mass media, hobbies, and crafts. Their primary goal is to make a consistent profit through the creation of experiences. In many cases, they are large and highly diversified operations, such as the Walt Disney organization, with its theme parks, resorts, and television, movies, Internet, and popular music components. From a social perspective, many for-profit businesses offer constructive, high-quality programs. However, in some cases—as in sectors of the entertainment industry—they are believed to contribute to youth violence, sexism, and racial hostility.

QUESTIONS FOR CLASS DISCUSSION OR ESSAY EXAMINATION

1. Identify the key recreation providers from the federal government as well as their core mission or purposes. Compare all the federal agencies and identify their commonalities and differences. Discuss with your classmates how these agencies collectively and individually influence the recreation landscape of the United States.

   _____

   _____

   _____

   _____

2. There appear to be different perspectives from providers of recreation opportunities from the federal level to the community level. Identify what you see as the major role at each level (federal, state, county, municipality). Second, identify what you see as common roles that cross three or more levels. Explain how you would justify to your community duplication of the roles of another agency (such as the National Park Service or your state park system).

   _____

   _____

   _____

3. Select a park and recreation agency from your hometown or a larger community close to your hometown and look at their website. Identify the types of services and programs that they offer. Is this a small town, medium-sized town, or large city? Or is it a county system? Identify the core services provided and assess the quality and quantity of their level of service. Explain why you assessed their services in the way you did.

_____

_____

_____

4. Explain the importance of nonprofits in the leisure-services industry. What do nonprofits bring to the leisure-services delivery system that make them unique and effective?

_____

_____

_____

5. Select a commercial recreation enterprise in your community. Identify what its core business is and how it delivers that business. Describe how its delivery model is different from a public and a nonprofit organization.

_____

_____

_____

ENDNOTES

1. Kraus, R. (1971). *Recreation and leisure in modern society*. New York: Appleton-Century-Crofts.
2. National Park Service. About us: Our mission. Retrieved February 25, 2021 from https://www.nps.gov/aboutus/index.htm
3. Stebbins, S. (2019, October 29). Here's how much land the government owns in your state. *USA Today*. Retrieved January 27, 2021, from https://www.usatoday.com/story/money/2019/10/29/how-much-land-government-owns-in-every-state/40453833/.
4. National Park Service. (2020). *National Park System*. Retrieved January 27, 2021, from https://www.nps.gov/aboutus/national-park-system.htm.
5. United States Forest Service. (n.d.). Managing the land. Retrieved April 15, 2020, from https://www.fs.usda.gov/managing-land.
6. Mitchell, B. A. (2011). Projecting America's best ideals: International engagements and the National Park Service. *George Wright Forum, 28*(1), 7–16. Retrieved October 26, 2013, from http://www.georgewright.org/281mitchell.pdf.
7. U.S. Department of the Interior. (2019, June 27). Visitor spending at national wildlife refuges boosts local economies by $3.2 billion. Retrieved November 30, 2019, from https://www.doi.gov/pressreleases/visitor-spending-national-wildlife-refuges-boosts-local-economies-32-billion.
8. U.S. Department of the Interior Bureau of Land Management. (n.d.). *Public land statistics*. Retrieved May 29, 2017, from https://www.blm.gov/about/data/public-land-statistics.
9. U.S. Department of Agriculture Farm Service Agency. (n.d.). *Conservation Reserve Program*. Retrieved May 29, 2017, from https://www.fsa.usda.gov/programs-and-services/conservation-programs/conservation-reserve-program/index
10. U.S. Department of Agriculture Farm Service Agency. (n.d.). *Conservation programs*. Retrieved January 27, 2021, from https://www.fsa.usda.gov/programs-and-services/conservation-programs/index.
11. Keener, K. (2020, January 2). *NEA receives $162 million in funding for 2020*. Art Critique. Retrieved March 31, 2020, from https://www.art-critique.com/en/2020/01/nea-receives-162-million-in-funding/.
12. National Endowment for the Arts. Initiatives. Retrieved March 1, 2021 from: https://www.arts.gov/initiatives
13. National Endowment for the Arts (2016). *2015 annual report* (p. 3). Retrieved January 27, 2021, from https://www.arts.gov/sites/default/files/2015%20Annual%20Report.pdf.
14. McLean, D. D. (2006). *The 2006 annual information exchange*. National Association of State Park Directors.
15. Illinois Association of Park Districts. (2019). *2019 annual report*. Author.
16. Pennsylvania Department of Conservation and Natural Resources. (2008, December 15). *Public dedication of land and fees-in-lieu for parks and recreation. A guide to using Section 503(11) of the*

Pennsylvania Municipalities Planning Code. Retrieved February 18, 2017, from http://www.dcnr.state.pa.us/cs/groups/public/documents/document/dcnr_002299.pdf.

17. King County, Washington, Department of Natural Resources and Parks. Retrieved November 18, 2012, from https://www.kingcounty.gov/environment/dnrp.aspx.

18. City of Henderson, Nevada. Retrieved April 16, 2020, from http://www.cityofhenderson.com/henderson-happenings/home.

19. Murray, J. (2017, December 7). Stacked floors, amazing views and two pools: See inside central Denver's new $44 million urban recreation center. *Denver Post.* Retrieved January 10, 2020, from https://www.denverpost.com/2017/12/07/denver-carla-madison-recreation-center/.

20. White Pine County, Nevada. (n.d.). *White Pine County Aquatic Center.* Retrieved February 8, 2017, from http://www.whitepinecounty.net/index.aspx?nid=471.

21. Seattle Parks and Recreation. (2020). *2020 approved budget.* Retrieved April 19, 2020, from https://www.seattle.gov/Documents/Departments/FinanceDepartment/20adoptedbudget/SPR.pdf.

22. Seattle Park District. (n.d.). *Programs for people.* Retrieved June 12, 2016, from http://www.seattle.gov/seattle-park-district/projects/programs-for-people.

23. AmeriCorps. (2018, November 13). *Volunteering in U.S. hits record high; worth $167 billion.* Retrieved January 27, 2021, from https://www.nationalservice.gov/newsroom/press-releases/2018/volunteering-us-hits-record-high-worth-167-billion.

24. U.S. Bureau of Labor Statistics. (2018, August 31). *Nonprofits account for 12.3 million job, 10.2 percent of private sector employment, in 2016.* Retrieved January 27, 2021, from https://www.bls.gov/opub/ted/2018/nonprofits-account-for-12-3-million-jobs-10-2-percent-of-private-sector-employment-in-2016.htm?view_full.

25. Boy Scouts of America. (2019). *2018 annual report.* Retrieved February 10, 2020, from https://ar2018.scouting.org/wp-content/uploads/2019/05/BSA-2018-AnnualReport_1.pdf.

26. Girl Scouts of the United States of America. (n.d.). *Who we are.* Retrieved April 1, 2020, from https://www.girlscouts.org/en/about-girl-scouts/who-we-are.html.

27. Boys & Girls Clubs of America. (n.d.). *Club impact.* Retrieved January 27, 2021, from https://www.bgca.org/about-us/club-impact.

28. Best Buddies. Retrieved January 27, 2021, from http://www.bestbuddies.org.

29. Best Buddies (2021). *Best buddies in Massachusetts & Rhode Island.* Retrieved March 1, 2021, from https://bestbuddies.org/mari/.

30. Young Men's Christian Association. (n.d.). *Organizational profile.* Retrieved October 22, 2013, from http://www.ymca.net/organizational-profile.

31. Sierra Club. Retrieved March 1, 2021, from https://www.sierraclub.org/about-sierra-club

32. Appalachian Mountain Club. Retrieved March 1, 2021, from https://www.outdoors.org/wp-content/uploads/pdf/AMC-Fact-Sheet.pdf

33. Little League Baseball. (n.d.). *Who we are.* Retrieved April 17, 2020, from https://www.littleleague.org/who-we-are/.

34. Niles, R. (2019, May). Disney extends its lead in global theme park attendance. *Theme Park Insider.* Retrieved April 17, 2020, from https://www.themeparkinsider.com/flume/201905/6792/.

35. Bell, T. (2019, May 22). *Global theme park attendance grew 5% in 2018, with Disney still on top.* Retrieved April 17, 2020, from https://www.wdwinfo.com/news-stories/global-theme-park-attendance-grew-5-in-2018-with-disney-still-on-top/.

36. Lange, D. *Amusement and theme parks—Statistics & facts.* Retrieved April 17, 2020, from https://www.statista.com/topics/2805/amusement-and-theme-parks/.

37. U.S. Department of the Interior, U.S. Fish & Wildlife Service. (2017, September 7). *New 5-year report shows 101.6 million Americans participated in hunting, fishing & wildlife activities.* Retrieved April 17, 2020, from https://www.doi.gov/pressreleases/new-5-year-report-shows-1016-million-americans-participated-hunting-fishing-wildlife.

38. Lange, D. (2020). *Recreational boating—Statistics & facts.* Retrieved April 27, 2020, from https://www.statista.com/topics/1138/recreational-boating/.

39. The Trust for Public Land. (2017, January 19). *In the Seattle metro, a new bike path gets kids to school the old-fashioned way.* Retrieved February 2, 2017, from http://www.tpl.org/blog/eastside-rail-corridor#sm.01lwp1261b52dtu110i23341oygox.

40. The Trust for Public Land. (2016, November 9). *A Cleveland's neighborhood long-awaited link to the lakefront.* Retrieved February 12, 2017, from http://www.tpl.org/blog/cleveland-greenways-link-lakefront#sm.01lwp1261b52dtu110i23341oygox.

41. Godbey, G. (2005, October). Providing more for older adults. *Parks and Recreation,* 76–81.

Chapter 7
Leisure as a Profession

"Recreation as a career still suffers from lack of public understanding….the recreation profession is often seen as a playground leader rather than as a municipal executive with considerable responsibilities and importance." (p. 116)[1]

-From the first edition of Kraus' Recreation and Leisure in Modern Society, published in 1971.

LEARNING OBJECTIVES

1. Understand and discuss the seven criteria outlined for professional practice.

2. Identify appropriate professional certifications.

3. Describe operational philosophies of recreation and leisure.

4. Design an outline of a plan to establish a career in leisure services.

Introduction

Recreation, parks, and leisure services have expanded greatly over the past several decades as a diversified area of employment. Today, several million people work in different sectors of this field, including amateur and professional sport, entertainment and amusement services, event planning, travel and tourism related businesses, and government and nonprofit community organizations.

As a distinct part of this larger group, several hundred thousand people are directly involved as recreation leaders, supervisors, managers, therapists, planners, and consultants in public, nonprofit, and commercial agencies. These individuals with a primary concern for the provision of recreation services are generally regarded as professionals on the basis of their job responsibilities, specialized training, and affiliations with professional associations.

The prevailing image of leisure-services professionals has been that of public, governmental recreation and park employees. The leading professional associations, as well as most textbooks and college curricula, reinforced this narrowly defined identity. However, the reality is that vast sectors of employment in recreation and leisure services are not government related but instead have to do with nonprofit community agencies; company-sponsored, commercial, and recreation therapy services; sport management; and travel and tourism programs. As such, they have their own professional associations, as well as goals, job functions, and strategies that differ from those of public recreation and park specialists.

Recreation as a Career

People have worked in recreation for many centuries in the sense that there have been professional athletes and entertainers throughout history. Musicians, tumblers, dancers, huntsmen, park designers, and gardeners were all recreation specialists meeting the leisure needs first of royalty and, ultimately, the public at large. However, the idea of recreation itself as a career field did not surface until the late 1800s, when public parks and playgrounds, along with voluntary social service and youth-serving organizations, were established.

After the beginning of the 20th century, courses in play leadership were developed by the Playground Association of America and were taken by many teachers. In the middle 1920s, the National Recreation Association provided a graduate training program for professional recreation and park administrators, and leisure as a distinct area of public service came to be recognized. This recognition increased during the Great Depression of the 1930s as several thousand individuals were assigned by the federal government to emergency posts providing community recreation programs and developing new parks and other facilities.

However, it was not until the development of separate degree programs in a handful of colleges that higher education in recreation and parks as a distinct career field came into being.

By the second half of the 20th century, careers in recreation and parks were seen as a growth area. A nationwide study of workforce requirements in the 1960s concluded that there would be a need for hundreds of thousands of new recreation and park professionals in the years ahead. The U.S. Department of Labor reported widespread shortages of leisure-services personnel in local government, hospitals, and youth-serving organizations. Several factors, such as the federal government's expanded activity in outdoor recreation and open space and the establishment of the National Recreation and Park Association, stimulated interest in this field. In the 1970s, as employment grew, curricula in recreation and leisure services gained increased acceptance in higher education to what it is today.

Scope of Employment Today

People spend free time participating in sport, arts, and nature activities; visiting museums, zoos, and aquariums; and attending special events, shows, and performances; as well as traveling to tourism destinations. With all of this recreation going on, people are needed to work in these and many other areas.

Employment opportunities in parks and recreation are highly diversified. Recreation workers are found in local parks and recreation agencies, on cruise ships, planning major festivals such as the Sundance Film Festival, planning promotional events for the Phoenix International Raceway, and working with people with disabilities in a recreation therapy setting. They can be found in all of the national parks from Acadia to Zion. They serve as park rangers,

Jobs in parks and recreation are quite varied—from working with the National Park Service to planning major special events to working with Special Olympics.
© spirit of america/Shutterstock.

interpreters, guides, and activity planners. Throughout this chapter, you will find vignettes of people working in the field of parks and recreation. Some of them are brand new to the field, and others have several years of experience. Each shares their typical responsibilities for the job. It is easy to see how diverse this profession is.

The educational backgrounds of people working in recreation vary. A plethora of summer and part-time positions require a high school diploma—or less as is the case with many lifeguards and camp counselors. However, these positions are not considered professional positions but rather a means to gain experience in order to obtain a professional position in the recreation field. As responsibilities increase in recreation-related jobs, so do degree requirements. Entry-level positions in the field such as after-school program supervisors, special-event planners, and facility supervisors may require a bachelor's degree, and middle- and upper-level management positions may require a master's degree.

Although data on the total number of jobs in recreation are limited, we do know that the tourism industry is one of the nation's largest employers, with 5.9 million people working in this industry.[2] The 2019 Bureau of Labor Statistics estimates indicate that there are 19,900 people employed as recreation therapists,[3] 417,100 in recreation,[4] and another 138,600 employed as event planners.[5] Furthermore, the National Park Service employs 20,000 people to take care of its 85 million acres of land;[6] state parks employ approximately 51,000 people full and part time.[7]

The Bureau of Labor Statistics expects the demand for most recreation jobs to grow much faster than average through 2029, with an expected growth of about 10% through this time.[8] They also predict that recreation therapy will see a growth that is much faster than average, with an increase of 8% over the next several years.[9] Part of what is driving this growth is the rate of retirement of baby boomers, previously discussed in other chapters. It is also the result of increased concern for health and wellness.

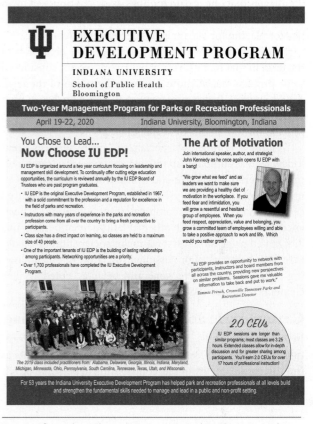

Training for parks and recreation positions does not stop with a degree. Professionals take advantage of programs such as the Indiana University Executive Development program to enhance their skills.
Courtesy of The Trustees of Indiana University.

EMILY MARTIN, SEASONAL INTERPRETIVE RANGER, NATIONAL PARK SERVICE

I work seasonally with the National Park Service (NPS), which means I'm only in the parks for 4 to 6 months of the year. The NPS is a vast, diverse organization, so a typical day can vary, but my responsibilities as an interpretive ranger boil down to three areas: visitor services, programming, and informal contact. Much of the job is customer service—staffing visitor centers, orienting people to the park, providing maps and other information, and being a front-line contact for visitors having issues. Programming lets me research, design, prepare, and present educational talks, walks, and demonstrations for both children and adults and is a favorite part of many interpretive rangers' jobs. Informal contact involves simply heading out into the park and facilitating positive, spontaneous interactions with people, whether that is answering questions or reminding them of park rules. Other tasks often depend on the nature of the site—for example, helping to run a historic farm, or doing basic resource monitoring. Although the job can be demanding, helping create an emotional connection between the visitor and the park is always what inspires me to do my best and make each interaction count.

Professional Identification in Recreation

What does being a professional mean? At the simplest level, it indicates that one is paid for one's work—as opposed to an amateur, who is not paid for it. Thus, an athlete who receives pay for playing for a team is classified as a professional.

However, this obviously is not a sufficient definition of the term in that many forms of paid work are not considered to be professional. A more complete definition of the term would suggest that a professional is one who has a high degree of status and specialized training and provides a significant form of public or social service.

Within a number of specialized leisure-services areas today, such as company-sponsored employee programs, recreation therapy, or fitness and health clubs, professionalism might be narrowly defined as the possession of a required certification based on a combination of education, experience, and examination. In other situations, membership in a designated professional association or society may be recognized as a hallmark of professionalism. However, the following seven criteria have generally been accepted as key elements of professionalism.

Criterion 1: Social Value and Purpose

In general, the goals, value, and purpose of organized community leisure-services agencies deal with such elements as improving the quality of life, contributing to personal development and social cohesion, helping to prevent socially destructive leisure pursuits, and protecting the environment. The goals, value, and purpose of organized community leisure-services agencies are described in another chapter.

Public and nonprofit leisure-services agencies have long been known for their social good. For example, the mission of the YWCA is to improve the lives of girls and women through programs to improve racial justice and civil rights, empowerment, and economic advancement and improve health and safety.[10]

People are willing to pay for their own personal leisure and are more reluctant to pay taxes to support leisure for the public good such as parks and trails.
© Jim Noetzel/Shutterstock.

CARLY MIKTUK, MANAGER OF DRIVER AND TEAM COMMUNICATIONS, KAULIG RACING (NASCAR)

A typical day for me varies during the week versus a race weekend. During the week, I am communicating with our entire team on relevant topics and happenings within the sport. I am also gathering information on our drivers and team and compiling this information into what we call a race preview or advance. The race preview consists of information on each specific driver, as well as their previous stats at the race track we are traveling to that upcoming weekend. If we have a special storyline we want to ensure makes it into the TV broadcast that weekend, that information is included in the race preview or written about in a press release. The race previews and press releases are then sent out to NASCAR media members, other sports media, and in-market media members.

I then prepare race-weekend schedules for each of our drivers. I book interviews and appearances for the upcoming race weekend to maximize our drivers' and team's public image. It is important to leverage relationships with media members, as they will be more apt to work with me on future projects and will want to schedule interviews. All appearances and interviews are scheduled around on-track action and competition.

While at the track during the weekend, I take the drivers to and from any appearances and interviews I booked earlier in the week, while also making sure the drivers have enough time to prepare for any competition-related obligations. Race day can be hectic, as sponsor and partner guests are present. I help entertain them between media obligations and appearances. During on-track activity, such as practice, qualifying, and the race, I am updating social media on what is happening during the race and what the drivers are communicating on the radios. Following the race, I make sure the drivers complete any media obligations mandated by NASCAR before we leave for the airport to go home.

Its member organizations provide safety, shelter, daycare, physical fitness and recreation programs, counseling, and other social, health, educational, and job-related services to millions of women and girls and their communities each year.

Although the public and nonprofit sectors are most often equated with social good, the commercial sector contributes to this as well and has its own social value and purpose. It may provide entertainment, support health and fitness, or expose people to other cultures, historic sites, or a multitude of other tourism-related destinations. This was never more evident than during the COVID-19 pandemic when many commercial recreation opportunities were closed and people missed vacations and other fun endeavors.

Criterion 2: Public Recognition

The rapid expansion of the leisure-services field over the past several decades does not necessarily mean that the public at large understands and respects it fully or that they regard it as a distinct area of professional service. To illustrate, most individuals today know what recreation is, and many regard it as an important part of their lives. Most are prepared to pay substantial portions of their income for recreational goods or services, such as memberships in health clubs, vacations, sport equipment, tickets to theater productions, and other leisure-related fees and charges. However, they are often less willing to pay taxes in support of public recreation and park facilities and programs than they are to spend privately for their own leisure needs.

A time-use study done by the Bureau of Labor Statistics found that 95.2% of people older than the age of 15 reported having some sort of leisure, whether it be socializing, sport, or exercising.[11] They also average 5.19 hours per day on leisure and sports.[12] In 2018, there were more than 813.2 million visitors to state parks.[13] The National Park Service reported over 327 million visitors in 2019.[14] Nearly 68 million people attend major league baseball games each year.[15]

Although these are just a minute portion of the leisure-services opportunities available, it demonstrates that a large portion of the population uses recreation services.

Even though the value of organized recreation service may be acknowledged through participation and use, how aware is the public at large of the leisure-service field as a profession? The likelihood is that most individuals recognize the roles of recreation professionals within specific areas of service. For example, they are likely to be familiar with the function of a recreation therapist in a hospital or nursing home or the function of a community center director, a park ranger, or a sport specialist in an armed forces recreation program. What they tend not to understand is that recreation represents a field of practice that requires special expertise and educational preparation in a college or university. At issue is the image of the recreation professional.

IMAGE OF THE PROFESSIONAL

Unless one is an actual participant in organized leisure activities, people are most likely unaware that these jobs and careers even exist. Even with participation, the career acknowledgment may not happen. People attending a major special event may enjoy the special event and return year after year, but they are unlikely to understand all of the planning and preparation that goes into that event. People have the luxury of enjoying recreation services, whereas the people who provide them remain behind the scenes. The public often does not see the people who cut the grass in the park, plan and plant the flowerbeds, develop the tournament schedule, or schedule the concerts in the park. In many instances, a park and recreation professional is out of sight if the event or program is running smoothly. This can lead to the public not equating what is being done to a true profession or career.

Another misconception about this profession is that anyone can do it. People think anyone can plan a 64-team softball tournament, organize a special event that attracts 100,000 people, or manage a pool. On the surface, these activities may not seem very difficult. However, they require an extensive amount of academic preparation, experience, and organizational skills. In addition, if recreation and leisure-service employees are to sharpen their identity and support, they must enrich their own competence through specialized professional study and by joining organizations that strengthen their field.

As a professional association, NRPA helps the public understand the value of parks and recreation in their communities.
Courtesy of National Recreation and Park Association.

JORDAN MORAHN, THERAPEUTIC RECREATION SPECIALIST, OSF SAINT ELIZABETH MEDICAL CENTER

As a Therapeutic Recreation Specialist on a Behavioral Health Unit, it is my duty to plan and implement recreation groups that meet the patient's needs during their admission. Once a patient is admitted to the unit, I meet with them within 24 hours to assess their needs and determine a short-term goal. A patient's typical length of stay is 3 to 5 days; therefore, goals need to be obtainable given the short amount of time. After meeting with the patient and assessing their needs, I input their assessment into their electronic medical record (EMR) and write a care plan based on their psychiatric diagnosis and recreational needs. The most common type of goal for patients on the Behavioral Health Unit focuses on using healthy recreational and leisure activities as a coping skill to decrease signs and symptoms of mental illness like depression, anxiety, suicidal ideations, or increased self-harming behaviors.

After meeting with all new patients and updating existing patient's progress, I implement the Recreation Therapy Group for all the patients. Treatment modalities for the group vary based on patient needs; however, common treatment modalities include therapeutic games (cards, dice, board games, trivia, music), therapeutic projects (bird houses, glitter jars, puzzles), physical activity like chair exercises, and leisure education where we focus on the "why" behind engagement in recreation and leisure. I also meet with patients before discharge to assess their progress toward their goal and provide additional resources for engagement in recreation after discharge.

CASE STUDY: Perceptions of a Profession

Interview five friends and/or family members. Ask them the following questions:

1. What are parks, recreation, and leisure services to you?
2. Did you know that someone could major in parks and recreation, sport, commercial recreation or tourism, or recreation therapy? Do you know anyone who has?
3. What kinds of jobs does someone get after they graduate with a degree in parks and recreation, sport, commercial recreation or tourism, or recreation therapy.

Questions to Consider

1. What did your friends and family say when you told them you would major in a leisure-services professional area?
2. What are their perceptions of the field?
3. What is an elevator speech and how are they used? Develop a 1–2 minute "elevator speech" about what this profession is and why it is important.

Criterion 3: Specialized Professional Preparation

A measure of the professional authority of any given field is the degree of specialized preparation that people must have to function in it.

Parks and recreation is no exception. There are many jobs in the field that require no education, but many of these are part time and most are low paying. To obtain a full-time, professional-level position, a post-high school education is often required. Two- and four-year degree programs, as well as master's degrees and doctoral degrees in parks and recreation related fields are available. These degrees provide the specialized training needed to hold entry-level and higher jobs.

PROFESSIONAL PREPARATION IN RECREATION AND PARKS

The early period of the development of higher education in recreation, parks, and leisure services is described elsewhere in this text. Over the past 5 decades, college and university curricula in recreation and parks have been developed on three levels: 2-year, 4-year, and graduate (master's degree and doctorate) programs.

Two-Year Curricula

During the late 1960s and early 1970s, many community colleges began to offer associate degree programs in recreation and parks. Typically, these sought to prepare individuals on para- or subprofessional levels rather than for supervisory or administrative roles. Most community

AMANDA ELSTON, EVENTS MANAGER, DESTIHL® BREWERY

Most of my days are a mix of working in the office and running the events at the venue. My day starts by checking my email to see any new leads that have come in, because it is important to respond to new leads as quickly as possible so you have a better chance of booking them. Then I check on any updates for events I currently have booked or answer any questions my clients have. Being quick and thorough with my responses helps my clients have trust in me and know their event will go off without a hitch.

Most of my events happen in the evening, so late afternoon when the staff arrives, we rally and go over all the details of the event before they start to set up. From there, I am available if the staff have any questions. I also make myself available when the host arrives. I communicate with the event host to see what questions they have and check in with them periodically with any updates. I trust my staff to have the bar, food, and room ready to go 15 minutes before the start of the event, and make sure to lend a hand if needed. During the event, I check in frequently with my lead server and bartender to see if there are any questions or concerns. I do not approach the host, or any member of the event, once the event starts unless there is an emergency that I think they need to know about. Finally, the day ends with making sure the staff cleans the space properly and the financials of the event are taken care of.

Of course, there are many small tasks in between such as meeting with hosts, making event signage, showing the event space to potential clients, creating custom menus, editing BEOs (banquet event orders), and taking inventory of event supplies. Every event is different; therefore, a day with a corporate event is very different from a day with a wedding. With corporate clients, I must be a little quicker, to the point, and factual; with wedding couples, I must be more patient, thorough, and available. It is important to read your clients and team and adjust accordingly so your days can be as efficient as possible, and your events can be successful!

colleges offered recreation majors a choice of two types of programs: terminal and transfer. *Terminal programs* are intended to equip students immediately for employment and give heavy emphasis to developing basic, useful recreation leadership skills, often within a specific field of practice. *Transfer programs* are intended for students who hoped to transfer to 4-year degree programs.

Four-Year Programs

The most widely found degree program in recreation and parks has been the 4-year bachelor's degree curriculum. Initially, most such programs consisted of specialized degree options in college departments of health, physical education, and recreation, although some were located in departments or schools of landscape architecture, agriculture, or forestry. Today, although many departments still are situated administratively in schools or colleges of health, physical education, and recreation, they have achieved a high level of curricular independence, with their own objectives, courses, degree requirements, and faculty.

Four-year programs typically have established degree options in areas such as recreation programming, resource management, outdoor recreation, recreation therapy, sport management, commercial recreation, and tourism. The normal pattern has been to require all department majors to take certain core courses representing the generic needs of all preprofessionals, including basic courses in recreation history and philosophy, programming, management, and evaluation and/or research, and then to have a separate cluster of specialized courses for each option.

What once started as a training ground for public parks and recreation professionals has grown to meet the changing demands of the field. There was growing academic awareness of the job opportunities in other recreation areas. As a result, a number of college and university programs changed their titles and departmental affiliations to reflect the new interest in commercial recreation, travel and tourism, sport management, hotel and resort management, and similar specializations. Typically, a considerable number of departments added the term *tourism* to their titles and established enriched programs in this area—in some cases in collaboration with schools of business in their institutions. In other cases, recreation therapy majors were transferred administratively to departments or schools of public health or healthcare services. As the most striking example of proliferation in this field, as of 2020 there were more than 500 independent departments of sport management designed to meet personnel needs in this growing field.[16] This is up from 300 in 2010.

Master's Degree and Doctoral Programs

Although it is generally agreed that the 4-year curriculum should provide a broad base of general or liberal arts education along with the core of essential knowledge underlying recreation service, the specific function of graduate education in this field is not as clearly defined. Some authorities have suggested that graduate curricula should accept only those students who already have a degree in recreation and should focus on providing advanced professional education within a specialized area of service. However, there tends to be little support for this position, and many graduate programs accept students from other undergraduate disciplines as well as those holding undergraduate degrees in recreation.

In general, authorities agree that master's degree work should involve advanced study in recreation and park administration or in some other specialized area of service, such as recreation therapy or sport management. The assumption is that individuals on this level are preparing for supervisory or managerial positions or, in some cases, roles as researchers or chief executive officers.

Doctoral programs in leisure services-related fields prepare graduates to teach and conduct research at the university level. Degree programs are typically a minimum of 3 years of study culminating with a major research project in the form of a dissertation. Students specialize in an area of interest and build a research line in that area.

SPECIALIZED BODY OF KNOWLEDGE

At the outset, many recreation and park degree programs were established as "minor" specializations in other areas of study, such as physical education. As such, they tended to lack theoretically based courses within the field of study. Over the past 4 decades, this deficiency has been corrected.

The knowledge and skills components of higher education in recreation, parks, and leisure studies are formulated in terms that are specifically applicable to the recreation field, although they may involve content taken from other scholarly disciplines or fields of practice.

Given the recent impressive growth in both research studies and publication of findings, it seems clear that the field has a legitimate body of knowledge that must be possessed by professionals. Indeed, within some areas of practice, there has been systematic study of the competencies and knowledge that entry-level practitioners should possess. These skills, knowledge, and abilities guide curricula so that students are equipped with the skills needed to get their first job.[17]

Increasingly, undergraduate curricula have been redesigned to include specific areas of knowledge and job performance based on standards of practice or certification examinations that have been developed by professional societies.

For undergraduates, a major element of the degree program is a culminating internship, and so students are able to gain work experience and implement the knowledge gained in the classroom. Although these vary from institution to institution, in general they require at least a semester of full-time commitment to work in an agency of high quality within the student's expressed field of professional interest. Such placements should extend far beyond an agency's using field work or internship students in routine or mundane roles as a source of cheap labor. Instead, they are meant to involve a full range of realistic job assignments and exposures, supervision by professional staff members, and preparation for entry-level positions.

ACCREDITATION IN HIGHER EDUCATION

The most significant effort that has been made to upgrade curricular standards and practices in recreation, parks, and leisure studies has come in the accreditation process.

Accreditation of a degree program involves meeting standards set by a larger governing body. These standards ensure that students are being exposed to standards of practices within the field.

The park and recreation accreditation program is administered by the Council on Accreditation of Parks, Recreation, Tourism and Related Professions (COAPRT). This group of academic faculty and practitioners in the field serves as the COAPRT Council, a nonprofit independent organization. A group of trained visitors go into universities to review their programs and make recommendations on accreditation to the council. Academic programs become accredited for a number of reasons. First, and usually most important, is to ensure program quality and uncover areas in need of improvement. A secondary reason is that students graduating from an accredited university may take the Certified Park and Recreation Professional examination upon completion of their degree (certification is discussed later).

Undergraduate baccalaureate programs in parks and recreation are eligible for accreditation. At this time graduate programs cannot go through the accreditation process. In this process, there are set accreditation standards and learning outcomes that programs must meet in the areas of administration, faculty, students, instructional resources, and learning outcomes. After completing a self-study of these areas, an outside review team visits the campus to judge how well standards are met. Suggestions for improving weaknesses are made with the understanding that these things are for the betterment of the degree program.

Accreditation began in the early 1980s with about 50 programs being accredited. There has been a steady increase in the number of programs being accredited, and this number has risen to 71 in 2020.[18]

In addition to accreditation from COAPRT, sport management has a Commission on Sport Management Accreditation (COSMA). Accreditation in sport management is available for both undergraduate and graduate degree programs. COSMA accredited its first two programs in 2010, and by 2020 there were 54 accredited sport management programs across the country.[19] Accreditation requires review of many of the same aspects of general parks and recreation programs, but these standards are sports specific in terms of curriculum and faculty.

Criterion 4: Existence of Related Professional Associations

Another important characteristic of professions in modern society is that they have strong organizations, shared values, and traditions.

In North America, professional recreation associations have been in existence for a number of years. Like their counterparts in other professions, recreation and park associations have the following functions: They (1) regulate and set standards for professional development; (2) promote legislation for the advancement of the field; (3) develop public information programs to improve understanding and support of the field by the general public; (4) sponsor conferences, publications, and field services to improve practices; and (5) press for higher standards of training, accreditation, and certification. There are a number of professional associations available for park and recreation professionals that provide those and other services.

NATIONAL RECREATION AND PARK ASSOCIATION

Because of the varied nature of professional service in recreation and parks and the strong role played by citizens' groups and nonprofessional organizations, many different associations were established through the years to serve the field. Five of these (the National Recreation Association, the American Institute of Park Executives, the National Conference on State Parks, the American Association of Zoological Parks and Aquariums, and the American Recreation Society) merged into a single body in 1965, with Laurance S. Rockefeller as president. Within a year or two, other groups, such as the National Association of Recreation Therapists and the Armed Forces Section of the American Recreation Society, merged their interests with the newly formed organization.

This national body, the *National Recreation and Park Association* (NRPA), is an independent, nonprofit organization intended to advance parks, recreation, and environmental conservation efforts that enhance the quality of life for all people.[20] This organization is arguably the broadest in scope for the recreation profession by embracing most of the professional categories listed earlier in the chapter. NRPA is directed by a board of trustees, which meets several times each year to guide its major policies.

NRPA plays a vigorous role in helping to bring about a fuller national consciousness of the value of recreation and leisure through various public information campaigns, publications, research efforts, and legislative presentations. The organization responds to thousands of inquiries and requests for technical assistance from practitioners, establishes national partnerships for local departments, oversees conferences and training opportunities, and provides numerous publications for members. In addition, NRPA representatives regularly testify before congressional subcommittees in support of legislation and funding proposals dealing with the environment, social needs, and similar national problems.

OTHER PROFESSIONAL ORGANIZATIONS

Although NRPA welcomes membership from all over the world, it is predominantly focused on the United States. The Canadian Parks and Recreation Association has much the same charge for parks and recreation professionals in Canada. They serve as advocates, build partnerships, promote the value of parks and recreation, and offer educational opportunities to its members.[21] For organized camps, the American Camp Association (ACA) strives to be the leading authority in child development, provides resources to camp managers and staff, holds annual conferences, and administers the ACA camp accreditation program, among other services.[22]

Other organizations that have made important contributions to this field include those listed in Table 7-1.

It is clear that no one organization can possibly speak for or represent the entire leisure-service field today. As each specialized area of recreation has become more active and successful, it has tended to form its own professional society to deal with its unique needs and interests.

Criterion 5: Credentialing, Certification, and Agency Accreditation

Credentials are qualifications that must be satisfied through a formal review process before an individual is permitted to engage in professional practice in a given field. Obviously, this is a very important criterion of professionalism. If anyone can call themselves a qualified practitioner in a given field—without appropriate training or experience—that field has very low standards and is not likely to gain or hold the public's respect.

Because the recreation and park field has been so diversified, no single standard or selection process has been devised for those who seek employment in it. However, within the field of recreation and parks, certification programs have been developed to increase the professionalism of the field as well as set some standards that all certified professionals should possess.

Certification in a profession indicates that a certain level of skill and knowledge has been attained. Certification in parks and recreation is no exception. Although there are several different certifications available for different specialties in the field, and arguably the most recognized are the Certified Park and Recreation Professional (CPRP) and the Certified Therapeutic Recreation Specialist (CTRS).

CERTIFIED PARK AND RECREATION PROFESSIONAL

The Certified Park and Recreation Professional program as we know it today has existed since 1990. To qualify to receive the CPRP designation one of the following criteria must be met:

■ Have received, or are set to receive (in their final semester), a bachelor's degree from a program accredited by COAPRT. Have a bachelor's degree or

TABLE 7-1 **Common Professional Associations in Recreation, Sport, and Tourism**

Purpose/Focus	Agency	Website
General Recreation	Canadian Parks and Recreation Association	http://www.cpra.ca/
	National Correctional Recreation Association	http://www.strengthtech.com/correct/ncra/ncra.htm
	National Recreation & Park Association	http://www.nrpa.org
	World Leisure Organization	http://www.worldleisure.org/
	Shape America Society of Health and Physical Educators	http://www.shapeamerica.org/
Outdoor/Camping	American Camp Association	http://www.acacamps.org/
	Association for Experiential Education	http://www.aee.org/
	Association of Outdoor Recreation and Education	http://www.aore.org/
	Canadian Parks and Wilderness Society	http://www.cpaws.org/
	National Association for Interpretation	http://www.interpnet.com/
	Society of Outdoor Recreation Professionals	http://www.recpro.org/
	Outdoor Industry Association	http://www.outdoorindustry.org/
	Student Conservation Association	http://www.thesca.org/
	Wilderness Education Association	http://www.weainfo.org/
	North American Association for Environmental Education	http://www.naaee.org/
Recreation Therapy	American Therapeutic Recreation Association	http://www.atra-online.com
	National Recreation & Park Association	http://www.nrpa.org/
Resorts/Commercial Recreation	International Association of Amusement Parks and Attractions	http://www.iaapa.org/
	National Ski Areas Association	http://www.nsaa.org/
	Resort and Commercial Recreation Association	http://www.rcra.org/
	American Hotel and Lodging Association	http://www.ahla.com/
	Club Managers Association of America	http://www.cmaa.org/

Purpose/Focus	Agency	Website
Special Events & Meeting Planning	Events Industry Council	https://www.eventscouncil.org/
	International Association of Venue Managers	http://www.iavm.org/
	International Festivals & Events Association	http://www.ifea.com/
	International Live Events Association	https://www.specialevents.com/ilea
	Meeting Professionals International	http://www.mpi.org/
	Professional Convention Management Association	http://www.pcma.org
	Association of Collegiate Conference and Events Directors-International	https://www.acced-i.org/
Sport	NIRSA: Leaders in Collegiate Recreation	https://nirsa.net/nirsa/
	North American Society for Sport Management	http://www.nassm.org/
	Sports Events & Tourism Association	https://www.sportseta.org/
Tourism	The International Ecotourism Society	http://www.ecotourism.org
	Tourism Industry Association of Canada	http://www.tiac-aitc.ca/
	World Travel & Tourism Council	http://www.wttc.org/
	World Tourism Organization	http://www.unwto.org/index.php
	American Society of Travel Advisors	http://www.asta.org/

© Jones & Bartlett Learning.

higher from any institution in recreation, park resources, or leisure services; and also have no less than 1 year of full-time experience in the field.
- Have a bachelor's degree in a major other than recreation, park resources, or leisure services; and also have no less than 3 years of full-time experience in the field.
- Have an associate's degree and have 4 years of full-time experience in the field.
- Have a high school degree or equivalent and have 5 years of full-time experience in the field.[23]

Once the criteria are met, an exam must be passed. The exam covers five broad content areas including the following:

- *Communication*: Public input, mission, marketing, partnerships, and planning

- *Finance*: Purchasing, program budgets, alternative funding, cash handling procedures, collecting financial data
- *Human resources*: Recruiting, hiring, and supervising staff and volunteers
- *Operations*: Risk management, facility management, customer service, external relationships, needs assessments, emergency management, maintenance
- *Programming*: Program leadership, planning, implementing and evaluating programs and events[24]

Once an individual receives certification, they must recertify every 2 years. Recertification requires individuals to receive 2.0 continuing education units (CEUs). One CEU is equivalent to 10 contact hours in an educational program. CEUs can be obtained from state, regional, and national conference educational sessions; university courses; or professional service points. Professional service experience points come from service given to the profession in the form of speaking at a conference, writing articles for a professional magazine, or serving on committees within the professional association.

Scanning the latest job search announcements, it is clear that more and more public parks and recreation departments are requesting applicants be certified. These employers see the value in obtaining a certain level of education and a commitment to staying current by continually attending workshops and conferences.

CERTIFIED THERAPEUTIC RECREATION SPECIALIST

Certification in recreation therapy is administered by the National Council for Therapeutic Recreation Certification (NCTRC). To obtain a CTRS certification, professionals may follow either an academic path or an equivalency path. The academic path is for people who have completed a bachelor's degree or higher with a concentration in recreation therapy. The equivalency option is for people without a degree specifically in recreation therapy, but a bachelor's degree in another area as well as full-time work experience in recreation therapy. Regardless of the path chosen, both require successfully passing the CTRS exam.[25]

Based on the 2014 job analysis study, the NCTRC Certification exam has the following five content areas: foundational knowledge (20%), assessment process (19%), documentation (18%), implementation (26%), administration of therapeutic recreation/recreation therapy service (10%), and advancement of the profession (7%).[26]

Both the CPRP and CTRS certification programs have resources available to help candidates prepare for the exams. Resources include practice exams, study guides, and in some cases study groups.

STANDARDS IN NONPUBLIC LEISURE-SERVICE AGENCIES

The NRPA and the NCTRC have been the prime movers in the attempt to strengthen professionalism in leisure-service agencies. In general, the employees in nonprofit and commercial agencies have not been identified as key players in the recreation certification movement. Hiring in such agencies therefore has not been influenced by the NRPA accreditation efforts or certification.

However, national organizations such as the Ys and Boys and Girls Clubs as well as commercial entities are obviously concerned with helping their local branches, businesses, or other direct-service units maintain a high level of staff competence. They do that through specialized training. For example, Meeting Professionals International (MPI) offers the MPI Academy where professionals can build their skills and knowledge base through in-person meetings, prerecorded webinars, and live stream workshops. MDI has also partnered with San Diego State University to offer the first master's degree in meeting and event management.[28]

OTHER CERTIFICATIONS

Because not all jobs in the leisure-service profession are best associated with the CPRP or CTRS certification, a number of others available may better reflect job responsibilities.

- *Certified meeting professional:* For people who plan meetings, conventions, and exhibitions.[29]
- *Certified playground inspector:* This certification is offered by the National Playground Safety Institute.[30]
- *Aquatics facility operator and certified pool operator:* These certifications focus on managing and operating aquatics facilities.
- *Certified special events professional (CSEP):* Awarded by the International Live Events Association, certification is earned through education, experience, and service to the industry.[31]
- *National Association for Interpretation:* Offers certifications in a number of outdoor-related areas including Certified Interpretive Guide, Certified Interpretive Host, Certified Interpretive Planner, Certified Interpretation Trainer, Certified Heritage Interpreter, and Certified Interpretive Manager.[32]
- *Certified Destination Management Executive:* This certification is often obtained by people working with convention and visitors bureaus.

CERTIFIED PARK AND RECREATION EXECUTIVE

In 2012 a new certification was unveiled—the Certified Park and Recreation Executive (CPRE). This exam establishes a national standard for managerial, administrative, and executive parks and recreation professionals and reflects mastery-level credentials. It is designed for upper-level administrators who seek to be directors or department heads.[27] There are currently 250 CPREs in the United States.

AGENCY ACCREDITATION PROCESS

Another example of the thrust toward fuller professionalism in the organized recreation, park, and leisure-service field is found in the accreditation process for local public departments initiated in the mid-1990s. For an agency to become accredited, it must examine all aspects of its operations, from maintenance to marketing, and adhere to carefully developed standards of excellence. An outside team of park and recreation practitioners visits the agency to see how well it is meeting the set standards and to offer suggestions for improvements to the agency. Currently, there are 172 accredited agencies.[33] Many of the directors of the accredited agencies have used accreditation as a benchmark for

improving services offered to the community and to show the public their tax-supported agency is using its resources wisely. For example, the City of Fort Collins Parks and Recreation Department used the accreditation process to measure themselves against best practices across the country, improve their day-to-day operations, and identify where they can change and grow.[34]

Agency accreditation is also done in the camping industry. The American Camp Association accredits camps that meet specific safety, health, and risk management aspects of a camp's operation. An onsite visitation team examines such areas as facilities, transportation, human resources, programs, staffing, and health and wellness.[35]

CASE STUDY: The Job Search

Using Table 7-1, select two professional associations that have job listings. Review the listings for four positions you would be interested in after graduation.

Questions to Consider

- What skills or experiences are required for these positions? What are some commonalities among the jobs?
- What education is needed for the positions? Are there any certifications that are needed? If so, which one(s)?
- What surprised you most about the jobs in the field?

ALLISON FLEISCHAUER CLAYTON, BUILDING OPERATIONS AND SAFETY ASSOCIATE, SOUTH CAROLINA AQUARIUM

A typical workday starts early in the morning at 6 a.m. when I relieve our overnight associates. At this time of the day, the view from my office is breathtaking, an additional perk to starting each morning so early; I am often greeted with a picturesque view of the sun rising over Charleston Harbor. Working mostly behind the scenes at the aquarium, I spend a significant portion of my time monitoring and ensuring that all of the automation and alarm systems supporting the facility are functioning properly. Then it is off to checking out the visitor experience. Walking around the entire facility and visiting each of our exhibits is vital to ensuring that everything is running smoothly. In early 2018, I developed a custom SharePoint site that allows the operations staff to document all operations responsibilities, from each activity through problem resolution. This enables all shifts to track situations and their current resolution status within the facility while ultimately providing a safer environment for the animals under our care.

The other portion of my role is safety. I am responsible for building access safety by issuing personal ID badges to staff, volunteers, and interns in addition to maintaining the safety portion of our accreditation with the Association of Zoos and Aquariums. Keeping this accreditation is vital to the operations of the aquarium, and my responsibilities include maintaining an online database of all the facility's incident reports. Additionally, I document, plan, and facilitate all required annual safety drills, including annual interactive refresher training on zoonotic diseases and bloodborne pathogens for all staff members.

Care for the animals is not the only concern in our safety group, as we also must address our staff and guests. I also serve as one of our resident CPR/First Aid/AED instructors training the other staff working in the facility should they ever need to administer aid. Each day at the South Carolina Aquarium is different, both with our guests and our animals. The wide range of animals we care for all have different and unique needs. Finally, it is my department's responsibility to ensure that the overall safety of the facility is continually monitored and maintained, from exact water temperatures and ozone levels to the proper functioning of tank machinery. The goal of all staff members supporting the aquarium is to allow the animals to live their best life while in our care.

Criterion 6: Code of Ethical Practice

An important measure of any profession is that it typically outlines the public responsibilities of practitioners and establishes a code of ethical behavior. In fields such as medicine and law, where the possibility of malpractice is great and the stakes are high, strict codes of ethics prevail.

In the field of leisure services, it might appear that any issues related to ethical practice are not as critical as in these other professions. However, in specialized areas such as recreation therapy, where patients or clients are likely to be physically, emotionally, or economically vulnerable, the opportunities for harmful, negligent, or unprofessional behavior are great. In other areas of leisure services as well, professionals should have a strong sense of obligation to those they serve, to their communities, and to the profession itself.

The American Therapeutic Recreation Association's Code of Ethics is outlined in 10 principles guiding practices such as justice, confidentiality and privacy, and competence.[36] The American Camp Association stresses integrity, truthfulness, fairness to all people, and an agreement to comply with relevant laws of the community. There is a Global Code of Ethics for Tourism that serves as guiding principles for tourism development. These 10 principles cover the economic, social, cultural, and environmental components of travel and tourism, including such things as sustainability, rights of workers and entrepreneurs in the tourism industry, and mutual understanding and respect between peoples and societies.[37]

INTERNATIONAL LIVE EVENTS ASSOCIATION (ILEA) PRINCIPLES OF PROFESSIONAL CONDUCT AND ETHICS

Special events are important—the last thing someone wants to worry about is the integrity of the special-events professional. That's why all ILEA members subscribe to the ILEA Principles of Professional Conduct and Ethics, listed here.

Each member of ILEA shall agree to adhere to the following:

- Promote and encourage the highest level of ethics within the profession of the special events industry while maintaining the highest standards of professional conduct.
- Strive for excellence in all aspects of our profession by performing consistently at or above acceptable industry standards.
- Use only legal and ethical means in all industry negotiations and activities.
- Protect the public against fraud and unfair practices, and promote all practices that bring respect and credit to the profession.
- Provide truthful and accurate information with respect to the performance of duties. Use a written contract clearly stating all charges, services, products, performance expectations, and other essential information.
- Maintain industry-accepted standards of safety and sanitation.
- Maintain adequate and appropriate insurance coverage for all business activities.
- Commit to increase professional growth and knowledge, to attend educational programs, and to personally contribute expertise to meetings and journals.
- Strive to cooperate with colleagues, suppliers, employees, employers, and all persons supervised, in order to provide the highest quality service at every level.
- Subscribe to the ILEA Principles of Professional Conduct and Ethics, and abide by the ILEA bylaws and policies.[38]

Courtesy of International Live Events Association.

Criterion 7: Existence of Extensive Professional Development Opportunities

A true profession has many avenues for professionals to develop their skills, knowledge, and abilities in their chosen career after their degrees are completed. Conferences, workshops, seminars, and institutes are held at the state, regional, and national levels, focusing on training opportunities in all areas of the profession. For example, the International Festivals & Events Association has an annual convention; an annual expo (trade show) featuring vendors for ticketing, crowd management, and equipment rental; and a webinar series covering such topics as sponsorship retention, dealing with severe weather, and maximizing revenue.[39] The National Intramural Recreational Sports Association offers workshops and institutes throughout the year such as National Women's Leadership Institute, Recreation Facilities Institute, and the Marketing Institute.[40]

Recreation is a changing profession and it is necessary to continually educate its practitioners so they continue to provide high-quality services. The importance of professional development is evident by the creativity being used during the COVID-19 pandemic. Because people cannot travel to conference sites, many organizations are running virtual conferences. Some keynote sessions will be run as webinars and others as breakout sessions so participants can interact and learn about key issues and trends in the field. An advantage of a virtual conference is the lower cost for many agencies because travel is eliminated. This will often result in more staff being able to participate in these learning opportunities.

In addition to workshops and trainings, most professional associations have monthly, quarterly, or annual publications with articles focusing on issues in the field. The Association for Experiential Education has the *Journal of Experiential Education;* the North American Society of Sport Management has the *Journal of Sport Management;* and the Resort and Commercial Recreation Association has the *Journal of Tourism Insights.*

KALI SANDERS, ENGAGEMENT COORDINATOR, CKY: CANOE KENTUCKY

Canoe Kentucky is the state's premier paddle-sports retail shop running one of the most successful rental/livery operations in Kentucky. As one of three full-time managers, my duties include all aspects of the business. There isn't a task or position that I haven't yet done. Daily tasks include such things as opening the store, getting computers ready for reservations, and prepping special rental inquiries (adaptive paddling, fishing kayaks, special requests). I assist with scheduling staff through our app called *When I Work*. I set "to-do lists" for our staff to complete throughout the day. I make phone calls to book reservations and rentals, discuss boat services, and provide information to people interested in buying kayaks/canoes and related supplies. There are just a couple of us with access to our social media, so I am also in charge of assisting with social media posts and responses. These can be tough to keep up with as we receive inquiries through our reservation software, emails, phone calls, Facebook, Instagram, and our website chat. On busy weekends I can be found helping drive boat trailers, loading/unloading canoes and kayaks, washing life jackets and paddles, and providing overall help where needed. I am around to assist with difficult customers and help orchestrate the flow of rental operations. I also assist with our Environmental Programs and Homeschool Adventure Programs, both of which have slowed down because of the coronavirus pandemic. Overall, in this field and in my position, I wear many hats and assist in all aspects of the business.

Current Level of Professional Status

When the seven accepted criteria of professionalism reviewed here are used as the basis for judgment, it is apparent that the recreation, parks, and leisure-service field has made considerable progress toward becoming a recognized profession.

Some elements are already securely in place, such as the development of a unique body of knowledge and the establishment of a network of college and university programs of professional preparation. As for the professional organization element, the NRPA and other national associations or societies represent a significant force for upgrading and monitoring performance in the recreation field, but their attempts to serve the interests of a wide variety of leisure-service agencies also illustrate the field's diversity of services. Realistically, many practitioners in such specialized disciplines as special-event planning, employee recreation, and varied aspects of commercial recreation tend to identify more closely with their separate fields than they do with the overall leisure-service field.

Professionalism in recreation, parks, and leisure services has increased greatly over the past several decades, along with the growing recognition of the field's value in modern society. Because of the immense scope of the diversified recreation field in terms of employment, it has the potential for becoming even more influential in contributing to community well-being in the years ahead.

Establish a Career in Leisure Services

Now that there is an understanding of what drives leisure services a profession, it is understandable that there might be questions about how students can make this a career field. A review of growth in this job market showed that the prospects are quite good.

As a student in leisure services, developing your career prospects starts today. Here are some guidelines to follow to help position yourself in a fast-growing job market.

1. Major in parks and recreation, tourism management, sport management, or a related field. The major will have many different titles and can be found in any number of academic colleges from business to education.

2. Build your transferable skills. Transferable skills are those skills that can be used across various jobs. Transferable skills include such things as excellent communication skills, ability to work well in a team, organizational skills, or time management. These skills can be used anywhere. For example, your experience as a server in a restaurant helps you learn about customer service, multitasking, and thinking on your feet. Working as a receptionist will build these same skills but in a different way. Do not discount the skills built in any job.

3. Meet with a career counselor on campus. They will help you explore your current interests as well as where you want to be in the future. They can also help you take a career assessment that will help you find a career that best meets your interests, skills, and goals.

4. Build the skills needed for an entry level position. In addition to transferable skills, develop the specific skills needed for the types of positions you want once your degree is completed. There are many ways to learn what these skills are. Check entry-level job descriptions you would eventually be interested in. Review them for required and desired qualifications. Look at the research on entry-level competencies (knowledge, skills, abilities, and other characteristics

needed for a particular field). For example, the field of public parks and recreation suggests that competencies needed by young professionals include such things as understanding financial processes (e.g., purchasing, budgets), understanding the hiring process, and the ability to schedule programs, leagues, and staff.[41] Meeting and event planners need to be able to develop plans for managing the movement of attendees, coordinating food and beverage services, and managing audiovisual and technical production.[42]

5. Get part-time jobs in the field. Having a part-time job in an afterschool program, as a lifeguard, or at the front desk in a hotel will be good ways to build your resume, show that you can hold a job, and develop a better understanding of professionalism and the work environment that can set you apart from your peers.

6. Build your network. Knowing people in the industry helps you make connections to others. It could be your current supervisor, a faculty member, or a peer you worked with. These people can serve as resources and references. Your professional network can give you leads on jobs, put in a good word for you, recommend you to people in their network, or offer career advice. Never underestimate the power of connections.

7. Find a mentor. In addition to building a network, find a mentor who can work with you individually and give career advice and guidance. This person can help build your network, but they will also be someone who gets to know you well and vice versa. A mentor can come from within your place of employment or outside of it. Someone inside the organization will know how it operates, but someone outside the organization can be a confidant about handling difficult work situations or when it is time to seek new employment. Mentors will change throughout your career as your needs change.

8. Volunteer your time at recreation or community center agencies and events. This can be a short-term 1-day event or a long-term program such as coaching youth baseball. These volunteer opportunities can expose you to the different aspects of the field, while also demonstrating that you are civic and socially minded.

9. Develop an academic and career plan. Start as early as your freshman year in college. This plan should include things to do to prepare you for your first full-time job. For example, Illinois State University Career Services developed a resource for students that guides them through academic achievement, building transferable skills, experiences and involvement, and networking. This guide is meant to help students start doing small things to better position themselves for academic and career success.

Specialized fields within parks and recreation include faith-based recreation, recreation therapy, travel and tourism, sport, outdoor recreation, and others. Explore these areas and try them out through volunteer, part-time, or full-time employment opportunities. Each one will build transferable skills that can be moved to a different area. The next several chapters look at the specialized fields within parks and recreation.

Need for a Sound Philosophical Basis

As discussed, several elements define a profession. Whereas these factors legitimize a profession, a profession has a philosophy that drives its values, ethics, ideas, and approach to service delivery. A sound philosophy of recreation and leisure also can serve the leisure-service field in ongoing policy formulation and program development.

Meaning of Philosophy

The term *philosophy* often conveys an image of ivory tower abstraction, divorced from practical or realistic concerns. Understandably, many practitioners are likely to be suspicious of any approach that appears to be overly theoretical, rather than pragmatic and action based. The nature of practitioners is to be in the here and now. They look for answers that assist them today and tomorrow, not 6 months or 3 years in the future. Philosophy, more often than not, provides more questions than answers. In far too many instances, it is easier to deal with the present than to anticipate the future and one's appropriate role in shaping that future.

The term philosophy has many definitions. As it applies to a profession, a philosophy is the most basic beliefs, principles, perceptions, and approach to delivering services. A philosophy will guide why the profession or agency exists, guide decision making, and even influence what programs are offered.

Throughout the text many trends and purposes of recreation have been presented. All of these are guided by one of the philosophies presented here.

Operational Philosophies of Recreation and Leisure

It is possible to identify several approaches or orientations found in leisure-service agencies today that may be called *operational philosophies*. These include the following: (1) the quality-of-life approach, (2) the marketing or entrepreneurial approach, (3) the human services approach, (4) the prescriptive approach, (5) the resource manager/aesthetic/ preservationist approach, (6) the hedonist/individualist approach, and (7) the benefits-based approach.

KEYS TO ACADEMIC *and* CAREER SUCCESS

STAGE 1: EXPLORE

ACADEMIC ACHIEVEMENT
- Always strive for academic success.
- Attend and actively participate in classes and get to know your professors.
- Meet with your academic advisor and faculty to discuss major requirements and your academic goals.
- Participate in and contribute to department-based introductory classes.
- Explore your academic and career interests online. Contact the Career Center for help.
- Attend available tutoring sessions and workshops as needed.

TRANSFERABLE SKILLS
- Develop your transferable skills, such as writing, communication, or public speaking. Seek a part-time job, internship, or other experiences to build your current skill set.

EXPERIENCES AND INVOLVEMENT
- Explore student organizations, volunteer, and seek leadership or civic engagement opportunities.
- Attend academic, career, and campus events.

NETWORKING
- Conduct an informational interview with professionals in your areas of interest.

STAGE 2: EXPAND

ACADEMIC ACHIEVEMENT
- Create an academic plan with your academic advisor and faculty.
- Meet with your career advisor to identify career opportunities that align with your interests.
- Explore options to study abroad.

TRANSFERABLE SKILLS
- Refine writing, communication, analytical, and other transferable skills through course work and involvement opportunities.

EXPERIENCES AND INVOLVEMENT
- Obtain a leadership role in an organization.
- Attend academic, career, and campus events.
- Apply for internships at HireARedbird.IllinoisState.edu.

NETWORKING
- Get to know faculty.
- Conduct a job shadow with a professional in your area of interest.
- Create LinkedIn and Hire-A-Redbird profiles; visit the Career Center to learn how.

STAGE 3: EXECUTE

ACADEMIC ACHIEVEMENT
- Inquire about earning academic credit for an internship or research opportunity in your department.
- Evaluate the status of your academic and career plans.
- Ask faculty to serve as references to help meet your career goals.

TRANSFERABLE SKILLS
- Leverage your acquired writing, communication, analytical, and other transferable skills.

EXPERIENCES AND INVOLVEMENT
- Relate your internship experience to your course work and career preparation.

NETWORKING
- Meet with a career advisor and faculty to discuss job-search strategies.
- Establish a professional social media presence.
- Continue to build your network at academic, career, and campus events.

STAGE 4: EMBARK

ACADEMIC ACHIEVEMENT
- Research specific academic and career opportunities (i.e., job search, graduate school, etc.).
- Meet with your career advisor to implement job-search strategies.
- Apply to graduate programs or jobs that align with your goals.

TRANSFERABLE SKILLS
- Update and finalize your resume and related professional documents to include your transferable skills.

EXPERIENCES AND INVOLVEMENT
- Attend academic, career, and campus events.

NETWORKING
- Network with faculty.
- Maximize your professional networks (i.e., LinkedIn, professional contacts, etc.).

Keys to Academic and Career Success.

CASE STUDY: Keys to Academic and Career Success

Using the four stages outlined in Keys to Academic and Career Success, map out a plan detailing things you can do to better position yourself for academic and career success.

Questions to Consider

- What can you do to enhance your academic achievement?
- What transferable skills do you currently have? What ones do you need to build? What experience and community involvement do you need to enhance your resume?
- Outline your current network. In what areas do you need to build this network? How will you do it?

JAMEEL JONES, DIRECTOR OF RECREATION, CHAMPAIGN (IL) PARK DISTRICT

Each day presents a different set of challenges, opportunities, reminders, and forward thinking, especially in the midst of COVID-19. Some of the challenges we face in our world today have taken a toll on our programs and how we offer them moving forward. We have found that virtual works for some, but not all, because of access and equipment issues. This becomes a matter of equity and accessibility, which is an ongoing concern. As we work to solicit feedback and information from our community on how we can best serve them, new opportunities have arisen to help them stay engaged with us. I work daily with our staff to provide as many offerings as we can, within safety guidelines, as the interest is still present. We are reminded each day how valuable our services are to our community and beyond in this field. It is a reminder that what we do is so important to our residents and their families. As we navigate these new and unprecedented times, we are adjusting how we do business, offer programs, schedule facilities and staff, and how we maintain our parks to meet the level of use they currently demand. We have to focus on sustained efforts to beautify our parks, improve our pathways in the parks, and update our amenities within the parks so they are safe, clean, and attractive! All of this is to provide the highest quality parks and recreation opportunities to our citizens that we can.

TWO EXAMPLES OF AGENCY MISSION STATEMENTS THAT DEMONSTRATE THE QUALITY OF LIFE PHILOSOPHY

Park Ridge Park District's mission is to enhance Park Ridge's quality of life by providing park and recreation opportunities for all residents while being environmentally and fiscally responsible.[43]

The Johnston Senior Center's mission is to enrich the quality of life and support independence and vitality for seniors.[44]

Quality-of-Life Approach

The *quality-of-life approach* has been the dominant one in the field of organized recreation service for several decades. It sees recreation as an experience that contributes to human development and to community well-being in various ways: improving physical and mental health, enriching cultural life, reducing antisocial uses of leisure, and strengthening community ties.

The quality-of-life orientation stresses the unique nature of recreation as a vital form of human experience—one that is engaged in for its own sake rather than for any extrinsic purpose or conscious social goal. Generally, proponents of this view have agreed that recreation satisfies a universal human need that has been made even more pressing by the tensions of modern urban society, the changed nature of work, and other social conditions.

Those holding this view argue that the pleasure, freedom, and self-choice inherent in recreation and leisure are their most vital contributions to the lives of participants. Quality-of-life advocates have tended to assume that public recreation should be supported for its own sake as an important area of civic responsibility and that adequate tax funds should be provided for this purpose. In today's era of intense competition for limited tax dollars, the quality-of-life issue remains important, yet the concept of full tax support for parks and recreation is recognized as no longer viable.

Marketing or Entrepreneurial Approach

The *marketing* or *entrepreneurial approach* is a business-oriented approach to providing organized recreation and park programs and services. Understandably, most commercial recreation agencies will function with this philosophy. They will focus on revenue generation substantial enough to fiscally sustain itself. However, the marketing or entrepreneurial approach to recreation and leisure is not just for the commercial sector but also for the public and nonprofit sectors. This philosophy evolved rapidly during the latter part of the 20th century as a direct response to the fiscal pressures placed on public and voluntary leisure-service agencies. Steadily mounting operational costs and a declining tax base during that time forced many recreation and park departments to adopt what has come to be known as the marketing or entrepreneurial approach to agency management. This approach is based on the idea that public, voluntary, or other leisure-service providers will flourish best if they adopt the methods used by commercial enterprises. It argues that they must become more aggressive and efficient in developing and promoting recreation facilities and programs that will reach the broadest possible audience and gain the maximum possible income.

Proponents of the marketing approach take the position that recreation and park professionals should not have to plead for tax-based support solely on the basis of the social value of their programs but rather should seek to become more independent as a viable, self-sufficient form of community service.

This self-sufficiency can come from either increasing participation in programs, thus generating more revenue, or

Commercial recreation.
© Sing Studio/Shutterstock.

looking at cost recovery policies. Agencies with a cost recovery approach look at how much programs actually cost and the fees that are charged. They establish a cost recovery benchmark where some programs will be priced to have expenditures higher than revenues (a loss), break even (revenues = expenditures), or where revenues exceed expenditures (a profit). For public agencies, programs operating at a loss can be offset with tax revenue. Nonprofit agencies could use fundraising or profits from other programs to cover costs, and commercial agencies will most likely eliminate programs that are not profitable.

Human Services Approach

In direct contrast to the marketing approach is the *human services approach* to organized recreation service. This approach regards recreation as an important form of social service that must be provided in a way that contributes directly to a wide range of desired social values and goals. The human services approach received a strong impetus during the 1960s, when recreation programs were generously funded by the federal government as part of the war on poverty and recreation was used to offer job training and employment opportunities for economically disadvantaged youth and adults.

The human services approach is similar to the quality-of-life approach in its recognition of the social value of recreation service. However, it does not subscribe to the latter's idealization of recreation as an inherently ennobling kind of experience, carried on for its own sake. Instead, within the human services framework, recreation must be designed to achieve significant community change and to use a variety of appropriate modalities.

This does not mean that recreation personnel should seek to be health educators, employment counselors, nutritionists, correctional officers, legal advisors, or housing experts. Rather, it implies that they must recognize the holistic nature of the human condition, provide such services when able to do so effectively, and cooperate fully with other practitioners in the various human services fields when appropriate.

Operating under this approach, many recreation departments have sponsored youth or adult classes in a wide range of educational, vocational, or self-improvement areas and also have provided daycare programs, special services for people with disabilities, roving leader programs for juvenile gangs, environmental projects, and numerous other functions of this type.

In its forceful emphasis on the need to meet social problems head on and achieve beneficial human goals, the human services approach to recreation and park programming may at times be at odds with the marketing approach to service. In the marketing approach, efficient management and maximum revenue are often the primary aims. In the human services orientation, social values and human benefits are emphasized.

Regardless of sector, some agencies may have enterprise facilities that generate a profit.
© FloridaStock/Shutterstock.

Prescriptive Approach

Of the orientations described here, the *prescriptive approach* is the most purposeful in the way it defines the goals and functions of the recreational experience. The idea that recreation should bring about constructive change in participants has been stressed in a number of textbooks on programming. Rossman and Schlatter suggest that leisure programs have goals that describe what change or experience will result from participation.[45]

The clearest cases of prescriptive recreation programs are found in recreation therapy. The prescriptive approach to leisure supports the idea that leisure is a part of health and that health and wellness do not totally involve the use of medical intervention. The prescriptive approach recognizes the needs of the participants such as improvement of social or motor skills. Recreation therapy professionals use a standard approach to developing programs that are prescriptive in nature. This approach is assessment, planning, implementation, evaluation, and documentation (APIED). The participant is assessed to determine their needs, a plan is developed to address these needs, the plan is then implemented and evaluated, and the entire experience is documented. The evaluation phase reverts to the assessment and the goals that resulted from the assessment.

Although it is similar to the human services approach in its emphasis on deliberately achieving significant social goals, the prescriptive approach differs in its reliance on the practitioner's expertise and authority. In contrast, a recreation professional working within a human services framework would be much more likely to value the input of community residents and to involve them in decision making.

Resource Manager/Aesthetic/Preservationist Approach

The unwieldy title *resource manager/aesthetic/preservationist approach* is used as a catch-all model to lump together three elements that are not synonymous but that exhibit a high degree of similarity. The *resource manager* obviously is concerned with managing, using, and protecting the outdoor environment. The balance between use, preservation, and protection is a difficult issue that is hotly contested by planners and stakeholders. The *aesthetic* position is one that values the appearance of the environment, both natural and artificial, and stresses the inclusion of cultural arts and other creative experiences within a recreation program. The *preservationist* seeks to maintain the physical environment not simply out of a respect for nature but to preserve evidence of a historical past and a cultural tradition.

This approach to recreation planning is more likely to be evident in agencies that operate extensive parks, forests, waterfront areas, or other natural or scenic resources. Thus, one might assume that it would chiefly be found in such government agencies as federal and state park departments that administer major parks and outdoor recreation facilities. However, this is not the full picture. Many urban recreation and park planners are responsible for large parks. Recent years have seen a growth of new

Many outdoor recreation agencies strive to balance managing, using, and preserving the natural environment.

© tusharkoley/Shutterstock.

Natural areas such as the Wakodahatchee Wetlands in Delray Beach, FL serve as a means to preserve wildlife and endangered species.

Courtesy of Deb Garrahy.

large urban parks in areas that are experiencing growing populations with economically advantaged residents. Often they may help to rehabilitate or redesign rundown waterfront areas, industrial sites, or gutted slum areas. In many cases, their purpose is to preserve or rebuild historic areas of cultural interest that will maintain or increase the appeal of cities for tourism and cultural programming. Preservation and restoration are the primary focuses for older parks whereas new development with revenue-producing facilities is becoming more common in newer or newly developed park and recreation agencies and communities.

Environmental Awareness

A key element in this approach is the deep reverence that many individuals have today for nature in its various forms. A common theme throughout this text is the need for nature and the lack of time children spend in nature. The value of the outdoor experience is extensive. It helps people understand a lost culture, face the challenge of adventure activities, find a spiritual connection, and experience the beauty and serenity of the outdoors.

However, environmental programming approaches cannot be carried out simply through a poetic evocation of the beauty and experience of nature. Political and economic realities also come into play when environmental decisions must be made.

State and national parks have seen dramatic budget cuts that have negatively affected park land and services. For example, the National Park Service has a $11.92 billion maintenance backlog in 2018, which is an increase of $313 million from 2017.[46]

If this trend continues, parks will stop some programming, open later in the season, reduce hours, turn to corporate sponsors, and continue to backlog maintenance.

Hedonist/Individualist Approach

The *hedonist/individualist approach* to recreational programming is concerned chiefly with providing fun and pleasure. It regards recreation as a highly individualistic activity that should be free of social constraints or moral purposes. The term *hedonist* is used to mean one who seeks personal pleasure, often with the implication that it is of a sensual, bodily nature. The term *individualist* is attached because this philosophical approach stresses the idea that each individual should be free to seek his or her own fulfillment and pleasure untrammeled by group pressures or social expectations.

Obviously, certain forms of leisure activity that have gained increased popularity in U.S. life fit this description. The accelerated use and generally freer acceptance of drugs, alcohol, gambling, and sex as a commercialized recreational pursuit, and other forms of sensation-seeking entertainment and play, illustrate the hedonist approach to leisure. These forms of play may best be described as morally marginal, in the sense that they are legal in some contexts or localities and illegal in others, regarded as acceptable leisure experiences by some population groups and condemned by others.

One form of morally marginal leisure that is a key component of the hedonist approach to recreation and leisure is the use of sex as a form of play or entertainment. Commercialized sex takes many forms, including prostitution and escort services; sex films, books, and magazines; the widespread rental of X-rated movies for home viewing; Internet pornography; and the increased showing of explicit sexual images and

---

CASE STUDY: How Do Values Drive an Organization?

The NRPA has built its mission and core values on three important functions that parallel some of the seven philosophies discussed here:

● Conservation: Protecting open space, connecting children to nature, and engaging communities in conservation practices.
● Health and Wellness: Leading the nation to improved health and wellness through parks and recreation.
● Social Equity: Ensuring all people have access to the benefits of local parks and recreation.

Review a complete description of these values at http://www.nrpa.org.

Questions to Consider

1. How is NRPA using these values?
2. How do the values compare to the philosophies discussed?
3. Review one of the position statements on these three values found online. Summarize the position.

---

themes on network television programs. Drug and alcohol use, gambling, legalized marijuana, and some forms of sexual activity are discussed in other chapters.

Although public, nonprofit, and other types of community-based leisure-service organizations generally do not sponsor substance abuse, gambling, or sex-oriented types of entertainment, such activities are widely available through commercial sponsorship and, in many cases, have governmental approval or tacit acceptance.

Benefits-Based Management Approach

The final philosophical approach to the design and implementation of recreation, park, and leisure-service programs is the *benefits-based approach*. Essentially, this approach holds that it is not enough to verbalize a set of desirable goals or mission statements or to carry out head counts of participation and tally the number of events sponsored by a leisure-service agency. Instead, governmental, nonprofit, therapeutic, armed forces, and other types of managed recreation agencies should more clearly define their roles and purposes in terms of community and participant benefits. A benefit is defined as something that is good for an individual.

Within this process, it is essential that target goals be defined in terms of concrete and measurable benefits. A benefits-based approach focuses on *outcomes* that measure long-term change or effect rather than *outputs* that simply describe a program.

Philosophical Approaches: No Pure Models

It should be stressed that although these seven approaches to the definition and management of organized leisure services are separate and distinct philosophical positions, it is unlikely that any single agency or government department follows one approach exclusively.

The changing nature of the political, economic, and social environment has forced parks and recreation agencies to reevaluate traditional approaches to delivering public parks and recreation. No single approach has been discarded, but some have fallen out of favor with politicians and professionals. Especially affected has been the human services approach. The availability of funding for parks and recreation has not kept up with inflation and in many cases has been significantly reduced. Yet agencies are expected to provide more programs and services and to maintain existing and new facilities, constituencies, and markets. The marketing or entrepreneurial approach, the fastest growing approach to delivery, has been embraced at all levels of government. Services remain available, using the human services approach, especially in major urban areas. In suburban areas, with higher family incomes, supersized recreation centers are replacing older neighborhood centers or are being created in the place of smaller centers. In growing urban fringe areas where recreation services or centers have never been present, or present as only a small operation, the supercenter is an attractive amenity for their growing population. Supercenters typically charge membership fees, charge higher prices for programs, cater to an upscale economic population, and are located in areas of the community where disadvantaged individuals may not have ready access. In addition, the supercenters have more of a club ambience than traditional recreation centers, representing a move away from the human services approach.

SUMMARY

Recreation, parks, and leisure services have grown immensely as a career field, with several million people now employed in organized recreation. Of this overall group, it is estimated that several hundred thousand individuals should be regarded as professionals because of their academic training, job functions, and organizational affiliations.

This chapter describes several important criteria of professionalism, including the following:

■ Having a significant degree of social value, in terms of providing benefits to individual participants and/or to community life
■ Being recognized by the public as a meaningful area of social service or as a legitimate occupational field
■ Requiring specialized professional preparation at the college or university level, based on a distinct body of theoretical and practical knowledge
■ Having profession-related associations that involve national and regional organizations that sponsor conferences, research, publications, and other efforts to upgrade practice and that promote collegiality and a sense of commitment among the practitioners
■ Having a credentialing system to ensure that only qualified individuals—usually identified through a system of certification—are permitted to undertake professional-level tasks

■ Having a code of ethics to ensure that responsible and effective service is provided to the public
■ Having extensive professional development opportunities

The recreation, parks, and leisure-services field has made substantial progress in most of these areas. As recreation and leisure become increasingly important aspects of life in the years ahead, the challenge to the leisure-service field will be to become even more highly professionalized by building on the foundation that has already been laid.

Students interested in a parks and recreation related career can start preparing for that career right now by taking several steps including such things as volunteering, building a network, and acquiring transferrable skills.

In addition to the criteria for professionalism, a profession also has a philosophical foundation. This chapter identifies seven distinct operational philosophies that influence the provision of organized recreation services today. These range from the quality of life and marketing orientations to a more recent model of service, the benefits-based management approach. Most leisure-services agencies use a mix of these philosophies in their policy development and program delivery. Given the current state of the profession, many agencies blend the benefits-based and marketing or entrepreneurial approaches to leisure-services delivery.

QUESTIONS FOR CLASS DISCUSSION OR ESSAY EXAMINATION

1. Several criteria are generally accepted as hallmarks of professionalism, such as having a social mandate or set of important social values or having a body of specialized knowledge. Select any four of these and discuss the extent to which you believe the recreation, park, and leisure-service field meets these criteria of professionalism.

2. What are the two certifications that are most prominent in parks and recreation? What are the criteria and requirements to obtain these certifications?

3. Several professional associations are listed. What associations would best match your future career interests?

4. There are nine guidelines to follow to help position yourself in a fast-growing job market. Select three of them and discuss how you could implement them so that they could affect your career after graduation.

5. Seven different philosophies and approaches to leisure are presented (for example, quality of life). Which of the seven approaches do you find most compatible with your own view?_____

_____

_____

_____

ENDNOTES

1. Kraus, R. (1971). *Recreation and leisure in modern society*. New York: Meredith Corporation.

2. National Travel and Tourism Office. (2019). *Fast facts: United States travel and tourism industry 2018*. Retrieved April 12, 2020, from http://travel.trade. gov/outreachpages/download_data_table/Fast_ Facts_2018.pdf.

3. Bureau of Labor Statistics. (2020, September 1). Summary: Recreational therapists. *Occupational Outlook Handbook*. Retrieved April 12, 2020, from https://www.bls.gov/ooh/healthcare/recreational-therapists.htm.

4. Bureau of Labor Statistics. (2020, September 21). Summary: Recreation workers. *Occupational Outlook Handbook*. Retrieved April 12, 2020, from https:// www.bls.gov/ooh/personal-care-and-service /recreation-workers.htm.

5. Bureau of Labor Statistics. (2020, September 1). Summary: Meeting, convention and event planners. *Occupational Outlook Handbook*. Retrieved April 12, 2020, from https://www.bls.gov/ooh/business-and-financial/meeting-convention-and-event-planners.htm.

6. National Park Service. (2020, December 10). *Frequently asked questions*. Retrieved January 12, 2021, from https://www.nps.gov/aboutus/faqs.htm.

7. America's State Parks. *2019 Outlook and Analysis Letter*. Retrieved February 13, 2021, from https:// extension.usu.edu/iort/ou-files/2019_outlook_and_ analysis_report_rfs.pdf.

8. Bureau of Labor Statistics. (2020, September 21). Summary: Recreation workers. *Occupational Outlook Handbook*. Retrieved April 12, 2020, from https:// www.bls.gov/ooh/personal-care-and-service /recreation-workers.htm.

9. Bureau of Labor Statistics. (2020, September 1). Summary: Recreational therapists. *Occupational Outlook Handbook*. Retrieved April 12, 2020, from https://www.bls.gov/ooh/healthcare/recreational-therapists.htm.

10. YWCA. (n.d.). *Our mission in action*. Retrieved April 12, 2020, from https://www.ywca.org/what-we-do /our-mission-in-action/.

11. Bureau of Labor Statistics. (2020). *Percent of the population engaging in selected activities, averages per day by sex and day. American Time Use Survey–2019 results*. Retrieved April 12, 2020, from https://www.bls. gov/charts/american-time-use/civ-pop-by-sex-and-day. htm.

12. Bureau of Labor Statistics. (2020). *Avg hrs per day— Leisure and sports (includes travel). American Time Use Survey–2019 results*. Retrieved April 12, 2020, from https://data.bls.gov/timeseries/ TUU10101AA01013585.

13. America's State Parks. *State park facts*. Retrieved April 12, 2020, from https://www.stateparks.org /about-us/state-park-facts/.

14. National Park Service. (2020, December 10). *Frequently asked questions*. Retrieved January 12, 2021, from http://www.nps.gov/aboutus/faqs.htm.

15. ESPN. (2019). *Major league attendance report*. Retrieved April 12, 2020, from http://www.espn.com /mlb/attendance/_/year/2019.

16. North American Society for Sport Management. (n.d.). *Sports management programs: United States*. Retrieved April 12, 2020, from http://www.nassm. org/Programs/AcademicPrograms/United_States.

17. Hurd, A. R., Barcelona, R., Zimmerman, J., & Ready, J. (2020). *Leisure services management* (2nd ed.). Champaign, IL: Human Kinetics Publishing.

18. Council on Accreditation of Recreation, Parks, Tourism and Related Professions. (2020). *Accredited programs directory*. Retrieved January 12, 2021, from https://accreditationcouncil.org/ Accredited-Programs-Directory.

19. Commission on Sport Management Accreditation (COSMA). (n.d.). *Directory of accredited programs*. Retrieved April 13, 2020, from https://www.cos-maweb.org/directory-of-accredited-programs.html.

20. National Recreation and Park Association. (n.d.). *Our mission*. Retrieved April 13, 2020, from https:// www.nrpa.org/ About-National-Recreation-and-Park-Association/.

21. Canadian Parks and Recreation Association. Retrieved April 13, 2020, from https://www.cpra.ca/.

22. American Camp Association. Retrieved April 13, 2020, from https://www.acacamps.org/.

23. National Recreation and Park Association. (n.d.). *CPRP eligibility*. Retrieved April 13, 2020, from http://www.nrpa.org/certification/CPRP/eligibility/.

24. Mulvaney, M. A. & Hurd, A. R. (2017). *Official study guide for the Certified Park and Recreation Professional Examination* (5th ed.) Ashburn, VA: National Recreation and Park Association.

25. National Council for Therapeutic Recreation Certification. (n.d.). *Certification standards*. Retrieved January 12, 2021, from https://www.nctrc.org/about-certification/certification-standards/.

26. National Council for Therapeutic Recreation Certification. (2020). *Information for the Certified Therapeutic Recreation Specialist® and new applicants*. Retrieved April 13, 2020, from https://www.nctrc.org/wp-content/uploads/2019/08/CertificationStandards.pdf.

27. National Recreation and Park Association. (n.d.). *Certified Park and Recreation Executive (CPRE) certification*. Retrieved April 13, 2020, from https://www.nrpa.org/certification/cpre/become-a-cpre/.

28. Meeting Professionals International. Retrieved April 13, 2020, from https://www.mpi.org/education/mpi-academy.

29. Events Industry Council. (n.d.). *About the Certified Meeting Professional (CMP) Program*. Retrieved April 13, 2020, from https://www.eventscouncil.org/CMP/About-CMP.

30. National Recreation and Park Association. (n.d.). *Certified Playground Safety Inspector certification*. Retrieved April 13, 2020, from https://www.nrpa.org/certification/CPSI/.

31. International Live Events Association. (n.d.). *Certified Special Events Professional (CSEP)*. Retrieved April 13, 2020, from https://www.ileahub.com/CSEP.

32. National Association for Interpretation. (n.d.). *Certification & training program*. Retrieved April 13, 2020, from https://www.interpnet.com/NAI/interp/Certification/nai/_certification/NAI_Certification.aspx?hkey=0c08ac07-c574-4560-940f-82fba3a22be9.

33. National Recreation and Park Association. (n.d.). *CAPRA accredited agencies*. Retrieved April 13, 2020, from https://www.nrpa.org/certification/accreditation/capra/accreditedagencies/.

34. Troxell, W., & Atteberry, D. (2019). *CAPRA: A tangible guidepost for the City of Fort Collins*. National Recreation and Park Association. Retrieved April 13, 2020, from https://www.nrpa.org/parks-recreation-magazine/2019/november/capra-a-tangible-guidepost-for-the-city-of-fort-collins/.

35. American Camp Association. (n.d.). *Introduction to accreditation*. Retrieved April 13, 2020, from http://www.acacamps.org/staff-professionals/accreditation-standards/accreditation/about-aca-accreditation.

36. American Therapeutic Recreation Association. (2009). *Code of ethics*. Retrieved April 13, 2020, from https://www.atra-online.com/page/Ethics.

37. World Tourism Association. (n.d.). *Global code of ethics for tourism*. Retrieved April 13, 2020, from https://www.unwto.org/global-code-of-ethics-for-tourism.

38. International Live Events Association. (n.d.). *Professional conduct and ethics*. Retrieved January 12, 2021, from https://www.ileahub.com/Meet-ILEA/Professional-Conduct-Ethics.

39. International Festivals & Events Association. (n.d.). *Education*. Retrieved April 13, 2020, from http://www.ifea.com/p/education.

40. National Intramural Recreational Sports Association. (n.d.). *Events and professional development*. Retrieved April 13, 2020, from http://nirsa.net/nirsa/grow/.

41. Hurd, A. R., Barcelona, R. J., Zimmerman, A. M., & Ready, J. (2020). *Leisure services management* (2nd ed.). Champaign, IL: Human Kinetics.

42. Events Industry Council. (2017). *Certified Meeting Professional international standards*. Retrieved May 10, 2020, from https://www.eventscouncil.org/Portals/0/EIC%20CMP-IS%202017_1.pdf.

43. Park Ridge Park District. (n.d.). *About us*. Retrieved April 13, 2020, from http://parkridgeparkdistrict.com/general.

44. Johnston Senior Center. (n.d.). *The Johnston Senior Center mission statement*. Retrieved April 13, 2020, from http://johnstonsc.net/2.html.

45. Rossman, J. R., & Schlatter, B. E. (2015). *Recreation programming: Designing leisure experiences* (7th ed.). Champaign, IL: Sagamore Publishing.

46. National Park Service. (2020, June 18). *Infrastructure: What is deferred maintenance?* Retrieved April 13, 2020, from https://www.nps.gov/subjects/infrastructure/deferred-maintenance.htm.

Chapter 8

Specialized Leisure-Services Areas

"Those who suffer from disability frequently find difficulty in meeting their recreative needs in constructive and varied ways, in part, because serious physical handicaps obviously limit the extent of participation. Much recreation deprivation of the disabled is, however, caused by the reluctance of society to permit them to engage in activity to the extent of their real potential."[1]
-From the first edition of Kraus' Recreation and Leisure in Modern Society, published in 1971

LEARNING OBJECTIVES

1. Demonstrate a basic understanding of the fields of recreation therapy, armed forces recreation, employee services recreation, campus recreation, private-membership recreation clubs, meetings and events, and faith-based recreation.

2. Explain the types of clientele that specialized leisure-services providers serve.

3. Name examples of organizations that provide specialized leisure services.

4. Describe career opportunities with the seven specialized leisure-services areas.

Introduction

One can participate in leisure in any number of ways. It can be as simple as playing catch in the backyard, walking through a park, or hanging out with friends. It can also be more complex and experienced through organized opportunities such as a pickleball league, camping, or international travel. Organized leisure and recreation can be found within three sectors—public, nonprofit, and commercial. These three sectors were discussed in previous chapters. However, there are some specialized leisure-services opportunities that warrant further exploration and often cross over all three sectors.

We now turn to seven categories of recreation services that meet more specialized needs and interests. These seven areas are recreation for people with disabilities; armed forces morale, welfare, and recreation services; employee recreation services; campus recreation; private-membership organizations; events and meetings; and faith-based recreation. Each of these areas serves a specific type of population or organization, with goals and program elements geared to meet its specific needs. These specialized areas and their terminology have also evolved considerably since the first edition as demonstrated in the opening quote about recreation participation for people with disabilities.

Recreation Therapy Services

The roots of today's use of recreation to improve health conditions in treatment settings can be traced back to Benjamin Rush, an American physician, and Florence Nightingale, a British nurse. Both of these figures were advocates of the early therapeutic value of recreation. Over the past 50 years, the expanded use of recreation and leisure in hospitals, physical rehabilitation, mental health, and long-term care settings has demonstrated its increased value as a treatment approach and the importance of having a recreation therapist on the treatment team. During this same period, there was tremendous growth in the provision of specialized or adapted recreation services in the community for people with disabilities.

This role in the recreation profession has a variety of names, including recreation therapist, therapeutic recreation specialist, inclusion specialist, and activity therapist, to name a few. The American Therapeutic Recreation Association (ATRA) defines recreation therapy as "a systematic process that utilizes recreation and other activity-based interventions to address the assessed needs of individuals with illnesses and/or disabling conditions, as a means to psychological and physical health, recovery and well-being." They go on to say that recreation therapy is "a treatment service designed to restore, remediate and rehabilitate a person's level of functioning and independence in life activities, to promote health and wellness as well as reduce or eliminate the activity limitations and restrictions to participation in life situations caused by an illness or disabling condition."[2] Although recreation therapy may involve enjoyable activities and seem like play and fun on the surface, it is much more complicated than that. There is a purpose behind the activities beyond fun. A recreation therapist works with clients to assess their needs, set goals, develop plans to reach those goals using recreation activities, and assess progress made. These goals will include such things as build physical strength, reduce stress, or manage anxiety or mental illness.

Early Development of Recreation Therapy

The history of past centuries provides a number of examples of the use of recreation in the treatment of psychiatric patients, in both Europe and America. The greatest impetus for recreation therapy, however, came in the 20th century in three types of institutions: hospitals and rehabilitation centers for those with physical impairments, hospitals for people with mental illness, and special schools for those with developmental disabilities.

After both World War I and World War II, there were waves of concern about the need to rehabilitate veterans who had sustained major physical injuries or psychological trauma while in service. As a consequence, the Veterans Administration and military hospitals developed comprehensive programs of rehabilitative services, including physical and occupational therapy, psychotherapy, social services, vocational training, guidance, and recreation. In such settings, recreation was perceived as being one of several techniques that contributed to patient recovery.

At the same time, recreation gained recognition as a form of allied or adjunctive service within such civilian institutions as special homes or schools for individuals with cognitive or other disabilities, nursing homes and long-term care institutions, and state or private psychiatric hospitals or mental health centers. Gradually, *recreation therapy*, as it came to be known, gained acceptance in the healthcare field. Colleges and universities initiated major curricula or degree options in this field, and professional societies developed standards for practice and accreditation and certification procedures for practitioners.

As the recreation therapy field grew in demand and stature, it could be found in a variety of settings including "inpatient and outpatient physical rehabilitation, inpatient and outpatient mental health, skilled nursing facilities and assisted living, adult day programs, park and recreation, adapted sports programs, acute care hospitals, pediatric hospitals and programs and school systems."[3]

Although all individuals need diverse recreation outlets, those with disabilities encounter barriers that those without disabilities do not, substantially narrowing their options for participation. In part this is because of significant and sometimes multiple disabling conditions that restrict physical, cognitive, and/or emotional functioning. Many times, however, the problems with access to recreation opportunities can be attributed to attitudinal, architectural, programmatic, and transportation barriers.

Smith et al.[4] explored the question of why persons with disabilities have been underserved by community recreation and leisure services. They suggest that in the first half of the 20th century the way society generally treated people during this period who did not fit the norm was to separate and hide them away, and this produced a similar philosophy within the evolving field of recreation. Examples include the "old folks homes" for older people who were indigent, warehousing people with cognitive disabilities in large institutions away from populated areas, and placing people with mental health problems in similarly remote "insane asylums." While attitudes toward vulnerable populations were shifting during the 1960s, 1970s, and early 1980s, there were other barriers for public parks and recreation departments to contend with, both real and perceived. These included lack of funding, inaccessible facilities, untrained staff, lack of knowledge to develop such programs, lack of accessible community transportation, continuing attitudinal barriers, and lack of awareness of the great need for recreation participation by people with disabilities.

In some cases, recreation and park departments barred people with disabilities from their programs, arguing that serving such people would impose a higher risk of accident lawsuits and increased insurance costs. We now know this is not true. In other cases, parents, relatives, and schools have sheltered people with disabilities excessively, or the individual's perceived lack of ability or fear of rejection by others has caused him or her to limit recreation participation.

Recreation Therapy Job Settings

Recreation therapy (RT) professionals can find themselves working in the public sector, private sector, and nonprofit sector. RT specialists can predominantly work in one of two areas of practice—clinical settings or community settings.

RT specialists in a clinical setting often work in nursing homes and hospitals. Nursing home RT staff plan programs to help residents with their long-term, day-to-day function. There may be programs to enhance memory skills, social skills, and fitness levels. In hospital settings, RT specialists work with patients in four main areas: acute care, outpatient care, psychiatric care, and rehabilitation hospitals.[5] Acute care hospitals are for people with more serious illnesses and injuries on a short-term basis. RT specialists work with patients to prepare them for discharge or their next facility, such as a nursing home or rehabilitation center. Once discharged, a patient may move to outpatient care where they receive RT services while living at home. Psychiatric care is available for people with mental illnesses. Psychiatric care can be in a standalone facility or part of a general hospital and can be short or long term. Last, rehabilitation centers

serve people with disabilities that have resulted from an illness such as a stroke or an accident. The RT specialist helps patients adjust to their disability and learn to use leisure to meet their needs. All of these clinical settings often have a treatment team that might include occupational therapists, physical therapists, social workers, physicians, and recreation therapists working together to help patients improve their health.

Not all people with disabilities need to experience leisure in a clinical setting. A far greater number of people with disabilities live in the community than live in hospital settings, and they have equally strong needs for recreation. Municipal parks and recreation agencies were given the charge to provide these much-needed services. Public parks and recreation agencies hire RT specialists to oversee programs specifically for people with disabilities or for inclusion purposes. People specializing in inclusion manage their own programs as well as assist staff in making programs and events accessible to people with disabilities. An inclusion specialist may help a program leader adapt a program so that someone who is deaf or who has a physical disability can participate with individuals who do not have a disability. The inclusion specialist most likely has extensive knowledge of the Americans with Disabilities Act,[6] which requires parks and recreation agencies to provide accessible services and access to all users. Community RT does not deliberately gear programs to achieve specific treatment or rehabilitative goals within a clinical framework, but those providing special or inclusive recreation do have important purposes. They value recreation as an important life experience for people with disabilities and seek to achieve positive physical, social, and emotional outcomes, making adaptations in programming, facilities, equipment, or leadership methods as appropriate.

Recreation Therapy Process

RT is unique in the recreation field in that it follows a clinical process, called the RT process, to help clients. The RT process has five parts: assessment, planning, implementation, evaluation, and documentation. In the profession, this is known as APIED (pronounced *a-pie-d*).

The assessment piece of the RT process is information gathering. It is necessary to understand where the client currently is in functioning, strengths, and needs. Documents are gathered from physicians, other therapists, others involved in the care of the client, and from the client and/or the family. RT specialists also use RT-specific assessment tools designed to measure any number of factors needed to enhance care and reach a desired outcome. Once the initial assessment is complete, an individual program plan is developed outlining client goals, programs, and the overall treatment plan. Implementation of the individual program plan is facilitated by the RT specialist in collaboration with the client. The RT specialist's level of

RT TREATMENT MODALITIES

A treatment modality is the activity used to bring about a change or to reach a client's goals. RT specialists use a plethora of activities and approaches to help clients. The most common modalities used in RT include (1) games, (2) exercise, (3) parties, (4) arts and crafts, (5) community integration activities, (6) music, (7) problem-solving activities, (8) sports, (9) self-esteem, and (10) activities of daily living. Some of these modalities are used more often with certain populations. For example, community integration, games, and exercise are often used for physical rehabilitation. Games, problem solving, and arts and crafts are more commonly used for people with mental health issues.

Kinney, J. S., Kinney, T., & Witman, J. (2004). Therapeutic recreation modalities and facilitation techniques: A national study. *Annual in Therapeutic Recreation*, 13, 59–79.

involvement varies depending on the needs of the client. Next, evaluation is the systematic process where the RT specialist gathers information to assess whether the treatment plan and outcomes are appropriate. This information is used to modify the plan if needed. This aspect of the RT process requires the evaluation of the client to assess the progress he or she is making on goals and outcomes. An evaluation is also done on the programs selected to ascertain their effectiveness for the individual.[7] Lastly, documentation is done throughout all other steps of the process to keep a record of the activities and progress of the client. This documentation tracks such things as level of participation, behaviors, response to interventions, or progress toward goals.

The APIED process is the crux of RT and requires the RT specialist and the participant to work together to establish what is in the best interest of the participant and how to achieve the goals created.

In 1981, the National Council for Therapeutic Recreation Certification (NCTRC) was established as an autonomous credentialing body to oversee the development and administration of the Certified Therapeutic Recreation Specialist (CTRS) professional certification. A research-based recreation therapy job analysis was performed and used to develop the certification exam, which was administered for the first time in November 1990. This exam and the requirements set by NCTRC to sit for the exam are the primary certification standards for both clinical and recreation applications of recreation therapy.

The most recent report by NCTRC in 2014 found the top-rated job tasks fall in the areas of professional relationships and responsibilities, document intervention services, implementation of interventions and/or programs, and assessment. The top-listed knowledge areas were foundational knowledge and the assessment process.[8]

Expansion of Sport and Outdoor Recreation Participation

At every level, people of all ages with physical or cognitive disabilities are taking part in varied forms of sport and out-

Assistive technology has helped people with disabilities enjoy a wide variety of recreation activities.
© Eric Rodolfo Schroeder/iStockphoto/Thinkstock/Getty Images.

door recreation. Many of these activities are promoted by organizations such as Adaptive Sports, USA, a multisport organization for athletes who compete annually in regional, national, and international games. Included among the competitive events for both men and women are archery, athletics (track and field), swimming, table tennis, and powerlifting. Thousands of young athletes also participate in Special Olympics events, and many others compete in marathons, bowling leagues, and other individual and team sports.

In terms of outdoor recreation, programs have become increasingly geared for individuals with disabilities. Like sports, there are organizations specifically designed for outdoor recreation pursuits. For example, Outdoors Without Limits educates people about outdoor recreation opportunities for people with disabilities. The National Sports Center for the Disabled offers programs in sport and outdoor recreation. For example, they currently offer whitewater rafting, canoeing, mountain biking, rock climbing, alpine skiing, and more for all ages.[9]

MORGAN'S WONDERLAND

Morgan's Wonderland, located in San Antonio, Texas, is a 25-acre amusement park designed specifically for people with disabilities. Gordon Hartman, whose daughter Morgan has a cognitive disability, raised $30 million to build this facility. Admission is free for people with disabilities. Everyone else is charged an admission fee. Amenities on the property include an event center and gymnasium, an interactive sensory village, butterfly-themed playground, Wonderland Express train, amphitheater, the first ever off-road adventure ride, a 36-foot-diameter carousel, music garden, water play area, and much more.[10]

CASE STUDY: Americans with Disabilities Act

The Americans with Disabilities Act of 1990 (ADA) is a civil rights law that prohibits discrimination based on disability. There are five sections of the act:

- *Title 1: Employment:* Qualified candidates cannot be discriminated against in the hiring process, employment, advancement, or discharge based on disability. Applies to agencies with 15+ employees.
- *Title 2: Public Services:* People with disabilities must have access to state and local government facilities and programs. This section also addresses accessibility of transportation such as on buses and trains.
- *Title 3: Public Accommodations (and Commercial Facilities):* People with disabilities may not be discriminated against with regard to use of public accommodations including hotels, resorts, restaurants, and recreation opportunities, among others. In addition, buildings must be compliant with the ADA Accessibility Guidelines. Public accommodations are exempt if the cost of compliance is too great (e.g., small businesses) or if the property is deemed historic. Private clubs and religious organizations are exempt from the law. Public accommodations can include such things as sign language interpreters, assistive listening devices, Braille publications, taped publications, telephone typewriter (TTY)/Telecommunications Device for the Deaf (TDD), and facility accessibility.
- *Title 4: Telecommunications:* Telecommunications companies must make their services available to people with disabilities. This is most focused on serving people who are deaf/hard of hearing and/or who have a speech impairment.
- *Title 5: Miscellaneous Provisions:* This section covers the technical aspects of the law such as immunity under ADA, retaliation against claims, and responsibilities for technical assistance.

In 2008, the definition of the term "disability" was adjusted, effectively making it easier for an individual seeking protection under the ADA to establish that he or she has a disability within the meaning of the ADA. The ADA defines a person with a disability as a person who has a physical or mental impairment that substantially limits one or more major life activity.

Questions to Consider

- Walk through a building on campus such as the campus recreation facility. What examples did you find that the facility and/or programs were accessible to people with disabilities?
- What aspects of the facility and/or programs were not accessible?
- Investigate the ADA and its impact on outdoor recreation. How do parks, trails, and bodies of water comply with ADA requirements? Do they have to? Why or why not?

Data from ADA National Network. (n.d.). What does *"regarded as" having a disability mean?* https://adata.org/faq/what-does-regarded-having-disability-mean; Americans with Disabilities Act. https://www.ada.gov; U.S. Equal Employment Opportunity Commission. (n.d.). *Fact sheet: Disability discrimination.* https://www.eeoc.gov/laws/guidance/fact-sheet-disability-discrimination

Use of Technology and Assistive Devices

Sophisticated technology is being brought into play to permit persons with disabilities to participate successfully in different leisure activities. For several decades, various modified instruments or pieces of equipment have been used to help people with disabilities take part in card and table games, arts and crafts, team and individual sport, and other pursuits. For example, for outdoor recreation there are adaptive gun and bow mounts for hunting, all-terrain tires for trails, and fishing pole holders. Adapted sports equipment includes ice hockey sledges, handcycles, mono- and bi-skis for alpine skiing, and Nordic cross-country skis.

Aerodynamic wheelchairs are now being used by racers with disabilities, and carbon-fiber prosthetic feet enable athletes with amputations to run almost as fast as athletes without disabilities. Research into the use of electrodes to stimulate the leg muscles of persons with spinal cord injuries is helping to maintain bone, joint, and muscle health, which has positive effects on cardiovascular functioning and recreation participation, and numerous other devices are being invented each year to facilitate independent functioning for people with disabilities. Electronic devices such as "aura interactor" strap-on vests enable deaf people to dance without straining to hear the music and help video game players who are blind to feel laser beams "bouncing" off the screen.

Cooperative Networks of Agencies

Because many community and nonprofit organizations lacked the staff resources or special facilities required to provide comprehensive leisure-services programs for persons with disabilities, the 1980s and 1990s saw a trend toward developing cooperative networks of such agencies. In such structures, two or more public or nonprofit human-service organizations—or a combination of both types—share their funding and facilities to provide needed recreation programs in a number of locations. For example, there are more than 20 independent special recreation associations (SRAs) in northern Illinois, based on revenue generated from special direct property taxes. Rather than each agency having its own staff trained in RT, they pool resources to provide a higher level of service for the communities involved. All SRAs are coordinated by boards representing the cooperating communities. They interface with municipal recreation and park departments and offer programming for persons with all types of disabling conditions in both integrated and segregated groupings. For example, the Fox Valley Special Recreation Association[11] is an extension of the Batavia, Fox Valley, Geneva, Oswego-land, St. Charles, Sugar Grove Park Districts, and South Elgin Parks and Recreation Department.

In another example of joint cooperation, Disability Partnerships is a 501(c)(3) that provides community-based services to people with physical disabilities. Their projects span affordable accessible housing, advocating for legislation that helps people with disabilities, and working with local healthcare providers to offer health and wellness programs to build strength, improve balance, and help people lead a healthy lifestyle.[12]

Increased Emphasis on Inclusion

In the late 1990s, instead of the term *special recreation*, professional organizations began to use the term *inclusion*, meaning simply the involvement and full acceptance of people with disabilities in a wide range of community settings. In 2009, a research team of inclusion experts examined best practices employed by agencies deemed to be successful at implementing inclusive service delivery. Best practices are tied to participant assessment, accommodation plans, behavioral interventions, inclusion support staff, preparing nondisabled peers, and numerous other criteria. The study found that successful agencies use best practices but implement them in highly individualized manners.[13]

The efforts of researchers, ATRA, NCTRC, agencies that deliver services, and recreation therapy practitioners have combined to broaden the scope of services, improve the quality of services, and make recreation therapy services available to more people with illnesses and disabling conditions than ever before. Many factors are still unfolding in the areas of healthcare, community recreation services, efficacy-based research, university RT programs, and credentialing, which will affect the future of RT.

Certification and Working in Recreation Therapy

The practice of RT as a treatment discipline has become increasingly sophisticated. The body of research knowledge has expanded, protocols for treatment approaches have been developed, university curricula have become broader in scope, and more populations are being served. There is also greater recognition of the discipline within healthcare systems and what it has to offer. Facilitating this is the reinforcement of standards by healthcare-accrediting bodies, such as the Commission on Accreditation of Rehabilitation Facilities. This accrediting organization has specific criteria for providing qualified recreation therapy services, which includes a requirement that said services be provided only by a CTRS.

Because recreation therapy jobs are in so many different settings, the job search requires looking on many different websites. At NRPA.org one will find community-based positions such as the Recreation Manager at Stepping Stones, Inc. in Cincinnati, Ohio and the Recreation Supervisor for Community Connections and Inclusion Services in Chandler, Arizona. The American Therapeutic Recreation Association has job listings for community-based recreation but also clinical positions such as Recreation Therapists for the Boise (Idaho) Veterans Affairs Medical Center or the South Texas Veterans Health Care System. Most of these positions require applicants to have their CTRS certification and experience working with people with disabilities.

Armed Forces Recreation

For many years, it has been the official policy of the military establishment to provide a well-rounded morale, welfare, and recreational program for the physical, social, and mental well-being of its personnel. During World War I, Special Services Divisions were established to provide social and recreational programs that would sustain favorable morale, curb homesickness and boredom, minimize fatigue, and reduce AWOL (absent without leave) and sexually transmitted disease rates.

Today, each branch of the armed forces has its own pattern of recreation sponsorship, although they are all under the same morale, welfare, and recreation (MWR) program, which is administratively responsible to the Office of the

Under Secretary for Personnel and Readiness. They serve several million individuals, including active duty, reserve, and retired military personnel and their dependents; civilian employees; and surviving spouses of military personnel who died in active duty. In addition, MWR services are also provided to Coast Guard personnel, who are not part of the Department of Defense, but the Department of Homeland Security.

Goals and Scope of Armed Forces Recreation Today

The U.S. Army Morale, Welfare, and Recreation exists because the U.S. Army states it "is committed to the well-being of the community of people who serve and stand ready to defend the nation, to enhance the lives of soldiers, their families, civilian employees, and military retirees."[14] The mission is to serve the needs, interests, and responsibilities of each individual in the Army community for as long as he or she is associated with the Army, no matter where he or she is.

Military recreation departments are structured and operate similarly to public parks and recreation agencies. They both offer a variety of programs for the community. The military community is far more defined and limited than a community such as a city or county. Potter and Ogilvie outline four major differences between MWR and community recreation.[15] First, the military community is quite transient and ever changing. Working in MWR requires staff to constantly focus on the changes in needs going on within the military community. Second, military communities are not always in the most stable parts of the world. They are in remote areas, combat zones, and less than desirable geographic locations. The staff, military personnel, and their families must be aware of these situations. Recreation can serve as a way to make life a little more stable for all involved. Third, MWR is exclusive in whom it serves. MWR provides services for active and retired military personnel and their families only. Last, MWR relies heavily on volunteers to carry out programs and events. Although municipal agencies also often rely on volunteers, MWR volunteers are transient, making it difficult to manage and recruit a consistent stream of volunteers.

Program Elements

SPORTS AND FITNESS

MWR sports and fitness programs include an extensive range of sport, fitness, social, outdoor recreation, and hobby leisure pursuits. In the Navy, for example, sports and fitness are offered at many different levels. The All-Navy Teams are for sailors with the skill to compete above the intramural level and represent the Navy at competitions such as the Armed Forces Sports Championships and the Department of Defense Sports Program.[16] For those not wanting this

level of competition, there are individual and intramural sport and fitness opportunities available.

In addition to sport, fitness is a primary focus of MWR. To improve fitness levels of personnel, the Air Force installed health and wellness centers (HAWC) on each base; these centers are well equipped and are staffed with leaders qualified to provide fitness and health risk assessments, exercise programming, weight counseling, stress management, smoking cessation assistance, and similar activities.

On some military bases, fitness is promoted through well-publicized and challenging special events. At the Marine Corps Base at Camp Lejeune, North Carolina, the Lejeune Grand Prix Series is labeled the ultimate fitness challenge, and features a number of competitive events that involve hundreds of service personnel and the community in a mud run, half marathon, sprint triathlon, duathlon, and other types of races. Proceeds from the events go to support Marine Corps Community Services facilities and programs.[17]

Many of the fitness programs are designed and carried out by certified fitness instructors so that the military personnel and their families receive high quality fitness and health guidance and programming.[18]

Many military bases have fitness and recreation centers on the premises. For those that do not, the Department of Defense has partnered with the local Ys to provide memberships.[19]

OUTDOOR RECREATION

Often, outdoor program activities are keyed to the location of a base. For example, Fort Carson, Colorado, offers such activities as ice climbing lessons, workshops, and trips; skiing and snowshoe trips; and rafting.[20] Responding to widespread interest in mountain climbing and rock climbing, this Army base constructed a 17,400-square-foot outdoor recreation center that features a 30-foot-high indoor climbing wall and a 60-foot outdoor wall with the look and feel of

Varying levels of health and wellness programs are major components of most MWR programs.

natural rock and climbing routes geared to different skill levels. Other bases offer instruction, equipment, and facilities for such water-based activities as fishing, wind-surfing, jet skiing, scuba diving, and similar pastimes.

FAMILY RECREATION

The Department of Defense has become increasingly aware of the need to provide varied family-focused programs to counter the special problems that may affect the spouses and children of military personnel.

All branches of the military have family programs. For example, the Marine Corps Community Services is committed to supporting both individual marines and family members with its fitness and wellness programs, as well as other services designed to enhance personal and family readiness such as the Family Team Building program that provides educational resources and services to foster personal growth and enhance the readiness of Marine Corps families.[21]

The Armed Forces prides itself on its Child and Youth Programs (CYP) that provide high-quality and affordable childcare and recreation programs that is readily available for military and Department of Defense families worldwide.[22] CYP serves infants to 18 year olds.

COMMUNITY RELATIONS

Many military bases in the United States and overseas place a high priority on establishing positive relationships between armed forces personnel and nearby communities. Civilian MWR personnel working around the globe in such settings as Europe, Korea, and Central America, and even Saudi Arabia, Turkey, and Africa, seek to provide a wealth of recreational experiences and positive intercultural experiences with local residents.

MWR programs are sometimes open to the general public. For example, Marine Corps Community Services Miramar Memorial Golf Course is open to the public. However, because of security and gate access at the course, player names must be submitted in advance to gain access. These players are also charged a higher fee than active duty soldiers, retirees, and their families.[23] There are also many services within MWR that help families acclimate to the communities in which they live. They do this by providing information about the community and participating in community events.[24]

RESORTS AND VACATIONS

The Armed Forces provides a full range of resorts and vacation destinations for all military members. Armed Forces Recreation Centers (AFRC) are affordable Joint Service facilities operated by the U.S. Army Community and Family Support Center and located in different areas, including Germany, Florida, and Hawaii. They offer a full range of resort hotel opportunities for members of all branches of the military service, their families, and other members of the

Total Defense Force. The resorts are self-supporting, funded by revenues generated internally from operations. These vacation destinations include such things as cabins in the woods, a resort on a beach, and locations worldwide.

Fiscal Support of Armed Forces Recreation

Military recreation has traditionally depended on two types of funding: *appropriated funds*, which are tax funds approved by Congress, and *nonappropriated funds*, which are generated on the military base through a combination of post exchange profits and revenue from fees, rentals, and other recreation charges. As such, not all recreation activities are free to military personnel and their families. Just like other public agencies, some programs are free and supported by tax dollars (appropriated funds) and others are used to generate revenue.

With growing federal government budget cutbacks and the need to maximize revenues from clubs, messes, post exchanges, and varied forms of commercial sponsorship or partnerships, MWR planners have initiated a range of new fiscal strategies. The effort has been to reduce the costs of operations, standardize procedures, and eliminate redundant programs or personnel. The Navy, for example, established 10 major regions to simplify the planning and supervision of programs, increasingly encouraged public/private projects, and established new planning processes to "reinvent" facility development and other projects.

Working in MWR

Those who work in MWR positions are often civilian employees of the federal government. MWR employees are hired as either part-time or full-time employees. Full-time employees receive a comprehensive benefits package (medical, dental, life insurance, spouse and dependent life insurance, long-term disability, retirement, a 401(k) savings plan, annual vacation time, sick leave, tuition reimbursement, etc.). Some positions will offer housing and utilities if the location is overseas as well as periodic flights back to the United States. Some MWR positions have a specific time commitment such as 2 years the person must remain in the job. Examples of full-time positions include a Recreation Assistant for Great Pond Outdoor Adventure in Great Pond, Maine; Child and Youth Program Assistants in Manama, Bahrain and Bethesda, Maryland, or a Fitness Specialist in Norfolk, Virginia.[25]

Employee Services and Recreation Programs

MWR provides recreation for its service members, and employee services and recreation programs provide recreation and related personnel services to employees and in some cases their families or other community residents.

EMPLOYMENT IN MWR

MWR employs 100,000 people worldwide. Entry-level positions are often in specialty areas such as sports, youth, or special events. To find jobs in MWR, see these websites:

- Coast Guard: https://www.usajobs.gov/Search/Results?k=Coast%20Guard
- Marines: https://careers.usmc-mccs.org/
- Navy: https://www.navymwr.org/careers
- Army: https://www.armymwr.com/m/emplyee-portal/human-resources/employment/
- Air Force: https://www.indeed.com/q-Air-Force-Morale,-Welfare-&-Recreation-Center-jobs.html

Background of Company-Sponsored Programs

Employee recreation (formerly called "industrial recreation") began in the 19th century but did not expand rapidly until after World War II. At this time, the National Industrial Recreation Association was formed. This professional association provided resources for people working in corporate recreation, and at this point the emphasis was on fitness and wellness. Later, this organization became the Employee Services Management (ESM) Association.

ESM Association is for staff who work in units that provide benefits to employees such as employee stores, community services, voluntary benefits, employee recognition programs, and recreation. Recreation services encompasses programs, wellness, travel services, and special events.[26]

Although the providers of employee services and recreation originally were manufacturing companies and other industrial businesses, today many different types of organizations also sponsor employee activities. They include such diverse groups as food market chains, airlines, insurance companies, hospitals, and government agencies.

Goals of Employee Recreation

The major goals of the institutions providing employee programs and services include improving employee and employer relations, directly promoting employee fitness and efficiency, recruitment and retention, and company image and community role.

IMPROVEMENT OF EMPLOYER–EMPLOYEE RELATIONS

Earlier in this country's industrial development, there was considerable friction between management and labor that often resulted in extended and violent strikes. A major purpose of industrial recreation programs at this time was to create favorable employer–employee relationships and instill a sense of loyalty among workers. It is believed that such programs tend to create a feeling of belonging and identification among employees and that group participation by workers at various job levels contributes to improved worker morale, increased harmony, and an attitude of mutual cooperation.

For example, the Ford Employees Recreation Association was established in 1947 "for the purpose of developing fellowship and understanding among the Michigan employees of Ford Motor Company through the promotion of social, physical, cultural and special programs."[27] In addition, U.S. Small Business Administration (SBA) employees and retirees have an Employee Recreation Association whose mission is to build community and camaraderie among SBA employees and retirees in the Washington, DC metropolitan area. The SBA Employee Recreation Association stands true to the purpose of the SBA and makes sure it uses small business vendors and service providers at all of its events and activities.[28]

DIRECTLY PROMOTING EMPLOYEE FITNESS AND EFFICIENCY

Corporations large and small today have become concerned about maintaining the health of their employees. One reason may be the skyrocketing costs of health insurance for employers. A major factor in this increase is the nation's obesity epidemic. Obesity accounts for more annual healthcare costs than drinking and smoking. The American Public Health Association estimates that obesity costs the United States $190.2 billion annually in healthcare costs. Obesity also costs employers $4.3 billion per year in absenteeism.[29]

For example,

> The McLean County (IL) Government Employee Wellness Program focuses on the health and wellbeing of county employees. Recognizing that employee wellness programs can contribute to improved wellness, reduced absenteeism, and medical plan expenses, programs are designed to help employees understand how to lead healthy lifestyles. Programs offered include wellness challenges, exercise cases, immunization clinics, and lunch and learn programs to learn about disease-related topics.[30]

Employers are also starting to recognize the health ramifications of employees not taking advantage of paid vacation time. At least 50% of employees do not take vacation time. This behavior can lead to fatigue, burnout, health problems, and reduced productivity. A significant number of employees can take a vacation, but it is unpaid time and not part of their benefits package. Unfortunately, many of these employees are in lower paying jobs. Others cannot afford to go anywhere on vacation; they have too much happening in their life or are afraid to be gone from work because there is not anyone there to do their job. A select number of companies are incentivizing employees to actually take vacation time by providing paid vacations.[31] Evernote provides a $1,000 vacation stipend annually so employees can travel wherever they want.[32] AirBnB pays their employees $2,000 to stay at any AirBnB site in the country. thinkParalax pays their employees $1,500 for a vacation but asks that one day of vacation be spent volunteering in the local community. The Motley Fool, a multimedia financial services firm, chooses one employee a month to send on a spontaneous trip by drawing their name out of a hat. If chosen, the employee can have no contact with the company while on vacation.[33]

RECRUITMENT AND RETENTION

An attractive program of recreation and related personnel services that can meet the needs of both the employee and his or her family is a persuasive recruitment weapon. Agencies advertise employee recreation opportunities as a perk of employment. It demonstrates the company's commitment to its employees and makes the company appear to be a great place to work.

In terms of retention, many companies find that successful employee programs help reduce job turnover. Litton Laser Systems in Apopka, Florida, now owned by Northrop Grumman, for example, credits its low employee turnover and high morale to its social activities committee (SAC), a group of employees who manage social, recreational, and sports events and other services for all company members and their families.

COMPANY IMAGE AND COMMUNITY ROLE

An important part of the recreation and services function involves external relations—the company's external, community-based role. Eli Lilly and Company established the Eli Lilly and Company Foundation, which awards grants to initiatives that match the philosophy of the company such as healthcare, culture, and youth development. The company also matches gifts to charities by employees and financially supports organizations where staff volunteer on a regular basis.[34]

Many large companies offer recreation programs for current employees, retirees, and families. These programs are one means of increasing employee morale.
© Photodisc/Getty Images.

CASE STUDY: Employee Recreation Improves Morale

Companies are increasingly understanding the power that employee perks have to boost morale in the workplace. Here are a few examples of innovative perks on the job provided by major corporations across the country. Many of those were recreation related, including:

- Google: Access to company bowling alley, bocce courts, gyms, unlimited free snacks.
- Morgan Stanley provides a chauffeured ride home for anyone working past 10:00 p.m.
- Smuckers: Onsite daycare, tuition assistance, and pet adoption assistance for fees paid to animal shelters or pet adoption centers for the adoption of cats or dogs.[a]
- Boeing: 12 paid holidays and a winter recess between Christmas and New Year's Day, matches employee contributions to charity up to $10,000.

Questions to Consider

- Find 5 more examples of innovative employee perks.
- Which of benefits would be important to you as an employee at a company?
- List the pros and cons of having an employee recreation program within a company.
- You have a company of 30 employees. Develop an employee recreation program.
- You have a company of 300 employees. How does your employee recreation program change from the one developed for 30 people?

[a]The J.M. Smucker Company. (n.d.). *Employee benefits overview*. Retrieved February 28, 2021, from https://www.jmsmucker.com/careers/why-smucker/employee-benefits

In other settings, the employee services program provides a means through which company executives can move purposefully to transform the business's internal and external image. In 2017 Target employees donated $13 million and 1 million volunteer hours to projects in their community. Target supports these efforts because it makes for safer, healthier, and stronger communities.[35]

Program Activities and Services

Many companies established extensive and well-equipped recreation and fitness centers and staffed them with qualified personnel. The Texins Activity Center in Dallas, serving employees of Texas Instruments, contains a multiuse gymnasium; strength and cardiovascular exercise areas; conference rooms; childcare rooms; club rooms; a natatorium with a six-lane, 25-lap pool; two aerobic studios; an indoor running track; and varied outdoor facilities. Other employers such as Double Encore and Airbnb offer alternative activities such as game rooms and company retreats.[36]

Scheduling Flexibility: Off-Shift Programming

Employee service and recreation managers must adapt to the special circumstances of their organizations and the changing needs of the employees they serve. Often this may involve providing a wide range of special courses designed for vocational or career development, cultural interest, or personal enrichment.

Some large corporations seek to meet the needs of their employees who work second and third shifts by scheduling facilities such as health clubs or weight rooms to be available at odd hours of the day and night. For example, Phillips Petroleum and Pratt and Whitney schedule morning and midnight softball and bowling leagues for off-shift workers and make gyms, tennis courts, and other facilities, as well as discount ticket operations, available to them at convenient times.

Innovation and Entrepreneurship

Just as in other sectors of the leisure-services field, employee service and recreation practitioners have experienced the need to become more fiscally independent by generating a fuller level of revenues through their offerings and by demonstrating their value in convincing terms.

The purposes of adopting businesslike values and strategies are (1) to enable employee programs to become less dependent on company financial support, and (2) to ensure that funds allocated to them by management yield significant, quantifiable benefits. A number of employee service and recreation directors in major corporations have been quite innovative in developing revenue sources based on businesslike ventures.

Working in Employee Services and Recreation

Various approaches to the management of employee service and recreation programs exist. In some, the company itself provides the facilities and leadership and maintains complete control of the operation. In other organizations, the company provides the facilities, but an employee recreation association takes actual responsibility for running the program. Other companies use combinations of these approaches. Frequently, profits from canteens or plant vending machines provide financial support for the program, as does revenue from moderate fees for participation or membership. Many activities—such as charter vacation flights—are completely self-supporting; others are fully or partly subsidized by the company.

There is not one specific place or professional association that lists jobs in employee services and recreation. Some are advertised internally within the company and do not require any recreation background. Others hire recreation professionals and list them on various job websites.

Campus Recreation

The nation's colleges and universities provide a major setting for organized leisure-services programs of involving millions of participants each year in a wide range of recreational activities. Although their primary purpose is to serve students, faculty, and staff members also may be involved in such programs on many campuses.

All institutions of higher education today sponsor some forms of leisure activity for their resident and commuter populations. Many of the larger colleges and universities have campus unions, departments of student affairs, or student centers that house a wide range of such activities. Frequently, a dean of student affairs is responsible for overseeing these programs, although intramural and recreational sports often may be administratively attached to a department or college of physical education and recreation or to a department of intercollegiate athletics.

The diversified leisure-services function may include operating performing arts centers (sometimes in cooperation with academic departments or schools in these fields), planning arts series, film programs, and forums with guest speakers, and similar cultural events. Student union buildings may include such specialized facilities as bowling alleys, coffee houses, game rooms, restaurants, bookstores, and other activity areas.

Rationale and Values of Campus Recreation Programs

Some campus recreation programs must justify their existence on campus as the mission of colleges and universities is primarily seen as academic in nature. Although students do come to college to study a specific discipline and obtain a degree, there are many other elements of higher education that make it special, and these things contribute to the overall educational process. This became quite evident during the COVID-19 pandemic. Most colleges and universities were primarily online during the 2020–2021 academic year. Students missed being in classes with their peers and interacting in person with faculty, but they also missed all of the other aspects of campus life, including service learning opportunities, internships, career development, cultural arts events, and campus recreation activities. All these things are part of the overall student experience and combined contribute to an essential function of higher education institutions: student success.

Participation in campus recreation can contribute to overall student success. Colleges and universities define student success differently, but it can be summarized as positive student outcomes in key areas of a student's academic career including retention (remaining at the university until graduation), graduation, the time it takes to complete the degree, student engagement in cocurricular activities, development of transferrable job skills and career readiness, a sense of belonging on campus, and overall student satisfaction. The National Intramural Recreational Sports Association (NIRSA), the professional association for campus recreation employees, worked with its members to develop seven evidence-based values of campus recreation participation that establish the rationale for its very existence and can lead to student success.

ACADEMIC SUCCESS

Research has shown the positive impacts campus recreation has on academic success. Academic success is often measured by grade point average (GPA) and graduation. Students who participate in intramural sports and club sports had a 6% higher retention rate than those who did not participate in campus recreation offerings.[37] Those participants are also more likely to have higher GPAs, credits completed, higher class standings, and higher graduation rates.[38]

PROFESSIONAL AND LEADERSHIP DEVELOPMENT

Campus recreation units employ full-time and part-time employees. Those part-time employees are often students within the university. Not only does campus recreation strive to hire high-quality students, but they spend a considerable amount of time orienting them to the job, training them for the skills they need, and providing professional development opportunities so they can grow as employees and leaders by building their transferable skills. These skills are valuable in campus recreation but also after the students graduate and enter the workforce.

Research has shown that campus recreation employees learn how to plan, organize, and prioritize their work; learn how to work in a team structure; and learn how to make decisions and solve problems. All of these skills will be beneficial regardless of the field of choice the campus recreation employees enter.[39]

DIVERSITY AND INCLUSION

Campus recreation provides a unique opportunity for students to work and play together. It provides inclusive spaces and programs that allow people from different backgrounds to come together and learn about each other, learn how to respect differences, and build networks and friendship that shape who these students will become.[40] Many colleges and universities have diversity statements that guide their entire operation and show their dedication to providing an inclusive and safe environment regardless of race, ethnicity, religion, spirituality, gender, gender identity/expression, age, sexual orientation, ability, socioeconomic status, or national origin, among others. This may mean offering nontraditional sports, prayer rooms, diversity and inclusion student advisory groups, gender-inclusive locker rooms, and adaptive equipment for people with disabilities.

RECRUITMENT AND RETENTION

When high school students tour colleges and universities to make their decisions, campus recreation facilities are often included, and featured, on the tours. Prospective students are excited to see all of the opportunities that are available and are encouraged to get involved as soon as possible. Early engagement in campus recreation helps build a sense of belonging on campus and builds friendships that make acclimation to college easier.[41] As previously discussed those who use campus recreation services and/or are employed in campus recreation are more likely to stay at the college or university and graduate.

ENGAGEMENT AND BELONGING

Campus recreation departments have as their goal to fully engage as many students as possible. Levels of engagement will vary from occasional users to regular users in many facets of the department. Engagement and belonging affect retention, but they also enhance mental health. A multitude of strategies are used to increase student engagement through campus recreation. For example, the University of Dayton launched their *On Your Path to 30* campaign, which encouraged students to engage in 30 minutes of physical activity each day. It resulted in a 15% increase in engagement.[42]

PHYSICAL HEALTH

The primary purpose that most users assigned to campus recreation is enhanced physical health. This can lead to lifelong physically active habits and improved health.[43] For many students it is an opportunity to try new activities to which they may not have had exposure while in high school. Not only are their many more options, but they are located on campus with easy, affordable access. Those who participate in campus recreation services have increased physical health and quality of life. They also sleep better, feel better, and function better.[44]

CASE STUDY: Campus Recreation and the Values Received

Review the recreational opportunities offered by the campus recreation unit on your campus. Look at the variety of offerings, cost of participation, and strengths and weaknesses of the offerings. Now, review three or four other universities that are either comparable to your institution or larger. Review the Rationale and Values of Campus Recreation Programs.

Questions to Consider

1. What did you notice about the offerings of campus recreation?
2. What is different about your campus offerings than the other universities reviewed?
3. What is your level of participation in campus recreation?
4. If you do not use campus recreation services, why not?
5. What do you get from your participation in terms of value? How does that compare to the Rationale and Values of Campus Recreation Programs?

MENTAL WELL BEING

A significant concern of most colleges and universities is the mental health and well-being of its students. Approximately 80% of college students feel overwhelmed by college, 50% feel their mental health is below average, and 40% of students with a mental health issue do not seek help.[45] The mental health issues most experienced by college students are anxiety and depression. Counseling services are often the first place where students are directed for help. In addition, campus recreation can provide opportunities to engage in activities that support and improve mental health and overall well-being of students.[46] Research on this topic indicates that students who participate in campus recreation are more likely to report improved feelings of well-being and improved psychosocial factors including such things as self-confidence, ability to make friends, respect for others, and multicultural awareness.[47]

Range of Campus Recreation Experiences

Campus recreation programs today are becoming more diversified, including a wide range of recreational sport, outdoor activities, entertainment and social events, cultural programs, activities for persons with disabilities, and various other services.

An outstanding example of college sport programming is found at Virginia Commonwealth University in Richmond, Virginia, which sponsors a host of recreational sport activities and events and fitness programs in six impressive campus facilities. Sports programs include a huge range of instructional, club, and intramural activities in such areas as individual, dual, and team sport; martial arts; and aquatics programs. Similar sport programs are offered throughout the United States.

Outdoor recreation, which includes clinics, clubs, and outings, may involve hiking, backpacking, camping, mountain climbing, scuba diving, sailing, skiing, and numerous other nature-based programs. There are a number of outstanding campus recreation programs with outdoor recreation

Campus recreation activities typically include intramural sports, special events, clubs, and fitness.
© Christian Bertrand/Shutterstock.

departments. The geography of the university obviously affects which programs are offered. It is not unusual for these universities to offer trips, rental gear, and do outdoor-related service projects. For example, Colorado State University offers snowshoeing trips, avalanche certification, and classes on ice and rock climbing.[48] University of Utah Campus Recreation rents outdoor equipment including camping equipment, mountain bikes, watercraft, and winter sports equipment.[49]

Many campuses sponsor large-scale one-time or short-term events These events include such things as 5K runs, sports competitions, and the National Girls and Women in Sports Day. San Diego State University (SDSU) offers late night fun fests such as Templo del Sol to acquaint new SDSU students to campus recreation offerings, campus carnivals, outdoor movies, and midnight study breaks.[50] Large-scale special events that students plan and carry out themselves—such as sports carnivals or other major competitions—are highlights of campus social programs. They involve extensive interaction among leaders and participants and an intense outpouring of energy as people share fun in a crowded school or college setting.

Students with disabilities are encouraged and assisted to participate in general campus recreation programs whenever possible. However, for those students who want programs with others with disabilities, special programs have been designed using modified equipment and adapted instructional techniques or rules.

Outstanding examples of such programs are those offered by the University of Illinois, which provides special teams in the areas of football, softball, basketball, swimming, and track and field for students with physical disabilities. Other activities, such as archery, judo, swimming, bowling, and softball, have been adapted for such special groups as people with visual impairments.

Many students also become involved in volunteer community projects such as repairing facilities, working with older adults, or helping with community special events. Such efforts are important for two reasons: (1) They illustrate how student-life activities may include a broad range of involvement beyond those that are clearly recognizable as recreational "fun" events; and (2) they serve to blend academic and extracurricular student experiences, increasing the individual's exposure to life and enhancing his or her leadership capability. For example, at Temple University the campus recreation department holds community service events such as Relay for Life and a swim-a-thon to benefit the Multiple Sclerosis Foundation.

Working in Campus Recreation

In addition to many part-time jobs for students, campus recreation employs full-time professional staff. Campus recreation is unique in that many universities follow the same employment structure in that most full-time staff start as graduate assistants in campus recreation. A graduate assistant works part time while completing a master's degree. Most of the jobs listed on bluefishjobs.com (campus recreation jobs website) have a master's degree preferred. Entry-level positions are often labeled as coordinator, then increases to assistant director and director. The director is the top position within the organization. Jobs are in the areas of facilities, fitness, special events, aquatics, intramurals, and more. Each position has its own unique job requirements and many transferrable skills such as the ability to multitask, work as a team, or adapt to change.

Private-Membership Recreation Organizations

A significant portion of recreational opportunities today is provided by private-membership organizations. As distinguished from commercial recreation businesses—in which any individual may simply pay an admission fee to a theme park, for example—private-membership bodies usually restrict use of their facilities or programs to individual members and their families and guests.

Within the broad field of sport and outdoor recreation, many organizations offer facilities, instruction, or other services for activities such as skiing, tennis, golf, boating, and hunting or fishing. Whereas some private-membership organizations are commercially owned and operated, others exist as independent, incorporated clubs of members who own their own facilities. For these clubs, policy is set by elected officers and boards, and the actual administration and operation of the club are carried out by paid employees.

An important characteristic of many private-membership organizations has been their social exclusiveness. Membership policies historically have sometimes screened out certain prospective members for reasons of religion, ethnicity, gender, economics, or other demographic factors.

It is important to recognize that although the ostensible function of such private organizations is to provide sociability as well as specific forms of leisure activity, the clubs also provide a setting in which the most powerful members of communities meet regularly to discuss business or political matters and often reach informal decisions or plans for action. Those who are barred from membership in such clubs are thus also excluded from this behind-the-scenes, establishment-based process of influence and power.

Despite recent changes, many private-membership organizations continue to represent exclusive enclaves of the rich and powerful. Country clubs are generally of two types: (1) nonprofit "equity clubs," owned and operated by members; and (2) commercially owned, for-profit clubs. Equity clubs can be established as either nonprofit or for-profit organizations. A common equity club is a destination club where people buy in to vacation homes. They have the right to use the homes but have no real ownership in the individual home. Commercially owned for-profit clubs are quite common. For example, ClubCorp owns more than 200 golf courses, country clubs, and city and stadium clubs. ClubCorp owns such clubs as the Firestone Country Club in Akron, Ohio (site of the Bridgestone Senior Players Championship since 1954) and Mission Hills Country Club in Rancho Mirage, California (home of the LPGA ANA Championship, formerly the Dinah Shore Golf Tournament), and claims more than 430,000 members.[51]

Residence-Connected Clubs

Other types of private-membership recreation organizations continue to flourish—particularly in connection with new forms of home building and marketing. Many real estate developers have recognized that one of the key selling points in home development projects is the provision of attractive recreational facilities. Thus, tennis courts, golf courses, swimming pools, health spas, and similar recreation facilities are frequently provided for the residents of apartment buildings, condominiums, or one-family home developments, whether the residents are families, singles, or retired persons.

An important trend in society has been the rapid growth of housing developments in the suburbs, with community associations that carry out such functions as street cleaning, grounds maintenance, security, and the provision of recreation facilities such as tennis courts, golf courses, and swimming pools. Once found chiefly in the Southwest, such developments and community associations now have spread throughout the United States. Although such real estate developments tend to be somewhat expensive and thus intended chiefly for more affluent homebuyers, there are exceptions. For example, a giant apartment development in Brooklyn, New York, known as Spring Creek Towers, was constructed in the mid-1970s to serve middle-income tenants drawn from varied ethnic populations—approximately half were African American, Hispanic, and Asian. Its 15,000 residents enjoy a 100,000 square foot sports club, pools, fitness facilities and classes, youth and senior programs and events, a shopping center, and parks and playgrounds. Spring Creek Towers is considered a self-contained community.[52]

In some cases, large condominium-structured apartment buildings also have extensive leisure facilities and programs. For example, in Philadelphia, one such building with 776 residential units has a bank, restaurant, 10 stores, doctors' and dentists' offices, garages, and two swimming pools, all under one roof. It also has a library, card room, fitness center, and numerous clubs and committees, including a welcoming committee, Weight Watchers, a writers' club, book club, and computer club.

Vacation Homes

A specialized form of residence-connected recreation is often found in vacation home developments. During the

---

CASE STUDY: Do Private Clubs Discriminate?

A number of lawsuits have claimed discrimination in the membership practices of private clubs. Many of these clubs have been able to maintain their membership policies even though civil rights laws make it illegal to discriminate based on race, gender, national origin, and other basis. However, these laws do not cover bona fide private clubs and religious organizations—these can discriminate on whatever basis they choose. Some states have extended the Civil Rights Act of 1964 and prevent private clubs from discriminating, closing this loophole in the law. Because not all states have done this, discrimination still exists. Here are a few examples.

- Burning Tree Club in Bethesda, Maryland, and Butler National Golf Club in Oak Brook, Illinois, continue to deny memberships to women on the basis of their sex. Burning Tree does not even have women's locker rooms.[a]
- In 2020 Scotland's Muirfield Golf Club agreed to finally allow female members when the British Open's organizing entity, the Royal and Ancient (R&A) announced that Muirfield would not host future British Opens so long as it maintained its men-only policy. This was a tremendous financial blow to the club.[a]
- Augusta National Golf Club just allowed women into the club in 2013. Before the first two women were admitted, Hootie Johnson, chairman of Augusta National, stated, "There may well come a day when women will be invited to join our membership, but that timetable will be ours and not at the point of a bayonet."
- In 2009, 60 African American children were turned away from a northeast Philadelphia private swim club despite the fact that they had paid the $1,900 fee. John Duesler, president of the Valley Swim Club, said they were turned away because "there was concern that a lot of kids would change the complexion . . . and the atmosphere of the club."[b]
- In 2018 five Black women filed suit against the Grandview Golf Club in Pennsylvania because police were called on them for playing too slowly. The women later filed suit claiming racial and gender discrimination. In 2020 the club failed to reply to the lawsuit resulting in a default judgment and assessment of monetary damages to the women.[c]
- Birgit Koebke and Kendall French, a lesbian couple registered as domestic partners under the California Domestic Partner Rights and Responsibilities Act of 2003, sued Heights Country Club because of discrimination. Club membership pertains to member spouses but not domestic partners. The California Supreme Court ruled that domestic partners should receive the same benefits as legal spouses and mandated the club provide the same benefits to all couples.[d]

Private clubs have been coerced into relaxing their discriminatory policies. For example, if clubs allow outside rentals of their facilities for events like weddings and parties, they are becoming more like public entities and could lose their private membership status and the legal protections that come with it. Cities will grant liquor licenses and tax deductions only to organizations with antidiscrimination policies.

Questions to Consider

- If members own a private club, should they be able to establish policies that intentionally or unintentionally discriminate against a group?
- Should clubs be required to allow legally married same sex couples? Why or why not?
- Is a high membership fee a form of discrimination? Why or why not?

[a]M. McCann. (2019, July 1). Why private golf clubs are legally still able to discriminate against women. *SI Golf*. Retrieved October 16, 2020, from https://www.si.com/golf/2019/07/01/private-golf-clubs-muirfield-augusta-women-discrimination#:~:text=As%20a%20starting%20point%2C%20the,color%2C%20religion%20and%20national%20origin
[b]A. Kilkenny. (2009, July 8). Philadelphia private swim club forces out black children. *Huffington Post*. https://www.huffpost.com/entry/philadelphia-private-swim_b_228253
[c]M. Miller. Pa. golf course fails to reply to federal sex and racial discrimination lawsuit filed by Black female golfers. *Pennsylvania Real Time News*. Retrieved August 24, 2020, from https://www.pennlive.com/news/2020/08/pa-golf-course-fails-to-reply-to-federal-sex-and-racial-discrimination-lawsuit-filed-by-black-female-golfers.html
[d]National Center for Lesbian Rights. *Koebke v. Bernardo Heights Country Club*. Retrieved April 28, 2021, from https://www.nclrights.org/our-work/cases/koebke-v-bernardo-heights-country-club/

1960s and 1970s, direct ownership and time-sharing arrangements for such homes became more popular, often in large-scale developments situated close to a lake or other major recreational attraction.

The baby boom, with millions of couples reaching the age and financial status at which they are able to afford vacation homes, has led to a rapid rise in the number of such developments. Nearly 6% of American households own a second home, typically within 150 miles of the primary residence. Most are located near recreation sites such as lakes or mountains.[53]

Vacation homes can be used only by the owners or can be rented out when not in use to help pay for the home. Some vacation home communities will not allow outside rentals, many of which are a bit more exclusive. When looking at the top vacation home communities, the Great Smoky Mountains is home to 2 of the top 10 vacation home locations—Sevierville, Tennessee, and Whittier, North Carolina. Florida is also a popular vacation home spot in Kissimee, Key West, and Dauphin.[54] These top sites are based on home sale prices and return on the investment when buying the vacation home.

Retirement Communities

Similarly, large retirement villages offer recreation and social programs for their residents. A vivid example may be found in Sun City, Arizona. Established in 1960, this community has about 42,000 residents. Sun City is the country's first planned retirement community. The recreation opportunities are extensive because the community has seven community centers with a pool in each one, eight golf courses, two bowling alleys, two lakes, a wide variety of programs, and more than 120 social and civic clubs.[55]

Many retirement communities offer extensive recreation facilities and programs and encourage residents to attend cultural events in the surrounding area. Others, as in Sarasota, Florida's Pelican Cove, have uniquely beautiful

Many retirement communities offer extensive recreation facilities and programs for their residents.
© Matthew Apps/Shutterstock.

natural surroundings, including a marina with easy access to open bay waters.

In numerous other retirement communities, such as Leisure World in Laguna Hills, California, such recreational facilities as pools, tennis courts, and riding stables often are found.

Meetings and Events

Professionals in the meeting and event planning industry are given the responsibility of planning corporate meetings, conventions, tradeshows, fundraisers, social events, and other types of large-scale special events. Although there are a plethora of different types of meetings and events to plan, there are four broad categories: conventions, corporate meetings, weddings, and community special events.

A convention is a large gathering of people with a specific interest or profession in common. Professional associations often plan annual conventions (also called conferences) where attendees gather to take part in workshops and tradeshows featuring products of interest to the industry. Convention venues are often secured several years in advance, and large conventions may be limited to cities with a large convention center that can accommodate the attendees. The National Recreation and Park Association holds its annual conference in the fall for over 8,000 delegates. Highlights of the conference include workshops on topics and trends in the field, committee meetings where the work of the association is done, special events in the evenings to enhance professional networking, social activities for informal networking, entertainment, and a tradeshow featuring products of interest to the professionals. The National Recreation and Park Association (NRPA) has event planners on staff who work with the convention site to ensure that everything is planned to the specifications of NRPA.

Larger corporations will hold regular meetings of the staff at various locations. These meetings can last for a single day or several days and be fairly small to several thousand. When planning corporate meetings there are several things that must be done for the meeting to be successful. The meeting planners will do such things as confirm dates and locations, find venues, sign contracts for services, secure hotel blocks, set the meeting itinerary, select the menu, establish registration processes, do event walk throughs prior to attendee arrivals, and troubleshooting during the meeting.

Weddings are a $165 billion industry with over 2.3 million weddings per year in the United States.[56] Wedding planners are hired to handle varying levels of tasks from the entire wedding to specific areas such as the wedding reception. Wedding planners work behind the scenes to reduce the stress for the wedding party and the families. A high-quality wedding planner will provide time- and money-saving strategies to make the day what the couple wants it to be. Wedding planners must be skilled in marketing their services to prospective spouses; developing proposals outlining service provision and costs; understanding wedding etiquette for such things as sending invitations, prenuptial parties, and who pays for which part of the wedding; how best to provide wedding services such as venue selection, flowers, catering, cakes, music, videography/photography, and much more.[57]

Community special events are the events that most people are familiar with. The Rose Bowl Parade in Pasadena, the Albuquerque Balloon Festival, and the Indianapolis 500 are all examples of large-scale special events that attract thousands and sometimes millions of people. Planning these events is a major undertaking and can be done by hiring an event planning company, having an internal staff to plan the event, or forming committees of community members to do the planning work.

Certifications and Working in Meeting and Event Planning

There are several different certifications that meeting and event planners can obtain. They include such certifications as a Certified Festival Executive from the International Festivals and Events Association, a Certified Meeting Professional from the Convention Industry Council, and a Certified Special Events Professional from the International Special Events Society.

In addition to certifications, successful event planners are able to build strong relationships with customers; develop a network of contacts in areas such as catering, entertainment, lodging, and more; are able to manage costs and understand contracts; manage stress and multitasking; and make decisions quickly when things go wrong.

Faith-Based Recreation

Many of us have a fairly fixed view of the role of churches in the community. In addition to places of worship, churches provide social activities for members through things like youth groups, community services for those in need such as foodbanks, religious education, and a support system for members, among others. What many do not necessarily think about is the role of recreation within the church. Faith-based recreation is not just for the mega church, but for churches of all sizes. Churches have used recreation and sports programs for outreach, discipleship, and personal growth.

Churches offer a wide variety of programming and facilities. For example, the Trinity Baptist Church in Raleigh, North Carolina, has a Recreation Outreach Center (ROC) that offers such activities as 5K races, special events, golf tournaments, men's softball and basketball leagues, and fitness classes.[58] The Cathedral of Christ the King in Atlanta, Georgia, offers sport leagues and fitness activities but also

afterschool programs, dance classes, comedy and improve classes, and youth science, technology, engineering, and math labs.[59] All of these activities have faith as the foundation.

Jewish Community Centers

Jewish community centers (JCC) provide recreation, sport, and social activities for the Jewish community throughout the world. The underlying purpose is to enhance Jewish culture and heritage. The JCC Association is a professional organization for the 350 JCCs in North America. Those JCCs employ 53,000 staff members with 12,000 being full-time skilled professionals, 24,000 part-time staff, and 17,000 seasonal summer staff. Program offerings are vast in JCCs. For example, the Arthur M. Glick JCC in Indianapolis, Indiana, is a large recreation center with an auditorium, tennis and racquetball courts, multiple gymnasiums, a café, and multiple indoor and outdoor pools. The Glick JCC is a membership-based organization and caters to those of the Jewish faith as well as others in the community.[60]

Faith-Based Camps and Conferences

Some churches own and/or operate land and facilities that are used for day or overnight camps and conferences. Camps will have a variety of activities and facilities. The sleeping quarters may be anything from tents to cabins to lodges. The other amenities can include lakes, pools, horseback riding, and archery, among others. Church camps and conference centers can be small scale or generate millions of dollars in revenue.

Church camps are not just for children and teens, some are designed with adults and families in mind. For example, the Whispering Winds Catholic Camp and Conference Center offers a Senior Moment Retreat for those 55+, Women's Retreat, and a men's getaway featuring darts, sandbag throwing, hatchet throwing, cornhole, a beer garden, worship time and speakers, zip lining, and football. All of these camps, whether for children or adults, focus on worship and their journey of faith.[61]

Conference centers allow churches to host their own meetings, trainings, and conferences as well as rent their facilities to other groups for these same purposes. Cohutta Springs Conference Center serves 25,000 people per year on its sprawling 800 acre complex. Meeting attendees can use the meeting rooms, amphitheatre, and recreational opportunities during breaks. The conference center can house visitors in cabins, chalets, and an RV park.[62]

Working in Faith-Based Recreation

Many think that working in church camps and conference is a great summer job for teens and college students and that it would be a lot of fun to set up leagues and events for the local church as a volunteer. Although this is true, there are also full-time positions for those who want to make faith-based recreation into a career. Full-time positions include such jobs as Manager of Food Services at Annunciation Heights in Estes Park, Colorado; Conference Center Manager at the Tennessee Baptist Conference Center in Newport, Tennessee; and Director of Programming at Camp Judson in North Springfield, Pennsylvania.[63]

Those interested in working in JCCs will find job postings in JCC Works (jccworks.com) such as Fitness Director, Director of Volunteer Services, and Director of Aquatics.

Many of these positions prefer degrees in recreation, Jewish communal service, sports management, nonprofit management, or a variety of other fields.[64]

The Association of Church Sports and Recreation Ministries offers certification as a Sport, Recreation, and Fitness Minister. The certification is a three-tier process and includes theological truths, philosophical principles, and methodological models.[65] Although many faith-based recreation programs are staffed with volunteers, some will have full-time staff to plan the activities.

SUMMARY

Seven specialized areas of leisure-services delivery described in this chapter illustrate the diversity of agencies that provide organized recreation opportunities today. In each case, they have their own goals and objectives, populations served, and program emphases—yet they are important elements within the overall leisure-services system and represent attractive fields of career opportunity for recreation, park, and leisure-services students today.

Recreation therapy service, in its two areas of professional emphasis—clinical and community-based special recreation—is probably the most highly professionalized of all the separate disciplines in the leisure-services field. It has a long history of professional development, with separate sections of state and national societies, early emphasis on certification, numerous specialized curricula, and a rich literature and background of research. With the possibility of lessened support being given to clinical recreation therapy in an era of cost cutting, hospital retrenchment, managed patient care, and deinstitutionalization, it is probable that community-based special recreation, with its emphasis on inclusion, will constitute an increasingly important element in recreation therapy.

Armed forces recreation professionals serve a distinct population composed both of large numbers of relatively young service men and women and their families. There is a growing need for recreation opportunities for those with temporary or permanent disabilities that came from being in the line of duty. MWR has many purposes including the physical, social, and mental welfare of its personnel and families. Military recreation has undergone major transformations in recent years, yet it continues to offer a wide range of attractive program opportunities and often has excellent facilities, both stateside and abroad.

Employee recreation and services today have gone far beyond their original emphasis on providing a narrow range of social and sports activities designed to promote company–worker relationships. They are carried on in many different kinds of organizations and include varied health- and fitness-related program elements, as well as such other personnel services as discount programs, company stores, community relationships, and other benefits-driven functions—all necessarily provided within a business-oriented framework that demands productivity and demonstrated outcomes.

Campus recreation is carried on within an educational setting and is designed to augment academic success, professional leadership development, diversity and inclusion, recruitment and retention, engagement and belonging, physical health, and mental well-being. It is highly structured in its job opportunities, starting as part-time student works, graduate assistants, and then to professional staff positions.

The private-membership association includes a wide range of country clubs, golf clubs, yacht clubs, and other social or business membership groups that often tend to be socially exclusive. They represent a growing trend in the United States today, with millions of families now living in residential developments that have their own community associations to provide services, including recreation. This tends to limit their interest in or dependence on public, tax-supported recreation services.

Events and meetings are a very broad form of specialized leisure services. Both events and meetings can be considered leisure and work—depending on what the focus of the event or meeting is. Events and meetings cross over most specialized leisure-services areas and the job prospects continue to grow.

The last type of organization described in this chapter, faith-based recreation encompasses a variety of leisure-services delivery models. Churches themselves can run recreation activities. There are recreation centers such as the Jewish community centers serving members of the religion as well as the community at large. Camps and conference centers provide programs and events for children and adults.

QUESTIONS FOR CLASS DISCUSSION OR ESSAY EXAMINATION

1. Differentiate between clinical-based recreation therapy and community-based recreation therapy.

2. Give specific examples of where recreation professionals could work within seven specialized leisure-services areas.

3. Describe the RT process.

4. List the benefits of employee recreation for the employer and the employee.

5. What role does campus recreation play on a college campus?

6. Describe private-membership recreation and give some examples of clubs. Explain the issues with member discrimination.

7. Make a convincing case to an employer that the benefits of an employee recreation program outweigh the financial costs of such a program.

8. Colleges and universities are spending millions of dollars on state-of-the-art facilities. Arguments for these this type of spending often center on the role campus recreation plays in the recruitment of new students. Explain your position regarding this type of spending—is it worth it? What about students who have no interest in campus recreation?

9. Discuss what an events and meeting planner does.

_____

_____

_____

10. Discuss the available certifications in the seven specialized leisure-services areas.

_____

_____

_____

11. Describe the different aspects of faith-based recreation.

_____

_____

_____

12. Of the seven specialized leisure-services areas, which are most similar and which are most different?

_____

_____

_____

ENDNOTES

1. Kraus, R. (1971). _Recreation and leisure in modern society_. Appleton-Century-Crofts.

2. ATRA. (n.d.). What is recreational therapy? Retrieved September 20, 2020, from https://www. atra-online.com/page/AboutRecTherapy.

3. ATRA. (n.d.). Where is recreational therapy provided? Retrieved September 20, 2020, from https://www.atra-online.com/page/AboutRecTherapy.

4. Smith, R. W., Austin, D. R., Kennedy, D. W., Lee, Y., & Hutchison, P. (2005). Inclusive and recreation: Opportunities for persons with disabilities (5th ed.). Urbana, IL: Sagamore

5. Williams, R. (2008). Places, models, and modalities of practice. In T. Robertson & T. Long (Eds.), _Foundations of therapeutic recreation: Perceptions, philosophies and practices for the 21st century_ (pp. 63–76). Human Kinetics.

6. Americans with Disabilities Act. Retrieved September 20, 2020, from www.ada.gov.

7. Long, T. (2008). The therapeutic recreation process. In T. Robertson & T. Long (Eds.), _Foundations of therapeutic recreation: Perceptions, philosophies and practices for the 21st century_ (pp. 79–97). Human Kinetics.

8. National Council for Therapeutic Recreation Certification. (n.d.). _NCTRC job analysis: 2014 Job Analysis Study_. Retrieved September 20, 2020, from http://nctrc.org/about-certification/national-job-analysis/.

9. National Sports Center for the Disabled. Retrieved September 20, 2020, from http://nscd.org.

10. Morgan's Wonderland. Retrieved September 20, 2020, from www.morganswonderland.com.

11. Fox Valley Special Recreation Association. _About FVSRA_. Retrieved September 20, 2020, from https://www.fvsra.org/about/mission-vision.aspx.

12. Disability Partnerships. Retrieved September 27, 2020, from http://www.disabilitypartnerships.org.

13. Miller, K. D., Schleien, S. J., & Lausier, J. (2009). Search for best practices in inclusive recreation: Programmatic findings. _Therapeutic Recreation Journal, 43_(1), 27–41.

14. U.S. Army MWR. _MWR history_. Retrieved September 27, 2020, from https://www.armymwr.com/commander/history.aspx.

15. Potter, C., & Ogilvie, L. (2013). Unique groups. In _Introduction to recreation and leisure_ (pp. 217–250). Human Kinetics.

16. Navy Installations Command. (n.d.). *All-Navy sports*. Retrieved September 27, 2020, from https://www.navyfitness.org/all-navy-sports.

17. U.S. Marine Corps. (n.d.). USAA Grand Prix Series. Retrieved October 3, 2020, from http://www.mccslejeune-newriver.com/grandprix/index.html.

18. Navy Installations Command. (n.d.). *Fitness.*. Retrieved September 27, 2020, from https://www.navyfitness.org/fitness.

19. Army MWR. (n.d.). *YMCA*. Retrieved September 27, 2020, from https://www.armymwr.com/programs-and-services/sports-fitness/ymca.

20. Fort Carson MWR. (n.d.). *Adventure Programs*. Retrieved October 3, 2020, from https://carson.armymwr.com/programs/adventure-programs-and-education.

21. Marine Corps Community Services Camp Lejeune. Marine Corps Family Team Building (MCFTB). Retrieved October 3, 2020, from https://usmc-mccs.org/services/family/marine-corps-family-team-building/.

22. Navy Child and Youth Programs. Retrieved October 3, 2020, from https://www.navycyp.org.

23. Marine Corps Community Services Miramar. (n.d.). *MCSS Miramar Memorial Golf Course*. Retrieved October 3, 2020, from www.mccsmiramar.com/golfcourse.html.

24. Fort Campbell MWR. (n.d.) *Army Community Service Outreach*. Retrieved October 3, 2020, from https://campbell.armymwr.com/programs/army-community-service-outreach.

25. Navy MWR. (n.d.). *Careers*. Retrieved September 27, 2020, from https://www.navymwr.org/careers.

26. Employee Services Management Association. Retrieved October 4, 2020, from https://www.linkedin.com/company/employee-services-management-association/about/.

27. Ford Employees Recreation Association. Retrieved October 4, 2020, from https://www.fera.org/faqs/.

28. U.S. Small Business Administration Employee Recreation Association. Retrieved October 4, 2020, from https://sbaemployeerec.org.

29. National League of Cities. (n.d.). *Economic costs of obesity*. Retrieved October 4, 2020, from http://www.healthycommunitieshealthyfuture.org/learn-the-facts/economic-costs-of-obesity/.

30. McLean County Health Department. (n.d.). *McLean County Government Employee Wellness Program*. Retrieved October 4, 2020, from https://health.mcleancountyil.gov/472/McLean-County-Government-Employee-Wellness-program

31. Titner, E. (n.d.). *The impact of 50% of American workers not taking vacation time*. Retrieved October 4, 2020, from https://www.thejobnetwork.com/the-impact-of-50-of-american-workers-not-taking-vacation-time/.

32. Evernote. Retrieved October 4, 2020, from https://evernote.com/careers.

33. Kuta, S. (2016, October 26). *These 9 companies pay for their employees' vacations*. Retrieved October 4, 2020, from https://www.simplemost.com/9-companies-that-pay-for-employees-vacations/.

34. Eli Lilly Foundation. (n.d.). *Strengthening communities*. Retrieved October 4, 2020, from https://www.lilly.com/social-impact/communities.

35. Target. (n.d.). *Volunteerism*. Retrieved October 4, 2020, from https://corporate.target.com/corporate-responsibility/volunteerism.

36. Harrison, K. (2014, February 19). The most popular employee perks of 2014. *Forbes*. Retrieved October 4, 2020, from http://www.forbes.com/sites/kateharrison/2014/02/19/the-most-popular-employee-perks-of-2014/.

37. McElveen, M., & Rossow, A. (2014). Relationship of intramural participation to GPA and retention in first-time-in-college students. *Recreational Sports Journal*, 38, 50–54.

38. Vasold, K. L., Deere, S. J., & Pivarnik, J. M. (2019). *Benefits of campus recreation: Results of the 2011–2016 recreation & wellness benchmark*. National Intramural-Recreational Sports Association.

39. Peck, A. Cramp, C., Croft, L., Cummings, T., Fehring, K., Hall, D., Hnatusko, P., & Lawhead, J. (2015). *Considering the impact of participation and employment of students in campus activities and collegiate recreation on the development of the skills employers desire most: A joint whitepaper from the National Association for Campus Activities and Leaders in Collegiate Recreation*. National Association for Campus Activities; National Intramural-Recreational Sports Association.

40. Elkins, D. J., Forrester, S. A., & Noël-Elkins, A. V. (2011). The contribution of campus recreational sports participation to perceived sense of campus community. *Recreational Sports Journal*, 35(1), 24–34.

41. Ibid.

42. Harbourne, E. (2017, July 18). *Special feature: An innovative way to increase student engagement*.

Retrieved October 10, 2020, from https://campusrec mag.com/increase-student-engagement-on-your-path-to-30/.

43. NIRSA. (n.d.). *The value of campus recreation: Powering student development through campus recreation.* Retrieved October 12, 2020, from https://nirsa.net/nirsa/value-of-campus-recreation/.

44. U.S. Department of Health and Human Services. (2018). *Physical activity guidelines for Americans* (2nd ed.). U.S. Department of Health and Human Services.

45. Petkovic, N. (2020, May 12). *Top 10 college student mental health statistics for 2019.* Health Careers. https://healthcareers.co/college-student-mental-health-statistics/.

46. NIRSA (n.d.).

47. Vasold, Deere, & Pivarnik (2019).

48. Colorado State University Campus Recreation. (n.d.). *Outdoor program.* Retrieved October 12, 2020, from https://csurec.colostate.edu/programs/outdoor-program/.

49. University of Utah Campus Recreation. (n.d.). *Equipment rental.* Retrieved October 12, 2020, from https://campusrec.utah.edu/programs/outdoor-adventures/rental/index.php.

50. San Diego State University. (n.d.). *Aztec Nights.* Retrieved October 12, 2020, from https://as.sdsu.edu/aztecnights/about.php.

51. ClubCorp. (n.d.). *Company profile.* Retrieved October 12, 2020, from https://www.clubcorp.com.

52. Spring Creek Towers. (n.d.). *About us.* Retrieved October 12, 2020, from http://www.springcreek towers.com/aboutus.html.

53. Lankarge, D., & Nahorney, V. (n.d.). The evolution of home ownership. HomeInsight. Retrieved October 16, 2020, from www.homeinsight.com/details.asp?url_id=7.

54. Kiesnoski, K. (2019, August 20). *Dreaming of a US vacation home? Here are the 10 best places to invest.* Retrieved October 16, 2020, from https://www.cnbc.com/2019/08/20/here-are-the-10-best-places-to-invest-in-a-us-vacation-home.html.

55. Sun City, AZ. (n.d.). *Activities.* Retrieved October 16, 2020, from www.suncityaz.org.

56. Association of Bridal Consultants. (n.d.). *Why this business?* Retrieved October 16, 2020, from http://www.bridalassn.com/whyThisBusiness.aspx.

57. Association of Bridal Consultants. (n.d.). *Professional Wedding Planner Program (PWP).* Retrieved October 16, 2020, from http://www.bridalassn.com/DocLib/PWP_Ad_Slick_3.10.16.pdf.

58. Trinity Baptist Church. (n.d.). *Recreation ministry.* Retrieved October 16, 2020, from https://tbcraleigh.com/ministries/recreation-ministry/.

59. Cathedral of Christ the King. (n.d.). *Youth recreation ministry.* Retrieved October 16, 2020, from https://cathedralctk.com/recreation-enrichment-ministry/.

60. Arthur M. Glick JCC. Retrieved October 16, 2020, from https://jccindy.org.

61. Whispering Winds Catholic Camp and Conference Center. Retrieved October 16, 2020, from https://www.whisperingwinds.org.

62. Cohutta Springs Conference Center. Retrieved October 16, 2020, from https://cohuttasprings.com.

63. Christian Camp and Conference Association. Retrieved October 18, 2020, from https://www.ccca.org/ccca/default.asp.

64. JCC Works. Retrieved October 16, 2020, from https://www.jccworks.com.

65. Association of Church Sports and Recreation Ministries. Retrieved October 16, 2020, from http://www.csrm.org.

Chapter 9

Outdoor Recreation and Natural Resources Management

"Today, if people are to survive, their communities must provide relief from the tensions of life, and must provide it within easy reach. The national, state, and county parks fill a real need… there are millions who no longer have the time or energy to seek these parks. For them, in spite of the rapid transit and freeways, whatever refreshment their spirits receive must come from the immediate surroundings where most if their lives are spent—the places they work, the places they live, and the roads between."[1]

-From the first edition of Kraus' Recreation and Leisure in Modern Society, published in 1971

LEARNING OBJECTIVES

1. Understand the legislation and history that shaped outdoor recreation.

2. Explain the different types of outdoor recreation programs and facilities.

3. Describe how sociodemographic variables impact outdoor recreation participation.

4. Summarize current issues affecting outdoor recreation and natural resources management.

Introduction

Outdoor recreation encompasses leisure pursuits that depend on the outdoor environment for their special appeal or character. Outdoor recreation can be provided by the federal, state, and local governments; through commercial and nonprofit organizations; and in local parks and recreation agencies. It is common to think about outdoor recreation in terms of fun activities such as hiking, camping, climbing, and fishing. Keep in mind there is a difference between outdoor recreation and recreation that is done outdoors. Outdoor recreation activities, such as those just listed, rely somehow on natural resources such as trees, wildlife, fish, soil, rivers, lakes, insects, and plants. So, playing a kickball game in the park is recreation but is not considered outdoor recreation for our discussion in this chapter. However, surfing, geocaching, birdwatching, sailing, scuba diving, and nature photography are considered outdoor recreation activities.

The purpose of this chapter is to introduce outdoor recreation, learn the broad history and legislation that shaped outdoor recreation, explore the types of programs and facilities where outdoor recreation can be found, examine the sociodemographics of outdoor recreation, and review a few issues the profession must address. Finally, career opportunities will be discussed to show potential professions within this complex discipline.

History and Legislation Shaping Outdoor Recreation

Outdoor recreation is steeped in an interesting history. A brief overview shows how land was first used and later protected by legislation for the generations to come.

Until the mid-1700s, open land was used mainly for farming, as pastures, or for hunting, and it was used more for survival than recreation. In the mid-1700s land began to be used for recreational activities such as hunting, fishing, skating, and tobogganing, and resorts were built for the wealthy. Recreation pursuits steadily grew,[2] and it was not until the mid-1800s that city parks started to be built on a regular basis. New York City's Central Park, designed by Frederick Law Olmstead and Calvert Vaux, is one of the nation's most well-known parks. Completed in 1876, this 840-acre park is in the heart of the city and caused considerable conflict between the classes when it was built. The elite wanted the park as a social space for other elites. The middle class wanted it as a place for art, nature, and beauty, and the working class wanted it for active recreation. The park was intentionally designed to accommodate all of those needs,[3] and continues to do so today.

Many other large cities began building similar spaces to accommodate the rapidly increasing migration from rural areas to cities.

The second half of the 19th century saw the rise in organized sports and outdoor recreation activities. It was at this time that there was a rise in concern about the depletion of wildlife because of hunting and the destruction of forests occurring as a result of construction of cities and towns. Several influential people such as John Muir, Gifford Pinchot (see conservation section in this chapter), and Theodore Roosevelt worked tirelessly to stop the destruction of natural resources and preserve lands for conservation and preservation. (See Chapter 4 case study.) In 1872 the first national park was established, Yellowstone National Park, under President Ulysses S. Grant. This set a precedent for setting aside public lands to protect natural resources. At this point, several key things happened with significant impact on outdoor recreation and our natural resources,[4,5,6] each one heavily influencing outdoor recreation today, as noted in the box, *Significant Milestones for Outdoor Recreation and Natural Resources.*

The history of outdoor recreation and natural resources is quite extensive and shows how today's natural resources have remained in existence. Much can be learned from the aggressive conservation and preservation of lands through national parks, forests, and wilderness areas as well as departments and legislation enacted to protect them.

Programs and Facilities

Outdoor recreation stretches far beyond just the activities one enjoys. It also has an important role in education and therapy. Outdoor recreation can be classified into several different program types including land- and water-based activities, experiential education, adventure therapy, environmental interpretation, and specialized recreation facilities.

Land-Based Programs

Land-based outdoor recreation opportunities are numerous and can fit any age or fitness level. Some may find themselves spelunking through limestone caverns in Washington state, climbing Mount Rainier, hiking the 2,190 miles of the Appalachian Trail, or camping in the Adirondacks.

Hiking is a popular land activity.
© Georgijevic/E+/Getty Images.

SIGNIFICANT MILESTONES FOR OUTDOOR RECREATION AND NATURAL RESOURCES

- 1873—Adirondack and Catskill Forest Preserves established in New York, making it the largest tract of land preserved to date.
- 1890—Yosemite National Park becomes the second national park to be established.
- 1902—Bureau of Reclamation was established to oversee water resource development, management, and protection.
- 1902—First National Wildlife Refuge was established at Pelican Island, Sebastian, Florida.
- 1905—40% of U.S. forests had been cleared for development.
- 1905—U.S. Forest Service was established and Gifford Pinchot was named the first chief.
- 1905—Bureau of Biological Survey was established (predecessor of the U.S. Fish and Wildlife Service in 1956) to conserve, protect, and enhance fish, wildlife, and natural habitats.
- 1906—The Antiquities Act allowed President Theodore Roosevelt to designate 15 million acres as national parks and monuments over the next 4 years; the act gave executive power to claim and protect areas of scenic wonder and natural beauty.
- 1908—President Theodore Roosevelt put together the National Conservation Commission to inventory U.S natural resources because of his concerns about their destruction.
- 1909—Illinois established the first state park system, followed by Indiana in 1919.
- 1916—The National Park Service was established and Stephen Mathers serves as the first director.
- 1924—Gila National Forest became the first designated wilderness area.
- 1925—The Appalachian Trail opened and was completed in 1937.
- 1930s—The Great Depression resulted in the establishment of the Public Works Administration, Works Progress Administration, and the Civilian Conservation Corps, directing 27,000 workers to undertake conservation projects and build recreation facilities (see case study in Chapter 4).
- 1937—Pittman-Robertson Act was established to tax sporting guns and ammunition for use in wildlife management efforts.
- 1944—The Flood Control Act required the U.S. Army Corps of Engineers to provide for recreation at the reservoirs it built.
- 1946—Bureau of Land Management was established to administer federal lands outside the National Park Service such as mineral estates, wilderness areas, wild and scenic rivers, national scenic and historic trails, and monuments.
- 1950—Dingell-Johnson Act established taxes on fishing equipment to fund fisheries management programs.
- 1958—Outdoor Recreation Resources Review Commission (ORRRC) was established by U.S. Congress; final reports issued in 1962 led to an expansion of outdoor recreation services at federal, state, and local levels.
- 1960s—This era saw many federal acts passed that still are in place today protecting the environment:
  - Multiple-Use Sustained Yield Act named outdoor recreation an official function of the U.S. Forest Service.
  - National Wilderness Preservation System Act was established to manage federally protected wilderness areas.
  - National Trails System Act was created to establish a system of national scenic trails, national historic trails, and national recreation trails in both urban and rural areas.
  - National Wild and Scenic Rivers Act was established to preserve certain rivers with outstanding natural, cultural, and recreational value in a free-flowing condition.
  - Land and Water Conservation Fund was established to provide public access to land and water areas for recreation and to preserve ecosystems for local communities.
- 1970—First Earth Day was held.
- 1973—Endangered Species Act was established to protect species from extinction.
- 2007—No Child Left Inside Act required schools to develop environmental education curricula.

The most popular land activity is hiking and can lead to many other activities for those who want more. Hiking means different things to different people. Those who walk a paved trail in the woods consider this hiking just as the person who hikes the Tahoe Rim on the boarder of California and Nevada. Hiking is an activity that can attract all income levels as the cost of hiking equipment is lower than many other outdoor activities. Moderate to medium level hiking can be done with no special equipment, but hikers may consider plenty of water, hiking boots, and layered clothing that is breathable. As the length and rigor of the hike increases so does the required equipment.

Those who want to expand their hiking experiences can backpack into the backcountry, camp along the way, and incorporate climbing into the excursion. Backpackers and climbers have a heightened need to plan trips ahead of time to get maps and study the area, be attuned to the weather conditions, be able to use a compass, and understand elevations. Those new to backpacking and climbing may best be served by hiring a guide through a local outfitter.

Not all land outdoor recreation is done in the warmer seasons. Snow and winter sports are also popular including such activities as snowshoeing, winter camping, cross country skiing, ice climbing, snowmobiling, and downhill skiing.

Water-Based Programs

Water-based recreationists might find themselves scuba diving in the Florida Keys, deep sea fishing in Cape Cod, kayaking the boundary waters, snorkeling in the Great Barrier Reef in Australia, or rafting down the Colorado River. Although land-based activities have varying levels of risk associated with them, water activities have an added layer of risk because of the dangers water can pose. Careful planning and safety precautions will provide the balance between maintaining the challenge and thrill of the activity versus the safety of the participants.

Water-based activities can be grouped into three categories: flat water, moving water (including whitewater), and open water.[7] Flat water activities are done in calm waters such as inland lakes and estuaries. These waters will not have significant waves or be choppy. These areas are ideal for beginners to sports such as flatwater kayaking, canoeing, or sailing. Flat water is also popular among those who enjoy fishing, either from a boat or the shore.

Moving waters flow at different speeds and affect the activities and the skill level needed to be successful. Slower moving rivers can offer a great experience for canoeing enthusiasts and faster ones can challenge even the most skilled whitewater rafters and kayakers. The International Scale of River Difficulty system uses a I to VI class designation measuring the difficulty in navigating the river. As the scale goes up, so does the difficulty.[8]

Open waters include oceans, seas, and large lakes like the Great Lakes that are unobstructed by islands, other lands, or the opposite shore. The water conditions in open waters can prove to be challenging. The speed of the boats and other watercrafts can be quite fast. Human powered boats such as kayaks, may not be visible to a large fishing boat traveling at a high rate of speed. Rip currents, tidal waves, tidal fluctuations, and sea life can also have an impact on a recreational experience.

The type of water may dictate the type of equipment needed. For example, depending on your purpose, you may want to purchase a recreational sit-on-top or sit inside kayak, which is better for lakes and fishing. A recreational kayak is a great model to start with to learn how to use it. Furthermore, it is slow and stable and easy to use in lakes and smooth water. Sea kayaks are very narrow, long, and tippy. Being tippy is an advantage in open water as it improves maneuverability. A kayak, like a lot of other recreational equipment for the water, is best researched with your end goals and use in mind.

Experiential Education

Experiential education, also referred to as adventure education, was first introduced by John Dewey as part of a progressive education movement. Dewey suggested that students would learn better if they were engaged through meaningful activities.[9] Adventure education uses outdoor activities to develop and enhance skills such as interpersonal and intrapersonal skills through experiential means. The activities push youth and adults beyond their perceived limits and teach them to solve problems and work together toward a common goal.[10] Experiential and adventure recreation allow us to observe our own actions and reactions to the activities, reflect on what the experience means, and what was learned from it.

One of the most well-known experiential education programs is Outward Bound. Outward Bound founder Kurt Hahn developed the nonprofit organization to teach through outdoor learning expeditions. With an emphasis on high achievement through active learning, character development, and teamwork, Outward Bound provides programs for all ages, from youth to adult. For example, teens (ages 14–16 and 16–18) can spend 15 days rafting and rock climbing between Redmond and Portland, Oregon. The program is described as

> an opportunity to challenge themselves physically and mentally while exploring amazing wilderness areas. The first days of your trip will be spent building critical skills in teamwork and the outdoors. At the world famous Smith Rock State Park, you will learn climbing techniques, as well as the basic gear, knots, and rope systems that keep you safe amidst the towering geologic formations. Along the wild and scenic Deschutes River, your team will learn paddling methods, river hydrology, raft captaining, and self-rescue techniques. The course also includes an emphasis on leadership, character development, and an ethic of service. Whether navigating through rapids, hiking long distances to reach climbs, or keeping calm when exposed to heights, wilderness travel is demanding. You do not need to have any previous experience but arriving physically fit and excited for the opportunity for personal development will enhance your experience and allow you to take full advantage of the expedition.[11]

This trip is designed to teach many technical skills including map and compass reading, knot tying, water safety and rescue, and basic first aid and is intended to infuse interpersonal skills such as empathy, positive risk taking, service, sense of social connection, and problem solving, among others.[12] Expeditions are designed to be short term or up to a semester long. Regardless of length, the underlying approach is to learn by doing.

Adventure Therapy

Adventure therapy uses adventure-based practices and therapeutic techniques to bring about positive behavioral changes.[13] Adventure therapy is also referred to as adventure-based counseling, therapeutic adventure, therapeutic camping, wilderness therapy, wilderness-adventure therapy, and outdoor behavioral healthcare.[14] Regardless of the title, experiential education is the premise behind adventure therapy and uses risk and physical and emotional challenges to promote "rehabilitation, growth, development, and enhancement of an individual's physical, social, and psychological well-being through the application of structured activities involving direct experience."[15] This can be done through such activities as cooperative games and problem solving, trust activities, low and high ropes courses, and expeditions like those provided by Outward Bound.

Adventure therapy can be part of a residential treatment program or an outpatient treatment plan. Adventure therapy can be the lone treatment method or used to supplement traditional therapy methods.[16] For example, the Newport Academy, located in multiple states on the east and west coasts, works with 12- to 22-year-olds who are struggling with mental health issues such as depression and anxiety, eating disorders, teen trauma, and substance abuse. Newport Academy uses a multitude of treatments including adventure therapy, music therapy, horticulture, and equine therapy. The adventure therapy programming includes rock climbing, paddle boarding, surfing, hiking, ropes course, and kayaking.[17] Although these activities are fun by themselves, they are part of the therapeutic intervention each participant needs, andthe activities are selected for the therapeutic value and the outcomes they can provide.

Environmental Interpretation

Environmental interpretation, also referred to as environmental education, is an educational activity that translates the technical, scientific, and complex characteristics of the environment into a nontechnical form that helps people create a sensitivity, awareness, understanding, enthusiasm, and commitment to the environment. It is hoped that these activities inspire a greater appreciation of the natural resource being learned about. Environmental interpretation combines the communication and education aspects of outdoor education. It may be through signage in the park explaining a grove of aspen trees in Rocky Mountain National Park, display boards identifying the flora and fauna in Indiana's Brown County State Park, posters about controlling invasive species in a community, leading classrooms through Helena National Forest in Montana to help students understand the process of reforestation (natural regeneration of tree plantings), or providing a conservation curriculum for older adults. Interpretation programs are common in such places as nature centers, state and national parks, museums, botanical gardens, aquariums, and wetlands.

National Park Service Rangers have interpretation as part of their job responsibilities where they work with the public to understand their surroundings. For example, the Rangers in Acadia National Park run programs including:[18]

■ Parks as Classrooms—Fieldtrips for school groups where topics vary by grade level.

■ Education Adventure Residential programs—Incorporate math, science, technology, social studies, language arts, physical education, health, and art through the environment. Students use actual scientific and cultural research taking place on site.[19]

■ Curriculum materials—Interpretative materials are developed for use in a classroom group or by a family. Topics include such things as ecosystem exploration, habitats, and fish migration. Many of these programs are designed for children as early as kindergarten with the purpose of sparking interest in the outdoors at a young age.

■ Traveling Trunks—Kits teachers can use to teach lessons about the environment to their classrooms if they are unable to bring the class to the park.

An overarching goal of environmental interpretation is to positively influence visitor behaviors through education to reduce negative impacts on the natural environment.

Specialized Recreation Facilities

Specialized facilities have been built to draw outdoor enthusiasts. Although not exhaustive, a few examples include climbing walls, challenge courses, urban whitewater rafting areas, and rental companies and outfitters.

CLIMBING WALLS

Climbing walls have become quite popular over the last two decades. They are being built in community centers and Young Men's Christian Association facilities, as part of playgrounds and health clubs, and at universities, among others. Climbing walls provide a way to learn the sport in a controlled environment and provide an experience for people who do not live near natural climbing areas. Some climbers use the walls as an opportunity to climb when they cannot get to an outdoor location, and some only climb on indoor walls and never outside.

There are currently over 10,000 climbing walls in the United States.[20] Climbing walls have a place for top rope climbing, which is climbing that occurs with the rope running from the climber to a fixed anchor and a belayer. Climbing walls will also have a bouldering area that provides small places to climb without ropes. Some will have areas for lead climbing (in which the climber clips the rope progressively through pieces of intermediate protection as they climb), rappel towers, artificial ice and mixed climbing areas, and areas devoted to cardiovascular and resistance training.[21] Climbing walls are judged based on their fun factor, challenge, aesthetics, and the ability to change routes. Most climbing wall businesses go beyond simply climbing opportunities, also offering classes, workshops, personal training, camps for children, clubs, and competitions. Climbing walls have also been built in creative locations such as an abandoned power plant, an old grain silo, and a rundown brick factory.

Ropes courses encourage personal growth through experiential learning.
© altanaka/Shutterstock.

Indoor climbing walls can be used to prepare for outdoor climbing or as their own recreational activity.
© Bertold Werkmann/Shutterstock.

CHALLENGE PROGRAMS AND COURSES

Challenge programs, also referred to as adventure education, provide opportunities for experiential learning through games, activities, and challenges. Challenge programs are often led by a trained facilitator because there are goals to participation. For example, a company may take its employees to an adventure challenge course to help them build better teamwork, develop leadership skills, enhance group dynamics, or build trust by being vulnerable in completing the challenges. The facilitator walks the group through each challenge and then debriefs with the group so they can reflect on what occurred and ensure the group meets their intended goals.

Challenge programs can be quite simple and done without much equipment, and they can be complex and use large-scale permanent equipment. Simple challenge programs may use natural elements in the area like a large tree stump where the group is asked to see how many people they can get off the ground and onto the stump. Those courses with permanent equipment will have it attached to trees, poles, or other structures. One of the most common types of permanent structures is a ropes course. Ropes courses can be low or high. Low ropes course activities are done from the ground up to about 12 feet. High ropes courses are often 15 to 50 feet in the air and bring a more intense level of challenges. Ropes courses will have proper safety equipment and trained staff to minimize injuries yet maintain a level of challenge to the activity.

In challenge programs, groups of people are given a real or imaginary scenario and asked to solve the problem through cooperation, creativity, careful planning, and maneuvering through differences. The group may work as one large group or broken into smaller one to see how each group approaches the problem differently. Challenge courses are rarely designed with only one solution. The creativity, problem solving, and teamwork are what makes challenge courses so effective and fun.

CASE STUDY: Adventure Challenges

Form groups of six to eight people in the class. Investigate outdoor adventure team building activities. Select an activity to facilitate with the rest of the class. Discuss the process of selecting the activity and the implementation.

URBAN WHITEWATER RAFTING CENTERS

Because not everyone has access to rivers for rafting, some communities bring the rivers to the people by building rafting centers that can be as calm as a lazy river, clear up to Category V rapids. Here are a few courses that can be found in the United States. Whitewater Express in Columbus, Georgia is the world's longest urban whitewater rafting course at 2.5 miles. Water speed can be controlled so that the mornings provide Class I–III rapids and the afternoons increase to Class III–V rapids for a wilder ride. RIVERSPORT Rapids in Oklahoma City was developed from a weed-filled drainage ditch and now serves the public as well as being a U.S. Olympic and Paralympic Training Site. Confluence Park in downtown Denver, Colorado was a polluted dump before it was cleaned up and boat chutes and locks added to control the water flow. Rafters can use the area for free or rent a kayak from a nearby outfitter.[22]

In addition to bringing a new activity to the community, many of these courses were built to refurbish rundown areas that were once eyesores. Because of the uniqueness of the course, they are sure to attract day trippers and tourists to the community.

RENTAL COMPANIES AND OUTFITTERS

Rental companies and outfitters have as their primary business to rent and sell outdoor equipment, plan and guide trips, and repair equipment. Rental companies and outfitters can be found as local businesses in a community, on university campuses, and within the armed forces morale, welfare, and recreation (MWR) units. They may also be located within a national or state park where they may be operated by park staff or contracted out to an outside vendor to provide a service.

To illustrate what rental and outfitting agencies do, here are a few examples from a public institution and two different types of businesses. The University of Utah Campus Recreation department rents equipment through its Outdoor Adventures unit. They rent equipment for water, snow, camping, biking, climbing (ice and mountain), and games such as slack line, washers, and cornhole.[23] REI Co-op is a nationwide business for the general public to purchase or rent outdoor equipment and clothing. Because it is a co-op, outdoor enthusiasts can purchase memberships that result in discounts, special access to member exclusive trips and equipment, and earn dividends on purchases. Nonmembers can purchase and rent from the store but do not receive the added benefits of membership. In addition to its sales and rental areas, REI sells used gear that members trade in.[24] Although REI is a large company, many rental companies and outfitters are smaller and locally owned. On the smaller end, Dive Right in Scuba is a local business in the Chicagoland area that sells a complete line of scuba and snorkeling gear, provides training to police and fire search and rescue teams, guides trips, and sells underwater camera and video equipment. Dive Right in Scuba provides extensive training from CPR and basic scuba to underwater navigation, master diver certification, and shipwreck diving.[25]

Outdoor recreation programs and facilities can be located on land and water, in urban and rural areas, done alone or in groups, and for fun or therapy. Each experience can be unique and tailored to the desires of the individual.

Sociodemographics in Outdoor Recreation

Sociodemographics are a means to identify people based on demographic or sociological characteristics. Demographics refer to individual quantifiable descriptors such as gender identity, age, race, and ethnicity. The more objective sociological factors include such things as household status and education. Using the combined sociodemographics better describes who a person is and what leisure activities they are more likely to engage in. Outdoor recreation has wide appeal across many sociodemographic factors. However, participation is not equal among different age groups, gender identities, races and ethnicities.

Age

As we age, our participation in outdoor recreation changes, much like it does for most other recreational activities. Some of this is because of the need for different levels of physicality, free time available, and exposure to new activities. Youth ages 6 to 17 make up 23% of all outdoor recreation participation and tend to participate in road, mountain, and BMX biking; running; camping; and hiking.[26] Currently, younger adults have a high level of participation in outdoor sports that became popular in the last 2 to 3 decades such as snowboarding, sport climbing, and mountain biking. Those in the 40- to 55-year-old age group prefer activities such as cross-country skiing, fishing, biking, visiting nature and cultural centers, and canoeing. After age 55 there is a significant decline in outdoor recreation participation, even for those activities popular for the 40- to 55-year-old groups. So, in general, as we age we do not continue our outdoor recreation pursuits as we once did.[27]

As expected, early exposure to outdoor recreation as children positively affects participation as adults. Approximately 38% of adults who were introduced to the outdoors during childhood grew up to enjoy outdoor activities as adults, and only 17% of adults who do not currently participate in any outdoor activities had outdoor experiences as children.[28]

Gender Identity

In general women participate in all leisure less than men. Much of this can be attributed to their role in the household, role as caregivers, and working outside the home in addition to these other two roles. So as expected, males participate in outdoor recreation more than females. Prepuberty is the only time in our lives that outdoor recreation participation gender differences do not exist. Women's outdoor recreation participation seems to surge a bit during and right after college. At the time of retirement women participate in outdoor recreation more than men because they live longer and are healthier. As adults, women participate more in activities such as nature walks, horseback riding, picnicking, ice skating, and visiting zoos and local parks. Men are more represented in activities such as backcountry camping, backpacking, river running, and snowmobiling. Males and females equally enjoy cross country skiing, hiking, and bird watching.[29] There is little research about gender identity and recreation participation that goes beyond the traditional male/female identities.

Race and Ethnicity

American demographics are rapidly shifting (Table 9-1). People who identify as non-Hispanic Whites make up a majority of the U.S. population at 59.7% but the overall percentage has continued to drop since 1950 as the United States becomes more diverse. The Hispanic population continues to grow and is currently at 18.7%, followed by Black U.S. residents making up 12.5% of the population, and the Asian population at 5.9%.[30] It is estimated that by 2030 these same trends will continue and by 2045 the Non-Hispanic White population will drop below 50%. The large number of older White people slows the demographic shifts as birthrates are

TABLE 9-1 **Estimated Demographic Shifts**				
Estimate and Projected U.S. Population by Race and Hispanic Origin, 1965–2065				
Year	**White**	**Black**	**Hispanic**	**Asian**
1965	84%	11%	4%	1%
2020	59.7%	12.5%	18.7%	5.9%
2065	46%	13%	24%	14%

Data from Frey, W. H. (2018, March 14). *The US will become "minority white" in 2045, Census projects.* Brookings Institution. Retrieved November 22, 2020, from https://www.brookings.edu/blog/the-avenue/2018/03/14/the-us-will-become-minority-white-in-2045-census-projects; Parker, K., Horowitz, J. M., Morin, R., & Lopez, M. H. (2015). *Multiracial in America: Proud, diverse, and growing in numbers.* Pew Research Center. Retrieved February 3, 2021, from https://www.pewsocialtrends.org/2015/06/11/multiracial-in-america/#fn-20523-2; and Pew Research Center. (2015). *Modern immigration wave brings 59 million to U.S., driving population growth and change through 2065: Views of immigration's impact on U.S. society mixed.* Retrieved February 3, 2021, from https://www.pewresearch.org/hispanic/2015/09/28/modern-immigration-wave-brings-59-million-to-u-s-driving-population-growth-and-change-through-2065/.

lower than death rates for White people. In 2020 Hispanic people, Black people, and Asian people make up the majority of people under age 18.[31] By 2027 that age range will grow to age 29 and under, and by 2033 to age 39 and under.[32] The next 2 decades will be transformative for the United States as the overall population will grow at a slower pace, it will age considerably, and it will become more racially diverse.[33]

This shift in demographics is exciting, and leisure services must change with these shifts to provide the services people want. It will be especially important for those working in outdoor recreation, because BIPOC are less likely to participate in outdoor recreation activities than people who are White.[34] With demographic shifts, there could be significant demand shifts for outdoor recreation and expanded opportunities to expose the outdoors to growing populations.

Outdoor participation among Latinx people has increased by an average of 1% over the past 5 years and among Asian people by 0.9%. Participation among Black and White populations have declined by an average of 0.4%. When Black and Latinx participants engaged in outdoor recreation, they did so at higher levels than both White and Asian people. Running was the most popular outdoor activity for all ethnicities except White populations, who participated in hiking at a higher rate.[35]

There are several nonprofit organizations whose mission it is to increase exposure to outdoor recreation for groups who are underrepresented in those pursuits. For example, Latino Outdoors is an organization whose mission is to "inspire, connect, and engage Latino communities in the outdoors and embrace *cultura y familia* as part of the outdoor narrative, ensuring our history, heritage, and leadership are valued and represented."[36] A growing segment of the U.S. Latinx population is second or even third generation born in the United States with at least one immigrant

parent. "That segment of the Latinx population is going to be more aware of opportunities that exist to engage with the outdoors," Luis Villa, Executive Director of Latino Outdoors says.[37] Despite the increase in participation, Latinx participants are still underrepresented. They make up 18.7% of the population but account for only 11% of the total participation in outdoor recreation.

The Black Outdoors (TBO) is a group whose mission is to increase awareness of and participation in outdoor recreational activity among Black people and other minoritized groups. TBO provides resources, education, and plans trips and activities to spark interest and increase participation.[38]

Despite these efforts and active participation in activities that are outdoors, White people use our national parks, national forests, and national wildlife refuges at far greater rates than other populations. Research in this area shows several barriers that can limit participation. First, access and affordability limit participation because many national recreation areas are not close to home, not located within cities, and can require financial means to pay for transportation, lodging, entrance fees, food, and equipment.[39] Second, early childhood experiences shape our love for the outdoors and desire to continue engagement with the natural environment. If that is missing as a youth, it is likely to be missing as an adult.[40] Third, cultural factors influence participation including cultural norms, value systems, and socialization practices.[41] Cultural factors provide a template for the activities that people should conform to and participate in. Communities can discourage activities that do not support the group's identity.[42] Fourth, the United States' history of discrimination and systemic racism still influence participation. Before the 1964 Civil Rights Act, Black people in the United States were banned or segregated from public recreation sites. This leads to lack of exposure to state and national parks and wildlife areas,[43] exacerbated by the limited number of staff who are Black, Asian, or Latinx. Approximately 83% of National Park Service employees are White, and 62% are male. The rest of the outdoor recreation industry is no different and lacks staff diversity.[44]

Demographic shifts, exposure, and access are positive indicators that participation in outdoor recreation will expand for all populations in the upcoming decades. Efforts to attract nontraditional users and staff from minoritized groups must be made.

Issues in Outdoor Recreation

Earlier we discussed historical and legislative efforts to protect our lands and water. Even with legislation and many local, state, and federal departments charged with managing these areas, much work is still needed. This section features some of the issues that outdoor recreation professionals and the general public face with their outdoor recreation resources.

Conservation vs. Preservation

Much of outdoor recreation is driven by the concepts of conservation and preservation. Both have a long and storied past and are infused in every piece of public land in the United States. Their initial conception can be traced back over 100 years to John Muir and Gifford Pinchot. Muir founded the Sierra Club and was instrumental in the creation of Yosemite, Grand Canyon, and Sequoia national parks.[45] Because of this and other work, Muir was known as the father of national parks and was a prolific writer and philosopher about the natural environment. Pinchot, known as the father of the forest, was the first chief of the U.S. Forest Service where he tripled the number of U.S. forests for conservation and recreational use. Pinchot saw forests as a social good because of the resources they

brought to the citizens.[46] At the turn of the century Muir and Pinchot worked tirelessly to get Congress to protect open space. Eventually the two men differed on their stance on how the protected lands should be used. Pinchot advocated for conservation and Muir preservation. Pinchot felt that the public lands should be used responsibly for recreation by the general public but also by industry for responsible logging and mining. Muir wanted the lands preserved with little or no industries profiting from its natural resources.[47]

Even though Muir was a mentor to Pinchot and they later were at odds on how to approach the use of public lands, conservation and preservation work together and both have a place even within the same park. Some national parks and forests will have areas that are managed using conservation principles and some areas that follow preservation principles.

Conservation principles promote sustainable and beneficial use of natural resources such as air, water, land, and wildlife. Conservation focuses mainly on renewable resources, or those resources that are replenished at a faster rate than they are used. Renewable resources include solar, geothermal, and wind power; carefully controlled and treated water; plants; sustainable agriculture; air; timber; wind; and animals.

Preservationists advocate for preserving the land as is, leaving lands unused and undeveloped. This is done to protect nonrenewable resources like fossil fuels (oil, natural gas, and coal), nuclear energy, earth minerals, and metal ores. Not only are lands preserved but so are cultural and historic sites and areas. For example, the National Historic Preservation Act of 1966 provides grants to Indian Tribes, Alaskan Natives, and Native Hawaiian Organizations preserve their unique cultural heritage and traditions[48] such as the preservation of a 16th-century pueblo and petroglyphs on mesa cliffs in New Mexico.[49]

CASE STUDY: Leave No Trace Center for Outdoor Ethics

The Leave No Trace Center for Outdoor Ethics focuses on educating people about the least resource intensive use of natural resources. Leave No Trace began by providing guidance for using the backcountry and the impact visitors can have. They developed the Leave No Trace Seven Principles to teach people how to conserve the environment for future generations. The seven principles include plan ahead and prepare, travel and camp on durable surfaces, dispose of waste properly, leave what you find, minimize campfire impacts, respect wildlife, and be considerate of other visitors.

Questions to Consider

1. Review the seven principles more in depth (https://lnt.org/why/7-principles). Summarize each of them.
2. Review the problems that the Leave No Trace Center for Outdoors Ethics attempts to solve (https://lnt.org/why/problems-we-solve/). Summarize the problems and connect them to the seven principles.
3. Review and summarize the educational programs offered by the Leave No Trace Center for Outdoors Ethics.

Data from Leave No Trace Center for Outdoor Ethics. (n.d.). *The 7 principles.* https://lnt.org/why/7-principles. © 1999 by the Leave No Trace Center for Outdoor Ethics: www.LNT.org

LAKE MICHIGAN PRESERVATION EFFORTS

Lake Michigan is the third largest Great Lake by surface and the second largest by volume and is a mix of bluffs, beaches, and marshlands touching many Midwestern towns and tourist communities. Climate change has caused surging water levels, which has resulted in collapsed bluffs, underwater sand dunes, disappearing beaches, and damaged homes, businesses, piers, trails, and sewer systems. Government officials, scientists, and engineers are working diligently in Wisconsin, Illinois, and Indiana to find solutions before the waters of Lake Michigan ruin all the parts of it that people love.

Recently, homeowners have stabilized their homes, built waterfront barriers, or just moved away. Sewer systems have been reinforced. Historical buildings have had to be relocated to preserve them before the shoreline erodes away because it loses about 6 inches per year. Because much erosion and damage come from wind, rainfall, and waves, work is being done to install offshore reefs and underwater break walls to reduce waves and the flow of sand and sediment away from the shoreline. It is hoped this will also restore some of the natural habitat that has been lost.

A goal of these preservation efforts is that they are designed to be as invisible as possible. Only time will tell if those efforts work and preserve one of our treasured Great Lakes and the surrounding communities.

Data from Briscoe, T. (2020, November 22). A determined fight for preservation. *Chicago Tribune*.

Land and Water Conservation Fund

The Land and Water Conservation Fund (LWCF) was established by Congress in 1964 as a way to safeguard natural resources and provide recreational opportunities. LWCF is funded by offshore oil and gas leases. The funding premise is that offshore drilling depletes resources, so funds generated from this are used to replenish other resources in order to conserve parks, wildlife refuges, forests, open spaces, trails, and wildlife habitats. Annually Congress can allocate up to $900 million for LWCF projects but has funded it at that level only one time. Even without full funding the impact of the LWCF is extensive. It has protected 8 million acres in all 50 states, $20 billion has been invested in communities since 1964, and 98% of U.S. counties have a park or open space funded by LWCF.[50]

LWCF is managed by the Department of the Interior, which explains funding use as "some of the funds are invested by agencies to protect federal lands for public outdoor recreation use and enjoyment—including national parks, national forests, and national recreation areas. Agencies also partner with landowners to support voluntary conservation activities on private lands. Some of the funds are distributed directly to states and local communities through grant programs. These grants enable state and local governments to establish baseball fields and community green spaces; to provide public access to rivers, lakes, and other water resources; to protect historic and cultural sites; and to conserve natural landscapes for public use and enjoyment."[51] The initial 50-year authorization of LWCF lapsed in 2015 and then again in 2018. However, it was reauthorized in 2019. In 2020 the Great American Outdoors Act was introduced and passed to fix the longstanding $12 billion maintenance backlog in our national parks, forests, and other public lands and to guarantee the full and dedicated funding of $900 million per year. This monumental legislation will help many communities, national parks, and other outdoor resources areas with development, preservation, and conservation efforts.

Negative Impacts of Recreation Use

The positive outcomes that people receive from being in the outdoors are immeasurable, but the negative impacts must also be considered. The negative recreation impacts are also referred to as user impacts, visitor impacts, or recreation resource impacts.[52]

Negative recreation impacts can come from overuse of wilderness areas, air pollution from the traffic going through a park, or engine exhaust from a boat. It can also come from poor policy decisions such as drilling for oil in the Arctic National Wildlife Refuge (see case study), inadequate or poorly trained staff, or unmet maintenance needs. Sample negative impacts are categorized in Table 9-2.

Our ecosystem is delicate, and it is imperative that we find a balance between maintaining the ecosystem and enjoying the natural environment. One way to balance this is by managing crowding. The level of crowding is measured in carrying capacity. Carrying capacity is the maximum number of people an area can accommodate without causing damage to the resources used or diminishing the experience. Carrying capacity is impacted by the number of users, intensity of use, habitat type, seasonality, and location of the resource. It is not easy to determine and is subjective.[53] Parks, beaches, rivers, and other areas can manage carrying capacity and crowding in a variety of ways including limiting the number of users in an area, charging an admissions fee to reduce visitors, educating the public

TABLE 9-2   Negative Impacts of Recreation Use

Resource	Negative Impact	Results
Soil	Trampling and overuse by humans and animals such as horses, bicycles, all-terrain vehicles	Eroding soil, loss of minerals and other organic materials, compacted soils that stop root growth, reduced infiltration of rainwater into the soil increases runoff, limited ability to support plant life
Water quality	Improper disposal of human waste into the water, aquatic species that deplete oxygen levels, chemical pollution	Shoreline erosion from boat wakes, flora and fauna death, drinking water contamination
Air quality	Pollution from motorized vehicles, campfire smoke, burning of oil and coal	Results in poor visibility and unhealthy air
Vegetation	Destroyed via trampling, gathering firewood, carving initials in trees, improper disposal of human waste and garbage	Death of vegetation or growth of invasive species, diminished protection of the underlying soil, shade, and food for animals
Wildlife	Poaching wildlife, damaging wildlife food supply, disrupting breeding by being in an animal's territory, feeding wildlife, bringing dogs into an animal's habitat	Reduction, death, and/or extinction of wildlife, reduced food source and shelter

Data from Moore, R. L., & Driver, B. L. (2005). *Introduction to outdoor recreation*. Venture Publishing; Ward, W., & Hobbs, W. (2012). *Environmental stewardship. Outdoor program administration: Principles and practice*. Human Kinetics.

CASE STUDY: Should Drilling Be Allowed in the Arctic National Wildlife Refuge?

A national wildlife refuge is a designation for certain protected areas managed by the U.S. Fish and Wildlife Service for the protection of wild animals, plants, and waters.[a] The Arctic National Wildlife Refuge is 19 million acres in northeastern Alaska. The area that will potentially be drilled in is a 1.5 million acre tract and is believed to contain one of the largest untapped onshore oil reserves in North America. The refuge is also home to polar bears; the porcupine caribou herd, which sustains the communities and way of life for the Indigenous Gwich'in and Iñupiat people who have deep and ancient connections to this land; musk oxen; Arctic fox; all three types of North American bear species; and over 270 other species.[b] Those opposed to drilling in the refuge are concerned that drilling would bring roads, airstrips, heavy machinery, noise, and pollution into the area; damage the refuge's fragile tundra ecosystem; and disrupt age-old migration and denning patterns for the animals.[b] It would also contribute to climate change and increase seismic activity. Those who support drilling in the refuge do so because of the oil that could be garnered, making the United States less dependent on foreign oil. Alaskan lawmakers have traditionally been in support of drilling because of the revenue it brings to the state, and thousands of Alaskans are employed in the oil industry, which are high-paying jobs. In August 2020, the Trump administration finalized plans to sell leases for companies to begin drilling, something that has been considered since the Reagan administration.[c] Several lawsuits are expected to be filed to try to stop the drilling, and the Biden administration may try to halt the sale of the leases.

Questions to Consider

1. Research the topic of drilling in the Arctic National Wildlife Refuge. Where does the situation currently stand?
2. Develop a list of pros and cons to drilling in the Arctic National Wildlife Refuge. Do you believe that drilling should occur? Why or why not?
3. Draft a letter to your representatives in the House and your senator advocating for your stance on this issue.
4. Research the impact of this drilling on the Indigenous Gwich'in and Iñupiat people. Summarize your findings.

[a] U.S. Department of the Interior. (2019, October 11). *Celebrating national wildlife refuges*. Retrieved November 24, 2020, from https://www.doi.gov/blog/celebrating-national-wildlife-refuges#:~:text=A%20national%20wildlife%20refuge%20is,America's%20 wild%20animals%20and%20plants.

[b] Plumer, B., & Fountain, H. (2020, August 17). Trump Administration finalizes plan to open Arctic refuge to drilling. *New York Times*. https://www.nytimes.com/2020/08/17/climate/alaska-oil-drilling-anwr.html

[c] The Wilderness Society. (n.d.). *Oil drilling: Arctic National Wildlife Refuge*. Retrieved November 24, 2020, from https://www.wilderness.org/wild-places/alaska/oil-drilling-arctic-national-wildlife-refuge#.

about the impact of their behaviors, or closing an area for a period of time.

Negative recreation impacts will occur if people are to use land, water, and air for recreation. Strong management practices can help control these negative impacts and keep outdoor areas open to the public for years to come.

Climate Change

Climate change is one of the world's most pressing ecological issues. It is defined as the long-term change in the normal climate patterns that an area experiences. This change could be an increase in the average amount of rain or snow an area gets or the average seasonal temperature increase over time.

The Earth's temperature has gone up 1° C in the last 100 years. Scientists suggest that although this may not seem significant, it is. A one-degree change causes snow and ice to melt; ocean levels to rise; and affects plant and animal life; causes droughts, wildfires and hurricanes; and causes food shortages for humans.[54]

The climate change that the world is experiencing is largely attributed to human actions and the increase in greenhouse gases emitted into the atmosphere. Greenhouse gases that are most problematic are water vapor (H_2O), carbon dioxide (CO_2), methane (CH_4), and nitrous oxide (N_2O). Carbon dioxide is the most prominent and comes from the burning of fossil fuels (coal, gas, and oil).[55] The second biggest cause of CO_2 emission is deforestation. Deforestation is the clearing or thinning of forests, usually to produce goods or to use the wood as heat. When trees are cut down, they release carbon that is normally stored for photosynthesis. Deforestation releases a billion tons of carbon into the atmosphere each year.[56] These greenhouse gases increase the global temperature, which is why climate change is often referred to as global warming.

Despite scientific evidence of the Earth's temperature changing, some around the world and in the United States do not believe climate change is real. Some reasons for this this include:[57]

■ The Earth is too complex for us to know the true extent of global warming.
■ Climate change is a natural evolution that will occur over time.
■ If scientists are not in agreement, then it must not exist.
■ People do not want to change and deny that there is a problem that they themselves are contributing to.
■ There are media and political biases; the media that people consume and the political ideologies to which they subscribe will influence their belief and understanding of climate change.

Some feel that climate change is a worldwide issue and one country cannot take full responsibility without the others doing the same. However, the United States emits 25% of all human-produced CO_2, followed by the 28 countries of the European Union (22%), China (13%), Russia (7%), Japan (4%), India (3%), and the rest of the world (26%).[58]

Even though this is a global issue, change starts at the grassroots level. Local, state, and national parks can begin to be change agents for global warming. Here are a few things that can be done at the local level:[59]

■ Cooling urban heat islands—parks with many trees can help reduce extreme heat, and park areas can be up to 17 degrees cooler than the parts of the city lacking trees.
■ Minimizing flooding and improving water quality— parks that install water-smart landscape features such as rain gardens can reduce storm runoff by as much as 90%, reducing the likelihood of flooding and filtering up to 95% of the pollutants out of the water.
■ Cleaning the air—an urban tree canopy in parks and along streets can reduce CO_2 and filter particulate matter from the air equal to removing 19 million cars from the streets.

The Trust for Public Land (TPL) has developed four guidelines to establish climate smart cities through weaving nature and natural functions into the built environment. They include:[60]

1. Connecting neighborhoods in the city with bike corridors to provide carbon free transportation options to popular destinations such as schools, parks, downtown areas, and neighborhoods. This enables people to walk or bike to learn, shop, and play.
2. Cool the community by building parks and planting shade trees to minimize the effects of heat waves and reduce indoor temperatures by as much as 10 degrees.
3. Absorb storm water runoff and recharge drinking supplies by building water-smart parks and playgrounds.
4. Protect cities that are vulnerable to climate driven devastation such as hurricanes and floods by establishing waterfront parks, wetlands, and healthy shorelines.

TPL has put these guidelines to use in cities such as New York City where they have converted asphalt playgrounds to areas with grass and vegetation. In south Los Angeles they have converted abandoned alleys into green, walkable parkways. Not only did these projects positively affect the environment, but they also improved aesthetics in these areas.

CASE STUDY: The Difference a Presidential Administration Can Make

The U.S. political impacts on environmental programs have been staggering based on which presidential administration is in office. A president will push an agenda on topics such as the environment, immigration, education, and many others. Environmentally, each has a differing degree of support for organizations such as the Environmental Protection Agency, climate change, and the Department of the Interior, home to the National Park Service, and U.S. Fish and Wildlife Service.

Questions to Consider

1. Research and summarize the environment plan/policies passed for the last four U.S. presidents. Answer the following questions:
   a. Compare and contrast the plans/policies passed. Which administration was most supportive of environmental issues? Who was the least supportive?
   b. Do you see any patterns based on political party? Support your answer.
2. Develop talking points supporting your arguments on whose plan you most support.
3. Review Representative Alexandria Ocasio-Cortez's Green New Deal plan. Summarize your findings. Outline things that you think could work and those that could not. Briefly justify your answers.

Working in Outdoor Recreation

By now it is evident that outdoor recreation is complex. The professional paths one can follow to make this a career are just as complex. To be a full time professional in outdoor recreation, students typically follow four pathways: natural resources, recreation and park administration, outdoor environmental education, and adventure leadership and adventure education.[61]

Natural resources management focuses on the scientific side of outdoor recreation with courses and training in areas such as biology, botany, ecology, and forest sciences. This path can lead to jobs such as environmental program manager, restoration ecologist, wildland manager, forester, or ranger.

Those who major in parks and recreation will have a focus on the program planning aspect of the profession. They may work as trip leaders, own their own equipment and outfitter company, serve as interpreters in outdoor areas, or work in nature centers. They may also manage outdoor recreation facilities such as campgrounds, climbing walls, and ski resorts.

Outdoor environmental education jobs will focus on teaching visitors to be environmentally literate, to understand the environment around them and how to better preserve or conserve it. This academic path will merge natural resources and parks and recreation and combine the scientific aspects and the program aspects so that the environmental educators can communicate knowledge of the outdoors. Study in this area can lead to interpretive work, teaching students about the outdoors on site within a park or forest, developing outdoor curriculum that infuses the outdoors in subjects such as math, science, language arts, and the fine arts.

Outdoor adventure leadership is very much a hands-on profession where staff lead participants through outdoor recreation activities, trips, and other adventures. They may teach rock climbing, plan expeditions, or work in adventure therapy agencies. Coursework will build high-level outdoor skills such as avalanche search and rescue, wilderness survival, all aspects of climbing (e.g., ice, alpine, rock), backcountry leadership, and outdoor adventure facilitation.

Although these four career paths have a fairly specific focus, students majoring in any of them build transferrable skills that allow them to work in many different areas within outdoor recreation. One way to continue to build skills while in college or afterwards is by acquiring certifications. Outdoor recreation has a wide variety of certifications available. For example, the Wilderness Education Association (WEA) offers certification as a Certified Outdoor Educator. WEA describes this certification as:

> The Certified Outdoor Educator (COE) credential recognizes the professional qualifications of individuals who work in programs that provide structured training and assessment/evaluation in outdoor leadership development. These professionals are committed to excellence and have proven their ability to deliver quality outdoor leadership experiences. In addition, COEs have also demonstrated proficiency in educating, evaluating, and assessing outdoor leadership training and development experiences based on the 6+1 standards....Outdoor Living, Planning and Logistics, Education, Risk Management, Environmental Integration, and Leadership *plus* Judgment and Decision-making.[62]

More information on certifications can be found in Chapter 7.

SUMMARY

Outdoor recreation involves leisure activities that depend on natural resources such as wildlife, rivers, and lakes. Outdoor recreation areas include local, state, and national parks; forests; and bodies of water such as rivers and lakes. These areas can be managed by the federal government such as the Department of the Interior, by the state Department of Natural Resources, or a local parks and recreation agency. Outdoor recreation can also be in the nonprofit and commercial sectors where you can find such businesses as rental companies and outfitters.

Protecting our natural resources has a long history and involved centuries of work by advocates such as John Muir, Gifford Pinchot, and Theodore Roosevelt. Their early work established the National Park Service and U.S. Forest Service and set aside 15 million acres of national parks and monuments in a short period of time.

Outdoor recreation activities can take place on land and in the water. Land-based popular activities include hiking, backpacking, and climbing. Land-based activities are not done only in the warmer months; there are also plenty of activities for those who like the colder weather such as winter camping, ice climbing, and snowshoeing. Water-based activities fall within three categories of water: flat water (smaller lakes and estuaries), moving water (whitewater), and open water (seas and large lakes). Each offers different opportunities for recreation activities with different challenges and equipment needs.

Sometimes outdoor recreation has an educational and therapeutic element to it. Experiential education uses outdoor recreation to engage learners through experiences. Engagement in meaningful activities can teach individuals about leadership, collaboration, problem solving, and more. Outward Bound is a well-known experiential education organization that teaches youth and adults through the outdoors. Adventure therapy uses experiential education to influence positive behavior changes. It uses risk and physical and emotional challenges to promote physical, social, and psychological well-being.

In addition to experiential education, environmental interpretation is a means of communication and learning about the natural environment. Interpreters are tasked with translating technical, scientific, and complex characteristics of the environment into nontechnical concepts that people use to better understand and care for the environment.

Specialized recreation facilities are numerous, but a few examples include climbing walls, challenge programs and courses, urban whitewater rafting centers, and rental companies and outfitters. Each provides a means for outdoor recreation participation, some in an alternative environment, and others in the natural environment. Indoor climbing walls and human-made rafting centers may be the only way that some people experience these activities.

Sociodemographic differences in outdoor recreation are evolving as our demographics continue to shift in the United States and Canada. There are differences in participation based on gender identity, age, race, and ethnicity. Some of this is because of early exposure to outdoor recreation, available opportunities, and resources such as time and money. The diversity of our population on all three of these factors will greatly influence outdoor recreation for years to come.

Although outdoor recreation is fun and brings many benefits for those who partake in the activities or use our parks, rivers, and forests, there are significant issues to consider that affect them daily. There is a conservation versus preservation philosophy that drives how we manage our natural resources. Conservationists promote sustainable and beneficial use of our renewable resources whereas preservationists want to leave the land unused and undeveloped, in its natural state. Both preservation and conservation can play a significant role in the same tract of land. Conservation and preservation efforts are sometimes funded through the LWCF. Part of conservation and preservation is to reduce or prohibit the negative impacts of recreation use on soil, water quality, air quality, vegetation, and wildlife. Part of these negative impacts can be managed by reducing carry capacity and managing the effects of climate change.

Outdoor recreation is quite complex as are the paths to a profession in this area. Often students will enter the profession by studying natural resources, recreation and park administration, outdoor environmental education, or adventure leadership and adventure education. These paths can lead to jobs as park rangers, interpreters, expedition guides, or facility managers.

QUESTIONS FOR CLASS DISCUSSION OR ESSAY EXAMINATION

1. Compare and contrast conservation and preservation.

_____

_____

_____

2. Summarize the sociodemographic differences in outdoor recreation participation.

_____
_____
_____

3. Differentiate experiential education and adventure therapy.

_____
_____
_____

4. What is the Land and Water Conservation Fund? How is it funded and what does it do?

_____
_____
_____

5. Discuss the four paths to a profession in outdoor recreation.

_____
_____
_____

6. Define climate change. Explain the impacts climate change is having on the world. Outline reasons people do not believe in climate change.

_____
_____
_____

ENDNOTES

1. Kraus, R. (1971). *Recreation and leisure in modern society* (p. 360). Appleton-Century-Crofts.
2. Ibrahim, H., & Cordes, K. A. (2008). *Outdoor recreation: Enrichment for a lifetime.* Sagamore Publishing.
3. Taylor, D. E. (1999). Central Park as a model for social control: Urban parks, social class and leisure behavior in nineteenth century America. *Journal of Leisure Research, 31*(4), 420.
4. Ibrahim & Cordes (2008).
5. Jensen, C. R., & Guthrie, S. P. (2006). *Outdoor recreation in America* (6th ed.). Human Kinetics.
6. Moore, R. L., & Driver, B. L. (2005). *Introduction to outdoor recreation.* Venture Publishing, Inc.
7. Stec, C., & Harrison, G. (2012). Water-based programming. In G. Harrison & M. Erpelding (Eds.), *Outdoor program administration: Principles and practices.* Human Kinetics.
8. Jensen & Guthrie (2006).
9. ARTA River Trips. (n.d.). *Difficulty scale.* Retrieved November 23, 2020, from https://www.arta.org/difficulty-scale/.
10. Harrison, G., & Erpelding, M. (2012). The Outdoor program administrator. In G. Harrison & M. Erpelding (Eds.), *Outdoor program administration: Principles and practice.* Human Kinetics.
11. Outward Bound. (n.d.). *Oregon rafting & rock climbing: Raft through desert canyons and climb volcanic peaks in the untamed wilderness of Oregon.* Retrieved November 21, 2020, from https://www.outwardbound.org/course/oregon-rafting-rock-climbing/369.
12. Ibid.
13. Jensen & Guthrie (2006).
14. Russell, K. C., & Hendee, J. C. (2000). *Outdoor behavioral healthcare: Definitions, common practice, expected outcomes, and a nationwide survey of programs* (Technical Report #26). Idaho Forest, Wildlife and Range Experiment Station.
15. Ewert, A., McCormick, B., & Voight, A. (2001). Outdoor experiential therapies: Implications for TR practice. *Therapeutic Recreation Journal, 35*(2), 107–122.
16. Association for Experiential Education. (n.d.). *Definition of adventure therapy.* Retrieved November 22, 2020, from https://www.aee.org/tapg-best-p-defining-adv-therapy.

17. Newport Academy. Retrieved November 22, 2020, from https://www.newportacademy.com/.

18. National Park Service. (n.d.). *Acadia National Park fall programs*. Retrieved November 22, 2020, from https://www.nps.gov/acad/learn/education/fall-programs.htm.

19. National Park Service. (n.d.). *Acadia National Park institutes and field schools*. Retrieved November 22, 2020, from https://www.nps.gov/acad/learn/education/classrooms/institutes-and-field-schools.htm.

20. Bicknell, J., & deBrun, G. (2012). Indoor climbing walls. In G. Harrison & M. Erpelding (Eds.), *Outdoor program administration: Principles and practices.* Human Kinetics.

21. Ibid.

22. Schroder, J. (2017, November 15). 5 amazing urban whitewater adventures. Retrieved November 24, 2020, from https://www.orbitz.com/blog/2017/11/5-amazing-urban-whitewater-adventures/.

23. University of Utah Campus Recreation. (n.d.). *Equipment rental*. Retrieved November 23, 2020, from https://campusrec.utah.edu/programs/outdoor-adventures/rental/index.php.

24. REI Co-op. (n.d.). *Used gear*. Retrieved November 23, 2020, from https://www.rei.com/used.

25. Dive Right in Scuba. Retrieved November 27, 2020, from https://www.diverightinscuba.com.

26. Outdoor Foundation. (2018). *Outdoor participation report 2018*. Retrieved February 1, 2021, from https://www.americantrails.org/images/documents/2018_outdoor_recreation_part.pdf.

27. Jensen & Guthrie (2006).

28. Outdoor Foundation (2018).

29. Jensen & Guthrie (2006).

30. PBS News Hour. (2020, January 2). *3 ways that the U.S. population will change over the next decade*. Retrieved November 22, 2020, from https://www.pbs.org/newshour/nation/3-ways-that-the-u-s-population-will-change-over-the-next-decade.

31. Ibid.

32. Frey, W. H. (2018, March 14). *The US will become "minority white" in 2045, Census projects*. Brookings Institute. Retrieved November 22, 2020, from https://www.brookings.edu/blog/the-avenue/2018/03/14/the-us-will-become-minority-white-in-2045-census-projects/.

33. U.S. Census Bureau. (2018, March 13). *Older people projected to outnumber children for first time in U.S. history*. Retrieved November 22, 2020, from https://www.census.gov/newsroom/press-releases/2018/cb18-41-population-projections.html.

34. Cordell, H. K., Betz, C. J., & Green, G. T. (2002). Recreation and the environment as cultural dimensions in contemporary American society. *Leisure Sciences, 24*, 13–41.

35. Outdoor Foundation (2018).

36. Latino Outdoors. Retrieved November 23, 2020, from https://latinooutdoors.org.

37. Sherwood, C. H. (2020, May 27). *Why Hispanic outdoor participation is on the rise*. Be Outdoors. Retrieved November 23, 2020, from https://www.outdoors.org/articles/amc-outdoors/why-hispanic-outdoor-participation-is-on-the-rise.

38. The Black Outdoors. (n.d.). *What to do? Where to go?* Retrieved November 22, 2020, from https://www.theblackoutdoors.com/getoutdoors.

39. Askew, R., & Walls, M. A. (2019, May 24). Diversity in the great outdoors: Is everyone welcome in America's parks and public lands? *Resources Magazine*. Retrieved November 22, 2020, from https://www.resourcesmag.org/common-resources/diversity-in-the-great-outdoors-is-everyone-welcome-in-americas-parks-and-public-lands/.

40. Ibid.

41. Floyd, M. F., & Stodolska, M. (2014). Theoretical frameworks in leisure research on race and ethnicity. In M. Stodolska, K. J. Shinew, M. F. Floyd, & G. J. Walker (Eds.), *Race, ethnicity and leisure* (pp. 9–19). Human Kinetics.

42. Scott, D., & Lee, K. J. J. (2018). People of color and their constraints to national parks visitation. *The George Wright Forum, 35*(1),73–82. Retrieved November 22, 2020, from http://www.georgewright.org/351scott.pdf.

43. National Park Service. (2016, March 22). *Civil Rights Act of 1964*. Retrieved November 22, 2020, from https://www.nps.gov/articles/civil-rights-act.htm.

44. Askew & Walls (2019).

45. National Park Service. (2018, May 13). *John Muir*. Retrieved November 22, 2020, from https://www.nps.gov/yose/learn/historyculture/muir.htm.

46. National Park Service. (2018, May 9). *Gifford Pinchot: The father of forestry*. Retrieved November 22, 2020, from https://www.nps.gov/articles/gifford-pinchot.htm.

47. Westover, R. H. (2016, March 22). *Conservation versus Preservation?* U.S. Forest Service. Retrieved November 22, 2020, from https://www.fs.usda.gov/features/conservation-versus-preservation.

48. National Park Service. (n.d.). *Tribal heritage grants.* Retrieved November 22, 2020, from https://www.nps.gov/thpo/tribal-heritage/index.html.

49. National Park Service. (2019, September 13). *National Park Service awards historic preservation grants to American Indian tribes, Alaskan Natives, and Native Hawaiian organizations.* Retrieved November 22, 2020, from https://www.nps.gov/orgs/1207/national-park-service-awards-historic-preservation-grants-to-american-indian-tribes-alaskan-natives-and-native-hawaiian-organizations2019.htm.

50. Trust for Public Lands. (n.d.). *Land and Water Conservation Fund.* Retrieved November 24, 2020, from https://www.tpl.org/lwcf.

51. U.S. Department of the Interior. (n.d.). *LWCF overview.* Retrieved November 24, 2020, from https://www.doi.gov/lwcf/about/overview.

52. Moore & Driver (2005)

53. Ibrahim & Cordes (2008).

54. Kann, D. (2019, September 4). *Trump's rollback of climate change regulations will be felt far beyond his presidency.* CNN. Retrieved November 29, 2020, from https://www.cnn.com/2019/09/04/politics/trump-climate-change-policy-rollbacks/index.html.

55. *Lallanilla, M. (2019,* January 3). *Greenhouse gases: Causes, sources and environmental effects.* Live Science. Retrieved November 29, 2020, from https://www.livescience.com/37821-greenhouse-gases.html.

56. Ibid.

57. Babu, S. (2016, October 16). *7 reasons why people don't believe in climate change.* Eco-Intelligent. Retrieved November 29, 2020, from https://eco-intelligent.com/2016/10/16/why-dont-people-believe-in-climate-change/.

58. Maslin, M. (2019, November 30). *Here are five of the main reasons people continue to deny climate change.* Science Alert. Retrieved November 29, 2020, from https://www.sciencealert.com/the-five-corrupt-pillars-of-climate-change-denial.

59. Schottland, T. (2019). Parks as a solution to climate change. *Parks and Recreation*, 54(4), 42.

60. Trust for Public Lands. (2018). *Climate-smart cities™.* Retrieved November 25, 2020, from https://www.tpl.org/how-we-work/climate-smart-cities.

61. Jensen, C.R. & Guthrie, S.P. (2006). Outdoor recreation in America (6th ed.). Champaign, IL: Human Kinetics.

62. Wilderness Education Association. https://www.weainfo.org/certified-outdoor-educator. Accessed November 29, 2020.

Chapter 10
Travel and Tourism

"Personal travel in automobiles is expected to continue as a major form of personal transportation, but the responsibility for much driving will be taken away from humans by computerized guidance systems that feed routing, weather, and road conditions to drivers by means of television-computers."[1] (pg. 458)

-From the first edition of Kraus' Recreation and Leisure in Modern Society, published in 1971

LEARNING OBJECTIVES

1. Define travel and tourism.

2. Understand the scope of tourism.

3. Identify and explain tourism and commercial recreation types.

4. Understand the role of travel and tourism within the commercial sector.

5. Describe technology advances in tourism.

Introduction

Travel and tourism is the world's largest industry. It spans the public, nonprofit, and commercial sectors; is highly affected by changing technology; and encompasses culture, history, the environment, religion, the arts, agriculture, sport, education, and additional areas. Tourism is big business and is not confined to this country, as it is a global industry. Although travel and tourism span all three sectors, they are arguably most connected to the commercial recreation sector. Commercial recreation often supports travel and tourism but also provides a wide array of recreational opportunities for the communities in which these businesses exist, positively affects the economic viability of the area, and can come in many shapes and sizes from small sole proprietorships to large corporations.

This chapter focuses on travel and tourism as well as the components that make up this massive industry. Before delving into the specifics, it is important to define what exactly travel and tourism are. On the surface, these may be easily defined, but think about the complexity. How far does one have to go to be considered a tourist? Do tourists have to stay overnight? Do tourists have to go outside of their home community? Does tourism have to be for pleasure or is business travel considered tourism?

Tourism is defined as "the activities of people traveling to and staying in places outside their usual environment, for leisure, business, or other purposes."[2] In this instance, a person's usual environment means the community in which that person lives. The World Tourism Organization puts a time stipulation on the definition of tourism by saying that people must not remain in the location for more than a year. From this definition traveling to conference, business meetings or other nonvacation purposes are considered tourism.

Crossley et al. do not separate commercial recreation and tourism because of the interconnectedness of these concepts.[3] They suggest that the tourism industry is made up of three parts: local commercial recreation, travel, and hospitality.

Local commercial recreation is the entertainment, activities and programs, and retail products and services within the community. It encompasses such venues and activities as theaters, festivals, water parks, golf courses, family entertainment centers, theme parks, and shopping (see Chapter 6, The Leisure-Service System).

The second piece of the industry is travel. *Travel* simply refers to the movement of people from one location to another. It may be carried out by plane, ship, railroad, bicycle, train, or other means. The last part of the commercial recreation and tourism industry is hospitality. *Hospitality* refers to the vast system of accommodations, food, and beverages that encompasses such things as hotels, resorts, RV parks, bars, and restaurants. Tangential to the industry are the facilitators who make tourism happen. Travel agents, travel information services, convention and visitors bureaus, and meeting planners are facilitators of this industry and play an important role in making tourism happen.

Scope of Tourism

Overall, the travel and tourism industry has been described as one of the world's largest businesses. Approximately 2.9% of the gross domestic product in the United States is generated by travel and tourism and creates $1.87 trillion in travel and tourism output.[4] It is the nation's second-largest employer, second only to health services. In 2018 travel and tourism directly accounted for 5.9 million jobs. These jobs include accommodations, transportation, food and beverage, retail, and entertainment and attractions.[5]

The tourism industry can be divided into international and domestic tourism. International tourism is both inbound and outbound. Inbound tourism is when visitors from one country come to visit another country. Outbound tourism is when residents of one country leave and visit a different country. The other type of tourism is domestic tourism, when travelers stay within their own country. According to the United States Travel Association, domestic and international travel accounted for $792.4 billion and business travel accounted for another $334.2 billion in spending in 2019.[6] Inbound international travel brings billions of dollars each year into the U.S. economy. These travelers accounted for 79.7 million people coming into the United States in 2018 and they spent $256.1 billion.[7] Travelers coming into and out of the United States can be affected by many events, including political and health issues. For example, the terrorist attack on the World Trade Center in New York City on September 11, 2001 had a significant impact on world travel, particularly travel to the United States. Within the first 20 months after the attack, the U.S. economy was negatively affected by more than $74 billion. Political factors such as 3 months of protests in Thailand culminating in a weeklong siege of the country's main airport (Suvarnabhumi), the political unrest in such places as Iraq, and the threats of terror attacks in Saudi Arabia and Indonesia can have a negative impact on tourism. In addition, health scares can negatively affect travel, including, for example, the Zika virus, severe acute respiratory syndrome (SARS), COVID-19, and cruise line–related illnesses.

International travelers come from a variety of locations, including Canada, Mexico, and the United Kingdom (Table 10-1). When these visitors come to the United States, they most often enter through New York, Miami, Los Angeles, and Orlando.[8]

People living in the United States are also traveling abroad at high rates, with more than 92.6 million people traveling to other countries each year. The top four international destinations visited by travelers from the United States include Mexico (36.2 million), Europe (17.7 million), Canada (14.4 million), and the Caribbean (8.7 million).[9]

CASE STUDY: COVID-19 and the Impact on Travel

At the time of the writing of this chapter the world is engulfed in the coronavirus (COVID-19). By the time this is over there could be millions of deaths and life as we know will have changed forever. It will have an impact on recreation, how we travel, where we go, how we interact with people, and so much more. It will have an economic impact on the world that will take decades to recover. Many businesses will close, especially small business. How the travel and tourism industry will recover is unknown.

Questions to Consider

1. How has COVID-19 affected the travel and tourism industry? Research what sort of economic impact the virus has had on the United States, Canada, and the world.
2. Has the travel and tourism industry been affected less or more than other industries? Why?
3. What has changed in the world since COVID-19?
4. Has the travel and tourism industry returned to prominence since COVID-19 began? Why? Why not?
5. If you or your family took a vacation during the height of the pandemic, what did you do? How was it different than it would have been before the pandemic?

TABLE 10-1   Visitors to the United States

2018 Visitors to the United States		
Rank	County	Arrivals
1	Canada	21.5 million
2	Mexico	18.4 million
3	United Kingdom	4.7 million
4	Japan	3.5 million
5	China	3.0 million
6	Brazil	2.2 million
7	South Korea	2.2 million
8	Germany	2.1 million
9	France	1.8 million
10	India	1.4 million

Data from National Travel and Tourism Office. (2018). *Fast facts: United States travel and tourism industry 2018*. Retrieved January 20, 2020, from http://travel.trade.gov/outreachpages/download_data_table/Fast_Facts_2018.pdf.

U.S. Residents Unwelcome Abroad?

Because of the high number of cases of COVID-19 in the United States and its continued difficulty in managing the outbreak, many countries have banned people from the United States from entering their countries by labeling them as high risk. Of the countries allowing U.S. visitors most have specific precautions in place such as testing upon arrival with a quarantine period.

Many different kinds of organizations provide tourism opportunities for visitors. Thousands of commercial sponsors of tourist attractions and transportation services, theme parks and water parks, cruise ships, charter airline operators, group tour managers, hotel chains, sport arenas, entertainment venues, casinos, zoos, aquariums, wild animal parks, and numerous other businesses satisfy the tourism market. Many government agencies manage parks, historical sites, oceanfront areas, and other kinds of events that attract millions of recreational visitors.

Similarly, many nonprofit organizations sponsor sport events, cultural programs, educational tours, religious pilgrimages, and other special travel programs that serve millions of tourists each year. Armed forces morale, welfare, and recreation units offer travel services to people in uniform, and industrial and other business entities frequently schedule charter flights for their employees. Local convention and visitors bureaus facilitate vacation travel and promote regional tourist attractions.

Impact on Communities

Tourism can have both positive and negative impacts on local communities. Crossley et al. outlined several positives and negatives for the local community.

Positive impacts on the community:

- Increases number of job opportunities
- Decreases individual property taxes by bringing in sales taxes and room taxes
- Increases property values
- Tourists stimulate the local economy
- Attracts new business
- Increases recreational opportunities for local residents

Negative impacts on the community:

- Increases number of jobs that are often lower paying and/or part-time jobs

---

CASE STUDY: Economic Impact: Where Does the Money Go?

Travel and tourism can have a tremendous economic impact on a community. There are direct, indirect, and induced expenditures that one must consider. Direct expenditures are those things purchased specifically for travel such as transportation, lodging, food, and activities. Indirect expenditures could be viewed as "respending" of the direct expenditures. They are the expenditures made for intermediate goods and services needed to do business with the tourist. For example, restaurants purchase food supplies from producers and souvenir shops purchase goods from suppliers. Part of the direct expenditure of food and souvenirs is used by the retailer to purchase the needed supplies, thus generating indirect expenditures. Lastly, there are induced expenditures. These expenditures account for the wages paid by companies to their employees in direct contact with tourists and how the employees later spend these wages within the community. For example, induced expenditures include purchases made by the hotel manager for her own personal consumption such as a new car, bicycle, or gym membership. So, each dollar spent on tourism can be seen as having a ripple effect in the community as it purchases a hotel room, pays for hotel linens and cleaning supplies, and pays staff who buy goods to sustain their own lives.

Questions to Consider

- Using a trip you have recently taken, list examples of direct, indirect, and induced expenditures.
- If there is an economic or other crisis in the United States and tourism dropped by 75%, what industries would be hurt?
- What are the advantages and disadvantages of being a major tourism community such as Las Vegas, Nevada, or Daytona Beach, Florida?

- Although property taxes are lower, the cost of housing may outdistance the average wages making it difficult for locals to live in the community
- Many commercial and tourism related businesses have a high failure rate leading to increased unemployment
- Local infrastructure (roads, sewers, utilities, etc.) are overburdened requiring more frequent replacement.
- Overuse of natural resources such as parks, lakes, and trails.
- Increases traffic year round or during peak seasons.
- Local residents can become disenchanted with their own communities

People who live in tourism-oriented communities must decide if the positives outweigh the negatives. Many are willing to deal with the increased traffic in their communities, especially if it is seasonal, because of the amenities within the community. For example, Estes Park, Colorado, is considered the base camp for Rocky Mountain National Park and sees thousands of visitors between May and October. Full-time jobs are somewhat hard to come by for the 5,858 residents of the community,[10] and the closest large retailers are 45 minutes away. However, living in the midst of the Rocky Mountains and seeing elk and other wildlife daily might offset these other concerns.

Links Between Public and Commercial Sponsors

It is becoming apparent that both public and commercial agencies have an important stake in promoting successful tourism programs today. In the past, tourism has been regarded as a commercial economic phenomenon rooted in the private business sector. Today, with cities, states, and entire nations competing to attract large numbers of tourists because of their contribution to the overall economy, both government agencies and private entrepreneurs have joined forces in planning and promoting tourist attractions.

At another level, many state and local governments have moved vigorously into cooperative ventures to sponsor and promote varied forms of tourist attractions, both to heighten their positive image and to draw needed revenues and bolster local employment. For example, and keeping with our Estes Park, Colorado, discussion, there are many commercial and public entities that partner with Rocky Mountain National Park (a federal public agency) including commercial sector horse riding stables, Green Jeep Tours, and private guided tours.

Tourism and Commercial Recreation Types

Tourists today seek to satisfy a remarkable range of personal interests and motivations. The following sections present an overview of some popular types of tourism and commercial recreation types that support the overall travel industry.

Cruises

Over the past 3 decades, the growing prosperity of many Americans has made it possible for greater numbers of vacationers to indulge themselves with more varied forms of travel. Luxury cruise ships are no longer simply a vehicle for getting from one place to another or for extended, leisurely ocean voyages. Instead, they have evolved into floating amusement parks, health spas, classrooms, and nightclubs. The major cruise companies have developed huge new vessels and are catering to younger and less affluent individuals by offering relatively inexpensive short-term trips.

Today, more than 80 cruise ship lines offer a remarkable variety of vacation options afloat, ranging from small sail-propelled schooners to giant, luxurious ocean liners. In many cases, their attractions include gourmet meals, early morning workouts, nightlife and gambling, language classes, deck games, and visits to exotic ports. The cruise industry estimated 26 million passengers in 2018.[11]

There are three major cruise line companies that dominate the industry: Carnival (39.4%), Royal Caribbean (20.2%), and Norwegian Cruise Lines (12.6%). These companies hold 72.2% of the industry market share, and the number of people taking cruises continues to increase each year. This is partially driven by larger capacity ships being built with a wider variety of amenities, more local ports, more destinations, and new on-board/on-shore activities that match demands of consumers.[12]

The cruise line industry shut down on March 14, 2020 when COVID-19 cases started to pop up on ships. At the time of this writing, it was estimated that it would be closed until at least late spring, 2021. In February 2021 Canadian Transport Minister Omar Alghabra issued a ban on cruise ships carrying 100 or more people from operating in Canadian waters until February 28, 2022 because of health risks to the country. This will be especially devastating to Seattle's billion dollar cruise industry as ships leaving their ports cannot get to Alaska without crossing into Canadian waters.[13] This 12-month shutdown is devastating to the industry with estimated daily losses of $110 million and 800 American jobs.[14]

Tourism involves transportation in many forms, and international tourism frequently involves air travel.
© Mikael Damkier/Shutterstock.

VARIETY OF CRUISE EXPERIENCES

As in the overall tourism field, cruise passengers' motivations and interests take many different forms. Although some travelers prefer luxurious, pampered, and relatively inactive trips, others enjoy excursions and activities that are demanding or that provide unusual leisure experiences. For example, travelers can take a food and wine cruise through New Zealand, Portugal, France, and South America featuring wine and food of the region. [15] The Ports of Apparitions Cruise stops in locations where passengers will search for ghosts and spirits, visit cemeteries, and hear paranormal presentations.[16]

Other specially designed cruises offer such themes as "clothing-optional" trips for "naturists," LGBTQIA+ (lesbian, gay, bisexual, transgender, queer/questioning, intersex, asexual/ally) cruises, golf cruises that combine shipboard lessons and stops at notable links, and cruises specifically for people with disabilities, as well as many other unique travel tours with sea and land adventures.

Cultural and Historical Interests

The term *cultural* may have two possible meanings when applied to tourism motivation. It may suggest interest in attending major performing arts festivals, visiting famous art museums, or having other kinds of aesthetic experiences. Another meaning involves interest in being exposed to new and different cultures.

Cultural tourism is experiencing places and activities that promote the unique heritage, arts, traditions, and history of a location. This can include museums, art galleries, tours, events, and more. Cultural tourism allows travelers to learn about the diversity and character of the place. Cultural tourism includes doing such things as visiting the National Museum of African American History and Culture in Washington, DC, a Broadway Show in New York, or Machu Picchu in Peru.

The purpose of cultural and historical tourism is to experience people and history in other places and countries because it helps us better understand and appreciate what currently exists and how that emerged. Cultural tourism may include destinations such as the Amish countryside in Pennsylvania, smaller communities throughout French Canada where the culture is determinedly Gallic, or visits to Indigenous lands throughout the West. It may also involve what Canadian authorities term "heritage tourism," with trips to see old mines, factories, or prisons that have been redesigned to provide today's visitors with a fuller understanding of the past.

Increasingly, festivals or holiday events commemorate famous battles of the past, scenes of the Civil War, or other historic events. Even rodeos, which illustrate the real-life work of cowboys in the American West, or lumberjack contests and similar competitions at state fairs, serve as experiences that make this kind of tourism meaningful.

Linked to this type of cultural and historic exploration, such organizations as American Youth Hostels or the Elderhostel movement, which serves older travelers, combine educational and cultural exposures with what are usually short-term stays in foreign lands or distant locations.

CULTURAL DISTRICTS

Cultural tourists have a tendency to be more affluent and educated, spend more and stay longer on their trips, and take more trips per year than noncultural tourists.[17] Despite these demographics, communities are beginning to see the value of cultural districts to attract outside visitors as well as bring the arts to their own residents. Cultural districts are defined areas within a city that serve as a hub for cultural activity. Including facilities and activities, they are often walkable neighborhoods that support local artists and art related nonprofit organizations. Cultural districts can have a significant impact on a community because of the economic impact the district can have by attracting business and visitors. They can also be a means to revitalize a neighborhood that has declined over the years.

The Pittsburgh Cultural District was formed by the Pittsburgh Cultural Trust, a nonprofit organization, in 1984.

Cruise ships continue to become more elaborate in the amenities offered to travelers.
© Bryan Busovicki/Shutterstock.

Cultural tourism involves experiencing the culture, whether it be indigenous or historical.
© WizData, Inc./Shutterstock.

ANCESTRAL TOURISM

Americans are particularly interested in their family history and spend millions of dollars annually on ancestral tourism. Ancestral tourism involves such experiences as traveling to historical sites, visiting international destinations where ancestors were known or suspected to originate, attending conferences and workshops on genealogy, and so forth. The industry has continued to grow as Americans turn inward toward an understanding of their roots.

It is a 14-block area near downtown Pittsburgh in what used to be the redlight district. It is now a bustling area with theatre, art galleries, public art displays, art education centers, plazas, and comedy clubs. Visitors can take walking or biking tours to see the entire district.[718]

Cultural tourism can take many forms. It can include visiting historical sites, touring an art gallery or watching a Broadway play. It can be a higher cost activity or free of charge; enjoyed alone or in groups; viewing others' work or creating your own. Regardless of the chosen activities, cultural tourism is as unique of an experience as the individuals themselves.

Sport Tourism

Sport tourism became a major force in the tourism marketplace beginning in the mid-1980s. There have always been major sporting events that draw tens of thousands and even millions of people.

Sport tourism has traditionally focused on two groups—participants and spectators. People travel to participate in such activities as softball tournaments, basketball tournaments, or to play golf. Arguably more common is travel to be a spectator at such events as the Super Bowl, NASCAR races, or the Kentucky Derby. Sport tourism has many different dimensions and means to experience sport. Here is an overview of the elements of sport tourism.

Sport Places

Sporting events and sport places both serve as attractions. The 1896 Olympic stadium sits in downtown Athens and receives more visitors than the now-closed Athens 2006 Olympic site. The College Football Hall of Fame, Professional Baseball Hall of Fame, and the National Collegiate Athletic Association (NCAA) Hall of Champions all draw many visitors. Visitations to sport facilities when teams are out of town or out of season are now commonplace. The Indianapolis Pacers/Indiana Fever and Bankers Life Fieldhouse charge an admission when visiting the fieldhouse, which goes to local charities. Yankee Stadium is probably the most visited baseball stadium in the United States because it holds a rich heritage of baseball greatness. Many avid baseball fans dream of seeing a game in every stadium in the United States.

Sporting Events

Major sporting events draw large numbers of tourists and have significant impacts on the local, regional, and national economies. The Indianapolis Motor Speedway, home of the Indianapolis 500, is the site of the oldest auto race in the world. The Indianapolis Motor Speedway operated a single race from 1911 to 1993. In 1994, the Brickyard 400, a major new NASCAR race, was initiated and is now called the "Big Machine Vodka 400 at the Brickyard." Six years later a Formula One race was added, making Indianapolis the race capital of the world. These events pale by comparison to mega sport events such as the Olympic Games. The 2012 London Summer Olympics drew 9 million people[19] and the 2016 Rio Olympics sold 7.5 million tickets.

Resorts

Resorts use sport as a means to attract tourists. For example, the Tourism Authority of Thailand uses resorts and their crystal-clear oceans to attract scuba divers. In addition, the country has more than 100 world-class golf courses with very reasonable greens fees. In the United States, golf and tennis resorts are abundant. The Kiawah Island Golf Resort in South Carolina boasts five championship golf courses and was ranked the number one tennis resort in the world by tennisresortsonline.com.[20] Resorts also cater to winter sports such as skiing and snowboarding. Some of these resorts are located in regions where climate dictates how often people visit. Resorts with winter sports as their main attraction rely on a large number of visitors during the cold months to sustain the resort year round.

Cruises and Tours

Cruises were previously discussed in this chapter. However, sport cruises add a different dimension and have themes such as baseball greats, fans of specific teams, running, cycling, and golf. Companies such as Sports Travel and Tours set up sports-oriented tours for individuals and groups. They offer Football Hall of Fame Enshrinement Fan packages, baseball road trips with stops at multiple baseball parks in a region, and Kentucky Derby Tours.[21]

CASE STUDY: COVID Postpones Tokyo 2020 Summer Olympics and Paralympics

The rapid spread of COVID 19 caused the International Olympic Committee (IOC), the International Paralympic Committee (IPC), the Tokyo 2020 Organizing Committee, the Tokyo Metropolitan Government, and the Japanese government to postpone the 2020 Summer Olympic and Paralympic Games in Tokyo. They were moved to July 23–August 8, 2021 and August 24–September 5, 2021. The "Here We Go" Task Force was formed to work through the implications and decisions to be made by the postponement. Here We Go is currently addressing a long list of issues raised by the postponement of the Olympic Games.[a] For example, the IOC Qualification Task Force has approved a series of amendments to the Tokyo 2020 qualification system principles. These include an extended qualification period and new deadlines:[b]

- The new qualification period deadline is June 29, 2021, and international federations can define their own qualification period deadlines should these be prior to this date
- The revised final sport entries deadline has now been set at July 5, 2021.

The revision of the qualification systems will be finalized as quickly as possible, to give certainty to the athletes and National Olympic Committees (NOCs). Those athletes who had previously qualified will retain their spots on the Olympic team, but only 57% of the spots had been filled at the time of the postponement. However, the NOC in each country is responsible for final determination of who will represent it at the games.[b]

Questions to Consider

1. Give examples of some of the things that the planning committee will have to consider with the rescheduling of the games. Discuss such things as ticketing, sponsors, facilities, and the media, among others.
2. Should the IOC have simply cancelled the games rather than postpone them? Why? Why not?
3. What are the implications if the games cannot be held in 2021?

[a]International Olympic Committee. (n.d.). *What are the main consequences of COVID-19 on the Olympic Games Tokyo 2020?* Retrieved September 15, 2020, from https://www.olympic.org/faq/competing-and-being-part-of-the-games/what-are-the-main-consequences-of-covid-19-on-the-olympic-games-tokyo-2020;
[b]International Olympic Committee. (2020). *Frequently asked questions about the Olympic Games Tokyo 2020.* Retrieved September 15, 2020, from https://www.olympic.org/news/ioc/tokyo-2020-q-a.

National and international sporting events, such as the Montreal Olympics, brand their events with logos promoting recognition among visitors, advertisers, and participants.
© meunierd/Shutterstock.

OUTDOOR/ADVENTURE SPORTS

The sale of outdoor sports equipment continually increases. This is an indicator of the popularity of outdoor adventure sports. Traditional outdoor vacations feature hiking, climbing, and fishing. People who are more adventurous can experience dog sledding, fly-in hiking, glacier tours, and heli-skiing, among other sports.

FANTASY CAMPS

Sport fantasy camps allow participants to train alongside current and previous professional sports players and often on the same fields and courts. These camps target diehard fans who want to be immersed in their favorite teams and play alongside players they have watched for years. Baseball offers many fantasy sport camps, usually during spring training. Participants wear the team jersey, get instruction from former players, and hear their name announced by legendary announcers. For $12,500 Duke fans over age 35 can participate in the K Academy with Coach Mike Krzyzewski and many former Duke players.[22] Other sports stars such as Wayne Gretzky, Michael Jordan, and Chris Evert offer their own fantasy camps as well.

Sport tourism has a major impact on the tourism industry whether the tourist is visiting a destination to participate or experience the attractions. Sport can be the reason to visit the community or a part of the overall vacation.

Religion-Based Tourism

Centuries ago, one of the motivations spurring international travel was pilgrimages. Today, religion-oriented travel is one of the industry's fastest-growing segments. Tours highlight Christian, Jewish, Muslim, and Buddhist places of importance.

Religious tourism, also called spiritual tourism, encompasses many aspects of religion. First, pilgrimages are quite

Religious-based tourism draws people to visit such places as St. Peter's Square in Vatican City.
© Sergii Figurnyi/Shutterstock.

common where individuals take long journeys to experience a location of religious significance. For example, Mecca in Saudi Arabia is the most sacred place for the Islamic religion. It is the place toward which all Muslims point themselves during their daily prayers, and they are encouraged to make the pilgrimage to Mecca at least once in their lifetime. Another popular pilgrimage destination is to the Western Wall in Jerusalem, which is a Jewish holy site and Santiago de Compostela in Spain, a Catholic pilgrimage site.

A second aspect of religious tourism is missionary travel where people travel to other locations as part of a religious group or church affiliation. On these trips, people help the local community with education, recreation, construction of needed facilities, healthcare, and economic development.

Third, conventions and crusades are held annually, bringing together people of specific religions for worship. For example, each summer 6,000 members of Jehovah's Witnesses gather in Bloomington, Illinois, for their district convention.

Last, religious tourism has a focus on visiting attractions and locations that have religious significance. Attractions such as the Basilica de Guadalupe in Mexico, the Vatican, or the Reclining Buddha in Thailand are popular to those within specific religions but also those outside of the religion.

Nauvoo, Illinois, has become an American religion-based tourism site. It was home to the Latter-Day Saints (Mormons) from 1839 to 1842 and has received increased tourism focus over the last 25 years as the Latter-Day Saints Church and nonprofit groups have restored much of the original area and in 2002 replaced the 1840 temple. Tourism here exceeds 1.5 million people annually.

Often, such trips are not narrowly denominational but bring members of various faiths together to explore their linked heritages and contrast their present beliefs and practices.

Health-Related Tourism

Recognizing that religious travel is for many people a means of obtaining spiritual well-being and emotional health, it should be stressed that for many other individuals health needs represent a primary motivation for travel. In Europe, particularly, visits to traditional health spas that are based on natural mineral springs are being gradually replaced by stays at more modern health and fitness centers. These destinations often combine varied forms of exercise, nutritional care, massage, yoga, and other holistic approaches to healthcare to provide a fuller range of services to visitors. Whereas weight reduction or recovery from alcohol or drug addiction is the primary focus of many such centers, others involve a much broader approach to achieving "wellness."

A recent trend related to health-motivated travel is medical tourism. In response to rising healthcare and insurance costs in their home countries, citizens from the United States and Great Britain are increasingly seeking less expensive medical and surgical care in developing countries such as India, Thailand, and Costa Rica. Although some may think that medical tourism is of lesser quality and focuses only on elective surgeries, this is not accurate, as many healthcare facilities are accredited and have highly trained specialists. Different funding structures and the lower cost of living in many countries when compared to the United States can result in up to an 80% savings on such procedures as cosmetic, dental, and cardiovascular surgeries.[23] Medical tourism packages usually include luxury room accommodations in hospitals and are often combined with flights, transportation, resort hotel bookings, interpreters, and airport concierge services.

Ecotourism and Adventure Travel

With the growth of environmental concerns and programs over the past few decades, ecotourism has emerged and is deeply concerned with the preservation and protection of the natural environment. The International Ecotourism Society (IETS) defines ecotourism as "responsible travel to natural areas that conserves the environment, sustains the well-being of the local people, and involves interpretation and education."[24]

Ecotourism may be carried out at various levels of personal challenge and comfort. For example, labeled as eco-luxurious, the South Africa Fair Trade Explorer trip includes stops in five cities including Cape Town. Travelers stay in eco-certified guest houses and experience wine tasting, whale watching, and birding while supporting local businesses that are helping their communities socially and environmentally. Many tours are done by bicycle or walking to enhance sustainability.[25]

A more rustic eco-vacation could have travelers camping in the Brazilian rainforest, learning about the indigenous people in the region. It could also mean hiking through national parks and visiting the volcanoes of Costa Rica or tracking primates in Rwanda.

The concept of ecotourism is entrenched in the principles of sustainable tourism. Sustainable tourism advocates tourism activities that are compatible with the ecological processes, sociocultural characteristics, and economic structure of the destination and that enhance the geographical character of a place.

As a variant of this approach, some tourist companies offer "action vacations" that provide the traveler the chance to visit foreign lands not simply to lie on a beach but to take part in an archaeological dig, study wildlife or the local environment systematically, teach English to children, or be involved in healthcare projects. As a result of heightened interest among tourists to make voluntary contributions to the communities they visit, a new form of tourism, *volunteer*

tourism, is gaining popularity across the globe. Tours catering to "volun-tourists" provide cultural immersion along with opportunities for self-fulfillment through volunteer work. For example, Restoration Works International, a California-based nonprofit group, offers tours focusing on the restoration of Buddhist monasteries in Nepal. Another nonprofit, Projects Abroad, plans trips for groups based on age and interest. There are trips for teens in high school, university students, gap year (18–19) young adults, professionals (30+), and those 50+. They will do such things as teach English to children, preserve ecosystems, and build sustainable farms in places like Madagascar, Bolivia, and Fiji.[26]

With less of a social service orientation and more of an adventure recreation focus, some vacations may involve high-risk adventure pastimes such as trail rides through

---

CASE STUDY: Defining Ecotourism

The International Ecotourism Society is about *uniting conservation, communities, and sustainable travel*. Those who implement, participate in, and market ecotourism activities should adopt the following ecotourism principles:[a]

- Minimize physical, social, behavioral, and psychological impacts
- Build environmental and cultural awareness and respect
- Provide positive experiences for both visitors and hosts
- Provide direct financial benefits for conservation
- Generate financial benefits for both local people and private industry
- Deliver memorable interpretative experiences to visitors that help raise sensitivity to host countries' political, environmental, and social climates
- Design, construct, and operate low-impact facilities
- Recognize the rights and spiritual beliefs of the indigenous people in your community and work in partnership with them to create empowerment

Ecotourism is touted as being a positive vacation option for those seeking a little more adventure, a different experience, and want to be environmentally conscious. However, there are some downsides to ecotourism that can cause harm to the very people ecotourism is designed to protect. The negatives include such things as follows:[b]

- As the popularity of a destination grows, resources become overused. For example, too many people can disrupt the natural habitats of wildlife. This negatively affects their mating and feeding habits.
- Ecotourism destinations are often in remote locations, requiring an increased carbon footprint to arrive by plane or motor vehicle.
- Developers see the potential revenue owing to increased traffic and build resorts, stores, and other amenities to cater to the crowds without regard for the impact on the community and environment. These developments send money back to the corporations and take it away from the local economy.
- Increased tourism causes inflated prices for food and services, which is passed on to the local residents who must pay this same inflated cost.
- Increased tourism increases the number of jobs in a community, but the jobs are often low paying in the service industry.

Questions to Consider

- What other positives and negatives can be associated with ecotourism?
- Overall, is ecotourism a positive or negative thing? Why?
- Investigate the pros and cons of ecotourism further. Have a class debate to argue your points on whether ecotourism is positive or negative thing.

[a]International Ecotourism Society. (n.d.). *Principles of ecotourism*. Retrieved February 4, 2021, from http://www.ecotourism.org/what-is-ecotourism
[b]Woods, A. (2018, March 21). *Problems with ecotourism*. USA Today. Retrieved February 4, 2021, from https://traveltips.usatoday.com/problems-ecotourism-108359.html

wild country, hang gliding, mountain climbing, or whitewater rafting on turbulent streams. Extreme versions of adventure tourism may involve the opportunity to track down tornadoes, offered as a package deal by a number of companies in the Midwest or Southwest regions of the United States during the tornado seasons of the year.[27]

Hedonistic Forms of Tourism

Still other forms of tourism are designed to provide hedonistic forms of pleasure to participants. Gambling clearly represents the most popular such activity, with millions of individuals traveling each year to major casinos throughout the world or enjoying gaming as a convenient amenity on ocean cruises or major airline flights.

At another level, thousands of young people each year roam through the Far East, including unscheduled, freewheeling trips through Thailand, Cambodia, and Nepal, partly to experience their exotic environments but also to take part in the drug culture that is readily available and inexpensive in these regions.

Finally, a form of pleasure-seeking tourism that has emerged throughout the world involves the search for sex. The sex industry has become extremely profitable, providing substantial revenues not only to individuals and the networks involved in human trafficking but to some nations that have come to depend on sex industry profits. Sex tourism thrives in countries such as Ukraine where the women are poor and unprotected by the government and law enforcement. Odessa is a Ukrainian port that has become a principal hub for international sex trade. This area is infused with police corruption and organized crime, making human trafficking and the sex industry thrive. In Costa Rica, prostitution is legal. However, prostitutes are supposed to register, be regularly examined by a doctor, and carry an identification card. Many do not, and so the sex industry is quite risky but rampant.[28]

Hosteling and AirBnB

Many travelers are choosing cheaper and/or more social travel options by staying in hostels or AirBnBs. Hostels are low-cost accommodations where people rent a bed in a dormitory-style facility. Guests share bathroom facilities and often have a common area for social interaction. Some hostels have private rooms for one to four people at an increased cost. En-suites are also becoming more popular. Prices for hostels vary depending on the location and amenities. For example, a hostel in Milan, Italy with rooms in a dorm with breakfast go for $25. A private room with two beds, breakfast, and sheets costs $68. A hostel two blocks from the beach in San Diego with the same amenities as Milan runs $32 per night. Hostels are most known for the social aspects. The common rooms entice conversations among guests. It is not unusual for people staying at hostels to get to know each other and go off for adventures together.

Hostels have traditionally been places in the countryside for young hikers to stop off for the night before continuing on their trek. Although this is a portion of the users of hostels, they are also starting to serve adults who want a simpler and less expensive place to stay. These people do not require the amenities of large-scale hotels such as room service and provided toiletries, and they can bring their own towels.

Part of the charm of hostels, in addition to the price, is that some can be quite unique. For example:

- *Stockholm af Chapman & Skeppsholmen (Sweden)*: This hostel is an old sailing ship.
- *Stockholm Långholmen (Sweden)*: Housed in a converted prison, this hostel was voted best hostel in Sweden in 2008. Inside this youth hostel visitors can see the prison museum, illustrating 250 years of prison history.
- *Point Montara Lighthouse (Montara, California)*: On the rugged California coast, 25 miles south of San Francisco, an historic 1875 fog signal station and lighthouse have been preserved and restored by Hostelling International—American Youth Hostels and the California Department of Parks and Recreation, in cooperation with the Coast Guard.[29]
- *Hoosville Hostel (formerly known as Everglades International Hostel)*: Described as a cozy laid-back hostel just 10 miles from the Everglades National Park and Biscayne National Park, the hostel offers Guided Everglades Tours, canoe rentals and bike rentals.[30]

AirBnBs often offer more privacy and a cozier atmosphere. Rather than renting a bed, AirBnBs offer a room in someone's home, a section of the home, or the entire home. AirBnB is less about socializing and more like a vacation rental at a lesser cost. AirBnB started in 2008 as a marketplace to connect hosts with unique spaces to rent with guests needing accommodations. Since its inception,

Hostels are low-cost, dormitory-style accommodations with shared bathroom facilities, and are often charming and unique.
© Stephen B. Goodwin/Shutterstock.

CASE STUDY: The Growth of Marijuana Tourism

In 2016 Colorado and Washington were the only states to allow licensed marijuana stores to legally sell marijuana without a prescription to people 21 and over. By April 2021, that number grew to 16 states with 36 legalizing it for medical use.[a] Washington continues to capitalize on marijuana tourism, seeing the revenue it can bring to the state. For example, the Original CannaBus Tour Company offers tours exploring Seattle's exploding cannabis culture, offering airport pickup and hotel drop-off with a stop at a legal recreational marijuana shop.[b] Kush Tourism promotes cannabis-related lodging, tours, and activities such as Seattle airport layover specials, tours of cannabis growing facilities, and cannabis-friendly painting classes.[c] Private clubs are opening catering to marijuana-using locals and tourists.

Questions to Consider

- What are the pros and cons of advertising marijuana tourism as a regular part of tourism activities and attractions through the state tourism bureau (Go-Washington) or local convention and visitors bureaus?
- If more states legalize marijuana, will advertisement of marijuana-related activities increase? Why or why not?
- As the first states in the market, look at how Washington and Colorado advertise marijuana-related activities. Compare and contrast their approaches to the newer states who have legalized marijuana. How are these states taking advantage of the tourism market?

[a]Berke, J., Gal, S., & Lee Y.J. (2021). Marijuana legalization is sweeping the US. See every state where cannabis is legal. Retrieved May 26, 2021, from https://www.businessinsider.com/legal-marijuana-states-2018-1
[b]DISA Global Solutions. Map of Marijuana Legality by State. Retrieved March 21, 2021, from https://www.businessinsider.com/legal-marijuana-states-2018-1.
The Original Cannabus. Retrieved February 4, 2021, from http://originalcannabus.com/2
[c]Kush Tourism. Retrieved February 4, 2021, from http://kushtourism.com

---

AirBnB has expanded from an air mattress in the home of AirBnB's founders to the ability to rent shared spaces, private rooms, and entire apartments all around the world. This company has rentals in 190 countries and over 34,000 cities. Hosts set the pricing, rules for rentals, who can stay, and when they can stay. Both hosts and guests rate the other, and so the quality of the rental as well as the quality of the guest is known. Some AirBnB options have become quite unique and include castles, boats, tree houses, tipis, and igloos. Travelers can stay in a glass tree house in Athens, Georgia, a 100-year-old houseboat docked under the Eiffel Tower, or in the St. Pancras Clock Tower guest suite in London.[31]

Food Travel

Food tourism is a growing phenomenon and a term that was first coined in 1998. The World Food Travel Association (WFTA) defines food tourism as "the pursuit and enjoyment of unique and memorable food and drink experiences, both far and near."[32]

Food tourism is quite vast and can include such activities as attending cooking schools, visiting cooking supply stores, going on culinary tours, attending food festivals, visiting farmers' markets, stopping at street food carts or microbrews, going to wineries and distilleries, or enjoying farm to table restaurants. The increase in food tourism is quite evident on television channels such as the Food Network and the Travel Channel. Andrew Zimmern consumes mainstream and exotic cuisine in all parts of the world, and Guy Fieri travels across the United States finding the best drive-ins, diners, and dives.

Some of the more extravagant food tourism happens with tours to well-known gastric regions. Here are a few examples:

- *The Hess Collection Mediterranean Wine Cruise*: Traveling from Barcelona to Rome, this 7-day cruise features the Hess Collection's Director of Winemaking, private parties, special tastings and winemaker's dinner, gourmet culinary program, and optional wine-focused shore excursions exclusive to the group.[33]
- *The Beery Soul of Ireland: Country Pubs & Craft Beer Galway to Dublin*: On a tour featuring the deeply rooted pub and music culture, travelers experience local craft beers in Dublin, Kilkenny, Doolin, and Galway including its pub culture, architecture, folklore, and history.[34]
- *Chiang Mai Thai Cooking School*: This internationally renowned cooking school in Thailand teaches tourists how to cook Thai food. Classes run for 1 to 5 days and feature topics such as introduction to Thai ingredients, making curry pastes, and vegetable carving.[35]

Train Travel

Travel by train has seen a significant growth in the past decade, especially among older travelers. It is viewed as a more relaxed paced form of transportation that avoids busy airports and crowded highways. Train travel allows travelers to rent sleeper cars, move about the train, and enjoy the scenery as travelers go from place to place. They can choose any number of interesting trips and destinations such as:

Train tourism incorporates train travel with tourism destinations, offering a different type of vacation experience.
© Leonard Zhukovsky/Shutterstock.

- *Napa Valley Wine Train:* A 36-mile 3-hour trip from Napa to St. Helena that allows passengers to jump on and off at different stops including overnight stays in wine country
- *America's Great National Parks Trip:* A 14-day tour through five national parks including Glacier, Yellowstone, Grant Tetons, Arches, and Canyonlands[36]
- *Belmond's Royal Scotsman:* A luxury train that winds through Scotland's castles, peaks, and lochs, includes a spa car and stops for golf, canoeing, pigeon shooting, and malt tasting tours[37]

Travel by train can be likened to cruises, but on land. Many have stops in different cities where travelers can choose different excursions, full course meals are provided, and private sleeping accommodations allow people to feel as if they are in a hotel.

Hotel/Motel Industry

The hotel/motel industry is a profession in and of itself. Students major in hotel management and spend their entire careers working in the field. There is a difference between hotels and motels including clientele and structure. Because hotels are most associated with the travel and tourism industry, they are the focus of this section. However, it is important to understand the differences between the two.

The term motel is coined from "motorist hotel" and is a place to stay for people who are traveling through cities and towns. Motels are often located right off major interstates or busy highways. Motel visitors are often passing through and not choosing this as their vacation destination. Motels are often small and have only a couple of floors with most doors facing outside rather than in an enclosed hallway like a hotel. Motels do not have the extra amenities like a hotel such as a swimming pool, breakfast, or bar/restaurant. Motels have the basic services and serve the short-term traveler.

The Federal Road Aid Act of 1916 caused a boom in the motel industry as rooms were added along the new highways and interstates being built. Another huge growth happened after World War II with increased use of the automobile. The motels not only were built near highways but on land that was much cheaper to buy, keeping motel costs lower.

When compared to motels, hotels are more often designated as vacation destinations and more likely to serve the guest who is staying for a few days or longer. They are designed to maximize comfort, and hotel guests expect the special amenities that are missing at a motel. With these amenities comes a higher price point. In addition, hotels are located in very desirable areas such as near a beach, in a downtown area, or in a nice area of town with multiple attractions external to the hotel.

The hotel industry uses classifications to identify its standing in the industry. These classifications are price, function, location, and market segment.[38] Many hotel chains have several different classifications in their portfolio, so they are able to attract a multitude of types of travelers. For example, Marriott Corporation has high-end hotels such as the Ritz-Carlton and the W hotel as well as midlevel hotels such as the Fairfield Inn and Four Points by Sheraton.

Price

Price is dictated by services provided and can be classified from limited-service hotels to full-service luxury hotels. Limited-service hotels resemble motels in that they do not often have pools, fitness facilities, or food and beverage options on the property. Limited-service rooms are tagged as budget or economy hotels by the common traveler. Full-service luxury hotels have extensive amenities, high-end restaurants, banquet facilities, a low guest room to staff ratio, and room rates considerably above the market area average. Hotels span the service continuum.[39]

Function

Hotels can be classified as either convention hotels or commercial hotels. Convention hotels are large to accommodate conventions. They are often 500+ rooms and offer many meeting spaces including large ballrooms and exhibit areas. These hotels have extended food and beverage capacity through multiple restaurants and catering services for banquets. Convention hotels are most often located close to convention centers, and some are even connected to them. Convention attendees can reserve rooms that are blocked for them at a reduced price. However, this price is still often quite high because attendees want to be close to the convention center and the company usually covers all or a portion of the room bill.

Commercial hotels are smaller, usually 100 to 500 guest rooms. These hotels have less public space for functions, fewer food and beverage areas, and limited recreation amenities. Commercial hotels are often in downtown areas near large business districts, restaurants, and shopping facilities. The room costs are higher than the same hotel would be in the suburbs because of the higher cost of land in downtown areas.[40]

Location

The location of a hotel serves as a means of classification. Hotels can be located in downtown areas as discussed previously, in the suburbs, near highway/interstate, and near airports. Suburban hotels tend to be a bit smaller (200–350 rooms). Highway/interstate hotels are even smaller than suburban hotels (100–250 rooms) and are located near travel corridors. Airport hotels are designed and located to aide air travel. They are used as a place to stay before early morning flights. Airport hotels (250–550 rooms) sometimes offer free or low-cost long-term parking options for anyone staying the night prior to their flight. They also provide airport shuttles for convenience to travelers.

Market Segment

Hotels can be classified by the group that it most attracts, that is, its market segment. There are a wide variety of market segments to consider including such things as executive conference centers, resorts, casino hotels, golf resorts, ski resorts, waterparks, and health spas.[41] For example, resorts attract vacationers who stay for several days and are looking for relaxation, escape, or to participate in the local attractions. Health spas are often also considered resorts and have many spa amenities such as dieticians, massage therapists, fitness centers, and physiologists.

Different market segments seek different types of rooms such as all-suite hotels, extended stay hotels, historic properties converted to hotels, bed and breakfasts, all-inclusive hotels, and boutique hotels. Boutique hotels are considered unique in their style and are often labeled as cozy or intimate.

Motels and hotels are a complex system and serve an important niche in the travel and tourism industry. This is a very brief overview of an industry that generates billions of dollars a year in revenue and has independent individual owners up to multibillion dollar corporations such as Marriott and Hilton.

Technology and Tourism

Technology has changed the way people plan their travel, move through the trip, and reflect on the experience. The Internet has now surpassed word of mouth as the primary source for location inspiration and travel information. When people are researching where to go, where to stay, and how to get there, they rely on many different websites and apps. For example, Tripadvisor.com website, which has 463 million unique monthly users,[42] allows tourists to post ratings of tourism businesses and discuss travel experiences with others. Websites and apps that monitor and alert you to flight price changes (e.g., FareCompare.com and hopper.com) and track flight performance (e.g., flight on time

---

CASE STUDY: A Traveler's Best App

Many travel magazines and websites select their top travel-related apps. Here are a few examples on the list of favorites:

- Tripadvisor: Checks hotel and restaurant reviews.
- HotelTonight: Finds last-minute discounted hotels with bookings available until 2:00 a.m.
- TripIt: Keeps your travel itineraries and allows them to sync to your personal calendar.
- Free Wi-Fi Finder: Locates free Internet hotspots in the area.
- Google Translate: Translates 103 languages, with 43 of those being voice activated.
- Kayak: Allows you to rebook cancelled flights and find hotels nearby.
- WhatsApp Messenger: Shares texts and pictures for free when traveling abroad, eliminating international charges.
- PackPoint: Creates packing lists based on number of children and adults and days traveled; takes into account temperature, destination, and laundry preferences; allows for custom lists.
- Flush: Find the public restrooms near you.
- Waze: Monitor traffic, police, accidents and other hazards while on a roadtrip.

Questions to Consider

- Develop your own travel app by creating an outline of the contents of the app. What would the app look like? Would it be a free app or have an associated charge? What makes your app different from what is already on the market?
- Do some research to find other apps that could be beneficial to people traveling domestically and internationally.

ratings, delay statistics, and cancellation history) are also becoming increasingly popular among travelers. Before arriving at a destination, the Internet allows travelers to research destinations and entertainment options, advance purchase tickets, hire a guide, book train tickets, rent a car, and many other things to make travel easier.

Technology also has a major impact during the trip. Social media has skyrocketed in the last several years where people post photos and commentary on Facebook, Twitter, and Instagram immediately. Photos can also be uploaded to such sites as Shutterfly to share. In addition, travelers are using travel blog sites such as travelblog.org to send notes or electronic postcards, photos, and sound recordings to others during the course of the trip. Smartphones are indispensable to many travelers. Smartphones are used in place of their cameras, and the global positioning system (GPS) features help travelers find destinations in a city or a national park. These same phones will keep track of tickets, allow you to pay tabs, or search for needed information in the moment. If traveling internationally, there are many apps that can help navigate a new country, such as those that translate the language or help understand money conversion. After the vacation, technology is used for reflection on the journey via photos, updating social media posts, or reviewing the accommodations and destinations via the appropriate websites. Regardless of the trip taken or destination visited, technology plays a key role in how it is planned and experienced.

SUMMARY

Travel and tourism involve huge sections of the leisure-service field, is provided by many different kinds of organizations, and has developed into a complex discipline in terms of job specialization and career opportunities. Tourism has a major economic impact on the United States and the rest of the world. Inbound and outbound travelers help stimulate economies domestically and abroad.

Travel and tourism represent diverse forms of leisure activity, with immense economic revenues. This chapter describes some of the most popular forms of tourism, such as cruises, cultural and historic interests, sport, religion, health, ecotourism, hedonism, hostels, food tourism, and train travel.

The Internet and smartphone apps have had a major impact on trip planning, the trip itself, and the post-trip reflection. The Internet and apps play an important role in researching destinations, navigating through them, and is a means to share experiences through posting commentaries on the trip or sharing photos with friends and family. Technological advances will continue to affect travel and tourism in the years to come.

QUESTIONS FOR CLASS DISCUSSION OR ESSAY EXAMINATION

1. Tourism may be carried on for many purposes: exploration of different environments, cultural or educational purposes, adventure and risk, or hedonism. Give examples of such forms of tourism, based on class members' experiences.

    _____
    _____
    _____

2. Select either sport tourism or cruises and describe their role today in the tourism industry, including current trends and new methods for appealing to the public.

    _____
    _____
    _____

3. Discuss the role of the Internet in tourism. How do you use the Internet for your travel plans?

    _____
    _____
    _____

4. Consider the different generations within your family. Which type of tourism would most appeal to each group? Which would be least appealing? Why?

    _____
    _____
    _____

5. Discuss the impact of the tourism industry on the world economy.

_____

_____

_____

6. Define cultural and historic tourism. Give examples of these types of destinations.

_____

_____

_____

7. Define ecotourism. Give examples of these types of destinations. Do you see this form of tourism increasing or declining in the future? Why?

_____

_____

_____

_____

ENDNOTES

1. Kraus, R. (1971). _Recreation and leisure in modern society_ (p. 458). Appleton-Century-Crofts.

2. Crossley, J. C., Rood, S., Brayley, R. E., Price-Howard, K., & Holdnak, A. (2018). _Introduction to commercial recreation and tourism: An entrepreneurial approach_ (7th ed.). Sagamore Publishing.

3. Crossley et al. (2018).

4. National Travel and Tourism Office. (2018). _Fast facts: United States travel and tourism industry 2018._ Retrieved January 20, 2020, from http://travel.trade.gov/outreachpages/download_data_table/Fast_Facts_2018.pdf.

5. Ibid.

6. U.S. Travel Association. (n.d.). _U.S. travel answer sheet._ Retrieved January 20, 2020, From https://www.ustravel.org/answersheet.

7. National Travel and Tourism Office (2018).

8. National Travel and Tourism Office. (n.d.). _International visitation and spending in the United States. 2018 overseas visitation estimates to the states, cities, and regions visited._ Retrieved January 20, 2020, from http://travel.trade.gov/outreachpages/inbound.general_information.inbound_overview.asp.

9. National Travel and Tourism Office. (n.d.). _Outbound overew. Monthly U.S. outbound air travel to international regions._ Retrieved January 20, 2020, from http://travel.trade.gov/outreachpages/outbound.general_information.outbound_overview.asp.

10. _Jobs in Estes Park._ (n.d.). Estes Park Information. Retrieved February 4, 2021, from https://www.estesparkinformation.com/jobs-in-estes-park/.

11. Cruise Market Watch. (n.d.). 2021 Worldwide Cruise Line Market Share. Retrieved September 15, 2020, from https://cruisemarketwatch.com/market-share/.

12. Cruise Market Watch. Retrieved January 20, 2020, from http://www.cruisemarketwatch.com.

13. Grimaldi, L. February 25, 2021 Cruise Lines Once Again Extend Sailing Start-Up Dates. Retrieved March 21, 2021 from https://www.northstarmeetingsgroup.com/News/Industry/Cruise-Lines-Suspend-Sailings-Coronavirus.

14. Hines, M. (2020, August 5). Exclusive: Cruise industry extends sailing suspension past CDC "no-sail" order, until Oct. 31. _USA Today._ Retrieved September 13, 2020, from https://www.usatoday.com/story/travel/cruises/2020/08/05/us-cruise-industry-extends-covid-19-suspension-until-oct-31/3296043001/.

15. The Cruise Critic. (2020). _Theme cruises 2020–2021._ Retrieved March 29, 2020, from https://www.cruisecritic.com/articles.cfm?ID=349.

16. Theme Cruise Finder. Retrieved March 29, 2020, http://themecruisefinder.com/.

17. Hargrove, C. (2014). _Cultural tourism: Attracting visitors and their spending. 2014 National Cultural Districts Exchange_ (p. 12). Americans for the Arts. Retrieved March 26, 2020, from https://www.americansforthearts.org/sites/default/files/pdf/2014/by_program/reports_and_data/toolkits/cultural_districts/issue_briefs/Cultural-Tourism-Attracting-Visitors-and-Their-Spending.pdf.

18. Pittsburgh Cultural Trust. Retrieved March 26, 2020, from https://trustarts.org.

19. CNN World. (2012, July 27). *London Olympics by the numbers.* Retrieved March 26, 2020), from http://www.cnn.com/2012/07/27/world/olympics-numbers.

20. Tennis Resorts Online. (n.d.). *Top 100 tennis resorts & camps for 2015.* Retrieved March 26, 2020, from http://www.tennisresortsonline.com/trofiles/top-100-tennis-resorts-and-camps.cfm#Resorts.

21. Sports Travel and Tours. Retrieved March 26, 2020, from http://www.sportstravelandtours.com/index.php.

22. K Academy. Retrieved March 26, 2020, http://kacademy.com.

23. Patients Beyond Borders. (2019). *Quick facts about medical tourism.* Retrieved March 26, 2020, from https://www.patientsbeyondborders.com/media.

24. International Ecotourism Society. (n.d.). *What is ecotourism?* Retrieved April 5, 2020, from https://ecotourism.org/what-is-ecotourism/.

25. Greenloons. (n.d.). *South Africa fair trade explorer.* Retrieved April 5, 2020, from https://greenloons.com/tour/south-african-fair-trade-explorer/.

26. Projects Abroad. (n.d.). *Volunteer abroad & internships.* Retrieved April 5, 2020, from http://www.projects-abroad.org.

27. Storm Chasing Adventure Tours. Retrieved April 5, 2020, from http://www.stormchasing.com.

28. The Real Costa Rica. (n.d.). *Adult entertainment in Costa Rica.* Retrieved April 5, 2020, from http://www.therealcostarica.com/travel_costa_rica/adult_entertainment_costa_rica.html.

29. Hostel World. Retrieved March 27, 2016, from http://www.hostelworld.com.

30. Hoosville Hostel. Retrieved April 5, 2020, from https://www.hoosvillehostel.com.

31. Airbnb. Retrieved February 4, 2021, from https://www.airbnb.com.

32. World Food Travel Association. (n.d.). *What is food tourism?* Retrieved April 5, 2020, from https://worldfoodtravel.org/what-is-food-tourism-definition-food-tourism/.

33. Food & Wine Trails. (n.d.). *The Hess Collection.* Retrieved April 5, 2020, from https://www.foodandwinetrails.com/cruises/hesscollection2020/#overview.

34. Beertrips.com. (n.d.). *Beer trips 2020.* Retrieved April 5, 2020, from http://www.beertrips.com/trips.html.

35. Chiang Mai Thai Cookery School. Retrieved April 5, 2020, from http://www.thaicookeryschool.com.

36. Trageser, C. (2020, October 13). *The best train trips to take across America.* Retrieved February 4, 2021, from https://www.travelandleisure.com/trip-ideas/bus-train/train-travel-usa.

37. Dekel-Daks, T. (2019, May 24). *Belmond's luxury sleeper train wants to take guests into the "wilds of Scotland."* Retrieved April 5, 2020, from https://www.departures.com/travel/belmond-royal-scotsman-train-bespoke-excursions.

38. Barrows, C. W., Powers, T., & Reynolds, D. (2012). *Introduction to management in the hospitality industry* (10th ed.). Wiley.

39. Ibid.

40. Ibid.

41. Hotel News Now. (2020, January 24). *Hotel industry terms to know.* Retrieved October 20, 2020, from https://www.hotelnewsnow.com/Articles/6217/Hotel-Industry-Terms-to-Know.

42. Tripadvisor. (n.d.). *About Tripadvisor.* Retrieved April 5, 2020, https://tripadvisor.mediaroom.com/us-about-us.

Chapter 11

Sport and the Leisure Industry

"Without question, participation in sports represents a major leisure interest for the great mass of Americans. There are many reasons for their popularity. They offer participants a chance to test themselves, by striving physically in a world that offers few other challenges. They provide means of sublimating aggression and hostility, and they offer both competition and cooperation on intense levels.... As part of an industrial society, sports have become big business. They are money-makers, sponsored by powerful commercial interests and promoted by mass media advertising, public relations, television, magazines, and newspapers."[1]
-From the first edition of Kraus' Recreation and Leisure in Modern Society, published in 1971

LEARNING OBJECTIVES

1. Understand the scope of the sport industry.

2. Identify and explain sport participation and sport spectating.

3. Discuss the four levels of team sport participation.

4. Describe the influence of media on sport.

5. Summarize current issues in sport and society.

Introduction

Sport, on its various levels, represents a major area of the leisure-services industry today and constitutes a powerful economic force through participation and spectatorship by people of every age and background.

Sport in American society is viewed from a narrow to broad perspective, based on who is defining sport. A day of watching ESPN might convince an individual that football, basketball, soccer, baseball, poker, golf, or other traditional team and individual contests are major sports. Changing television channels might convince someone else that hunting and fishing are major sports. Watching the Olympic games broadens the idea of sport to include winter and summer sports that may or may not be common in North America. Our society tends to focus on sports that are portrayed in sporting magazines, in the broadcast media, on the Internet, and that are frequented in local communities. University and professional sport programs have strengthened the image of traditional sport programs. More than 100,000 people may attend a college football game while far fewer may attend a college cross-country meet or a golf match.

From a participant perspective, when talking about sport one must also think about fitness. The line between sport and fitness often seems blurred. Like sport, fitness can be viewed both narrowly and broadly based on the perspective of the individual and society as a whole. The fitness industry focuses on health, exercise, and overall wellness of the body. Fitness activities can overlap with sport as many sports can build one's fitness level such as soccer and basketball. Other recreation activities can be done for enjoyment and have a significant fitness component such as hiking, biking, or walking, but not everyone would consider all of these to be sports.

Defining sport is somewhat difficult to do. What some conceive as a sport others may not. Sport can be broadly defined as physical activity that is governed by rules where the participants play for enjoyment and/or competition. It can also be defined as activity that requires physical exertion and skills in a form of competition—either against oneself or a team. The Global Association of International Sports Federations (GAISF) defines sport more narrowly as follows:[2]

- The sport proposed should include an element of competition.
- The sport should not rely on any element of "luck" specifically integrated into the sport.

Sports—in both participation and spectator involvement and regardless of age—are a major leisure activity in the United States.
© Rob Hainer/Shutterstock.

CASE STUDY: Is it a Game or is it a Sport?

What is seen as a sport has expanded over the last couple of decades, much of this because of the advent of sport specific television channels that need to fill 24 hour a day programming. For example, ESPN now televises cornhole championships and poker tournaments.

The definitions of sport provided call into question whether or not any competition that is on television and advertised as a sport is really a sport. Consider esports, or electronic sports. Esports are multiplayer video games played for competition and watched by spectators. Esports players can be amateurs or professionals. These players argue that they are as much athletes as race car drivers because of the skill, fast reflexes, and dexterity needed to operate the controller. Others argue that cornhole is a sport because it requires hand-eye coordination and depth perception, much like horseshoes, shuffleboard, and lawn bowling.

Questions to Consider

1. What is the difference between a sport and a game?
2. Are esports a sport or game? Why?
3. Make an argument for and against hunting and fishing being classified as a sport.
4. Should esports players be given college scholarships and other services like collegiate athletes? Why or why not?

Data from Steinberg, L. (2018, July 28). *What defines a "sport"?* Retrieved November 15, 2020, from https://www.forbes.com/sites/leighsteinberg/2018/07/28/what-defines-a-sport/#6fb2919b2d66.

- The sport should not be judged to pose an undue risk to the health and safety of its athletes or participants.
- The sport proposed should in no way be harmful to any living creature.
- The sport should not rely on equipment that is provided by a single supplier.

This definition may eliminate some sports that the more broader definition would encompass. For example, hunting and fishing could be classified as a sport under the broader definition but not by the GAISF who classifies chess as a sport. Others may see this as a game rather than a sport.

The Centers for Disease Control and Prevention define physical fitness as "a set of attributes that people possess or achieve that relate to the ability to perform physical activity and is comprised of skill-related, health-related, and physiological components." Fitness also is composed of healthy muscle strength and endurance, cardiorespiratory endurance, body composition, and flexibility so fitness activities would provide these elements that can be sport or nonsport activities.[3]

In this chapter, the broadest possible view of sport is adopted and explored from the participant and spectator perspectives, structure of organized sport, and all levels of competition from youth to professional.

Sport for Participants

Sport participation is seen as an opportunity for members of society to engage in socially positive and healthy activity that contributes to society. Communities across the United States sponsor sport activities and have done so through most of the 20th century and now into the 21st century. Sport as leisure has grown as the population and economy have grown, and sport participation and sport events vary from region to region. In the 1950s, soccer clubs were difficult to find for any age group. Today youth soccer represents one of the continuously fast-growing sports. In secondary schools, universities, and professional leagues, soccer has found a place in mainstream sport.

Sport, as a component of leisure experiences, is an integral part of many communities. It is expressed in youth sport programs, adult leagues, and senior (older adult) leagues and programs and has extended to include what were once called nontraditional sport activities. Government agencies no longer attempt to serve as the primary provider of leisure sport opportunities. Nonprofits and for-profit organizations are actively engaged in the provision of sport activities for people of all ages.

Participation in Sport and Fitness Activities

Sport can range from casual to serious participation, from passive to active involvement, and from noncompetitive participation to competitive. One of the accepted ways of determining leisure involvement is to measure participation. Participation measures give a sense of involvement and commitment to a sport activity.

SPORT FOR INDIVIDUALS WITH DISABILITIES

Sport as a leisure and competitive activity has a strong following by people with disabilities. Even before the wars in Iraq and Afghanistan, sport involvement by athletes with disabilities was strong, as was evidenced by the presence of a variety of competitions, at all skill levels, up through the Paralympics, which began in 1960 for the summer games and 1976 for the winter games.[4] A leader in the provision of sports for people with disabilities is Move United. Move United was formed after a merger of Disabled Sports USA and Adaptive Sports USA.[5] The goal of the organization is to improve the lives of wounded warriors, and youth and adults with disabilities by providing sports and recreation opportunities. Some of the sports participants can enjoy include snow skiing, water sports (such as water skiing, sailing, kayaking, and rafting), cycling, climbing, horseback riding, golf, and social activities.

SPORT AS A HOBBY

Sport participation is a large component of leisure involvement. Participation is defined in many ways. It does not necessarily involve active engagement in sport activities. In the 1930s and beyond, collecting sport cards (e.g., baseball cards, football cards) was and continues to be a form of sport involvement, albeit from the hobby perspective. Today's fantasy sport teams are similar to collecting baseball cards and fit into the concept of a hobby. Purists might argue the point, especially when professional teams and sport broadcasters and their websites devote considerable attention to fantasy teams, yet they do fit the description of a hobby.

A selection of the most popular sport and fitness activities and participation levels are identified in Table 11-1. A number of the pastimes listed might better be described as outdoor recreation pursuits, such as exercise walking or camping. Others, such as skiing, swimming, or even fishing, are usually engaged in as noncompetitive recreation, although they may represent part of school or college competition or large-scale tournaments.

There are many ways to measure sport involvement and many groups collecting information about how people participate in sport. The measure of sport participation comes from multiple sources, including the National Sporting Goods Association, the Sport and Fitness Industry Association, the Outdoor Foundation, and the Physical Activity Council. In this sense, we allow those who sell sports products to help define sport.

Measuring the number of participants in organized sport is much easier than identifying numbers participating in recreation leagues, pickup games, and the like. Any number of participants identified will be limited by the source of the information. For example, Little League measures only baseball players participating in their sanctioned programs. Their programs represent just a small part of the total youth participating in baseball in any given year. The measures that are available do provide indicators of how many people are involved in formalized sport activities on an annual basis.

Sport is sometimes seen as an activity that will prepare youth for adulthood. In a similar vein, some continue to participate in sport because it demonstrates or extends their competence, and perceived competence is a primary motivation factor for teens. Between high school and college, participation in physical activity declines considerably, and following college it continues to decline. Sport participation must compete for an individual's time with work, family,

Early involvement in developmental sport programs can lead to sport participation for a lifetime.
© Rawpixel.com/Shutterstock.

TABLE 11-1   2016 Participation in Sport Activities (in millions)—Ranked by Total Participation

Activity	Total Number (9.1 is 9,100,000)	Males	Females
Exercise walking	105.70	46.028	59.672
Exercising with equipment	57.1	27.710	29.390
Swimming	45.618	21.679	23.939
Aerobic exercising	45.591	16.413	29.179
Running/jogging	44.946	23.808	21.137
Hiking	423.927	21.694	21.234
Camping (vacation/overnight)	40.410	21.865	18.545
Workout at club	37.8	17.846	19.854
Bicycle riding	36.188	21.007	15.181

Data from ProQuest (2016). ProQuest Statistical Abstract of the U.S. 2016 Online Edition (Table 12578; Participants In Selected Sports Activities: 2016 [By Sex, Age, And Income]). Retrieved May 22, 2020.

and other social activities as individuals enter the workforce and see work as a primary motivator as opposed to recreation. Yet, recreational sport leagues flourish across the United States with millions of participants.

Reasons individuals continue to participate in leisure sport activities are varied but include the opportunity for affiliation with others, improving one's appearance, taking up a new or continuing challenge, competition, enjoyment, positive health, social recognition, stress management, and weight management, to name a few.[6] What we do know is that participation in strenuous and team sports, such as baseball, basketball, and football declines as people age and switch to less physically stressful small-group or individual activities. As might be expected, there are exceptions to the decline in sport activities. Among older adults, for example, competitive sports continue to flourish, even if the numbers participating are a smaller percentage of their age group. Those participating in master sporting events are in better health, have experienced less physical decline than the older adult population as a whole, are motivated, and frequently were involved in sport throughout their life. Some half and full marathons list masters as age 40 or above, and many international competitions use 35+. United States Masters Swimming is for those swimmers 18+.

Team Sport Participation

If any activity defines mainstream American sport, it is organized team sports, beginning with T-ball and soccer for 3-, 4-, and 5-year-olds and continuing throughout people's lives. Actual participation numbers in organized team sports are available only where governing organizations are present and data are collected, and participation is highest among high school students (see Table 11-2) and has grown steadily.

Collegiate sport participation declines dramatically, but this is expected because the number of available opportunities to participate in sport teams declines dramatically. Table 11-3 shows the participation levels in intercollegiate athletics. The number does not represent recreational sport involvement at the collegiate level, which is far higher. In addition to extensive intercollegiate sport facilities, today's college campuses have one or more recreational sport facilities that cater to the general student population. Over the last 30 years, universities have recognized the importance of participation in sport by students who are not engaged in intercollegiate athletics.

According to the Sports and Fitness Industry Association, among noncollegiate athletes, some team sports such as basketball, baseball, and soccer continue to grow, whereas football is on the decline. Those sports that are growing among youth can be attributed to grassroots programs such as Major League Baseball's (MLB's) Play Ball and the National Basketball Association's (NBA's) Jr. NBA.[7]

The most significant change over the past 5 years has been based on casual versus core participation. Casual participants play multiple sports whereas core participants play only one or two. The United States is seeing a growth in casual team sports and a decline in core team sports except

TABLE 11-2	High School Athletic Participation		
Year	**Boys Participating**	**Girls Participating**	**Total**
2018–19	4,534,758	3,402,733	7,937,491
2017–18	4,565,580	3,415,306	7,980,886
2016–17	4,563,238	3,400,297	7,963,535
2015–16	4,544,574	3,324,326	7,868,900
2005–06	4,206,549	2,953,355	7,159,904
1995–96	3,634,052	2,367,936	6,001,988
1985–86	3,344,275	1,807,121	5,151,396
1975–76	4,109,021	1,645,039	5,754,060
1971–72	3,666,917	294,015	3,960,932

Note: Title IX was passed on June 23, 1972.

Top 10 Boys Sports Participants			Top 10 Girls Sports Participants		
1	Football	1,006,013	1	Outdoor track and field	488,267
2	Outdoor track and field	605,354	2	Volleyball	452,808
3	Basketball	540,769	3	Basketball	399,067
4	Baseball	482,740	4	Soccer	394,105
5	Soccer	459,077	5	Softball–fast pitch	362,038
6	Cross-country	269,295	6	Cross-country	219,345
7	Wrestling	247,410	7	Tennis	189,436
8	Tennis	159,314	8	Swimming and diving	173,088
9	Golf	143,200	9	Competitive spirit	161,358
10	Swimming and diving	136,638	10	Lacrosse	99,750

Data from National Federation of State High School Associations. (2019). *NFHS Annual Report: 2018-19.* https://www.nfhs.org/media/3609710/2018-19-nfhs-annual-report.pdf

College students are more likely to participate in recreational sports than intercollegiate sports.
© sirtravelalot/Shutterstock.

for ice hockey, lacrosse, gymnastics and rugby, presumably because they all require high levels of basic skills and commitment.[8]

Fast-growing adult sports include pickleball and ultimate frisbee. Both of these sports attract adults more than youth, especially pickleball, which is a modified version of tennis and draws an older crowd.

Structure of Sport Participation Opportunities

Sport participation opportunities are found in a multitude of levels and can vary by age, interest, and skill level. People can participate in recreation leagues, in developmental programs to learn skills such as T-ball, or on high school teams; compete at the college level; or go on to be a professional athlete. Each of these areas could consume a whole chapter or even course on the topic. This is just a brief overview of the scope of four overarching structures.

RECREATIONAL AND DEVELOPMENTAL OPPORTUNITIES

Of the four structures, recreation and developmental sports is arguably the most diverse in the age, skill level, and sport opportunities available. Young children can begin learning sport skills at home, but many partake in developmental classes, clinics, and leagues as young as 3 to 5 years of age. For example, the McFetridge Sports Center offers Pee Wee Tennis starting at 4 years of age. Classes focus on developing skills and use modified

TABLE 11-3 Collegiate Participation in Organized Sport

Association	Participants	Number of Teams	
		Men	Women
National Collegiate Athletic Association	498,691	24	24
National Association of Intercollegiate Athletics	77,000	11	11
National Junior College Athletic Association	59,196	13	13
California Community College Athletic Association	24,000	12	12
Total	**658,887**	**60**	**60**

Data from California Community College Athletic Association. (n.d.). *Welcome to the CCCAA*. Retrieved October 25, 2020, from http://www.cccaasports.org/about/about; National Association of Intercollegiate Athletics. (n.d.). *Why choose the NAIA?* Retrieved October 25, 2020, from https://www.naia.org/why-naia/index; National Collegiate Athletic Association. (n.d.). *NCAA demographics database*. Retrieved October 25, 2020, from http://www.ncaa.org/about/resources/research/ncaa-demographics-database; National Junior College Athletic Association. (n.d.). *Student-athlete participation statistics*. Retrieved October 25, 2020, from https://www.njcaa.org/about/history/SA_Participation/index

THE EXPLOSION OF WORLD CHAMPIONSHIPS

At the beginning of the 20th century, there was one world game that was widely recognized—the Olympic Games. The Olympic Games represented the equivalent of world games for many sports. The Olympic Games still brings together athletes from many sports and from most of the countries of the world, remaining the premiere example of the purpose and focus of world game—or championship—events. During the 20th century, and especially beginning in the 1950s, more sport governing bodies created their own global (or world) championship.

The diversity of world championships is almost staggering. In 1896, there were five world championships; by 1920, there were still fewer than 30 world championships. In 2020, there were over 500 different competitive sporting events including championships in badminton, canoeing, darts, beach handball, women's baseball and men's softball, inline hockey, table tennis, snooker (billiards), and many more.

Many of these sporting events have big name recognition. Football (known as soccer in the United States) is a good example. The FIFA (Fédération Internationale de Football Association) World Cup involves 3 years of competition between national teams to qualify. For example, the 2022 FIFA World Cup involves qualifying rounds for the six continental zones. Qualifying participants began competing in the playoffs in June 2019, with the finals to be held in Qatar in 2022. A total of 211 teams (1 per country) will compete for 32 slots in the finals before a champion is declared.[9]

equipment including smaller courts and nets and tennis balls with reduced compression to reduce the bounce and speed of the ball.[10] Little League has created age-appropriate levels for children to progress through and learn baseball and softball skills including T-ball (5–7 years old), coach pitch, minor league, and major league. Little League stresses that the early baseball/softball programs should be fun and help the child fall in love with the game, provide opportunities for kids to learn and grow, develop teamwork and social skills, and begin to learn the basic fundamentals of the game. As players develop they move on to more advanced and competitive leagues to build technical skills and improve performance and gain confidence. In these advanced leagues competition begins to develop and skill differentiation between players is more evident.[11]

Some youth players in sports such as basketball, baseball, hockey, and soccer will begin at a young age and want more competition and skill development than they feel they can get from leagues in their communities. To get this they choose to join club teams. Club teams are formed in communities and players must try out to be placed on the team. Only highly skilled players will make the elite teams, sometimes called travel teams. These teams travel from city to city to play other teams and can be quite expensive as the players are expected to cover the cost of tournament entry fees, facility fees, hotel rooms, and travel to and from tournaments and practices. The cost of participating in these teams can average $100–$500 per month per child, and for some elite teams such as volleyball the cost can climb to $10,000 per year. Many players and parents see travel leagues as the most beneficial path to a college scholarship. The thought of a college scholarship is justification for

many parents to pay this kind of money for their young players if they can afford it.[12]

As people age, their need for sport changes. Recreational sport continues throughout the lifespan but may take on a different form of the sport. For example, baseball/softball players may finish playing in high school but not have the talent to play in college. In college there are intramural league opportunities for most any sport one desires, and these teams often remain quite competitive. For those who are most competitive there are often club sports within the university that travel to play other university club teams. These club teams are structured much like club teams for high school age players but often with defrayed costs by limiting travel, overnight stays, expensive tournament fees, and families traveling along.

Postcollege sport leagues can see even more evolution. Using our baseball/softball example, there are a limited number of baseball and fast pitch softball leagues after

CASE STUDY: Club Sports: Pay to Play, Part 1

Club sports are expensive, but many college athletes were once club sport players. A 2017 National Collegiate Athletic Association (NCAA) survey of 21,233 athletes found that the following played club sports:

Sport	Women	Men
Soccer	95%	93%
Basketball	92%	89%
Swimming	90%	88%
Baseball/softball	94%	87%
Ice hockey	91%	86%
Football	N/A	24%
Track and field	32%	31%

Ninety-five percent of the NCAA athletes also played on their high school teams, meaning many are playing the sport year round and narrowed their sport down to one specialized sport versus being a multisport athlete.

Questions to Consider

1. Develop the pros and cons of a youth/teens trying out for a club team. What are the pros and cons of the player being selected for a club team?
2. What are the advantages and disadvantages of sport specialization and of being a multisport athlete?
3. Would you want your son/daughter to specialize or be a multisport athlete? Why? Why not?

Data from Moore, J. (2017, May 17). Do you have to play club sports to get recruited?. *USA Today High School Sports*. https://usatodayhss.com/2017/do-you-have-to-play-club-sports-to-get-recruited

---

CASE STUDY: Club Sports: Pay to Play, Part 2

Twenty-one percent of children in the United States live in households below the federal poverty level. These same children do not have access to a $400 bat or ball glove, the best shoes, bags to carry equipment, or even enough food to maintain the good nutrition an athlete needs. Household income is the primary driver of youth athletics participation. Children ages 6 to 12 with household incomes of less than $25,000 per year are three times more likely to be inactive or play no sports.

In addition to financial lack of access to club sports, the cost of recreational sports can be expensive as well, especially those with specialized facilities and equipment such as golf, hockey, or swimming. Less expensive sports can prove to have just as many barriers when there is no open space available to play soccer, the basketball courts in low-income neighborhoods are run down, or there is no track on which to run. Add to this, schools in low-income districts are less well funded, more likely to drop physical education programs, and may require kids to pay to play on high school sports teams.

Community recreation leagues are available through local parks and recreation departments and the YMCA. Many of these agencies will have scholarships for low-income families. This provides an opportunity to play, but these leagues allow everyone to play, regardless of skill level. Young athletes with high skills may not receive the level of competition they need to further develop, especially if the most wealthy, talented players move on to club sports.

Questions for Consider

1. Should club sports and the opportunities they provide be limited to those who can afford it? Why or why not?
2. What sport opportunities do players from low-income families have? Are club sports another way of widening the gap between those who have access to a college education and those who do not? Why or why not?
3. In addition to college scholarships, what else do children who are low income miss out on because they do not have the means to participate in sport?

Data from Flanagan, L. (2017, September 28). What's lost when only rich kids play sports?. *The Atlantic*. https://www.theatlantic.com/education/archive/2017/09/whats-lost-when-only-rich-kids-play-sports/541317

---

college. It is at this point these players may switch to a different game such as slow-pitch softball as these leagues are abundant in communities across the country. Sports leagues may be modified for older players including leagues for people aged 35+ all the way up to 70+. Some softball leagues for older adults will adapt the game to protect players. For example, a pitching screen may be used to protect the pitcher, implementation of a five-run rule, allowing sliding only at second and third base, and limiting the types of bats that may be used because of the speed of the ball coming off the bat. Community parks and recreation departments will adapt rules in consultation with the players, but there are several national and international governing bodies that have their own rules, leagues, and tournaments including the National Senior Games Association, United States Specialty Sports Association Senior Softball, Senior Softball USA, and the International Senior Softball Association.

Recreational and developmental sport provides sport, both team and individual, throughout the lifespan. Sport begins with developmental aspects to learn the sport in ways that are age appropriate, and sport changes to accommodate the impacts of aging, yet still providing a fun and exciting activity for all ages and abilities.

INTERSCHOLASTIC SPORTS

Interscholastic sports, often referred to as high school sports, attract 52% (7.8 million) of all high school students.[13] Each state and Washington, DC, has a governing body that oversees high school sports. These governing bodies are members of the National Federation of State High School Associations (NFSH) and serve 19,500 high schools.[14] The federation writes playing rules and regulations for amateur sports at the high school level, issues guidance on national issues, and provides education for students, parents, officials, and administrators. In addition to high school sports, the NFSH has expanded to include the arts, speech, debate, and theatre. Interscholastic sports have a significant financial impact and contribute over $15 billion to the economy and employ 300,000 coaches and administrators.

Some high schools have come under fire for cutting sports and music programs as cost-saving methods. The sports budget in high schools is quite low (1%–3%) compared to the overall budget, and sport participation by students has many benefits including higher grades, higher achievement test scores, and higher educational expectations beyond high school; enhanced school engagement and sense of belonging, positive youth development and opportunities for learning a number of life skills and values not typically taught in classroom education; and better physical and mental health.[15]

Working in interscholastic sports often means being either a coach or an athletic director. Coaches can be teachers within the school or an outside hire. Most coaches are part time, and for teachers, coaching responsibilities are in addition to their teaching duties. The athletic director most likely also comes from within the school and is a teacher. This may be a full-time job for a teacher in the school or they may have split responsibilities of teaching and overseeing the athletics program.

INTERCOLLEGIATE ATHLETICS

College sports in the United States is a unique phenomenon that many other countries do not have. Many colleges and university programs can build considerable fan bases and brand loyalty to teams and players, sell logoed items, and have a significant media presence for games, playoffs, and tournaments.

The NCAA is the largest governing body of intercollegiate athletics with over 1,098 college and university members with 19,886 teams.[16] The NCAA establishes rules and regulations that guide play, recruitment, academics, practice and playing seasons, championships, and amateur status. The NCAA has three divisions that are based on the number of sports sponsored, size of the athletic department budget, type of sports offered (team vs. individual), attendance and seating capacity in arenas, and whether the program offers scholarships.[17] In Division I football there are two subdivisions: Football Bowl Subdivision and Football Championship Subdivision.

NCAA oversight is through the Board of Governors (BoG). The BoG deals with policy, strategic planning, member-wide votes, resolving litigation, and budget. Under the BoG, Division I has its Board of Directors, and Division II and III have the President's Council. Those groups set policy and direction for the division, make recommendations to the BoG, and handle responsibilities delegated by the BoG.[18]

The NCAA is not the only governing body within intercollegiate athletics. The National Association of Intercollegiate Athletics (NAIA), open to 2- and 4-year institutions in the United States and Canada, has 250 member institutions with 77,000 student athletes. It prides itself on being more cost effective than NCAA membership, autonomy, and sensible and simple rules and regulations.[19] The National Christian College Athletic Association (NCCAA) serves Christian liberal arts institutions and bible colleges. Two-year colleges can be members of the National Junior College Athletic Association, the California Community College Association, or the Northwest Athletic Conference. Tribal colleges and universities can be members of these organizations but can also join the American Indian Higher Education Consortium.[20]

Most colleges and universities belong to an athletic conference. Conferences provide opportunities for its member schools to compete against other schools like them, somewhat leveling the playing field, also referred to as competitive balance. Conferences also enhance the financial status of its members through maintaining competitive games. When games are competitive, the excitement draws fans when the winner is not already assumed. When conferences sign contracts for media rights, sponsorships, and licensing, a portion of the revenue is distributed to conference members. Furthermore, when teams are successful on the national level, the whole conference benefits from revenue streams.[21]

For example, the NCAA Men's Basketball National Championship funds the entire NCAA, as well as provides a lot of money to conferences. The NCAA profits about $700 million per year from the tournament. They keep about 60% to fund their operations and distribute approximately $290 million to the conferences. The amount depends on how far teams advance in the tournament. Conferences will earn about $1.67 million over 6 years for not winning a single game. Those teams that advance to the final four will earn about $8.3 million each for their respective conferences. The conferences are urged to distribute the revenue evenly among all members, but the conference determines actual distribution.[22] The schools in the power five conferences—Atlantic Coast Conference (ACC), Big 10, Big 12, Pacific-12 (Pac-12), and Southeastern Conference (SEC)—receive a significant amount of money each year, but it is a smaller portion of their total budgets than in a smaller conference like the Missouri Valley. For example, in March 2018 the Loyola Chicago Ramblers unexpectedly made it to the final four. The Missouri Valley schools will earn more from this tournament success than they will from their ESPN annual contracts, and the earnings constitute about 65% of the conference's revenues. The Missouri Valley has done well with tournament revenue mainly because of Wichita State University (WSU) teams regularly advancing in the tournament.[23] However, WSU left the Missouri Valley in 2017 to join the American Athletic Conference (AAC). The move "extends our conference's national footprint, enhances our national profile, and strengthens our position as a leader in intercollegiate athletics" according to their athletic director. It will also increase their media rights contracts as well as potentially increasing their seeding in the NCAA tournament by coming from a more highly competitive conference.[24]

Medium- and large-sized colleges and universities can have extensive staff working within them. The most visible staff are the coaches and athletic training staff. The administration of the athletics department starts at the top with the athletics director. The person in this position oversees all aspects of the division of intercollegiate athletics. They are considered the chief executive officer and have the responsibility of hiring and firing coaches and managing department heads in areas such as compliance, media relations, ticketing, academic support, and facilities and events. Often these areas are managed by associate or assistant athletic directors. It is

CASE STUDY: Disparities Between Men's and Women's NCAA Basketball Tournament Revealed

The 2021 NCAA Men's and Women's basketball tournament revealed drastic differences in how the men's teams and women's teams are treated and the financial imbalance that exists for participating teams. For example:

- The men's teams had access to a full gym with top quality weight equipment. The women were given a single rack of hand weights and yoga mats.
- Men's teams received catered meals and the women were fed pre-packaged meals.
- The women's final four logo is gendered (reading "women's final four") while the men's just says "final four," perpetuating the idea that men's basketball is the norm, while women's basketball is of lesser value than the men's.
- The Twitter handles and hashtags are also gendered @MarchMadness is reserved for the men and @NCAAwbb for the women along with the hashtag #MarchMadness for the men and #ncaaW and #WFinalFour for the women.
- The men are being given PCR COVID tests while the women receive the antigen tests, which are cheaper and less accurate.
- The women's #1 seeds (South Carolina, NC State, UConn, and Stanford) have an average budget of just over $6 million per team. Those same institutions spent an average of almost $9 million on each of their men's teams in 2019.
- The top four seeds in the 2021 men's tournament (Baylor, Gonzaga, Illinois, and Michigan) spent an average of $10 million in 2019 on the teams, compared with $5.7 million on average for their women's teams.

Probably the biggest differences come in the payouts to teams. All of the men's teams will all collect money whether they win a game or not. Getting to the men's final four means an infusion of $10 million to the school and its conference. The women's final four participants will receive $0, the same amount the other women's team participants receive.

Media contracts are different for the two tournaments. The men's tournament has a contract worth $770 million and the women's contract is worth $500 million and includes 24 other NCAA championships. Television viewership is up for the women's consistently sold out final four and for the games leading up to the final four, where more than 3 million viewers watched Baylor defeat Notre Dame 82-81 in the 2019 championship game.

Questions to Consider

1. Should there be a difference in what amenities (e.g., food, hotels) the men's teams and women's teams receive for participating in the tournament? Why or why not?
2. Should the women's teams receive revenue for participating in the tournament? Why or why not?
3. Should differences in size of budget exist between men's and women's college athletic teams? Why or why not?
4. Why have these differences existed for decades and have never been made public by past players and coaches?

Data from Azzi, A. (2021). All of the disparities at the 2021 NCAA women's basketball tournament. NBC Sports. Retrieved March 21, 2021, from https://onherturf.nbcsports.com/2021/03/19/ncaa-womens-mens-basketball-weight-rooms-discrepancies; Caron, E. (2021). March Madness daily: Men's vs women's NCAA tournament money. Sportico. Retrieved March 21, 2021, from https://www.sportico.com/leagues/college-sports/2021/march-madness-mens-womens-ncaa-tournament-money-1234625281; Jenkins, S. (2021). NCAA's message to women's basketball players: You're worth less. The Washington Post. Retrieved March 21, 2021 from https://www.washingtonpost.com/sports/2021/03/19/ncaa-womens-basketball-unequal

not uncommon for one these division heads to be the senior associate athletic director, designating them to be the second in command behind the athletic director. One of these division heads will also be the senior women's administrator (SWA). The NCAA designated this role within institutions to ensure that there was a high-ranking female administrator involved in decision making within athletics and to ensure women's sports are represented within the department. The desire to work in college athletics is great, making it a competitive industry. Many people working in these institutions start as graduate assistants working toward a master's degree, gain experience, and then move into entry-level positions. Although this is common, there are exceptions. The skills needed are specific to each job and may attract people with education and experience in sport management, accounting, media relations, communication, and law, among others.

PROFESSIONAL SPORTS

Professional sport separates itself from the others in that the athletes are paid to play. This compensation comes in the form of a salary but also endorsements, performance bonuses, and sponsorships. It is easy to see the most popular professional sports such as football, baseball, basketball, and golf, but many others exist such as ultimate fighting, boxing, soccer, auto racing, and cricket.

Professional sports have a similar structure throughout the different sports. They have a league commissioner who runs the league, a board of governors composed of team owners, and team central administration. The leagues themselves are structured differently based on the sport. For example, the Women's National Basketball Association (WNBA) has two conferences—eastern and western—for its 12 teams. The National Football League (NFL) is one

---

CASE STUDY: Paying College Athletes

For years there have been discussions centering around whether or not college athletes should be paid to play in college. Athletes such as LeBron James and Senators Chris Murphy and Bernie Sanders argue that athletes should be paid to play because the university makes money from ticket sales and media rights that they help generate. Others argue that coaches make exorbitant salaries that could be reduced and passed on to players and that being a student athlete is like working a full-time job. Student athletes are not able to work during the season, even to help defray those costs not covered by the institution.

Mark Emmert, NCAA president, disagrees with paying student athletes, stating that they are student athletes playing against other student athletes and not employees playing against other employees. Those opposed to paying athletes argue that athletes receive tuition and fee waivers as well as room and board waivers.

In California the Fair Pay to Play Act was introduced, which would allow student athletes in institutions that make more than $10 million in media rights revenue each year to be paid for the institution using their likeness. They would also be allowed to hire an agent to represent them in business deals, without losing their eligibility to play college sports, which is similar to Olympic athletes.

Emmert has argued that if California schools allow college athletes to make money, they would have an unfair advantage over schools in other states and has warned that these schools would be barred from competing in NCAA championships. Emmert says that if this passes and California schools opt to pay athletes, they will be barred from competing in NCAA-sanctioned events because it would give an unfair advantage to those schools who could pay players.

Questions to Consider

1. Should student athletes be paid? Develop arguments both for and against this issue.
2. If student athletes are paid, should they all be paid, or should just some athletes be paid? Support your argument.
3. How are smaller, less lucrative leagues going to be able to manage paying athletes when they have limited budgets?
4. How will schools outside of the power five conferences compete with those schools? Will it be the end of the "Cinderella teams"? Why or why not?
5. Find out how many student athletes there are in your university. Set a stipend for these athletes and determine how much paying athletes would cost. Where will your university get revenue? Is it a self-sustaining athletics department or does it get money from the university to operate (e.g., money from tuition-based student fees)?

Data from Hess, A. (2019, September 11). *Majority of college students say student-athletes should be paid, survey finds.* Retrieved November 1, 2020, from https://www.cnbc.com/2019/09/11/student-athletes-should-get-paid-college-students-say.html; Robinson, A. (2020, May 6). *Should college athletes be paid? An expert debate analysis.* Retrieved November 8, 2020, from https://blog.prepscholar.com/should-college-athletes-be-paid-why; Top 10 Reasons College Athletes Should Be Paid. (2020, February 13). Retrieved November 8, 2020, from https://www.collegesportsmadness.com/article/18319

---

league with two conferences—the American Football Conference and the National Football Conference, each with four regional divisions. Major League Baseball also has two leagues (National and American) with three divisions in each league. They also have an extensive minor league system used to develop players for the major leagues. For example, the Chicago Cubs have within its system the Iowa Cubs (AAA), the Tennessee Smokies (AA), the Myrtle Beach Pelicans (A-Advanced), the South Bend Cubs (A), and the Eugene Emeralds (Rookie League).[25] Like MLB, the NBA also created a developmental league, the Gatorade League (G-League), to help young players, coaches, and referees to develop in hopes of making an NBA team.

Professional team sport has four unique labor elements that set it apart from other levels of sport—collective bargaining, free agency, salary caps, and drafts.[26] Collective bargaining is essentially the formation of player unions with the ability to negotiate a basic labor contract. The labor contract outlines minimum salaries, benefits, and working conditions. Individual players have their own contracts that go beyond receiving the basics outlined in the collective bargaining agreement.

Once players complete their current individual contract, they can enter into free agency. Free agency allows players to move to another team without penalty; free agency guidelines are a negotiated element of the collective bargaining agreement. It also allows players to play for the team that is willing to pay them the most. Because free agency can quickly escalate salaries, there is a need for salary caps to control this and create a more competitive balance.

Salary caps set a ceiling on the salaries teams have on their payrolls. This establishes parity among teams in smaller and larger communities and owners with varying degrees of resources that they can invest in teams. It stops teams that have the most resources from buying all the best players and dominating the sport. The NFL ($198.2 million), National Hockey League (NHL; $82 million), and the WNBA ($1.3 million) have hard salary caps that cannot be exceeded. The

NBA has a soft $109 million cap that allows teams some exceptions to keep long-time players to maintain their fan base. MLB is the only major professional team that does not have a salary cap because of their strong collective bargaining agreement.

Lastly, player drafts are a means to add new players in an equitable way. Usually teams with worse records get their first choice of players who are entered into the draft.[27] The WNBA uses a lottery selection system to determine the order of the first four selections for the four teams who did not make the playoffs on the previous season. After those four teams, the remaining teams select in inverse order based on their 2-year cumulative record. The 2020 WNBA draft was held virtually because of COVID-19; it was the most watched WNBA draft ever and the most watched in ESPN history. A part of this historic draft was WNBA Commissioner Cathy Engelbert naming Alyssa Altobelli, Gianna Bryant, and Payton Chester as honorary draft picks. These Mamba Sports Academy teammates, who played on a youth basketball team coached by Kobe Bryant, tragically died in a helicopter accident in January 2020 with Bryant.[28] Like intercollegiate athletics, those wanting to work in professional sport are numerous, creating extensive competition for jobs. Leagues and teams will have executive officers, chief financial officers, marketing and sales staff, general counsel (lawyers), general managers, coaches, and training staff. One of the unique positions in professional sport is player development. These staff members work with player personnel (identifying, evaluating and developing players), medical staff and team support, coaching staff, player education and relations, video support staff, and stadium and facilities staff.[29] People working in professional sport have varying backgrounds, much like intercollegiate athletics. It is not uncommon to see former athletes in front office jobs.

RACIAL INTEGRATION OF PROFESSIONAL SPORT

Many have come to know Jackie Robinson as the first Black major league player, when it was actually Moses Fleetwood Walker and his brother Weldy Walker who played for the Toledo Blue Stockings in 1884. When they retired in 1889, there became an unwritten "gentlemen's agreement" that Black players were not allowed in MLB. That held true until 1947 when Robinson began playing for the Brooklyn Dodgers, breaking the modern era color barrier.[30] In the time between the Weldy brothers and Robinson playing for the Dodgers, the Negro National League was formed where most team owners, managers, coaches, and umpires were Black. Once Robinson joined the Dodgers, Black fans were allowed into MLB games and the Negro National League later folded in the 1960s.[31] Although the integration of baseball is often the more widely known history in professional sports, the NFL was integrated in 1946 by Kenney Washington, and Chuck Cooper was drafted in the NBA in 1950.[32]

FEMALE ATHLETES DEMAND EQUAL PAY

In March 2019 the United States Women's Soccer team filed suit against the United States Soccer Federation (USSF) claiming that the Women's National Team (WNT) should be paid equally to their male counterparts.[33] They asserted that their pay structure violates the Equal Pay Act and Title VII of the Civil Rights Act of 1964. The WNT won the World Cup in 2018 (the men's team failed to qualify), which fueled fan support for equal pay.

The USSF argued that the WNT averaged $220,747 per game in total payments compared to $212,639 per game for the men. The USSF also argued that the four plaintiffs, Carli Lloyd, Alex Morgan, Megan Rapinoe, and Becky Sauerbrunn, earned more in total than their male counterparts.[34]

Parts of the lawsuit were dismissed by a California federal judge arguing that the collective bargaining agreement for the WNT was different from the Men's National Team (MNT) agreement. The WNT agreement gave up higher performance bonuses for a greater base compensation package and guaranteed a higher number of contract players. The judge ruled they cannot later claim the contract was unfair because of the choices they made in collective bargaining.[35]

NG BREAKS MLB GENDER BARRIER

The Miami Marlins MLB team hired Kim Ng in November 2020 making her the first female to serve as a general manager for any men's professional team. Ng started as an intern with the Chicago White Sox, which led to a role as the team's assistant director of baseball operations. She also spent time with the Dodgers and Yankees, holding assistant general manager positions twice. Ng stated, "When I got into this business, it seemed unlikely a woman would lead a major league team, but I am dogged in the pursuit of my goals." Administrative positions in men's professional sports continue to be heavily dominated by White men. At the beginning of the 2020 season, only four people of color led baseball operations departments in contrast to the 40% of the players who are people of color.

Kepner, T., & Wagner, J. (2020, November 13). Miami Marlins hire Kim Ng, breaking a baseball gender barrier. *New York Times*. https://www.nytimes.com/2020/11/13/sports/baseball/kim-ng-miami-marlins.html.

Sport Spectators

It has been said, "If there is sport, there are spectators." People enjoy watching sport activities, albeit the number of spectators varies from sport to sport and by individual and group interest. A bass fishing tournament draws far fewer spectators than does a collegiate or professional football game. Yet, both of these sports have strong print and electronic media followers.

Spectators have been described in a variety of ways. An overarching approach to understanding spectators focuses on motivation, or why people choose to watch sports and how they react to the sports they watch. Underwood and colleagues suggest, "Spectator sports are a unique group experience characterized by a sense of belonging that spectators feel and an inherent bias against out-group members. . . . For these individuals, sports are not merely a form of entertainment and recreation, but provide a sense of community and family."[36]

Giulianotti developed a taxonomy or classification for spectators.[37] He classified spectators as supporters, followers, fans, and flâneurs. His study, although focusing on English football (soccer) clubs with a corporate identity, has the potential to be related to American professional sports. The four categories are based on two continua, the first being attraction to the team (called hot and cool), with hot focused on an intense loyalty. Cool fans are at the other end of the continuum, exhibiting loyalty that is neither intense nor binding. The second continuum is a traditional consumer focus, or a cultural versus a market-centered approach.

A supporter is a traditional hot spectator with deep personal understanding and a strong commitment to the team. Giulianotti suggests supporters have a "relationship with the club that resembles those with close family and friends."[38] Followers are also traditionalists and can be described as knowledgeable spectators with a strong interest in the game but not with a single team. As a result, single teams have minimal impact on their identity as a follower.

Fans are hot consumers. They are not traditionalists, but their focus is with a single team. "The individual fan experiences the . . . traditions, its star players, and fellow supporters through a market-centered set of relationships."[39] Consumption of market products and the display of those products is a driving force. Fans, because they are not traditionalists, are more transient in their loyalty to a team. If teams do not perform to their expectations, they may change their loyalty to another team. Finally, flâneurs have an almost aloof relationship with a team. Giulianotti suggests flâneurs may be more impressed with branding, such as logos, tattoos, and the like. They are transient, switching affiliations like surfing websites.

At a sporting event, or viewing a sporting event on television, all of these types of fans are present. The centerfield bleachers of the Chicago Cubs is composed of all four types but most probably supporters and fans. The individual sporting Oakland Raiders tattoos, car stickers, T-shirts, and hats has a higher probability of being a flâneur, fan, or supporter. The typologies suggested can provide insights into how and why spectators are involved in sport. It can give clues to researchers, sport franchises, and commercial enterprises about how sport might be marketed and whom to target. Not only does the sport industry closely monitor the different levels of spectators, so do businesses outside of sport. The importance businesses attribute to major spectator sports is evident in associated business-related use of statistical data collected from fans who attend, watch, and follow teams and athletes. Attendance figures, average attendance, and percentages of stadium capacity filled are important indicators of fan support and influence the financial commitment that advertisers, partners, and governments are willing to invest in a team or individual. Similar to television shows, sports broadcasts are tracked for penetration into a given market, average ratings, peak ratings, and responses. This is discussed in greater detail in the next section.

Measuring attendance at sporting events can be challenging.
© Grindstone Media Group/Shutterstock.

Attendance at Sporting Events

For years the hallmark of a spectator's commitment to sport was attendance at sporting contests. To some degree, that remains true today for collegiate and professional sport franchises, although the cost of attendance has increased considerably.

Measuring attendance is, at best, problematic. Teams can count tickets sold, distributed, and given away. Estimated attendance is also a common approach, although less so than in the past. A surfing contest, for example, may not have formal tickets; people just show up and attendance must be estimated. This was common for many sporting events for a long time and continues to be the norm in smaller or less formally organized events. However, sport has become more formal and is following business models with more exact measurements expected. Regardless, it is difficult to get a handle on spectator attendance at park and

TABLE 11-4	Attendance at Selected Sporting Events				
Sport	**2000**	**2007**	**2011**	**2016**	**2019**
MLB	74,340,000	80,759,000	75,504,000	73,159,000	68,478,648
Minor league baseball			41,279,000	37,345,000	36,883,218
NCAA men's basketball	28,949,000	33,396,000	32,781,000	32,382,000	24,707,552
NCAA women's basketball	8,825,000	11,121,000	11,211,000	11,367,000	8,103,579
NBA	12,134,000	20,272,000	21,841,000	13,351,000	21,933,429
NHL	18,800,000	20,862,000	20,928,000	13,440,000	22,186,851
NCAA football	39,059,000	48,752,000	46,699,000	49,058,000	34,602,770
NFL	20,954,000	22,256,000	20,959,000	17,509,000	16,894,856
Indianapolis 500					Approx. 300,000
Tour de France					Approx. 15 million in person; 3.5 billion on television
Total	**203,061,000**	**237,418,000**	**271,202,000**	**247,611,000**	

Data from ESPN. (n.d.). *MLB attendance report–2019*. Retrieved October 26, 2020, from http://www.espn.com/mlb/attendance/_/year/2019; ESPN. (n.d.). *NBA attendance report–2019*. Retrieved October 26, 2020, from http://www.espn.com/nba/attendance/_/year/2019; ESPN. (n.d.). *NFL attendance–2020*. Retrieved October 26, 2020, from http://www.espn.com/nfl/attendance; Glaspie, A., & Ayello, J. (2019, May 26). IMS President Doug Boles on Indy 500 attendance: "Down from where we were in 2018." *Indianapolis Star*. https://www.indystar.com/story/sports/motor/indy-500/2019/05/26/indy-500-crowd-attendance-down-2018/1244754001; *National Collegiate Athletic Association. NCAA statistics*. Retrieved October 26, 2020, from https://stats.ncaa.org/rankings/change_sport_year_div; Pledge Sports. (n.d.). *These are the 5 biggest sporting events in the world*. Retrieved October 26, 2020, from https://www.pledgesports.org/2017/04/these-are-the-5-biggest-sporting-events-in-the-world recreation–sponsored programs, local youth leagues, and informal sport settings. Organized sports do a better job of counting "in attendance" spectators. Table 11-4 depicts attendance over the past 2 decades at selected collegiate and professional sporting events. Professional baseball, including minor and major leagues, has the highest total attendance on a yearly basis. Professional baseball also has the largest number of teams and annual games.

Media Use and Spectators

Media long ago changed how people view their role as a spectator. An MLB game was first broadcast via radio in 1921, and in 1935 the Chicago Cubs became the first team to broadcast their entire schedule on the radio. Radio broadcasts allowed people to be spectators during the contest when they were not present. No one could anticipate what the next 85 years would bring to professional, collegiate, and high school sports. The explosion of opportunities for spectators to watch sport over the last 10-plus years has been nothing short of spectacular.

ESPN became the first "all-sports" television network, beginning in 1979 on a limited basis and becoming a 24-hour broadcast station in 1980. Beginning in the late 1990s, professional sports leagues began to establish their own television networks and financed them, in part, with viewer subscriptions through cable and satellite carriers. The league networks, although in competition with major networks, did not sever their existing contracts but instead expanded the availability for spectators to watch every game of their favorite teams. The ability for people to watch sports of any kind on television has expanded dramatically over the last 20 years. In 2018 ESPN reached 86 million households, followed by Fox Sports with 83.2 million, the NFL Network with 67.6 million, and the MLB network with 58.5 million households reached. Other networks have emerged in the last several years, including the Tennis Network (54.5 million), Golf Channel (70 million), and the Big Ten Network (57 million).[40]

In 2020, the Super Bowl was the largest viewed sporting event, with more than 99.9 million U.S. viewers watching the game on the Fox network. Viewers increased to 102 million when counting those watching a Spanish-language simulcast and those watching a live stream on Fox, NFL, and Verizon platforms.[41] This is the single largest American market sporting event. By contrast, the 2018 World Cup final was watched by over 884 million live viewers worldwide.[42]

The 2016 Rio Olympics, a multiweek event, was watched by 3.5 billion viewers worldwide down from 4.8 billion viewers for the 2012 London Olympic Games. This does not represent separate viewers because many viewers tuned in more than one time and sometimes more than once a day. The opening ceremony for the 2016 Olympics had 342 million viewers.[43] Estimates of actual viewers are always just that, an estimate based on historical statistical models. Actual numbers are impossible to identify because one or many people may watch a single television. Numbers of households subscribing, however, are a verifiable number, although they do not show actual numbers watching in a home. Americans are able to watch television in many different ways. Watching delayed broadcasts of television after recording a program, viewing from one of many sources on the Internet, or purchasing a broadcast to watch later are all common.

The most significant trend for spectators is the use of the Internet by viewers. Streaming is growing at incredible rates. Most cable and satellite television providers give access to live sports streaming to their customers. Some networks like ESPN offer free streaming services for the cable and satellite subscribers and sell subscriptions to others without it. There are low-cost and free options available. These services often have low-quality video and pop-up ads, but they are an option for those without cable or satellite subscriptions.

High television ratings lead to fierce negotiations between league officials and network executives when television contracts are about to expire or new media packages (Internet broadcasting, pay per view, and so forth) are available for bid.

Television allows sports fans to be spectators at home.
© Vasyl Shulga/Shutterstock.

COVID-19 IMPACT ON STREAMING

The NFSH has its own network that streams high school sports across the country. Those who are unable to attend the events in person because of COVID-19 restrictions or other reasons can watch high school competitions on television. The NFSH network is a subscription service that costs $69.99 per year or $10.99 per month.

Data from NFHS Network. Retrieved November 3, 2020, from https://www.nfhsnetwork.com/.

Streaming has further increased spectatorship of sporting events.
© Master1305/Shutterstock.

All major professional sports teams and a large percentage of major college teams have medium to large revenue contracts with television and cable networks. For example, the 2016 NCAA basketball championship was broadcast on a cable-only network for the first time. Turner and CBS Sports and the NCAA agreed to an $8.8 billion dollar contract that will run until 2032 to broadcast the NCAA basketball championship. CBS and Turner networks (TBS, TNT, and truTV) broadcast the first round through the elite 8. The final four and title game will alternate between CBS and Turner, though the last NCAA final game on Turner saw a 40% decline in viewers.[44] Major League Baseball signed a multiyear broadcasting agreement with Turner Sports for a reported $470 million.[45] College conferences now bid for their own television rights. For example, the Southeast Conference has television deals worth $300 million.[46]

FRANCHISE VALUES AND PLAYER SALARIES

The importance and magnitude of spectator sport are also evident in franchise financial worth and player salaries. Franchises in most major leagues have seen their values appreciating significantly in the last 5 to 10 years, with price tags reaching as high as $4 billion.

To help determine the fair market value of sport franchises, *Forbes* magazine conducts an annual survey evaluating factors such as the team's annual operating income, the size of the market the team operates in, stadium value, roster value, and so forth. By 2020, all 32 NFL teams were valued in excess of $2 billion. The top three teams are the Dallas Cowboys ($5.7 billion), New England Patriots ($4.4 billion), and the New York Giants ($4.3 billion).[47] The New York Yankees baseball team is valued at $5 billion, the highest-valued MLB franchise followed by the Los Angeles Dodgers ($3.4 billion) and Boston Red Sox ($3.3 billion).[48]

Players' values also have exceeded industry analysts' projections. Athletes earn money from many different sources including playing contracts, prize money, endorsements, appearance fees, product sales, and facility designs (e.g., golf courses), among others. The top paid male athletes in the world for 2020 saw a new sport move to the top because of COVID-19. The pandemic caused salary cuts for some sports such as soccer to make way for tennis player Roger Federer to take over the top spot. The other top earning male athletes include Cristiano Ronaldo (soccer), followed by Lionel Messi (soccer), Neymar (soccer), LeBron James (basketball), and Stephen Curry (basketball).[49] The highest paid female athlete in 2020 was Naomi Osaka (tennis) followed by Serena Williams and Ashleigh Barty (tennis). Female athletes in tennis are much more likely to be the highest paid athletes as 9 of the top 10 female athletes are in tennis. Furthermore, tennis players do well with endorsements. For example, Serena Williams made $4 million in prize money in 2019 but had $32 million in endorsements.[50]

PUBLIC SUBSIDY OF SPORT FACILITIES

Over the last 20 years, cities have invested billions of dollars into the construction and maintenance of sport facilities primarily to retain or attract professional sport teams and to attract more spectators. Numerous teams today are housed in stadiums paid for wholly or in part by public taxes. In 2016, the Los Angeles Rams moved from St. Louis based on the promise of a new stadium estimated at $1.9 billion. When San Diego failed to pass a bond issue to build their Chargers a new stadium, the team announced they were moving to Los Angeles in 2017, joining the Rams. The Oakland Raiders moved to Las Vegas, Nevada, in 2020 on the promise of a $1.9 billion stadium with a significant amount paid for by an increased hotel and motel room tax.

ATTENDANCE COSTS OF SPECTATOR SPORTS

The increasing cost of attending a sport event is one of the factors that creates discomfort for sport fans and their families. Attending a sporting event for any one of the male major leagues today can be a personal account–draining proposition.

The Fan Cost Index (FCI), a survey conducted annually by Chicago-based Team Marketing Report, a sport marketing company, provides a comparable measure of how much a family of four likely will spend attending a professional sporting event. The survey assesses the costs of two average-price adult tickets, two average-price children's tickets, four of the cheapest soft drinks, two of the cheapest beers, four hot dogs, two programs, parking, one game program, and two of the cheapest-size caps.

The 2019 FCI reported that the most expensive place to attend an NFL game is the Los Angeles Chargers SoFi stadium ($820.56) followed by the Chicago Bears Soldier Field ($647.52) with an NFL average FCI of $539.09.[51] By contrast, the average ticket price for the entire NFL was $101.92.[52]

Broadcasting sporting events has become a major source of income for sport teams and their sponsors.
© Fotosr52/Shutterstock.

As a comparison, the FCI average for MLB was $234.38 and for the NBA was $339.02.[53,54]

Costs of tickets has outpaced inflation and has made it difficult for many families to experience games together. The *Los Angeles Times* asked the 11 major sports teams in LA and Orange County whether a family of four could attend a game for under $100 including tickets, parking, food, and beverage. Only the Angels (MLB) could meet that threshold at $54. The Sparks (WNBA) offered a family pack for $110, and the Ducks (NHL) offered a $120 family pack excluding parking.[55] Both the NFL and MLB have seen declining attendance over the past several years. Many people state that they would rather watch the game at home than pay the high prices.

These high ticket prices coupled with a decline in interest by today's youth in sport may prohibit many children from becoming lifelong fans.[56] To counter this and build their fan base, some teams are doing targeted promotions to bring young fans in. For example, the Baltimore Orioles and the Oakland As offer free tickets to children on special days.

Issues in Sport and Society

Because sport is infused throughout our lives in a plethora of ways, many issues arise that affect individuals and society. One cannot talk about sport without thinking of the moral value and civic pride it brings, sport as big business, the pressure for children to compete, corruption, and the prevalence of injury.

Sport as a Source of Moral Values and Civic Pride

It was widely believed that sport has several important values: (1) contributing to health and physical fitness as a form of rigorous training, conditioning, and exercise; (2) building personal traits such as courage and perseverance,

self-discipline, and fair play; (3) encouraging social values linked to obeying rules and dedication to team goals, as well as providing a channel for social mobility, especially for individuals from disadvantaged backgrounds; and (4) serving as a force to build group loyalty, cohesiveness, and positive morale in schools and colleges and in communities throughout the nation.

Beyond these values, sport obviously has immense appeal, both for participants and for the vastly large audience of fans who often attach themselves to their favorite teams, wearing their colors or uniforms, cheering them enthusiastically, traveling to spring practice or "away" games, and contributing as loyal alumni to the recruitment or support of star athletes. This fervor and degree of commitment to sport embeds itself in the fiber of our individual lives, communities, and society. Sport helps communities come together for a common cause whether it is supporting the local college football team or traveling to watch the high school girls soccer team play against their conference rivals in a neighboring town. Sport can often be a significant part of civic pride and a reason to come together in solidarity.

Sport as Big Business

Sport has become a large enterprise in the United States and across the world. Nations embrace major sporting events, cities and states embrace collegiate and professional sports teams, and communities mark their calendars by interscholastic sports contests. In higher education, sport management programs are appearing in business schools and the more traditional physical education and recreation programs.

We have discussed ticket sales, game attendance, the value of teams and players, and media contracts in terms of revenues but not the sale of sports-related brands, equipment, apparel, footwear, and related services and activities. Not surprisingly, Nike is the most valuable sport brand in the world and is valued at $36.8 billion, over twice the value of the next largest sports brand, ESPN. These two companies have the majority control of the sport brand. Retail companies like Dick's Sporting Goods, Bass Pro Shops, and the Sports Authority sell billions of dollars' worth of products each year to help companies such as Nike grow further.[57]

The global sports industry is estimated to be valued between $480 and $620 billion and is the second fastest growing industry. Here are a few examples of the economic impact that sport has in the United States:[58]

- $17 billion was spent in 2018 on sport sponsorships.
- Revenues for esports reached $1.1 billion in 2019.
- The sports analytics market was valued at $56 million in 2018.
- Media rights will reach $23.8 billion in revenue by 2022 and represent 30% of all sports revenues.
- Sport gambling is estimated to be valued at $40 billion.
- $75 billion was invested in sport startups in 2019.

Pressure to Compete

Sports for children too often have been influenced by adult pressures to win at all costs. As a result, youngsters often feel excessive pressure to compete and to win, and the experience is no longer fun for them. Studies show that many children about to enter their teen years quit organized sport at this point or shift to a much more relaxed, recreational approach to games.

Linked to such pressures, adults frequently encourage overaggressive and violent play, as well as tactics that ignore sportsmanship and condone rule breaking. In extreme cases, parents may verbally or physically abuse players, parents, or coaches of rival teams and even attack officials who have made decisions ruling against them.[59]

In the not too distant past, the influence of high-pressure sports occurred at the secondary school level as university coaches began to make contact with athletes and parents, inviting them to elite training camps that were financed by sport manufacturers. Now, in many cases parents and coaches are no longer the influencing factor in assisting young players to make decisions. High-pressure sport competition has moved down to the youngest ages, often with parents becoming the motivating force for involvement. Table 11-5 shows just a few of the many national championships for youths that are sponsored mostly by sports

The cost of attending sporting events in person sometimes makes attendance cost prohibitive for families.
© gary718/Shutterstock.

TABLE 11-5   Youth Sport National Championships

National Championship	Age Group	Gender	Sponsor
Future Champions Golf Callaway Junior World Golf Championship	6 years and under	boys/girls	Callaway Golf
Amateur Athletic Union Basketball National Championships	8 years and under	boys/girls	Amateur Athletic Union (AAU)
Junior Pee Wee Pop Warner Super Bowl	8–11 years with weight limits	boys	Pop Warner Football
Junior Pee Wee Cheer and Dance Championships	8–11 years	girls	Pop Warner Cheer and Dance
Amateur Athletic Union Junior Olympic Swimming Meet	8-18	boys/girls	Amateur Athletic Union
Little League Baseball World Series	9–12 years	boys/girls	Little League Baseball
Little League Softball World Series	9–12 years	girls	Little League Softball
Amateur Athletic Union Girls Junior National Volleyball Championships	12U-18U	Girls/boys	Amateur Athletic Union

Data from Lumpkin, A. (2009). Sports as a Selection of Society. University of Kansas. http://aahperd.confex.com/aahperd/2009/webprogram/.

organizations. Some individuals call this movement in sport the "professional model" or more specifically the "professionalization of youth sports." Gould reflected, "the adoption of a 'professional model' within sport organizations is the single biggest problem we face in contemporary youth sports. It is adversely affecting the motivation of young people, exposing them to risks of injury, destroying an appreciation of sport, and often turning them away from sport and a recognition of the benefits of lifelong physical activity at the very time we need to turn them on to it."[60]

CORRUPTION OF SPORT

Corruption and bribery are sometimes infused into sport. Even the Olympic Games, traditionally viewed idealistically as amateur sport at its best, were revealed in 1999 as having involved widespread bribery in the awarding of the 2000 Summer Olympics to Sydney, Australia, and the 2002 Winter Olympics to Salt Lake City.[61] The bribery continued into the awarding of the 2020 Tokyo Olympics bids when Haruyuki Takahashi used $8.2 million to provide gifts for International Olympics Committee members.

Beyond corruption at this level, the constant disclosure of prohibited performance-enhancing drugs and "blood doping" being used in international sport has helped to destroy public confidence in such events as the major cycling event, the Tour de France, and other competitions.[62] Most recently, the Russian Olympic team was banned from the 2020 Tokyo Olympics and the 2022 Beijing games for doping. The ban also excludes them from competition in most major international competition through 2023 including FIFA's World Cup, the Youth Olympic Games, Paralympics, world championships, and other major sporting events subject to the World Anti-Doping Code.[63]

College athletics are also not immune to scandal and NCAA infractions. For example, in 2017–18 the Federal Bureau of Investigation brought forth a corruption scandal in Division I men's basketball including Adidas and several major programs associated with the company including University of Arizona, Auburn, and University of Louisville, among others. Ten people including assistant coaches, a financial planner, and an Adidas executive were arrested on charges of bribery, money laundering, and wire fraud.[64] The first sanctions were handed out to Oklahoma State men's basketball team, which now has a 1-year ban from participating in the NCAA tournament, reduced scholarships, and fines for Lamont Evans, a former assistant coach who accepted $22,000 in bribes to direct players to a specific financial advisor.[65]

Other problems surrounding sport on all levels have involved physically dangerous and even life-threatening conditioning practices, concussions, playing with debilitating injuries and hazing in high school and college sport such as ice hockey or wrestling, which has included physical, emotional, and even sexual abuse.[66]

PREVALENCE OF INJURY

One of the most relevant issues in youth sport is the prevalence of concussions and other significant injuries. Concussions can lead to traumatic brain injury (TBI), hospitalization, and partial or permanent disability.[67] The issue of concussions was brought to the forefront when a number of professional sport athletes lives were negatively affected as a result of multiple concussions during their career. The awareness has resulted in changes in sport at all levels. The Centers for Disease Control and Prevention estimate 3.8 million sports- and recreation-related concussions each year as well as 1.7 million TBIs sustained in sport each year.[68] Most children do not receive medical attention for a TBI, although this is changing as awareness is raised among coaches and parents. Youth football has been the focal point for concussion news reports, but data suggest concussions are spread across the whole spectrum of youth sport. For example, soccer is the most common risk for females (50% chance of a concussion). Some studies report that 50% of high school athletes and 70% of college athletes failed to report a concussion.

In addition to the number of concussions, 40% of high school athletes who suffer concussions return to the field of play prematurely, thus putting themselves at greater risk for more severe injuries.[69]

Concussions are just one form of injury for players. Youth in particular are increasingly sustaining injuries typically experienced by adults, such as anterior cruciate ligament (ACL) and rotator cuff injuries caused by overuse. ACL injuries in children under age 18 have risen about 2.3% per year for 20 years, and girls are more likely than boys to sustain ACL injuries (52%).[70] Rotator cuff tears or pain are caused by repeated overhand throwing, using poor throwing technique, or insufficient rest for the shoulder. Little League baseball provides guidelines for the number of pitches per day by age and the amount of rest needed to minimize injuries in young athletes.

Careers in Sport

The career options in sport are vast. Many were discussed within the sections detailing sport structure at the developmental and recreational level, interscholastic sports, intercollegiate athletics, and professional sports. There are a few more careers that deserve further discussion. They can be loosely categorized into sport venues, event management, and facility operations; sport law; and sport marketing and sales. The positions in each area overlap with the other categories, and this is especially true for those in sport marketing and sales. Sport industry jobs can be found in facilities, with specific teams, and with sport organizations such as the Olympic Games.

Sport Venues, Event Management, and Facility Operations

Sport venues span from very traditional facilities such as Lucas Oil Stadium (Indianapolis Colts), the Enterprise Center (St. Louis Blues), and public and private golf courses. When not in use by the team, these facilities are often home to other events and activities. For example, the Enterprise Center regularly hosts NCAA hockey and basketball playoffs such as the Missouri Valley basketball tournament, concerts, trade shows, and more. In addition to these traditional venues, some sports require more specialized facilities such as Churchill Downs (horseracing), Indy 500 Motor Speedway, and the Lexus Velodrome in Detroit, Michigan.

Jobs in sport venues, event management, and facilities operations span a wide array of tasks based on the sport involved, the additional events held, the clientele/users, and the specificity of the facility. For example, the Chattanooga Lookouts Double A baseball team has positions in areas such as ticket operations, stadium operations, groundskeeping, sales, and food and beverage.[71] It is also typical to have staff who oversee event planning, security, parking and traffic, lighting and sound, marketing and public relations, and business managers who deal with contracts, budgeting, and human resources management.

Sport Law

Some choose to focus on the legal side of the sport industry by focusing their law career on it or serving as a sports agent. Those specializing in sport law will work with clients on such things as licensing their brands, protecting their likenesses from being inappropriately used (for example in advertising and video games); seeking restitution for sports injuries; negotiating player contracts for athletes, venues, sponsorships, and media rights; protecting trademarks slogans, and likenesses; and negotiating labor union contracts.

Sports agents often have a background in sport management or sports law. Agents deal with professional player contracts, handle athlete endorsements and appearances, provide guidance on establishing positive public relations, and manage the financial side of the athlete. Not only are agents expected to have a thorough understanding of the law, but they must also understand the sport to know the athlete's value to the team and the sport. Agents seek the best deal possible for their client and must negotiate contracts on a regular basis.

Agents are often paid based on a percentage of the contract earned by the athlete. Some leagues limit the amount the agent can make. For example, the NFL and NBA limit the agent to 3% of the athlete's playing contract. The agent can also expect to collect 3% to 10% of the athlete's endorsements as well.[72]

Sport Marketing and Sales

It is in sport marketing and sales that many young professionals begin their careers and move through the ranks to higher level positions. Sport marketing and sales professionals are responsible for promoting team events and athletes, selling products licensed by teams such as jerseys and hats, managing consumer behaviors, selling tickets, managing the media including social media and other digital platforms, acquiring corporate sponsors, and working on community relations, among others.

Sport marketing can be seen from two perspectives—marketing *of* sport and marketing *through* sport. Marketing of sport focuses on attracting and maintaining consumers of the sport product whether it is season ticket sales or creating team promotional events. Those nonsport companies such as a car dealership or a beer company promote their own product through sport by being a sponsor or using an athlete as a spokesperson. Both approaches have the same end goal in mind: to convince consumers to use their resources (e.g., time, money) to engage with their product.

Educational background for sport marketing professionals varies. Some positions require a business degree, sport management degree, or related field. The sport marketing and sales industry is quite competitive, and applicants may have an advantage if they already have a master's degree versus a bachelor's degree. Experience, even part time, can be beneficial depending on the job. Furthermore, sport marketing and sales professionals should plan to build their interpersonal skills, organizational skills, and technical skills. Interpersonal skills require the individual to be people oriented; be able to network with other professionals; and have solid negotiation, presentation, and public speaking skills. Organizational skills focus on strategic planning, staff supervision, and management skills. Finally, technical skills needed include excellent written communication, budgeting, and comprehension of target marketing.[73]

SUMMARY

In this chapter, the discussion of sport has progressed beyond its primacy as a leisure activity. Sport is viewed from the participant and spectator perspectives. It reviews the structure of recreational and developmental sport, interscholastic sport, intercollegiate athletics, and professional sport. Spectator involvement in sport continues to grow. The availability of expanded television coverage through cable and satellite networks; creation of league networks for MLB and the NFL; the growth of Internet content through the use of live streaming; and increased interest in international sporting events such as World Cup Soccer and the Summer and Winter Olympics, have resulted in the highest number of spectators in history.

Yet it sometimes remains difficult to measure the actual number of spectators, especially when including electronic media.

The maturation of professional sport leagues on an international scale, and especially in the United States, has resulted in the integration of business models in sport. In short, sport has become big business, and like any business enterprise, it is expected to return a profit for the owners and shareholders. The individual worth of a growing number of professional sport teams exceeds $1 billion, including international teams such as the Manchester United Football Club. Sport as big business will drive the future of professional and collegiate sports for the near future. Although little was discussed regarding the value and business aspects of collegiate sports, they too have entered an era when they must be partially or fully self-supporting.

Finally, this chapter discusses a few issues in sport and includes the discussion of sport as a source of moral values and civic pride, issues and concerns with youth sport participation and the pressure to compete, youth sports injuries, and corruption of sport. Infused throughout the chapter are other financial topics such as the cost of club sport participation, rising cost of media contracts, growth of the financial value of sport brands, and working in the sport industry.

Sport is a major influence in society. It is a topic of discussion at work, over the Internet, and among friends, and yet for all its engagement and involvement, only a moderate percentage of the population actually engages in sport participation or spectating.

QUESTIONS FOR CLASS DISCUSSION OR ESSAY EXAMINATION

1. Define what the word "sport" means to you. Include as part of the definition characteristics that you think a "sport" must have. List five different sports that meet your definition. List "sports" that don't fit your definition but may be seen as a sport to others. Explain why they are not sports to you.

_____

_____

_____

2. Compare and contrast sport and fitness.

_____

_____

_____

3. In a group, determine how many members of your group actually watch sporting events. Use the broadest possible definition of "watch" to include the news, ESPN, other sport channels, the newspaper, or mobile devices. Then ask how they most frequently watch sports—live attendance, on live television, live on a mobile device, record the event to watch later, or watch just the highlights on a television or mobile device. What is the most common way to watch a sporting event in your group? Is it consistent across other groups in the class?

_____

_____

_____

4. Identify your motivations for participating in sport or exercise. Ask, "Why do I participate? What do I expect to get from my participation? Is it important to me? Why (yes or no)? What prevents me most from participating in sport or fitness? Do I do it for myself or as part of a group?"

_____

_____

_____

5. Summarize the four levels of sport and how they are structured.

_____

_____

_____

6. Discuss the three broad areas of sport careers. Which one would you most want to work in? Why?

_____

_____

_____

ENDNOTES

1. Kraus, R. (1971). *Recreation and leisure in modern society* (p. 320). Appleton-Century-Crofts.

2. Global Association of International Sports Federations. Retrieved May 17, 2020, from https://worldlacrosse.sport/worldlacrosse/gaisf/.

3. Centers for Disease Control and Prevention. (2017, February 17). *National Health Interview Survey. Glossary.* Retrieved October 25, 2020, from https://www.cdc.gov/nchs/nhis/physical_activity/pa_glossary.htm#:~:text=Related%20Pages,done%20in%20one's%20leisure%20time.

4. Official Website of the Paralympic Movement. Retrieved October 25, 2020, from http://www.paralympic.org.

5. Move United. Retrieved October 25, 2020, from https://www.moveunitedsport.org.

6. All Star Activities. (n.d.). *Why should your child participate in sports.* Retrieved October 25, 2020, from http://www.allstaractivities.com/sports/sports-why-participate.htm.

7. Lefton, T. (2019, February 18). Team sports show growth trend in 2018. *Sports Business Journal.* Retrieved October 25, 2020, from https://www.sportsbusinessdaily.com/Journal/Issues/2019/02/18/Sports-and-Society/SFIA.aspx.

8. Ibid.

9. FIFA World Cup. Retrieved October 25, 2020, from https://www.Fifa.com.

10. McFetridge Sports Complex. Retrieved November 1, 2020, from http://mcfetridgesportscenter.com/tennis/tennis-programs/.

11. Little League. (n.d.). *Balancing expectations that are both age appropriate and realistic.* Retrieved November 1, 2020, from https://www.littleleague.org/university/articles/balancing-expectations-that-are-both-age-appropriate-and-realistic/.

12. Smith, J. (2017, August 1). Paying to play: How much do club sports cost? *USA Today High School Sports.* Retrieved November 1, 2020, from https://usatodayhss.com/2017/paying-to-play-how-much-do-club-sports-cost.

13. Forsyth, E. W., Martin, T. G., & Whisenant, W. A. (2018). Interscholastic athletics. In P. M. Pedersen & L. Thibault (Eds.), *Contemporary sport management* (6th ed., pp. 143–165). Human Kinetics.

14. National Federation of State High School Associations. (n.d.). *About us.* Retrieved November 1, 2020, from https://www.nfhs.org/who-we-are/aboutus.

15. National Federation of State High School Associations. (n.d.). *The case for high school activities.* Retrieved November 1, 2020, from https://www.nfhs.org/articles/the-case-for-high-school-activities/#chapter1.

16. National Collegiate Athletic Association. (n.d.). *What is the NCAA?* Retrieved November 8, 2020, from http://www.ncaa.org/about/resources/media-center/ncaa-101/what-ncaa.

17. Staurowsky, E.J., Abney, R., & Watanabe N. M. (2018). Intercollegiate athletics. In P. M. Pedersen & L. Thibault (Eds.), *Contemporary sport management* (6th ed., pp. 167–183). Human Kinetics.

18. Ibid.

19. National Association of Intercollegiate Athletics. (n.d.). *Why choose the NAIA?* Retrieved November 7, 2020, from https://www.naia.org/why-naia/index.

20. Staurowsky, Abney, & Watanabe (2018).

21. Perline, M. M., Stoldt, G. C., & Vermillion, M. C. (2012, January 3). The effects of conference realignment on national success and competitive balance: The case of Conference USA men's basketball. *The Sport Journal.* Retrieved November 8, 2020, from https://thesportjournal.org/article/the-effects-of-conference-realignment-on-national-success-and-competitive-balance-the-case-of-conference-usa-mens-basketball/.

22. Hobson, W. (2014, March 18). Fund and games. *Washington Post.* Retrieved November 8, 2020, from https://www.washingtonpost.com/graphics/sports/ncaa-money/.

23. Southard, D. (2018, March 28). How Loyola's Final Four run has financially benefited the Missouri Valley Conference. *The Des Moines Register.* Retrieved November 8, 2020, from https://www.desmoinesregister.com/story/sports/college/2018/03/28/loyola-chicago-final-four-run-benefited-missouri-valley-conference-drake-uni-basketball-mvc-hoops/466678002/.

24. Associated Press. (2017, April 7). Shocking move: Wichita State leaves Missouri Valley for American Athletic Conference. *Omaha World Herald.* Retrieved November 8, 2020, from https://omaha.com/sports/shocking-move-wichita-state-leaves-missouri-valley-for-american-athletic-conference/article_156072ff-07e5-5b00-b223-6420dfcea836.html.

25. Major League Baseball. (n.d.). *Teams by name.* Retrieved November 8, 2020, from https://www.milb.com/about/affiliations.

26. McDowell, J., Kim, A. C. H., & Brison, N. T. (2018). Professional sport. In P. M. Pedersen & L. Thibault (Eds.), *Contemporary sport management* (6th ed., pp. 185–203). Human Kinetics.

27. Ibid.

28. Women's National Basketball Association. (2020, April 21). WNBA delivers most-watched draft in 16 years. Retrieved November 8, 2020, from https://www.wnba.com/news/wnba-delivers-most-watched-draft-in-16-years/.

29. McDowell, Kim, & Brison (2018).

30. Ibid.

31. Negro Leagues Baseball Museum. (n.d.). *Negro Leagues history*. Retrieved November 8, 2020, from https://nlbm.com/negro-leagues-history/.

32. McDowell et al. (2018).

33. Cater, F. (2020, May 2). *Federal judge dismisses U.S. women's soccer team's equal pay claim*. NPR. Retrieved November 8, 2020, from https://www.npr.org/2020/05/02/849492863/federal-judge-dismisses-u-s-womens-soccer-team-s-equal-pay-claim.

34. Hays, G. (2020, May 1). Judge sides with U.S. Soccer in USWNT's equal pay lawsuit. ESPN. Retrieved November 8, 2020, from https://www.espn.com/espnw/sports/story/_/id/29125363/judge-sides-us-soccer-uswnt-equal-pay-lawsuit.

35. Ibid.

36. Underwood, R., Bond, E., & Baer, R. (2001). Building service brands via social identity: Lessons from the sports marketplace. *Journal of Marketing: Theory and Practice, 9*(1), 1–12.

37. Giulianotti, R. (2002). Supporters, followers, fans, and flaneurs: A taxonomy of spectator identities in football. *Journal of Sport and Social Issues, 26*(1), 25–46.

38. Ibid.

39. Ibid.

40. Bucholtz, A. (2018, September 10). *Nielsen coverage estimates for September see gains at ESPN networks, NBCSN, and NBA TV, drops at MLBN and NFLN*. Retrieved February 5, 2021, from https://awfulannouncing.com/espn/nielsen-coverage-estimates-september-espn-nbcsn-nbatv-mlbn-nfln.html.

41. Coster, H. (2020, February 3). *Super Bowl TV audience rises slightly to 99.9 million viewers*. Reuters. Retrieved November 3, 2021, from https://www.reuters.com/article/us-football-nfl-superbowl-ratings/super-bowl-tv-audience-rises-slightly-to-99-9-million-viewers-idUSKBN1ZX2LI.

42. Fédération Internationale de Football Association. (2018, December 21). *More than half the world watched record-breaking 2018 World Cup*. Retrieved November 3, 2020, from https://www.fifa.com/worldcup/news/more-than-half-the-world-watched-record-breaking-2018-world-cup.

43. Fischer, B. August 18, 2016. Global TV Viewers Of Opening Ceremony Flat From 2012, IOC Says. Retrieved March 21, 2021 from https://www.sportsbusinessjournal.com/Global/Issues/2016/08/18/On-The-Ground-In-Rio/Global-viewership.aspx.

44. Bonesteel, M. (2016, April 12). CBS and Turner Sports lock down NCAA tournament through 2032. *Washington Post*. Retrieved November 3, 2020, from https://www.washingtonpost.com/news/early-lead/wp/2016/04/12/cbs-and-turner-sports-lock-down-ncaa-tournament-through-2032/.

45. Brown, M. (2020, June 14). With TBS renewal, MLB could see $2 billion annually from national TV contracts. *Forbes*. Retrieved November 3, 2020, from https://www.forbes.com/sites/maury-brown/2020/06/14/with-tbs-renewal-mlb-could-see-2b-annually-from-national-tv-contracts.

46. Carp, S. (2020, January 8). *Report: SEC closing in on "US$300m-a-year" ESPN broadcast deal*. Retrieved November 3, 2020, from https://www.sportspromedia.com/news/sec-football-tv-rights-espn-abc-cbs.

47. Ozanian, M. K., & Badenhausen, K. (2020, September 10). The NFL's most valuable teams 2020: How much is your favorite team worth? *Forbes*. Retrieved November 3, 2020, from https://www.forbes.com/sites/mikeozanian/2020/09/10/the-nfls-most-valuable-teams-2020-how-much-is-your-favorite-team-worth.

48. Forbes. (2020). *The business of baseball*. Retrieved November 3, 2020, from https://www.forbes.com/mlb-valuations/list/#tab:overall.

49. Bengel, C. (2020, May 29). *Roger Federer tops Forbes' 2020 list of the world's 100 highest-paid athletes*. Retrieved November 3, 2020, from https://www.cbssports.com/general/news/roger-federer-tops-forbes-2020-list-of-the-worlds-100-highest-paid-athletes/.

50. Badenhausen, K. (2020, August 17). Highest paid female athletes 2020: 50 years after creation of women's tours, tennis dominates earnings list. *Forbes*. Retrieved November 13, 2020, from https://www.forbes.com/sites/kurtbadenhausen/2020/08/17/

the-highest-paid-female-athletes-2020-center-court-takes-center-stage/.

51. Hartweg, C. September 5, 2019. *Team Marketing Report.* (2020, September 1). 2019 Fan Cost Index. Retrieved March 21, 2021, from https://static.clubs.nfl.com/image/upload/v1568214703/bengals/matpgustvpitdmf8wakl.pdf.

52. Gough, C. (2020, October 5). *Average ticket price in the NFL by team 2019.* Retrieved November 3, 2020, from https://www.statista.com/statistics/193595/average-ticket-price-in-the-nfl-by-team/.

53. Gough, C. (2020, June 19). *Fan Cost Index of MLB teams 2019.* Retrieved November 3, 2020, from https://www.statista.com/statistics/202611/fan-cost-index-of-the-major-league-baseball/#statisticContainer.

54. Statista Research Department (2016, January 31). *Fan Cost Index of NBA teams 2015/16 season.* Retrieved November 3, 2020, from https://www.statista.com/statistics/202628/fan-cost-index-of-the-national-basketball-association/.

55. Shaikin, B. (2019, December). Good luck getting a family of four into a professional sport for $100—not in good seats, but any seats. *Los Angeles Times.* Retrieved November 2, 2020, from https://www.latimes.com/sports/story/2019-12-26/most-affordable-tickets-prices-dodgers-lakers-clippers-rams-chargers.

56. Perreault, O. (2020, January 9) *Professional sports are pricing out middle class fans.* TicketNews. Retrieved November 2, 2020, from https://www.ticketnews.com/2020/01/pro-sports-pricing-out-fans/.

57. Statista Research Department. (2020, September 1). *Sporting goods industry—Statistics & facts.* Retrieved November 13, 2020, from https://www.statista.com/topics/961/sporting-goods/.

58. Sports Industry Insights. Retrieved November 13, 2020, from https://medium.com/qara/sports-industry-report-3244bd253b8.

59. Kozlowski, J. (1999, November). Sport league held liable for brutal attack on coach. *Parks and Recreation,* 45–52.

60. Gould, D. The professionalization of youth sports: It's time to act! *Clinical Journal of Sport Medicine, 19*(2), 81–82.

61. Sullivan, R. (1999, January 25). How the Olympics were bought," *Time,* 38.

62. Lemonick, M. (1998, August 10). Le tour des drugs. *Time,* 76.

63. Maese, R. (2019, December 9). *Russia banned from 2020 Olympics and 2022 Beijing Games.* Retrieved November 7, 2020, from https://www.washingtonpost.com/sports/2019/12/09/russia-banned-tokyo-olympics/.

64. Lavigne, P., & Schlabach, M. (2020, January 31). *FBI informant to provide more info to NCAA investigators after sentencing.* Retrieved November 13, 2020, from https://www.espn.com/mens-college-basketball/story/_/id/28609696/fbi-informant-provide-more-info-ncaa-investigators-sentencing.

65. Witz, B., & Zagoria, A. (2020, June 5). Oklahoma State punished by N.C.A.A. for role in basketball recruiting scandal. *New York Times.* Retrieved November 13, 2020, from https://www.nytimes.com/2020/06/05/sports/ncaabasketball/oklahoma-state-ncaa-punishment.html.

66. ESPN. (n.d.). *Sports hazing incidents.* Retrieved November 7, 2020, from https://www.espn.com/otl/hazing/list.html.

67. Headcase. (n.d.). Sports concussion statistics. Retrieved November 7, 2020, from http://www.headcasecompany.com/concussion_info/stats_on_concussions_sports.

68. Ibid.

69. Ibid.

70. Jenco, M. (2017, February 22). Rate of pediatric ACL tears increasing 2.3% annually. *AAP News.* Retrieved November 13, 2020, from https://www.aappublications.org/news/2017/02/22/ACLTear022217.

71. Chattanooga Lookouts Baseball. Retrieved November 2, 2020, from https://www.milb.com/chattanooga/team/staff.

72. Gentile, M. (2018, June 28). The average sports agent's commission. *Houston Chronicle.* Retrieved October 28, 2020, from https://work.chron.com/average-sports-agents-commission-21083.html

73. Lahey, C., Lubenetski, J., & Smith, D. (2018). Sport management and marketing agencies. In P. M. Pedersen & L. Thibault (Eds.), *Contemporary sport management* (6th ed.). Human Kinetics.

Chapter 12
Future Perspectives

"If we are to cope effectively with the changing physical and social environment of the future, and to provide leadership in an age of unbelievably rapid change, we must do so with entirely new concepts and approaches to providing leisure literacy and recreational opportunity to America's masses. This, then, is the challenge of the future."[1]
-From the first edition of Kraus' Recreation and Leisure in Modern Society, published in 1971

LEARNING OBJECTIVES

1. Identify the skills and attitudes needed to be a leisure-services professional with an eye to the future.

2. Describe key societal trends and their impact on the leisure-services industry.

3. Explain key issues and opportunities for the leisure-services industry moving forward.

4. Reflect on leisure services in the postpandemic landscape.

5. Articulate your reasons for pursuing a career in the field of leisure services.

Introduction

Read this quotation, from a book written by Marshall McLuhan and Quentin Fiore discussing how the present age of rapid change is affecting our society:

> It is forcing us to reconsider and re-evaluate practically every thought, every action, and every institution formerly taken for granted. Everything is changing…and they're changing dramatically…innumerable confusions and a profound feeling of despair inevitably emerge in periods of great technological and cultural transitions. Our "Age of anxiety" is, in great part, the result of trying to do today's job with yesterday's tools—with yesterday's concepts.[2]

Do you think this description accurately captures the current state of rapid change in our society? Well, so did Hugh Davis when he used McLuhan and Fiore's 1967 quotation in his 1968 article for *Parks & Recreation* magazine titled, "Recreation Planning in the Technological Age"![3] Indeed, even the first edition of this text, published in 1971, stated that the "challenge of our future" was coping with an "age of unbelievably rapid change," as you see in quotation opening this chapter. In short, for the past 50 years, at least, all generations of professionals in the field of leisure services have felt that they were living and working in uniquely uncertain and fluctuating times. Our current age is no different. Perhaps, then, we should reframe our thinking to accept that the field of leisure services is situated in a dynamic society, meaning that being flexible and adaptable are key skills that leisure professionals will always need. Further, the most effective leisure-services professionals embrace the excitement of rapid change and always have an eye to the future—of our field and of our society.

The new century, now almost to its second quarter, is already experiencing new challenges, opportunities, and approaches to the leisure mosaic. Former traditional models of leisure are changing in many communities; traditional approaches to the provision of recreation services are changing; opportunities for leisure are more abundant than at any time in recorded history; governments and people are rethinking the role of parks, recreation, and leisure in the national fabric; and nonprofits are expanding services while commercial enterprises are engaging in new and creative leisure opportunities. The United States has experienced several cycles of economic growth and decline over the past half century, including, most recently, significant economic disruptions surrounding the events of the Great Recession in the early 2000s and the COVID-19 pandemic. Such economic fluctuations impact debates about what government can do, should do, and what citizens are willing to pay for. The relevant question of the 21st century is how do public parks, recreation, and leisure provide effective services and programs in an era of uncertainty? What is the appropriate role and responsibility of urban, suburban, and rural recreation agencies, as well as nonprofit and commercial organizations? This chapter discusses

Parks and recreation facilities are frequently debated in public hearings.
© Yurico/Shutterstock.

issues, opportunities, challenges, and changes in the American fabric that influence parks, recreation, and leisure.

How should the major priorities of organized recreation service in the United States be determined? In what ways can or should government provide more effective and efficient services? What are the key responsibilities of organized recreation toward people with physical and mental disabilities, toward those who are aging, or toward those who may have had inadequate opportunities in the past because of their gender, race, or ethnic background? How is the millennial generation changing our perception of, operation of, and access to parks and recreation?

How has technology affected the planning, delivery, operation, and marketing of parks and recreation—in the public, nonprofit, and commercial sectors? Social media, smartphones, tablets, and a whole host of technology supported by rapidly emerging apps have changed the way people look at, use, and embrace their world. Long-held assumptions about how information is shared and exchanged are no longer valid. How will leisure-services professionals respond and anticipate such changes in the years ahead?

And, of course, how will the COVID-19 pandemic, which still rages at the time of this writing, affect the leisure-services profession moving forward? How will changing social and economic conditions in the coming decades affect the public's leisure values and patterns of participation, and how can recreation, parks, and leisure-services professionals and organizations respond effectively to the challenges, and opportunities, of the future?

These are key questions we will explore in this chapter. Our aim is to help you think through how to be a flexible and adaptable professional, with an eye to the future of our field. Then, we will address the question we asked at the outset of this text, what is your "why" for wanting to pursue a career in the field of leisure services?

Becoming a Leisure-Services Professional with an Eye to the Future

Those who read this text—primarily college and university students in recreation, park, tourism, sport, and leisure-studies curricula—are looking ahead to careers in the future. What will the next quarter of the 21st century bring in terms of demographic, social, and economic changes that can have a radical impact our perceptions, expectations, and demand for our leisure? If we do aim to be flexible and adaptable professionals with an eye to the future, what does that look like? Let's discuss some of the things that will most help you achieve that mindset.

Maintaining Sight on Core Principles amid Change

Even as you strive to become a leisure-services professional with an eye to the future, it's essential to keep hold of some core principles that can guide our work through times of rapid change. For recreation, parks, and leisure-services practitioners, it is possible to identify a number of key principles that should be used to guide their professional operations today. First, it is assumed that such individuals—no matter what their fields of specialization—regard recreation and leisure as important to human growth and community development. A contemporary philosophy of organized leisure services therefore should deal with such important issues as the place of recreation and leisure in modern life, the role of government, the development of experience-based programming, and building relationships with partners to meet social needs.

Place of Recreation and Leisure in the Modern Community

In U.S. society, our view of recreation and leisure as social phenomena and areas of community involvement is influenced by our governmental systems. In our Constitution and in court decisions that have influenced government policy through the years, we have accepted the view that, on various levels, government has the responsibility for providing certain major services to citizens. These include functions related to safety and protection, education, health, and other services that contribute to maintaining the quality of life of all citizens.

Linked to this system of governmental responsibility is our general acceptance of the concepts of the worth and dignity of all human beings and the need to help each person become the most fully realized individual that they are capable of being. Through government and through many voluntary community associations, we have accepted the responsibility for providing needed services and opportunities for people at each stage of life and for those who have been underserved.

Needs of Individual Citizens

Recreation and leisure are important aspects of personal experience in modern life for the physical, social, emotional, intellectual, and spiritual benefits they provide. Positive leisure experiences enhance the quality of a person's life and help each person develop to the fullest potential. To make this possible, agencies across the leisure-services system should provide recreation resources, programs, and, where appropriate, leisure education to help people understand the value of free time when constructively and creatively used.

Government's Responsibility

In addition to providing personal benefits, vibrant recreation and leisure systems in a community help a community to meet health needs, gain economic benefits, and maintain community morale. On each level (local, state, and federal), appropriate government agencies should therefore be assigned the responsibility for maintaining a network of physical resources for leisure participation, including parks, playgrounds, centers, sport facilities, and other special recreation facilities. Government should be responsible for planning, organizing, and carrying out programs, under proper leadership, for all age levels.

Government cannot and should not seek to meet all of the leisure needs of the community. It must recognize that other types of community organizations—including voluntary, private, commercial, therapeutic, industrial, and educational groups—sponsor effective recreation programs, which are often designed to meet specialized needs or more advanced interests. Therefore, its unique role should be to provide a basic, and socially just, floor of recreational opportunity, to fill the gaps that are not covered by other organizations, and to provide coordination and overall direction to community leisure-services programs.

There has been a growing body of opinion that local government recreation and park agencies should take less responsibility for the direct provision of program activities, particularly when limited by fiscal constraints, and should move instead into the role of serving as an advocate for recreation and leisure in community life and providing coordinating or facilitating assistance to other agencies. There is an ongoing debate regarding how much service can be provided, who should be the director or primary provider, who should pay and who should not pay, and at what level services should be provided.

Influence of the Nonprofit Sector

The nonprofit sector has accepted an increasingly significant role in the provision of recreation and leisure-based social services. An important part of the effort has focused on youth-serving agencies in historically underserved neighborhoods. There are several reasons why nonprofits have taken an increasing role. First, this is not a new model for nonprofits to assume but rather a continuation and expansion of services when members of the community realize that the government cannot provide needed services. Second, more individuals are willing to give to nonprofits, are able to give substantial sums of money, and are willing to give to their community. Nonprofits are frequently seen as more desirable and effective organizations to address social ills than is government. Finally, government has recognized its inability to meet all of the needs of a community and either encourages nonprofits and/or works jointly with them.

INFLUENCE OF THE COMMERCIAL SECTOR

The commercial sector serves a unique and increasing role in the provision of recreation and leisure opportunities. Its engagement is infrequently focused on a particular social group or those who are economically disadvantaged; instead it looks at the broad sector of recreation opportunities for the masses. The services can be broad, such as resorts, theme parks, cruise lines, and the like, or very narrow, such as river tours, backcountry excursions, flights over and into wilderness areas, and specialized recreation services such as bike shops, tours, and races; shooting ranges and hunting ranches; and mountain climbing manufacturers, schools, and expeditions. Online delivery of rec-

reation experiences is expanding, as evidenced by the rapid growth of virtual technology. The breadth of involvement by the commercial sector is staggering. Commercial enterprises are often seen as innovative, able to react to trends, and appropriate providers for certain mass and specialized recreation services.

Embracing a Mindset of Innovation

Two decades into the 21st century there remains much discussion about the role of parks and recreation in our society. Whatever discussions were held in the early part of this century, the recession earlier in the century and the uncertain economic landscape beyond the COVID-19 pandemic have changed the ability and willingness of government to deliver parks, recreation, and leisure services, programs, and facilities. Nonprofits and commercial enterprises are equally challenged by these economic realities.

The "business as usual" model that dominated the latter part of the 20th century and the early part of this century has been challenged in ways not anticipated. The impact on the public parks and recreation sector's ability to provide services and facilities is the most significant in 50 years. Local and state governments and park and

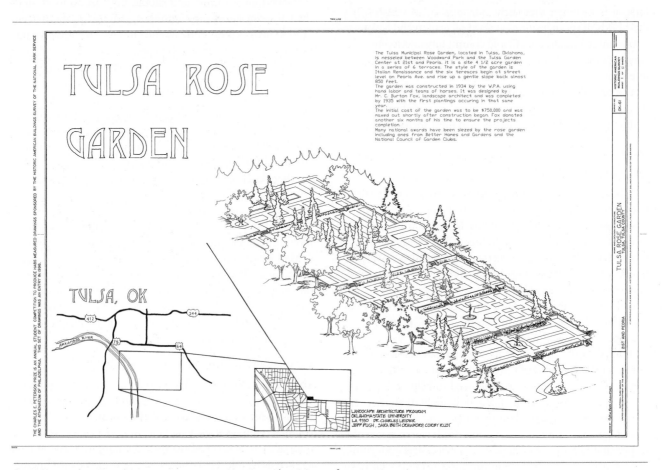

Designing park settings incorporates past experiences and anticipates future expectations.
Courtesy of the Library of Congress, Prints and Photographs Division.

recreation agencies have adapted to new organizational models and mandates. As a result, they are changing the vision of their role in their communities.

Traditional forms of leisure are growing but at a slower rate than the population. New diverse forms of leisure, often individual or Internet based, are growing outside of traditional program areas. Academic programs and curricula based on a 20th-century model no longer prepare students and professionals for the challenges of this century. Recognition of a social responsibility ethic grounded in community engagement structured in the context of a "do-more-with-less" government reality is what students and professionals are already dealing with. Leisure-services professionals must endure challenges to our social fabric, mores, and openness as a society. The awareness of environmental and social justice in society and how public parks and recreation will address these issues are paramount to the profession's future.

Many contemporary authorities in the leisure-services field emphasize that bringing about needed changes will require a new wave of entrepreneurship. Recreation and park professionals in all spheres of service need to think more imaginatively and innovatively and be content experts in leisure, politically astute in government, and able to build coalitions across disparate groups. They need to cultivate an organizational and professional climate that is interactive, community focused, and politically and socially responsible.

Developing Abilities to Identity Potentially Meaningful Trends

There has been no single national effort by parks and recreation organizations to address the 21st century's impact on parks and recreation; individual organizations have focused on trends that affect themselves. The broader societal impact has been left for others to deal with. The U.S. Forest Service operates an outdoor recreation trends center; states generate 5-year comprehensive outdoor recreation plans that are of varying quality with some to significant trend analysis. Many municipalities have master plans for development and have strategic plans. In both instances, trend analysis may be a small or significant part of the plan. Some state parks and recreation associations, especially California's, make efforts to keep their members abreast of trends. The problem facing trend analysis in leisure services is the diversity of the profession itself. Some trends cross boundaries between urban recreation, outdoor recreation, city parks and recreation departments, state park systems, national parks, and nonprofits, but there are many other trends that do not. National trends paint a broad picture, whereas regional and local trends may be significantly different. Making assumptions that trends will occur as predicted is equally dangerous. In 2004, the economy looked as if it would continue to be positive. In October 2007, the economy collapsed around the housing market and had a worldwide ripple effect on global investment banks and international, national, and local economies. Unemployment reached levels not seen since the depression of the 1930s. By 2016 the economy had recovered from the recession, but the damage inflicted on public and nonprofit agencies was still present and has altered how people see the roles of government and nonprofits. And then came 2020, with the COVID-19 pandemic and its sweeping impacts on worldwide economies and our profession.

How then do leisure services organizations focus on trends that have some basis of validity? There are those who are considered futurists and have a track record of success. Trends, at their best, are educated guesses about the future. They are influenced by those who are suggesting them—their knowledge, biases, and creative ability to anticipate change.

Though we look to trend analysis experts to help us understand what the future might hold, leisure-services professionals can employ a variety of strategies that allow them to identify potentially meaningful trends that could lead to new opportunities and challenges in their work. Here are some ways that leisure-services professionals with an eye to the future can ensure they stay on top of the meaningful trends that may affect their work:

- Be a news consumer. Subscribe to daily news summary apps, such as the Skimm, to easily keep up with what's going on in the world.
- Regularly read press releases from sources such as the U.S. Census Bureau and the Pew Research Center to stay up to date with trends in our country's population demographics and national opinions.
- Attend professional conferences both within your specific area of interest and in related fields to hear what professionals are talking about.
- Leverage the power of social media, particularly Twitter, to follow the commentary of professional organizations or thought leaders in your field.
- Subscribe to publications related to your specific field and related fields (email newsletters, professional magazines, etc.).
- Maintain an active professional network and check in frequently about what other professionals are hearing and experiencing.
- Develop your skills of keen observation and observe everything around you.

If leisure-services professionals regularly engage in these practices, they will start to see patterns and themes emerge in what seems to be on people's minds and what's happening in our society. In doing so, they will be able to identify and leverage relevant trends in a proactive, rather than reactive, manner.

Meaningful Societal Trends Affecting Leisure Services

Leisure-services professionals who have an eye to the future will identify a whole host of trends. For example, here's a list of potentially meaningful trends for leisure-services professionals to consider as they enter the second quarter of the 21st century:

- Parks and recreation professionals must embrace rapid societal change as the norm and learn to anticipate needed service provision.
- Demographic complexity, as demonstrated by shifting social issues of gender identity, lifestyle, and life stage, require parks and recreation agencies to rethink for whom, what, and how they offer programs.
- The trend toward greater public participation in decision making is a reality, and public agencies must be on the cutting edge of the movement.
- Obesity is increasingly a major societal health crisis. Partnering in community-based efforts is critical to overcoming the obesity crisis, as is focusing on the broader issue of individual and community wellness.
- Public agencies are receiving smaller shares of available public dollars for operations, maintenance, and repairs.
- Public agency success depends on an organization's ability to build relationships and establish networks and coalitions with other community-based organizations.
- Federal leadership in the recreation and parks movement will become more narrowly focused, as the challenges of an aging society, globalization, international commitments, tax revolts, and other unforeseen mandates reduce the ability to support the broad range of traditional services.
- Park and recreation agencies need to enhance their technological competence to introduce new generations to the outdoors, fitness, community engagement, and expanded leisure opportunities.
- An understanding of current users, nonusers, potential users, and their motivation is the foundation for anticipating change and meeting the needs of the current and future generations.
- Public agencies must provide environmental leadership at the local level.
- Embracing the role of a community change agent through engagement on issues focusing on quality of life, community visioning, creation of public places and spaces, and building whole and healthy communities in partnership with community, regional, and national organizations.
- Public park and recreation agencies are increasingly moving beyond the quality of life role and becoming partners in community economic development, often providing impetus for regional and multistate sport, recreation, and cultural events.
- There is a mandate to embrace tourism, the world's largest economy, on a local, regional, and national level in new and creative ways. Public agencies can be the catalyst for community and regional tourism development.

Clearly, a single professional or agency cannot hope to address every trend they identify nor should they. Part of being a flexible and adaptable professional is to know how to focus on the trends that are most relevant to their work and will have the most positive impact on their ability to serve their clients or participants. Four current societal trends that have been and will, for the foreseeable future, require leisure-services professionals to continue to innovate and evolve the way we do our work are demographic shifts, environmental realities, technology advances, and changing ideas about time.

Demographic Shifts and Population Diversity

Demographic shifts and population diversity are two of the major issues today. Public agencies, accustomed to serving single or fixed cultural groups, have discovered that the demographic dynamic is rapidly changing. Immigration and migration (movement within the United States) is changing the makeup, population size, and diversity of communities. We are part of an aging society, the concept of the traditional family is no longer useful, and children and teens face increasing challenges. Understanding these trends and their impacts are part of the leisure profession's responsibilities. Examples of some key population shifts, both geographic and generational, include the following:

- More than 59% of all Americans live in the South and West, and that number is growing.
- Hispanic people are projected to make up 24% of the population by 2065.[4]
- Millennials, young adults born after 1980, have become the largest generation, surpassing baby boomers. They are the generation to watch.
- The United States has moved from a rural to a metropolitan nation, with four of five Americans now living in metropolitan areas (84%).
- Millennials are making key personal choices regarding resource and energy consumption and family size, taking into consideration ecological and environmental impacts and sustainability.[5]

Shifts are cultural, geographic, demographic, and environmental. The shifts have important impacts on the delivery of parks, recreation, and leisure services. In the early stages of migration from the urban core to the suburbs, loss of free time was measured in commuting time. It was assumed most commuting was done from the suburbs to the urban core. More recently, the commute has stretched both ways, with increasing numbers of people choosing to live in the urban core and work in the suburbs. Beyond the urban core, the exurbs have become the new growth area, outpacing growth within cities. Land in this area has been developed twice as fast as in the urban and suburban cores. In addition, in 2011 urban areas occupied over 2.5 times as many acres in the United States than they did in 1959.[6]

Immigrant residents represented 14.7% of the population in 1910, 5.4% in 1960, and 12.9% in 2010. In 1960, the largest percentage of the immigrant population came from Europe. In 2010, it was Latin America, followed by Asia.[7] The immigrant population held relatively steady at 8%–12% of the total population from 1860 to 2000, but between 2000 and 2050 it is projected that the major growth in population will come from immigrants. The United States is the third most populous nation in the world behind China and India. The steady growth in population and diversity has increasing impacts on recreation demand, participation, and types of programs.

THE GENERATIONS

America is a land of generations. In recent years, the terms *baby boomer*, *Gen X*, *Millennials*, and *Generation Z* have garnered much public press. Only more recently has the term *generations* taken on a marketing connotation. Some authors have adjusted the names to fit marketing terminology. In Table 12-1, you will see four of these generations and how their percentage of total United State population has shifted over time.

It is important to note that the scientific validity of the concept of generations as distinct, identifiable categories has recently and increasingly come under criticism, with scholars suggesting that other models, such as the social constructionist perspective or the life development perspective, may be more valid and useful to discuss. We use the concept of generations here as one way to discuss temporal changes over time in the United States. An exploration of genera-

tions is a way to think about American history and how culture, war, poverty, technology, social movements, education, and other influences affect individuals within generations, their attitudes, expectations, and leisure participation. A similar perspective of generations can be applied to the history, challenges, influences, and actions within parks, recreation, and leisure.

ETHNIC AND RACIAL DIVERSITY

As previously shared, the United States is becoming more diverse. The immigration of Europeans has lessened dramatically, replaced by the immigration of people who identify as Latinx, as well as those who immigrate from Asian, Middle Eastern, and African countries. The 2010 U.S. Census showed a growing diversity. The Hispanic population is the largest minority in the United States. Between 2000 and 2010 the Hispanic population grew 43%, from 35.5 million to 50.5 million. The total estimated U.S. population is depicted in Table 12-2.

Research into the influence of race and ethnicity has received greater attention over the last decade. Most important, it has shown that race and ethnicity are a factor in levels of recreation participation, types of activities engaged in, and comfort levels with the natural environment. Some early research set the stage for a better understanding of why there are differences. For example, a study by Virden and Walker reports that White people found a forest environment more pleasing and safer than did people who identify as African American or Hispanic.[8] Hibbler and Shinew identified four factors that explain the differences in leisure patterns. The four reasons are (1) the limited socioeconomic resources of many African American people; (2) a historical pattern of oppression and racial discrimination toward African American people; (3) distinct cultural differences between African American and European American people; and (4) feelings of discomfort and constraint by African American people in public leisure settings.[9]

There is a growing realization that integration of immigrants in our society is a complex issue. They are more

TABLE 12-1   Generations of Americans

Generation	Birth Years in 2016	Percentage of Total Adult Population		
		2015	2036	2050
Millennials	Born 1977–1995	30.9%	43.0%	57.7%
Gen X	Born 1965–1976	27.0%	31.8%	36.5%
Baby Boomers	Born 1946–1964	30.7%	23.9%	5.8%
Silent Generation	Born 1937–1945	11.5%	1.3%	0.0%

Data from Fry, R. (2016). *Millennials overtake Baby Boomers as America's largest generation.* Pew Research Center. http://www.pewresearch.org/fact-tank/2016/04/25/millennials-overtake-baby-boomers/.

THE MILLENNIAL GENERATION

The Pew Research Center (pewresearch.org) has actively tracked the generations for years. The Millennial generation has just supplanted the baby boomer generation as the largest generation. Coming in a period of rapid technological and social change, this generation is facing opportunities and challenges and is redefining America in their own image. Pew conducted a study of Millennials and arrived at six conclusions:

- Millennials have fewer attachments to traditional political and religious institutions, but they connect to personalized networks of friends, colleagues, and affinity groups through social and digital media.
- Millennials are more burdened by financial hardships than previous generations, but they're optimistic about the future. Millennials are the first in the modern era to have higher levels of student loan debt, poverty, and unemployment and lower levels of wealth and personal income than their two immediate predecessor generations had at the same age. Yet, they are extremely confident about their financial future.
- Singlehood sets Millennials apart from other generations. Just 26% of Millennials are married. When they were at the age that Millennials are now, 36% of Gen Xers, 48% of Baby Boomers, and 65% of the members of the Silent Generation were married.
- Millennials are a racially diverse generation. Some 43% of Millennial adults identify with a race other than White.
- Millennials are less trusting of others than older Americans are. In a survey, only 19% say that most people can be trusted.
- Few Millennials believe that Social Security will provide them with full benefits when they are ready to retire, but most oppose cutting current benefits as a way to fix the system.

Drake, B. (2014, March 7). *6 new findings about Millennials*. Pew Research Center. Retrieved February 8, 2021, from http://www.pewresearch.org/fact-tank/2014/03/07/6-new-findings-about-millennials/.

TABLE 12-2 2019 Race and Ethnicity of the United States Population

Race/Ethnicity	% Total Population
White alone	76.3%
Black or African American alone	13.4%
Asian alone	5.9%
American Indiana and Alaska Native alone	1.3%
Native Hawaiian or other Pacific Islander alone	0.2%
Two or more races	2.8%
Hispanic or Latino of any race	18.5%
Total	**100.0%**

Data from U.S. Census Bureau. (2019). *QuickFacts*. https://www.census.gov/quickfacts/fact/table/US/RHI125219.

New immigrants bring with them their own culture and customs.
Courtesy of Martha Reed.

space for land; wildlife; passive-, individual-, or family-based recreation; and conservation. People who identify as Hispanic and Asian tend to come to outdoor areas in larger family groups for social purposes. African American, White, and Hispanic people all shared similar views toward social-setting attributes such as sharing experiences, being by oneself, and so forth. Research has made progress in explaining differences in race and ethnic decisions and preferences for leisure, but the field still needs further development.[10,11]

AGE DIVERSITY

Generations are represented by age diversity. The baby boomer generation, as a percentage of the total population, is staggering in its size and impact. In addition, the population

ethnically diverse, may have complex intergenerational changes, and are growing rapidly in number. Beyond immigrant and generational issues, different ethnic groups view leisure at once similarly and differently. People who identify as African American prefer shopping, going to church, and open spaces that serve active recreation-related functions. People who identify as White show a greater preference for open distribution has changed dramatically over the last 50 years with its influence on society and government already significant. Births are declining and immigration and births among first- and second-generation Latinx people are higher than the national average for all other ethnic groups.

In 1967, the median age in the United States was 29.5 years. In 2015, the median age increased to 37.8 years. America is an aging society and it suggests that we are moving from an economy where there are more workers than retirees to a society where there are insufficient workers to maintain retirees. At the same time, the patterns of baby boomers in terms of retirement have been fluctuating. In 2018, baby boomers ages 65 to 72 were staying in the labor force in record rates compared to previous generations at the same age.[12] Then, between 2019 and 2020, the annual increase in the number of retired baby boomers doubled from the year before, partially because of the effects of the COVID-19 pandemic on the work force.[13]

AGING SOCIETY

The United States has an aging society. For the first time in history, Americans are reaping the benefits of advances in science, technology, healthcare, nutrition, and affluence. The life expectancy of Americans has nearly doubled in the past century; in 1900, the life expectancy was 47 years, and by 2000, it had risen to 77. Individuals living into their late 80s and mid-90s is no longer uncommon. This population represents the most financially independent aging group in history. The 55-plus age group controls more than 75% of the country's wealth.

Between 2012 and 2050, the growth of an older population will expand dramatically. By 2050, the 65 and older population is expected to grow to 83.7 million, almost double the 2012 population.[14] It is suggested that 20% of the workforce could focus on providing services to and caring for the aging population. In some states, particularly in the Midwest and Northeast, healthcare is already the largest industry.

Yet, can we expect the boomers, as they enter retirement, to do the same as earlier older adults? The answer is no. They will make their own mark on society and do it their way, which is a continuation of their lifelong contributions to

change society. The early assumption was that boomers would go into full retirement as so many other generations have. Changes in the economy, retirement benefits, concerns about Social Security and Medicare, healthcare costs, longevity, and overall health have changed perceptions about retirement. In a 2015 Census Bureau report, 20% of the population over age 65 worked at least 1 to 14 hours a week, with 57.6% of the 65- to 69-year-old male population working an average of 35 or more hours a week, whereas 36% of women of the same age range worked. Overall, 36% of the 65- to 69-year-old population worked, whereas only 12.4% of the 70 or older population were employed.[15]

The end of mandatory retirement in 1986 allowed many older adults to continue to work and contribute to the workforce. Simultaneous with the end of mandatory

More and more adults are celebrating the "new old," which is a new generation of seniors who are aging on their own terms.
© digitalskillet/Shutterstock.

 POVERTY AND OLDER AMERICANS

Seniors are not only not exempt from poverty but sometimes are more susceptible to poverty. In general, minoritized groups experience higher levels of poverty, and the same pattern holds true when looking only at the older adult population. In a 2016 report from multiple federal agencies (*Older Americans: Key Indicators of Well-Being*), the prevalence of poverty among those 65 and over has lowered since a 1966 report showed that 29% of older Americans lived at or below the poverty level. This was the highest rate among any population in the United States. By 2014 that number had dropped to 10%, but minoritized populations continued to lag. Minoritized groups were more likely to live at or below the poverty level. Among Asian men, 13% were at this level, and 16% of Asian women. Older Latinx men and women were at 16%, older Black men were at 17%, and older Black women were at 21%.

Data from Federal Interagency Forum on Aging-Related Statistics. (2016). *Older Americans: Key indicators of well-being.* Federal Interagency Forum on Aging-Related Statistics. Retrieved February 4, 2021, from https://agingstats.gov/docs/LatestReport/Older-Americans-2016-Key-Indicators-of-WellBeing.pdf.

CASE STUDY: Serious Leisure Contributes to Successful Aging

Serious leisure is a concept first proposed by sociologist Robert Stebbins in 1982, who contended that "serious leisure is the systematic pursuit of an amateur, hobbyist, or volunteer core activity that people find so substantial, interesting and fulfilling that . . . they launch themselves on a (leisure) career centered on acquiring and expressing a combination of its special skills, knowledge, and experience".[a] In the context of Maslow's hierarchy of needs, serious leisure fulfills multiple need and growth roles for individuals, ranging from belonging to creativity. Stebbins sees serious leisure as a substitution for work for those who may have left the workforce, whether voluntarily or involuntarily, yet he says serious leisure is not a livelihood and one should not get caught up in seeing serious leisure as a substitute for work. Serious leisure carries with it "numerous pleasant expectations and memories, doing so to a degree only rarely found in work."[b]

As part of his description of serious leisure, Stebbins identified six qualities, or descriptors, that are present. In some ways, they are similar to life challenges and do not always represent positive emotions, but they do represent challenges individuals must face in the pursuit of serious leisure. There are linkages to Maslow's hierarchy of human needs at the creativity level as well as Csikszentmihalyi's flow theory. The six qualities are as follows:

Serious leisure activities help older adults maintain successful aging.
© Photodisc/Getty Images.

- The occasional need to persevere to overcome difficulties
- The presence of a career that involves achievement, occurring through stages of development and involvement
- A significant personal effort focusing on unique acquired knowledge, skill, or training
- Eight durable benefits including social interaction and belongingness, self-expression, self-enrichment, enhancement of self-image, feelings of accomplishment, lasting physical products, self actualization, and renewal
- A strong identity formed among participants in their chosen pursuits
- A unique ethos formed related to the activity resulting in a special social world[c]

Today's aging population, as reported elsewhere in this text, no longer conforms to the concept of a slow downward spiral or the notion that involvement, physical activity, and learning are not part of acceptable retirement activities. Rather, as the baby boomer population ages, this group is challenging all of the notions of what is appropriate for an aging population. Involvement, engagement, physical activity, and extended work or work-related activities are becoming the norm. Linked with predictors of successful aging, serious leisure is showing promise as a way to enrich successful aging. Rowe and Kahn identified three factors crucial to successful aging: "low probability of disease and disease-related disability, high cognitive and physical functional capacity, and active engagement with life."[d]

Brown and colleagues studied older adults involved in a dance program and identified six themes related to the qualities of serious leisure.[e] They found *perseverance* among the participants as they learned how to dance. The perseverance was manifested among the participants in attitude and behaviors as they attempted to master basic and advanced dancing steps. Second, the notion of a *leisure career* included achievement or involvement among the participants. For those so engaged, "the concept of a leisure career reflects the successful aging components of learning, involvement, and keeping active."[f] The third quality and theme involved *considerable personal effort* to acquire specific knowledge of the leisure activity. The characteristic of a *unique ethos* reflects directly upon the development of a new and specialized social world, resulting in a strong social network, both of which are recognized components of successful aging. The *benefits of involvement* in serious leisure as they relate to this study involved self-actualization, self-enrichment, self-expression, feelings of accomplishment, enhancement of self-image, regeneration of self, self-gratification, lasting physical products, and social interaction and belongingness. The benefits of involvement may have the most long-lasting impact on the participants and successful aging. *Identity formulation*, another quality, comes from the other five characteristics and the researchers found the participants formed a strong identity with their pursuits. More important, it suggests the power of serious leisure as a contributor to successful aging.

Questions to Consider

- After reading the description of the features of serious leisure, would you classify any of the activities you do as serious leisure? If so, how does that activity meet the characteristics of serious leisure?
- Think about the activities of the older adults in your life. Would you classify any of the activities they do as serious leisure? If so, how does that activity meet the characteristics of serious leisure? Conduct an interview with that person to determine how that activity has benefited them.
- Explain why serious leisure is important to successful aging. Do you see any potential downsides of serious leisure for older adults?

[a] Stebbins, R. (2007). *Serious leisure* (p. 5). Transaction Publishers.
[b] Stebbins, R. (2001). Serious leisure. *Society, 38*(4), 55.
[c] Stebbins (2007). *Serious leisure* (p. 5). Transaction Publishers.
[d] Rowe, J. W., & Kahn, R. L. (1997). Successful aging. *The Gerontologist, 37*(4), 433.
[e] Brown, C. A., McGuire, F. A., & Voelkl, J. (2008). The link between successful aging and serious leisure. *International Journal of Aging and Human Development, 66*(1), 82.
[f] Ibid.

retirement, the Social Security system retirement ages were raised to 66 and 67. Between 1990 and 2010, there was a 20.8% increase in the number of men working between ages 62 and 64, a traditional retirement period. Overall, the workforce of men and women ages 60 to 64 grew from 52.8 million to 58 million. Baby boomers do not see retirement as a period of relaxation and reduced lifestyle but rather a continuation of challenges and personal growth—but on their own terms. The decision to retire is based more on the ability to do what they want and having the resources to do it than it is on the need to retire in a more traditional sense.

The aging of Americans has significant implications for recreation participation and delivery. Demands for recreation and leisure will increase, but not necessarily for traditional services. Many baby boomers will be better able to pay for services and activities and will be more demanding of creative and nontraditional services. Leisure-services professionals will be challenged to determine how to serve baby boomers. The new aging population cannot be considered older adults in the traditional sense. The days of senior centers, bingo, cards, Friday afternoon movies, and bus tours will not be over but will fail to attract the large number of older adults who see themselves as independent. They are already more active, have a more mobile lifestyle, are healthier, have a longer life expectancy, and use technology as a compensation for particular deficiencies, and will do so even more in the future. They are as diverse as any group in society and are changing the way recreation is considered

for an aging population. Cities are establishing separate senior service departments or integrating them into existing government organizations. There will be a need to continue to provide traditional services to those older adults who desire them, but many will seek new experiences and greater challenges. This group uses their financial resources to remain involved; to engage in travel, sport, and active leisure; and to continue their involvement in family and society.

Recent research holds promise for improving recreation programming for baby boomers and other older adults. Some research suggests that older adults will focus on more meaningful relationships at the expense of less important relationships. Fitness programs are growing and being adapted to the needs of older adults' health, mobility, and strength levels. Healthy older adults may benefit from activities that focus on goal selection and optimization. Older adults with more limited health should benefit from adapted and facilitated activities.[16] Regardless of the approach taken, public parks and recreation agencies need to understand that older adults are more diverse and have higher expectations than any previous generation.

THE CHANGING FAMILY

Over the last 30 years, family structure and definition have changed more than in the previous 200 years. The United States has seen increasing visibility and acknowledgment of the wide variety of family structures in our society.

World War II changed the United States as a society. Women had experienced an influx into the workforce; soldiers coming home from the war had the GI Bill and gained more education than any generation before them. The 1960s and 1970s saw a change in societal mores, values, and perceptions. For decades, the traditional nuclear family was defined and promoted as having a stay-at-home mother, a single-income source, three or more children, family dinners, church on Sunday, and marriage as a lifetime commitment. In 1960, this picture of the traditional nuclear family comprised only 45% of American households. The 2000 U.S. Census reported for the first time that less than one-quarter (23.5%) of American households consisted of a married man and woman and one or more of their children.[17] The percentage remained unchanged in the 2010 census.

Today's families are characterized in a variety of ways. It may be as a traditional nuclear, an adoption with no marriage, single mom, two dads, two moms, single dad, no children, multigenerational, or other endless combinations.

Children growing up in single-parent homes frequently have fewer opportunities and financial resources than do children growing up in two-parent homes, even if both parents are in the workforce. The Annie E. Casey Foundation reported in 2020 that 23.9 million children are in single-parent families and that the disparity of opportunities, based on ethnicity and race, is dramatic.[18] Figure 12-1 depicts the differentiation of single-parent families by race and ethnicity. The presence of high levels of single-parent homes among minoritized groups mirrors poverty rates and suggests the importance of providing recreation programs, after-school programs, and other social support services to these children.

Today, less than 25% of American households are composed of a single wage earner, meaning 75% of households are dependent on two or more wage earners. This places greater stresses on families, parents, and children. The notion of the mother as the primary caregiver has changed. Fathers are becoming more involved in the lives of their children—from changing diapers to taking time off for sick children. The roles of fathers are in transition as larger numbers of men are indicating a desire to be more nurturing with their children. Mothers traditionally assumed the extra burden of the home, work, and child rearing and now are more frequently sharing these duties with others.

The challenge for recreation and family service agencies is to determine how to serve the new permeable family. Traditional after-school programs may no longer work when parents expect to pick up children later in the day. Many agencies have gone to extended after-school programs, frequently partnering with schools to mix education, tutoring, and recreation.

Child Well-Being

Between 1950 and 2008, Americans experienced the most sustained economic growth of any time in history. For the most part, U.S. children are growing up in relative luxury compared to their grandparents, who grew up in relative luxury compared to their grandparents.

The youth population (ages 0–19) has been declining as a percentage of the total population for several decades: 28.56% in 2000 and 26.9% in 2010. In 1960, near the end of the baby boomer generation, youth represented 38.49% of the population. The Pew Research Center projects that this trend will continue through at least 2060.[19] Youth population since 2000 is not declining as a total number but only as a percentage of the total U.S. population.

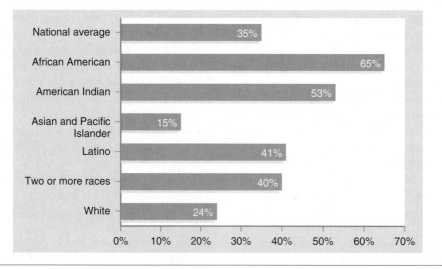

FIGURE 12-1 Percentage of children in single-parent families by race and origin

Data from The Annie E. Casey Foundation. (2020). *2020 KIDS COUNT data book* (p. 8). https://www.aecf.org/m/resourcedoc/aecf-2020kidscountdatabook-2020.pdf

The shift to an urban society continued to increase, with more than 80% of children living in urban areas, including the suburbs and exurbs. Generations of contact and grounding with a rural environment have been replaced by city parks, community recreation centers, YMCAs, YWCAs, Boy Scouts, Girl Scouts, Camp Fire USA, and other organizations. In many cases, these organizations changed their orientation from a rural to an urban perspective. Today's camps are less likely to be overnights away from home than they are to be day camps in parks or on nonprofit-owned properties, usually in or near the neighborhood where the children live. State park organizations nationwide have reported decreases in the number of children participating in outdoor recreation–based activities and attending parks and recreation areas in rural areas.

Yet there are also greater challenges facing today's youth than at any time in modern history. Numerous groups are investigating children and the issues they face. Three such organizations at the forefront are:

Social service organizations offer support to homeless families.
© Vladislav Gajic/Shutterstock.

- Forum on Child and Family Statistics (www.childstats.gov), a federal interagency forum focusing on collecting, analyzing, and reporting data on issues related to children and families.
- Child Trends (www.childtrends.org), a nonprofit organization focusing on trends affecting children and providing research, a databank of trends and indicators, and best practices.
- Kids Count (www.kidscount.org), a major initiative of the Annie E. Casey Foundation that tracks the status of children on a state-by-state basis. It measures the educational, social, economic, and physical well-being of children and reports results in a variety of research publications. It also has funded projects in many states.

A major area of concern of public and private agencies is youth well-being. Child well-being has been variously described as those conditions affecting children in the United States. The Forum on Child and Family Statistics uses 41 national indicators of child well-being under seven domains: Family and Social Environment, Economic Circumstances, Health Care, Physical Environment and Safety, Behavior, Education, and Health.[20] The Annie E. Casey Foundation sponsors the Kids Count report on the well-being of America's youth, which is updated every other year. It measures items such as children's access to healthcare, environmental conditions, economic growth of families, education, safety and risky behaviors, and family and community factors.[21]

Poverty is the most pervasive and abusive condition affecting children in the United States. UNICEF, in The State of the World's Children 2016 report, said:

"Trapped in a cycle of disadvantage, children from the poorest households…are effectively pre-selected for heightened risks of disease, hunger, illiteracy and poverty based on factors entirely outside their control."[22]

Almost 12 million youth under the age of 18 in the United States, or 17% of all youth, were living in poverty in 2019.[23] The economic recession had a significant impact on

NATIONAL CHILD AND YOUTH WELL-BEING INDEX

The National Child and Youth Well-Being Index (CWI) is an important resource and has provided information on the well-being of children and youth since 1975. The index is composed of 28 key indicators focusing on family economic well-being, safe/risky behavior, social relationships, emotional/spiritual well-being, community engagement, educational attainment, and health. The 2014 report looks at 2013 and compares it with previous years. Concerns remain about family income. It has not returned to the 2000 pre-recession level. Safe/risky behavior has improved, with a decline in teenage births per thousand; violent crime victimizations for ages 12 to 19 years went down; and children were found to be more connected to their communities. The number of children in single-parent homes has not decreased, but grown larger. Obesity has shown a slight decline in children since the mid-1980s. Overall, child and youth well-being is marginally up. It rose rapidly from 1993 to 2003 and then stabilized, fluctuating after 2003 through 2013.

Data from Duke Center for Child and Family Policy. (2014). *Child and Youth Well Being Index (CWI) report*. Retrieved February 4, 2021, from http://childandfamilypolicy.duke.edu/wp-content/uploads/2014/12/Child-Well-Being-Report.pdf.

families as unemployment grew to more than 10% nationally and more than 13% in some regions, suggesting that the number of children living in extreme poverty (half the poverty level) would climb to between 4.5 and 6.3 million. This was up from 2.5 million in 2008. Children in poverty remain a significant national concern.

Leisure is a commodity in the lives of children that is essential and developmental. Leisure professionals have addressed concern for child well-being. Government and nonprofit agencies are working together to serve historically underserved youth by providing interventions, services, and opportunities. The challenges are significant and public agencies are attempting to balance needs while simultaneously serving more affluent populations of taxpayers who demand services and are willing to pay for them. Urban parks and recreation agencies are expanding their partnerships with social service nonprofits and government organizations to meet the needs of historically underserved youth and families. This includes joint programming, provision of facilities, redirecting individuals to social service agencies, expanding existing services, and developing innovative interventions targeting specific populations.

TEENS AND TWEENERS: MOVERS OF CHANGE

Any discussion of children is incomplete without a discussion of teens and tweeners. The Harris Poll regularly tracks trends among teens and has become an important source for information about this age group. Many other organizations watch trends in teens for various reasons, including market forces, college directions, family issues, social stresses, and so forth.

Any study of teens must also include tweens, the age group from 8 to 12 years of age. Tweens are between being children and teens and the 5-year time frame represents a period of dramatic physical, emotional, and social growth. For example, take a look at Table 12-3 to see how these two age groups differ in opinions on certain behaviors. These groups are different and create sometimes challenging dynamics in family lifestyles.

Teens' interaction patterns change between 12 and 18 years. They begin to rely more heavily on their peers, are trend conscious, and react to peer pressure. The Harris Poll and Pew Internet Initiative found teens to be major users of the Internet; teens have become the innovators in social networking. Social networking sites have become increasingly important communication sources for teens. They are putting more and more of their lives online for others to see, comment on, and to expand their network of relationships. The Pew Internet and American Life Project tracks teen activities online. Table 12-4 reports teen usage of different social media apps.

Social networking and cell phone use are up for teens.
© Syda Productions/Shutterstock.

TABLE 12-3	Differences in Tweens and Teens' Attitudes and Values	
Statement	**Percentage of 11–12 year olds agreeing with the statement (Tweens)**	**Percentage of 16–17 year olds agreeing with the statement (Teens)**
It is OK to smoke if a person finds it enjoyable.	11%	26%
Sex before marriage is OK if a couple loves each other.	25%	58%
Abortion is all right, if having a baby will change your life plans.	18%	31%
Friendship would not change if they discovered that a friend was gay or lesbian.	33%	55%

Modified from The Harris Poll. (2010). *Big changes in tweens' and teens' attitudes and values over two decades* . https://theharrispoll.com/wp-content/uploads/2017/12/Harris-Interactive-Poll-Research-Social-Tweens-Attitude-2010-02.pdf.

TABLE 12-4 U.S. Teen (13–17) Reported Use of Social Media Applications

Rank	Social Media Platform	Percentage Using
1	YouTube	85%
2	Instagram	72%
3	Snapchat	69%
4	Facebook	51%
5	Twitter	32%
6	Tumblr	9%
7	Reddit	7%
8	None of the above	3%

Note: Figures add to more than 100% because respondents were able to select more than one response.
Data from Anderson, M., & Jiang, J. (2018, May 31). *Teens, social media, and technology 2018*. Pew Research Center. Retrieved February 4, 2021, from https://www.pewresearch.org/internet/2018/05/31/teens-social-media-tetechnology-2018/.

access to a smartphone, from which they can access such social media platforms.[24] U.S. tweens spent close to 5 hours per day and teens spent over 7 hours per day on screen media in 2019, and those figures do not include time spent on screens for school work.[25] Smartphones provide opportunities for talking, texting, emailing, and, more important, teens see them as a primary tool for staying connected to their friends. Teens themselves have a variety of views about the impact of screen use on them. For example, a Pew Research study indicated that 31% of teens thought social media had a mostly positive impact, 24% indicated a mostly negative impact, and 45% said it had neither a positive or negative impact. Those who reported positive impacts said the main reasons were because social media allowed them to connect with friends and family, to easily find news and information, and to meet others with the same interests. Those reporting negative impacts indicated the main reasons were because social media resulted in bullying and rumor spreading, harmed relationships and in person contact, and provided an unrealistic view of others' lives.[26] Clearly, tweens' and teens' access to technology and social media is a prime consideration for this age group.

Engaging tweens and teens in parks and recreation is challenging, at best, and daunting if they are not involved in the planning. Too many organizations continue to provide traditional activities for youth, and although beneficial, this fails to draw and provide the services needed. These youth now see the cell phone as an entertainment device, not just a communication device. They expect to be able to communicate with their current friends, make new friends, and engage in social groups, all online. Organizations that capture the desire for community engagement and strengthen opportunities for social inclusion will find greater involvement by youth and simultaneously meet some of their needs.

The Environment

Americans struggle to think beyond their borders. As a group, they, for the most part, fail to see a global picture as it relates to the environment. Americans are not alone in this narrow view of the world, yet they seem to epitomize a lack of concern for the environment. Whether it be a loss of open space, the continued purchasing of gas-guzzling vehicles, or a supersized approach to living and buying, our indifference is, rightly so, considered by some of the world community as selfish and inexcusable.

Outdoor recreation activities such as camping, biking, backpacking, boating, hunting, fishing, skiing, and mountain climbing depend heavily on parks, forests, and water areas operated chiefly by public recreation and park agencies. The concern of many people regarding the health of the nation's outdoor resources stems from more than the need for outdoor recreation spaces. A recent poll conducted by the National Recreation and Park Association found that more than four in five of the Americans surveyed thought that local governments should set aside land simply to preserve the natural landscape. As May and Ozbenian reflected on the poll result, they said:

> So why do Americans value undeveloped land? People value wild natural areas with limited evidence of humans because they provide a source of inspiration, wonder and escape from busy urban environments. Undeveloped green space also plays an important role in maintaining physical and mental health. These areas can serve as "living classrooms" and provide important educational opportunities and as "living laboratories" for scientists to study areas with minimal human alteration. The Wilderness Act also acknowledges the importance of protecting undeveloped areas for their scenic or historical value.[27]

For such reasons, the environmental movement receives strong support from many recreation advocates and organizations. At the same time, it is recognized that such activities as fishing and hunting are part of a bigger scene requiring clean—and safe—air and water and wise use of the land.

Growing national concern about the need to protect the environment was buttressed by the 1962 report of the Outdoor Recreation Resources Review Commission. During the following 2 decades, there was a wave of federal and state legislative action and funding support in the United States that was designed to acquire open space; to protect imperiled forests, wetlands, and scenic areas; to help endangered species flourish; and to reclaim the nation's wild rivers and trails. This movement was threatened during the early 1980s, when a new administration sought to reduce park and open space funding, eliminate conservation programs and environmental regulations, and subject the outdoors to renewed economic exploitation. In the mid-1990s, and again under the second Bush administration in the early- and mid-2000s, the effort to open protected wilderness areas to increased oil drilling, cattle grazing, lumbering, and other commercial uses gained strong political support. The recent administration of President Trump has further complicated America's progress toward environmental commitment and action.

Organizations such as the nonpartisan League of Conservation Voters, National Audubon Society, National Wildlife Federation, Wilderness Society, Sierra Club, and Nature Conservancy have been in the forefront of the continuing battle to protect the nation's natural resources. Numerous outdoor recreation organizations have joined with such groups, and the struggle will clearly continue to be an important political issue in the years ahead.

As the world celebrated Earth Day 2010, 40 years after the first Earth Day in 1970, it was clear that North American air was cleaner and its water purer than it had been for many past decades. Earth Day has gained an international following as demonstrated by the 40th anniversary efforts that included a goal of a "Billion Acts of Green": One million students abroad participated in community green activities, an effort to plant 1 million trees in 16 countries was initiated, 400 elected officials in 40 countries held dialogues with community members about the creation of sustainable green economies, 22,000 worldwide partners, and much more. In 2016, Earth Day was celebrated with 50,000 partners in 196 countries, engaging 1 billion people.

In the United States there was more protected open space in national parks and wildlife areas, yet there is still

cause for concern. Many Americans continue to purchase large, inefficient vehicles, but smaller, more efficient vehicles are a growing segment of the auto industry. Government agencies at a variety of levels are increasingly embracing the presence of global climate change and have joined the international community in efforts to reduce impacts on the environment. At the same time, Americans' environmental ethic continues to evolve. Attendance at state and national parks fluctuates, children's exposure to the natural envrionment is inconsistent, and technology is making our relationship with nature more complex. America's connection with the outdoors and the environment is clearly in a time of significant flux. In response, organizations, individuals, researchers, and governments are finding ways to make people aware of the importance of the outdoors in their lives. Governments and schools are creating campaigns and educational requirements introducing and encouraging families and youth to return to the natural environment.

ENVIRONMENT AND POPULATION

The United States represents less than 5% of the world's population and consumes almost 17% of the world's energy. If the global population had consumption patterns similar to the average American, it would take five Earths to support the human population.[28]

Population growth at current levels has the potential to negate efforts to reduce impact on the climate. Even as federal, state, and local governments move forward with plans to reduce greenhouse emissions, the continued rapid growth of population in high-density population centers and centers of ecological vulnerability may offset gains in addressing climate change. Figure 12-2 compares

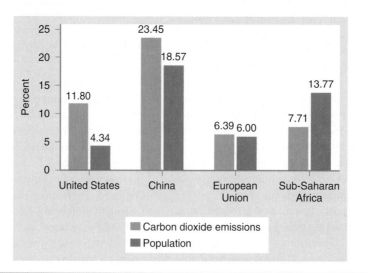

FIGURE 12-2 2016 CO$_2$ emissions and populations for select regions
Data from Climate Watch and The World Bank.

the proportion of worldwide CO_2 Emissions for the United States, China, the European Union, and Sub-Saharan Africa compared to each region's proportion of the worldwide population. As you can see, the United States has the largest disparity between its CO_2 emissions and its population. Further, Americans produce 4.5 pounds of garbage per day, compared to 2.98 pounds in the United Kingdom.[29]

The Brookings Institute labeled our nation as a "metro nation," emphasizing that our country is made up of major metropolitan areas that "encompass large cities, old and new suburbs, and even exurban and rural areas that, by virtue of their interwoven labor and housing markets, share common economic destinies" (p. 8).[30] The 192 largest metro areas in the United States contain 77% of the country's population and 85% of its gross domestic product (GDP).[31] The McDonalds influence on U.S. culture to supersize everything has moved from french fries to houses, shopping centers, recreation centers, and land and resource consumption. The impact on recreation is not lost. Demand for recreation facilities, park areas, and access to these is growing in metropolitan and adjacent areas. Congestion in this country's premiere natural resources has been well documented by the National Park Service, and similar patterns are occurring at the state and community levels.

CLIMATE CHANGE

Humans have affected the environment as never before. The 1997 Kyoto Protocol (named after an international conference convened in Kyoto, Japan) is often credited as the most significant environmentally based international agreement of the 20th century. The essence of the agreement was for developed nations to reduce their greenhouse gases (CO_2 emissions) to 5% below their 1990 levels and for less developed countries to be allowed to make a lesser contribution to reductions. In 2015, the Paris Agreement effectively replaced the Kyoto Protocol, committing parties to limit warming to below 2° C, compared to preindustrial temperature, and to strive for 1.5° C if possible.[32] Though the United States was among the almost 200 nations that signed the agreement under the Obama administration, it formally withdrew from the agreement under the Trump administration, the only nation to do so.

Individual countries have moved forward with developing and implementing initiatives to counteract these climate trends. New Zealand, for example, now generates two thirds of its energy from renewable resources. Korea is building a smart grid power system to assist regions in becoming self-sufficient with renewable energy. Saudi Arabia is home to the world's largest thermal power plant and Germany is the largest solar energy producer in the world. Also, in the wake of the U.S. withdrawal from the Paris Agreement, individual U.S. cities and states have renewed their commitment to combating climate change.

There remain many individuals who do not believe that humans are the primary influencer of climate change, but the body of evidence continues to grow and individuals and

CLIMATE CHANGE BY THE NUMBERS

Here are some facts and projections to illustrate the current realities of climate change:

- Global temperatures are projected to reach 1.5 degrees Celsius above preindustrial levels between 2030 and 2052.[33] Such a rise would bring significant impacts such as increased frequency and intensity of storms, droughts, floods, heat waves, and more.[34]
  - Increasing global temperatures are projected to have a negative impact on annual catch for marine fisheries worldwide.[35]
  - Populations most at risk for experiencing disproportionately adverse effects of climate changes are the populations that are already some of the most vulnerable, such as minoritized groups, indigenous peoples, island developing nations, and developing countries.[33]
  - Global warming increases the frequency of heat-related and ozone-related deaths.[35]
- In the last 800,000 years, the highest concentration of carbon dioxide in the atmosphere was 300 parts per million. In 2019, the average was 409.9 parts per million. The last time the rate was so high was more than 3 million years ago.[36]
- Between 2005 and 2017, 41 U.S. states actually increased their GDP while reducing their CO_2 emissions. Investment in clean energy generates more jobs than fossil fuels.[34]
- The warmest 20 years on record have occurred in the last 22 years.[35]

350.ORG – COMMUNITY-LED MOVEMENT TO COMBAT CLIMATE CHANGE

350.org is "an international movement of ordinary people working to end the age of fossil fuels and build a world of community-led renewable energy for all." Founded in 2008 in the United States by a group of university friends, it went global in 2011. They named their organization 350 to represent the level of concentration of carbon dioxide in the atmosphere considered safe (350 parts per million). The current level is over 400 ppm. The organization operates under five values: (1) We are bold, creative, and strategic; (2) We work for justice; (3) We care for and trust one another; (4) We are stronger when we collaborate; (5) We are transparent and accountable. The organization sees climates change as not just an environmental issue, but also as asocial justice and economic issue, because "…the people suffering the most [from climate change] are the ones who have done the least to cause the problem." These core values focus the organization on their three-step approach to reach their mission:

1. Accelerate the transition to a new, just clean energy economy by support community-led energy solutions.
2. Stop and ban all oil, coal and gas projects from being built through local resolutions and community resistance.
3. Cut off the social license and financing for fossil fuel companies — divest, desponsor, and defund.

This three-step approach focuses on community-level, local action to create cumulative, lasting change.

At the 2015 Paris Climate Change Conference, 350.org was instrumental in organizing a major demonstration the weekend before the conference began that included thousands of youth from across the world. They self-reported 785,000 people taking to the streets in 175 countries and 2,300 events. In September 2019, the organization helped mobilize over 7.6 million people taking place in over 6,000 events worldwide in the largest ever Global Climate Strike.

Reproduced from 350.org. (n.d.). *Website statement.* https://www.nyxt.nyc/350org/.

organizations are beginning to recognize the importance of responding to and providing leadership on climate change. Nonprofits have taken the lead on making Americans aware of the potential damage of climate change. Some nonprofits, such as the Environmental Defense Fund, Greenpeace, and the Nature Conservancy, have long histories in the environmental movement. Others, including the Center for Climate and Energy Solutions, Pew Center on Global Climate Change, and the Alliance for Climate Protection, U.S. Climate Action Network, The Climate Reality Project, 350. org, Friends of the Earth, and the Coalition for Environmentally Responsible Economies (Ceres) are less well known, but all are playing key roles in changing attitudes about climate change.

The federal government has created a Global Change Research Program (www.globalchange.gov) composed of 13 departments and agencies. The agency existed under another name from 2002 through 2008 and reports directly to the president. Its function is to coordinate and integrate federal research on changes in the global environment with potential implications for society. The agency produces regular reports, including *2009 Global Climate Change Impacts in the United States*, identifying anticipated national and global impacts. In 2014 the *National Climate Assessment Report* was released. The report reaffirms the primary influence of human activity on global climate change and the already visible impacts, such as Hurricane Sandy in late 2012, rising sea levels, and melting of glaciers and arctic sea ice. The perceived impacts are not just on temperatures, but more broadly on environmental patterns, agricultural capability, human health, water supplies, transportation, and energy, to identify some of the more significant issues.[37]

Climate change, if continued unabated, will have profound impacts on our country's prized natural treasures: our National Parks. These impacts may be felt most in the National Parks in the west, as Saunders and Easley explain here:

> Many scientists think the American West will experience the effects of climate change sooner and more intensely than most other regions. The West is warming faster than the East, and that warming is already profoundly affecting the scarce snow and water of the West. In the arid and semiarid West, the changes that have already occurred and the greater changes projected for the future would fundamentally disrupt ecosystems. The region's national parks, representing the best examples of the West's spectacular resources, are among the places where the changes in the natural environment will be most evident. As a result, a disrupted climate is the single greatest threat to ever face western national parks.[38]

WHERE PEOPLE LIVE: URBAN, SUBURB, EXURB

History has recorded the decline of rural populations, the growth of cities, industrialization, postindustrialization, the growth of suburbs and exurbs, the decline of the inner city, and

Development consumes almost 2000 acres of agricultural land daily.
© Jack Cronkhite/Shutterstock.

Climate change affects our daily lives, including rush hour traffic in crowded areas.
© Rorem/Dreamstime.com.

A METROPOLITAN REVOLUTION

Metropolitan areas are traditionally defined by size, as prescribed by the U.S. Census Bureau. This designation has served well but hardly begins to address what a metropolitan area is. Nationally and internationally, metropolitan areas are growing at a steady pace. One source suggested that, internationally, 1 million people move to a metropolitan space every 5 days! The Brookings Institute suggests, "A city's true measure goes beyond human-made structures and lies deeper than daily routine." They are "defined by the quality of the ideas they generate, the innovations they spur, and the opportunities they create for people."[41] Urban recreation, park, cultural, and sport organizations have great opportunities to provide services in a metropolitan region. There is frequently a wealth of opportunities, but they are not always equally distributed among the population. Public and nonprofit organizations are the primary source of support for minoritized populations in metropolitan areas. In recent years, these organizations have partnered with corporations and other social service organizations to bring opportunities to historically underserved areas.

Katz, B., & Bradley, J. (2013). *The metropolitan revolution: How cities and metros are fixing our broken politics and fragile economy.* Brookings Institution Press.

the simultaneous revitalization of cities and urban areas. In the 1950s, people began to commute into the city. In the 21st century, commuting has become a norm for millions of people, but urbanites are as likely to commute to the suburbs to work as suburbanites are to commute to cities' business centers. In 2019, the average travel time to work was 27 minutes.[39] In 2018, the average American commuter spent 225 hours a year commuting to and from work. That's the equivalent of over 9 days![40]

Beyond the suburbs are the exurbs, difficult to define, but an easy area to describe. They exist beyond the suburbs in traditionally rural areas, which are now dotted with individual homes on acreage or subdivisions and may include cities of 50,000 or more people. They are adjacent to large metropolitan areas and their distinctive feature is the residents' choice of place over people, where the primary commonality is the need to commute to work. The exurbs are growing population areas because individuals are more

willing to increase travel time for a perceived improved quality of life.

OPEN SPACE LOSS AND THE ENVIRONMENT

The environment is coming under increasingly difficult challenges, both as a part of national policy and among Americans as a whole. In Iowa, the state government gives new homeowners 5 years of tax relief if they purchase a new home on previously open space or farmland. Between 2001 and 2016, almost 11 million acres of agricultural land was either developed or compromised.[42] Americans experienced an average daily loss of almost 2,000 acres of farmland during that time period. Land converted for development occurs at twice the rate of population growth. We have become a nation of sprawl represented by low-density development in the suburbs and exurbs. The exurbs are growing at a rate almost three times that of urban areas.

FFA ADAPTS TO RURAL POPULATION DECLINE

The National FFA organization, originally the Future Farmers of America, traditionally represented rural farming America. As families moved to urban areas and farms became larger and corporate, membership began to decline and FFA recognized the need to rethink who their membership base was. FFA realized that its future lay in attracting not only traditional rural youth but also urban youth. They looked at the larger agricultural marketplace and began to adapt. The traditional farm-related programs were expanded to include business, marketing, science, communications, education, horticulture, production, natural resources, and other related fields. Today, FFA has almost 650,000 members in all 50 states plus U.S. Puerto Rico and U.S. Virgin Islands. As it grew into urban areas, it also began attracting a more ethnically diverse membership base. FFA is an example of a youth-based organization who has done some work meet new demographic realities.

Belz, A. (2019). FFA FFA failing to connect with farming needs of the future, says alum working at U. Retrieved from https://www.startribune.com/ffa-failing-to-connect-with-farming-needs-of-the-future-ag-teacher-says/510459102/; National FFA Organization. (2021). https://www.ffa.org/

Youth prefer computers to the outdoors. Parents are afraid to send their children outdoors because they too have lost their outdoor ethic. As a society, Americans have almost fully transitioned from a generation raised on or near farms to a generation raised in an urban environment. Like a zoo or museum, the outdoors is a place to visit and see but not to partake of. Scares such as polluted beaches, Lyme disease, wasting disease in elk, and others have encouraged parents already unfamiliar with the outdoors to keep their children home. Attendance at national parks, national forests, state parks, and other rural recreation and preservation areas has been fluctuating at a time when the population is increasing. This has been reflected in Congress as it has become more difficult to secure funds for parks and recreation lands. For example, the Arctic National Wildlife Refuge is continuously under attack by politicians and oil interests in an effort to open the area to increased oil production.

Many national associations focusing on the environment are encouraging individuals to express concern and demand action. Often this action is local and even bounded by the property owned. The National Wildlife Federation encourages individuals to certify their backyards for wildlife. The Audubon Society encourages individuals to take the healthy yard pledge by reducing pesticides, conserving water, planting native species, protecting water quality, and supporting birds and other wildlife. Many of the same organizations that are promoting local environmental awareness and action are also active at the national and international levels.

IMPACT OF NATURE ON PEOPLE'S LIVES: ISSUES OF WELLNESS, WELL-BEING, AND HUMAN DEVELOPMENT

The environmental concerns discussed earlier go beyond issues associated only with the environment. It has become personal for many who have recognized that the absence of involvement with nature negatively affects human growth and development, especially among youth. Numerous researchers have begun to link environmental and ecological issues to health and well-being outcomes for individuals and society as a whole.

Richard Louv, with the publication of *No Child Left in the Woods: Saving Our Children from Nature-Deficit Disorder*, became the spokesperson for a growing movement to reconnect children with nature. The term *nature-deficit disorder*, referred to as human environment interaction in the research literature, captured the imagination and has become a rallying cry to address the issues of children, and adults, who are becoming more separated from nature with every generation. Daily contact with nature has become the exception rather than the norm. There are a number of reasons for the decline in contact with nature, including the loss of natural areas in and near urban areas, the absence of parks close to where people live, the overscheduling of children, safety concerns, more homework, and fear of stranger-danger.[43]

The correlation of the absence of nature in our lives with the developmental growth of children has raised a concern among public health officials, child development specialists, urban environmentalists, and parks and recreation practitioners. The National Parks Service has recently updated its Healthy Parks Healthy People strategic plan, which emphasizes the idea that parks are important to our nation's health. In the plan, they state, "Despite research that shows the health benefits derived from spending time in nature, Americans spend an average of 93% of time indoors each day and only 21% of adults get the recommended 2½ hours of physical activity per week" (p. 1). Some of the promising practices to promote health in parks that they outline in the plan are park prescriptions, park-based fitness challenges, community gardens, nature play zones, and more.[44]

Nearby nature refers to the presence or absence of nature in close proximity to an individual. Parks and natural areas in urban environments are seen as important contributors to the opportunity of individuals, and especially youth, to experience nature. The backyard, neighborhood, and areas where individuals, work, play, and go to school are also important. Research is beginning to show that the presence of nearby nature has an impact on individual wellness and well-being. The ideal situation is for individuals to have regular contact with natural areas, but, in the absence of those opportunities, nearby nature in urban environments can have positive mediating effects on individuals.

CHILDHOOD EXPERIENCES WITH NATURE AND ITS INFLUENCE ON ADULT BEHAVIOR AND ATTITUDES

There are indicators that adults who had positive childhood experiences with wild nature have a more positive attitude about the environment than those who had experiences with domesticated nature. Wild nature involves being in an outdoor setting where hiking, camping, hunting, and related activities can occur and these are usually away from urban areas. Domestic nature is more reflective of nearby nature in that it is at or close to home and may involve flowers, planting trees, shrubs, a garden, or caring for indoor plants. The frequency of involvement in such activities is also important. A single camping experience has little long-term impact, whereas repeat camping experiences influence future environmental attitudes and visits.[45] However, although it would be expected that frequent visits to wild nature as a child would carry over to adult behaviors, that is not necessarily the case. However, lack of visits to wild nature as children is a predictor that as adults they are less likely to visit wild nature. The research suggests that adults who continue to visit wild nature do so for opportunities for physical activity and emotional and spiritual renewal.[46]

Kellert's work regarding nature and childhood development is groundbreaking. His identification of direct, indirect, and vicarious experiences with nature frame much of the research currently conducted. Where the previous paragraphs discussed wild nature and domestic nature, Kellert frames the same descriptions as direct, indirect, and vicarious contact with nature. Table 12-5 describes each of the types of contact with nature with examples. Similarly to other research, he found that direct contact has the most

significant impact on individuals, regardless of age; indirect contact has a lesser impact but is still positive; and vicarious contact has an influence but one considerably less than direct or indirect contact.[47]

The importance of childhood experiences with nature is increasingly evident and cannot be ignored. As others have suggested, the absence of experiences with nature, at any level, causes potential health, wellness, and well-being issues for children and adults, but especially for children. In 2008, politicians reacted to the need to provide children with nature experiences when the U.S. House of Representatives Education and Labor Committee voted in June to send the *No Child Left Inside Act* (HR 3036) to the House floor for a full vote. The legislation was unsuccessful, but the message was clear.

Children need to experience the outdoors, not be protected from it.
© Van Truan/Fotolia.com.

TABLE 12-5	Types of Contact with Nature	
Type of Contact	**Description**	**Examples**
Direct	Interaction with large self-sustaining features and processes in the natural environment	Relatively unmanaged areas such as forests, creeks, sometimes a backyard or park
Indirect	Involves actual contact with nature occurring in highly controlled environments dependent on ongoing human management and intervention	Highly structured, organized and planned occurring in zoos, botanical gardens, nature centers, museums, parks
Vicarious	Symbolic experiences of nature not involving contact with actual living organisms or environments, but rather with the image, representation, or metaphorical expression of nature	A teddy bear, various cartoon and book characters, Mickey Mouse, Lassie, films focusing on nature, television programs such as on the Discovery Channel

Data from Kellert, S. R. (2007). *Building for life: Designing and understanding the human–nature connection.* Island Press.

CLIMATE CHANGE AND RECREATION: CONSEQUENCES AND COSTS

Americans who like to play outdoors may soon find that climate change–induced warming trends around the nation will put some of their favorite recreational retreats in jeopardy—from trout streams to waterfowl preserves, from ski areas to mountain biking trails, and from beaches to forested parkland. "Climate impacts on natural resources are pervasive," write Daniel Morris and Margaret Walls in a background paper titled, *Climate Change and Outdoor Recreation Resources*. Their paper highlights the stresses climate change will put on water resources, which could result in reduced mountain snowpack levels; increased drought conditions across public lands; decreased waterflows into streams, reservoirs, and wetlands; and weakened forests more susceptible to fire and insect infestations.

Walls, a senior fellow at Resources for the Future (RFF), and Morris, an RFF research assistant, included a number of possible scenarios, among them:

- *Snowpack:* Extended warm seasons may result in more rainfall than snow, which would reduce skiing and snowboarding opportunities, particularly in comparatively warmer areas in California, Nevada, Arizona, and New Mexico.
- *Fresh waterways:* Reduced snowpack and more rain in winter months would mean earlier spring runoff into streams and reservoirs. That could mean less fresh water flowing in the summer months, when sport fishing and boating are most popular. Fishing depends on water temperature, streamflow levels, and ecological quality, and boating is more sensitive to lake, reservoir, and stream levels.
- *Noncoastal wetlands:* Stretching across 216 million acres of the northern plains and Canada, these wetlands are rich sources of many species of ducks and other waterfowl. By one estimate, lower water levels caused by climate change in the Upper Great Lakes could reduce regional duck populations by nearly 40% in the area.
- *Beaches:* Rising sea levels over time could reduce the size of beachfront recreation areas, national seashores, and coastal waterways, the authors find. A full 85% of tourism-related revenues in the United States are generated by coastal states.
- *Forests and parks:* Tree cover, particularly in the western United States, is already feeling the impact of climate change, particularly as a result of drought. Insects have decimated millions of acres of evergreens in the Rocky Mountain region, and dryness has fueled damaging wildfires. Tree die offs also resulted in closures of campgrounds, trails, and picnic areas in public parks.

What is clear, the authors conclude, is that impacts from climate change will affect such leisure pursuits as skiing, camping, boating, fishing and hunting, outdoor sports such as golf, and wildlife viewing. That prospect may require more assertive efforts by public officials to adapt policies that will help preserve outdoor recreation areas.

"Longer and warmer summers are expected to increase the demand for outdoor recreation, from hiking, fishing, hunting, and camping to simple beach visits," the authors write. "This makes it all the more important that government policy at all levels develop climate adaptation programs and funding" (p. 21).

BENEFITS AND OUTCOMES OF CONTACT WITH NATURE

Our understanding of the benefits and outcomes of contact with nature is growing as additional research is conducted. Forty years ago, few people outside of leisure scientists and landscape architects explored the importance of outdoor recreation. Today, the list of those researching this area includes experts in public health, early childhood education, child psychology, urban planning, medicine, psychology, and sociology, among others. A number of authors discuss the benefits and outcomes of participation in natural settings. Table 12-6 depicts what Maller calls the contributions of parks to human health and well-being. The categories expressed in Table 12-6 are generally agreed upon by researchers, even if different terms are used.

Leisure-services agencies have the opportunity to take the lead in providing direct and indirect contact with nature for individuals. The approach demands creativity and a willingness to challenge the norm. Godbey provided a list of policy recommendations for enhancing direct and indirect contact with nature, including planning for outdoor recreation in urban areas involving schools and recreation and park departments, public health, transportation, public utilities, hospitals, and nonprofit environmental organizations.[48] Maller et al. stated, "Parks, in fact, are an ideal catalyst for the integration of environment, society, and health (which have been demonstrated to be inextricably linked) by promoting an ecological approach to human health and well-being based on contact with nature."[49]

Public parks and recreation organizations, environmental- and outdoor-based nonprofits, and federal land management and protection agencies traditionally have been proponents of protection and rationality. The organizations

TABLE 12-6   A Summary of the Contributions of Parks to Human Health and Well-Being

Component of Health	Contribution of Parks
Physical	Provide a variety of settings and infrastructure for various levels of formal and informal sport and recreation, for all skill levels and abilities (e.g., picnicking, walking, dog training, running, cycling, ball games, sailing, surfing, photography, birdwatching, bushwalking, rock climbing, camping).
Mental	Make nature available for restoration from mental fatigue, solitude and quiet, artistic inspiration and expression, and educational development (e.g., natural and cultural history).
Spiritual	Preserve the natural environment for contemplation, reflection, and inspiration; invoke a sense of place; facilitate feeling a connection to something beyond human concerns.
Social	Provide settings for people to enhance their social networks and personal relationships, from couples and families to social clubs and organizations of all sizes, from casual picnicking to events days and festivals.
Environmental	Preserve ecosystems and biodiversity, provide clean air and water, maintain ecosystem function, and foster human involvement in the natural environment (Friends of Parks groups, etc.).

Reproduced from Maller, C., Henderson-Wilson, C., Pryor, A., Prossor, L., & Moore, M. (n.d.). *Healthy parks healthy people: The health benefits of contact with nature in a park context: A review of relevant literature* (2nd ed.). Deakin University and Parks Victoria.

A family camping trip allows family members to benefit from their connections to the wilderness.

© Oleg Kozlov/Dreamstime.com.

sometimes have been at odds, especially at the national level when the executive branch of government has been perceived as unfriendly to the environment. Local government has a mixed response to environmental issues and city, county, and state agencies have not provided the level of leadership that once was common. Park and recreation agencies can provide leadership by example in their communities in the 21st century.

Impacts of Technology

Technology has changed the way we communicate. As little as 30 years ago, mail was the most common communications method. There was only one long-distance telephone company. Long-distance telephone calls were expensive and usually reserved for special occasions or for business enterprises. Most families subscribed to a morning newspaper and watched the network news on one of three commercial channels. They listened to one or two local radio stations and only in larger markets was there a variety of music available on the radio. Indeed, the rate at which technology changes is so rapid, that it makes predicting its impacts challenging, as illustrated in Table 12-7.

Today Americans, on average, spend more waking time communicating and using media devices such as the television, computers, and smartphones, than any other activity. The smartphone is an example of how technology has affected individuals, families, work, and communities. Even older adults use their cell phones to make contact while traveling, even if most of the time the phone sits turned off while at home. As late as 2002 a cell phone was primarily a phone. People carried cell phones and digital handheld devices for scheduling, note taking, and the like. Today's smartphones have replaced these two devices and expanded their level of services. In 2019, 96% of Americans had cell phones and 81% had smartphones.[50] Smartphones

TABLE 12-7   A Comparison of 2005 and 2017 Trends and Reality

2005	2017
Americans love their toys, and baby boomers expect "amenity-rich" experiences.	Millennials, now the largest generation, are digital natives, and what was a desire in previous generations is now an expectation.
Technology will continue to affect how we work and how we plan.	The boundaries around information technology are fading as technology becomes integral to almost every business function and social relationship.
Each generation is better educated, more adept with, and more dependent on technology than the previous generation.	Privacy and security linked to personal data concerns are growing as companies are mining more and more data of customers.
Technological advances affect the affordability, accessibility, and required skill level of many recreation activities.	Technology has created an "ambient user experience" allowing individuals to preserve their experiences across traditional boundaries of time and space.
Technology allows "mass customization."	Technology allows "built-to-order" personal customization.
New activities will be developed around innovative devices and procedures.	Americans have become cable cutters—in 2015 24% of Americans did not have cable TV—a trend that is growing.
Technology creates entirely new recreation uses.	Technology has allowed the development and growth of adventure recreation opportunities not even dreamed of by previous generations—this growth will continue to expand.
People tend to self-define and organize around their chosen form of recreation.	This continues to be true, but organization has become seamless for many activities through the use of technology.
Each group tends to want (demand) their own exclusive allocation of resources.	Technology has created an awareness for specialized activities and has less community involvement.

© Jones & Bartlett Learning.

dominate the market. Some continue to use a cell phone primarily as a phone, but many more use it as an email client; note taker; camera (still and video); calendar; a link to online services such as Twitter, Facebook, the global positioning system (GPS); game console; newsreader; address finder with map; and much more. For one in five American adults, the smartphone is their only source of at-home Internet.[51]

The Pew Internet and American Life project states that mobility changes the way people interact with each other and the ways they use their computer. We have reached a level where businesses and others expect to have broadband always on or be always connected. Questions remain unanswered about the impact of continual information exchange on individuals. For example, does it stress social norms, or cause continuous partial attention? In Pew's typology, the sophisticated user of technology has mobile access and

becomes an elite, replacing home access as an elite status. Many of today's teens and young adults see being always connected as a necessity and a right. Citizens can attend town meetings, business meetings, and the like without leaving their home or office. They can attend these meetings from anywhere with their mobile devices. Skype became the first free or low-cost Internet-based international telephone service. It has had a major impact on the developing world.

In 2000, only 52% of American adults used the Internet; in 2019, that number was up to 90%. The number of users varied by age, gender, ethnicity, income. According to the Pew Research Center:[52]

- Men and women used the Internet almost equally.
- Rural users lagged behind urban and suburban users.
- Internet use increases with the amount of education, with college graduates being the highest users.

- In 2016, there were almost no differences in use due to race, but since then Black and Hispanic users have fallen behind White users.
- Seniors—those over 65—have the lowest rate of use (73%), whereas the 18 to 29 and 30 to 49 age groups are almost equal in their use at or almost at 100%.
- Internet use rates increase as people's salaries increase, with a 15% use gap between the lowest and highest salary Americans.

Social media has defined use of mobile devices. About 7 of every 10 individuals use social media. Peak users of social media are 18- to 29-year-olds, closely followed by the 30 to 49 age group. Social media is widely used among individuals to keep up to date, to see what is going on, to pass along information and gossip, and to stay in touch with their friends.[53] During the 2016 and 2020 presidential races, social media was highlighted as a key source of information, even when that information was proven to be false.

A number of implications result from technology that parks and recreation professionals need to consider. They include, but are not limited to, the following:

- Teens are less engaged in traditional recreation activities than their predecessors. They are more engaged in technology-based activities such as creating Web pages, posting photos and videos on social network sites, watching videos online, modifying music, sharing music, and being involved with their peers through texting and social media platforms.
- There is greater competition for an individual's time. The notion of "free time" is almost a lost term. Technology has made this generation the most connected in history.
- Community members want active involvement, even if it is through the Internet. They do not want to be talked to but talked with. The same is true for

participating in programs offered by public and nonprofit agencies.

- Communicating images, program information, and building brands is far more difficult because of the plurality of communications alternatives. Sending home flyers through the public schools, sending brochures out in the mail, and advertising on traditional television stations will no longer reach the desired public. Knowledge about how different groups communicate, where they get their information, and how that information is determined to be important becomes essential for public agencies attempting to reach community members.
- Understanding that the old "word-of-mouth" model is magnified a hundred- or even thousandfold is essential. Administrators used to believe that one person could influence five to eight people they came in

With a perceived lack of leisure time, Americans feel the need to multitask.
© PeterMooij/Shutterstock.

FINDING LEISURE AND FUN IN THE "GIG ECONOMY"

Characterized by individuals who operate as independent contractors, the "gig economy" is the digital platform economy, and it has been growing faster than traditional payroll employees. Examples of gig economy include Uber, TaskRabbit, Managed by Q, and WashClub. Increasing numbers of people are entering this marketplace for a variety of reasons. Reportedly, the gig economy has outperformed the traditional job market over the last few years.

Why engage in the gig economy? For many it is an economic reality. They need the additional funds to make ends meet or to stabilize their income. Others participate because they can't find a job anywhere else. But, surprisingly, a large group of participants, as measured by the Pew Research Center (42%), reported they did it because it was fun and something to do in their spare time.

What does this mean for leisure? Has "killing time" and "extra income" become a fun activity? Could it be classified as a leisure activity? It begs the question of the need to educate individuals about the value of leisure time vs work time. What starts as fun can quickly turn into a burden as the money generated from the gig economy ventures moves from fun to essential.

Data from Pew Research Center. (2017). *Why join the gig economy? For many, the answer is 'for fun.'* http://www.pewresearch.org/fact-tank/2016/11/18/why-join-the-gig-economy-for-many-the-answer-is-for-fun/.

LEISURE-SERVICES AGENCIES GET THEIR GROOVE ON WITH TIKTOK

TikTok, a social media app dedicated to short-form, user-created, music-based videos, started as three different apps in the mid-2010s then hit global expansion in 2018. The app has over 2 billion downloads and 800 million active users.[a] Leisure-services agencies had started to leverage the power of the app to reach their audience before the COVID-19 pandemic, and the use became even more prominent during the pandemic. Lafayette Parks and Recreation Department in Lafayette, Indiana, has used their TikTok account to share fun videos to encourage people to get outside to their parks during the pandemic. They also did a TikTok video that featured their returning lifeguards dancing as a call for lifeguard applications.[b] Professional sports teams and individual professional athletes have used their TikTok accounts to engage with their fans. The National Basketball Association, in particular, adopted TikTok early on and ramped up its use during the pandemic, with more than 33 million followers.[c] TikTok itself has been focusing on travel and tourism, creating the #TikTokTravel campaign to encourage creators to share content about travel. The hashtag has attracted over 400,000 videos and 1.7 billion views. Tourism boards around the world are joining the campaign, sharing their own content about their destinations.[d]

[a] Tidy, J., & Smith Galer, S. (2020, August 5). *TikTok: The story of a social media giant*. BBC News. Retrieved February 9, 2021, from https://www.bbc.com/news/technology-53640724.

[b] Melin, C. (2020, November 27). *Lafayette Parks and Recreation takes fun approach to community outreach*. Retrieved February 9, 2021, from https://www.wlfi.com/content/news/Lafayette-Parks-and-Recreation-takes-fun-approach-to-community-outreach-573215791.html.

[c] NBA. (2021). NBA. Retrieved June 15, 2021 from, https://twitter.com/NBA.

[d] TikTok. (2019, June 6). *TikTok celebrates a new journey with #TikTokTravel*. Retrieved February 9, 2021, from https://newsroom.tiktok.com/en-us/tiktok-celebrates-a-new-journey-with-tiktoktravel/.

contact with. Today that one person can influence thousands and even hundreds of thousands without ever making physical contact with people. Images of organizations and their public goodwill can be positively or negatively influenced by minor as well as major events.

- Public parks and recreation agencies must learn to think and act in a digital age. Members must embrace technology as an important part of their operation, but more important, they must understand how their community members have embraced technology, whether they be 92 or 2. This suggests professionals need to be flexible and able to transition between digital natives, digital immigrants, and digital refusers.

Technology is influencing recreation and leisure in ways that were never imagined. As parks and recreation professionals embrace technology, they do so from multiple perspectives: Professionals need to ask: (1) How can technology help me?; (2) How can I use technology to help our community, residents, and program participants?; (3) How do I reach those who we are not reaching or those who chose not to take advantage of our services?; and (4) How do we position ourselves to make the most of technology today and in the future?

The Changing Conceptions of Time

The growth of individual discretionary time, sometimes referred to as free time or time without obligation, has long been considered a major influence on the increased participation in recreation activities. Between 1900 and 1995, the growth in leisure time was steady, if not spectacular. Freedom from an agrarian economy, increased holidays, paid vacations, and shorter workweeks combined to give people more opportunities for participation in recreation than at any other time in history. A debate about the actual availability of free time began in the early 1980s and continues. Today the 40-hour workweek is nonexistent for many. Manufacturing firms frequently mandate 20 or more hours of overtime for their employees. Corporate executives, mid-level managers, supervisors, and service employees experience a 24/7 (24 hours a day, 7 days a week) work life. The digital age has made everyone more accessible. The introduction of electronic communications exemplified by the iPhone has made the Internet available anywhere and any time. Smartphones now provide continuous connectivity. Business travelers use their smartphones until flight attendants ask everyone to turn off their electronic devices, and then they turn off the cell phone function and use the device to take notes, work offline, watch videos, read books, and listen to music. Vacations no longer provide time away from work, just time away from the office.

The availability of discretionary time is based on age, education, gender identity, and the presence or absence of a disability. Children, those who are unemployed, and retirees have considerably more discretionary time than do individuals who are in the workforce. Children have less discretion about what they might participate in and older adults' physical, mental, or economic condition may limit their ability to participate in some recreation activities. Professionals and those with a college education typically work fewer hours than those in nonprofessional jobs, such as in the service industry, manufacturing, construction, and the like. Many individuals with severe disabilities have limited opportunities to explore a range of recreation activities but have long enforced hours of free time.

The Bureau of Labor Statistics maintains annual data on how people use their time. The American Time Use Survey is released annually and measures the average amount of time per day that individuals worked, did household activities, cared for household children, participated in educational activities, and engaged in leisure and sports activities. Personal care, including sleep, is the largest consumer of individual time. During the weekdays, work is the largest waking time-consumer, with leisure and sports a close second. On weekends, leisure and sports are the largest activity time is spent on, although about half of this time is spent watching television. (See Table 12-8.)

Several issues related to the perception of time have become more apparent in recent years. *Time deepening, time shifting, time compression*, and *time famine* have entered the vocabulary of researchers, leisure providers, and the general public. Time deepening suggests more efficient use of the time available by engaging in several activities simultaneously, such as driving and talking on the cell phone, or watching a television show and knitting at the same time.

Time shifting refers to the viewing of broadcast media, such as network television, at times and in ways other than the intended time and method, such as broadcast news at 6:00 p.m. Almost 15% of all viewing is now done at times other than scheduled times. Time compression is a perspective that relates to acceleration of time and making experiences seem shorter. It is related to technology and some suggest it is the driver of lifestyle changes. Going on a picnic with the family used to be an all-day activity where the focus was on the family. Today mom and dad bring their cell phones, talk to other people, make plans, respond to email, and so forth, while children play with their handheld game devices. At the end of the day, the family feels they have had little time together. Time famine is present when an individual has insufficient time to accomplish all of the tasks required for work, leisure, and necessities. Time famine is particularly prevalent among people in jobs demanding large amounts of a person's available time.

Layered on top of time compression, time famine, time shifting, and time deepening is technology and how it has

TABLE 12-8   Average Hours per Day Spent in Selected Activities, 2019 Annual Averages

Activity	Weekday Hours	Percentage	Weekend Hours	Percentage
Leisure and sports	4.64	19.5%	6.44	27.1%
Work and work-related activities	4.63	19.5%	1.26	5.3%
Personal care activities	9.35	39.3%	10.25	43.1%
Household activities	1.62	6.8%	2.17	9.1%
Eating and drinking	1.13	4.7%	1.29	5.4%
Purchasing goods and services	0.70	2.9%	0.85	3.6%
Caring for and helping household members	0.51	2.1%	0.43	1.8%
Educational activities	0.56	2.3%	0.21	0.9%
Organizational, civic, and religious activities	0.21	0.9%	0.48	2.0%
Telephone call, postal mail, and email	0.17	0.7%	0.13	0.5%
Other activities, not classified elsewhere	0.27	1.1%	0.29	1.2%

Data from U.S. Bureau of Labor Statistics. (n.d.). *Graphics for economic news releases: Average hours per day spent in selected activities by sex and day.* https://www.bls.gov/charts/american-time-use/activity-by-sex.htm.

changed people's lifestyles. Social networking tools such as Facebook, Twitter, Instagram, blogging, and the ability for smartphones to "push" email and other information to consumers means that people no longer have empty free time. In a sense, free time, or time with no obligation, has ceased to exist for some people. With the implementation of these mobile technologies, people attempt to maximize the content available in every minute, increasing the pace of their lives. The inability to keep up with all of the available information results in increased anxiety, stress, and feelings of time famine.

The feelings of time compression and time famine lead many to believe that they have less time available than preceding generations did. With the exception of a small percentage of people, most people have more discretionary time available today than at any time in history. The term *real time* is one reflection of today's perception of time. Real time "applies not to any device but to the technologically transformed context of everything we do. Real time is characterized by the shortest possible lapse between idea and action, between initiation and result."[54]

Opportunities and Issues for the Field of Leisure Services Moving Forward

The beginnings of the 21st century held little indication of how the latter part of the first decade would bring changes that may have long-term influences on the profession. At the community level, public parks and recreation programs are being challenged to survive in many communities. What defined economic growth at the start of this century did not define economic growth midway through the second decade of this century. Reduction of services, closing of facilities and parks, furloughs, and elimination of staff are becoming accepted tools to deal with the economic declines over the first two decades of the 20th century. Nonprofits are finding ways to secure funding particularly challenging while simultaneously attempting to provide desperately needed services to a large number of unemployed and underemployed. Recreation providers have had to rethink the delivery of services and programs.

The first decade of the 21st century gradually saw a turnaround in state and local government as economies began to grow once again. However, the damage of the great recession has yet to be overcome. Governments, whose primary source of income comes from taxes, typically take longer to recover (up to 3 to 5 years) from a recession than commercial enterprises. There is always a lag in tax collections, making it difficult for city, county, and state governments to respond. Pensions of state and local government employees have changed forever. Investments in programs and services, organization of departments, and staffing of park and recreation programs continue to lag.

The unanswered question facing the leisure-services profession is what the future will look like. However, by looking at the past we can glean some ideas for the future. The recent recession may be the worst since the Depression of the 1930s, but there are parallels in the 1960s and 1970s that we can draw on. Organizations will recover, tax income will increase, staff will be expanded, new facilities and services will be designed, built, and operated. It has happened before and it will happen again. That is the one constant that economists agree on. However, how governments, nonprofits, and commercial enterprises structure and deliver their services most assuredly will change from what has been done in the past. New models are already emerging, partnerships are becoming more common, and new sources of revenue generation will be created. More difficult decisions regarding service levels, land acquisition, staffing, organizational focus, and future direction are receiving greater attention from policy makers.

In the 1930s, leisure and recreation were seen as critical to the success of the New Deal and to society. Whether that will be the same today is unknown, but early trends suggest it is unlikely. Public safety continues to receive the majority of available tax dollars. People want to feel safe. Recreation and leisure, essential elements of quality of life, fall much lower on individual taxpayers' perception of need. After almost 100 years, one might expect that the profession would have done a better job of positioning itself. The conclusion to that statement remains to be seen.

Growth of Special Interest Groups

Throughout this chapter are discussions on the influences of the Internet, media, and social networking on leisure and recreation. As these influences have affected how leisure and recreation services are delivered, they have also affected how people interact and react to the debate about services, needs, and future directions. Social networking has allowed individuals and small organizations to influence policy, decision

Public park and recreation agencies are embracing partnerships with fitness and health organizations.
© Paul McKinnon/Shutterstock.

making, and planning. Before the Internet, special interest groups were not always well organized and struggled to make their voices heard at local and national levels. That has changed considerably as small, local, and traditional groups, such as the Sierra Club, National Trust for Historic Preservation, and the Environmental Defense Fund, have embraced the use of the Internet as a social networking tool. At their websites one can join; sign up for a newsletter; download specialized information; discover what is going on in the community; find information for special events, trips, and activities; be alerted to proposed local, state, and federal changes in laws and rules; and provide financial support. Where an organization previously would send out letters or make phone calls, both time consuming, it can now send email, texts, and tweets alerting interested parties about issues and request support for targeted funding.

The explosion of involvement by special interest groups is having a profound impact on how public agencies, at all levels, look at their delivery of services. For the most part, special interest groups have a positive impact on recreation and leisure. Organizations can more effectively coordinate with the groups, track involvement, and draw upon their interests. Figure 12-3 depicts types of social interest groups that might affect recreation, leisure, and parks. Each of the descending branches identifies a major type of special interest group. Twenty years ago, this same mind map might

have had only two or, at most, three trunks. Special interest groups are challenging recreation and leisure organizations to rethink and expand their view of services and programs.

Commodification of Leisure

The contrast in leisure opportunity among people from high and low socioeconomic backgrounds is heightened by what has been termed the "commodification" of leisure. Increasingly, varied forms of play today are developed in complex, expensive forms by profit-seeking businesses. More and more, giant conglomerates such as Time Warner, Disney, and Viacom have taken control of huge corporations that run music, television, and movie businesses. These conglomerates also own sports stadiums, professional sports teams, cruise ships, theme parks, and other leisure enterprises.

Ogden, Utah, proposed a $38 million indoor recreation center with an Olympic-sized pool plus a large water park, an indoor velodrome, and six tennis courts. Such investments are a drain on local economies if they are not heavily marketed (which they often are not) and operated like a commercial enterprise and not like a city-owned facility. There are good and bad examples of such facilities across the country. Public agencies should be wary of facilities that are based on high revenue projections, realizing they are often out of reach of many of their citizens.

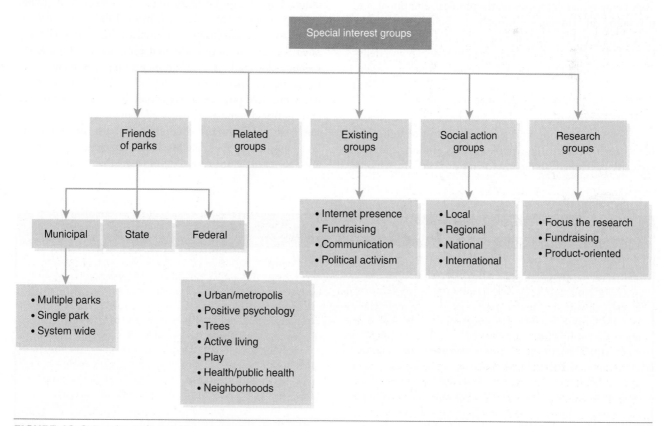

FIGURE 12-3 Typology of special interest groups
© Jones & Bartlett Learning.

Lippke shared concerns about the effects of commercialization of leisure on individuals and society. He suggested individuals "are subtly and not so subtly encouraged to indulge themselves in a consumption binge that, temporarily at least, distracts them from the cares and concerns of everyday life."[55] The problem lies not with the distraction but with the use of such leisure-time activities to replace what leisure theorists have called personal development, creativity, and flow. Lippke suggested that the commercialization of leisure promotes a lack of self-development, and an increase in the inability of persons to direct their own lives as they become dependent on external stimulators. Commercialization of recreation has created a competition for everyone to have the same things, or what one author calls, "sneer group pressure." Advertisers and sellers of commercialization create expectations among potential buyers that life should be "filled with glamorous, exciting, or dramatic moments."[56]

Integration into the Health, Fitness, and Well-Being Movements

A key trend continuing in U.S. society is public interest in well-being, exercise, and physical fitness programs. Well-being, discussed previously, is being embraced by the leisure profession in recognition of the need for and importance of individuals improving their lives beyond just the physical. Well-being research focuses on the physical, emotional, and psychological domains through a holistic approach. Research on well-being is increasing, and the leisure field is but one of many disciplines engaged in research and delivery of programs. Other fields including psychology, medicine, environmental studies, and sociology have linked well-being to leisure and recreation and park places.

Realizing that modern life is frequently inactive, sedentary, beset by tensions, and subject to a host of unhealthy habits such as overeating, smoking, and drinking, popular concern developed about improving one's health, vitality, and appearance through healthy eating and exercise. Participation in such activities as walking, aerobics, swimming, running and jogging, racket sports, and similar vigorous pursuits has more than physiological effects. It also has psychological value: Those who exercise regularly look and feel better physically and mentally. Experts conclude that fitness is not a passing trend; the public's desire to be healthy and physically attractive is supported by continuing publicity, social values, personal vanity, and solid business sense.

Research shows that the most successful fitness programs are likely to be those that provide an ingredient of recreational interest and satisfaction. The National Recreation and Park Association recognizes the value of fitness and health and sponsors local involvement in Step Up to Health: Start in the Parks, a nationwide fitness program delivered by local park and recreation agencies. Each agency is to develop fitness programs that encourage employee and community participation. Sandy, Utah held a sprint triathlon that included a 400-yard swim, a 9-mile bike ride, and a 5-kilometer run. Columbus, Georgia sponsors two annual festivals, one in the spring and one in the fall, to encourage fitness in the parks. The Decatur, Illinois Park District hosted a teen fitness summit. The Robert Wood Johnson Foundation has focused much of its effort on a healthy communities initiative. They recognize that although many are served well in communities, there are those who are not served well. It may be poverty, transportation, lack of care facilities, housing, recreation, or public transportation that impedes an individual and neighborhood's ability to achieve a healthy community. They have championed the need to have parks that promote health by documenting that parks play a significant role in human health including spiritual, mental, and physical health. In addition, parks promote physical activity, they help children flourish, and combat chronic disease. It is all about being outdoors in a safe environment where children and adults can relax, play, and enjoy one another. The research is replete with the restorative power of nature, regardless of where that nature occurs.[57]

SITTING IS THE NEW SMOKING

Reports of the obesity crisis are increasing in the media. A recent report suggested that within a few years obesity will outpace smoking as the leading cause of death in the United States. "Sitting Is the New Smoking" is the rallying cry of researchers as they attempt to alert the public to the dangers of prolonged sitting, overeating, and lack of exercise. Americans sit an average of 9.3 hours per day. Some research has suggested that uninterrupted sitting may be an overlooked risk factor for cancer and other conditions associated with increased inflammation and insulin levels. What is more alarming is that research is beginning to suggest that going to the gym a few times a week or even working out every day may not overcome the effects of sitting. In addition to incorporating movement when not at work, health experts recommend taking 5 minute breaks from sitting every 30 minutes to do some movement. It appears that increasing numbers of researchers are encouraging people to change their daily routine to include more walking and climbing stairs and less sitting. Standing, although not sitting, does not replace walking. The evidence suggests all Americans need to engage in more activity, at all ages.

Active Life Utah. (2017). *Beware of the chair*. Retrieved from https://www.activelifeutah.com/beware-of-the-chair/

Leisure-services organizations have always been associated with social movement, but over the last 30 years they have expanded their understanding and role of recreation and leisure in the community. Increased focus on better trails, fitness, wellness, happiness, and community engagement have contributed to the broader perspective of how public parks and recreation crosses many community boundaries and can be an active and effective contributor to community growth and development.

Growth of the Experience Economy

Researchers and recreation providers have often talked about the recreation experience and have done so in generic terms. More recently, the discussion of experience has become broader, especially among economists and market specialists. The context of experience was from the provider and the focus was on giving a service to the individual or group. The focus was on delivery and process. The central point of the structure in recreation programs was the program itself and the process of moving it from concept to delivery to a potential end user. It worked for many years and is still the core of much of what recreation providers do, but society has changed, and so have the expectations of receivers of traditional recreation experiences. As far back as 1970, Toffler suggested the emergence of an experience industry. In 1999 Pine and Gilmore published *The Experience Economy*, focusing on a new economic model, superseding the traditional service model. They propose that engaging the customer through experience is necessary to create value in an increasing competitive business environment. Moving beyond traditional recreation concept of experience, they saw experience as an economic offering.[58]

Experience requires two key components. The first is the participation or involvement by an individual, and an understanding that experiences are internal in nature, making them individualized and each participant unique. This concept is not far from how leisure researchers have discussed experiences, especially the Csikszentmihalyis and their discussion of optimal experiences.[59] The second component was a common component of developing recreation programs but almost always from a group perspective. The new concept of experience argues that each consumer is unique. We each bring different backgrounds, values, attitudes, and beliefs to the situation; we experience it through our individualized "rose-colored glasses." The idea of individual experiences resulted from the convergence of three major forces: "(1) new technology to fuel innovative experiences; (2) a more sophisticated, affluent, and demanding consumer base; and (3) escalating competitive intensity."[60]

Redesigning the process of creating a recreation experience, moving it from a group to individual experience opportunity, is the foundation for change. Outcomes focus on participant perception of value. "Value may be reflected in many ways. Among these expressions of value are participants'

decisions to commit time to the offering; their willingness to persist in participation; their decisions to accept social, psychological, and physical risks associated with participation; or their decision to spend money that, in many settings, is necessary to secure rights to engage in the offering."[61] Creating value for the participants is grounded in the development of program delivery models.

Application to the recreation and leisure industry is important and gaining momentum across the industry—from public agencies to large commercial recreation enterprises. In many instances the commercial sector has understood and applied the concept of individual experiences better than the public and nonprofit sectors. The provision of experiences will continue to grow. Its adherents are expanding and academic programs are embracing the concept.

Maturation of the Organized Leisure-Services Field

The nature of municipal, state, and federal governments has changed dramatically in the nearly 140 years of organized recreation in the United States. Today's city government is markedly different from that of previous generations. Government is more dependent on alternative income sources and less reliant on taxes. Public parks and recreation agencies have, of necessity, become entrepreneurial. Where few fees once existed, now public agencies are dependent on fees and charges to make up as much as 90% of their operating budgets. Parks and recreation agencies are hard pressed to serve all of those who either desire or have a need for services. Nonprofit and commercial agencies fill the gap in many instances. In today's environment of rapidly changing demand for different types of leisure activities, public, commercial, and nonprofit organizations strive to respond, but often public and nonprofits do not have the resources, financial capital, or ability to respond. Commercial enterprises typically respond more quickly to what initially may appear as fringe activities such as paintball, skateboarding, laser tag, and the like.

Maturation does not suggest the organized leisure-services field is not changing, but rather that growth in the public and nonprofit sector is constrained by available funds, politics, public interest, and the perceived opportunity for growth. Public and nonprofit agencies have developed an infrastructure of parks, recreation centers, sports fields, cultural centers, and other types of facilities. The traditional programming focus of public and nonprofit agencies remains in place, although it is frequently unable to grow with public demand. Where communities once built a 50-meter swimming pool, today they build a small to medium water park, except when politicians or other influential groups intervene and demand a traditional or old-fashioned approach. The leadership is changing and new, younger leaders are emerging. Values are being reassessed, commitments rethought, demands evaluated, and expectations challenged.

As the economic and political climate of public agencies has changed over the last half-decade, there is a recognition of all involved that government must change. What has been accepted for years as a government responsibility, especially in the parks and recreation profession, is now under debate. The change, as described earlier, began decades ago, and public agencies must rethink how they operate and redefine themselves within the context of the political, economic, and public perceptions of expectations, importance, and relevance.

Acknowledgment of the Economic Impact of Leisure Services

Many think of recreation as free time, something done when not working; for example, an activity, event, or trip that may or may not be planned. Even in the leisure research literature that perception is reinforced. Yet, for a large segment of the United States economy, recreation is a major factor in individual and family expenditures. Between 2000 and the final quarter of 2019, personal spending on recreation rose from 699.3 million dollars to 1.2 billion dollars. Even in the fourth quarter of 2020, when the United States remained in the grips of the pandemic, personal spending on recreation was 1.2 billion dollars.[62]

Let's look at one sector of leisure services to better understand the economic impact our field can and does have on the economy. In 2019, the outdoor recreation industry accounted for over $450 billion of the national GDP (2.1%).[63] In 2017, the outdoor recreation industry accounted for $887 billion of annual consumer spending, which was almost double the contributions of the pharmaceuticals industry. This consumer spending was divided between $700 billion in trip and travel spending and $184 billion in outdoor recreation product spending. Some interesting numbers: Americans spend $20 billion on trail sports gear, $14 billion on water sports gear, and $97 billion on cycling and skateboarding gear. Further, the outdoor recreation industry generated 7.6 million jobs, more than the computer technology, construction, and finance and insurance industries. Outdoor recreation generates $125 billion in tax revenue at the local, state, and federal levels.[64] So anyone who says that the leisure-services industry is frivolous hasn't looked at the numbers!

The recreation, sport, and tourism industries are essential components of local, state, and national communities. The Idaho state government, for example, recently recognized the tremendous economic impact of recreation on the state-wide economy when they passed Idaho House Bill 204, which invests significant money to enhancing state parks, outdoor recreation, and tourism efforts. In the Governor's office press release for the signing of the bill, the Governor reported that Idaho saw 7.7 million visitors in 2020.[65] Indeed, in 2017, outdoor recreation accounted for 3% of Idaho's state GDP.[66] Idaho provides just one example of the essential role recreation can play in local, state, and national economies. What makes recreation an economic force is, in part, the variety and type of commercial enterprises that provide equipment, supplies, travel, lodging, guides, instructors, lessons, and the like directly to the industry and are supported by other commercial enterprises.

THE ECONOMIC IMPACT OF LEISURE SERVICES

Here are some specific examples of the economic impacts that outdoor recreation can have on the economy:

- Attendees of the annual Red Rock Rendezvous, a climbing event outside Las Vegas, contribute over $1 million to the local economy.
- Out-of-state tourists to Florida generated $115 billion in direct spending in 2016.
- The Head of the Hooch rowing regatta generates $5.5 million in economic impact for the city of Chattanooga, Tennessee.
- Saltwater beach activities in Florida, not including fishing, generated $7.9 million in visitor spending.
- Users of the Miami Valley Trail system in southwest Ohio generate $13 million in economic impact for communities in that area.
- In Vail, Colorado, the GoPro Mountain Games generates $7.2 million in economic impact for that community.
- Domestic and international travelers to Alaska spent $2.9 billion in 2018.
- The festivals in New Orleans in 2016 generated $904 million in economic impact for the city.

This list could go on and on. Do a quick Internet search for other facts about the economic impact of the leisure-services industry. What do you find?

Office of Cultural Economy. (2016). *2016 New Orleans cultural economy snapshot*. https://www.nola.gov/cultural-economy/documents/2016-ce-snapshot-electronic-en/; Outdoor Industry Association. (2017). The outdoor recreation economy. Retrieved February 4, 2021, from https://outdoorindustry.org/wp-content/uploads/2017/04/OIA_RecEconomy_FINAL_Single.pdf; Seidel, V., Barker, A., Diamond, C., & Osario, D. (2017); *Economic impact analysis of outdoor recreation in Florida*. https://floridadep.gov/sites/default/files/Economic-Study-Appx-A-w-tags.pdf; and U.S. Travel Association. (2018); and *The economic impact of the travel industry*. https://www.ustravel.org/economic-impact.

Take, for example, the bed-and-breakfast industry that directly employs support staff to clean rooms; maintenance staff or specialists to deal with equipment upkeep and repairs; marketing firms or collaborations to sell their product; tour companies to provide special services to guests; food vendors for meals prepared on site; cleaning supplies from building maintenance services; and they pay local, state, and federal taxes. Expand the concept of the local bed-and-breakfast to that of the local bait shop, or the bicycle shop, the sporting goods store, local tour companies, sporting goods companies, specialized recreation services, both local and online, and suddenly the real impact of the recreation industry is significant.

Recreation is a major contributor to the economy. It plays significant roles, often built around small to midsized local vendors. Larger enterprises are expanding in the marketplace and in some instances, such as sporting goods stores and outdoor supply stores, may come to dominate the market, yet the small local and regional retail merchant remains a key player.[67] Recreation expenditures are subject to prevailing economic conditions, and like much of the economy, rise and fall based on individual perceptions of the economy. However, over the last 20 years, before the COVID-19 pandemic, the recreation, sport, and tourism industry has grown at a steady rate.

Surge of Esports

Esports was rapidly growing in popularity prior to the COVID-19 pandemic and since the pandemic has hit, esports continues its surge into relevance to leisure services in a variety of sectors. In 2019, global esports annual revenues exceeded $1 billion, a number that is nearly 8 times the revenue generated in 2012.[68] We are seeing esports teams and leagues becoming popular in a variety of sectors, but particularly in public parks and recreation and collegiate recreation and athletics. Some people may be, and are, resistant to the idea of esports in traditional recreation settings because there are many myths about esports such as esports are "just games," video games are bad for health, and that esports is just about gaming. What we know, however, is that esports can provide meaningful development of social skills, can promote cognitive development, and are much more than "just games." Further, esports can offer a powerful way for agencies to connect with the hard-to-reach teen audience and other populations that don't traditionally use their services. Read this story from an article in *Parks & Recreation* magazine about how esports might just open up new audiences:

> The story that most resonated with me was one I heard from Nate Williams, director of Excelsior Springs (Missouri) Parks and Recreation. On March 9, 2019, the park agency hosted an esports tournament to play Smash Bros on the Nintendo Switch.

> One of its participants was a child with special needs. When the tournament concluded, the participant's mother approached the staff and told them how she could never cheer on her son since he didn't play any of the traditional sports. However—thanks to the agency's esports offerings—for the first time that day, she got to see her son play and cheer him on like all the other moms do.

> With this single act that offered a child a chance to compete, if not on the traditional field of play but a virtual one, esports just helped make a case for true inclusion and how it positively impacted that child (and his family's life). At the end of the day, isn't that what parks and recreation is all about?[69]

As of October 2019, 15 states recognized esports as a varsity sport[70] and there are over 400 university programs competing at the intercollegiate level. The rate of growth of college esports has accelerated in the last decade. Over 72% of the current programs began competing in 2018 or 2019.[71] Esports continue to evolve as well, as virtual reality and artificial intelligence technology continues to advance. As Bhatt argued, "Esports will be a disruptor to the traditional model of park and recreation offerings and agencies will have two choices: You can either be the force for change or you will be forced to change."[72]

Looking Beyond the COVID-19 Pandemic to the Postpandemic Landscape

As we write this newest edition of this text, the COVID-19 pandemic continues to devastate the United States. Hundreds of thousands of Americans are dying, countless people have lost their jobs, and many are experiencing mental health impacts from it all. We hope, as you are reading this, that those tides have turned in a positive direction. Regardless, it's hard to predict what the long-term impacts of the pandemic will be on the field of leisure services. We have certainly seen disheartening impacts on jobs, particularly seasonal positions in many sectors and all positions particularly in professional sports, hospitality, and events but are hopeful that these impacts will be reversed postpandemic. We would be remiss if we did not directly address the pandemic in a chapter about future perspectives; however, we are still in the midst of the pandemic so it's unclear exactly what the postpandemic landscape will look like. So, we decided that instead of trying to forecast the uncertain future, we would highlight the voices of leisure-services professionals from across the field to hear what they have learned and what they think the future may hold. These professionals, who have been working in the field on the front line of the pandemic, had many insights to share that offer a snapshot of the resiliency, creativity, and innovation our field continues to display. Here is the list of leisure-services professionals we heard from:

- Leanna Bordner, Deputy Athletics Director & Senior Woman Administrator, Illinois State University
- Doug Damery, Director, Town of Normal Parks & Recreation
- Jayne DeLuce, President & CEO, Visit Champaign County
- Joe DeLuce, Executive Director, Champaign Park District
- Jill Eichholz, Program Manager, Bloomington Parks Recreation & Cultural Arts
- Michael Hernbrott, Manager, Bloomington Ice Center
- Austin Hochstetler, Associate Principal, PROS Consulting, Inc.
- Crystal Howard, President and CEO, Bloomington-Normal Area Convention and Visitors Bureau
- Tim Jaskiewicz, Risk Management Consultant, Park District Risk Management Agency
- Jameel Jones, Director of Recreation, Champaign Park District
- Nicole Kohler, SOAR Program Manager, Bloomington Parks Recreation & Cultural Arts
- Rebecca Krzyszkowski, Recreation Supervisor, City of Brentwood
- Mackenzie Morgan, Senior Coordinator of Conferences and Events, Society of Women Engineers
- Mike Pederson, Owner, Dive Right In Scuba
- Dawn Pote, Executive Director, Campus Recreation and Student Fitness Center, Illinois State University
- Heather Richardson, Support Services Supervisor, Western DuPage Special Recreation District
- Jamie Sennett, Director, Alumni Engagement, Illinois State University
- Kelly Shook, Marketing Coordinator, Sunriver Realty
- Samantha Rupkey, professional in the sports industry
- Kara Snyder, Assistant Dean of Marketing, Communications, and Constituent Relations, College of Applied Science and Technology, Illinois State University
- Brycen Turnbull, Park Ranger, National Parks Service
- Tiffany P. White, Recreation Specialist, City of Grand Prairie

What Leisure-Services Professionals Have Learned About Themselves

The first question we asked the professionals was "What is one thing you've learned about yourself as a professional during the pandemic that you will hold on to after the pandemic is over?" The professionals' answers to this question reflected two themes. First, professionals overwhelmingly discussed that they learned, or relearned, how adaptable and resilient they are. For example, Leanna Bordner shared, "I have learned that while you say you can adapt and adjust at the drop of a hat, you really have to live it, own it, respect it, and go with it. I have learned I am more resilient that I thought myself to be, and for that I am proud." Many of the professionals not only discussed recognizing their own adaptability and resilience but also the adaptability and resilience of the leisure-services field as a whole. Many saw this adaptability and resilience as an opportunity to discover new approaches to their work. Further, they focused their adaptability and resilience on their desire to continue to serve their audience. Heather Richardson explained, "Recreation professionals have always said that we are very flexible as we often find ourselves in situations where we need to think on our feet. Well, this pandemic has shown just how true that statement is with recreation programs continuing to serve their communities and bring albeit modified experiences, some wonderful programs and opportunities to those that they serve."

The second theme discussed by the professionals in regard to what they learned about themselves during the pandemic was how important connection is to the work that they do. Some discussed being reminded how much they relied on the in-person interactions with their colleagues as they navigated their work. They also shared that they felt that connection with both coworkers and their audience provided them with a sense of well-being that they sought to replicate using technology during the pandemic. For some, the pandemic highlighted their strengths at making such connections. For example, Jamie Sennett shared, "For me, I have really relied on my communication skills and my ability to create relationships with people. The lack of communication skills for some was really highlighted in a virtual environment. Some did well, some really struggled. I also took pride in my ability to form relationships, but it is very different in a virtual space. This skill really came in handy as that is the nature of our work." Kara Snyder used this reflection to look forward, saying, "One of the most important things that I learned during the pandemic was how to prioritize people on your team. We are nothing without our health (both physical and mental). I made an effort to check in with team members and really see how they were doing every meeting. Pre-pandemic, my focus was entirely on the agenda and achieving goals. I made a conscious effort to shift gears and prioritize people over tasks."

WHAT DID I LEARN ABOUT MYSELF AS A PROFESSIONAL DURING THE COVID-19 PANDEMIC?

Reflections from Mike Bassett, Certified Therapeutic Recreation Specialist, New Hampshire Department of Corrections

I learned that the possibilities for Rec Therapy are endless. When the pandemic hit in Spring 2020, I was working at Northeast Passage, a nonprofit dedicated to empowering people living with disabling conditions through sports and recreation. I was really impressed with my team's ability to adapt our collaborative creativeness. All of our clinical Rec Therapists were operating large caseloads at the time we received the news that we'd be immediately stopping in person sessions. That day, all of us got together on a Zoom session and we were all at home talking together, problem solving, generating resource lists, and just figuring out ways to support each other.

When the news came that I'd be moving to telehealth platform, I was pretty scared. I went from having the nation's largest adapted equipment rental inventory, unlimited access to our community resources, and access to different green spaces to conduct my sessions to asking my clients what items they have in their home for our sessions. I'm proud to say that I'm a person who is very open minded, even pre-COVID, but being forced to step out of my comfort zone to be able to accommodate the lack of access to supplies or equipment that my clients had on hand at home certainly impacted my skills as a Rec Therapist forever.

Being a professional during this pandemic also highlighted the importance of engaging my own personal leisure interests. As a recreational professional, we really emphasize the importance of self-care and how it correlates to overall quality of life and COVID has really taken all of that to the extreme. I'm a very active person. I live very active lifestyle. To go from that lifestyle—being very active, engaging my body every day in a certain way—to being required to live a very stagnant lifestyle, that was really hard for me. I tried some different things but being physically active is my most preferred way of recharging my batteries and I knew that at some point not being physically active was going to have an impact on my ability to serve my clients.

Normally, I would be hiking from when the second snowboarding season ends all the way through summer and fall right up into when the next snowboarding season begins again. In 2020, I wasn't able to go on my first hike of the year until May! That was the first time I got to go out and be active and really push myself physically. That's where my creativity comes from. When I left the mountain that day, I had 10 or 11 new ideas for virtual sessions that I hadn't explored yet.

I had spent 2 months, or a little more, prescribing recreation and engaged living to my clients, but I wasn't taking my own prescription!

So what did I learn as a professional during the pandemic?

Take the best care of myself so I can take the best care of my clients.

What Changes Will Persist Postpandemic

The second question we asked the professionals was "What is one adjustment you've had to make during the pandemic in how you've delivered your services that you think should or will persist into the post-COVID landscape?" One theme that emerged in the professionals' responses was a renewed attitude toward the importance of partnerships in order to meet new challenges. Rebecca Krzyszkowski provided an illuminating example of this theme:

> Overseeing sports programs during the pandemic has been a challenge, as restrictions have not allowed full competition to take place. Cancelling all of my sport programs has pushed me to be creative and think of new ideas, such as esports. Our department has recently met with a new local esports organization, Nerd Street Gamers, that is looking to partner with our Parks and Recreation department for future programs. We are excited to partner with this organization in hopes of offering programs such as teen sport tournaments (Madden, NFL, NHL, etc.) and adult leagues (Madden, NFL, NHL, League of Legends, Fortnite, etc.) during and post COVID.

Another theme that the professionals discussed was the idea that postpandemic, there will remain an increased emphasis on cleaning and safety, particular in regard to facilities management. Several professionals shared that they are confident that the cleaning and sanitation protocols put in place during the pandemic will persist beyond it. Further, some professionals talked about continuing to implement safety protocols after the pandemic such as decreased crowd limits, rethinking public spaces, and youth participant dropoff happening outside the building. Doug Damery also shared that he sees future impact on the actual design of buildings, saying, "Design of renovation and new projects may think about sanitation issues, reducing, the need for certain high contact areas such as doors, and the ability to better socially distance within certain programming spaces."

A third theme in the professionals' responses was that they see possible changes to work practices moving forward. The professionals discussed that the increased use of technology to make their work more efficient will likely persist beyond the pandemic. They predict that they will continue to use videoconferencing tools to conduct staff meetings, virtual interviews, and client meetings. Heather Richardson also sees applications in staff training, sharing, "We have created and are working on building a video library of training topics allowing us to significantly scale back our in-person training to just what is absolutely needed to be presented in person, which allows new staff to watch the videos and review the information on their own time at a pace that works for them. Again there is value in this as we are very well aware that staff zone out and do not pay attention for the duration of a content heavy staff training, so giving staff the ability to break that up and obtain that information section by section can be helpful in the long run." A few professionals also discussed the need to rethink the typical workweek and think more flexibly about when and how people work. In particular, many of the professionals shared that remote work, in some capacity, will persist beyond the pandemic now that people see that it can work for some people and some tasks. Samantha Rupkey explained her hopes this way, "The past year has shown that working from home is possible for many organizations and should be utilized. My hope is that employees feel empowered to stay home when sick and that businesses continue to put the health and safety of employees first whether amidst a global pandemic or not."

By far the most prominent theme in the professionals' responses to our second question was that virtual programming is here to stay. Many professionals discussed the reality that the pandemic has demonstrated that programming that would have previously been thought of as impossible to host virtually can work, and work well, in a virtual environment. Jamie Sennett shared, "We have provided virtual professional development opportunities, light-hearted entertainment, virtual tours of campus, creative outlets, education about civic engagement and even how to support their own mental health. We have done these things in the past, but only in the form of articles and events. Switching to virtual events and webinars has allowed us to rethink our work and we have found it works. It is here to stay." Further, the pandemic restrictions have provided opportunities to consider new types of programming, like activity boxes that community members can do at home, new types of events they hadn't previously offered, and blended programming with in-person and virtual components. Mackenzie Morgan discussed these ideas in relation to an annual conference she helps organize, explaining, "The main adjustment that we had to make at the Society of Women Engineers was giving

our members the same professional development and networking that they have always had in-person at conferences. This inevitably caused us to announce that our already scheduled New Orleans conference would move virtual. After seeing our attendance soar from 16,000+ attendees at the 2019 in-person Annual Conference to 18,000+ attendees at the 2020 Virtual Annual Conference, we know as a society that we will always need to have a virtual component."

The professionals saw great benefit in retaining virtual programming as a way to bring down barriers for participation and reach wider audiences. Nicole Kohler said, "I believe the biggest benefit to this platform has been that caretakers, parents, and siblings have been able to participate in these activities alongside our participants so the whole household benefits from recreational activities." Similarly, Heather Richardson explained, "We have expanded our reach and have seen incredible growth in a number of our programs. Through conversations with families we have learned that transportation/scheduling difficulties, location of programs (we work with nine different park districts and unfortunately cannot offer every program in every community), other family member's schedules and many other reasons often stand in the way of participants joining programs they are interested in. Additionally, often times in-person programs have a cap on how many people can attend due to room capacity, staffing needs, bus capacity and other factors. However, when meeting on Zoom the capacity is often significantly larger offering us the opportunity to include more people."

Final Hopeful Thoughts about the Postpandemic Landscape

We received numerous impactful responses from the professionals about what they've learned about themselves and our field. We wish we could share them all. We did want to share a few full responses with you, as they contain valuable insights for leisure-services professionals who wish to have an eye to the future:

- Nicole Kohler: Working in recreation is anything but routine or repetitive and requires those working in the field to be flexible. I believe that recreation professionals were well prepared to be creative, innovative, flexible, and concerned about the well-being of their consumers with the onset of a pandemic. I have learned, however, as a professional working in this type of environment, nothing is more important than human connection, both for myself, the staff I lead, and the families I serve in the community. Working through a pandemic has taught me to be intentional about connecting with people and to rid some of the hurry and hustle in my life to make room for cultivating relationships.
- Rebecca Krzyszkowski: As a parks and recreation professional during a pandemic, I've learned what it

truly means to think on my feet and have patience. Although many professionals may believe they already possess these transferable skills, a pandemic will truly put them to the test…The constant change of events is stressful, but I really learned how to take a deep breath, relax, and be patient. Although the pandemic has negatively impacted many people, it has really brought the value and importance of being part of a parks and recreation department to light. Our community has 100% relied on us to keep outdoor facilities, parks, and trails open safely for physical, mental, and emotional health.

- Dawn Pote: In the midst of uncertainty, you never go wrong making decisions that are in line with your values and the values of your organization. Too much of what we do seems legalistic and focused on a "right or wrong" answer to each situation. There is never one "right" or one "wrong." One of the best pieces of advice I was given (and that I share often) is that there are no wrong decisions. You take all of the information you have and you make the right decision based on the values and what you know. If more information becomes available that changes your original decision, it does not mean your first decision was wrong. It was right for that time. Everyone will interpret information differently. When mitigations came out, there was not a definitive way to do things. I counted on established networks of colleagues (such as directors of institutions in the state), professional organizations (National Intramural-Recreational Sports Association, American College of Sports Medicine, Association of Outdoor Recreation and Education), and institutional partners to determine what was best for our university and our needs. There were so many elements (risk management, reputation, internal and external expectations) that no one person could or should be making decisions in a bubble.

- Austin Hochstetler: I think an easier answer someone would give is something along the lines of "overcoming adversity" or "adaptability." However, and albeit those are true, I've learned more about my own ability to problem solve during the pandemic. As a consultant, we are continually tasked to identify a community's needs, barriers, challenges, etc., and then propose solutions as a result. The pandemic has challenged our way of thinking when it comes to financial sustainability, recreation program delivery, and frankly, what "community need" really is. Therefore, this pandemic time has allowed me to grow more in my critical thinking along with identifying different types of corresponding solutions.

- Samantha Rupkey: The pandemic stripped my job down to its very core. Working from home, I was not able to collaborate in-person amongst my colleagues and did not have access to my grand office building or the perks it offered. When those aspects of the job are taken away, the actual work of the job is revealed. This year has helped me realize that at the end of the day, the foundation of a career is truly about the good work that I'm producing and the mission of the company that I'm tied to.

- Michael Hernbrott: The ability to ignore the white noise of everyone's opinion and to focus on the reality of the challenges. From the start, our main mission was simple. Keep our doors open and keep our consumers and employees as safe as possible. There have been challenges but having that mission focused every decision back to it. The mission may change when this challenge is over but having that mission statement at the core always makes the process easier.

- Mike Pederson: That no hurdle is too high. I've always told myself and others that life is full of speed bumps, some are bigger than others. This pandemic has been the biggest hurdle yet, that took a lot of teamwork, guessing, and forward thinking to get over. A few scars, scratches, but we got over it! There is truly nothing that worrying did to get us through this, so don't worry about problems. Just put your head down, and make it happen!

As we've demonstrated throughout this text, the leisure-services industry as a whole is vital to the well-being and economy of our communities and leisure-services professionals seem to have adaptability ingrained in their nature. As you can see in the professionals' responses, these features of our profession have allowed these professionals to adapt and innovate in ways that will continue to expand the value of what we do as they keep their eyes to the future. We are eager to see what the postpandemic landscape holds for us all.

What's Your "Why"?

You have reached the end of your journey through this text so it is time to answer the question "What is your 'why' for pursuing a career in leisure services?" We do not expect you to have it all figured out; indeed, your "why" will evolve throughout the rest of your education and throughout your career. But, you can, we hope, start to articulate your "why" based on the parts of this text that have most resonated with you, that would most motivate you to do the often challenging and exhausting work of a leisure-services professional. This "why" will be different for each person—some of you may be motivated by the health benefits of our field or by the potential for our field to achieve social justice or by the economic impact of our field or by a particular sector of our field or by your own personal experience with play, recreation, and leisure or by some combination of ideas. So take a few minutes to sit down and try to write a paragraph that would explain to someone else why you want to pursue this field.

How will articulating your "why" help you moving forward? First, continuing on the theme of this chapter, reflecting on your "why" will better able you to be a professional who keeps an eye to the future—your future. It will keep you grounded as you figure out what types of career paths you want to explore. Second, it will allow you to advocate for our field to others who may see leisure services as a luxury or as frivolous. Your "why" will be one powerful way you can speak persuasively to people about the value of our field because it moves people beyond the surface nuts and bolts of what we do to realize the impact of what we do. Our field does, indeed, have tremendous impact and, as a result, leisure-services professionals have a tremendous responsibility, as

Daniel Dustin reminded in his message to leisure-services professionals:

> Every day, we must respect the power we have to make a difference, apply that power with the dignity it deserves, and proceed with the understanding that every little thing we do or say is replete with rippling effects that reverberate far and wide. In all likelihood, we will never know how much of a difference we are making in this world, but rest assured we are making a difference. That fact of life, and faith in ourselves, should be enough to sustain us through good times and bad. To that end, I wish you the very best of success in all the "little things" you do to build a happier, healthier, and more civilized United States of America.[73]

SUMMARY

This chapter moves from the past and the present to focus on contemporary issues, challenges, and the future of leisure and recreation.

The chapter began by focusing on skills and attitudes that leisure professionals with an eye to the future should develop. Professionals should keep their sights on core principles of our field amid change, be willing to embrace innovation and an entrepreneurial spirit, and develop their skills in identifying and leveraging potentially meaningful trends.

The chapter then moved on to discuss several trends currently affecting U.S. society that have implications for the practice of leisure services moving forward. The United States is undergoing a variety of rapid demographic shifts that will alter the landscape of our audience moving forward. Real threats to the environment necessitate specific

actions in our field. And the ever-evolving technologies and attitudes toward time in our society will have an impact on future leisure services in a variety of ways.

Other opportunities and issues that were presented in the chapter focus on the growth of special interest groups, the commodification of leisure, the well-being movement, growth of the experience economy, the maturation of leisure services as a field, the economic impact of leisure services, and the surge of esports. All of these issues are cause for concern or opportunity for the leisure-services profession.

The chapter explored what the post-COVID-19 pandemic landscape may look like from the voices of current leisure-services professionals. It ended with a call to readers to articulate their "why" for pursuing a career in leisure services.

QUESTIONS FOR CLASS DISCUSSION OR ESSAY EXAMINATION

1. What are the skills and attitudes a leisure professional with an eye to the future possesses? Which of those do you feel like you are already strong in? Which do you feel like you can grow in? How will you take steps to grow in those areas?

2. Based on your reading of this chapter, what do you see as a major concern that you feel should be addressed by public park and recreation agencies? Explain and justify your response.

3. Choose one of the societal trends discussed in the chapter: changing demographics, the environment, technology, and time. How does that trend affect the future delivery of recreation, park, tourism, and other related leisure systems?

4. Choose one of the topics from the opportunities and issues section of the chapter. Think about the sector or career path you're interested in pursuing in leisure services. Generate three specific ideas for how a leisure-services professional in your chosen sector could leverage (use) that topic to improve their services.

---

5. What stood out to you the most from the responses of the professionals about the postpandemic landscape? Have you seen the professionals' predictions about changes in the leisure-services profession happening? How so?

---

6. Write a paragraph that explains why you want to pursue a career in leisure services. Share your paragraph with someone in your life who you think may be skeptical about the value of our field. How did they react?

ENDNOTES

1. Kraus, R. (1971). *Recreation and leisure in modern society*. Appleton-Century-Crofts

2. McLuhan, M., & Fiore, Q. (1967). *The medium is the massage*. Penguin Random House.

3. Davis, H. C. (1968). Recreation planning in the technological age. *Parks & Recreation*, 22.

4. Pew Research Center. (2016, March 31). *10 demographic trends that are shaping the U.S. and the world*. Retrieved February 4, 2021, from http://www.pewresearch.org/fact-tank/2016/03/31/10-demographic-trends-that-are-shaping-the-u-s-and-the-world/.

5. Markham, V. D. (2008). *U.S. population, energy and climate change* (p. 7). Center for Environment and Population.

6. U.S. Department of Agriculture. (2019, August 20). *Major land uses*. Retrieved February 4, 2021, from https://www.ers.usda.gov/topics/farm-economy/land-use-land-value-tenure/major-land-uses/.

7. United States Census Bureau. (2010). *America's foreign born in the last 50 years*. Retrieved February 4, 2021, from https://www.census.gov/programs-sur-veys/sis/resources/visualizations/foreign-born.html.

8. Virden, R. J., & Walker, G. J. (1999). Ethnic/racial and gender variations among meanings given to, and preferences for, the natural environment. *Leisure Sciences, 21*(3), 219–239.

9. Hibler, D. K., & Shinew, K. J. (2002). Moving beyond our comfort zone: The role of leisure service providers in enhancing multiracial families' leisure experiences. *Parks and Recreation, 37*(2), 26.

10. Ho, C., Sasidharan, V., Elmendorf, W., Willits, F. K., Graefe, A., & Godbey, G. (2005). Gender and ethnic variations in urban park preferences, visitations, and perceived benefits. *Journal of Leisure Research, 37*(), 281–306.

11. Shinew, K. J., Floyd, M. F., & Parry, D. (2004). Understanding the relationship between race and leisure activities and constraints: Exploring an alternative framework. *Leisure Sciences, 26*, 188–191.

12. Fry, R. (2019, July 24). *Baby boomers are staying in the labor force at rates not seen in generations for people their age*. Pew Research Center. Retrieved February 4, 2021, from https://www.pewresearch.org/fact-tank/2019/07/24/baby-boomers-us-labor-force/.

13. Fry, R. (2020, November 9). *The pace of Boomer retirements has accelerated in the past year*. Pew Research Center. Retrieved February 4, 2021, from https://www.pewresearch.org/fact-tank/2020/11/09/the-pace-of-boomer-retirements-has-accelerated-in-the-past-year/.

14. Ortman, J. M., Velkoff, V. A., & Hogan, H. (2014). *An aging nation: The older population in the United States: Population estimates and projections*. U.S. Census Bureau. Retrieved February 4, 2021, from https://www.census.gov/prod/2014pubs/p25-1140.pdf.

15. Kromer, B., & Howard, D. (2015, October 23). *Working in America: New tables detail demographics of work experience.* U.S. Census Bureau. Retrieved February 4, 2021, from https://www.census.gov /newsroom/blogs/random-samplings/2015/10 /working-in-america-new-tables-detail-demographics -of-work-experience.html.

16. Burnett-Wolle, S., & Godbey, G. (2005). Active aging 101. *Parks and Recreation*, 30–40.

17. U.S. Census Bureau. (2002). *Your gateway to Census 2000.* Retrieved February 4, 2021, from http://www.census.gov/main/www/cen2000.html.

18. The Annie E. Casey Foundation. (2020). *2020 KIDS COUNT data book* (p. 8). Baltimore, MD. Retrieved March 17, 2021, from https://www.aecf.org/m/ resourcedoc/aecf-2020kidscountdatabook-2020.pdf.

19. Taylor, P. (2014, April 10). *The next America.* Pew Research Center. Retrieved February 4, 2021, from https://www.pewresearch.org/next-america.

20. Forum on Child and Family Statistics. (2020). *America's children in brief: Key national indicators of well-being, 2020.* Retrieved February 4, 2021, from https://www.childstats.gov/americaschildren/index.asp.

21. Annie E. Casey Foundation. (2020). Kids Count Data Center. Retrieved February 4, 2021, from https://datacenter.kidscount.org.

22. UNICEF. (2016). *The state of the world's children 2016.* Retrieved February 4, 2021, from https://www. unicef.org/reports/state-worlds-children-2016.

23. Annie E. Casey Foundation (2020).

24. Anderson, M., & Jiang, J. (2018, May 31). *Teens, social media, and technology 2018.* Pew Research Center. Retrieved February 4, 2021, from https://www.pewresearch.org/internet /2018/05/31/teens-social-media-technology-2018/.

25. Siegel, R. (2019, October 29). Tweens, teens and screens: The average time kids spend watching online videos has doubled in 4 years. *Washington Post.* Retrieved February 4, 2021, from https://www.washingtonpost.com/technology /2019/10/29/survey-average-time-young-people -spend-watching-videos-mostly-youtube-has -doubled-since/.

26. Anderson & Jiang (2018).

27. May, M., & Ozbenian, S. (2017, March 2). Wild and wonderful: Making a case for undeveloped open spaces. *Parks & Recreation.* Retrieved February 4, 2021, from https://www.nrpa.org/parks-recreation- magazine/2017/march/wild-and-wonderful-making-a- case-for-undeveloped-open-spaces/.

28. Center for Sustainable Systems University of Michigan. (2020). *U.S. environmental footprint.* Retrieved February 4, 2021, from http://css.umich. edu/factsheets/us-environmental-footprint-factsheet.

29. Center for Sustainable Systems University of Michigan (2020).

30. Brookings Institution. (2007). *Metro nation: How U.S. metropolitan areas fuel American prosperity* (p. 8). Retrieved February 4, 2021, from https://www.brookings.edu/wp-content/uploads /2016/06/MetroNationbp.pdf.

31. Berube, A., Crump, S., & Friedhoff, A. (2020, March 5). *Metro monitor 2020.* Brookings Institution. Retrieved February 4, 2021, from https:// www.brookings.edu/interactives/metro-monitor-2020/.

32. CNN. (2020, April 8). *Kyoto Protocol fast facts.* Retrieved February 4, 2021, from https://www.cnn. com/2013/07/26/world/kyoto-protocol-fast-facts /index.html.

33. Intergovernmental Panel on Climate Change. (2018). *Special report: Global warming of 1.5°C.* Retrieved from https://www.ipcc.ch/sr15/chapter/spm/.

34. Hersher, R. (2020). *U.S. officially leaving Paris Climate Agreement.* Retrieved from https://www.npr. org/2020/11/03/930312701/u-s-official-leaving-paris- climate-agreement.

35. World Meteorological Organization. (2018). *The state of the global climate in 2018.* Retrieved from http:// ane4bf-datap1.s3-eu-west-1.amazonaws.com/ wmocms/s3fs-public/ckeditor/files/ raft_Statement_ 7_February.pdf?5.6rzIGwBm5lwDSTPbgprB2_ EgrjzRVY.

36. Lindsey, R. (2020). *Climate change: Atmospheric carbon dioxide.* Retrieved from https://www.climate. gov/news-features/understanding-climate/ climate-change-atmospheric-carbon-dioxide.

37. U.S. Global Change Research Program. (2020). Retrieved February 4, 2021, from https://www.global change.gov.

38. Saunders, S., & Easley, T. (2006). *Losing ground: Western national parks endangered by climate change.* Rocky Mountain Climate Organization and the Natural Resources Defense Council. https://www. nrdc.org/sites/default/files/gw.pdf

39. United States Census Bureau. (2019). *Communing characteristics by sex.* Retrieved February 4, 2021,

from https://data.census.gov/cedsci/table?q=Commu ting&tid=ACSST1Y2019.S0801&hidePreview=false.

40. Ingraham, C. (2019, October 7). Average commute time reached a new record last year. *Washington Post*. Retrieved February 4, 2021, from https://www.washingtonpost.com/business/2019/10/07/ nine-days-road-average-commute-time-reached-new -record-last-year/.

41. Katz, B., & Bradley, J. (2014, December 11). *The metropolitan revolution*. Brookings Institution. Retrieved February 4, 2021, from https://www. brookings.edu/book/the-metropolitan-revolution-2/.

42. Farmland Information Center. (2016). *Farms under threat: The state of the states*. Retrieved February 4, 2021, from https://farmlandinfo.org/statistics/ farms-under-threat-the-state-of-the-states/.

43. Charles, C., Louv, R., Bodner, L., & Guns, B. (2008). *Children and nature 2008: A report on the movement to reconnect children to the natural world (p. 13)*. Children's Nature Network.

44. U.S. Department of the Interior National Parks Service. (2018). *Healthy Parks Healthy People 2018–2023 strategic [plan (p. 1)*. Retrieved February 4, 2021, from https://www.nps.gov/subjects/healthand- safety/upload/HP2-Strat-Plan-Release-June_2018.pdf.

45. Godbey, G. (2009). *Outdoor recreation, health, and wellness: Understanding and enhancing the relation- ship (p. 27)*. Resources for the Future.

46. Thompson, C. W., Aspinall, P., & Montarzino, A. (2008). The childhood factor: Adult visits to green places and the significance of childhood experience. *Environment & Behavior, 40*(1), 111–143.

47. Kellert, S. R. (2007). *Building for life: Designing and understanding the human–nature connection*. Island Press.

48. Godbey (2009).

49. Maller, C., Townsend, M., St. Leger, L., Henderson- Wilson, C., Pryor, A., Prosser, L., & Moore, M. (2009). Healthy Parks, Healthy People: The health benefits of contact with nature in a park context. *George Wright Forum, 26*(2), 57. Retrieved February 4, 2021, from http://www.georgewright.org/262maller.pdf.

50. Pew Research Center. (2019, June 12). *Mobile fact sheet*. Retrieved February 4, 2021, from https:// www.pewresearch.org/internet/fact-sheet/mobile/.

51. Ibid.

52. Pew Research Center. (2019, June 12). *Internet/ broadband fact sheet*. Retrieved February 4, 2021,

from https://www.pewresearch.org/internet /fact-sheet/internet-broadband/.

53. Pew Research Center. (2019, June 12). *Social media fact sheet*. Retrieved February 4, 2021, from https://www.pewresearch.org/internet/fact-sheet /social-media/.

54. Wajcman, J. (2008). Life in the fast lane? Toward a sociology of technology and time. *British Journal of Sociology, 59*(1), 59–76.

55. Lippke, R. L. (2001). Five concerns regarding the commercialization of leisure. *Business and Society Review, 106*(2), 107–126.

56. Ibid.

57. Robert Wood Johnson Foundation. (n.d.). *Healthy communities*. Retrieved February 4, 2021, from http://www.rwjf.org/en/our-focus-areas/focus-areas /healthy-communities.html.

58. Pine, B. J., II, & Gilmore, J. H. (1999). *The experience economy*. Harvard Business School Press.

59. Csikszentmihalyi, M., & Csikszentmihalyi, I. S. (Eds.). (1988). *Optimal experiences: Psychological studies of flow in consciousness*. Cambridge University Press.

60. Knutson, B. J., Beck, J. A., Kim, S. H., & Cha, J. (2006). Identifying the dimensions of the experience construct [Electronic Version]. *Journal of Hospitality & Leisure Marketing, 15*(3), 31–47.

61. Ellis, G. D., & Rossman, J. R. (2008). Creating value for participants through experience staging: Parks, recre- ation, and tourism in the experience industry. *Journal of Park and Recreation Administration, 26*(4), 1–20.

62. Bureau of Economic Analysis. (2020). *Consumer spending*. Retrieved March 17, 2021 from https://www.bea.gov/national/consumer_spending.htm.

63. Bureau of Economic Analysis. (2020). *Outdoor recreation satellite account, U.S. and states, 2019*. Retrieved February 4, 2021, from https://www.bea. gov/sites/default/files/2020-11/orsa1120_1.pdf.

64. Outdoor Industry Association. (2017). *The outdoor recreation economy*. Retrieved February 4, 2021, from https://outdoorindustry.org/wp-content/uploads/2017 /04/OIA_RecEconomy_FINAL_Single.pdf.

65. Office of the Governor. (2021). *"Building Idaho's Future": Gov. Little signs bill investing in outdoor recreation and state parks*. Retrieved March 17, 2021, from https://gov.idaho.gov/pressrelease/ building-idahos-future-gov-little-signs-bill-invest- ing-in-outdoor-recreation-and-state-parks/.

66. Idaho Business for the Outdoors. (2019). *Outdoor recreation's importance continues to grow nationally and in Idaho*. Retrieved March 17, 2021, from https://www.idahobo.org/blog/2019/10/14/idahos-outdoor-recreation-economy-accounts-for-approximately-3-of-state-gdp.

67. Salazar, K. (2011, August 22). *The economic power of outdoor recreation*. Retrieved February 4, 2021, from https://obamawhitehouse.archives.gov/blog/2011/08/22/economic-power-outdoor-recreation.

68. Ayles, J. (2019, December 3). Global esports revenue reaches more than $1 billion as audience figures exceed 433 million. *Forbes*. Retrieved February 4, 2021, from https://www.forbes.com/sites/jamesayles/2019/12/03/global-esports-revenue-reaches-more-than-1-billion-as-audience-figures-exceed-433-million/?sh=c28e67e13298.

69. Bhatt, N. (2019, September 1). Esports: The next big thing for parks and rec. *Parks & Recreation*. Retrieved February 4, 2021, from https://www.nrpa.org/parks-recreation-magazine/2019/september/esports-the-next-big-thing-for-parks-and-rec/.

70. McKenzie, L. (2019, October 16). *Leveling up esports on campus*. Inside Higher Ed. Retrieved February 4, 2021, from https://www.insidehighered.com/news/2019/10/16/bringing-esports-campus.

71. Grand Canyon University. (2020, March 24). *College esports across the United States*. Retrieved February 4, 2021, from https://www.gcu.edu/blog/gcu-experience/college-esports-across-united-states.

72. Bhatt (2019).

73. Dustin, D. (2015, November 1). The work we do. *Parks & Recreation*. Retrieved February 4, 2021, from https://www.nrpa.org/parks-recreation-magazine/2015/november/the-work-we-do/.

Index